Speech, Conduct, & the First Amendment

TEACHING TEXTS IN LAW AND POLITICS

David A. Schultz
General Editor

Vol. 14

PETER LANG
New York • Washington, D.C./Baltimore • Bern
Frankfurt am Main • Berlin • Brussels • Vienna • Oxford

Howard Schweber

Speech, Conduct, & the First Amendment

PETER LANG
New York • Washington, D.C./Baltimore • Bern
Frankfurt am Main • Berlin • Brussels • Vienna • Oxford

Library of Congress Cataloging-in-Publication Data
Schweber, Howard H.
Speech, conduct, and the First Amendment / Howard Schweber.
p. cm. — (Teaching texts in law and politics; v. 14)
Includes bibliographical references and index.
1. Freedom of speech—United States. 2. United States.
Constitution. 1st Amendment. I. Title. II. Series.
KF4772 .S39   342.73'0853—dc21   2002028508
ISBN 978-0-8204-5295-1
ISSN 1083-3447

Bibliographic information published by **Die Deutsche Bibliothek**.
Die Deutsche Bibliothek lists this publication in the "Deutsche
Nationalbibliografie"; detailed bibliographic data are available
on the Internet at http://dnb.ddb.de/.

The paper in this book meets the guidelines for permanence and durability
of the Committee on Production Guidelines for Book Longevity
of the Council of Library Resources.

© 2003, 2014 Peter Lang Publishing, Inc., New York
29 Broadway, 18th floor, New York, NY 10006
www.peterlang.com

All rights reserved.
Reprint or reproduction, even partially, in all forms such as microfilm,
xerography, microfiche, microcard, and offset strictly prohibited.

Printed in the United States of America

To my teachers, past and present.

Table of Contents

Acknowledgments xi

Introduction 3

I.   **"Congress Shall Make No Law..."** 5

   A. *Preferred Liberties* 5
   B. *Historical Background to the First Amendment* 7
   C. *The Search for a Unified Reading* 15
   D. *Some Useful Terms* 25

II. **"...Abridging the Freedom of Speech": From Clear and Present Danger to the Categorical Approach** 31

   A. *Libel and the Meaning of Sedition* 31
   B. *The Focus on Circumstances: The "Clear and Present Danger" Test, 1919–1969* 38
   C. *The Categorical Approach: Fighting Words, Obscenity, and Libel* 46
   D. *General Principles* 57
      1. *Regulation of Speech in a Public Forum* 58
      2. *Limited Forums* 66

III. **The Categorical Approach Revisited: Libel, Obscenity and Indecency, Sexual Harassment, and Hate Speech** 72

   A. *Libel* 74
   B. *Obscenity and Privacy* 74
      1. *Defining Obscenity* 74
      2. *Protecting Privacy* 80
      3. *Special Protections for Children* 85
   C. *Indecency and Public Spaces* 89
   D. *Sexual Harassment* 106
   E. *Hate Speech: Reconsidering the Categorical Approach* ... 109

F.	*Commercial Speech*	118
G.	*Campaign Contributions and Expenditures*	123

IV. Speech-Plus and Expressive Conduct; Compelled Speech and the Right of Association 127

A.	*Speech-Plus and Expressive Conduct*	127
B.	*Compelled Speech and the Right of Association*	145
	1. *Compelled Speech*	145
	2. *Association and Compelled Association*	150

V. "Congress Shall Make No Law Respecting an Establishment of Religion..." 164

A.	*Subsidies for Religious Activities*	168
B.	*Endorsement*	189
	1. *Public Prayers*	190
	2. *Public Displays*	203
	3. *Revisiting the Question of Legislative Intent: Endorsement and School Curricula*	210
C.	*The Establishment Clause and the Problem of Accommodation*	216

VI. "...Or Prohibiting the Free Exercise Thereof" 218

A.	*What is a "Religion"?*	225
B.	*What is a "Law Prohibiting the Free Exercise" of Religion?*	230

VII. Government as Speaker; Access Cases 258

A.	*Government as Speaker*	259
B.	*Access to Public Facilities*	272
C.	*Access to Public Support*	278

VIII.	**Freedom of the Press**	292
	A. *Prior Restraints*	292
	B. *Libel and Invasion of Privacy*	301
	C. *Limits on Newsgathering*	321
	D. *Reporter's Privilege*	328
	E. *The Special Case of Broadcast Media: The Rise and Fall of the Equal Time Doctrine*	333
IX.	**Rights of Assembly and Petition**	340
	A. *Assembly*	340
	B. *Petition*	344
X.	**Three Views of the First Amendment; the First Amendment and the Problem of Equality; the Future of the First Amendment**	362
	A. *Approaches to Understanding the First Amendment*	362
	1. *The Affirmative Approach*	363
	2. *The Negative Approach*	366
	3. *Test Cases: Access and Association*	368
	4. *Another View: The Activist Approach*	371
	B. *The First Amendment and the Problem of Equality*	373
	C. *The Future of the First Amendment*	394
Table of Cases		401
Sources		415
Index		419

Acknowledgments

Thomas I. Emerson, "Toward a General Theory of the First Amendment," 72 *Yale Law Journal*, 878 (1963). Copyright 1963 by the Trustees of Yale University. Reprinted by permission of the Yale Law Journal Company and William S. Hein Company.

William Marshall, "What Is the Matter with Equality?: An Assessment of the Equal Treatment of Religion and Nonreligion in First Amendment Jurisprudence," 75 Ind. L. J. 193 (2000). Copyright 2000 by the Trustees of Indiana University. Reprinted by permission.

Congress shall make no law respecting an establishment of religion, or prohibiting the free exercise thereof; or abridging the freedom of speech, or of the press, or the right of the people peaceably to assemble, and to petition the Government for a redress of grievances.

Introduction

This book reviews the development and the current state of the First Amendment. My intention in writing this book was to create a text that could be used by teachers in courses on law or political science. It is my hope that this is also a book that will be useful to readers wishing to give themselves an introductory education to the First Amendment outside the context of a university. At the same time, however, this book is not an introduction to constitutional law and reasoning generally. It is assumed that the reader is familiar with the American Constitution, the court system and the special role that courts play in constitutional interpretation, the basic approaches to interpreting the Constitution—original intent, original understanding, strict construction, intrepretivism—and so on. A few terms specific to the First Amendment are defined at the end of the first chapter, but terms such as certiorari, appellate court, brief, and motion are presumed to be familiar.

As a teacher myself, I am familiar with some of the problems that arise when one tries to design a text of this kind. For example, should the author—like the teacher in a classroom—attempt to present a veil of neutrality that treats the material like specimens of natural objects to be described and classified? Or should the author's own views appear, thus giving the teacher or reader a voice to which they can respond? Either of these approaches runs the risk of leaving a reader with the erroneous impression that there is a verifiable correct answer to the questions about the First Amendment, rather than conflicting and competing interpretations grounded in different approaches to the special problem of textual interpretation that are presented by a constitution. In this book I have tried to avoid both the pretense that there is an "objective" answer to constitutional questions and the false argument that there can be a single, authoritative interpretation. Instead, I have attempted to include arguments from several different perspectives, by including excerpts of both court cases and secondary materials that reflect a range of different approaches to constitutional interpretation. In some places, I have also presented my own interpretations of the patterns that emerge across a range of cases. My intent has been to provide readers and teachers, alike, with interesting ideas that they can engage and evaluate; in other words, my goal has been to write a book that would provoke a valuable discussion.

These considerations also led to certain decisions in organizing the discussion, deciding on what cases and materials to include, and how to edit the excerpts that are included. The book is organized in terms of the various clauses of the First Amendment. This seems to me the organization which nonspecialists, in particular, would find most natural. Thus, while there is certainly considerable attention paid to shifts in Court personnel and ideology, this is not a book that is designed for Court-watchers, judicial biographers, or lawyers, but rather a discussion intended for an audience of interested students of the American Constitution. In selecting cases for inclusion, I have attempted to pick out those that, when read together, make sense of the development of the prevailing judicial thinking in each area. As a result, in comparison with a traditional casebook, in this book fewer cases are excerpted but the excerpts are often a bit longer. Dissenting and concurring opinions are included where those opinions expressed ideas that either later became adopted as binding precedent, or where arguments were raised that articulate important perspectives on the issues that might otherwise go unnoticed. It is by no means the case that all opinions are excerpted or even acknowledged; for one thing, it was considered important to keep this book down to a reasonable length. Similarly, in contrast with an official case report, the excerpts in this book only identify all the different justices' positions in a case where that information appears relevant to appreciating the final outcome. Finally, highly technical areas of constitutional law are given somewhat short shrift here, despite their obvious interest. For example, readers who want to understand the current state of the law concerning the prerogatives and responsibilities of journalists, or the intricacies of campaign finance law, should not consider the materials presented in this book to be anything more than introductions to the basic constitutional issues involved in each of these areas.

The journals that have been kind enough to permit me to make use of articles originally appearing in their pages have been acknowledged already. I should be remiss, however, if I did not acknowledge the signal contributions of David Schultz, the editor of the series in which this book appears, and Lynn Schweber, my wife and the finest manuscript editor I know. In addition, Jill Wieber provided valuable research assistance. I should also like to acknowledge the various teachers, friends, and colleagues who have contributed to my understanding of the First Amendment. Most of all, however, the understandings that are reflected in these pages have grown out of the conversations I have had with my students, colleagues, and teachers; my greatest debt is owed to them.

I. "Congress Shall Make No Law..."

A. *Preferred Liberties*

When Justice Cardozo wanted to explain why some rights were more "fundamental" than others, he turned to the rights of "freedom of thought and speech." "Of that freedom," he wrote, "one may say that it is the matrix, the indispensable condition, of nearly every other form of freedom. With rare aberrations a pervasive recognition of that truth can be traced in our history, political and legal." *Palko v. Connecticut*, 302 U.S. 319 (1937). In the 1940s, it became common to speak of the First Amendment's freedoms of speech and religion as occupying a "preferred position" in the pantheon of constitutionally guaranteed liberties. *Jones v. Opelika*, 316 U.S. 584, 608 (1942) (Stone, J., dissenting). And since 1928, when judges look to find the basis for a right of privacy in the Constitution, more often than not they follow the lead of Justice Brandeis and look to the First Amendment.

> The makers of our Constitution undertook to secure conditions favorable to the pursuit of happiness. They recognized the significance of man's spiritual nature, of his feelings and of his intellect. They knew that only a part of the pain, pleasure and satisfactions of life are to be found in material things. They sought to protect Americans in their beliefs, their thoughts, their emotions and their sensations. They conferred, as against the Government, the right to be let alone—the most comprehensive of rights and the right most valued by civilized man. *Olmstead v. United States*, 277 U.S. 438, 478 (1928) (Brandeis, J., dissenting).

But why? Why is the First Amendment so central to the scheme of constitutional liberties? A related question is, What connects the different elements of the First Amendment? The First Amendment includes freedom of speech, of religious exercise, of the press, of petition, and of assembly, plus a proscription against the government's acting in a way tending toward the establishment of religion. This is by far the most diverse set of propositions contained in any single amendment or section of the Constitution; what connects them? The answers to these two questions are presumably related. That is, the freedoms protected by the First Amendment are thought in some way to define the necessary conditions for a larger conception of "liberty," and the establishment of a religion by government is in some way thought to raise a uniquely dangerous threat to that liberty.

These questions provide the starting point for the discussion of this book. How one answers these questions says a great deal about how one answers the next questions that necessarily arise: How shall we understand the words of the First Amendment, and what are the limiting principles that apply to its guarantees? Someone who does not feel that the First Amendment's protections define "preferred freedoms," and who does not find a unifying purpose that connects the diverse elements of the First Amendment, is likely to read each particular guarantee narrowly. Conversely, someone who shares Cardozo's view that protection of thought and speech is "the indispensable condition, of nearly every other form of freedom" is likely to be sympathetic to a broad and unified interpretation of the text. Either of these positions, it should be pointed out, can be derived from any number of different approaches to reading the Constitution, whether these are based on historical practices and understandings, modern philosophical commitments, or legal and judicial traditions.

One approach that is sadly not possible is to simply read the words literally. As Henry Louis Gates Jr. puts it, the argument that "the First Amendment means what it says...is a dependable and well-rehearsed argument whose only flaw is that it happens to be entirely false and nobody ever believed it anyway."[1] The attempt to read the language of the First Amendment strictly, without any interpretation, leads to meanings that are both impossibly narrow and impossibly broad. Take the simplest clause of all: "Congress shall make...no law...abridging the freedom of speech." Read strictly, this might permit a law making it a crime to speak in any setting in which anyone can hear you, since the language refers only to "speech," not to hearing. In other words, read this way the First Amendment is satisfied if you can speak freely only when locked in a soundproof closet. The words also would not guarantee any right to write or print your words, to send them through the mails or post them, to display them, or in any other way to make them known to others. Obviously, this is not an outcome that would be acceptable under any theory of the Free Speech Clause, and from the very beginning it has been understood that a right to speak implies a right to hear, even though there is no mention of hearing speech anywhere in the actual text. As Justice Douglas put it, "[T]he State may not, consistent with the spirit of the First Amendment, contract the spectrum of available knowledge. The right of freedom of speech and press includes not only the right to utter or to print, but the right to distribute, the right to receive, the right to read; and freedom of inquiry, freedom of thought, and freedom to teach—indeed the freedom of the entire university community." *Griswold v. Connecticut*, 391 U.S. 145 (1965).

It is equally unsatisfying, however, to read the Free Speech Clause absolutely. There is probably no area of conduct that has been traditionally regulated as extensively as speech. Libel, fraud, blackmail, and treason are all crimes whose central components involve communication, but no one has seriously suggested that the First Amendment should be understood to protect those particular kinds of expressions. Similar problems are attendant on any attempt to "simply read the words" of the other clauses of the First Amendment. Referring to the Religion Clauses, Justice Black famously said, "I read 'no law...abridging' to mean no law abridging," *Smith v. California*, 361 U.S. 147 (1959), but that is more useful as decorative rhetoric than as an analytical approach. Constitutional questions are raised when government has enacted a law, and the question is whether that law is constitutionally permissible. To say, then, that government may "make no law respecting an establishment of religion" means just what it says is not helpful. When they review a particular law judges have to decide whether it "respects" an "establishment" of "religion"; these are terms whose meaning is far from self-evident.

Ultimately, the problem with trying to read the words of the First Amendment "to mean what they say" is that there are simply too few of them for all the things that need to be said. The entire amendment, covering all the broad range of topics that it does, comprises only forty-five words. As a result, some principles of interpretation will always be required, and the questions with which this essay began remain inescapable. Before we turn to an examination of the arguments that have been made about each of the clauses of the First Amendment, however, it is worthwhile taking a few moments to consider the historical background of the amendment and to introduce some key concepts that will appear frequently in the discussions that follow.

B. *Historical Background to the First Amendment*

The elements that are grouped together in the First Amendment undoubtedly reflect the historical experience of seventeenth-century England. During that time, religious and political dissension was repressed by the Star Chamber, whose extrajudicial proceedings, use of coercion, and inquisitorial mandates made it a symbol of tyranny for the early American settlers. The Puritans of New England, in particular, conceived of their separation from England as an escape from tyranny and an opportunity to create a new kind of society. (Contemporaneous Virginia settlements were commercial enterprises with no explicit religious purposes.) In terms of religious practice, the Puritans were, above all, devoted to the ideals of Congregationalism, expressed in the principle of "every church on its own bottom," which meant no centralized authority dictating liturgical practice or church organization. Thus the idea in Massachusetts was that any community could form its own church, and the state would have nothing to say in the matter. Conversely, churches were expected to keep out of the business of civil government. These principles were embodied, for example, in the Massachusetts *Body of Liberties* of 1641, America's first constitution. Among other provisions, the *Body of Liberties* declared that censure by a church could not affect a person's civil privileges, that ministers could not hold political office, that one church could have no say in the affairs of another, that the state could not prohibit a group of people from forming their own church, and that no one could be obliged to attend any particular church. Ministers were to be supported by public funds, but this appears to be primarily an effort to avoid the creation of a wealthy and politically powerful clergy, such as was known in England.

Nevertheless, the leaders of Massachusetts were certainly not inclined to tolerate the presence of Baptists, Quakers, or Catholics in their midst. Laws against both blasphemy and heresy were enacted, justified by the claim that Providence depended on maintenance of orthodoxy. This was similar to the version of religious toleration that was espoused by Milton in 1644: "I mean not tolerated Popery, and open superstition, which as it extirpates all religions and civil supremacies, so it self should be extirpate, provided first that all charitable and compassionate means be us'd to win and regain the weak and the misled."[2]

This balance between state and church did not please everyone. New Haven was settled by Puritans who found the Massachusetts government insufficiently devoted to preserving religious law. Conversely, Roger Williams departed from Massachusetts and settled Rhode Island in protest against the extent to which the state was involved in religious matters. Williams spoke of "a wall of separation between the garden of the Church and the wilderness of the world," and declared that "it is the will and command of God that...a permission of the most pagan, Jewish, Turkish, or anti-christian consciences and worships, be granted to all men in all nations and countries." "An enforced uniformity of religion," he wrote, "confounds the civil and religious."[3] Thus the issues of freedom of conscience, freedom of religion, and the proper relationship between civil and clerical authority were at the heart of the earliest American political conflicts and the first attempts at American constitutionalism.

Another element in the early history of the First Amendment is the development and new prominence of modes of scientific reasoning that, not coincidentally, began in England during the same early years of the seventeenth century. Francis Bacon defined the project of scientific reason as the dispelling of "myths" that prevented humans from seeing the truths of the natural and social world. Bacon was not a scientist, but rather the foremost lawyer and judge of his day, and his project was about law and politics as much as it was about reformulating the study of physics or chemistry. This, too, accorded with the Calvinist tradition that described the natural world as the "second book of revelation" and denied the special authority of priests to interpret its meaning or that of written scripture. Thus by the end of the seventeenth century American colonists had experienced the political consequences of a century of English traditions that shared a commitment to freedom of thought as the necessary condition for the improvement of society, whether from a pietistic or naturalistic foundation. In the eighteenth century, these traditions were joined by Enlightenment vocabularies that emphasized the political importance of free thought, critical reason, and unrestricted inquiry. These early historical roots provide the sources for the basic arguments that are most often heard in defense of the principles of the First Amendment: That freedom of thought is required for the pursuit of truth, that religious freedom is essential to political freedom, that freedom to speak critically and to question is essential to reason. Above all, the traditions of English dissenting Protestantism, scientific reasoning, and Enlightenment politics all shared a rejection of the possibility that the answers to the most profound questions can be known in advance or dictated by authority figures.

All of these themes can be seen clearly at work in the thinking of Thomas Jefferson and James Madison. Madison wrote the section of the Virginia *Declaration of Rights* concerning religious liberty, which states that "all men are equally entitled to the free exercise of religion, according to the dictates of conscience."[4] In 1785, he wrote a "Memorial and Remonstrance Against Religious Assessments" in opposition to a bill that would have used state funds to pay religious teachers. "The Religion...of every man must be left to the conviction and conscience of every man; and it is the right of every man to exercise it as these may dictate. This right is in its nature an unalienable right...because the opinions of men, depending only on the evidence contemplated by their own minds cannot follow the dictates of other men." Madison argued that this one issue was an exception to the general rule of democracy because religion, uniquely, was a matter separate from society. "True it is, that no other rule exists, by which any question which may divide a Society, can be ultimately determined, but the will of the majority; but it is also true that the majority may trespass on the rights of the minority." Tyranny of the majority, in turn, was a concern not only between religions but because it might diminish the equality of the believer and nonbeliever. "Whilst we assert for ourselves a freedom to embrace, to profess and to observe the Religion which we believe to be of divine origin, we cannot deny an equal freedom to those whose minds have not yet yielded to the evidence which has convinced us."[5]

Madison was motivated both to shield government from religion, and to shield religion from government. In his *Remonstrance*, he enumerated a long list of concerns, including the divisive effect of religion once it was permitted to enter into political debates and the corrupting effect of civil authority on the purity of religion itself. Later, as President, Madison vetoed bills that would have incorporated the Episcopal Church in Washington, D.C., and another that would have set aside federal land for a Baptist Church. After his retirement, Madison wrote that in his view the Establishment Clause prohibited presidential religious proclamations and the employment of military and governmental chaplains. "Religion flourishes in greater purity," he wrote, "without than with the aid of Government," a sentiment that echoed the feelings of Roger Williams more than a century earlier.[6]

Jefferson's feelings, despite his other disagreements with Madison, were similar on the issue of religious freedom. Himself a deist rather than a believing Christian, Jefferson was unwilling to see the government compel the support of religious teachings. In 1785, the same year as Madison's *Remonstrance* quoted above, Jefferson authored "A Bill for Establishing Religious Freedom." "[T]o compel a man to furnish contributions of money for the propagation of opinions which he disbelieves...is sinful and tyrannical; that even forcing him to support this or that teacher of his own religious persuasion, is depriving him of the comfortable liberty of giving his contributions to the particular pastor, whose morals he would make his pattern." Jefferson had a keen interest in the scientific tradition, and he drew on that tradition in making his arguments. "[O]ur civil rights," he said, "have no dependence on our religious opinions, any more than our opinions in physics or geometry." Like Madison, Jefferson also warned of the corrupting influence that political support might have on religion. "It tends only to corrupt the principles of that religion it is meant to encourage, by bribing with a monopoly of worldly honours and emoluments, those who will externally profess and conform to it."[7] In 1802, in a letter to the Baptist

Association of Danbury, Connecticut, Jefferson revived Roger Williams's metaphor of the wall of separation.

> Believing with you that religion is a matter which lies solely between man and his God, that he owes account to none other for this faith or his worship, that the legislative powers of government reach actions only, and not opinions, I contemplate with sovereign reverence that act of the whole American people which declared that their legislature should "make no law respecting an establishment of religion, or prohibiting the free exercise thereof," thus building a wall of separation between church and State."[8]

With these latter comments Jefferson pointed to the crucial connection between religious freedom and freedom of thought generally, and to the argument that religious freedom is an aspect of a general right to privacy.

Specific issues of free speech outside the context of religion also played important roles in early American history. Returning to seventeenth-century Massachusetts, for example, we find in the *Body of Liberties of 1641* a guarantee of a right to publish "remonstrances" against actions taken by the government "in case they cannot in Judgement and conscience consent to that way the Major vote or suffrage goes." Like the principles of separation between religious and civil authority, this was a highly limited right, but it points to the desire to escape the tyranny of the English system. During the debates on the First Amendment, Madison made it clear that he considered the right of free speech to be something that reached beyond the freedoms guaranteed in the British system. "[T]heir Magna Charta does not contain any one provision for the security of those rights, respecting which the people of America are most alarmed. The freedom of the press and rights of conscience, those choicest privileges of the people, are unguarded in the British constitution."[9]

Madison's great concern was to protect the rights to freedom of speech against state governments. "I think there is more danger of those powers being abused by the State Governments than by the Government of the United States. The same may be said of other powers which they possess, if not controlled by the general principle, that laws are unconstitutional which infringe the rights of the community."[10] This accorded with Madison's general concern that state governments' actions ought to be restrained by the Constitution. Madison had supported, for example, a proposal that the Congress ought to have the power to strike down any state law "interfering...with the general interests and harmony of the Union." In 1789, the Select Committee charged with drafting a bill of rights adopted Madison's language verbatim in proposing that Article I be amended to include a provision that "no State shall infringe the equal rights of conscience, nor the freedom of speech or of the press...." But this argument was one which Madison and his friends did not win. "This is offered, I presume," said Thomas Tucker, "as an amendment to the constitution of the United States, but it goes only to the alteration of the constitutions of particular States. It will be much better, I apprehend, to leave the State Governments to themselves."[11] As a result, states were left unencumbered by constitutional guarantees of free speech (or any of the other rights in the Bill of Rights) until after the adoption of the Fourteenth Amendment in 1868.[12]

Jefferson, too, took a broad view of the freedom of speech, writing in a 1789 letter to Madison that he would have liked to see Article IV of the Constitution include the following provision: "The people shall not be deprived or abridged of their right to speak, to write, or otherwise to publish any thing but false facts affecting injuriously the life, property, or reputation of others or affecting the peace of the confederacy with foreign nations." Similarly, in his proposed draft of a constitution for Virginia, Jefferson had included a provision that "[p]rinting presses shall be subject to no other restraint than liableness to legal prosecution for false facts printed and published."[13] As Jefferson's comments suggest, the issues of personal and seditious libel provided the connection between the freedom of speech and the freedom of the press in this period.

In English law, the press was thought to be free from prior restraints imposed by the Crown. This was the case in the common law. James Wilson, second only to Madison as a legal scholar among the members of the Constitutional Convention and justice of the first Supreme Court, placed the dangers of libel at the heart of the freedom of the press in a speech at the Pennsylvania Ratifying Convention in 1787:

> I presume it was not in the view of the honorable gentleman to say there is no such thing as a libel, or that the writers of such ought not to be punished. The idea of the liberty of the press, is not carried so far as this in any country—what is meant by the liberty of the press is, that there should be no antecedent restraint upon it; but that every author is responsible when he attacks the security or welfare of the government, or the safety, character and property of the individual. With regard to attacks upon the public, the mode of proceeding is by a prosecution.[14]

Benjamin Franklin seemed to agree in 1789: "If by the Liberty of the Press were understood merely the liberty of discussing the propriety of public measures and political opinions, let us have as much of it as you please: But if it means the Liberty of affronting, calumniating, and defaming one another, I, for my part, own myself willing to part with my share of it when our legislators shall please so to alter the law, and shall cheerfully consent to exchange my liberty of abusing others for the privilege of not being abus'd myself."[15]

Madison was unusual among his contemporaries in embracing a more absolute notion of the freedom of the press. In his challenge to the Alien and Sedition Acts enacted by President John Adams, which criminalized "seditious libel" of the government, he argued that the common law rule could not suffice for America:

> [T]his idea of the freedom of the press, can never be admitted to be the American idea of it: since a law inflicting penalties on printed publications, would have a similar effect with a law authorizing a previous restraint on them. It would seem a mockery to say, that no law should be passed, preventing publications from being made, but that laws might be passed for punishing them in case they should be made.

Madison pointed out that the British rule restrained only the Crown, but not Parliament, and proposed that the role of the Constitution in limiting the authority of legislatures was at the root of the different meaning of "freedom of the press." "In the British government, the danger of encroachments on the rights of the people, is understood to be confined to the executive magistrate.... In the United States, the case is altogether different. The people, not the government, possess the absolute sovereignty. The legislature, no less than the executive, is under limitations of power.... The state of the press, therefore, under the common law, cannot in this point of view, be the standard of its freedom in the United States."[16] Again, Madison's fear of legislatures, state and federal, as the threat to freedom were at the heart of his devotion to a strong version of press freedoms that reached beyond English tradition.

Jefferson occasionally made statements that suggested that he shared Madison's view and joined him in opposing the Alien and Sedition Acts, but more often he adopted a common law view. When he and his allies were using the press to challenge Adams's Federalists, that was one thing. But when Jefferson himself became president, and thus the target of his own opposition press, his attitude changed considerably. The press attacks on his administration, he wrote in a letter, were "pushing its licentiousness and its lying to such a degree of prostitution as to deprive it of all credit.... I have therefore long thought that a few prosecutions of the most prominent offenders would have a wholesome effect in restoring the integrity of the presses." And he repeated this theme in his Second Inaugural Address in 1805:

> During this course of administration, and in order to disturb it, the artillery of the press has been leveled against us, charged with whatsoever its licentiousness could devise or dare. These abuses of an institution so important to freedom and science, are deeply to be regretted...they might, indeed, have been corrected by the wholesome punishments reserved and provided by the laws of the several states against falsehood and defamation.[17]

Thus Jefferson's earlier objections to the Alien and Sedition Acts were, at most, directed only at the creation of a federal law punishing publication of false criticisms of the government; he had no such objections to the same power being exercised by state governments.

The right of petition has at its roots the idea of a final remedy in the event of a failure in the laws. Turning to William Blackstone's *Commentaries on the Laws of England* (1765), we find the following declaration: "If there should be any uncommon injury, or infringement of the rights before mentioned, which the ordinary course of law is too defective to reach, there still remains a fourth subordinate right appertaining to every individual, namely, the right of petitioning the king, or either house of parliament, for the redress of grievance."[18] This right, in other words, was a right of political participation, the prerogative of a constituent of seeking the assistance of the government in the furtherance of his interests which the courts had failed to vindicate. Similarly, the right of peaceful assembly was an attempt to ensure that people would be able to organize themselves into politically active groups, preserving the possibility of access to the political process.

Out of these differing views, and many others besides, came the modern First Amendment. For the first century and a half of its history, however, the First Amendment applied only to the federal government. As far as the federal Constitution was concerned, states were free to establish religions, silence speech, and control the press to their hearts' content, and in various ways they often did so. It was only with the adoption of the Fourteenth Amendment after the Civil War that there began to be arguments that the guarantees of rights in the Constitution might apply against the states as well, under a theory called the "incorporation doctrine." This was a theory which said that the Fourteenth Amendment's guarantees of equal protection and due process against actions by state governments implicitly meant that state governments were bound by the First Amendment and the other guarantees of the Bill of Rights. The idea of incorporation is a contentious one, but for purposes of this book it is sufficient to observe that the history of the First Amendment begins in earnest in 1925 in *Gitlow v. New York*, 268 U.S. 652 (1925), when the United States

Supreme Court declared that the First Amendment protects the liberties of Americans against infringement from all government forces and applies equally in all parts of the nation.

C. *The Search for a Unified Reading*

This brief historical sketch is offered in an attempt to provide some coherence as well as context to the First Amendment. Legal writers have long debated whether there is a sound basis for reading the different parts of the First Amendment as a unitary whole, and even whether such a reading is desirable. During the debates over the adoption of the amendment, in fact, some speakers objected that including a right to assemble or petition would diminish the apparent importance of the rights to freedom of speech and press. "What," said Theodore Sedgwick of Massachusetts, "shall we secure the freedom of speech, and think it necessary, at the same time, to allow the right of assembling? If people freely converse together, they must assemble for that purpose; it is a self-evident, unalienable right which the people possess...it is derogatory to the dignity of the House to descend to such minutiae."[19]

In a famous article written in 1965, Thomas Emerson reviewed the general theories and attempted to describe a way of thinking about the First Amendment that would tie all its pieces together. His primary focus is on the freedom of speech, but consider whether and to what extent these arguments also apply to the other elements of the First Amendment.

Thomas I. Emerson, *"Toward a General Theory of the First Amendment"*

The first task is to bring together all the basic considerations which must enter into any formulation of first amendment doctrine that goes beyond the merely verbal level. The fundamental purpose of the first amendment was to guarantee the maintenance of an effective system of free expression. This calls for an examination of the various elements which are necessary to support such a system in a modern democratic society. Some of these elements found early articulation in the classic theory of free expression, as it developed over the course of centuries; others are the outgrowth of contemporary conditions. More specifically, it is necessary to analyze (I) what it is that the first amendment attempts to maintain: the function of freedom of expression in a democratic society; (II) what the practical difficulties are in maintaining such a system: the dynamic forces at work in any governmental attempt to restrict or regulate expression; and (III) the role of law and legal institutions in developing and supporting freedom of expression.

These three elements are the basic components of any comprehensive theory of the first amendment viewed as a guarantee of a system of free expression.

The second task is to formulate legal doctrine which takes into account these basic factors, which gives legal effect to the fundamental decisions made in adopting the first amendment, and which provides the courts with guidelines sufficiently specific and legal in character as to enable them to perform their judicial function in supporting the system. We must therefore undertake (IV) a statement of the general principles upon which such legal doctrine must be based, and (V) an attempt at a formulation of some detailed rules of law that should govern the various types of first amendment problems which arise in our society today.

Within the confines of this article, of course, it is not possible to do more than sketch broadly the various propositions put forward, stating them in abbreviated, at times conclusory and indeed tentative form....

The right of the individual to freedom of expression has deep roots in our history. But the concept as we know it now is essentially a product of the development of the liberal constitutional state. It is an integral part of the great intellectual and social movement beginning with the Renaissance which transformed the Western world from a feudal and authoritarian society to one whose faith rested upon the dignity, the reason and the freedom of the individual. The theory in its modern form has thus evolved over a period of more than three centuries, being applied under different circumstances and seeking to deal with different problems. It is sufficient for our purposes to restate it in its final, composite form, as it comes to us today.

The values sought by society in protecting the right to freedom of expression may be grouped into four broad categories. Maintenance of a system of free expression is necessary (1) as assuring individual self-fulfillment, (2) as a means of attaining the truth, (3) as a method of securing participation by the members of the society in social, including political, decision-making, and (4) as maintaining the balance between stability and change in the society. We consider these in their affirmative aspects, without regard at this time to the problems of limitation or reconciliation with other values.

Individual Self-Fulfillment

The right to freedom of expression is justified first of all as the right of an individual purely in his capacity as an individual. It derives from the accepted premise of Western thought that the proper end of man is the realization of his character and potentialities as a human being. Man is distinguished from other animals principally by the qualities of his mind. He has powers to reason and to feel in ways that are unique in degree if not in kind: The capacity to think in abstract terms, to use language, to communicate thoughts and emotions, to build a culture. He has powers of imagination, sight and feeling. It is through development of these powers that man finds his meaning and his place in the world.

The achievement of self-realization commences with development of the mind. But the process of conscious thought by its very nature can have no limits.

An individual cannot tell where it may lead nor anticipate its end. Moreover, it is an *individual* process. Every man is influenced by his fellows, dead and living, but his mind is his own and its functioning is necessarily an individual affair.

From this it follows that every man—in the development of his own personality—has the right to form his own beliefs and opinions. And, it follows, that he has the right to express these beliefs and opinions. Otherwise they are of little account. For expression is an integral part of the development of ideas, of mental exploration and of the affirmation of self. The power to realize his potentiality as a human being begins at this point and must extend at least this far if the whole nature of man is not to be thwarted.

Hence suppression of belief, opinion and expression is an affront to the dignity of man, a negation of man's essential nature. What Milton said of licensing of the press is equally true of any form of restraint over expression: it is "the greatest displeasure and indignity to a free and knowing spirit that can be put upon him."

The right to freedom of expression derives, secondly, from basic Western notions of the role of the individual in his capacity as a member of society. Man is a social animal, necessarily and probably willingly so. He lives in company with his fellow men; he joins with them in creating a common culture; he is subject to the necessary controls of society and particularly of the state. His right to express his beliefs and opinions, in this role as a member of his community, follows from two fundamental principles. One is that the purpose of society, and of its more formal aspect the state, is to promote the welfare of the individual. Society and the state are not ends in themselves; they exist to serve the individual. The second is the principle of equality, formulated as the proposition that every individual is entitled to equal opportunity to share in common decisions which affect him.

From these concepts there follows the right of the individual to access to knowledge; to shape his own views; to communicate his needs, preferences and judgments; in short, to participate in formulating the aims and achievements of his society and his state. To cut off his search for truth, or his expression of it, is thus to elevate society and the state to a despotic command and to reduce the individual to the arbitrary control of others. The individual, in short, owes an obligation to cooperate with his fellow men, but that responsibility carries with it the right to freedom in expressing himself.

Two basic implications of the theory need to be emphasized. The first is that it is not a general measure of the individual's right to freedom of expression that any particular exercise of the right may be thought to promote or retard other goals of the society. The theory asserts that freedom of expression, while not the sole or sufficient end of society, is a good in itself, or at least an essential element in a good society. The society may seek to achieve other or more inclusive ends—such as virtue, justice, equality, or the maximum realization of the potentialities of its members. These problems are not necessarily solved by accepting the rules for freedom of expression. But, as a general proposition, the society may not seek to solve them by suppressing the beliefs or opinions of individual members. To achieve these other goals it must rely upon other methods: the use of counter-expression and the regulation or control of conduct which is not expression. Hence the right to control individual expression, on the ground that it is judged to promote good or evil, justice or injustice, equality or inequality, is not, speaking generally, within the competence of the good society.

The second implication, in a sense a corollary of the first, is that the theory rests upon a fundamental distinction between belief, opinion and communication of ideas on the one hand, and different forms of conduct on the other. For shorthand purposes we refer to this distinction hereafter as one between "expression" and "action." As just observed, in order to achieve its desired goals, a society or the state is entitled to exercise control over action—whether by prohibiting or compelling it—on an entirely different and vastly more extensive basis. But expression occupies a specially protected position. In this sector of human conduct, the social right of suppression or compulsion is at its lowest point, in most respects non-existent.

This marking off of the special area of expression is a crucial ingredient of the basic theory for several reasons. In the first place, thought and communication are the fountainhead of all expression of the individual personality. To cut off the flow at the source is to dry up the whole stream. Freedom at this point is essential to all other freedoms. Hence society must withhold its right of suppression until the stage of action is reached. Secondly, expression is normally conceived as doing less injury to other social goals than action. It generally has less immediate consequences, is less irremediable in its impact. Thirdly, the power of society and the state over the individual is so pervasive, and construction of doctrines, institutions and administrative practices to limit this power so difficult, that only by drawing such a protective line between expression and action is it possible to strike a safe balance between authority and freedom.

Attainment of Truth

In the traditional theory, freedom of expression is not only an individual but a social good. It is, to begin with, the best process for advancing knowledge and discovering truth.

Considered in this aspect, the theory starts with the premise that the soundest and most rational judgment is arrived at by considering all facts and arguments which can be put forth in behalf of or against any proposition. Human judgment is a frail thing. It may err in being subject to emotion, prejudice or personal interest. It suffers from lack of information, insight, or inadequate thinking. It can seldom rest at the point any single person carries it, but must always remain incomplete and subject to further extension, refinement, rejection or modification. Hence an individual who seeks knowledge and truth must hear all sides of the question, especially as presented by those who feel strongly and argue militantly for a different view. He must consider all alternatives, test his judgment by exposing it to opposition, make full use of different minds to sift the true from the false. Conversely, suppression of information, discussion, or the clash of opinion prevents one from reaching the most rational judgment, blocks the generation of new ideas, and tends to perpetuate error. This is the method of the Socratic dialogue, employed on a universal scale.

The process is a continuous one. As further knowledge becomes available, as conditions change, as new insights are revealed, the judgment is open to reappraisal, improvement or abandonment. The theory demands that discussion must be kept open no matter how certainly true an accepted opinion may seem to be. Many of the most widely acknowledged truths have turned out to be erroneous. Many of the most significant advances in human knowledge—from Copernicus to Einstein—have resulted from challenging hitherto unquestioned assumptions. No opinion can be immune from challenge.

The process also applies regardless of how false or pernicious the new opinion appears to be. For the unaccepted opinion may be true or partially true. And there is no way of suppressing the false without suppressing the true. Furthermore, even if the new opinion is wholly false, its presentation and open discussion serve a vital social purpose. It compels a rethinking and retesting of the accepted opinion. It results in a deeper understanding of the reasons for holding the opinion and a fuller appreciation of its meaning. The only justification for suppressing an opinion is that those who seek to suppress it are infallible in their judgment of the truth. But no individual or group can be infallible, particularly in a constantly changing world.

It is essential to note that the theory contemplates more than a process for arriving at an individual judgment. It asserts that the process is also the best method for reaching a general or social judgment. This is true in part because a social judgment is made up of individual judgments. It will therefore be vitally conditioned by the quality of the individual judgments which compose it. More importantly, the same reasons which make open discussion essential for an intelligent individual judgment make it imperative for rational social judgments. Through the acquisition of new knowledge, the toleration of new ideas, the testing of opinion in open competition, the discipline of rethinking its assumptions, a society will be better able to reach common decisions that will meet the needs and aspirations of its members.

Participation in Decision-Making

The third main function of a system of freedom of expression is to provide for participation in decision-making through a process of open discussion which is available to all members of the community. Conceivably the technique of reaching the best common judgment could be limited to an elite, or could be extended to most members of the society excluding only those who were felt to be clearly unworthy. In its earlier forms the theory was often so restricted. But as the nineteenth century progressed it came to be accepted that all men were entitled to participate in the process of formulating the common decisions.

This development was partly due to acceptance of the concept that freedom of expression was a right of the individual, as discussed previously. But it was also inherent in the logic of free expression as a social good. In order for the process to operate at its best, every relevant fact must be brought out, every opinion and every insight must be available for consideration. Since facts are discovered and opinions formed only by the individual, the system demands that all persons participate. As John Stuart Mill expressed it, "If all mankind minus one, were of one opinion, and only one person were of the contrary opinion, mankind would be no more justified in silencing that one person, than he, if he had the power, would be justified in silencing mankind."

But in addition to these reasons, the right of all members of society to form their own beliefs and communicate them freely to others must be regarded as an essential principle of a democratically-organized society. The growing pressures for democracy and equality reinforced the logical implications of the theory and demanded opportunity for all persons to share in making social decisions. This is, of course, especially true of political decisions. But the basic theory carried beyond the political realm. It embraced the right to participate in the building of the whole culture, and included freedom of expression in religion, literature, art, science and all areas of human learning and knowledge.

In the field of political action, as just mentioned, the theory of freedom of expression has particular significance. It is through the political process that most of the immediate decisions on the survival, welfare and progress of a society are made. It is here that the state has a special incentive to repress opposition and often wields a more effective power of suppression. Freedom of expression in the political realm is usually a necessary condition for securing freedom elsewhere. It is in the political sector, therefore, that the crucial battles over free expression are most often fought.

As the general theory makes clear, freedom of discussion in public affairs serves an important function regardless of whether the political structure of a nation is democratic or not. Every government must have some process for feeding back to it information concerning the attitudes, needs and wishes of its citizens. It must, therefore, afford some degree of freedom at least to some of its citizens, to make known their wants and desires. Indeed in a more formal aspect—as a petition for redress of grievances—this right of communicating to the government in power was one of the earliest forms of political expression. The Magna Carta and the Bill of Rights of 1689, for instance, were promulgated in response to such petitions. In general, the greater the degree of political discussion allowed, the more responsive is the government, the closer is it brought to the will of its people, and the harder must it strive to be worthy of their support.

The crucial point, however, is not that freedom of expression is politically useful, but that it is indispensable to the operation of a democratic form of government. Once one accepts the premise of the Declaration of Independence —that governments derive "their just powers from the consent of the governed"—it follows that the governed must, in order to exercise their right of consent, have full freedom of expression both in forming individual judgments and in forming the common judgment. Together with the argument for freedom of religious belief, this proposition was the one most frequently and most insistently urged in support of freedom of expression.

The proponents of freedom of political expression often addressed themselves to the question whether the people were competent to perform the functions entrusted to them, whether they could acquire sufficient information or possessed sufficient capacity for judgment. The men of the eighteenth century, with their implicit faith in the power of reason and the perfectibility of man, entertained few doubts on this score. Political theorists of the nineteenth and twentieth centuries have been more cautious. And there was some disagreement as to whether the right of political expression could safely be extended to societies which had not reached a certain point in the development of education and culture. But these problems were actually questions concerning the viability of democracy itself. And once a society was committed to democratic procedures, or rather in the process of committing itself, it necessarily embraced the principle of open political discussion.

Balance Between Stability and Change

The traditional doctrine of freedom of expression, finally, embodies a theory of social control. The principle of open discussion is a method of achieving a more adaptable and at the same time more stable community, of maintaining the precarious balance between healthy cleavage and necessary consensus. This may not always have been true, and may not be true of many existing societies. But where men have learned how to function within the law, an open society will be the stronger and more cohesive one.

The reasons supporting this proposition can only be stated here in summary form. In the first place, suppression of discussion makes a rational judgment impossible. In effect it substitutes force for logic. Moreover, coercion of expression is likely to be ineffective. While it may prevent social change, at least for a time, it cannot eradicate thought or belief; nor can it promote loyalty or unity. As Bagehot observed, "Persecution in intellectual countries produces a superficial conformity, but also underneath an intense, incessant, implacable doubt."

Furthermore, suppression promotes inflexibility and stultification, preventing the society from adjusting to changing circumstances or developing new ideas. Any society, and any institution in society, naturally tends toward rigidity. Attitudes and ideas become stereotyped; institutions lose their vitality. The result is mechanical or arbitrary application of outworn principles, mounting grievances unacknowledged, inability to conceive new approaches, and general stagnation. Opposition serves a vital social function in offsetting or ameliorating this normal process of bureaucratic decay.

Again, suppression of expression conceals the real problems confronting a society and diverts public attention from the critical issues. It is likely to result in neglect of the grievances which are the actual basis of the unrest, and thus prevent their correction. For it both hides the extent of opposition and hardens the position of all sides, thus making a rational compromise difficult or impossible. Further, suppression drives opposition underground, leaving those suppressed either apathetic or desperate. It thus saps the vitality of the society or makes resort to force more likely. And finally it weakens and debilitates the majority whose support for the common decision is necessary. For it hinders an intelligent understanding of the reasons for adopting the decision and, as Mill observed, "beliefs not grounded on conviction are likely to give way before the slightest semblance of an argument." In short, suppression of opposition may well mean that when change is finally forced on the community, it will come in more violent and radical form.

The argument that the process of open discussion, far from causing society to fly apart, stimulates forces that lead to greater cohesion, also rests upon the concept of political legitimation. Stated in narrower and perhaps cruder terms, the position is that allowing dissidents to expound their views enables them "to let off steam." The classic example is the Hyde Park meeting where any person is permitted to say anything he wishes to whatever audience he can assemble. This results in a release of energy, a lessening of frustration, and a channeling of resistance into courses consistent with law and order. It operates, in short, as a catharsis throughout the body politic.

The principle of political legitimation, however, is more broadly fundamental. It asserts that persons who have had full freedom to state their position and to persuade others to adopt it will, when the decision goes against them, be more ready to accept the common judgment. They will recognize that they have been treated fairly, in accordance with rational rules for social living. They will feel that they have done all within their power, and will understand that the only remaining alternative is to abandon the ground rules altogether through resort to force, a course of action upon which most individuals in a healthy society are unwilling to embark. In many circumstances, they will retain the opportunity to try again and will hope in the end to persuade a majority to their position. Just as in a judicial proceeding where due process has been observed, they will feel that the resulting decision, even though not to their liking, is the legitimate one.

In dealing with the problem of social control, supporters of free expression likewise emphasize that the issue must be considered in the total context of forces operating to promote or diminish cohesion in a society. By and large, they theorize, a society is more likely to be subject to general inertia than to volatile change. Hence resistance to the political order is unlikely to reach the stage of disorder unless a substantial section of the population is living under seriously adverse or discriminatory conditions. Only a government which consistently fails to relieve valid grievances need fear the outbreak of violent opposition. Thus, given the inertia which so often characterizes a society, freedom of expression, far from causing upheaval, is more properly viewed as a leavening process, facilitating necessary social and political change and keeping a society from stultification and decay.

Moreover, the state retains adequate powers to promote political unity and suppress resort to force. For one thing it shares the right to freedom of expression with its citizens. While there may be some limits on this power, the state is normally in a much better position to obtain information and in a much more authoritative position from which to communicate its official views than the ordinary citizen or group of citizens. More importantly, the state possesses the authority to restrict or compel action. The right with which we are concerned, as already noted, extends only to expression; when the stage of action is reached the great power of the state becomes available for regulation or prohibition. And finally the state has not only the power but the obligation to control the conditions under which freedom of expression can function for the general welfare. This includes not only responsibility for eliminating grievances which may give rise to disorder but also a responsibility for maintaining economic and social conditions under which the ground rules of democracy can operate.

Proponents of the theory acknowledge that the process of full discussion, open to all, involves some risks to the society that practices it. At times there may be substantial delay in the working out of critical problems. There can be no ironclad guarantee that in the end a decision beneficial to society will be reached. The process, by encouraging diversity and dissent, does at times tend to loosen the common bonds that hold society together and may threaten to bring about its dissolution. The answer given is that the stakes are high and that the risks must be run. No society can expect to achieve absolute security. Change is inevitable; the only question is the rate and the method. The theory of freedom of expression offers greater possibilities for rational, orderly adjustment than a system of suppression. Moreover, they urge, as the lesson of experience, that the dangers are usually imaginary; that suppression is invoked more often to the prejudice of the general welfare than for its advancement. To this they add that the risks are the lesser evil, that the alternatives are worse, that the only security worth having is that based on freedom.

Thus, the theory of freedom of expression involves more than a technique for arriving at better social judgments through democratic procedures. It comprehends a vision of society, a faith and a whole way of life. The theory grew out of an age that was awakened and invigorated by the idea of a new society in which man's mind was free, his fate determined by his own powers of reason, and his prospects of creating a rational and enlightened civilization virtually unlimited. It is put forward as a prescription for attaining a creative, progressive, exciting and intellectually robust community. It contemplates a mode of life that, through encouraging toleration, skepticism, reason and initiative, will allow man to realize his full potentialities. It spurns the alternative of a society that is tyrannical, conformist, irrational and stagnant. It is this concept of society that was embodied in the First Amendment.

It is not within the scope of this article to demonstrate the soundness of the traditional theory underlying freedom of expression, or its viability under modern conditions. The writer believes that such a demonstration can be made. But the significant point here is that we as a nation are presently committed to the theory, that alternative principles have no substantial support, and that our system of freedom of expression must be based upon and designed for the realization of the fundamental propositions embodied in the traditional theory.

Emerson's four principles of justification for the First Amendment are: assuring individual self-fulfillment, pursuing the search for truth, securing social and political participation, and maintaining the balance between stability and change. His discussion covers not only the rationale for a principle of free speech, but also many of the traditional philosophical arguments in favor of freedoms of religion, the press, assembly, and petition. Freedom of religion, for example, is viewed both as a critical element of self-fulfillment and as part of the search for truth. The eradication of religious tests for office is an obvious example of an effort to secure broad political participation, and few forces are as disruptive of a political regime as the frustration of a suppressed religious minority. Similarly, a free press is justified as an element of the search for truth, a necessary precondition for political participation, and a safety valve for dissent. Is a free press also a necessary condition for self-fulfillment? To a person for whom reading and writing are part of the path toward self-fulfillment, the answer is "yes."

As was noted earlier, when Justice Douglas was looking for ways to explain the constitutional source for a right to privacy, one of the things on which he focused was the First Amendment. "In *NAACP v. Alabama*, we protected the 'freedom to associate and privacy in one's association,' noting that freedom of association was a peripheral First Amendment right.... In other words, the First Amendment has a penumbra where privacy is protected from governmental intrusion." *Griswold v. Connecticut*, 391 U.S. 145 (1965). This kind of "discovery" of implied rights is, arguably, a natural consequence of the attempt to read the different provisions of the First Amendment as a unified whole. Emerson thought so, explaining the connection later in the essay quoted above:

> There are certain types of conflict between freedom of expression and interests that may be considered predominantly private in character. These may involve one or both of two elements. The first is where the injury to the individual is direct and peculiar to him, rather than one suffered in common with others.... The second is where the interest is an intimate and personal one, embracing an area of privacy from which both the government and one's neighbors ought to be excluded.... [W]hen we are dealing with a question of personal privacy, we are in an area, like that of belief, where the interest involved should receive a paramount measure of protection.

Emerson's attempt to provide a unified theory of the First Amendment, in fact, has been criticized on the grounds that it leads to the discovery (or invention) of new rights not specifically named in the text. Thus the meaning not only of the First Amendment but of the Constitution generally is at stake when we consider how we will go about interpreting the text. In the chapters that follow, we will review some general principles and also examine each of the clauses of the First Amendment in turn.

D. *Some Useful Terms*

In the discussions that follow, there are a number of technical terms that appear repeatedly. The following short definitions are offered to help make it easier to follow the arguments for different approaches to understanding the First Amendment. It is important to realize, however, that the precise meaning and scope of each of the terms below is itself often a matter of dispute and interpretation. What follows, therefore, are less definitions than descriptions of the ways key words and phrases are used to denote concepts that are useful when talking about the First Amendment.

Overbreadth. A law is "overbroad" if it restricts First Amendment speech as well as unprotected speech. The idea is not that such a law was designed to deprive people of their constitutional rights, but that it has that effect nonetheless because it reaches too far. Such a law is unconstitutional by virtue of being insufficiently precise. The basic principle is that it is not permissible to ban protected speech in order to get at unprotected speech.

Chilling effect. Even if a law does not infringe on First Amendment free speech rights, it may nonetheless be unconstitutional because it has the effect of discouraging people from engaging in protected speech out of fear that they might be subject to prosecution. Once again, the issue is that the law is insufficiently precise, but in this case the objection goes beyond the actual reach of the law to the way it is likely to be understood by the public. This is a more subtle form of overbreadth, one that occurs when, for example, the definition of "obscenity" is so vague that a person might not be able to tell whether their book/picture/act is or is not subject to criminal penalties. A law that has a "chilling effect" is hence constitutionally suspect, and potentially unconstitutional (if the effect is sufficiently severe) because it has the effect of preventing protected speech in practice, even if formally it only addresses unprotected speech. This is a form of constitutional analysis unique to the First Amendment. There is no constitutional harm, for example, in drivers failing to drive at the maximum allowable speed on a highway. In no other context is there a principle that laws should not discourage behavior that comes right up to the edge of criminality. But there is perceived to be a constitutional harm when speakers do not have the freedom, in actual practice, to engage in the full range of speech that is protected by the First Amendment.

Expressive conduct and speech plus. "Expressive conduct" refers to actions that communicate a message, but that do so through behavior that does not obviously meet the definition of "speech" as that term is used in the First Amendment. Flag burning, artistic performances, or the wearing of political symbols are all examples of expressive conduct. These are protected against government interference as forms of expression, like pure speech, but the rules for determining whether the government has gone too far are different. "Speech plus" is different from expressive conduct because it refers to a situation in which there is both speech and action, but the two are distinguishable. The classic example of speech plus is picketing. There is the expression of the message on the signs carried by the picketers, but there is also the conduct of walking in front of the entrance to a business. In these situations, courts will distinguish between efforts to suppress the message and efforts to regulate the conduct, a distinction that is impossible where the conduct is, itself, the means of expressing the message.

Secondary effects. This refers to circumstances that are associated with a certain mode of speech but that are not actually caused by the speech itself. The most common example is the regulation of adult entertainment centers on the grounds that such establishments tend to attract crowds, criminal activities, noisy people, etc. Another famous example concerns a law prohibiting young men from burning their draft cards as an act of protest (an example of expressive conduct). That law was found to be intended to prevent the secondary effects of disrupting the selective service process, rather than aimed at the suppression of the protest itself. When a law is justified entirely on the basis of limiting secondary effects, it is not a law "aimed at" suppressing expression, and is therefore more likely to be found constitutional.

Incidental burdens. "Incidental burdens" are the effects that occurs when laws limit the exercise of constitutional rights as a consequence of a more general prohibition. A law which proscribed public assemblies on Sundays, for example, would have an "incidental burden" on Christian practice, just as a law prohibiting public burning has an "incidental effect" on a certain form of political expression. In the context of the Free Exercise Clause, in particular, the question of whether a law should be found unconstitutional based on the incidental burdens that it imposes on religious practice has been hotly debated in recent years. *However*, it is perfectly possible that there could be evidence that persuades a court that a law that purports to impose only incidental burdens on speech was actually designed to suppress speech in the first place. This is what is called a "pretext" case, as in the example of a city hosting a national political convention that conveniently enacts a law prohibiting public burning two weeks before the convention begins, or a prohibition on public assemblies on Sunday enacted by a town that wants to discourage a revival meeting from taking place. In either of these situations, a court would be likely to find that the burdens that had been placed on First Amendment freedoms were not the incidental effects of general prohibitions at all, and therefore would strike down the laws as unconstitutional.

Public forum. Generally speaking, the authority of government is greatest in public areas and least in the most private areas. This is not a matter of a right to privacy, it is a much more fundamental statement about the nature of government. But First Amendment rights, the rights that prevent the government (local, state, or federal) from acting, are *strongest* in the public sphere. They are especially strong in a place that is a "traditional public forum." The theory is that a public forum is the traditional locus for political debate, cultural exchange, and truth-seeking disputation, and is therefore the context in which the need to preserve freedom of thought and communication is greatest. It is also, not coincidentally, the environment in which government is most likely to try to suppress speech in one form or another. Courts have found "traditional public forums" in public streets, parks, shopping centers, and public buildings. So, for example, a 1937 New Jersey law prohibiting the Congress of Industrial Organizations (an umbrella group of industrial unions) from meeting in public buildings was struck down as an unconstitutional restraint on access to a public forum. Some courts have also talked about something called a "quasi-public forum," which is an intermediate case between public and private. There is also something called a "limited public forum." This is a forum that is created for a specific purpose, such as political debate or commercial advertising. The government is permitted to limit access to a limited public forum to the kinds of speech that fit the purpose for which the forum was created in the first place. So if one imagines a limited public forum created to give merchants an opportunity to present their wares (a city trade center, for example), the government would be able to exclude political parties from setting up a display in that space, but not to pick and choose among merchants based on their political affiliation.

Time, place, and manner restrictions. A public forum is not utterly free of state authority; it is only the case that the state may not single out a particular voice or message either for favorable treatment or for suppression. So long as government's regulations are content-neutral, however, there can always be laws governing the "time, place, and manner" in which a public forum is employed for First Amendment purposes. So, for example, a regulation that prohibits sleeping in parks in Washington, D.C., was held to be perfectly constitutional even though it had the effect of preventing protesters from spending the night in a park across from the White House (see *Incidental Burden*, above). Similarly, in 1989 New York could restrict the use of loudspeakers in a rock concert in Central Park (*Ward v. Rock Against Racism*); the U.S. Post Office can ban solicitation (*U.S. v. Kokinda* [1990]); religious groups can be prohibited from proselytizing in airports (*Lee v. International Society for Krishna Consciousness* [1992]); and permits may be required for parades (*Poulos v. New Hampshire* [1953]).

Facial versus "as applied" challenges. A facial challenge to a statute is a claim that a law is unconstitutional as it is written, in all situations. An example of a facially unconstitutional law would be one that criminalized statements critical of government officials. An "as applied" challenge refers to the application of a possibly constitutional law in an unconstitutional manner. An example would be a law against "incitement to riot," and a prosecution under that law brought against a peaceful speaker who was criticizing government officials. In the latter case it is not the law itself, but rather the application of the law to a particular defendant, that is unconstitutional.

Notes

1. Henry Louis Gates, Jr. "War of Words: Critical Race Theory and the First Amendment," in Henry Louis Gates, Jr., Anthony P. Griffin, Donald E. Lively, Robert C. Post, William B. Rubenstein, Nadine Strossen, and Ira Glasser, *Speaking of Race, Speaking of Sex* (New York: New York University Press, 1994), pp. 20–21.

2. John Milton, *Aeropagitica* (New York: Payson & Clark, Ltd., 1927), p. 39.

3. Roger Williams, "Mr. Cotton's Letter Lately Printed, Examined and Answered, 1644" and "The Bloody Tenent, of Persecution, for Cause of Conscience, 1644," in Reuben Aldridge Guild, ed., *Complete Writings of Roger Williams* (Providence, RI: Russell & Russell, 1963), vol. I, p. 392; Samuel L. Caldwell, ed., *Complete Writings of Roger Williams* (Providence, RI: Narragansett Club), vol. III, pp. 3–4.

4. *Virginia Declaration of Rights of 1776*, Article 16.

5. James Madison, "Memorial and Remonstrance" (1785), in Saul K. Padover, ed., *The Complete Madison* (New York: Harper & Bros., 1953), pp. 299–306, 302.

6. James Madison, letter to Edward Livingstone (July 10, 1822), in Marvin Meyers, ed., *The Mind of the Founder: Sources of the Political Thought of James Madison* (Hanover, NH: University Press of New England for Brandeis University Press, 1981), pp. 338–41, 340.

7. Thomas Jefferson, "A Bill for Establishing Religious Freedom" (1779), in Saul K. Padover, ed., *The Complete Jefferson* (New York: Duell, Sloan & Pearce, 1943), pp. 946–47.

8. Thomas Jefferson, "Reply to the Danbury Baptist Association" (letter to Nehemiah Dodge, Ephraim Stephens, and Stephen S. Nelson, A Committee of the Danbury Baptist Association. of the State of Connecticut, January 1, 1802), in H. A. Washington, ed., *The Writings of Thomas Jefferson* (Washington, DC: Taylor and Maury, 1854), vol. VIII, p. 8.

9. "Massachusetts Body of Liberties of 1641 (Liberty 75)," in Daniel R. Coquillette, ed., *Law in Colonial Massachusetts 1630–1800* (Boston: Publications of the Colonial Society of Massachusetts, 1984). The *Body of Liberties of 1641* is considered by scholars to be one of the most important inspirations for the Constitution, and some of the parallels (a due process clause, an equal protection clause, rights of free speech, conscience, and assembly) are quite striking. (See Donald Lutz, *The Origins of American Constitutionalism* (Baton Rouge: Louisiana State University Press, 1988), pp. 32–33. The *Body of Liberties* is sometimes confused with a set of laws proposed by the Rev. John Cotton but never adopted. These proposed laws, collected under the title *Moses, His Judicials*, were published in London by William Aspenwall in 1641. For many years, historians believed that Cotton's draft—which was much more theologically grounded than the *Body of Liberties of 1641*—was the real thing, leading to an unwarranted assumption that Puritan governance was essentially theocratic. Cotton, "An Abstract of the Lawes of New England, as they are now established," in Peter Force, ed., *Tracts and Other Papers Relating Princially to the Origin, Settlement, and Progress of the Colonies in North America* (Washington, DC: Peter Force, 1844) vol. III, pp. 59 et. seq.

10. "House Debate, 8 June," *Annals of Congress*, vol. I, pp. 434–36, in Philip B. Kurland and Ralph Lerner, eds., *The Founders' Constitution* (Chicago: University of Chicago Press, 1987), vol. V, p. 128.

11. Thomas Tucker, August 17, 1789, in David J. Currie, *The First Freedoms: Church and State in America to the Passage of the First Amendment* (New York: Oxford University Press, 1986), p. 204.

12. James Madison, *The Debates in the Federal Convention of 1787 Which Framed the Constitution of the United States of America* (New York: Prometheus Books, 1997), p. 456.

13. Thomas Jefferson, letter to James Madison (March 15, 1789), in Julian P. Boyd, ed., *The Papers of Thomas Jefferson* (Princeton: Princeton University Press, 1950), vol. XV, p. 660; "Draft of a Fundamental Constitution for the Commonwealth of Virginia," (1786, published as appendix to "Notes on Virginia"), in Saul K. Padover, ed., *The Complete Jefferson* (New York: Duell, Sloan & Pearce, 1943), pp. 110, 119.

14. James Wilson, "Speech at the Pennsylvania Ratifying Convention" (1787), in Leonard W. Levy, *Freedom of the Press From Zenger to Jefferson* (New York: Bobbs-Merrill, 1966), p. 130.

15. Benjamin Franklin, "An Account of the Supreme Court of Judicature of the State of Pennsylvania," (article in the *Pennsylvania Gazette*, September 12, 1789), in Leonard W. Levy, *Freedom of the Press From Zenger to Jefferson* (New York: Bobbs-Merrill, 1966), p. 156.

16. James Madison, "Report of the Committee" (1799), in Marvin Meyers, ed., *The Mind of the Founder: Sources of the Political Thought of James Madison* (Hanover, NH: University Press of New England for Brandeis University Press, 1981), pp. 329–31.

17. Thomas Jefferson, letter to Thomas McKean (February 19, 1803), "Second Inaugural Address," in Paul Leicester Ford, ed., *The Works of Thomas Jefferson* (New York: G.P. Putnam and Sons, 1905), pp. 451–52.

18. William Blackstone, *Commentaries on the Laws of England* (1765) (Chicago: University of Chicago Press, 1979), vol. I, pp. 138–39.

19. Philip B. Kurland and Ralph Lerner, *The Founders' Constitution* (Chicago: University of Chicago Press, 1987), vol. V, p. 129.

II. "...Abridging the Freedom of Speech": From Clear and Present Danger to the Categorical Approach

A. *Libel and the Meaning of Sedition*

In chapter 1, it was observed that a literal reading of the Free Speech Clause is impossible. To take one example that was dear to the hearts of eighteenth-century gentlemen, no one would seriously argue that the First Amendment prevent states from punishing libel. The problem becomes filling in the meaning of the term "libel." In English common law, libel meant simply saying things that might injure the reputation of another. Since gentlemen and ladies were the class of persons most invested in the protection of their reputations, and most able to demonstrate pecuniary losses as a result of injuries to those reputations, libel was a peculiarly class-bound offense. There was also a category of "seditious libel," statements injurious to the reputations of the Crown or Parliament rather than an individual. Blackstone explained that libel actions could be prosecuted by the government in criminal proceedings, as well as in private lawsuits for damages, on the theory that "the direct tendency of these libels is the breach of the public peace by stirring up the objects of them to revenge, and perhaps to bloodshed." (The term "bloodshed" refers primarily to the risk of duels rather than rebellion.) In a criminal prosecution for either personal or seditious libel, the truth of the statements at issue would be no defense. "[I]t is immaterial, with respect to the essence of a libel, whether the matter of it be true or false, since the provocation, and not the falsity, is the thing to be punished criminally." Blackstone did recognize truth as a defense, however, in a civil lawsuit, "for, if the charge be true, the plaintiff has received no private injury...whatever offence it may be against the public peace."[1]

The definition of criminal libel, and its limits, was among the most hotly contested free speech issues in the early years of the Republic. Seventeenth-century writers from John Locke to Roger Williams took it for granted that statements questioning the legitimacy of the civil government could be criminally punished. It was only in the 1700s that Whig writers in England began to promote the idea that the government's power to suppress seditious speech reached too far. *Cato's Letters* was the name of a collection of essays, written by Thomas Gordon and John Trenchard, that first appeared in London newspapers between 1720 and 1723 and were later reprinted many times and were widely read in America. The most famous essay was "Of Freedom of Speech: That the same is inseparable from Public Liberty." Free speech, wrote Cato, was "the Right of every Man, as far as by it he does not hurt and controul the Right of another." In "An Enquiry Into the Nature and Effects of Liberty," the writer explained that liberty depended in the first instance on freedom of thought. "True and impartial liberty is...the right of every man to pursue the natural, reasonable, and religious dictates of his own mind; to think what he will, and act as he thinks, provided he acts not to the prejudice of another." As for criticisms of the government, "Only the wicked Governors of Men dread what is said of them." "A libel is not the less a libel for being true.... There are some Truths not fit to be told; where, for example, the discovery of a final fault may do mischief.... But this doctrine only holds true as to private and personal failings; and it is quite otherwise when the Crimes of Men come to affect the publick."[2] This distinction pointed toward a conception of truth as a defense, since a good governor could only be libeled by a falsehood, and accurate statements criticizing a bad governor would benefit the state by checking his actions. "Publick truths ought never to be kept secrets.... Every man ought to know what it concerns all to know. Now, nothing upon earth is of a more universal nature than government; and every private man upon earth has a concern in it."[3] In addition, a bad governor lacked the virtues of a true magistrate and so did not deserve the law's protection. As for the danger of disorder, Cato argued that the state was far more threatened by suppression and the risk of tyranny than by the opinions that accusations against its representatives might encourage.

In America, *Cato's Letters* were first published by Benjamin Franklin, and later republished in John Zenger's *New-York Weekly Journal*. Zenger was a prominent critic of Royal Governor Cosby and had founded his journal in 1733 as a vehicle for criticizing the administration and the conservative, royalist political faction that it represented. Chief among the writers for Zenger's journal was James Alexander, who wrote essays throughout the 1730s extending the arguments of the English Whigs in the American context and challenging the authority of Governor Cosby. Alexander and his political ally William Smith were Zenger's original counsel, but the judge, appointed by Cosby, summarily disbarred them. Instead, Zenger was represented by an out-of-towner, a Pennsylvania lawyer named Andrew Hamilton who was the most famous trial lawyer in the colonies. Hamilton attempted a daring tactic; he denied none of the facts of the case, but appealed eloquently to the jury to simply ignore the law and find Zenger innocent on the grounds that truthful criticisms of a political figure ought not to be the subjects of criminal punishment.

Hamilton won the case, but the legal significance of the trial itself was not great. The law did not change; in fact, Hamilton made no effort to argue that the law should be changed, only that the jury should refuse to apply it in the case at hand. There is little question that the jury accepted this argument primarily because Governor Cosby was a heartily disliked figure. Thus, apart from some suggestion concerning the relation between judge and jury, the Zenger case had little significance as a legal precedent. As a political precedent, however, it was greatly influential. James Alexander wrote a narrative description of the trial that was printed and reprinted, and a public perception grew that a basic principle had been established. This principle received legal recognition in the context of the most important discussion of free speech and sedition in early American history, the controversy surrounding the enactment of the Alien and Sedition Acts of 1798. The laws were enacted by the Federalists, in response to attacks on John Adams's presidency and his pro-British policies. The Alien Act restricted immigration, and the Sedition Act imposed penalties on "false, scandalous writing against the government of the United States," a formulation that implies the acceptance of truth as a defense.

From the beginning, the Acts were controversial, and the arguments that they provoked outline the state of American political theories of free speech at the turn of the century. On the one hand, supporters of the Acts insisted that they were well within the traditional scope of governmental authority. A congressional committee produced a report defending the constitutionality of the acts on the basis of four arguments: 1) that freedom of speech did not mean "a license for every man to publish what he pleases without being liable to punishment"; 2) that laws protecting speech did not cover "scandalous and malicious writing against the government"; 3) that the Sedition Act merely restated the common law already in force; and 4) that the religion clauses of the First Amendment were absolute, while the free speech clause only spoke of laws "abridging"—rather than "respecting"—the freedom of speech, so that the First Amendment created no new rights of free speech, it only prevented Congress from infringing on those rights recognized at common law.

On the other side of the debates were the *Virginia Resolutions* of 1798 and 1799–1800, and the *Kentucky Resolution* of 1798, authored by Madison and Jefferson, respectively. Compared with the common law at issue in *Zenger*, the Sedition Act was singularly progressive; conviction required criminal intent, a jury would make the determination of guilt, and the truth of the statements at issue would, if proved, provide a complete defense. Madison, however, used the issue as an opportunity to restate arguments he had been making since the days when he wrote the first drafts of the First Amendment. In Madison's version, the amendment would have applied to states as well as the federal government, and would have defined the scope of its protections in the broadest possible terms: "[N]o State shall violate the equal rights of conscience, or the freedom of the press." He had lost the argument in 1789, but in the *Virginia Resolutions* he reaffirmed his position in declaring his opposition to the Sedition Act. "[T]his is a power, which more than any other ought to produce universal alarm; because it is levelled against that right of freely examining public characters and measures, and of free communication thereon, which has ever been justly deemed the only effectual guardian of every other right."[4]

Jefferson's objections, however, were limited to his concern for the prerogatives of states against the federal government. As was noted in the previous chapter, when he himself became president he spared no energy in urging state courts to prosecute his Federalist critics for seditious libel. In 1803 he wrote to the governor of Pennsylvania, enclosing a critical newspaper article about his administration and recommended prosecution of the authors.[5] In 1804, New York prosecuted Federalist editor Harry Croswell for writing that Jefferson had paid to have Washington and Adams anonymously denounced. Croswell was convicted under the law (rather than the outcome) of the Zenger case, and on appeal Alexander Hamilton argued that "[t]he liberty of the press consists in the right to publish, with impunity, truth, with good motives, for justifiable ends, though reflecting on government, magistracy, or individuals." *People v. Croswell*, 3 Johns Cas 337, 340 (N.Y. 1804). Although prosecutions of Federalists continued for several years thereafter, from that time forward the basic principle was that the definition of libel permitted truth as a defense.

The fact that "true" statements could not be prosecuted as seditious libel, however, hardly settled the questions that were raised by the conduct of both Federalist and Antifederalist political prosecutions. For one thing, to prove the truth of a matter is often a difficult prospect. And for another, statements of opinion cannot readily be characterized as "true" or "untrue" at all, a problem Madison had commented upon in his *Virginia Resolution*: "[I]t must be obvious to the plainest minds, that opinions, and inferences, and conjectural observations, are not only in many cases inseparable from the facts, but may often be more the objects of the prosecution than the facts themselves...and that opinions and inferences, and conjectural observations, cannot be subjects of that kind of proof which appertains to facts, before a court of law."[6] Moreover, while the redefinition of libel was significant both in itself and as an indicator of a legal philosophy, it was not a matter of First Amendment doctrine insofar as the states were concerned. Throughout the nineteenth and early twentieth centuries states remained free to suppress even "true" speech, and they did so.

From the early 1800s to the Civil War, the issue that dominated free speech debates was the issue that dominated all political discussions: slavery. Southern states enacted laws criminalizing abolitionist speech, and in addition relied on a long tradition of public silence on the subject. In the 1830s, "vigilance committees" began to be formed across the South, with a mandate to look for and stamp out any expression of sentiments that would deny the legitimacy of slave ownership or challenge the order of slave society. The process of suppression was aided by the federal government's prohibitions on sending "incendiary" materials through the mails. In 1835, when a South Carolina mob destroyed a shipment of abolitionist mail, a debate arose over a proposed law that would have barred the delivery of such materials to southern addresses. Ultimately, Congress rejected the proposed law, but throughout the South state laws were passed that contradicted the federal rule, and federal postal authorities cooperated in blocking "incendiary" mail. The same precedent would be relied upon during the Civil War, when the postmaster general used his authority to block delivery of pro-southern mails.

In the North, meanwhile, attempts to suppress abolitionist speech were carried out by private parties. Abolitionists were the targets of violent attacks aimed at silencing their voices. William Lloyd Garrison, in Boston (as abolitionist a city as any in the nation) was publicly beaten, and in southern Illinois Elijah Lovejoy was murdered by a pro-slavery mob. Moreover, a gag rule in Congress prevented the introduction of any bill seeking to abolish the institution of slavery in the years prior to the Civil War. These were largely political rather than legal controversies, but they pointed to the extent to which the idea that public spaces had to be secured for the exercise of free speech—i.e., that government has an affirmative obligation to ensure the conditions of free expression—was not yet an accepted element of American political thought.

The Civil War itself was a period of crisis for free speech, as the Lincoln administration, after months of vituperative attacks from "Copperhead" speakers, newspapers, and organizations, issued orders to limit disloyal speech. In May 1863, Ohio Democrat Clement L. Valladingham was arrested for interfering with recruitment and convicted of treason, pursuant to Lincoln's order suspending the right of habeas corpus. Lincoln justified the conviction by insisting that not only treasonous speech, but even nonsupport of the government in time of war was an act that required response. "The man who stands by and says nothing when the peril of his government is discussed cannot be misunderstood. If not hindered, he is sure to help the enemy...." Stung by criticism of his actions, Lincoln wrote to a friend, "Must I shoot a simple-minded soldier boy who deserts, while I must not touch a hair of a wily agitator who induces him to desert?.... I insist that in such cases [these laws] are constitutional wherever the public safety does require them, as well in places to which they may prevent the rebellion extending, as in those where it may be already prevailing."[7]

In the late nineteenth and the early twentieth century, the two largest areas of government suppression of speech were the beginning of efforts to stamp out "obscenity" and the effort to silence political radicalism, especially in the context of labor organization. The federal Comstock Act of 1873 made it a crime to ship "obscene" materials across state lines. The definition of "obscene" was generally drawn from an 1868 English case, *Regina v. Hicklin* L. R. 3 Q. B. 360 (1868), that covered any words that had a tendency to "deprave or corrupt" any listener, regardless of age or condition. State governments, too, got into the act, passing numerous laws making it a crime to possess or sell or produce materials that fit this very broad definition of "obscenity." In the same period, criminal libel and sedition laws became prevalent once again, this time primarily in response to the challenges of a growing industrial labor movement. The Knights of Labor in the late 1800s and the Industrial Workers of the World (the "Wobblies," forerunners of the Congress of Industrial Organizations) of the early 1900s agitated for laws prohibiting child labor, limiting working hours, regulating working conditions and, above all, granting collective bargaining rights to wide classes of unskilled workers (as opposed to the craft unions of the American Federation of Labor, which focused on highly skilled employees in narrowly defined fields).

These broad movements were closely associated with political radicalism, particularly a uniquely American version of socialism called "syndicalism." In an effort to respond to these political challenges, as well as to serve the interests of financially powerful corporate employers, states passed numerous "antisyndicalism" laws and laws designed to prevent workers from forming unions, holding meetings, picketing, or going on strike. The Industrial Workers of the World, in particular, responded to laws restricting public agitation with tactics that would be seen again in the Free Speech student movements of the 1960s. When a city passed a law prohibiting public speaking, for example, a favorite IWW tactic was to stand on a box and recite the Declaration of Independence until the speaker was arrested. Another speaker would then take the place of the first one, and so on, sometimes until the local jails were full.

As World War I approached, many labor radicals opposed the war as a conflict between the interests of capital, a war begun by the rich but fought by the working classes. The political radicalism of the industrial labor organizations increased the hostility of both the state and federal governments. In 1917 Congress passed the Espionage Act, a close cousin to the Sedition Act of 1798. The Espionage Act, as amended in 1918, made it a crime to attempt to foment insubordination or disloyalty among soldiers or to interfere with recruitment. In addition, twenty states adopted "criminal syndicalism" acts between 1917 and 1920. There were thousands of prosecutions under these laws, both during the war and afterward, motivated by the perceived danger of bolshevism in the aftermath of the Russian Revolution.

To the extent that these suppressions were carried out by state governments, they involved no significant discussion of constitutional issues, for the straightforward reason that the First Amendment had never been ruled to apply to the states at all. The story of free speech as a constitutional doctrine does not begin in earnest until 1919, when the Espionage Act was reviewed by the Supreme Court, and in 1925, for the first time, the First Amendment was held to apply to the states. The historical controversies, however, made clear what the basic questions would be: First, when can government suppress speech, and does that determination depend on the nature of the speech (e.g., libel), or the circumstances of the suppression (e.g., wartime)? Second, is there a general right of access to public spaces, the mails, or printed publications, i.e., a right to be heard that accompanies the right to speak? These two questions—what speech does the First Amendment not reach, and what is the extent of the right to be heard that is associated with the right to speak—run through the cases that define the jurisprudence of Free Speech to this day. To a great extent, the other clauses of the First Amendment—religion, press, petition, assembly—can be thought of as special cases of these two basic questions about the freedom of expression.

B. *The Focus on Circumstances: The "Clear and Present Danger" Test, 1919–1969*

The category of seditious libel was grounded in the idea that such speech had the potential to foment unrest. The suppression of such speech was thus based on an appeal to the public interest in order rather than the private reputations of prominent figures. This was the element that translated "seditious libel" into "sedition," giving rise to doctrinal justifications for punishing politically radical speech. Through the first half of the twentieth century, however, the focus of the analysis increasingly shifted from the speech itself toward the circumstances in which it was uttered. The danger of unrest became the issue requiring proof, rather than the content of the speech. As Justice Holmes put it, "the character of every act depends upon the circumstances in which it is done." Under this approach, otherwise protected speech might be subject to prosecution in special circumstances. The most obvious set of special circumstances, then as now, was war.

The Court's interpretation of free speech began with a set of four cases involving convictions under the Espionage Act in 1918. The first and most famous of these was *Schenck v. United States,* 249 U.S. 47 (1919). Schenck was secretary of the Socialist Party, and in that capacity he produced a mailing urging men eligible for the draft to resist conscription. The leaflet recited a portion of the Thirteenth Amendment (abolishing slavery), and proposed that the conscription act was unconstitutional. "If you do not assert and support your rights," read the text, "you are helping to deny or disparage rights which it is the solemn duty of all citizens and residents of the United States to retain." Up to that time, the scope of the federal government's authority to restrict speech was determined by the *Hicklin* "bad tendency" test for obscenity (discussed earlier). In *Schenck*, Justice Oliver Wendell Holmes Jr. extended the application of the bad tendency test beyond the context of obscenity, stating that the constitutionality of prosecutions under the law was "whether the statements...had a natural tendency to produce the forbidden consequences." In the same opinion, however, Holmes also described another, different approach:

> We admit that in many places and in ordinary times the defendants in saying all that was said in the circular would have been within their constitutional rights. But the character of every act depends upon the circumstances in which it is done. The most stringent protection of free speech would not protect a man in falsely shouting fire in a theatre and causing a panic.... The question in every case is whether the words used are used in such circumstances and are of such a nature as to create a *clear and present danger* that they will bring about the substantive evils that Congress has a right to prevent" (emphasis added).

These comments were dicta (not part of the holding of the case). Holmes was writing for the majority, and the conviction of Schenck was upheld based on the majority's application of the bad tendency test. But Holmes's comments pointed to a very different outcome. After all, it is hardly plausible that a mailed leaflet has the kind of immediate endangering effect of "shouting fire in a theatre and causing a panic." Holmes's new approach, then, had the effect of limiting the authority of government to restrict speech to cases of immediate danger. The other cases from that term involved the conviction of Eugene Debs for speaking against the war in such a way that "[the] natural and intended effect [of his speech] would be to obstruct recruiting," and the conviction of the writer of articles critical of the war for impeding the war effort "by words of persuasion...in quarters where a little breath would be enough to kindle a flame." *Debs v. United States*, 249 U.S. 211 (1919); *Frohwerk v. United States*, 249 U.S. 204 (1919).

By the beginning of the 1919 term, Holmes and Brandeis had concluded that the bad tendency test was wrong. Together, they dissented in three cases considering convictions for seditious speech in that year. *Schaefer v. United States*, 251 U.S. 466 (1919); *Pierce v. United States*, 252 U.S. 239 (1919); *Abrams v. United States*, 250 U.S. 616 (1919). In *Abrams*, the majority upheld the conviction of a member of the Communist Party for the crime of distributing leaflets objecting to the United States' military intervention in Russia (in 1919 American forces landed at Archangel and Murmansk in an effort to overthrow the communist government and reinstate the Tsarist regime), and calling for a general strike. Holmes, writing a dissenting opinion in which Brandeis joined, created one of the most enduring metaphors in the canon of free speech jurisprudence, the "marketplace of ideas":

> Persecution for the expression of opinions seems to me perfectly logical. If you have no doubt of your premises or your power and want a certain result with all your heart you naturally express your wishes in law and sweep away all opposition.... But when men have realized that time has upset many fighting faiths, they may come to believe even more than they believe the very foundations of their own conduct that the ultimate good desired is better reached by free trade in ideas—that the best test of truth is the power of the thought to get itself accepted in the competition of the market, and that truth is the only ground upon which their wishes safely can be carried out. That at any rate is the theory of our Constitution. It is an experiment, as all life is an experiment. Every year if not every day we have to wager our salvation upon some prophecy based upon imperfect knowledge. While that experiment is part of our system I think that we should be eternally vigilant against attempts to check the expression of opinions

that we loathe and believe to be fraught with death, unless they so imminently threaten immediate interference with the lawful and pressing purposes of the law that an immediate check is required to save the country.

In Holmes's conception, the guarantee of free speech is above all an admission that the answers to the most important questions can never be known with certainty, and therefore that the search for truth cannot justify the imposition of orthodoxy on public discourse. This is an interpretation that would connect the Free Speech Clause immediately and directly to the Establishment Clause; in the case of religion, too, there can never be certain knowledge of one true faith, and hence there can never be an adequate justification for the "establishment" of religion by government (see discussion, chapter 5).

In 1925, for the first time, the Court held that the First Amendment had been "incorporated" by the Fourteenth Amendment, and therefore applied to the states. The incorporation of the First Amendment was announced in the course of upholding the conviction of Benjamin Gitlow, a member of the New York state legislature from the Socialist Party. Gitlow published a pamphlet which predicted a future communist revolution. He was charged and convicted under New York's Criminal Anarchy Act of 1902, receiving a sentence of five to ten years in prison. The conviction was upheld by a vote of 7 to 2. Writing for the majority, Justice Edward Sanford responded to Holmes' arguments against the bad tendency approach:

> Such utterances...threaten breaches of the peace and ultimate revolution. And the immediate danger is none the less real and substantial, because the effect of a given utterance cannot be accurately foreseen. The State cannot reasonably be required to measure the danger from every such utterance, in the nice balance of a jeweler's scale. A single revolutionary spark may kindle a fire that, smoldering for a time, may burst into a sweeping and destructive conflagration. *Gitlow v. New York*, 268 U.S. 652 (1925).

Holmes and Brandeis dissented, reiterating their commitment to the "clear and present danger" test. "It is said that this manifesto was more than a theory, that it was an incitement. Every idea is an incitement. It offers itself for belief and if believed it is acted on.... Eloquence may set fire to reason. But whatever may be thought of the redundant discourse before us it had no chance of starting a present conflagration."

Two years later, in *Whitney v. California,* Holmes dissented again, this time when the Court upheld the conviction of a communist under California's antisyndicalism act. Brandeis, concurring with the outcome, made one of the most famous statements against the "bad tendency" test for the suppression of speech. 'Fear of serious injury cannot alone justify suppression of free speech and assembly. Men feared witches and burnt women." Turning to the specific charge at issue, he urged the Court to recognize a distinction between the promulgation of ideas, advocacy, and attempts to promote conduct. "The wide difference between advocacy and incitement, between preparation and attempt, between assembling and conspiracy, must be borne in mind. In order to support a finding of clear and present danger it must be shown either that immediate serious violence was to be expected or was advocated, or that the past conduct furnished reason to believe that such advocacy was then contemplated." *Whitney v. California*, 274 U.S. 357 (1927).

During the 1930s the Court continued to apply the "bad tendency" test, but did so in a way that increasingly limited the power of states to restrict "the liberty to discuss publicly and truthfully...matters of public concern." In the 1940s, under the leadership of Chief Justices Harlan Stone and Fred Vinson (1941–44 and 1946–53, respectively), the "clear and present danger" test was finally formally adopted. Statutes were found to be unconstitutional not only "as applied" but also on facial challenges in cases that often mixed free speech issues with concerns about the free exercise of religion, such as a series of rulings striking down laws that restricted the distribution of religious as well as political literature (e.g., *Cantwell v. Connecticut*, 310 U.S. 296 (1940); *Murdock v. Pennsylvania*, 319 U.S. 105 (1943). See discussion, chapter 4.) One case from this period established the principle that the First Amendment prohibits "compelled speech" as well as compelled silence in the case of a Jehovah's Witness who refused to recite the Pledge of Allegiance. *West Virginia Bd. of Ed. v. Barnette*, 319 U.S. 624 (1943.) In all these cases, the Court found the states' justifications for restricting or compelling speech to be inadequate based on the lack of any immediate danger to safety or public order. "The First Amendment," wrote Justice Stone in 1942, "is not confined to safeguarding freedom of speech and freedom of religion against discriminatory attempts to wipe them out. On the contrary, the Constitution, by virtue of the First and Fourteenth Amendments, has put those freedoms in a *preferred position*." *Jones v. Opelika*, 316 U.S. 584 (1942).

In the 1940s, however, the fear of communism once again became a driving force in American politics. The Smith Act (the "Alien Registration Act of 1940") was the first federal sedition law enacted in peacetime since the Sedition Act of 1798. The Smith Act made it a crime to belong to any organization that advocated the forceful overthrow of the American government, a description designed to target the American Communist

Party. In 1950, Congress passed the McCarren Act (the "Internal Security Act of 1950"), which required all members of the Communist Party to register with the Attorney General. Congressional investigations and hearings were held at which Senator Joseph McCarthy insisted that the government—including the State Department and the Army—were heavily infiltrated by communists. "I have a list," he said over and over, "of 400 known communists in the State Department," a list that was never produced. People were sent to prison for refusing to answer the question, "Are you now or have you ever been a Communist," or, after answering that question in the affirmative, for refusing to name other communists, past and present. Hollywood and the American universities blacklisted hundreds of suspected subversives (or "fellow travelers" of subversives), and even so revered a figure as J. Robert Oppenheimer, "the father of the bomb," was stripped of his security clearance.

In retrospect, there is little question either that there were, in fact, Soviet efforts to place agents in the United States government, or that the vast majority of individuals targeted and often ruined by the investigations were innocent or harmless. The heavy focus on actors and screenwriters may be taken as one indication that the red-hunters' talk of national security masked a deeper fear. Much of the rhetoric and actions of the McCarthy era suggest that the government was engaged in a contest for the soul of the nation. That is, communism as an idea was conceived of as carrying the kind of "bad tendencies" that had marked the earliest definitions of unprotected speech. In fact, there were real security issues at stake—there are disputes to this day about how much the Soviet H-bomb effort may have benefited from stolen secrets—but they were not explored in the highly publicized prosecutions of the Hollywood Eleven, the summary dismissal of teachers in high schools, or the targeting of the volunteers who had fought against the Nazi-backed forces in Spain alongside communist forces as "premature anti-Fascists." To this day, immigrants to the United States are required to swear that they are not communists...including infants from other countries being adopted by American parents. (Parents in international adoptions are also required to swear that their infant children are not homosexuals.)

Against this background, the Supreme Court considered a series of cases involving the convictions of communists under state sedition laws. The first case was *American Communications Ass'n. V. Douds*, 339 U.S. 382 (1950). *Douds* involved a challenge to a provision of a federal labor statute that required union members to file affidavits swearing that they "were not now and had never been" communists. (Similar loyalty oaths were required of schoolteachers.) Justice Vinson used that case to announce the revival of the "clear and present danger" test, but in a form less restrictive than that which Holmes and Brandeis had proposed. "When the effect of a statute or ordinance upon the exercise of the First Amendment freedoms is relatively small and the public interest to be protected is substantial, it is obvious that a rigid test requiring a showing of imminent danger to the security of the Nation is an absurdity." The implication of the formulation is that the clear and present danger test requires balancing the threat to free speech against the public purpose, rather than a strict rule.

The next year, in *Dennis v. United States*, the Court confirmed this understanding. Eugene Dennis and ten other leading members of the American Communist Party were convicted of conspiring to violate the Smith Act. Chief Justice Vinson, for the majority, attempted to make the Smith Act fit into the clear and present danger formula by drawing a series of distinctions. First, he argued that "discussion" was different from "advocacy." "[The Smith Act] is directed at advocacy, not discussion.... Congress did not intend to eradicate the free discussion of political theories, to destroy the traditional rights of Americans to discuss and evaluate ideas without fear of governmental sanction. Rather, Congress was concerned with the very kind of activity in which the evidence showed these petitioners engaged." The absence of any indication that such advocacy was anywhere near achieving its aims was irrelevant to the interpretation of the phrase "clear and present danger." "Obviously, the words cannot mean that before the Government may act, it must wait until the putsch is about to be executed, the plans have been laid and the signal is awaited. If Government is aware that a group aiming at its overthrow is attempting to indoctrinate its members and to commit them to a course whereby they will strike when the leaders feel the circumstances permit, action by the Government is required." *Dennis v. United States*, 341 U.S. 494 (1951).

At the same time, however, Chief Justice Vinson's opinion in *Dennis* also made it clear that something more was required than the kind of fanciful hypothesis ("a single revolutionary spark") that had justified the convictions in *Gitlow* and *Whitney*. The Court instead adopted a standard that had been proposed by Judge (and future Justice) Learned Hand when the case had been before the New York Court of Appeals (that state's highest court): "whether the gravity of the 'evil,' discounted by its improbability, justifies the invasion of free speech as is necessary to avoid the danger." This formulation, wrote Vinson, "is as succinct and inclusive as any other we might devise at this time. It takes into consideration those factors which we deem relevant, and relates their significance. More we cannot expect from words."

Justices Black and Douglas dissented. Justice Black focused on the fact that the convictions were for conspiracy. "These petitioners were not charged with an attempt to overthrow the Government. They were not charged with overt acts of any kind designed to overthrow the Government. They were not even charged with saying anything or writing anything designed to overthrow the Government." The charge of conspiracy, he wrote, essentially meant that the convictions were based on the bare fact of organizing a political party whose later activities would be "to use speech or newspapers and other publications in the future to teach and advocate the forcible overthrow of the Government." This, wrote Black, was "a virulent form of prior restraint." Justice Douglas focused on the majority's distinction between speech and advocacy. "[I]f the books themselves are not outlawed, if they lawfully remain on the library shelves, by what reasoning does their use in a classroom become a crime?.... The Act, as construed, requires the element of intent—that those who teach the creed believe in it. The crime then depends not on what it taught but on who the teacher is. That is to make freedom of speech turn not on *what is said*, but on the *intent* with which it is said. Once we start down that road we enter territory dangerous to the liberty of every citizen." *Dennis v. United States*, 341 U.S. 494 (1951).

In 1957, the Court again reviewed the constitutionality of the Smith Act. In the interim, Justices Warren, Brennan, Harlan, and Whittaker had joined the Court. Despite these changes in personnel, the Court again upheld the statute. In his opinion for the Court, however, Justice Harlan explicitly called for abandoning the clear and present danger test in favor of a balancing test that looked at each situation in terms of the relative weights of government interests and individual liberties. *Yates v. United States*, 354 U.S. 178 (1957). Four years later, the Court heard a trio of cases challenging the Smith Act. In each case the act was upheld, but in each case the rationale and the majority by which it was upheld became increasingly precarious. *Scales v. United States*, 367 U.S. 203 (1961); *Communist Party of the United States v. Subversives Activities Control Board*, 367 U.S. 1 (1961); *Deutch v. United States*, 367 U.S. 456 (1961). In the last case, however, the majority overturned a contempt conviction based on a witness's refusal to answer the questions of the House Un-American Activities Committee.

In 1969 the Court finally did away with the clear and present danger test in *Brandenburg v. Ohio*. This time the speaker was not a communist, but a Klansman. This time, the background to the case was not the fear and hysteria of the McCarthy era, but rather the chaos and upheaval of the late 1960s. And this time, Justices Black and Douglas heard the position that they had taken eighteen years earlier in their *Dennis* dissent adopted as the governing interpretation of the First Amendment. The new standard, after Brandenburg, would be that "the constitutional guarantees of free speech and free press do not permit a State to forbid or proscribe advocacy of the use of force or of law violation except where such advocacy is directed to inciting or producing imminent lawless action and is likely to incite or produce such action."

BRANDENBURG v. OHIO

SUPREME COURT OF THE UNITED STATES

395 U.S. 444 (1969)

PER CURIAM

...The Ohio Criminal Syndicalism Statute was enacted in 1919. From 1917 to 1920, identical or quite similar laws were adopted by 20 States and two territories. In 1927, this Court sustained the constitutionality of California's Criminal Syndicalism Act, Cal. Penal Code, the text of which is quite similar to that of the laws of Ohio. *Whitney v. California*, 274 U.S. 357 (1927). The Court upheld the statute on the ground that, without more, "advocating" violent means to effect political and economic change involves such danger to the security of the State that the State may outlaw it. But Whitney has been thoroughly discredited by later decisions. See *Dennis v. United States*, 341 U.S. 494, at 507 (1951). These later decisions have fashioned the principle that the constitutional guarantees of free speech and free press do not permit a State to forbid or proscribe advocacy of the use of force or of law violation except where such advocacy is directed to inciting or producing imminent lawless action and is likely to incite or produce such action. As we said in *Noto v. United States*, 367 U.S. 290, 297-298 (1961), "the mere abstract teaching...of the moral propriety or even moral necessity for a resort to force and violence, is not the same as preparing a group for violent action and steeling it to such action." A statute which fails to draw this distinction impermissibly intrudes upon the freedoms guaranteed by the First and Fourteenth Amendments. It sweeps within its condemnation speech which our Constitution has immunized from governmental control.

Measured by this test, Ohio's Criminal Syndicalism Act cannot be sustained. The Act punishes persons who "advocate or teach the duty, necessity, or propriety" of violence "as a means of accomplishing industrial or political reform"; or who publish or circulate or display any book or paper containing such advocacy; or who "justify" the commission of violent acts "with intent to exemplify, spread or advocate the propriety of the doctrines of criminal syndicalism"; or who "voluntarily assemble" with a group formed "to teach or advocate the doctrines of criminal syndicalism." Neither the indictment nor the trial judge's instructions to the jury in any way refined the statute's bald definition of the crime in terms of mere advocacy not distinguished from incitement to imminent lawless action.

Accordingly, we are here confronted with a statute which, by its own words and as applied, purports to punish mere advocacy and to forbid, on pain of criminal punishment, assembly with others merely to advocate the described type of action. Such a statute falls within the condemnation of the First and Fourteenth Amendments. The contrary teaching of *Whitney v. California*, supra, cannot be supported, and that decision is therefore overruled.

The end of the clear and present danger test (and the bad tendency test before it) meant the end of a catch-all theory that would permit protected speech to lose its protection based on an appeal to unspecified historical circumstances. The cases had all involved advocacy of political doctrines, but the reasoning—shouting fire in a crowded theater—reached a far greater range of potential applications. The circumstances-based approach did not disappear entirely, however; where "advocacy" produces a likelihood of "imminent lawless action," that advocacy could still be made the subject of criminal prosecution. In addition, there remained a whole range of situations in which, as Justice Douglas put it in his *Brandenburg* concurrence, "speech is brigaded with action." Finally, there remained whole categories of expression that had never been considered the proper subjects of First Amendment protection; after all, the demise of seditious libel did not mean that one had a constitutionally protected right to commit ordinary libel, nor treason, nor fraud, nor blackmail. These questions—what is the dividing line between "speech" and "conduct"? and what categories of speech do not deserve constitutional protection?—define the jurisprudence of the Free Speech Clause after *Brandenburg*.

C. *The Categorical Approach: Fighting Words, Obscenity, and Libel*

Long before the attempts to define the circumstances in which government had the authority to silence speech, it was well recognized that there were certain discrete categories of speech that the First Amendment simply did not reach. For the most part, the definition of these categories was left to traditional common law understandings, so that most of the categories of unprotected speech in 1900 would have been familiar to an Englishman of two or three hundred years earlier. Others, however, were more novel, such as the bad tendency test for "obscenity" devised by an English court in

Regina v. Hicklin and adopted in America. While historically there was a long tradition of banning certain works on the theory that they were morally questionable, the notion that this had to do with sex was a construction of the Victorian era. (By contrast, for example, the Catholic Church's awarding of its imprimatur was most often concerned with theological orthodoxy.)

With the extension of the First Amendment to the states beginning in 1925 (*Gitlow*), however, courts began to wrestle with the problem of defining the limits of these definitions. For one thing, could states or the federal government define new categories of unprotected speech, or were these categories fixed? The same question can be asked about the boundaries of each category of unprotected speech: can they be changed with time, or are they, too, permanently fixed? Finally, even if one can agree on a set of constitutionally permissible categories of unprotected speech, and on the constitutional limits to the definitions of those categories, what are the limitations on states' power to regulate speech within those categories? Each of these questions points to the problem of variation between states' laws and those of the federal government. Certainly it is not the case that all states must have identical laws; whatever the limitations the First Amendment might place on the authority of states to regulate speech, there is no constitutional requirement that states may not regulate *less* speech than is constitutionally permissible. Therefore there cannot be a single template to which every government can be compelled to conform. Instead, what is required is a clear limit, so that courts will be able to determine which, if any, of hundreds of different statutes cross the line into impermissible regulation of free speech. That clear limit, however, requires a "line" that, itself, is based somehow in the First Amendment. What general principles could be articulated that might guide courts in determining the constitutionality of a given state's definition of a category of unprotected speech? Even before the decline of the circumstances-based approach, the Supreme Court had begun to develop a categorical approach that attempted to answer these questions.

In 1942 the Court declared a general principle that is employed to this day to explain the existence of unprotected categories of speech. A Jehovah's Witness named Chaplinsky was convicted under a statute making it a crime to "address any offensive, derisive or annoying word to any other person who is lawfully in any street or other public place, nor call him by any offensive or derisive name, nor make any noise or exclamation in his presence and hearing with intent to deride, offend or annoy him, or to prevent him from pursuing his lawful business or occupation." Chaplinsky had been handing out literature and making speeches in which he described organized religion as "a racket." In response to complaints from local citizens, a city marshal named Bowering warned Chaplinsky to get out of the street, but he refused. The crowd became noisy, and rather than dispel or restrain the crowd, a policeman took Chaplinsky with him to the police station in order to protect him. On the way there, they met the marshal who had earlier warned Chaplinsky to get off the street. At that point, the stories differ. Chaplinsky testified that he asked Bowering to arrest the people who had been harassing him, and that in response the marshal cursed at him, and that at that point Chaplinsky called him a "Fascist." The marshal's testimony was that, without provocation, Chaplinsky called him "a God damned racketeer" and "a damned Fascist," and said that "the whole government of Rochester are Fascists or agents of Fascists." At that point, Chaplinsky was arrested.

In their review of the case, the Supreme Court had to decide whether the law criminalizing "offensive, derisive, or annoying" speech was within the bounds of the First Amendment. Earlier, in another case involving a Jehovah's Witness, Justice Roberts had commented that "[r]esort to epithets or personal abuse is not in any proper sense communication of information or opinion safeguarded by the Constitution." *Cantwell v. Connecticut*, 310 U.S. 296 (1940) (discussed in chapter 6). That was only dictum, however, and did not establish any binding rule. In *Chaplinsky v. State of New Hampshire*, 315 U.S. 568 (1942), the Court formalized the principle that government was free to restrict "well-defined and narrowly limited classes of speech" that are "no essential part of any exposition of ideas, and are of such slight social value as a step to truth that any benefit that may be derived from them is clearly outweighed by the social interest in order and morality." Chief among these classes of speech, according to Justice Murphy's majority opinion, are "fighting words," "those which by their very utterance inflict injury or tend to incite an immediate breach of the peace." "The test is what men of common intelligence would understand would be words likely to cause an average addressee to fight."

CHAPLINSKY v. STATE OF NEW HAMPSHIRE

315 U.S. 568 (1942)

JUSTICE MURPHY delivered the opinion of the Court.

It is now clear that "Freedom of speech and freedom of the press, which are protected by the First Amendment from infringement by Congress, are among the fundamental personal rights and liberties which are protected by the Fourteenth

Amendment from invasion by state action." Freedom of worship is similarly sheltered. Appellant assails the statute as a violation of all three freedoms, speech, press and worship, but only an attack on the basis of free speech is warranted. The spoken, not the written, word is involved. And we cannot conceive that cursing a public officer is the exercise of religion in any sense of the term. But even if the activities of the appellant which preceded the incident could be viewed as religious in character, and therefore entitled to the protection of the Fourteenth Amendment, they would not cloak him with immunity from the legal consequences for concomitant acts committed in violation of a valid criminal statute. We turn, therefore, to an examination of the statute itself.

Allowing the broadest scope to the language and purpose of the Fourteenth Amendment, it is well understood that the right of free speech is not absolute at all times and under all circumstances. There are certain well-defined and narrowly limited classes of speech, the prevention and punishment of which has never been thought to raise any Constitutional problem. These include the lewd and obscene, the profane, the libelous, and the insulting or "fighting" words—those which by their very utterance inflict injury or tend to incite an immediate breach of the peace. It has been well observed that such utterances are no essential part of any exposition of ideas, and are of such slight social value as a step to truth that any benefit that may be derived from them is clearly outweighed by the social interest in order and morality. Resort to epithets or personal abuse is not in any proper sense communication of information or opinion safeguarded by the Constitution, and its punishment as a criminal act would raise no question under that instrument.

The state statute here challenged comes to us authoritatively construed by the highest court of New Hampshire. It has two provisions—the first relates to words or names addressed to another in a public place; the second refers to noises and exclamations. The court said: "The two provisions are distinct. One may stand separately from the other. Assuming, without holding, that the second were unconstitutional, the first could stand if constitutional." We accept that construction of severability and limit our consideration to the first provision of the statute. On the authority of its earlier decisions, the state court declared that the statute's purpose was to preserve the public peace, no words being "forbidden except such as have a direct tendency to cause acts of violence by the person to whom, individually, the remark is addressed." It was further said: "The word 'offensive' is not to be defined in terms of what a particular addressee thinks...."

The test is what men of common intelligence would understand would be words likely to cause an average addressee to fight.... The English language has a number of words and expressions which by general consent are "fighting words" when said without a disarming smile.... Such words, as ordinary men know, are likely to cause a fight. So are threatening, profane or obscene revilings. Derisive and annoying words can be taken as coming within the purview of the statute as heretofore interpreted only when they have this characteristic of plainly tending to excite the addressee to a breach of the peace.... The statute, as construed, does no more than prohibit the face-to-face words plainly likely to cause a breach of the peace by the addressee, words whose speaking constitute a breach of the peace by the speaker—including "classical fighting words," words in current use less "classical" but equally likely to cause violence, and other disorderly words, including profanity, obscenity and threats."

We are unable to say that the limited scope of the statute as thus construed contravenes the constitutional right of free expression. It is a statute narrowly drawn and limited to define and punish specific conduct lying within the domain of state power, the use in a public place of words likely to cause a breach of the peace.... This conclusion necessarily disposes of appellant's contention that the statute is so vague and indefinite as to render a conviction thereunder a violation of due process. A statute punishing verbal acts, carefully drawn so as not unduly to impair liberty of expression, is not too vague for a criminal law.

Nor can we say that the application of the statute to the facts disclosed by the record substantially or unreasonably impinges upon the privilege of free speech. Argument is unnecessary to demonstrate that the appellations "damn racketeer" and "damn Fascist" are epithets likely to provoke the average person to retaliation, and thereby cause a breach of the peace.

The refusal of the state court to admit evidence of provocation and evidence bearing on the truth or falsity of the utterances is open to no Constitutional objection. Whether the facts sought to be proved by such evidence constitute a defense to the charge or may be shown in mitigation are questions for the state court to determine. Our function is fulfilled by a determination that the challenged statute, on its face and as applied, does not contravene the Fourteenth Amendment.

The specific category of unprotected speech defined in *Chaplinsky*, fighting words, has had a checkered history. *Chaplinsky* has never been formally overruled—it was cited with apparent approval in *R. A. V. v. City of St. Paul, Minnesota* (discussed in chapter 3) in 1992—but at a minimum its breadth was significantly diminished by *Brandenburg*, so that punishable fighting words must be not only those commonly understood to be likely to cause an average person to fight, but rather words that, uttered in context, presented an "imminent danger" of fighting. Thus fighting words appear more in the surviving vestiges of the circumstances-based test for permissible suppression of speech rather than as a distinct content category. Prior to *Brandenburg*, moreover, the test was most often applied to uphold convictions for talking back to police officers, a narrow and specific situation, and one in which the justifying rationale for the category is arguably the weakest (presumably, the average police officer is expected to be less rather than more likely than the average citizen to respond to words by fighting).

The underlying principle of *Chaplinsky* was not specifically about fighting words; rather, it was the proposition that classes of unprotected speech are unprotected because "they are no essential part of any exposition of ideas, and are of such slight social value as a step to truth that any benefit that may be derived from them is clearly outweighed by the social interest in order and morality." That proposition propels the search for truth to the forefront of First Amendment values, and embraces the model of a "marketplace of ideas" that was first proposed by Oliver Wendell Holmes Jr. in his dissenting opinion in *Abrams*. If the justifying principle for permitting the greatest possible range of speech was that the search for truth had no fixed answers, then it followed conversely that the one sensible argument for excluding speech would be that it did not contribute to that process. The formulation of *Chaplinsky* was picked up in 1957 when the Supreme Court revisited the question of what kinds of expression could be suppressed as "obscene." In *Roth v. United States*, heard with a companion case, *Alberts v. California*, 354 U.S. 476 (1957), Justice Brennan for the majority (Black, Douglas, and Harlan, dissenting), abandoned the nearly infinitely elastic *Hicklin* "bad tendency" test in favor of a standard drawn directly from *Chaplinsky*:

> All ideas having even the slightest redeeming importance—unorthodox ideas, controversial ideas, even ideas hateful to the prevailing climate of opinion—have the full protection of the guaranties, unless excludable because they encroach upon the limited area of more important interests. But implicit in the history of the First Amendment is the rejection of obscenity as utterly without redeeming social importance. This rejection for that reason is mirrored in the universal judgment that obscenity should be restrained, reflected in the international agreement of over 50 nations, in the laws of all of the 48 states, and in the 20 obscenity laws enacted by the Congress from 1842 to 1956. This is the same judgment expressed by this Court in *Chaplinsky v. New Hampshire*.

From the outset, then, the categorical approach to content based restrictions on speech was grounded in the claim that a single philosophical principle underlay each of the proscribable categories, and that the reach of those categories would be limited by the extent to which that principle could be invoked.

A third important category of proscribable speech that was developed prior to *Brandenburg* was a special case of libel. Joseph Beauharnais was the president of the White Circle League, a racist organization in Illinois. In January 1950, he arranged for volunteers to pass out pamphlets on the streets of Chicago calling for white citizens to resist "the further encroachment, harassment and invasion of white people, their property, neighborhoods and persons, by the Negro..." Below was a call for "One million self respecting white people in Chicago to unite," with the statement added that "[i]f persuasion and the need to prevent the white race from becoming mongrelized by the negro will not unite us, then the aggressions...rapes, robberies, knives, guns and marijuana of the negro, surely will." Other, similar language followed, and attached to the pamphlet was an application for membership in Beauharnais' organization. He was convicted of violating a Chicago municipal ordinance that prohibited the sale or distribution of any publication which "portrays depravity, criminality, unchastity, or lack of virtue of a class of citizens, of any race, color, creed or religion which said publication or exhibition exposes the citizens of any race, color, creed or religion to contempt, derision, or obloquy or which is productive of breach of the peace or riots." The penalty was a fine of $200, which Beauharnais appealed all the way to the Supreme Court.

In reading the excerpt below, modern readers should remember that the phrase "race riots" did not refer to the kind of violence that erupted in African-American urban neighborhoods in the "long hot summer" of 1968 or in Los Angeles in 1992 following the verdict in the Rodney King trial. In the early 1950s, "race riots" referred to the long-established tradition of attacks by gangs of armed whites, often aided by police deputies, against African-American neighborhoods. In 1921, a mob estimated at 10,000 invaded an African-American neighborhood in Tulsa, Oklahoma, killing more than forty people and destroying thirty-five blocks of the city. The events in East St. Louis, Chicago, and Cicero referred to in the *Beauharnais* opinion were of a lesser scale, but were equally violent.

The decision was 5 to 4, with Justices Black, Douglas, Reed, and Jackson dissenting. Justice Frankfurter, ever the opponent of absolutist readings of constitutional rights, wrote the opinion.

BEAUHARNAIS v. ILLINOIS

SUPREME COURT OF THE UNITED STATES

343 U.S. 250 (1951)

JUSTICE FRANKFURTER delivered the opinion of the Court.

> Libel of an individual was a common-law crime, and thus criminal in the colonies. Indeed, at common law, truth or good motives was no defense. In the first decades after the adoption of the Constitution, this was changed by judicial decision, statute or constitution in most States, but nowhere was there any suggestion that the crime of libel be abolished. Today, every American jurisdiction—the forty-eight States, the District of Columbia, Alaska, Hawaii and Puerto Rico—punish libels directed at individuals. "There are certain well-defined and narrowly limited classes of speech, the prevention and punishment of which have never been thought to raise any Constitutional problem. These include the lewd and obscene, the profane, the libelous, and the insulting or 'fighting'

words—those which by their very utterance inflict injury or tend to incite an immediate breach of the peace. It has been well observed that such utterances are no essential part of any exposition of ideas, and are of such slight social value as a step to truth that any benefit that may be derived from them is clearly outweighed by the social interest in order and morality. Resort to epithets or personal abuse is not in any proper sense communication of information or opinion safeguarded by the Constitution, and its punishment as a criminal act would raise no question under that instrument." Such were the views of a unanimous Court in *Chaplinsky v. New Hampshire.*

No one will gainsay that it is libelous falsely to charge another with being a rapist, robber, carrier of knives and guns, and user of marijuana. The precise question before us, then, is whether the protection of "liberty" in the Due Process Clause of the Fourteenth Amendment prevents a State from punishing such libels—as criminal libel has been defined, limited and constitutionally recognized time out of mind—directed at designated collectivities and flagrantly disseminated. There is even authority, however dubious, that such utterances were also crimes at common law. It is certainly clear that some American jurisdictions have sanctioned their punishment under ordinary criminal libel statutes. We cannot say, however, that the question is concluded by history and practice. But if an utterance directed at an individual may be the object of criminal sanctions, we cannot deny to a State power to punish the same utterance directed at a defined group, unless we can say that this is a wilful and purposeless restriction unrelated to the peace and well-being of the State.

Illinois did not have to look beyond her own borders or await the tragic experience of the last three decades to conclude that willful purveyors of falsehood concerning racial and religious groups promote strife and tend powerfully to obstruct the manifold adjustments required for free, ordered life in a metropolitan, polyglot community. From the murder of the abolitionist Lovejoy in 1837 to the Cicero riots of 1951, Illinois has been the scene of exacerbated tension between races, often flaring into violence and destruction. In many of these outbreaks, utterances of the character here in question, so the Illinois legislature could conclude, played a significant part. The law was passed on June 29, 1917, at a time when the State was struggling to assimilate vast numbers of new inhabitants, as yet concentrated in discrete racial or national or religious groups—foreign-born brought to it by the crest of the great wave of immigration, and Negroes attracted by jobs in war plants and the allurements of northern claims. Nine years earlier, in the very city where the legislature sat, what is said to be the first northern race riot had cost the lives of six people, left hundreds of Negroes homeless and shocked citizens into action far beyond the borders of the State. Less than a month before the bill was enacted, East St. Louis had seen a day's rioting, prelude to an outbreak, only four days after the bill became law, so bloody that it led to Congressional investigation. A series of bombings had begun which was to culminate two years later in the awful race riot which held Chicago in its grip for seven days in the summer of 1919. Nor has tension and violence between the groups defined in the statute been limited in Illinois to clashes between whites and Negroes.

In the face of this history...we would deny experience to say that the Illinois legislature was without reason in seeking ways to curb false or malicious defamation of racial and religious groups, made in public places and by means calculated to have a powerful emotional impact on those to whom it was presented. There are limits to the exercise of these liberties [of speech and of the press]. The danger in these times from the coercive activities of those who in the delusion of racial or religious conceit would incite violence and breaches of the peace in order to deprive others of their equal right to the exercise of their liberties, is emphasized by events familiar to all. These and other transgressions of those limits the States appropriately may punish....

It may be argued, and weightily, that this legislation will not help matters; that tension and on occasion violence between racial and religious groups must be traced to causes more deeply embedded in our society than the rantings of modern Know-Nothings. Only those lacking responsible humility will have a confident solution for problems as intractable as the frictions attributable to differences of race, color or religion. This being so, it would be out of bounds for the judiciary to deny the legislature a choice of policy, provided it is not unrelated to the problem and not forbidden by some explicit limitation on the State's power. That the legislative remedy might not in practice mitigate the evil, or might itself raise new problems, would only manifest once more the paradox of reform. It is the price to be paid for the trial-and-error inherent in legislative efforts to deal with obstinate social issues. "The science of government is the most abstruse of all sciences; if, indeed, that can be called a science which has but few fixed principles, and practically consists in little more than the exercise of a sound discretion, applied to the exigencies of the state as they arise. It is the science of experiment." Certainly the Due Process Clause does not require the legislature to be in the vanguard of science—especially sciences as young as human ecology and cultural anthropology.

Long ago this Court recognized that the economic rights of an individual may depend for the effectiveness of their enforcement on rights in the group, even though not formally corporate, to which he belongs. Such group-protection on behalf of the individual may, for all we know, be a need not confined to the part that a trade union plays in effectuating rights abstractly recognized as belonging to its members. It is not within our competence to confirm or deny claims of social scientists as to the dependence of the individual on the position of his racial or religious group in the community. It would, however, be arrant dogmatism, quite outside the scope of our authority in passing on the powers of a State, for us to deny that the Illinois legislature may warrantably believe that a man's job and his educational opportunities and the dignity accorded him may depend as much on the reputation of the racial and religious group to which he willy-nilly belongs, as on his own merits. This being so, we are precluded from saying that speech concededly punishable when immediately directed at individuals cannot be outlawed if directed at groups with whose position and esteem in society the affiliated individual may be inextricably involved.

We are warned that the choice open to the Illinois legislature here may be abused, that the law may be discriminatorily enforced; prohibiting libel of a creed or of a racial group, we are told, is but a step from prohibiting libel of a political party. Every power may be abused, but the possibility of abuse is a poor reason for denying Illinois the power to adopt measures against criminal libels sanctioned by centuries of Anglo-American law. While this Court sits it retains and exercises authority to nullify action which encroaches on freedom of utterance under the guise of punishing libel....

Libelous utterances not being within the area of constitutionally protected speech, it is unnecessary, either for us or for the State courts, to consider the issues behind the phrase "clear and present danger." Certainly no one would contend that obscene speech, for example, may be punished only upon a showing of such circumstances. Libel, as we have seen, is in the same class.

We find no warrant in the Constitution for denying to Illinois the power to pass the law here under attack. But it bears repeating—although it should not—that our finding that the law is not constitutionally objectionable carries no implication of approval of the wisdom of the legislation or of its efficacy. These questions may raise doubts in our minds as well as in others. It is not for us, however, to make the legislative judgment. We are not at liberty to erect those doubts into fundamental law.

Like *Chaplinsky*, *Beauharnais* has never been explicitly overruled, but as in the case of *Chaplinsky* it is an open question whether this case remains good law following *Brandenburg* and, especially, *R. A. V. v. City of St. Paul, Minnesota* (discussed in chapter 3). Justice Frankfurter's opinion raises a great number of issues that remain central to debates over the validity of the categorical approach to this day. Frankfurter's analysis challenges the metaphor of a marketplace of ideas, with its concomitant assumption that "truth" may be found in unexpected places. Frankfurter, instead, insists that we—or our legislatures—are permitted to declare that while we may not know any singular and certain truth, we are quite certain that some ideas are false. "[W]e would deny experience," he wrote in *Beauharnais*, "to say that the Illinois legislature was without reason in seeking ways to curb false or malicious defamation of racial and religious groups," echoing the assurance of Justice Brennan in *Roth* that it was a matter of "universal judgment that obscenity should be restrained."

Justices Frankfurter and Brennan were pointing toward an approach to thinking about the protections of the Free Speech Clause somewhat different from the categorical approach. In its simplest form, the categorical approach involves the delineation of unprotected categories and a universal standard of protection for all other expression. The categories of unprotected expression are sometimes described as not being "speech" at all, as when Justice Rehnquist described the act of flag-burning as "the equivalent of an inarticulate grunt or roar that, it seems fair to say, is most likely to be indulged in not to express any particular idea, but to antagonize others." *Texas v. Johnson*, 491 U.S. 397 (1989) (Rehnquist, C. J., dissenting).

Another approach is to justify the definition of unprotected categories based on their "secondary effects"; that is, not because of the content of the expression itself, but because of the effects that content are expected to produce. It is important to distinguish "secondary effects," exemplified by the *Hicklin* description of a tendency to corrupt an audience, from a "heckler's veto." The latter phrase refers to a situation like the one in *Chaplinsky*, where it is the antagonism of an audience, and the possibility that their reactions will be violent, that is used to justify silencing speech. In that situation, the government is in the position of giving effect to the hecklers' desire to silence the speaker, so that the test for protection will turn on the degree to which the speech in question is unpopular. "The argument amounts to little more than the self-defeating proposition that to avoid physical censorship of one who has not sought to provoke such a response by a hypothetical coterie of the violent and lawless, the States may more appropriately effectuate that censorship themselves." *Cohen v. California*, 403 U.S. 15 (1971). In *Chaplinsky*, the Court tried to avoid this situation by describing fighting words as "epithets" and "face-to-face words," which has been understood to mean that an expression cannot be characterized as fighting words based on public dislike of the idea expressed, but only if it constitutes "a direct personal insult or an invitation to exchange fisticuffs." *Texas v. Johnson*, 491 U.S. 397 (1989). In addition, the First Amendment does not give a speaker the right to deliberately antagonize a crowd. *Terminiello v. Chicago*, 337 U.S. 1 (1949). Within those limits, however, government is required to do everything within its power to protect a speaker against a heckler's veto.

Regardless of the justification, the categorical approach posits the existence of categories of expression that are exceptions to a more general rule protecting "[a]ll ideas...unorthodox ideas, controversial ideas, even ideas hateful to the prevailing climate of opinion"(*Roth*). In other cases, however, the Court and commentators have distinguished between "core speech" and other expression that is more peripheral to the purposes of the Free Exercise Clause. That is, within the broad universe of protected speech, it is argued that some speech is more valued than others. "Core speech" usually is taken to refer, at a minimum, to the advocacy of political ideals. But does the First Amendment extend an equal level of protection to speech that is valued purely for its entertainment value? In addition, "ideas" and "expression" need not be viewed as completely coextensional; may government restrict the way an idea is expressed without infringing on the freedom to express the idea?

The concept of "core" and "peripheral" protected expression is most clearly in play in cases involving expressive conduct. As the example of flag-burning suggests, "expression" has come to be seen as a much broader category than that which is ordinarily understood by the term "speech." It is generally the case that there are, or ought to be, different rules governing the authority of the government to regulate expressive conduct than for regulating "pure speech." There is an entire line of cases, for example, addressing challenges to government's authority to regulate exotic (usually nude) dancing. The Court has never held that such forms of expression are entirely without constitutional protection, but various justices have articulated their sense that this is not "core speech." (See discussion, chapter 3.) These justices are expressing a sense that there is a hierarchy within the universe of protected expression, one that sets a higher value on expression that serves a public, political purpose than on expression that is engaged in for the sake of private entertainment. The contrary philosophy is one that sees the guarantee of free speech as fundamentally a statement about a sphere of privacy into which government may not intrude. The most famous statement of this understanding is the statement by Justice Brandeis that is quoted at the beginning of the Introduction. Thus the way different justices approach the protection of free speech reflects their fundamental understanding of the nature and purpose of the First Amendment generally.

D. *General Principles*

There are some general principles that define the authority of the government to regulate expression. First, the extent of government's authority depends on the setting in which it occurs. Generally speaking, the freedom to express one's self is the greatest in the most public places. This is the idea of a "traditional public forum," which is that the traditional "core" functions of the First Amendment are most at stake in the traditional settings of public discourse—that is, the town square. Holmes did not choose the metaphor of a "marketplace" by coincidence; since before the time of Socrates it has been the tradition that the open market in the city square is the place for the exchange of news, opinions, and ideas. As a result, the authority of government to regulate speech is least where the "forum" of the speech is most public. This produces a kind of a paradox, since in every other area government's authority is traditionally greater in public than in private settings. Leaving aside special categories of unprotected speech, in a purely public setting the government's general police powers are at their zenith, but the scope of expression subject to those powers is almost nil; conversely, in a purely private setting little, if any, speech is protected, but the government's authority is nearly nonexistent. Since the First Amendment is a check on government power, it does little to limit the authority of private parties to restrict speech in private settings. So, on the one hand, the First Amendment does not prevent a homeowner from saying, "You don't talk that way in my house!," but on the other hand the police have no role to play in enforcing that edict.

More important, the First Amendment does not prohibit government from enacting laws to protect private homes against the invasion of unwanted messages. In 1970, the Supreme Court upheld a California law that gave the owners of mailboxes (which are not necessarily the same as owners of homes) the ability to block unwanted solicitations. *Rowan v. Post Office Dept.*, 397 U.S. 728 (1970). The same principle was at work in a decision upholding a ban on sound trucks whose political messages, broadcast from public streets, blared into the homes of area residents. The Court reasoned that a person inside the affected houses "is practically helpless to escape this interference with his privacy by loudspeakers." *Kovacs v. Cooper*, 336 U.S. 77 (1949). In 1951, the Court also upheld a law that prohibited salesmen from entering private property without permission, although that case turned in part on the argument that commercial speech was entitled to less protection than religious or political speech. *Breard v. Alexandria*, 341 U.S. 622 (1951).

1. *Regulation of Speech in a Public Forum*

The comparison between private and public property is at the heart of the development of the public forum doctrine. In 1897, the Supreme Court reviewed a case involving a challenge to a Massachusetts law requiring a permit for "any public address" on public property. Writing for the Massachusetts Supreme Court, future Justice Holmes had upheld the statute, stating that the government's restriction of access to public property "is no more an infringement of rights of a member of the public than for the owner of a private house to forbid it in the house." *Massachusetts v. Davis*, 162 Mass. 510 (1895). The Supreme Court affirmed Holmes's decision in *Massachusetts v. Davis*, 167 U.S. 43 (1897). In 1939, however, Justice Roberts revisited the question in two cases. In the first, the Court overturned a New Jersey law that required a permit for any open air meeting. "Wherever the title of streets and parks may rest, they have immemorially been held in trust for the use of the public and, time out of mind, have been used for purposes of assembly, communicating thoughts between citizens, and discussing public questions. Such use of the streets and public places has, from ancient times, been a part of the privileges, immunities, rights, and liberties of citizens." *Hague v. CIO*, 307 U.S. 496 (1939).

Later in the same term, Roberts explained that this traditional right meant that where government sought to regulate expression in "the streets and public places," the courts should apply a closer form of scrutiny than would otherwise be required. *Schneider v. New Jersey*, 308 U.S. 147 (1939) involved an antilittering ordinance that prohibited the distribution of leaflets. Roberts had no problem with the legislature's desire to prevent littering, but its choice of means was found to be insufficiently narrowly tailored to its ends to satisfy the level of constitutional scrutiny required in a case of this type. "We are of the opinion that the purpose to keep the streets clean and of good appearance is insufficient to justify an ordinance which prohibits a person rightfully on a public street from handing literature to one willing to receive it. Any burden imposed on the city authorities in cleaning and caring for the streets as an indirect consequence of such distribution results from the constitutional protection of the freedom of speech and press.... There are obvious methods of preventing littering. Amongst these is the punishment of those who actually throw papers on the street." In the 1960s, legislatures seeking to curtail the activity of civil rights organizers enacted laws prohibiting the distribution of leaflets. These laws were held to be unconstitutional as applied to the steps of a state capitol building, the streets surrounding a state capitol, and the sidewalk in front of a courthouse. *Edwards v. South Carolina*, 371 U.S. 229 (1963); *Cox v. Louisiana*, 379 U.S. 536 (1965); *Cox v. Louisiana*, 379 U.S. 559 (1965).

Even in a traditional public forum, it is not the case that government has no authority to regulate expression. State and local authorities, as well as the federal government, are always free to impose "time, place and manner" restrictions so long as these restrictions are "content neutral." Each of these phrases requires some explanation. "Time, place, and manner" restrictions refer to rules limiting the means by which a message is expressed, rather than the message itself. Classic examples include bans on the use of sound trucks, noise restrictions that limit the volume of music at outdoor concerts, and rules prohibiting overnight stays in public parks. *Kovacs v. Cooper*; *Ward v. Rock Against Racism*, 491 U.S. 781 (1989); and *Clark v. Community for Creative Non-Violence*, 468 U.S. 288 (1984). These laws were all upheld because they were not in any way directed at the particular speakers or message that was at issue in the particular cases, but rather were generally applicable rules designed to promote legitimate goals unrelated to the suppression of expression.

"Content neutrality" means that these rules must not distinguish between one kind of expression and another based on its underlying message or subject matter. In 1972, the Court heard a case challenging a law that banned picketing within 150 feet of a school building "except the peaceful picketing of any school involved in a labor dispute." The law was challenged by a postal employee who had been conducting a solitary vigil outside a Chicago high school carrying a sign accusing the school of having a "black quota" for its students. Justice Marshall, writing for the majority, found the law's focus on a particular content area to be impermissible. "The operative distinction is the message on a picket sign. But, above all else, the First Amendment means that government has no power to restrict expression because of its message, its ideas, its subject matter, or its content.... In this case, the ordinance itself describes impermissible picketing not in terms of time, place and manner, but in terms of subject matter.... If peaceful labor picketing is permitted, there is no justification for prohibiting all nonlabor picketing, both peaceful and nonpeaceful." *Chicago Police Dept. v. Mosley*, 408 U.S. 92 (1972).

The Court in *Mosley* focused on the principle that for the government to distinguish between speech on the basis of content violated not the First Amendment alone, but also the Equal Protection Clause of the Fourteenth Amendment. "[U]nder the Equal Protection Clause, Chicago may not maintain that other picketing disrupts the school unless that picketing is clearly more disruptive than the picketing Chicago already permits. If peaceful labor picketing is permitted, there is no justification for prohibiting all nonlabor picketing, both peaceful and nonpeaceful." A similar result was reached in *Carey v. Brown*, 447 U.S. 455 (1980), striking down a law prohibiting picketing of residences except those that were "used as a place of business...involved in a labor dispute." The reliance on the Equal Protection Clause challenges the justification for the hierarchical approach that treats some protected speech as more protected than others. Nonetheless, the language of equal protection continues to appear in Court opinions, suggesting an unresolved tension at the very heart of free speech doctrines. (See discussion, chapter 10.)

In the 1960s and 1970s, the issues that provided the context for these discussions were labor activism or antiwar protests. In the 1990s, the issue that challenged the Court to define the precise limits of the state's power to protect the order of the streets was raised by anti-abortion activism.

These were not cases that involved consideration of secondary effects, but rather the belief that the primary effects of expression were harmful. The source of the challenge was the disruptive and frequently violent tactics that were embraced by the anti-abortion movement during this period. In response to these activities, states and localities enacted statutes designed to protect doctors, clinics, and patients from harassment. In 1988, the Township of Brookfield, Wisconsin, responded to the situation of one of its citizens, a doctor who performed abortions among other medical services. Anti-abortion protesters had for months made a practice of gathering on the sidewalk outside Dr. Frisby's house chanting slogans, blocking his driveway, and picketing. Death threats that named the doctor, his wife, and their children were also delivered to the house. After several months of this activity, the township enacted a statute prohibiting picketing directly in front of a private residence. The organizations that had sponsored the protests challenged the statute, but the Supreme Court upheld it as constitutional. Justice O'Connor, writing for the majority, had no difficulty in identifying the government's compelling interest in the case. "The state's interest in protecting the well-being, tranquility, and privacy of the home is certainly of the highest order in a free and civilized society." *Frisby v. Schultz*, 487 U.S. 474 (1988).

In 1994, the Court again considered the attempts of a government to control the protests of the anti-abortion movement. *Madsen v. Women's Health Center* involved an attempt by a Florida judge to contain anti-abortion protests in the area of a clinic in Melbourne, Florida, and around the homes of clinic employees. In 1992, a state court judge had granted an injunction prohibiting protesters from blocking access to the clinics, but six months later the judge found that the initial injunction had not been effective:

> The court found that, despite the initial injunction, protesters continued to impede access to the clinic by congregating on the paved portion of the street—Dixie Way—leading up to the clinic, and by marching in front of the clinic's driveways. It found that as vehicles heading toward the clinic slowed to allow the protesters to move out of the way, "sidewalk counselors" would approach and attempt to give the vehicle's occupants antiabortion literature. The number of people congregating varied from a handful to 400, and the noise varied from singing and chanting to the use of loudspeakers and bullhorns.... Doctors and clinic workers, in turn, were not immune even in their homes. Petitioners picketed in front of clinic employees' residences; shouted at passersby; rang the doorbells of neighbors and provided literature identifying the particular clinic employee as a "baby killer." Occasionally, the protesters would confront minor children of clinic employees who were home alone.

The judge therefore ordered a more sweeping set of restrictions that included prohibitions on a list of specific activities: entering the premises of the clinic; blocking access to the clinic; demonstrating within a "buffer zone" thirty-six feet around the clinic property; demonstrating "[d]uring the hours of 7:30 a.m. through noon, on Mondays through Saturdays, during surgical procedures and recovery periods...[by] singing, chanting, whistling, shouting, yelling, use of bullhorns, auto horns, sound amplification equipment or other sounds or images observable to or within earshot of the patients inside the Clinic"; "physically approaching any person seeking the services of the Clinic unless such person indicates a desire to communicate by approaching or by inquiring of the [petitioners]"; demonstrating within three hundred feet of the residence of clinic staff or blocking access to their residences; and harassing or physically abusing patients or clinic staff.

The majority, in an opinion written by Chief Justice Rehnquist, found the injunction to consist of content neutral regulations restricting the expressive uses of a traditional public forum (excluding the restrictions on trespass). "There is no suggestion in this record that Florida law would not equally restrain similar conduct directed at a target having nothing to do with abortion; none of the restrictions imposed by the court were directed at the contents of petitioner's message." Instead of the usual "reasonableness" review for "time, place, and manner" regulations, however, Rehnquist applied a stricter standard on the grounds that an injunction was different from a statute. "There are obvious differences, however, between an injunction and a generally applicable ordinance. Ordinances represent a legislative choice regarding the promotion of particular societal interests. Injunctions, by contrast, are remedies imposed for violations (or threatened violations) of a legislative or judicial decree. Injunctions also carry greater risks of censorship and discriminatory application than do general ordinances.... Accordingly, when evaluating a content-neutral injunction, we think that our standard time, place, and manner analysis is not sufficiently rigorous. We must ask instead whether the challenged provisions of the injunction burden no more speech than necessary to serve a significant government interest." *Madsen v. Women's Health Center*, 512 U.S. 753 (1994).

Applying this standard, the majority upheld certain portions of the injunction (those involving limitations on harassment, noise, and interference with the clinic operations or the peace of private homes, and the portion of the buffer zone restricting activities on public property), but struck down others (those prohibiting displays of images, "physical approach" of persons entering the clinic, and the portion of the buffer zone restricting the use of private property). In each instance, the analysis turned on the question of how much the expression at issue would interfere with the proper functions of the clinic, and how much effort would be required on the part of persons associated with the clinic to avoid that disruption. Thus the restrictions on noise were upheld because "[h]ospitals, after all, are not factories or mines or assembly plants. They are hospitals, where human ailments are treated, where patients and relatives alike...need a restful, uncluttered, relaxing, and helpful atmosphere." By contrast, the restriction on the display of images was struck down. "The only plausible reason a patient would be bothered by "images observable" inside the clinic would be if the patient found the expression contained in such images disagreeable. But it is much easier for the clinic to pull its curtains than for a patient to stop up her ears, and no more is required to avoid seeing placards through the windows of the clinic."

Justice Stevens joined the majority in upholding some provisions of the injunction, but dissented from Chief Justice Rehnquist's announcement of a stricter standard for review of injunctions than of content neutral standards. Justice Scalia wrote a dissenting opinion, in which he was joined by Justices Kennedy and Thomas, arguing that the majority should not have sustained any of the injunction. Scalia argued that the peculiar nature of an injunction meant that such an order could never be content neutral, and that the level of scrutiny should therefore always be more strict than that described in the majority opinion. "When a judge, on the motion of an employer, enjoins picketing at the site of a labor dispute, he enjoins (and he knows he is enjoining) the expression of pro-union views. Such targeting of one or the other side of an ideological dispute cannot readily be achieved in speech-restricting general legislation except by making content the basis of the restriction; it is achieved in speech-restricting injunctions almost invariably." Furthermore, observed Scalia, an injunction was the product of a single judge, often one angered by previous disobedience to his or her orders. "They are the product of individual judges rather than of legislatures—and often of judges who have been chagrined by prior disobedience of their orders. The right to free speech should not lightly be placed within the control of a single man or woman." *Madsen v. Women's Health Center*, 512 U.S. 753 (1994).

In its 2000 term, the Court revisited the issue of government attempts to control violence at clinics that provided abortion services. *Hill v. Colorado*, 530 U.S. 703 (2000). In 1993 the Colorado legislature had enacted a law that made it a crime to block access to a health clinic. In addition, the law also made it a crime "to knowingly approach within eight feet of another person, without that person's consent, for the purpose of passing a leaflet or handbill to, displaying a sign to, or engaging in oral protest, education, or counseling with such other person" in the area in front of a health care facility. Unlike the airport cases, this law limited protected speech in "quintessential public forums." The key question, therefore, was whether the statute was content neutral. The Court found that it was:

> All four of the state court opinions upholding the validity of this statute concluded that it is a content-neutral time, place, and manner regulation. Moreover, they all found support for their analysis in *Ward v. Rock Against Racism*, 491 U.S. 781 (1989). It is therefore appropriate to comment on the "content neutrality" of the statute. As we explained in Ward: "The principal inquiry in determining content neutrality, in speech cases generally and in time, place, or manner cases in particular, is whether the government has adopted a regulation of speech because of disagreement with the message it conveys." The Colorado statute passes that test for three independent reasons. First, it is not a "regulation of speech." Rather, it is a regulation of the places where some speech may occur. Second, it was not adopted "because of disagreement with the message it conveys." This conclusion is supported...the statute's restrictions apply equally to all demonstrators, regardless of viewpoint, and the statutory language makes no reference to the content of the speech. Third, the State's interests in protecting access and privacy, and providing the police with clear guidelines, are unrelated to the content of the demonstrators' speech. As we have repeatedly explained, government regulation of expressive activity is "content neutral" if it is justified without reference to the content of regulated speech. *Hill v. Colorado*, 530 U.S. 703 (2000).

Since the law was determined to be a content neutral time, place, and manner regulation, the appropriate level of scrutiny involved asking whether the law served a legitimate state interest and was not aimed at suppressing expression. The precedent on which the majority relied for this proposition was *Ward v. Rock Against Racism*, upholding a noise ordinance limiting the volume of concerts in Central Park.

The majority found a legitimate state interest by extending the reasoning of *Madsen* and *Frisby*. In those two cases, content neutral regulations of expression in a public forum had been upheld on the grounds that they had the effects of interfering with the legitimate uses of nonpublic facilities (a hospital and a private home, respectively). In *Hill*, the majority extended that reasoning to include a legitimate state interest in preventing interference with the peaceful use of public streets and sidewalks. Justice Stevens explained the state's interest as the vindication of an individual's right to peaceful passage on the public thoroughfares:

> The right to free speech, of course, includes the right to attempt to persuade others to change their views, and may not be curtailed simply because the speaker's message may be offensive to his audience. But the protection afforded to offensive messages does not always embrace offensive speech that is so intrusive that the unwilling audience cannot avoid it.... The right to avoid unwelcome speech has special force in the privacy of the home, and its immediate surroundings, but can also be protected in confrontational settings.... How far may men go in persuasion and communication, and still not violate the right of those whom they would influence? In going to and from work, men have a right to as free a passage without obstruction as the streets afford, consistent with the right of others to enjoy the same privilege. We are a social people, and the accosting by one of another in an inoffensive way and an offer by one to communicate and discuss information with a view to influencing the other's action, are not regarded as aggression or a violation of that other's rights. If, however, the offer is declined, as it may rightfully be, then persistence, importunity, following and dogging, become unjustifiable annoyance and obstruction which is likely soon to savor of intimidation. From all of this the person sought to be influenced has a right to be free.... While the freedom to communicate is substantial, the right of every person 'to be let alone' must be placed in the scales with the right of others to communicate. It is that right, as well as the right of "passage without obstruction," that the Colorado statute legitimately seeks to protect.

The logic of the case follows that of cases upholding laws prohibiting "aggressive panhandling." *Gresham v. Peterson*, 225 F.3d 899 (7th Cir., 2000); *Smith v. City of Ft. Lauderdale*, 177 F.3d 954 (11th Cir., 1999); *Loper v. New York City Police Dept.*, 999 F.2d 699 (2d Cir., 1993).

Justices Scalia and Kennedy authored furious dissenting opinions. Their primary objection, apart from the fact that the case involved the always provocative issue of abortion, was to the provision of the law prohibiting anyone from approaching within eight feet of "an unwilling recipient" in an attempt to offer them a leaflet or "oral protest, education, or counseling." With regard to this part of the statute, Scalia challenged the majority's conclusion of content neutrality:

> The Court asserts that this statute is not content-based for purposes of our First Amendment analysis because it neither (1) discriminates among viewpoints nor (2) places restrictions on "any subject matter that may be discussed by a speaker." But we have never held that the universe of content-based regulations is limited to those two categories, and such a holding would be absurd. Imagine, for instance, special place-and-manner restrictions on all speech except that which "conveys a sense of contentment or happiness." This "happy speech" limitation would not be "viewpoint-based"—citizens would be able to express their joy in equal measure at either the rise or fall of the NASDAQ, at either the success or the failure of the Republican Party—and would not discriminate on the basis of subject matter, since gratification could be expressed about anything at all.... The

> vice of content-based legislation—what renders it deserving of the high standard of strict scrutiny—is not that it is always used for invidious, thought-control purposes, but that it lends itself to use for those purposes. A restriction that operates only on speech that communicates a message of protest, education, or counseling presents exactly this risk. When applied, as it is here, at the entrance to medical facilities, it is a means of impeding speech against abortion. *Hill v. Colorado*, 530 U.S. 703 (2000).

Justice Scalia's fanciful "happy speech" hypothetical aside, his argument points to the problem of defining "content." The majority conceives of content as subject matter. Justice Scalia would include purpose, form ("poetry"), and emotional state. Whether in a different case a majority of the Court would accept that definition is a matter for speculation.

In general, then, the rules for traditional public forums can be summarized as follows: government may regulate the time, place, and manner of expression in a content neutral way, based on the secondary effects of expression. Regulations of this type will be reviewed under a "reasonableness" standard. Any other restriction on expression will be reviewed under a strict scrutiny standard. (See discussion, chapter 1.)

2. Limited Forums

Some cases do not fall neatly onto a scale running from public to private. In modern life, private property does not refer only to individual homes but also to large spaces frequented by the public. Conversely, public property exists not only in the form of open city parks, but also in mailings sent by government agencies, in airports, and on military bases. Are all of these "traditional public forums"?

To deal with these situations, the Court over time developed a new formulation: "limited purpose public forums," or "limited public forums." This is a category somewhere in between public and private. The theory behind this category comes from *Lehman v. City of Shaker Heights* (1974), which upheld a ban on political advertisements in city transit vehicles. The Court in that case found that the inside walls of buses and subway cars were not a public forum, but rather served a more limited and specific purpose. "Here, we have no open spaces, no meeting hall, park, street corner, or other public thoroughfare. Instead, the city is engaged in commerce.... The car card space, although incidental to the provision of public transportation, is a part of the commercial venture.... In these circumstances, the managerial decision to limit car card space to innocuous and less controversial commercial and service oriented advertising does not rise to the dignity of a First Amendment violation. Were we to hold to the contrary, display cases in public hospitals, libraries, office buildings, military compounds, and other public facilities immediately would become Hyde Parks open to every would-be pamphleteer and politician. This the Constitution does not require." The analysis focused both on the purpose for which the forum had been created (here, the operation of a commercial venture), and the circumstances of its operation. "Users [of the transit system] would be subjected to the blare of political propaganda. There could be lurking doubts about favoritism, and sticky administrative problems might arise in parceling out limited space to eager politicians." *Lehman v. City of Shaker Heights*, 418 U.S. 298 (1974).

The same principle was applied to shopping malls in *Pruneyard Shopping Center v. Robins*, 447 U.S. 74 (1980). In 1968, the Court had declared a shopping mall to constitute a public forum. *Amalgamated Food Employees Union v. Logan Valley Plaza*, 391 U.S. 308 (1968) (affirming the right of a labor union to picket a store located in a mall). In two later cases, however, the opposite conclusion had been reached. *Lloyd Corp. v. Tanner*, 407 U.S. 551 (1972); *Hudgens v. NLRB*, 424 U.S. 507 (1976) (the latter case overruling *Amalgamated Food Employees Union*). In *Pruneyard*, finally, the Court suggested that shopping malls might be another example of a "limited public forum." The case involved a California mall owner's attempts to exclude political activists from handing out leaflets on his property. The Court, relying on *Lloyd*, found that the activists had no First Amendment right of access to the mall area, but that they did have such a right under the state constitution (a determination previously reached by the California Supreme Court, which the Supreme Court was bound to follow). However, the mall owners went further. They argued that their own First Amendment rights were at stake because by being compelled to allow the distribution of political literature they were in essence being required to join in the message of those leaflets, a violation of the principle that the First Amendment prohibits compelled speech. (See discussion, chapter 4.) In that context, the Court described the mall owners' concerns as unfounded based on the same circumstances that had been at issue in *Lehman*. "[T]he shopping center by choice of its owner is not limited to the personal use of appellants. It is instead a business establishment that is open to the public to come and go as they please. The views expressed by members of the public in passing out pamphlets or seeking signatures for a petition thus will not likely be identified with those of the owner."

Pruneyard is a complicated case, because it turns on the prerogatives of property owners to limit access to their private property, and to the consequent limitations on the powers of government to dictate the use of that property. What is important about *Lehman* and *Pruneyard* for First Amendment purposes is the recognition of a category that is neither purely public nor private. When such "limited forums" are created by the state, rather than by the acts of private property owners, then the importance of such forums, and the principles that govern their regulation, come clearly into focus. In *Perry Education Ass'n. v. Perry Local Educators' Ass'n.*, 460 U.S. 37 (1983), the conclusion was that teachers' mailboxes are not public forums, and therefore could be limited to union mailings sent by the duly elected union but still closed to those sent by a rival union. But the fullest explication of the "limited forum" idea came in *United States v. Kokinda*, 497 U.S. 720 (1990). A group of volunteers affiliated with the Democratic Party set up a table on the sidewalk outside a post office in order to distribute literature and solicit contributions. The sidewalk in question was located entirely on post office property, connecting the parking lot to the entrance of the building. They were arrested for violation of a statute that prohibited solicitations on post office property.

The Court, in an opinion by Justice O'Connor, began by stating the significance of the forum for the evaluation of the statute at issue. "Since *Lehman*, the Court has adopted a forum analysis as a means of determining when the Government's interest in limiting the use of its property to its intended purpose outweighs the interest of those wishing to use the property for other purposes.... [T]he extent to which the Government can control access depends on the nature of the relevant forum." O'Connor concluded that the location and purpose of the sidewalk made it something other than a traditional public forum.

> The postal sidewalk at issue does not have the characteristics of public sidewalks traditionally open to expressive activity. The municipal sidewalk that runs parallel to the road in this case is a public passageway. The Postal Service's sidewalk is not such a thoroughfare. Rather, it leads only from the parking area to the front door of the post office.... [T]he postal sidewalk was constructed solely to provide for the passage of individuals engaged in postal business. The sidewalk leading to the entry of the post office is not the traditional public forum sidewalk." *United States v. Kokinda*, 497 U.S. 720 (1990)

Instead, the sidewalk was a limited forum, and its use could be limited to the purpose (access to the post office) for which it was constructed. This analysis accorded with the outcomes of earlier cases finding that sidewalks in military bases were not public forums (*Greer v. Spock*, 424 U.S. 828

[1976]), in contrast to the sidewalk surrounding the Supreme Court building (*United States v. Grace*, 461 U.S. 171 [1983]) or an ordinary pedestrian sidewalk (*Frisby v. Schultz*, 487 U.S. 474 [1988]). Thus *Kokinda* extended the *Lehman* analysis that focused on the purposes and circumstances of a particular forum to determine its status as "public" or "limited."

In the case of a limited forum, government would be entitled to enact reasonable regulations to prevent disruption of the purpose for which the forum was created. These regulations can be content specific, so long as they are viewpoint neutral. "[C]ontrol over access to a nonpublic forum can be based on subject matter and speaker identity so long as the distinctions drawn are reasonable in light of the purpose served by the forum and are viewpoint neutral." Examples of such acceptable content specific but viewpoint neutral restrictions related to the purpose of the limited forum include limiting a public meeting to discussions of school board business, prohibiting political advocacy organizations from participating in a charity drive in a federal office building while permitting participation by charitable groups, or prohibiting political advocacy within one hundred feet of a polling place. *City of Madison Joint School District v. Wisconsin Employment Relations Commission*, 429 U.S. 167 (1976); *Cornelius v. NAACP Defense and Education Fund*, 473 U.S. 788 (1985); *Burson v. Freeman*, 504 U.S. 191 (1992). In the cases where the government has created a limited forum for the purpose of permitting expressive activity, that activity may nonetheless be limited in accordance with the purpose of the forum based on the identities of the participants. Thus use of a limited forum created in a school may be limited to students. *Widmar v. Vincent*, 454 U.S. 263 (1981).

The specifics of what limitations are and are not permitted in the case of a limited public forum turn on the degree to which those limitations are related to the forum's purpose. *International Society for Krishna Consciousness v. Lee*, 505 U.S. 672 (1992) involved a challenge to a rule prohibiting "continuous or repetitive" solicitation or distribution of literature in airport terminals. The rule was upheld as reasonable on the grounds that such terminals are limited public forums with commercial (i.e., nonexpressive) purposes. "We have on many prior occasions noted the disruptive effect that solicitation may have on business," wrote Chief Justice Rehnquist. "In addition, face-to-face solicitation presents risks of duress that are an appropriate target of regulation." Four justices—Kennedy, Blackmun, Stevens, and Souter—concurred in the result, but felt that the airline terminals should have been considered traditional public forums.

Justice O'Connor concurred in the result, agreeing with the majority that the terminals were not public forums, but writing separately to emphasize her conviction that even in the case of nonpublic fora attempts by the government to restrict expression had to be reviewed with considerable scrutiny. As a result, while O'Connor agreed with the outcome in the case of the statute prohibiting solicitation, she dissented from the conclusion that the law prohibiting distribution of literature was similarly valid. That precise issue was considered later in the same term. This time, a majority formed of Kennedy, Blackmun, Stevens, Souter, and O'Connor concluded that the ban on distribution of literature (without solicitation for money) was unconstitutional. Chief Justice Rehnquist and Justices Scalia, Thomas, and Kennedy dissented. "Leafletting," wrote Rehnquist for the dissenters, "presents risks of congestion similar to those posed by solicitation. It presents, in addition, some risks unique to leafletting. And of course, as with solicitation, these risks must be evaluated against a backdrop of the substantial congestion problem facing the Port Authority and with an eye to the cumulative impact that will result if all groups are permitted terminal access. Viewed in this light, I conclude that the distribution ban, no less than the solicitation ban, is reasonable." *Lee v. International Society for Krishna Consciousness*, 505 U.S. 830 (1992).

The disagreements in the two *Krishna Consciousness* cases gives a hint of the contentiousness and the philosophical stakes involved in the disputes over the proper definition of a "traditional public forum." The basic framework of analysis, however, remains the tripartite scheme described by Chief Justice Rehnquist in the first *Lee* case. "[R]egulation of speech on government property that has traditionally been available for public expression is subject to the highest scrutiny. Such regulations survive only if they are narrowly drawn to achieve a compelling state interest. The second category of public property is the designated public forum, whether of a limited or unlimited character—property that the state has opened for expressive activity by part or all of the public. Regulation of such property is subject to the same limitations as that governing a traditional public forum. Finally, there is all remaining public property. Limitations on expressive activity conducted on this last category of property...need only be reasonable, as long as the regulation is not an effort to suppress the speaker's activity due to disagreement with the speaker's view." *International Society for Krishna Consciousness v. Lee*, 505 U.S. 672 (1992).

Notes

1. William Blackstone, *Commentaries on the Laws of England (1769)*. (Chicago: University of Chicago Press, 1979), vol. IV, p. 150.

2. Thomas Gordon and John Trenchard, "Discourse Upon Libels" (1722), and "Reflections Upon Libeling" (1721), in Ronald Hamowy, ed., *Cato's Letters, or Essays on Liberty, Civil and Religious, and Other Important Subjects* (Indianapolis: Liberty Fund, 1995), vol. I.

3. Thomas Gordon and John Trenchard, "The Right and Capacity of a People to Judge of Government" (1721), in Philip B. Kurland and Ralph Lerner, eds., *The Founders' Constitution* (Chicago: University of Chicago Press, 1987), vol. I, p. 46.

4. James Madison, *Virginia Resolution of 1799–1800*. One of the best places to find the text of this and related documents is the "Avalon" web site maintained by Yale University. http://www.yale.edu/lawweb/avalon/virres.htm.

5. Thomas Jefferson, letter to Thomas McKean (February 19, 1803), in Paul Leicester Ford, ed., *The Works of Thomas Jefferson* (New York: G.P. Putnam and Sons, 1905), pp. 451–52.

6. James Madison, *Virginia Resolution* of 1799–1800, http://www.yale.edu/lawweb/avalon/virres.htm, p. 2.

7. Abraham Lincoln, letter to Erastus Corning (June 12, 1863), in *The Annals of America* (Chicago: Encyclopaedia Britannica, 1968), vol. IX, pp. 426–27.

III. The Categorical Approach Revisited: Libel, Obscenity and Indecency, Sexual Harassment, and Hate Speech

The discussion of public and limited forums in the previous chapter referred to the principles that govern the constitutional limits on government's authority to regulate protected speech. As noted earlier, however, many of the disputes about free speech concern the definition and treatment of those special categories of unprotected speech. These issues arise in one of two ways; either when government tries to enact statutes criminalizing expression, or when the courts—themselves agencies of government—try to determine what kinds of expression can be the basis for recovery in a civil suit. Common examples of the former case include laws criminalizing the sale and distribution of pornography, or laws criminalizing hate speech. The latter category often arises in terms of the definition of libel, or sexual harassment. Courts apply the First Amendment both to review the definitions of categories and to review the application of that definition to a particular case.

The basic question is whether the definition of a category of unprotected speech is "overbroad"—that is, whether expression that must be given First Amendment protection has been included within the definition. The existence of the overbreadth doctrine demonstrates the difference between the Free Speech Clause and other provisions of the Constitution. In ordinary situations, a person who can constitutionally be made subject to a law cannot challenge the law on the grounds that it might be unconstitutional if it were applied to someone else. So, for example, a company cannot challenge an employment regulation on the theory that the same regulation might violate the Religion Clauses if it were applied to a church. But where a challenged law is one regulating speech, the courts will listen to an argument that the law is unconstitutional because it impermissibly regulates protected expression, even if the person bringing the challenge cannot make the case that their own expression, in the particular case, was protected. *Broadrick v. Oklahoma*, 413 U.S. 601 (1973). It is not even necessary that the law will, in fact, result in people suffering punishments for engaging in protected speech. An overbroad regulation of speech can be found to be unconstitutional based on its "chilling effect," the tendency to cause people to refrain from engaging in protected expression for *fear* of prosecution. Writing laws in a way that induces "self-censorship" is treated as another form of government suppression of expression. *Gertz v. Robert Welch, Inc.*, 418 U.S. 323 (1974).

This principle requires lawmakers to define the boundaries of speech categories clearly to avoid even threatening protected speech. "While a sweeping statute, or one incapable of limitation, has the potential to repeatedly chill the exercise of expressive activity by many individuals, the extent of interference of protected speech can be expected to decrease with the declining reach of the regulation." *New York v. Ferber*, 458 U.S. 747 (1982). Thus the combination of overbreadth and chilling effects results in a requirement that the boundaries of unprotected categories of speech be carefully delineated. The overbreadth doctrine, however, is not limitless. To succeed, such a challenge requires that the overbreadth be "substantial." In a dissenting opinion in *Broadrick* that was later adopted as the authoritative statement of the overbreadth principle, Justice Brennan argued that a law should not be found unconstitutional "merely because it is possible to conceive of a single impermissible application." The requirement of substantial overbreadth applies equally to cases involving laws that regulate pure speech and those that regulate expressive conduct (discussed below). Therefore, categories of unprotected speech must be drawn in ways that do not "substantially" chill protected expression.

The difficulty with these rules is that they seem to beg the most important question. What is the source of legislatures' authority to define unprotected categories of speech in the first place, and what are the constitutional principles that determine whether such a category is permissible? Regulation of protected expression, after all, is required to be content neutral; what defines the categories of content that may be singled out consistent with the Free Speech Clause? There is no very clear answer to this question, but some principles do emerge from a review of cases in which the Supreme Court has rejected or upheld categorical definitions of unprotected content. First, the category must be viewpoint neutral. Both in its intent and its effects, the legal definition of a category of unprotected speech must not single out one side of a debate, or one perspective on an issue, for regulation. Second, the justification for the creation or recognition of a category of unprotected expression must be one that falls within the traditional "police" powers of government. To take one easy case, there is no problem with laws criminalizing threats or extortion because those are categories of expression that are uniquely employed to steal, and the prevention of theft is a traditional and legitimate function of government. Beyond these two principles, however, one has to look at the actual treatments of different cases to get a sense of the thinking that goes into this critical area of free speech jurisprudence.

A. Libel

As noted earlier, one of the most traditional categories of unprotected speech is libel. The constitutional limitations on the legal definition of libel turn on a distinction between public and private figures. The law of libel has primarily been explored by the courts in the particular context of the freedom of the press (see discussion, chapter 8). Where the issue is ordinary libel by a private person, the First Amendment requires, above all, preservation of the defense of truth that was first declared in the 1735 *Zenger* case (see chapter 1). In *Gertz v. Robert Welch*, 418 U.S. 323 (1974), a five-member majority concluded that this required not only that truth be available as a defense in a libel action, but that the standards of liability must be drawn in a way that avoids chilling the expression of statements that a person believes, but cannot prove, to be true. As a result, publication of an erroneous statement cannot be the basis of libel. "[P]unishment of error runs the risk of inducing a cautious and restrictive exercise of the constitutionally guaranteed freedoms of speech and press. [The] First Amendment requires that we protect some falsehood in order to protect speech that matters." As a result, states are prohibited from imposing "liability without fault." The law of libel must be written in a way that protects the innocent and unintentionally false statement from becoming the basis for liability. Beyond that limitation, however, states are free to design their libel laws in whatever way they see fit.

B. Obscenity and Privacy

1. Defining Obscenity

As far back as the English *Regina v. Hicklin* case of 1868, there has been a recognition that "obscene" materials define a category of unprotected speech. Defining that category has proved a difficult task. The first attempt was *Roth v. United States*, 354 U.S. 476 (1957) (announced with a companion case, *Alberts v. California*), which involved convictions for violation of a federal law prohibiting the shipment of obscene materials through the mails. Justice Brennan, writing for a six-member majority in *Roth*, (seven in *Alberts*), described the basis for excluding obscenity from the protected categories of speech. "[I]mplicit in the history of the First Amendment is the rejection of obscenity as utterly without redeeming social importance. This rejection...is mirrored in the universal judgment that obscenity should be restrained." Brennan noted, however, that "[s]ex and obscenity are not synonymous." "Obscenity" referred only to materials that dealt with sex in "a manner appealing to prurient interest." The majority therefore rejected the *Hicklin* "tendency to corrupt" standard as overbroad. "The *Hicklin* test, judging obscenity by the effect of isolated passages upon the most susceptible persons, might well encompass material legitimately treating with sex, and so it must be rejected as unconstitutionally restrictive of the freedoms of speech and press." Instead, the Court in *Roth* adopted the following test: "whether to the average person, applying contemporary community standards, the dominant theme of the material taken as a whole appeals to prurient interest."

Justice Douglas, joined by Justice Black, dissented. "The First Amendment, its prohibition in terms absolute, was designed to preclude courts as well as legislatures from weighing the values of speech against silence. The First Amendment puts free speech in the preferred position." Justice Harlan also dissented, arguing that while state suppression of obscenity might be acceptable, the establishment of a federal standard invited censorship. "[I]t seems to me that no overwhelming danger to our freedom to experiment and to gratify our tastes in literature is likely to result from the suppression of a borderline book in one of the States, so long as there is no uniform nation-wide suppression of the book, and so long as other States are free to experiment with the same or bolder books. Quite a different situation is presented, however, where the Federal Government imposes the ban." *Roth v. United States*, 354 U.S. 476 (1957).

The *Roth* standard produced a great deal of criticism and controversy, not least because it seemed to permit government to declare a good number of important erotic artistic and literary works to be obscene. In 1964, Justice Stewart famously ridiculed the *Roth* standard while proposing a somewhat less than precise alternative. "I shall not today attempt further to define the kinds of material I understand to be embraced within that short-hand description; and perhaps I could never succeed in intelligibly doing so. But I know it when I see it, and the motion picture involved in this case is not that." *Jacobellis v. Ohio*, 378 U.S. 184, 195 (1964) (the film in question was of a classic D. H. Lawrence story). In 1966, the Court added a new requirement. Material could be regulated as obscene only if it was not only prurient, but also "utterly without redeeming social value." *Memoirs v. Massachusetts*, 383 U.S. 413 (1966). This was a move that took the original justification for treating obscenity as unprotected and made it the limiting principle of the category as well. The idea that an unprotected category extends no further than its justifying principle emphasizes the extent to which the logic of free speech requires categories of unprotected speech to be defined narrowly.

The *Memoirs* standard resolved little, however. Through the late 1960s and into the early 1970s, obscenity cases took up a disproportionately large amount of the Court's docket. There were more than sixty obscenity cases on the docket in the 1971–72 term, for example. In 1973, the Court created a definition of obscenity that, with minor variations, has remained in place to this day. The catalyst for the new standard was President Nixon's appointment of Chief Justice Warren Burger to the Court in 1969. Burger had long been a critic of the *Roth* standard, but his objection was that it protected too much obscene material against regulation rather than too little. In the process, Burger moved away from the idea that, in the First Amendment context, the justifying principle for describing a category of unprotected speech also describes the limits of that category, as in a 1972 memorandum in which he wrote that "a little 'chill' will do some of the 'pornos' no great harm and...might be good for the country," a phrase reminiscent of Jefferson's comment that "a few prosecutions [for seditious libel] would have a wholesome effect in restoring the integrity of the presses."[1] In *Miller v. California*, over the vehement objections of Justice Brennan, Chief Justice Burger was able to assemble a five-member majority in support of an opinion that pulled the Court away from the libertarianism of *Memoirs* to a standard that gave states and localities more latitude.

Miller was convicted of violating a California statute by distributing obscene materials in the mail. He had sent a mass mailing to advertise four books, which had reached a restaurant in Newport Beach. Chief Justice Burger described the events with palpable indignation:

> The envelope was opened by the manager of the restaurant and his mother.... While the brochures contain some descriptive printed material, primarily they consist of pictures and drawings very explicitly depicting men and women in groups of two or more engaging in a variety of sexual activities, with genitals often prominently displayed. This case involves the application of a State's criminal obscenity statute to a situation in which sexually explicit materials have been thrust by aggressive sales action upon unwilling recipients who had in no way indicated any desire to receive such materials." *Miller v. California*, 415 U.S. 15 (1973).

At trial, the judge instructed the jury that Miller could be found guilty if the materials were obscene according to "the contemporary standards of the State of California."

Chief Justice Burger's approach in *Miller v. California* was to rely on local communities to define obscenity according to their own standards. In this way, neither the most restrictive nor the most liberal standards in the nation would be imposed on communities in which they would be inappropriate. "[O]ur Nation is simply too big and too diverse for this Court to reasonably expect that...standards could be articulated for all 50 States in a single formulation.... It is neither realistic nor constitutionally sound to read the First Amendment as requiring that the people of Maine or Mississippi accept public depiction of conduct found tolerable in Las Vegas, or New York City." As this mixed geographical metaphor demonstrates, the identification of entire states as "communities" casts doubt on the validity of the idea of shared norms and values. The geographical unit employed in *Miller* was the entire State of California, a "community" that today comprises approximately 12 percent of the population of the United States. It is difficult to imagine that the majority would have accepted an argument that a farming community in upstate New York must accept the same standards as the residents of Times Square. Instead, the state-based "community standards" approach appears to be an invocation of principles of federalism. "People in different States vary in their tastes and attitudes, and this diversity is not to be strangled by the absolutism of imposed uniformity." *Miller v. California*, 415 U.S. 15 (1973).

As for the question of literary value, Burger reduced the bar to requiring only that material deemed obscene be shown to lack "serious" value. Thus the new standard would depend on satisfying a three-part test:

> [W]e now confine the permissible scope of such regulation to works which depict or describe sexual conduct. That conduct must be specifically defined by the applicable state law, as written or authoritatively construed. A state offense must also be limited to works which, taken as a whole, appeal to the prurient interest in sex, which portray sexual conduct in a patently offensive way, and which, taken as a whole, do not have serious literary, artistic, political, or scientific value. The basic guidelines for the trier of fact must be: (a) whether "the average person, applying contemporary community standards" would find that the work, taken as a whole, appeals to the prurient interest; (b) whether the work depicts or describes, in a patently offensive way, sexual conduct specifically defined by the applicable state law; and (c) whether the work, taken as a whole, lacks serious literary, artistic, political, or scientific value....

Justices Douglas, Brennan, Stewart, and Marshall dissented from the outcome in *Miller*. Douglas pointed to the danger of local control. "[The new] test would make it possible to ban any paper or any journal or magazine in some benighted place." In addition, Douglas objected to the imposition of any judicially determined standard for obscenity.

> I do not think we, the judges, were ever given the constitutional power to make definitions of obscenity. If it is to be defined, let the people debate and decide by a constitutional amendment what they want to ban as obscene and what standards they want the legislatures and the courts to apply. Perhaps the people will decide that the path towards a mature, integrated society requires that all ideas competing for acceptance must have no censor. Perhaps they will decide otherwise. Whatever the choice, the courts will have some guidelines. Now we have none except our own predilections. *Miller v. California*, 415 U.S. 15 (1973).

Later cases have determined that the state-as-community's standards govern the application of the first two planks of the test for obscenity. "Appeal to prurient interest" is determined in terms of mainstream sexual interests, unless the material in question is published in a way that targets a particular minority. *Mishkin v. New York*, 383 U.S. 502 (1966). The "community" in question is the community of adults, unless children were the "intended recipients" of the materials in question, *Ginsberg v. New York*, 390 U.S. 629 (1968). Aside from these qualifications, the Court appears to use the term "average" to indicate some kind of a mathematical mean. When confronted with the question of choosing among the most and least sensitive members of a community, the Court somewhat confusingly declared that the sensibilities of both should be considered. "Especially sensitive" members of the community may not be the focus of jurors' definition of community standards, but may be included in some aggregated way in the equation. "The community includes all adults who constitute it, and a jury can consider them all in determining relevant community standards." *Pinkus v. United States*, 436 U.S. 293 (1978).

There remained the question of defining the third part of the three-part *Miller* standard. The most important was the question of defining "serious literary, artistic, political, or scientific value." Was value something to be determined by appeals to community standard, or was it an objective, national standard that limited the ability of communities to define obscenity? In *Pope v. Illinois* (1987), the Court focused on the third prong of the *Miller* test and determined that "serious...value" should be an objective test. "The proper inquiry is not whether an ordinary member of any given community would find serious literary, artistic, political, or scientific value...but whether a reasonable person would find such value in the material, taken as a whole." In practice, this ruling has meant that the question of "value" is determined by the expert testimony of art critics or literary scholars who represent an objective standard of evaluation. In a curiously ambiguous concurrence, Justice Scalia suggested the possibility that he would favor abandoning the judicial role in defining the limits of obscenity altogether, declaring, "De gustibus non es disputandum." ("There is no debating about taste.") *Pope v. Illinois*, 481 U.S. 497 (1987). These words, of course, might be read to imply either that states should be free to regulate anything they choose to define as obscenity, or, conversely, that the First Amendment precludes defining any material as obscene. Justice Scalia's opinions in other cases, such as *Barnes v. Glen Theatre*, 501 U.S. 560 (1991), (discussed in chapter 4), suggest that the former interpretation of his intentions is more likely correct. Regarding the first prong of the *Miller* test, "community standards" have been held to be reflected by the members of a jury rather than requiring evidence of actual local practice. The result is that material commonly available for sale in a community may nonetheless be declared "obscene" if that is the prevailing sense of the community's standards among a group of jurors.

At the beginning of his analysis in *Miller*, Chief Justice Burger took pains to observe that the facts of the case lent themselves to permitting regulation of expression. "This Court has recognized that the States have a legitimate interest in prohibiting dissemination or exhibition of obscene material when the mode of dissemination carries with it a significant danger of offending the sensibilities of unwilling recipients or of exposure to juveniles." At the end of his majority opinion, Burger reiterated the point:

> Under the holdings announced today, no one will be subject to prosecution for the sale or exposure of obscene materials unless these materials depict or describe patently offensive "hard core" sexual conduct specifically defined by the regulating state law, as written or construed. We are satisfied that these specific prerequisites will provide fair notice to a dealer in such materials that his public and commercial activities may bring prosecution. If the inability to define regulated materials with ultimate, god-like precision altogether removes the power of the States or the Congress to regulate, then 'hard core' pornography may be exposed without limit to the juvenile, the passerby, and the consenting adult alike....

Justice Brennan, dissenting, emphasized the fact that his analysis might have been different if he had not found the statute at issue to be facially overbroad. "I [have] had no occasion to consider the extent of state power to regulate the distribution of sexually oriented material to juveniles or the offensive exposure of such material to unconsenting adults." *Miller v. California*, 415 U.S 15 (1973). These comments point to two particular issues that arise in the context of the regulation of obscenity: the right to privacy, and the protection of children.

2. Protecting Privacy

Even before *Miller*, the Court had confronted the question of how far the government might go to suppress obscenity, however defined. The limit on state authority turned out to be the discovery that the First Amendment embodies a right to privacy. *Stanley v. Georgia* involved a police search of a home looking for evidence of bookmaking. In the course of the search, police officers found two unmarked reels of film and a projector. They set up the projector and viewed the films there in Mr. Stanley's home, then arrested him for possession of obscenity. In a unanimous opinion written by Justice Marshall, the Court struck down the Georgia law under which Stanley had been prosecuted.

STANLEY v. GEORGIA

SUPREME COURT OF THE UNITED STATES

394 U.S. 557 (1969)

JUSTICE MARSHALL delivered the opinion of the Court.

..."The makers of our Constitution undertook to secure conditions favorable to the pursuit of happiness. They recognized the significance of man's spiritual nature, of his feelings and of his intellect. They knew that only a part of the pain, pleasure and satisfactions of life are to be found in material things. They sought to protect Americans in their beliefs, their thoughts, their emotions and their sensations. They conferred, as against the Government, the right to be let alone—the most comprehensive of rights and the right most valued by civilized man." *Olmstead v. United States*, 277 U.S. 438, 478 (1928) (Brandeis, J., dissenting). See *Griswold v. Connecticut*....

These are the rights that appellant is asserting in the case before us. He is asserting the right to read or observe what he pleases—the right to satisfy his intellectual and emotional needs in the privacy of his own home. He is asserting the right to be free from state inquiry into the contents of his library. Georgia contends that appellant does not have these rights, that there are certain types of materials that the individual may not read or even possess. Georgia justifies this assertion by arguing that the films in the present case are obscene. But we think that mere categorization of these films as "obscene" is insufficient justification for such a drastic invasion of personal liberties guaranteed by the First and Fourteenth Amendments. Whatever may be the justifications for other statutes regulating obscenity, we do not think they reach into the privacy of one's own home. If the First Amendment means anything, it means that a State has no business telling a man, sitting alone in his own house, what books he may read or what films he may watch.

Our whole constitutional heritage rebels at the thought of giving government the power to control men's minds. And yet, in the face of these traditional notions of individual liberty, Georgia asserts the right to protect the individual's mind from the effects of obscenity. We are not certain that this argument amounts to anything more than the assertion that the State has the right to control the moral content of a person's thoughts.... Whatever the power of the state to control public dissemination of ideas inimical to the public morality, it cannot constitutionally premise legislation on the desirability of controlling a person's private thoughts.

Perhaps recognizing this, Georgia asserts that exposure to obscene materials may lead to deviant sexual behavior or crimes of sexual violence. There appears to be little empirical basis for that assertion. But more important, if the State is only concerned about printed or filmed materials inducing antisocial conduct, we believe that in the context of private consumption of ideas and information we should adhere to the view that "among free men, the deterrents ordinarily to be applied to prevent crime are education and punishment for violations of the law...." Given the present state of knowledge, the State may no more prohibit mere possession of obscene matter on the ground that it may lead to antisocial conduct than it may prohibit possession of chemistry books on the ground that they may lead to the manufacture of homemade spirits....

Finally, we are faced with the argument that prohibition of possession of obscene materials is a necessary incident to statutory schemes prohibiting distribution. That argument is based on alleged difficulties of proving an intent to distribute or in producing evidence of actual distribution. We are not convinced that such difficulties exist, but even if they did we do not think that they would justify infringement of the individual's right to read or observe what he pleases. Because that right is so fundamental to our scheme of individual liberty, its restriction may not be justified by the need to ease the administration of otherwise valid criminal laws.

We hold that the First and Fourteenth Amendments prohibit making mere private possession of obscene material a crime....

Stanley stands for the principle that privacy concerns are central to the limitations that the Free Speech Clause imposed on government's efforts to suppress obscenity. The reference to social scientific evidence is intriguing, as it implies that a sufficiently strong empirical showing of a relationship between the private viewing or obscene materials and antisocial conduct might lead to a different result. Nonetheless, thirty years later Stanley continues to stand for the proposition that so long as children are not involved, the authority of the state to restrict obscenity stops at the front door. That, however, is essentially the only restriction on the authority of government. For example, although both the majority and the dissenters in *Miller* referred to the issue of unwilling viewers, in reality the power of the state to restrict obscenity in public has never been limited by that concept. Thus the Court has upheld the power of government to punish the sale of obscene materials to willing customers. In *Miller*, Chief Justice

Burger had written the 5-4 opinion that enlarged the category of obscenity. That same year, in *Paris Adult Theatre I v. Slaton*, 413 U.S. 49 (1973), Burger wrote another 5-4 opinion, (Brennan, Stewart, Marshall, and Douglas dissenting), that upheld the authority of Atlanta to ban the presentation of obscene films to adult viewers in public theaters despite the absence of either unwilling viewers or children. "There is a right of the Nation," he wrote, "and of the States to maintain a decent society." In addition, this time the Georgia legislature was permitted to reach the very conclusions that had been left open in *Stanley*. "Although there is no conclusive proof of a connection between antisocial behavior and obscene material, the legislature of Georgia could quite reasonably determine that such a connection does or might exist." Finally, Chief Justice Burger argued that there were no privacy issues involved because the movies in question were being shown in theaters rather than in a private home. Fourteen years later, in *Pope v. Illinois*, 481 U.S. 497 (1987), the Rehnquist Court similarly upheld the convictions of the operators of two adult bookstores for selling obscene literature to a willing, adult undercover agent.

The Court has also upheld convictions for sending obscene materials through the mail. Furthermore, federal law contains a principle known as the "continuing offense doctrine," which means that if the mails are used in the commission of the crime, the crime continues to occur in each place where the mails travel. This has the result that if materials are sent through the mail, the sender may be subject to criminal prosecution under anti-obscenity laws if the materials in question meet the *Miller* "patently offensive" standard in *any community through which* the mail passes, regardless of whether the shipper is aware of the existence of such a community or its standards. *United States v. Hamling*, 418 U.S. 87 (1974). Chief Justice Rehnquist's justification for upholding the statute was the rather strained notion that existing state criminal laws already subjected senders of obscene materials to prosecution in jurisdictions through which the materials might pass, so that the federal law did not create any new liability. This analysis is difficult to explain, particularly since federal law makes it a crime for anyone in an intervening jurisdiction to view the contents of a package sent through the mails, so that it is only by the illegal conduct of a third party that the "obscene" materials would be viewed in the jurisdiction in which they were unprotected in the first place.

The peculiar outcome of the continuing offense doctrine is that a person may produce constitutionally protected materials in one place, and send them to another place where they are constitutionally protected, yet find himself subject to prosecution on the grounds that the same materials were not constitutionally protected in some third venue through which the mail trucks happened to pass along their route. In *Smith v. United States*, 431 U.S. 291 (1977), that logic was employed to uphold the conviction of an Iowa man for shipping materials from one place in Iowa to another place in Iowa, in response to a specific request (abandoning the *Miller* presumption that the relevant "community" is the state). The trial court found that neither the community of the sender nor that of the recipient would have defined the material in question as "obscene," but federal authorities succeeded in finding a town in between in which they were able to convince a jury that local community standards warranted a criminal conviction. Thus the *Miller* principle has progressed far from its original justification of protecting people against unwanted exposure to obscenity, to protecting the sensibilities of persons who might view obscene materials in the course of illegally examining other people's mail.

If it is a crime to intercept someone's mail, it is equally a crime to eavesdrop on an electronic transmission, but in *Sable Communications of California v. Federal Communications Commission*, 492 U.S. 115 (1989), the Court ruled that Congress's authority over interstate commerce permitted it to ban interstate dial-a-porn services. This did not entail the creation of a national standard of obscenity, according to the Court. "Sable is free to tailor its messages, on a selective basis, if it so chooses, to the communities it chooses to serve. While Sable may be forced to incur some costs in developing and implementing a system for screening the locale of incoming calls, there is no constitutional impediment to enacting a law which may impose such costs on a medium electing to provide these messages." The *Sable* decision established two crucial principles in the application of the *Miller* standards to electronic transmissions. First, materials may be defined as obscene under the "community standards" of the place where the message is received as well as those of the place from which the message is transmitted. (The applicability of the continuing offense doctrine, which would make every transmission subject to the most restrictive standard that exists anywhere, was not discussed in the case.) If the materials at issue are obscene under either standard, the federal government is free to criminalize the act of transmission, regardless of the age or desires of the recipient. Second, it is incumbent on the commercial provider of the materials to ascertain the "community standards" that are operative in every place to which it wants to send materials.

Sable and *Hamling* also point to the proposition that the project of defining obscenity goes beyond protecting the sensibilities of the viewer.

Instead, the authority of government to define this unprotected category is grounded in the authority of government to make statements about the character of the community. It is difficult to think of any other context in which the standards of local majorities are permitted to define, rather than be limited by, the reach of a constitutionally protected right. Certainly no other unprotected category of speech depends for its definition on the sensibilities of local majorities.

The degree to which the protections of the First Amendment vary with geography is especially problematic in the context of the Internet. While the Supreme Court has never considered the question, it was a key issue in *United States v. Thomas*, 74 F.3d 701 (6th Cir. 1996) (cert. den.). The case involved a California couple who maintained an electronic bulletin board devoted to the commercial delivery of images scanned from adult publications. Acting on a tip, a postal inspector in eastern Tennessee signed up for the service, paid his fee, and downloaded a number of images. He then forwarded the materials to the U.S. Attorney for Eastern Tennessee, who filed a criminal complaint against the Thomases under Title 18 statutes forbidding the interstate commercial shipment or transmittal of obscene materials.

The Thomases challenged their conviction on two grounds: first, that the relevant community for the "community standards" element of the *Miller* test should not be the Eastern District of Tennessee, but rather the community of Internet users; and, second, that the statute ought not to be applied to them because their actions did not constitute "sending" the images in question across state lines. The Sixth Circuit made short work of both arguments by simply applying the rules from *Sable*: that the sender bears the burden of ensuring that recipients are not located in communities whose standards would deem the transmitted materials obscene, and that utilization of electronic transmission falls within the ambit of the federal statute.

The facts in *Thomas* make it a relatively easy case for the appellate court to fit into the mold of existing pornography law. In the first place, in addition to the transmission of images the Thomases sent the plaintiff a number of videotapes via U.P.S., making the issue of defining "sending" moot (as well as settled, arguably, by the ruling in *Sable*). Furthermore, the Sixth Circuit took pains to point out that in this particular case the sender was aware of the address of the recipient, since to obtain a password for the "Amateur Action" bulletin board the plaintiff was obliged to send in (by mail) a photostat of his driver's license. Thus the court would have had no trouble in situating the case into the framework established in *Sable*.

Instead, however, the court relied on cases holding that the federal mailing statute covers wire transfers of money, making an analogy to the end product of the GIF transmission rather than to its medium of communication. "The beginning of the transaction is money in one account and the ending is money in another. The manner in which the funds were moved does not affect the ability to obtain tangible paper dollars or a bank check from the receiving account." Effectively, the rule in *Thomas* was the same as in *Sable*: anyone wishing to provide obscene materials via electronic transmission on a commercial basis is responsible for determining the "community standards" of the venue in which the materials are to be received. For accepting an application from eastern Tennessee, Mr. and Mrs. Thomas were sentenced to thirty-seven and thirty months in prison, respectively. Their conviction was upheld by the Court of Appeals, and the Supreme Court denied certiorari.

The First Amendment may protect one's right to possess obscene materials in the privacy of one's home, but it does not protect any right to buy, sell, transport, distribute, or receive such materials. In an extreme case, as Justice Douglas put it, the guarantee of *Stanley* could be reduced to a right to view obscene literature "only if one wrote or designed a tract in his attic and printed or processed it in his basement, so as to be able to read it in his study." *United States v. 12,200 Ft. Reels*, 413 U.S. (1973) (Douglas, J., dissenting). (The peculiar name of the case identifies it as one involving goods seized by customs officials at the point of importation). In fact, even that might not be protected if the material in question involves child pornography.

3. *Special Protections for Children*

The possibility that minors might have access to obscene materials has been one of the recurring concerns of the Court. One of its early important cases on the subject, however, made it clear that the overbreadth doctrine precludes protecting minors by infringing on the rights of adults. *Butler v. Michigan*, 352 U.S. 380 (1957) concerned a criminal conviction for the sale, to an adult, of materials "having a potentially deleterious influence upon youth." Before the Supreme Court, the State of Michigan argued that the law was justified as an effort to protect minors in the state. Justice

Frankfurter, no libertarian when it came to speech issues generally, was not impressed by the state's argument:

> The State insists that, by thus quarantining the general reading public against books not too rugged for grown men and women in order to shield juvenile innocence, it is exercising its power to promote the general welfare. Surely, this is to burn the house to roast the pig...we have before us legislation not reasonably restricted to the evil with which it is said to deal. The incidence of this enactment is to reduce the adult population of Michigan to reading only what is fit for children. It thereby arbitrarily curtails one of those liberties of the individual, now enshrined in the Due Process Clause of the Fourteenth Amendment, that history has attested as the indispensable conditions for the maintenance and progress of a free society." *Butler v. Michigan*, 352 U.S. 380 (1957).

Where adults' access to obscene materials is not impaired, however, whatever limited elements of the *Stanley* principle remain give way in cases involving either child pornography or the exposure of children to obscene materials. Child pornography, it should be noted, is a broader category than obscenity. Nonobscene sexual films, in particular, may be criminalized on a theory different from the one seen in *Miller*. Instead of the protection of society, the justification for the special treatment of this category is the protection of the participants. In *New York v. Ferber*, Justice White framed the question: "Could the New York State Legislature, consistent with the First Amendment, prohibit the dissemination of material which shows children engaged in sexual conduct, regardless of whether such material is obscene?" His answer, on behalf of a unanimous Court, was "yes":

> The distribution of photographs and films depicting sexual activity by juveniles is intrinsically related to the sexual abuse of children in at least two ways. First, the materials produced are a permanent record of the children's participation and the harm to the child is exacerbated by their circulation. Second, the distribution network for child pornography must be closed if the production of material which requires the sexual exploitation of children is to be effectively controlled.... The most expeditious if not the only practical method of law enforcement may be to dry up the market for this material by imposing severe criminal penalties on persons selling, advertising, or otherwise promoting the product. *New York v. Ferber*, 458 U.S. 747 (1982).

White went on to explicitly separate this analysis from the *Miller* tests for obscenity. "[A] work which, taken on the whole, contains serious literary, artistic, political, or scientific value may nevertheless embody the hardest core of child pornography. It is irrelevant to the child who has been abused whether or not the material has...value." To the extent that the portrayal of minors engaged in sexual conduct was required—say, in a staging of

Romeo and Juliet—"a person over the statutory age who perhaps looked younger could be utilized."

The analysis, finally, applied only to films and similar media. "[T]he nature of the harm to be combated requires that the state offense be limited to works that visually depict sexual conduct by children below a specified age." Finally, in response to an overbreadth challenge, White declared the *Broadrick* principle that only "substantial" overbreadth posed a problem for the First Amendment. "We seriously doubt," he wrote, "that...arguably impermissible applications of the statute amount to more than a tiny fraction of the materials within the statute's reach." The rationale of *Ferber* defined the case of child pornography as different from the issues involved in *Stanley*, so that mere possession of child pornography in one's home may be criminalized without offending the First Amendment. *Osborne v. Ohio*, 495 U.S. 103 (1990).

In *Osborne*, there was no danger of overbreadth because the statute at issue contained exceptions for materials possessed for "bona fide" purposes, a parent or guardian's possession of pictures of their own child, or photographs taken with the written consent of the parent or guardian. Other statutes, however, continue to raise potential overbreadth issues. *Massachusetts v. Oakes*, 491 U.S. 576 (1989) involved the conviction of a man for taking photographs of his fourteen-year-old stepdaughter under a Massachusetts law that made it a crime to "pose or exhibit" nude children for purposes of pictures, moving or otherwise. The constitutionality of the law was never addressed, because while the case was pending Massachusetts amended it to cover only those photographs taken with "lascivious intent," and a plurality of the Court voted to remand the case for reconsideration rather than ruling on the merits of Oakes' overbreadth challenge. Justice Brennan, in a dissenting opinion joined by Justices Marshall and Stevens, noted that the original form of the statute (which was echoed in other state statutes) would make it a crime for "parents to photograph their infant children or toddlers in the bath or romping naked on the beach," and would similarly ban the display of artistic photos. "Many of the world's great artists—Degas, Renoir, Donatello, to name but a few—have worked from models under 18 years of age, and many acclaimed photographs have included nude or partially clad minors." Scalia, joined by Blackmun, disagreed that the risk of overbreadth was substantial. "I would estimate that the legitimate scope [of the law] vastly exceeds the illegitimate."

The other unresolved question about the regulation of child pornography arises out of a federal statute, 18 U.S.C. § 2256(8), which makes it a crime not only to possess pictures of children engaged in sex acts, but also pictures that "appear to be of a minor engaging in sexually explicit conduct," or even materials that have been "advertised, promoted, described, or distributed in such a manner that conveys the impression that the material...contains a visual depiction of a minor engaging in sexually explicit conduct." Thus, slightly incredibly, it is a federal crime to possess a film that has been promoted by advertisements that falsely suggest that adult actors portraying minors would engage in depictions of sexual conduct. Similar state laws have been changed by legislatures in the face of court challenges, following the lead of Massachusetts in *Oakes*. In *Camfield v. City of Oklahoma*, 248 F.3d 1214 (2001), an Oklahoma judge determined that the movie *The Tin Drum*—winner of the 1997 Academy Award for best foreign film and co-winner of the Palme d'Or at the Cannes Film Festival—contained scenes of child pornography. Police officers went to video stores around Oklahoma City and obtained the names and addresses of patrons who had rented the movie, then went to those persons' houses to seize the videos. Michael Camfield had rented the movie because he was at work preparing a challenge to the judge's order for the ACLU. While the case was pending on appeal, however, the Oklahoma legislature changed the law to cover only pictures that showed minors "engaged in" or "observing" sexual acts, rather than mere "portrayals."

The federal statute has resulted in inconsistent rulings by the circuits. A panel of the Ninth Circuit ruled the "portrayal" and "promotion" rules went too far, while the Fifth Circuit has ruled that the law is constitutional. *Free Speech Coalition v. Reno*, 198 F.3d 1083 (9th Cir. 1999); *United States v. Fox*, 248 F.3d 394 (5th Cir. 2001). Both courts cited *Ferber*, which points to the problem; the justifications for excluding child pornography from constitutional protection offered in *Ferber* follow two distinct and different tracks. On the one hand, the Court in that case said that the rationale for creating a category called "child pornography" was the protection of children involved in the production of such materials, a principle which would not justify criminalizing mere portrayals. On the other hand, the Court also said that the government had a compelling interest in criminalizing such materials in order to shut down the market in real child pornography, a rationale which is not only not limited to child performers, it is arguably not limited to real performers at all, so that computer-generated images would suffice. In the hands of lower court judges, moreover, the state's interest in combating the market in child pornography reaches beyond visual representations and distribution of material entirely. In 2001, a twenty-two-year-old man in Ohio was sentenced to seven years in prison for possession of a journal that he had written himself which contained descriptions of sex acts with children. There was no indication that he intended to show the journal to anyone else; he was found to have violated a statute that made it a crime to possess materials that portray sex acts involving minors, a description that arguably covers a huge range of literature and art ranging from Indian temple carvings to the plays of William Shakespeare. In 2002, the Supreme Court struck down the law as overbroad on the grounds that it went far beyond *Ferber* and *Miller*, criminalizing nonobscene materials, including recognized works of great art. Justice Kennedy, writing for the majority, explained why Congress had gone too far. "The Government cannot ban speech fit for adults simply because it may fall into the hands of children. The evil in question depends upon the actor's unlawful conduct, conduct defined as criminal quite apart from any link to the speech in question. This establishes that the speech ban is not narrowly drawn. The objective is to prohibit illegal conduct, but this restriction goes well beyond that interest by restricting the speech available to law-abiding adults." *Ashcroft v. Free Speech Coalition*,122 S. Ct. 1389 1403 (2002). The vote was 7-2, Justices Rehnquist and Scalia dissenting. (Justice O'Connor also dissented in part but concurred in the holding.)

C. *Indecency and Public Spaces*

In the previous chapter, we observed that one of the reasons that content-based speech restrictions are permitted in limited forums is that the audience for such speech may be captive. In general, the authority of government to protect people *against* speech depends on the existence of an important privacy interest, such as the right to control the messages that come into one's home (*Frisby v. Schultz*, 487 U.S. 474 [1988]) or mailbox (*Rowan v. Post Office Dept.*, 397 U.S. 728 [1970]). In public, unless speech falls into an unprotected category, government is generally not permitted to restrict expression based on content. But courts have developed a kind of shadow category called "indecency" that exists in a gray area around the boundary of obscenity. May government restrict the expression of indecent-but-not-obscene messages? In 1970, the first important answer to this question was "no." Paul Cohen entered a Los Angeles County courthouse wearing (and then carrying) a jacket that bore the words "Fuck the Draft" on the back. He was arrested, convicted, and sentenced to thirty days in jail for violating a law that made it a crime to "maliciously and willfully disturb...the peace and quiet of any neighborhood or person...[by] offensive conduct."

COHEN v. CALIFORNIA

SUPREME COURT OF THE UNITED STATES

403 U.S. 15 (1970)

JUSTICE HARLAN delivered the opinion of the Court.

...In order to lay hands on the precise issue which this case involves, it is useful first to canvass various matters which this record does not present.

The conviction quite clearly rests upon the asserted offensiveness of the words Cohen used to convey his message to the public. The only "conduct" which the State sought to punish is the fact of communication. Thus, we deal here with a conviction resting solely upon "speech," not upon any separately identifiable conduct which allegedly was intended by Cohen to be perceived by others as expressive of particular views but which, on its face, does not necessarily convey any message and hence arguably could be regulated without effectively repressing Cohen's ability to express himself. Further, the State certainly lacks power to punish Cohen for the underlying content of the message the inscription conveyed. At least so long as there is no showing of an intent to incite disobedience to or disruption of the draft, Cohen could not, consistently with the First and Fourteenth Amendments, be punished for asserting the evident position on the inutility or immorality of the draft his jacket reflected.

Appellant's conviction, then, rests squarely upon his exercise of the "freedom of speech" protected from arbitrary governmental interference by the Constitution and can be justified, if at all, only as a valid regulation of the manner in which he exercised that freedom, not as a permissible prohibition on the substantive message it conveys. This does not end the inquiry, of course, for the First and Fourteenth Amendments have never been thought to give absolute protection to every individual to speak whenever or wherever he pleases, or to use any form of address in any circumstances that he chooses. In this vein, too, however, we think it important to note that several issues typically associated with such problems are not presented here.

In the first place, Cohen was tried under a statute applicable throughout the entire State. Any attempt to support this conviction on the ground that the statute seeks to preserve an appropriately decorous atmosphere in the courthouse where Cohen was arrested must fail in the absence of any language in the statute that would have put appellant on notice that certain kinds of otherwise permissible speech or conduct would nevertheless, under California law, not be tolerated in certain places. No fair reading of the phrase "offensive conduct" can be said sufficiently to inform the ordinary person that distinctions between certain locations are thereby created. n3 n3 It is illuminating to note what transpired when Cohen entered a courtroom in the building. He removed his jacket and stood with it folded over his arm. Meanwhile, a policeman sent the presiding judge a note suggesting that Cohen be held in contempt of court. The judge declined to do so and Cohen was arrested by the officer only after he emerged from the courtroom.

In the second place, as it comes to us, this case cannot be said to fall within those relatively few categories of instances where prior decisions have established the power of government to deal more comprehensively with certain forms of individual expression simply upon a showing that such a form was employed. This is not, for example, an obscenity case. Whatever else may be necessary to give rise to the States' broader power to prohibit obscene expression, such expression must be, in some significant way, erotic. *Roth v. United States*, 354 U.S. 476 (1957). It cannot plausibly be maintained that this vulgar allusion to the Selective Service System would conjure up such psychic stimulation in anyone likely to be confronted with Cohen's crudely defaced jacket.

This Court has also held that the States are free to ban the simple use, without a demonstration of additional justifying circumstances, of so-called "fighting words," those personally abusive epithets which, when addressed to the ordinary citizen, are, as a matter of common knowledge, inherently likely to provoke violent reaction. *Chaplinsky v. New Hampshire*, 315 U.S. 568 (1942). While the four-letter word displayed by Cohen in relation to the draft is not uncommonly employed in a personally provocative fashion, in this instance it was clearly not "directed to the person of the hearer." No individual actually or likely to be present could reasonably have regarded the words on appellant's jacket as a direct personal insult. Nor do we have here an instance of the exercise of the State's police power to prevent a speaker from intentionally provoking a given group to hostile reaction. There is, as noted above, no showing that anyone who saw Cohen was in fact violently aroused or that appellant intended such a result.

Finally, in arguments before this Court much has been made of the claim that Cohen's distasteful mode of expression was thrust upon unwilling or unsuspecting viewers, and that the State might therefore legitimately act as it did in order to protect the sensitive from otherwise unavoidable exposure to appellant's crude form of protest. Of course, the mere presumed presence of unwitting listeners or viewers does not serve automatically to justify curtailing all speech capable of giving offense. While this Court has recognized that government may properly act in many situations to prohibit intrusion into the privacy of the home of unwelcome views and ideas which cannot be totally banned from the public dialogue, e. g., *Rowan v. Post Office Dept.*, 397 U.S. 728 (1970), we have at the same time consistently stressed that "we are often 'captives' outside the sanctuary of the home and subject to objectionable speech." The ability of government, consonant with the Constitution, to shut off discourse solely to protect others from hearing it is, in other words, dependent upon a showing that substantial privacy interests are being invaded in an essentially intolerable manner. Any broader view of this authority would effectively empower a majority to silence dissidents simply as a matter of personal predilections.

In this regard, persons confronted with Cohen's jacket were in a quite different posture than, say, those subjected to the raucous emissions of sound trucks blaring outside their residences. Those in the Los Angeles courthouse could effectively avoid further bombardment of their sensibilities simply by averting their eyes. And, while it may be that one has a more substantial claim to a recognizable privacy interest when walking through a courthouse corridor than, for example, strolling through Central Park, surely it is nothing like the interest in being free from unwanted expression in the confines of one's own home. Given the subtlety and complexity of the factors involved, if Cohen's "speech" was otherwise entitled to constitutional protection, we do not think the fact that some unwilling "listeners" in a public building may have been briefly exposed to it can serve to justify this breach of the peace conviction where, as here, there was no evidence that persons powerless to avoid appellant's conduct did in fact object to it, and where that portion of the statute upon which Cohen's conviction rests evinces no concern, either on its face or as construed by the California courts, with the special plight of the captive auditor, but, instead, indiscriminately sweeps within its prohibitions all "offensive conduct" that disturbs "any neighborhood or person."

Against this background, the issue flushed by this case stands out in bold relief. It is whether California can excise, as "offensive conduct," one particular scurrilous epithet from the public discourse, either upon the theory of the court below that its use is inherently likely to cause violent reaction or upon a more general assertion that the States, acting as guardians of public morality, may properly remove this offensive word from the public vocabulary.

The rationale of the California court is plainly untenable. At most it reflects an undifferentiated fear or apprehension of disturbance [which] is not enough to overcome the right to freedom of expression. We have been shown no evidence that substantial numbers of citizens are standing ready to strike out physically at whoever may assault their sensibilities with execrations like that uttered by Cohen. There may be some persons about with such lawless and violent proclivities, but that is an insufficient base upon which to erect, consistently with constitutional values, a governmental power to force persons who wish to ventilate their dissident views into avoiding particular forms of expression. The argument amounts to little more than the self-defeating proposition that to avoid physical censorship of one who has not sought to provoke such a response by a hypothetical coterie of the violent and lawless, the States may more appropriately effectuate that censorship themselves....

The constitutional right of free expression is powerful medicine in a society as diverse and populous as ours. It is designed and intended to remove governmental restraints from the arena of public discussion, putting the decision as to what views shall be voiced largely into the hands of each of us, in the hope that use of such freedom will ultimately produce a more capable citizenry and more perfect polity and in the belief that no other approach would comport with the premise of individual dignity and choice upon which our political system rests.

To many, the immediate consequence of this freedom may often appear to be only verbal tumult, discord, and even offensive utterance. These are, however, within established limits, in truth necessary side effects of the broader enduring values which the process of open debate permits us to achieve. That the air may at times seem filled with verbal cacophony is, in this sense, not a sign of weakness but of strength. We cannot lose sight of the fact that, in what otherwise might seem a trifling and annoying instance of individual distasteful abuse of a privilege, these fundamental societal values are truly implicated. That is why "wholly neutral futilities...come under the protection of free speech as fully as do Keats' poems or Donne's sermons," and why "so long as the means are peaceful, the communication need not meet standards of acceptability."

Against this perception of the constitutional policies involved, we discern certain more particularized considerations that peculiarly call for reversal of this conviction. First, the principle contended for by the State seems inherently boundless. How is one to distinguish this from any other offensive word? Surely the State has no right to cleanse public debate to the point where it is grammatically palatable to the most squeamish among us. Yet no readily ascertainable general principle exists for stopping short of that result were we to affirm the judgment below. For, while the particular four-letter word being litigated here is perhaps more distasteful than most others of its genre, it is nevertheless often true that one man's vulgarity is another's lyric. Indeed, we think it is largely because governmental officials cannot make principled distinctions in this area that the Constitution leaves matters of taste and style so largely to the individual.

Additionally, we cannot overlook the fact, because it is well illustrated by the episode involved here, that much linguistic expression serves a dual communicative function: it conveys not only ideas capable of relatively precise, detached explication, but otherwise inexpressible emotions as well. In fact, words are often chosen as much for their emotive as their cognitive force. We cannot sanction the view that the Constitution, while solicitous of the cognitive content of individual speech, has little or no regard for that emotive function which, practically speaking, may often be the more important element of the overall message sought to be communicated. Indeed, as Mr. Justice Frankfurter has said, "one of the prerogatives of American citizenship is the right to criticize public men and measures—and that means not only informed and responsible criticism but the freedom to speak foolishly and without moderation."

Finally, and in the same vein, we cannot indulge the facile assumption that one can forbid particular words without also running a substantial risk of suppressing ideas in the process. Indeed, governments might soon seize upon the censorship of particular words as a convenient guise for banning the expression of unpopular views. We have been able, as noted above, to discern little social benefit that might result from running the risk of opening the door to such grave results.

It is, in sum, our judgment that, absent a more particularized and compelling reason for its actions, the State may not, consistently with the First and Fourteenth Amendments, make the simple public display here involved of this single four-letter expletive a criminal offense. Because that is the only arguably sustainable rationale for the conviction here at issue, the judgment below must be Reversed

DISSENT: JUSTICE BLACKMUN, with whom THE CHIEF JUSTICE and JUSTICE BLACK join.

...Cohen's absurd and immature antic, in my view, was mainly conduct and little speech.... Further, the case appears to me to be well within the sphere of *Chaplinsky v. New Hampshire*, where Mr. Justice Murphy, a known champion of First Amendment freedoms, wrote for a unanimous bench. As a consequence, this Court's agonizing over First Amendment values seems misplaced....

The extent to which government is proscribed from excluding indecent expression from public spaces is exemplified by *Erznoznik v. City of Jacksonville*, 422 U.S. 205 (1975), in which by a vote of 6 to 3 the Court ruled that a city could not prevent a drive-in theater from showing films that included nudity on a screen which could be seen from adjacent homes and from the street. Justice Powell concluded that the outcome was determined by *Cohen*: "the screen of a drive-in theatre is not so obtrusive as to make it impossible for an unwilling individual to avoid exposure to it.... Thus, we conclude that the limited privacy interest of persons on the public streets cannot justify this censorship of otherwise protected speech on the basis of its content."

Although the government may not exclude indecency from public spaces, it is free to regulate the time, place, and manner of such expression. Unlike the regulation of other forms of protected speech, moreover, the regulation of indecent expression need not be content neutral. In *Young v. American Mini-Theatres*, 427 U.S. 50 (1976), the Court considered a challenge to a Detroit statute that prohibited "adult motion picture theatres" and "adult book stores" within one thousand feet of a variety of other "regulated uses," including liquor stores, other theaters or bookstores, pool halls, and pawn shops. Justice Stevens wrote an opinion for only a four-vote plurality that upheld the ordinance. Justice Powell concurred in the judgment, but viewed the law in question as purely a "land use regulation," and Justices Stewart, Brennan, Marshall, and Blackmun dissented. The basic principle behind the plurality's analysis was that the expression in question was protected, but not very. "[T]here is surely a less vital interest in the uninhibited exhibition of material that is on the border line between pornography and artistic expression than in the free dissemination of ideas of social and political significance." That observation made all the difference, since "[e]ven within the area of protected speech, a difference in content may require a different governmental response."

According to Stevens, regulations that singled out particular content could nonetheless survive constitutional scrutiny so long as they were viewpoint neutral. "[T]he regulation of the places where sexually explicit films may be exhibited is unaffected by whatever social, political, or philosophical message the film may be intended to communicate; whether the motion picture ridicules or characterizes one point of view or another, the effect of the ordinances is exactly the same." In closing, Stevens returned to his basic premise. "Moreover, even though we recognize that the First Amendment will not tolerate the total suppression of erotic materials that have some arguably artistic value, it is manifest that society's interest in protecting this type of expression is of a wholly different, and lesser, magnitude than the interest in untrammeled political debate...." As a result, the ordinance could be upheld so long as the city council had demonstrated a legitimate basis unrelated to the suppression of a message. Such a basis was found in the danger of "secondary effects," a phrase explained by Justice Stevens in a footnote. "The Common Council's determination was that a concentration of 'adult' movie theaters causes the area to deteriorate and become a focus of crime, effects which are not attributable to theaters showing other types of films. It is this secondary effect which these zoning ordinances attempt to avoid, not the dissemination of 'offensive' speech. In contrast, in *Erznoznik v. City of Jacksonville*, the justifications offered by the city rested primarily on the city's interest in protecting its citizens from exposure to unwanted, 'offensive' speech." The fear of secondary effects of less protected speech, ruled the plurality, justified the regulations at issue.

The dissenters rejected the idea that there was a category of "less protected protected speech." Justice Stewart accused the majority of abandoning the "cardinal principles" of content neutrality.

> "The kind of expression at issue here is no doubt objectionable to some," wrote Justice Stewart, "but that fact does not diminish its protected status any more than did the particular content of the 'offensive' expression in *Erznoznik...Cohen v. California*, [or] *Brandenburg v. Ohio*.... What this case does involve is the constitutional permissibility of selective interference with protected speech whose content is thought to produce distasteful effects. It is elementary that a prime function of the First Amendment is to guard against just such interference. By refusing to invalidate Detroit's ordinance the Court rides roughshod over cardinal principles of First Amendment law, which require that time, place, and manner regulations that affect protected expression be content neutral except in the limited context of a captive or juvenile audience. In place of these principles the Court invokes a concept wholly alien to the First Amendment." *Young v. American Mini-Theatres*, 427 U.S. 50 (1976).

Despite the fact that its holding was supported only by a plurality, *Young* stands for the proposition that less protected speech may be singled out for zoning regulation on the basis of its secondary effects. Most famously, in *Renton v. Playtime Theatres, Inc.*, 475 U.S. 41 (1986), the *Young* principle was used to uphold a zoning ordinance that prohibited adult theaters from being located within one thousand feet of a residential zone, church, park, or school. The precise meaning of "secondary effect" is not clear, but the plurality's distinction between *Young* and *Erznoznik* makes it clear that such effects cannot be a result of the message itself. In a similar vein, government may require booksellers to take reasonable efforts to prevent minors from having access to indecent materials. The meaning of "reasonable efforts" is undetermined. In one case, booksellers argued that compliance with a state statute would require them to get rid of up to 20 percent of their stock, but the Court did not reach the issue in its analysis. *Virginia v. American Booksellers Association*, 484 U.S. 383 (1988).

The category of indecency became a series of cases involving nude dancing. Such performances have been consistently found to be nonobscene under the *Miller* test, yet the Supreme Court has upheld statutes banning such performances. In *Barnes v. Glen Theatre*, 501 U.S. 560 (1991), the Court upheld an ordinance enacted by the City of South Bend, Indiana, that prohibited totally nude dancing. Chief Justice Rehnquist, in a plurality opinion joined only by Justices O'Connor and Kennedy, began his analysis with an assertion that undercuts the logic of the categorical approach almost entirely. "[N]ude dancing of the kind sought to be performed here is expressive conduct within the outer perimeters of the First Amendment, though we view it as only marginally so." The idea of an "outer perimeter" of protected speech automatically suggests its opposite, speech that is at the center or "core" of the Free Speech Clause. What else might be in that "outer perimeter," and is there an hierarchy of other categories between the core and the periphery of protected expression? These cases were ultimately analyzed and decided as examples of expressive conduct rather than "pure speech," so they will be discussed in detail in the next chapter.

In 1986, the Court heard a case that involved indecent pure speech. Once again, however, the case involved special circumstances; the speech at issue was offered by a high school student at a school assembly during a student election. In an opinion by Chief Justice Burger, the Court found that the school had the authority to punish the student based on the special concerns involved in running a public school:

> [P]ublic education must prepare pupils for citizenship in the Republic.... It must inculcate the habits and manners of civility as values in themselves conducive to

> happiness and as indispensable to the practice of self-government in the community and the nation.... These fundamental values of habits and manners of civility essential to a democratic society must, of course, include tolerance of divergent political and religious views, even when the views expressed may be unpopular. But these "fundamental values" must also take into account consideration of the sensibilities of others, and, in the case of a school, the sensibilities of fellow students. The undoubted freedom to advocate unpopular and controversial views in schools and classrooms must be balanced against the society's countervailing interest in teaching students the boundaries of socially appropriate behavior.... The inculcation of these values is truly the work of the schools. The determination of what manner of speech in the classroom or in school assembly is inappropriate properly rests with the school board.... This Court's First Amendment jurisprudence has acknowledged limitations on the otherwise absolute interest of the speaker in reaching an unlimited audience where the speech is sexually explicit and the audience may include children. *Bethel School District No. 403 v. Fraser*, 478 U.S. 675 (1986).

Once again, in its treatment of indecent speech justices of the Court suggest the possibility that some protected speech is less protected than others, but as in other cases since *Cohen*, the decision upholding regulation of indecency relied on the special circumstances of the forum.

Broadcast media present a special set of circumstances. The regulation of indecent (as opposed to obscene) materials in the context of radio and television was dealt with in a case that involved the FCC's attempts to prevent Pacifica Radio from airing, ironically, a comedy routine about words that are not permitted on television. In general, the regulation of radio and television are justified by the fact that operators are licensed by the government, and are granted local monopolies over broadcast frequencies. *Red Lion Broadcasting Co. v. FCC*, 395 U.S. 367 (1969). Such regulation, however, cannot itself run afoul of the First Amendment. Nonetheless, in *FCC v. Pacifica*, 438 U.S. 726 (1978) the Court found that the government had adequate justification in banning the use of "filthy words" under a federal statute forbidding the use of "any obscene, indecent, or profane language by means of radio communications." Justice Stevens wrote the majority opinion, from which Justices Brennan, Stewart, Marshall, and White dissented.

Stevens began his analysis in *Pacifica* by arguing that the words at issue in the FCC's order were low-value protected speech. "While some of these references may be protected, they surely lie at the periphery of First Amendment concern.... Invalidating any rule on the basis of its hypothetical application to situations not before the Court is 'strong medicine' to be applied sparingly and only as a last resort. We decline to administer that medicine to preserve the vigor of patently offensive sexual and excretory speech." Reaching all the way back to 1919, Stevens then appealed to Justice Holmes's idea in *Schenck* that circumstances determine the degree of protection to which particular content is entitled. "[T]he character of every act depends upon the circumstances in which it is done.... The question in every case is whether the words used are used in such circumstances and are of such a nature as to create a clear and present danger that they will bring about the substantive evils that Congress has a right to prevent." Coming ten years after *Brandenburg*, this represented a somewhat startling revival of long-dormant doctrine, but Justice Stevens made it clear that in its new version the *Schenck* test applied only to indecent expression. "[I]t is undisputed that the content of Pacifica's broadcast was 'vulgar,' 'offensive,' and 'shocking.' Because content of that character is not entitled to absolute constitutional protection under all circumstances, we must consider its context in order to determine whether the Commission's action was constitutionally permissible." Stevens found, finally, that the character of broadcast media justified restrictions on content that would not have been acceptable in a public forum:

> [T]he broadcast media have established a uniquely pervasive presence in the lives of all Americans. Patently offensive, indecent material presented over the airwaves confronts the citizen, not only in public, but also in the privacy of the home, where the individual's right to be left alone plainly outweighs the First Amendment rights of an intruder. Because the broadcast audience is constantly tuning in and out, prior warnings cannot completely protect the listener or viewer from unexpected program content. To say that one may avoid further offense by turning off the radio when he hears indecent language is like saying that the remedy for an assault is to run away after the first blow. One may hang up on an indecent phone call, but that option does not give the caller a constitutional immunity or avoid a harm that has already taken place.

Second, radio broadcasts were "uniquely accessible to children, even those too young to read." Since bookstores and movie theaters could be prevented from allowing minors to view indecent material, Stevens reasoned that the same restrictions could be applied to radio stations. "[T]he government's interest in the well-being of its youth and in supporting parents' claim to authority in their own household justified the regulation of otherwise protected expression. The ease with which children may obtain access to broadcast material...amply justify special treatment of indecent broadcasting." *FCC v. Pacifica*, 438 U.S. 726 (1978).

In his dissent, Justice Brennan pointed out some holes in the majority's analysis. In the first place, he suggested that the view of radio broadcasters as unwanted invaders in the home was overstated:

> Although an individual's decision to allow public radio communications into his home undoubtedly does not abrogate all of his privacy interests, the residual privacy interests he retains vis-à-vis the communication he voluntarily admits into his home are surely no greater than those of the people present in the corridor of the Los Angeles courthouse in Cohen who bore witness to the words "Fuck the Draft" emblazoned across Cohen's jacket.... [U]nlike other intrusive modes of communication, such as sound trucks, the radio can be turned off,—and with a minimum of effort. As Chief Judge Bazelon aptly observed below, "having elected to receive public air waves, the scanner who stumbles onto an offensive program is in the same position as the unsuspecting passers-by in Cohen...he can avert his attention by changing channels or turning off the set." Whatever the minimal discomfort suffered by a listener who inadvertently tunes into a program he finds offensive during the brief interval before he can simply extend his arm and switch stations or flick the "off" button, it is surely worth the candle to preserve the broadcaster's right to send, and the right of those interested to receive, a message entitled to full First Amendment protection.
>
> The Court's balance, of necessity, fails to accord proper weight to the interests of listeners who wish to hear broadcasts the FCC deems offensive. It permits majoritarian tastes completely to preclude a protected message from entering the homes of a receptive, unoffended minority.... As surprising as it may be to individual Members of this Court, some parents may actually find Mr. Carlin's unabashed attitude towards the seven 'dirty words' healthy, and deem it desirable to expose their children to the manner in which Mr. Carlin defuses the taboo surrounding the words. Such parents may constitute a minority of the American public, but the absence of great numbers willing to exercise the right to raise their children in this fashion does not alter the right's nature or its existence. Only the Court's regrettable decision does that.

The dissenters took sharp issue with the Court's imposition of majoritarian standards of decency as the limiting factor in the analysis of free speech rights. Brennan accused his colleagues of showing "a depressing inability to appreciate that in our land of cultural pluralism, there are many who think, act, and talk differently from the Members of this Court, and who do not share their fragile sensibilities." The Court, he argued, was throwing its weight behind the majority's efforts to silence nonconformists. "In this context, the Court's decision may be seen for what...it really is: another of the dominant culture's inevitable efforts to force those groups who do not share its mores to conform to its way of thinking, acting, and speaking." *FCC v. Pacifica*, 438 U.S. 726 (1978). Nonetheless, the principle was established that "intrusive" media were subject to special restraints.

In 1996, Congress undertook its broadest effort to devise standards governing the transmission of indecent materials. The Communications Decency Act ("CDA," Title V of the Telecommunications Act of 1996) was an effort to establish rules for the Internet, while section 505 of the Act created new rules governing cable television. In reviewing both statutes, the Court applied strict scrutiny in a way that was noticeably missing in *Pacifica*, treating cable and the Internet as public forums rather than as invasive technologies.

Section 505 required cable stations that primarily showed sexually oriented programing to either scramble their signals or restrict the hours of their operation. Playboy Entertainment challenged the law, arguing that a "well-promoted blocking program" (whereby individual households could choose to have specific stations blocked) was a less restrictive but equally effective alternative. The Court accepted Playboy's argument. Justice Kennedy, writing for the majority (Rehnquist, Scalia, O'Connor, and Breyer dissenting), explained the difference between cable television and radio:

> There is, moreover, a key difference between cable television and the broadcasting media, which is the point on which this case turns: Cable systems have the capacity to block unwanted channels on a household-by-household basis. The option to block reduces the likelihood, so concerning to the Court in Pacifica, that traditional First Amendment scrutiny would deprive the Government of all authority to address this sort of problem. The corollary, of course, is that targeted blocking enables the Government to support parental authority without affecting the First Amendment interests of speakers and willing listeners—listeners for whom, if the speech is unpopular or indecent, the privacy of their own homes may be the optimal place of receipt. Simply put, targeted blocking is less restrictive than banning, and the Government cannot ban speech if targeted blocking is a feasible and effective means of furthering its compelling interests. This is not to say that the absence of an effective blocking mechanism will in all cases suffice to support a law restricting the speech in question; but if a less restrictive means is available for the Government to achieve its goals, the Government must use it. *United States v. Playboy Entertainment Group*, 529 U.S. 803 (2000).

Justice Thomas concurred, but wrote that he would have found at least some of the materials being broadcast obscene, and hence subject to regulation. "[G]overnmental restriction on the distribution of obscene materials receives no First Amendment scrutiny."

Justice Scalia dissented on the grounds that regardless of whether the material in question was obscene, it was subject to regulation on the grounds that the speech in question had little social value:

> We have recognized that commercial entities which engage in "the sordid business of pandering" by "deliberately emphasizing the sexually provocative aspects of [their nonobscene products], in order to catch the salaciously disposed," engage in constitutionally unprotected behavior. This is so whether or not the products in which the business traffics independently meet the high hurdle we have estab-

lished for delineating the obscene.... We are more permissive of government regulation in these circumstances because it is clear from the context in which exchanges between such businesses and their customers occur that neither the merchant nor the buyer is interested in the work's literary, artistic, political, or scientific value.

Although the example cited by Scalia concerned commercial advertising, he made it clear that his argument reached further than that. "The test applies equally to the improbable case in which a collector of indecent materials wishes to give them away, and takes out a classified ad in the local newspaper touting their salacious appeal. Commercial motive or not, the circumstances of...dissemination are relevant to determining whether [the] social importance claimed for [the] material [is]...pretense or reality." The focus on advertising may be misleading; the speech at issue in the case, of course, was not advertisements for programs but the programs themselves. Thus Scalia's argument seems to be the general proposition that indecent materials may be regulated where the Court finds them to lack social value based on the "circumstances of [their] dissemination." This was precisely the argument that the majority was unwilling to accept. As Justice Thomas put it, "The Government...asks us to dilute our stringent First Amendment standards to uphold § 505 as a proper regulation of protected (rather than unprotected) speech. I am unwilling to corrupt the First Amendment to reach this result. The 'starch' in our constitutional standards cannot be sacrificed to accommodate the enforcement choices of the Government." *United States v. Playboy Entertainment Group*, 529 U.S. 803 (2000).

Congress's attempt to regulate the Internet was similarly unsuccessful. The CDA made it a federal crime to use a computer service to send or display "in a manner available to a person under 18 years of age any comment, request, suggestion, proposal, image, or other communication that, in context, depicts or describes, in terms patently offensive as measured by contemporary community standards, sexual or excretory activities or organs, regardless of whether the user of such service placed the call or initiated the communication." The drafters of the CDA tried to avoids running afoul of the principle declared in *Butler*, that adults should not be held to the standards of children, by the inclusion of specified defenses for "good faith, reasonable, effective, and appropriate actions under the circumstances to restrict or prevent access by minors...by requiring use of a verified credit card, debit account, adult access code, or adult personal identification number." These defenses were quite sweeping;

for instance, in the *Thomas* case there could have been no prosecution under the CDA.

Nonetheless, in *Reno v. ACLU*, 521 U.S. 844 (1997), the Court struck down the law on grounds of overbreadth and the chilling effect that it was likely to have on protected speech. The government argued that the CDA was constitutional on the basis of three key precedents: *Ginsberg*, *Pacifica*, and *Sable*. Justice Stevens, who had earlier written the opinion in *Pacifica*, distinguished the situation of cyberspace from that of radio by virtue of the facts that the Internet is not "invasive," bandwidth is not a scarce commodity to which monopolies are granted by the government, and there is no extensive history of government regulation of Internet activities. Similarly, he found that the law upheld in *Ginsberg* was different from the CDA in that it had only targeted commercial transactions with minors, and had thus left open the possibility that parents might provide their minor children with such materials as they deemed fit. "Under the CDA, by contrast, neither the parents' consent—nor even their participation—in the communication would avoid the application of the statute." *Renton* was distinguished on the grounds that the zoning ordinance at issue in that case had been a content neutral regulation aimed at curbing the secondary effects of speech rather than its message. By contrast, the CDA "is a content-based blanket restriction on speech, and, as such, cannot be properly analyzed as a form of time, place, and manner regulation." As a result, the Court applied strict scrutiny to the CDA, and found the law to be unconstitutional on grounds of overbreadth. Note, in particular, Stevens's discussion of a chilling effect. "Could a speaker confidently assume," he asks, "that a serious discussion about birth control practices, homosexuality...or the consequences of prison rape would not violate the CDA?"

RENO v. AMERICAN CIVIL LIBERTIES UNION

SUPREME COURT OF THE UNITED STATES

521 U.S. 844 (1997)

JUSTICE STEVENS delivered the opinion of the Court, in which SCALIA, KENNEDY, SOUTER, THOMAS, GINSBURG, and BREYER joined. O'CONNOR filed an opinion concurring in the judgment in part and dissenting in part, in which REHNQUIST, C. J., joined.

> ...[S]ome of our cases have recognized special justifications for regulation of the broadcast media that are not applicable to other speakers. In these cases, the Court relied on the history of extensive government regulation of the broadcast

medium, the scarcity of available frequencies at its inception, and its "invasive" nature.

Those factors are not present in cyberspace. Neither before nor after the enactment of the CDA have the vast democratic fora of the Internet been subject to the type of government supervision and regulation that has attended the broadcast industry. Moreover, the Internet is not as invasive as radio or television. The District Court specifically found that "communications over the Internet do not 'invade' an individual's home or appear on one's computer screen unbidden. Users seldom encounter content by accident." It also found that "almost all sexually explicit images are preceded by warnings as to the content," and cited testimony that "odds are slim that a user would come across a sexually explicit site by accident...."

Finally, unlike the conditions that prevailed when Congress first authorized regulation of the broadcast spectrum, the Internet can hardly be considered a "scarce" expressive commodity. It provides relatively unlimited, low-cost capacity for communication of all kinds. The Government estimates that "as many as 40 million people use the Internet today, and that figure is expected to grow to 200 million by 1999." This dynamic, multifaceted category of communication includes not only traditional print and news services, but also audio, video, and still images, as well as interactive, real-time dialogue. Through the use of chat rooms, any person with a phone line can become a town crier with a voice that resonates farther than it could from any soapbox. Through the use of Web pages, mail exploders, and newsgroups, the same individual can become a pamphleteer. As the District Court found, "the content on the Internet is as diverse as human thought." We agree with its conclusion that our cases provide no basis for qualifying the level of First Amendment scrutiny that should be applied to this medium....

Regardless of whether the CDA is so vague that it violates the Fifth Amendment, the many ambiguities concerning the scope of its coverage render it problematic for purposes of the First Amendment. For instance, each of the two parts of the CDA uses a different linguistic form. The first uses the word "indecent," while the second speaks of material that "in context, depicts or describes, in terms patently offensive as measured by contemporary community standards, sexual or excretory activities or organs." Given the absence of a definition of either term, this difference in language will provoke uncertainty among speakers about how the two standards relate to each other and just what they mean. n37 Could a speaker confidently assume that a serious discussion about birth control practices, homosexuality, the First Amendment issues raised by the Appendix to our *Pacifica* opinion, or the consequences of prison rape would not violate the CDA? This uncertainty undermines the likelihood that the CDA has been carefully tailored to the congressional goal of protecting minors from potentially harmful materials.

---

n37 The statute does not indicate whether the "patently offensive" and "indecent" determinations should be made with respect to minors or the population as a whole. The Government asserts that the appropriate standard is "what is suitable material for minors." But the Conferees expressly rejected amendments that would have imposed such a "harmful to minors" standard. The Conferees also rejected amendments that would have limited the proscribed materials to those lacking redeeming value.

The vagueness of the CDA is a matter of special concern for two reasons. First, the CDA is a content-based regulation of speech. The vagueness of such a regulation raises special First Amendment concerns because of its obvious chilling effect on free speech. Second, the CDA is a criminal statute. In addition to the opprobrium and stigma of a criminal conviction, the CDA threatens violators with penalties including up to two years in prison for each act of violation. The severity of criminal sanctions may well cause speakers to remain silent rather than communicate even arguably unlawful words, ideas, and images. As a practical matter, this increased deterrent effect, coupled with the "risk of discriminatory enforcement" of vague regulations, poses greater First Amendment concerns than those implicated by...civil regulation....

The Government argues that the statute is no more vague than the obscenity standard this Court established in *Miller v. California*.... Because the CDA's "patently offensive" standard (and, we assume arguendo, its synonymous "indecent" standard) is one part of the three-prong *Miller* test, the Government reasons, it cannot be unconstitutionally vague. The Government's assertion is incorrect as a matter of fact. The second prong of the *Miller* test—the purportedly analogous standard—contains a critical requirement that is omitted from the CDA: that the proscribed material be "specifically defined by the applicable state law." This requirement reduces the vagueness inherent in the open-ended term "patently offensive" as used in the CDA. Moreover, the *Miller* definition is limited to "sexual conduct," whereas the CDA extends also to include (1) "excretory activities" as well as (2) "organs" of both a sexual and excretory nature....

In contrast to *Miller* and our other previous cases, the CDA thus presents a greater threat of censoring speech that, in fact, falls outside the statute's scope. Given the vague contours of the coverage of the statute, it unquestionably silences some speakers whose messages would be entitled to constitutional protection. That danger provides further reason for insisting that the statute not be overly broad. The CDA's burden on protected speech cannot be justified if it could be avoided by a more carefully drafted statute.

We are persuaded that the CDA lacks the precision that the First Amendment requires when a statute regulates the content of speech. In order to deny minors access to potentially harmful speech, the CDA effectively suppresses a large amount of speech that adults have a constitutional right to receive and to address to one another. That burden on adult speech is unacceptable if less restrictive alternatives would be at least as effective in achieving the legitimate purpose that the statute was enacted to serve.

In evaluating the free speech rights of adults, we have made it perfectly clear that "sexual expression which is indecent but not obscene is protected by the First Amendment." Indeed, *Pacifica* itself admonished that "the fact that society may find speech offensive is not a sufficient reason for suppressing it." It is true that we have repeatedly recognized the governmental interest in protecting children from harmful materials. But that interest does not justify an unnecessarily broad suppression of speech addressed to adults. As we have explained, the Government may not "reduce the adult population...[to] only what is fit for children." "Regardless of the strength of the government's interest" in protecting children, "the level of discourse reaching a mailbox simply cannot be limited to that which would be suitable for a sandbox...."

In arguing that the CDA does not so diminish adult communication, the Government relies on the incorrect factual premise that prohibiting a transmission whenever it is known that one of its recipients is a minor would not interfere with adult-to-adult communication. The findings of the District Court make clear that this premise is untenable. Given the size of the potential audience for most messages, in the absence of a viable age verification process, the sender must be charged with knowing that one or more minors will likely view it. Knowledge that, for instance, one or more members of a 100-person chat group will be a minor—and therefore that it would be a crime to send the group an indecent message—would surely burden communication among adults.

The District Court found that at time of trial existing technology did not include any effective method for a sender to prevent minors from obtaining access to its communications on the Internet without also denying access to adults. The Court found no effective way to determine the age of a user who is accessing material through e-mail, mail exploders, newsgroups, or chat rooms. As a practical matter, the Court also found that it would be prohibitively expensive for noncommercial—as well as some commercial—speakers who have Web sites to verify that their users are adults. These limitations must inevitably curtail a significant amount of adult communication on the Internet. By contrast, the District Court found that "despite its limitations, currently available user-based software suggests that a reasonably effective method by which parents can prevent their children from accessing sexually explicit and other material which parents may believe is inappropriate for their children will soon be widely available."

The breadth of the CDA's coverage is wholly unprecedented. Unlike the regulations upheld in *Ginsberg* and *Pacifica*, the scope of the CDA is not limited to commercial speech or commercial entities. Its open-ended prohibitions embrace all nonprofit entities and individuals posting indecent messages or displaying them on their own computers in the presence of minors. The general, undefined terms "indecent" and "patently offensive" cover large amounts of nonpornographic material with serious educational or other value. n44 Moreover, the "community standards" criterion as applied to the Internet means that any communication available to a nation-wide audience will be judged by the standards of the community most likely to be offended by the message. The regulated subject matter includes any of the seven "dirty words" used in the *Pacifica* monologue, the use of which the Government's expert acknowledged could constitute a felony. It may also extend to discussions about prison rape or safe sexual practices, artistic images that include nude subjects, and arguably the card catalogue of the Carnegie Library.

n44 Transmitting obscenity and child pornography, whether via the Internet or other means, is already illegal under federal law for both adults and juveniles. In fact, when Congress was considering the CDA, the Government expressed its view that the law was unnecessary because existing laws already authorized its ongoing efforts to prosecute obscenity, child pornography, and child solicitation.

For the purposes of our decision, we need neither accept nor reject the Government's submission that the First Amendment does not forbid a blanket prohibition on all "indecent" and "patently offensive" messages communicated to a 17-year-old—no matter how much value the message may contain and regardless of parental approval. It is at least clear that the strength of the Government's interest in protecting minors is not equally strong throughout the coverage of this broad statute. Under the CDA, a parent allowing her 17-year-old to use the family computer to obtain information on the Internet that she, in her parental judgment, deems appropriate could face a lengthy prison term. Similarly, a parent who sent his 17-year-old college freshman information on birth control via e-mail could be incarcerated even though neither he, his child, nor anyone in their home community, found the material "indecent" or "patently offensive," if the college town's community thought otherwise.

The breadth of this content-based restriction of speech imposes an especially heavy burden on the Government to explain why a less restrictive provision would not be as effective as the CDA. It has not done so. The arguments in this Court have referred to possible alternatives such as requiring that indecent material be "tagged" in a way that facilitates parental control of material coming into their homes, making exceptions for messages with artistic or educational value, providing some tolerance for parental choice, and regulating some portions of the Internet—such as commercial web sites—differently than others, such as chat rooms. Particularly in the light of the absence of any detailed findings by the Congress, or even hearings addressing the special problems of the CDA, we are persuaded that the CDA is not narrowly tailored if that requirement has any meaning at all....

D.   *Sexual Harassment*

While obscenity and indecency are categories that have a century of tradition behind them (although it is not clear how or whether they would have been understood at the time of the ratification of the First Amendment), in the 1970s Congress recognized a newly defined category of unprotected speech: sexual harassment. The concept of sexual harassment was simple; like blackmail, or threats of violence, sexually harassing speech was a form of expression that had destructive and coercive effects on its target. The sexual harasser, by this reasoning, was not expressing a message, he (usually) was perpetrating an act upon an unwilling victim. Based on its authority to regulate employment as an aspect of both interstate commerce and the Fourteenth Amendment's guarantee of equal protection, Congress created Title VII of the 1964 Civil Rights Act prohibiting discrimination in employment. In *Meritor Savings Bank v. Vinson*, 477 U.S. 57 (1986), the court unanimously held that Title VII prohibits sexual harassment in the workplace as well as discrimination in hiring. This ruling set the stage for consideration of the implications of sexual harassment law for the First Amendment.

HARRIS v. FORKLIFT SYSTEMS, INC.

SUPREME COURT OF THE UNITED STATES

510 U.S. 17 (1993)

JUSTICE O'CONNOR delivered the opinion for a unanimous Court. SCALIA, J., and GINSBURG, J., filed concurring opinions.

...Teresa Harris worked as a manager at Forklift Systems, Inc., an equipment rental company, from April 1985 until October 1987. Charles Hardy was Forklift's president. The Magistrate found that, throughout Harris' time at Forklift, Hardy often insulted her because of her gender and often made her the target of unwanted sexual innuendos. Hardy told Harris on several occasions, in the presence of other employees, "You're a woman, what do you know" and "We need a man as the rental manager"; at least once, he told her she was "a dumb ass woman." Again in front of others, he suggested that the two of them "go to the Holiday Inn to negotiate [Harris'] raise." Hardy occasionally asked Harris and other female employees to get coins from his front pants pocket. He threw objects on the ground in front of Harris and other women, and asked them to pick the objects up. He made sexual innuendos about Harris' and other women's clothing.

In mid-August 1987, Harris complained to Hardy about his conduct. Hardy said he was surprised that Harris was offended, claimed he was only joking, and apologized. He also promised he would stop, and based on this assurance Harris stayed on the job. But in early September, Hardy began anew: While Harris was arranging a deal with one of Forklift's customers, he asked her, again in front of other employees, "What did you do, promise the guy...some [sex] Saturday night?" On October 1, Harris collected her paycheck and quit.

Harris then sued Forklift, claiming that Hardy's conduct had created an abusive work environment for her because of her gender. The United States District Court for the Middle District of Tennessee...found this to be "a close case," but held that Hardy's conduct did not create an abusive environment. The court found that some of Hardy's comments "offended [Harris], and would offend the reasonable woman," but that they were not "so severe as to be expected to seriously affect [Harris'] psychological well-being....

Title VII of the Civil Rights Act of 1964 makes it "an unlawful employment practice for an employer...to discriminate against any individual with respect to his compensation, terms, conditions, or privileges of employment, because of such individual's race, color, religion, sex, or national origin." As we made clear in *Meritor Savings Bank v. Vinson*, 477 U.S. 57 (1986), this language "is not limited to 'economic' or 'tangible' discrimination. The phrase 'terms, conditions, or privileges of employment' evinces a congressional intent to strike at the entire spectrum of disparate treatment of men and women in employment, which includes requiring people to work in a discriminatorily hostile or abusive environment. When the workplace is permeated with "discriminatory intimidation, ridicule, and insult," that is "sufficiently severe or pervasive to alter the conditions of the victim's employment and create an abusive working environment," Title VII is violated. This standard, which we reaffirm today, takes a middle path between making actionable any conduct that is merely offensive and requiring the conduct to cause a tangible psychological injury. As we pointed out in *Meritor*, "mere utterance of an...epithet which engenders offensive feelings in a employee," does not sufficiently affect the conditions of employment to implicate Title VII. Conduct that is not severe or pervasive enough to create an objectively hostile or abusive work environment—an environment that a reasonable person would find hostile or abusive—is beyond Title VII's purview. Likewise, if the victim does not subjectively perceive the environment to be abusive, the conduct has not actually altered the conditions of the victim's employment, and there is no Title VII violation.

But Title VII comes into play before the harassing conduct leads to a nervous breakdown. A discriminatorily abusive work environment, even one that does not seriously affect employees' psychological well-being, can and often will detract from employees' job performance, discourage employees from remaining on the job, or keep them from advancing in their careers. Moreover, even without regard to these tangible effects, the very fact that the discriminatory conduct was so severe or pervasive that it created a work environment abusive to employees because of their race, gender, religion, or national origin offends Title VII's broad rule of workplace equality. The appalling conduct alleged in *Meritor*, and the reference in that case to environments "so heavily polluted with discrimination as to destroy completely the emotional and psychological stability of minority group workers," merely present some especially egregious examples of harassment. They do not mark the boundary of what is actionable....

This is not, and by its nature cannot be, a mathematically precise test. We need not answer today all the potential questions it raises, nor specifically address the EEOC's new regulations on this subject. But we can say that whether an environment is "hostile" or "abusive" can be determined only by looking at all the circumstances. These may include the frequency of the discriminatory conduct; its severity; whether it is physically threatening or humiliating, or a mere offensive utterance; and whether it unreasonably interferes with an employee's work performance. The effect on the employee's psychological well-being is, of course, relevant to determining whether the plaintiff actually found the environment abusive. But while psychological harm, like any other relevant factor, may be taken into account, no single factor is required....

The significance of the decision in *Harris* was that it not only affirmed Congress' authority to regulate a category of expression called "sexual harassment," it also made it clear that the category stood on its own. That is, the harm of harassment in the workplace was that it occurred at all, not that it led to some other, independently cognizable psychological harm of the sort that would support a lawsuit. The difficulty, however, is in defining the boundaries of this category of expression. What makes harassment "sexual" in a case less obvious than that of Teresa Harris? In *Oncale v. Sundowner Offshore*, 118 S.Ct. 998 (1998), the Court held that an action for sexual harassment could be maintained under Title VII where the harassers and the victim were all male, and the victim was not homosexual. What made the expression a basis for liability, in other words, was its content, not the identity of the listener or the personal relationship between the parties involved. The *Oncale* decision, written by Justice Scalia, focused on the issue of statutory interpretation rather than the First Amendment, but the treatment of sexual harassment as a form of discrimination based on sex emphasizes the extent to which this category of expression is treated as "nonspeech."

E. Hate Speech: Reconsidering the Categorical Approach

No category is more controversial than that of "hate speech." The roots of this category can be found in the idea of "group libel" in *Beauharnais*, but the more common formulation treats hate speech as an outgrowth of the *Chaplinsky* "fighting words" concept. The arguments in favor of recognizing such an unprotected category are familiar from those earlier cases: racist insults and sexual taunts cause injury to the listener and to society at large, contribute nothing to the exposition of ideas, and violate fundamental democratic norms. The problem for hate speech, as it was for obscenity, is in drafting a description of such speech that does not suffer from overbreadth. In the case of obscenity, the Court has been willing to grant communities the autonomy to make the determination of what "offends... standards," limited by an objective (i.e., expert) evaluation of artistic value. Confronted by the same challenge in the case of hate speech regulation, however, the Court reached the opposite conclusion.

In 1990, the Jones family moved into a neighborhood of St. Paul, Minnesota. They were the first African-American family in the neighborhood, and they immediately encountered racial hostility from some of their neighbors. Their tires were slashed, racial epithets were yelled at their children, a car window was broken. On June 21, two teenagers burned a cross on the Joneses' front lawn. The teens were convicted of violating a St. Paul ordinance which read as follows: "Whoever places on public or private property a symbol, object, appellation, characterization or graffiti, including, but not limited to, a burning cross or Nazi swastika, which one knows or has reasonable grounds to know arouses anger, alarm or resentment in others on the basis of race, color, creed, religion or gender commits disorderly conduct and shall be guilty of a misdemeanor." One of the convicted teens challenged the law on the grounds that it violated the First Amendment's guarantee of free speech.

Reviewing the statute, the Court found it unconstitutional by a vote of 9 to 0. The unanimity of the outcome, however, hid deep divisions within the Court over the analysis that was contained in Justice Scalia's majority opinion. Four justices—White, Blackmun, O'Connor, and Stevens—agreed that the St. Paul ordinance was overbroad, but argued that there was nothing wrong in principle with a city's attempt to criminalize hate speech, on the grounds that such speech fit into the recognized unprotected category of "fighting words." Justice Scalia, by contrast, wrote an opinion that radically reconfigured the categorical approach to analyzing free speech cases.

The precise argument that Scalia makes is complex, and difficult to follow. First, he states that the phrase "unprotected speech" really had never meant unprotected speech, only speech that is less valued and hence less protected than other speech. He then goes on to describe an approach to evaluating statutes that regulated unprotected speech, finding that there is a fundamental requirement of viewpoint neutrality. Thus, while speech may be defined as "unprotected" (or less protected) by virtue of its content, government is not permitted to single out a subset of that unprotected speech on the basis of its viewpoint. That does not mean, however, that government may never single out a subset of unprotected speech for regulation. Government is free to focus on a subset of an unprotected category of speech so long as there is no "realistic possibility that official suppression of ideas is afoot." If the subset of the unprotected category is chosen on a content neutral basis (e.g., in certain media or limited markets), or on an essentially random basis (Scalia uses the example of "obscene films starring blue-eyed actresses,") then there is no constitutional problem.

What is not clear is the connection that Justice Scalia draws between singling out a subset of unprotected speech based on its content, and doing the same thing based on viewpoint. For example, Scalia describes two forms of content-based regulation of some-but-not-all of a category of unprotected speech that would not be problematic: laws that singled out particularly egregious examples of the unprotected category, and laws that singled out a subset of an unprotected category because of secondary effects associated with that speech. These permissible content-based restrictions are themselves limited by the requirement of viewpoint neutrality, but beyond that they seem to be exceptions that entirely swallow the rule against content-based subcategory regulation. In the end, therefore, Scalia's analysis is understood to require viewpoint neutrality in the regulation of unprotected categories of expression.

Justice Scalia's analysis was controversial for two distinct reasons. First, as the four concurring justices pointed out, it was an entirely novel way of thinking about unprotected categories of expression that cast doubt on the continuing validity of the categorical approach *per se*. If unprotected speech is not absolutely unprotected, is "protected speech" absolutely protected? Or are sharp categorical definitions blurring into the kind of hierarchy of values that was seen to be at work in the indecency cases? More specifically, although Justice Scalia cites *Chaplinsky*, does the category of "fighting words" survive *R. A. V.* intact? The second basis of controversy has to do with Scalia's application of his viewpoint neutrality analysis to the statute at issue in the case. The concurring justices accused Scalia of employing false analogies and a distortion of existing categories to find viewpoint discrimination where there was none. Thus, while there was unanimous agreement that the St. Paul ordinance was unconstitutional, there was only a narrow five-member majority that was willing to join in Justice Scalia's revision of the categorical approach.

R. A. V. v. CITY OF ST. PAUL, MINNESOTA

SUPREME COURT OF THE UNITED STATES

505 U.S. 377 (1992)

JUSTICE SCALIA delivered the opinion of the Court, in which REHNQUIST, C. J., and KENNEDY, SOUTER, and THOMAS joined. JUSTICE WHITE filed an opinion concurring in the judgment, in which BLACKMUN and O'CONNOR joined, and in which STEVENS joined except as to Part I - A. JUSTICE BLACKMUN filed an opinion concurring in the judgment. JUSTICE STEVENS filed an opinion concurring in the judgment, in Part I of which WHITE and BLACKMUN joined.

...In construing the St. Paul ordinance, we are bound by the construction given to it by the Minnesota court.... Accordingly, we accept the Minnesota Supreme Court's authoritative statement that the ordinance reaches only those expressions that constitute "fighting words" within the meaning of *Chaplinsky*. 464 N. W. 2d, at 510-511. Petitioner and his amici urge us to modify the scope of the *Chaplinsky* formulation, thereby invalidating the ordinance as "substantially overbroad." We find it unnecessary to consider this issue. Assuming, arguendo, that all of the expression reached by the ordinance is proscribable under the "fighting words" doctrine, we nonetheless conclude that the ordinance is facially unconstitutional in that it prohibits otherwise permitted speech solely on the basis of the subjects the speech addresses.

The First Amendment generally prevents government from proscribing speech...or even expressive conduct...because of disapproval of the ideas expressed. Content-based regulations are presumptively invalid.... From 1791 to the present, however, our society, like other free but civilized societies, has permitted restrictions upon the content of speech in a few limited areas, which are "of such slight social value as a step to truth that any benefit that may be derived from them is clearly outweighed by the social interest in order and morality." We have recognized that "the freedom of speech" referred to by the First Amendment does not include a freedom to disregard these traditional limitations.... Our decisions since the 1960s have narrowed the scope of the traditional categorical exceptions for defamation...and for obscenity...but a limited categorical approach has remained an important part of our First Amendment jurisprudence.

We have sometimes said that these categories of expression are "not within the area of constitutionally protected speech," or that the "protection of the First Amendment does not extend" to them. Such statements must be taken in context, however, and are no more literally true than is the occasionally repeated shorthand characterizing obscenity "as not being speech at all." What they mean is that these areas of speech can, consistently with the First Amendment, be regulated because of their constitutionally proscribable content (obscenity, defamation, etc.)—not that they are categories of speech entirely invisible to the Constitution, so that they may be made the vehicles for content discrimination unrelated to their distinctively proscribable content. Thus, the government may proscribe libel; but it may not make the further content discrimination of proscribing only libel critical of the government....

Our cases surely do not establish the proposition that the First Amendment imposes no obstacle whatsoever to regulation of particular instances of such proscribable expression, so that the government "may regulate [them] freely." That would mean that a city council could enact an ordinance prohibiting only those legally obscene works that contain criticism of the city government or, indeed, that do not include endorsement of the city government. Such a simplistic, all-or-nothing-at-all approach to First Amendment protection is at odds with common sense and with our jurisprudence as well. It is not true that "fighting words" have at most a "de minimis" expressive content, ibid., or that their content is in all respects "worthless and undeserving of constitutional protection"; sometimes they are quite expressive indeed. We have not said that they constitute "no part of the expression of ideas," but only that they constitute "no essential part of any exposition of ideas."

The proposition that a particular instance of speech can be proscribable on the basis of one feature (e.g., obscenity) but not on the basis of another (e.g., opposition to the city government) is commonplace, and has found application in many contexts. We have long held, for example, that nonverbal expressive activity can be banned because of the action it entails, but not because of the ideas it expresses—so that burning a flag in violation of an ordinance against outdoor fires could be punishable, whereas burning a flag in violation of an ordinance against dishonoring the flag is not.... Similarly, we have upheld reasonable "time, place, or manner" restrictions, but only if they are "justified without reference to the content of the regulated speech...." And just as the power to proscribe particular speech on the basis of a noncontent element (e.g., noise) does not entail the power to proscribe the same speech on the basis of a content element; so also, the power to proscribe it on the basis of one content element (e.g., obscenity) does not entail the power to proscribe it on the basis of other content elements.

In other words, the exclusion of "fighting words" from the scope of the First Amendment simply means that, for purposes of that Amendment, the unprotected features of the words are, despite their verbal character, essentially a "nonspeech" element of communication. Fighting words are thus analogous to a noisy sound truck: Each is, as Justice Frankfurter recognized, a "mode of speech"; both can be used to convey an idea; but neither has, in and of itself, a claim upon the First Amendment. As with the sound truck, however, so also with fighting words: The government may not regulate use based on hostility—or favoritism—towards the underlying message expressed....

Even the prohibition against content discrimination that we assert the First Amendment requires is not absolute. It applies differently in the context of proscribable speech than in the area of fully protected speech. The rationale of the general prohibition, after all, is that content discrimination "raises the specter that the Government may effectively drive certain ideas or viewpoints from the marketplace." But content discrimination among various instances of a class of proscribable speech often does not pose this threat.

When the basis for the content discrimination consists entirely of the very reason the entire class of speech at issue is proscribable, no significant danger of idea or viewpoint discrimination exists. Such a reason, having been adjudged neutral enough to support exclusion of the entire class of speech from First Amendment protection, is also neutral enough to form the basis of distinction within the class. To illustrate: A State might choose to prohibit only that obscenity which is the most patently offensive in its prurience—i.e., that which involves the most lascivious displays of sexual activity. But it may not prohibit, for example, only that obscenity which includes offensive political messages. And the Federal Government can criminalize only those threats of violence that are directed against the President—since the reasons why threats of violence are outside the First Amendment (protecting individuals from the fear of violence, from the disruption that fear engenders, and from the possibility that the threatened violence will occur) have special force when applied to the person of the President. But the Federal Government may not criminalize only those threats against the President that mention his policy on aid to inner cities. And to take a final example, a State may choose to regulate price advertising in one industry but not in others, because the risk of fraud (one of the characteristics of commercial speech that justifies depriving it of full First Amendment protection) is in its view greater there. But a State may not prohibit only that commercial advertising that depicts men in a demeaning fashion.

Another valid basis for according differential treatment to even a content-defined subclass of proscribable speech is that the subclass happens to be associated with particular "secondary effects" of the speech, so that the regulation is justified without reference to the content of the speech. A State could, for example, permit all obscene live performances except those involving minors. Moreover, since words can in some circumstances violate laws directed not against speech but against conduct (a law against treason, for example, is violated by telling the enemy the nation's defense secrets), a particular content-based subcategory of a proscribable class of speech can be swept up incidentally within the reach of a statute directed at conduct rather than speech. Thus, for example, sexually derogatory "fighting words," among other words, may produce a violation of Title VII's general prohibition against sexual discrimination in employment practices. Where the government does not target conduct on the basis of its expressive content, acts are not shielded from regulation merely because they express a discriminatory idea or philosophy.

These bases for distinction refute the proposition that the selectivity of the restriction is "even arguably conditioned upon the sovereign's agreement with what a speaker may intend to say." There may be other such bases as well. Indeed, to validate such selectivity (where totally proscribable speech is at issue) it may not even be necessary to identify any particular "neutral" basis, so long as the nature of the content discrimination is such that there is no realistic possibility that official suppression of ideas is afoot. (We cannot think of any First Amendment interest that would stand in the way of a State's prohibiting only those obscene motion pictures with blue-eyed actresses.) Save for that limitation, the regulation of "fighting words," like the regulation of noisy speech, may address some offensive instances and leave other, equally offensive, instances alone.

Applying these principles to the St. Paul ordinance, we conclude that, even as narrowly construed by the Minnesota Supreme Court, the ordinance is facially unconstitutional. Although the phrase in the ordinance, "arouses anger, alarm or resentment in others," has been limited by the Minnesota Supreme Court's construction to reach only those symbols or displays that amount to "fighting words," the remaining, unmodified terms make clear that the ordinance applies only to "fighting words" that insult, or provoke violence, "on the basis of race, color, creed, religion or gender." Displays containing abusive invective, no matter how vicious or severe, are permissible unless they are addressed to one of the specified disfavored topics. Those who wish to use "fighting words" in connection with other ideas—to express hostility, for example, on the basis of political affiliation, union membership, or homosexuality—are not covered. The First Amendment does not permit St. Paul to impose special prohibitions on those speakers who express views on disfavored subjects.

In its practical operation, moreover, the ordinance goes even beyond mere content discrimination, to actual viewpoint discrimination. Displays containing some words—odious racial epithets, for example—would be prohibited to proponents of all views. But "fighting words" that do not themselves invoke race, color, creed, religion, or gender—aspersions upon a person's mother, for example—would seemingly be usable ad libitum in the placards of those arguing in favor of racial, color, etc. tolerance and equality, but could not be used by that speaker's opponents. One could hold up a sign saying, for example, that all "anti-Catholic bigots" are misbegotten; but not that all "papists" are, for that would insult and provoke violence "on the basis of religion." St. Paul has no such authority to license one side of a debate to fight freestyle, while requiring the other to follow Marquis of Queensbury Rules.

What we have here, it must be emphasized, is not a prohibition of fighting words that are directed at certain persons or groups (which would be facially valid if it met the requirements of the Equal Protection Clause); but rather, a prohibition of fighting words that contain (as the Minnesota Supreme Court repeatedly emphasized) messages of "bias-motivated" hatred and in particular, as applied to this case, messages "based on virulent notions of racial supremacy." One must wholeheartedly agree with the Minnesota Supreme Court that "it is the responsibility, even the obligation, of diverse communities to confront such notions in whatever form they appear," but the manner of that confrontation cannot consist of selective limitations upon speech. St. Paul's brief asserts that a general "fighting words" law would not meet the city's needs because only a content-specific measure can communicate to minority groups that the "group hatred" aspect of such speech "is not condoned by the majority." The point of the First Amendment is that majority preferences must be expressed in some fashion other than silencing speech on the basis of its content....

St. Paul and its amici defend the conclusion of the Minnesota Supreme Court that, even if the ordinance regulates expression based on hostility towards its protected ideological content, this discrimination is nonetheless justified because it is narrowly tailored to serve compelling state interests. Specifically, they assert that the ordinance helps to ensure the basic human rights of members of groups that have historically been subjected to discrimination, including the right of such group members to live in peace where they wish. We do not doubt that these interests are compelling, and that the ordinance can be said to promote them. But the "danger of censorship" presented by a facially content-based statute requires that that weapon be employed only where it is "necessary to serve the asserted [compelling] interest." The existence of adequate content-neutral alternatives thus "undercuts significantly" any defense of such a statute, casting considerable doubt on the government's protestations that "the asserted justification is in fact an accurate description of the purpose and effect of the law." The dispositive question in this case, therefore, is whether content discrimination is reasonably necessary to achieve St. Paul's compelling interests; it plainly is not. An ordinance not limited to the favored topics, for example, would have precisely the same beneficial effect. In fact the only interest distinctively served by the content limitation is that of displaying the city council's special hostility towards the particular biases thus singled out. That is precisely what the First Amendment forbids. The politicians of St. Paul are entitled to express that hostility—but not through the means of imposing unique limitations upon speakers who (however benightedly) disagree....

Justice Scalia's observation that the defendants in the case might have been charged under a variety of statutes bore fruit. R. A. V. and three of his fellows were charged with violation of federal civil rights laws for their acts of burning a cross on the Joneses' lawn and in two other locations. These laws fit the description of "a prohibition of fighting words that are directed at certain persons or groups (which would be facially valid if it met the requirements of the Equal Protection Clause)." The federal statute at issue declares that whoever "by force or threat of force willfully injures, intimidates or interferes with...any person because of his race, color, religion, sex, handicap...familial status...or national origin and because he is...occupying...any dwelling" commits a violation of fair housing laws. The defendants argued that this law must be found to be unconstitutional by the analysis in R. A. V., but the Eighth Circuit disagreed:

> The government argues that the convictions at issue do not violate the First Amendment because J. H. H. and R. A. V. were convicted for using cross-burning as a means to threaten and to intimidate the Jones family. The government points out that 18 U.S.C. § 241 and 42 U.S.C. § 3631 are not directed toward protected speech, but are directed only at intentional threats, intimidation, and interference with federally guaranteed rights. The government further emphasizes that the statutes punish any threat or intimidation, or conspiracy to threaten or to intimidate, violating the statutes regardless of the viewpoint guiding the action. This, the government contends, distinguishes prosecution under these statutes from prosecution pursuant to the St. Paul ordinance invalidated in R. A. V. We agree.... *United States v. J. H. H.*, 22 F.3d 821 (8th Cir. 1994).

The court also ruled that in addition to testimony concerning statements by the defendants, expert testimony could be admitted to explain the significance of symbols such as burning crosses, as well as testimony by the victims (the Jones family) to explain the threat that they understood to be implied by the presence of a burning cross on their lawn.

In 1993, the Court heard a case challenging a Wisconsin law that did not make hate speech a crime in itself, but instead made a motive of racial animus a factor in determining the appropriate sentence after conviction for another offense. The Court, in a unanimous opinion written by Chief Justice Rehnquist, upheld the statute:

> Nothing in our decision last Term in R. A. V. compels a different result here.... [W]hereas the ordinance struck down in R. A. V. was explicitly directed at expression (i.e., "speech" or "messages"), the statute in this case is aimed at conduct unprotected by the First Amendment. Moreover, the Wisconsin statute singles out for enhancement bias-inspired conduct because this conduct is thought to inflict greater individual and societal harm. For example, according to the State

and its amici, bias-motivated crimes are more likely to provoke retaliatory crimes, inflict distinct emotional harms on their victims, and incite community unrest. The State's desire to redress these perceived harms provides an adequate explanation for its penalty-enhancement provision over and above mere disagreement with offenders' beliefs or biases.... Finally, there remains to be considered Mitchell's argument that the Wisconsin statute is unconstitutionally overbroad because of its "chilling effect" on free speech.... We must conjure up a vision of a Wisconsin citizen suppressing his unpopular bigoted opinions for fear that if he later commits an offense covered by the statute, these opinions will be offered at trial to establish that he selected his victim on account of the victim's protected status, thus qualifying him for penalty enhancement.... [This] is simply too speculative a hypothesis to support Mitchell's overbreadth claim. *Wisconsin v. Mitchell*, 508 U.S. 476 (1993).

(There is some irony in the fact that the defendants in *Mitchell* were African-Americans convicted of targeting white victims based on their race, but of course the rule of the case extends beyond its facts.)

Mitchell has thus far been the Supreme Court's last word on the subject of hate speech. In 1996, the Eleventh Circuit upheld the conviction of several Ku Klux Klan members for violation of the same federal statutes that had been at issue in *J. H. H.* by cross-burning. Like the Eighth Circuit, the Eleventh Circuit focused on the idea that the defendants were being punished for the conduct, not their viewpoint:

The defendants contend that their conviction and punishment for burning a cross on the Ruffins' front lawn violated their First Amendment rights. Relying primarily upon the Supreme Court's decision in *R. A. V. v. City of St. Paul, Minn.*, they argue that they are being punished for a symbolic expression of their beliefs and for their association with the Ku Klux Klan. We disagree. The defendants have been convicted and are being punished for engaging in an activity—threatening, intimidating, and interfering with the rights of the Ruffins and using fire to do so—which the government may regulate without violating the First Amendment. *United States v. Stewart*, 65 F.3d 918 (11th Cir. 1996).

Despite the continuing division between the circuits in their interpretations of *R. A. V.*, the Supreme Court denied certiorari in *Stewart*. 516 U.S. 1134 (1996).

Thus, the precise meaning of *R. A. V.* remains somewhat ambiguous. Where hate speech can be described as a form of conduct, or where hate speech is singled out on the basis of the persons to whom it is addressed, rather than its content, the behavior involved can be punished without invoking First Amendment concerns. Whether any regulation aimed at suppressing hateful speech can survive constitutional scrutiny, however, remains unclear. Despite Justice Scalia's attempts at reassurance, it is difficult to formulate a definition of hate speech that is "an ordinance not limited to the favored topics." Moreover, it is not entirely clear that categories such as sexual harassment remain analytically viable in light of the requirement of viewpoint neutrality. In 2000, the Court declined to hear an appeal from an injunction issued against a supervisor who had been found guilty of sexual and racial harassment. The injunction prevented him from, among other things, "using any derogatory racial or ethnic epithets directed at, or descriptive of, Hispanic/Latino employees." Justice Thomas dissented from the denial of certiorari, citing *R. A. V.*

> Attaching liability to the utterance of words in the workplace is likely invalid for the simple reason that this speech is fully protected speech. No one claims that the words on the "exemplary list" (to be drafted by the trial court on remand) qualify as fighting words, obscenity, or some other category of speech currently recognized as outside the scope of First Amendment protection. Even if these words do constitute so-called "low-value speech," the content-based nature of [the injunction]—which bars speech based upon "race, religious creed, color, national origin, ancestry, physical disability, mental disability, medical condition, marital status, sex, age, or sexual orientation," but not because of political affiliation, union membership, or numerous other traits—renders it invalid under our current jurisprudence. *Avis Rent A Car System v. Aguilar*, 529 U.S. 1138 (2000).

F. Commercial Speech

Commercial speech is an interesting middle category, neither unprotected like obscenity nor fully protected like political expression. As a result, commercial speech ends up looking very much like indecency in its treatment, a connection that appeared in Justice Scalia's emphasis on the commercial aspects of certain forms of indecency in his dissenting opinion in *United States v. Playboy Entertainment Group*.

Prior to the 1970s, commercial speech was generally treated as unprotected. The government's unquestioned authority to prevent fraudulent advertising, predatory pricing, and other forms of commercial misconduct was understood to imply a similar power to regulate advertising. In the mid-1970s, however, a five-member majority of the Court repeatedly determined that "truthful and nonmisleading commercial messages about lawful products and services" was protected speech. *Bigelow v. Virginia*, 421 U.S. 809 (1975) involved a challenge to a Virginia statute that made it a crime to "encourage or prompt the procuring of abortion or miscarriage." A newspaper was convicted of violating the law by running a paid advertisement that read, in part, "UNWANTED

PREGNANCY, LET US HELP YOU. Abortions are now legal in New York. There are no residency requirements." Justice Blackmun characterized the content of the advertisement as protected speech:

> The advertisement published in appellant's newspaper did more than simply propose a commercial transaction. It contained factual material of clear "public interest." Portions of its message, most prominently the lines, "Abortions are now legal in New York. There are no residency requirements," involve the exercise of the freedom of communicating information and disseminating opinion. Viewed in its entirety, the advertisement conveyed information of potential interest and value to a diverse audience—not only to readers possibly in need of the services offered, but also to those with a general curiosity about, or genuine interest in, the subject matter.... The relationship of speech to the marketplace of products or of services does not make it valueless in the marketplace of ideas. *Bigelow v. Virginia*, 421 U.S. 809 (1975).

In dissent, Justice Rehnquist (joined by Justice White) described the advertisement as "a classic commercial proposition" containing "slight factual content."

In a 1976 case, the Court found that a state's blanket ban on advertising the price of prescription drugs violated the First Amendment. Justice Blackmun, writing for the majority (Rehnquist, again, dissenting), explained the basis for treating advertising as "speech":

> Advertising, however tasteless and excessive it sometimes may seem, is nonetheless dissemination of information as to who is producing and selling what product, for what reason, and at what price. So long as we preserve a predominantly free enterprise economy, the allocation of our resources in large measure will be made through numerous private economic decisions. It is a matter of public interest that those decisions, in the aggregate, be intelligent and well informed. To this end, the free flow of commercial information is indispensable. *Virginia Bd. of Pharmacy v. Virginia Citizens Consumer Council, Inc.*, 425 U.S. 748 (1976).

Other cases struck down blanket bans on advertising by lawyers, contraceptive advertising, bans on "For Sale" signs posted in yards, and bans on advertising abortion-related services. *Bates v. State Bar of Ariz.*, 433 U.S. 350 (1977); *Carey v. Population Services Int'l*, 431 U.S. 678 (1977) (contraceptive advertising); *Linmark Associates, Inc. v. Willingboro*, 431 U.S. 85 (1977) (ban on "For Sale" signs on homeowners' lawns). Still, the Court continued to recognize a difference between advertising and other forms of speech, permitting states to require warnings, disclaimers, and other informative elements. The Court justified these restrictions on the "commonsense differences" between commercial advertisements and other types of protected expression. Drawing a distinction from early in the history of libel, justices cited the fact that advertisements purport to present facts, rather than opinions, and furthermore observed that commercial speech was unlikely to be vulnerable to the chilling effects of regulation.

In 1980, these considerations were articulated in a single, four-part test written by Justice Powell. "At the outset, we must determine whether the expression is protected by the First Amendment. For commercial speech to come within that provision, it at least must concern lawful activity and not be misleading. Next, we ask whether the asserted governmental interest is substantial. If both inquiries yield positive answers, we must determine whether the regulation directly advances the governmental interest asserted, and whether it is not more extensive than is necessary to serve that interest." *Central Hudson Gas & Elec. Corp. v. Public Serv. Comm'n of N.Y.*, 447 U.S. 557 (1980) (striking down a prohibition on advertisements by utilities). The majority in the case focused on the particular concerns associated with outright bans on commercial speech, "unless the expression itself was flawed in some way, either because it was deceptive or related to unlawful activity."

In 1996, the Court revisited the issue. Rhode Island had a long-established law prohibiting advertisements for alcohol that included prices. The theory behind the prohibition was that it would preclude stores from increasing their sales by offering low prices, which in turn would limit the consumption of alcohol by keeping its price high.

44 LIQUORMART, INC. v. RHODE ISLAND

SUPREME COURT OF THE UNITED STATES

517 U.S. 484 (1996)

JUSTICE STEVENS delivered the opinion of the Court.

> ...When a State regulates commercial messages to protect consumers from misleading, deceptive, or aggressive sales practices, or requires the disclosure of beneficial consumer information, the purpose of its regulation is consistent with the reasons for according constitutional protection to commercial speech and therefore justifies less than strict review. However, when a State entirely prohibits the dissemination of truthful, nonmisleading commercial messages for reasons unrelated to the preservation of a fair bargaining process, there is far less reason to depart from the rigorous review that the First Amendment generally demands....
>
> The special dangers that attend complete bans on truthful, nonmisleading commercial speech cannot be explained away by appeals to the "commonsense distinctions" that exist between commercial and noncommercial speech.

Regulations that suppress the truth are no less troubling because they target objectively verifiable information, nor are they less effective because they aim at durable messages. As a result, neither the "greater objectivity" nor the "greater hardiness" of truthful, nonmisleading commercial speech justifies reviewing its complete suppression with added deference.

It is the State's interest in protecting consumers from "commercial harms" that provides "the typical reason why commercial speech can be subject to greater governmental regulation than noncommercial speech." Yet bans that target truthful, nonmisleading commercial messages rarely protect consumers from such harms. Instead, such bans often serve only to obscure an "underlying governmental policy" that could be implemented without regulating speech. In this way, these commercial speech bans not only hinder consumer choice, but also impede debate over central issues of public policy.

Precisely because bans against truthful, nonmisleading commercial speech rarely seek to protect consumers from either deception or overreaching, they usually rest solely on the offensive assumption that the public will respond "irrationally" to the truth. The First Amendment directs us to be especially skeptical of regulations that seek to keep people in the dark for what the government perceives to be their own good. That teaching applies equally to state attempts to deprive consumers of accurate information about their chosen products....

In this case, there is no question that Rhode Island's price advertising ban constitutes a blanket prohibition against truthful, nonmisleading speech about a lawful product. There is also no question that the ban serves an end unrelated to consumer protection ....

We can agree that common sense supports the conclusion that a prohibition against price advertising, like a collusive agreement among competitors to refrain from such advertising, will tend to mitigate competition and maintain prices at a higher level than would prevail in a completely free market. Despite the absence of proof on the point, we can even agree with the State's contention that it is reasonable to assume that demand, and hence consumption throughout the market, is somewhat lower whenever a higher, noncompetitive price level prevails. However, without any findings of fact, or indeed any evidentiary support whatsoever, we cannot agree with the assertion that the price advertising ban will significantly advance the State's interest in promoting temperance....

The State also cannot satisfy the requirement that its restriction on speech be no more extensive than necessary. It is perfectly obvious that alternative forms of regulation that would not involve any restriction on speech would be more likely to achieve the State's goal of promoting temperance. As the State's own expert conceded, higher prices can be maintained either by direct regulation or by increased taxation. Per capita purchases could be limited as is the case with prescription drugs. Even educational campaigns focused on the problems of excessive, or even moderate, drinking might prove to be more effective.

As a result, even under the less than strict standard that generally applies in commercial speech cases, the State has failed to establish a "reasonable fit" between its abridgment of speech and its temperance goal. It necessarily follows that the price advertising ban cannot survive the more stringent constitutional review that *Central Hudson* itself concluded was appropriate for the complete suppression of truthful, nonmisleading commercial speech....

Justice Stevens's opinion was joined by Justices Kennedy and Ginsburg. Justices Thomas, Scalia, O'Connor, Rehnquist, Souter, and Breyer all concurred with the outcome, but wrote separately to propose variations on the majority's analysis. Justice Thomas argued that the *Central Hudson* four-part test was inappropriate. "In cases such as this, in which the government's asserted interest is to keep legal users of a product or service ignorant in order to manipulate their choices in the marketplace, the balancing test adopted in *Central Hudson*...should not be applied, in my view. Rather, such an "interest" is per se illegitimate and can no more justify regulation of "commercial" speech than it can justify regulation of "noncommercial" speech." Justice O'Connor, joined by Chief Justice Rehnquist and Justices Souter and Breyer, approved of the application of the *Central Hudson* test, but proposed that the fourth prong ought to read strictly:

> The State has other methods at its disposal—methods that would more directly accomplish this stated goal without intruding on sellers' ability to provide truthful, nonmisleading information to customers.... The ready availability of such alternatives—at least some of which would far more effectively achieve Rhode Island's only professed goal, at comparatively small additional administrative cost—demonstrates that the fit between ends and means is not narrowly tailored. Too, this regulation prevents sellers of alcohol from communicating price information anywhere but at the point of purchase. No channels exist at all to permit them to publicize the price of their products." *44 Liquormart, Inc. v. Rhode Island*, 517 U.S. 484 (1996).

The exact status of commercial speech, then, remains somewhat unclear. A solid majority of the Court continues to favor application of the four-part *Central Hudson* test, with considerable support for reading the last prong strictly. The emphasis on alternative channels puts the analysis in line with the secondary effects test described above (but see discussion of nude dancing in the next chapter), while the overall effect of the *Central Hudson* approach is akin to the "reasonableness" test for content neutral regulation of time, place, and manner generally. Advertising may thus be thought of as "public" speech, and hence as something akin to a public forum. Given the fact that government retains the power to suppress misleading or burdensome advertisements, perhaps a closer analogy would be to something like a limited forum whose purpose is to facilitate "a predominantly free enterprise economy."

G. Campaign Contributions and Expenditures

The First Amendment issues involved in the regulation of campaign contributions and expenditures is a technical topic about which there have been many cases and much debate. The desire to regulate campaigns has been fostered by concerns that the high cost of campaigning makes government vulnerable to corruption. The need for money for campaigning, goes the reasoning, drives politicians to court individuals and groups that are wealthy enough to make significant contributions, in return for which those persons have special access to—if not direct influence over—the process of policymaking. This fear may be described as the remnant of one of the earliest principles of eighteenth-century republicanism, that great wealth corrupts democracy. Antifederalist writers, in particular, worried aloud that the accumulation of great fortunes would create inequality and the corruption of political virtue.[2] The first Kentucky Convention of 1784 adopted a resolution that no person should be granted more land than they needed for themselves and their family.[3] Even if there is no actual advantage gained by donating large sums, the perception that "money talks" is often cited as one of the reasons for a low level of civil engagement among Americans. Other concerns about campaign financing are more prosaic. Elected officials complain that the unrestricted costs of campaigns produce fund-raising contests that take significant portions of their time away from the business of governance.

In the 1970s, responding to a series of scandals involving illegal campaign fund-raising by the Nixon campaigns, Congress enacted a series of laws designed to clean up the process of political campaigns (the Federal Election Campaign Act, enacted in 1971 and amended in 1974). Among other things, these laws limited both campaign contributions and expenditures. These provisions were challenged by representatives of both parties on the basis that the expenditure of money to promote a political message is a form of speech, and core political speech, at that. In 1976 the Court established limits on Congress's ability to regulate campaign financing in *Buckley v. Valeo*, 424 U.S. 1 (1976). The law at issue limited contributions to any one candidate by individuals and groups to $1,000, and contributions by political committees to $5,000, with an annual cumulative limit of $25,000. In addition, expenditures by individuals or groups "relative to a clearly identified candidate" were limited to $1,000, and personal expenditures by candidates were also limited. The opinion was per curiam, and it was accompanied by five separate opinions concurring in part and dissenting in part, written by Justices Burger, White, Marshall, Rehnquist, and Blackmun. Justice Stevens did not participate; thus out of eight sitting members of the Court, only three joined in the opinion in its entirety.

The holding distinguished between the provisions of the law regulating contributions, and those regulating expenditures. The Court began by rejecting an argument that what was at stake was expressive conduct rather than pure speech. "The Act's contribution and expenditure limitations operate in an area of the most fundamental First Amendment activities.... The expenditure of money simply cannot be equated with such conduct as destruction of a draft card." Based on the conclusion that the expenditure of money is "speech," the Court struck down the expenditure limitations. "[V]irtually every means of communicating ideas in today's mass society requires the expenditure of money.... The electorate's increasing dependence on television, radio, and other mass media for news and information has made these expensive modes of communication indispensible instruments of effective political speech." *Buckley v. Valeo*, 424 U.S. 1 (1976).

Conversely, restrictions on campaign contributions were upheld. "By contrast...a limitation upon the amount that any one person or group may contribute to a candidate or political committee entails only a marginal restriction upon the contributor's ability to engage in free communication. The quantity of communication by the contributor does not increase perceptibly with the size of his contribution, since the expression rests solely on the undifferentiated, symbolic act of contributing." The Court in *Buckley* also upheld disclosure requirements, a system of limited public financing ("matching funds"), and limits on individual contributions. Chief Justice Burger dissented with the portion of the ruling that upheld portions of the Act; Justice White dissented from the conclusion that expenditure limitations violated the First Amendment; Justice Blackmun argued that there was no principled basis for distinguishing between expenditures and contributions; and Justice Marshall dissented from the conclusion that restrictions on a candidate's own expenditures violate the First Amendment.

Even before the ruling in *Buckley*, political organizations had realized that the way around the limitations was to form independent political organizations called Political Action Committees. One of the most successful fundraising PACs was the National Conservative Political Action Committee, formed in 1975 to raise and expend funds to promote the election of political conservatives. Accused by the Federal Election Commission and the Democratic Party (in separate suits) of violating campaign finance laws during the 1980 Reagan presidential campaign,

NCPAC argued that restrictions on expenditures by independent organizations violated the First Amendment. The rule at issue provided that if a candidate accepts public financing, independent PACs could not expend more than $1,000 to further that candidate's election. The idea of the law was to create an incentive to accept public financing as a way of diminishing the importance of private fund raising in elections.

The cases reached the Court as *Federal Election Comm'n. v. NCPAC* and *Democratic Party of the United States v. NCPAC*, both at 470 U.S. 480 (1985). In a 5-4 opinion written by Justice Rehnquist, the Court ruled that the law regulating expenditures by independent PACs was unconstitutional (Justices White, Marshall, and Brennan dissented, Justice Stewart dissented in part). Rehnquist ruled that the expenditures by PACs produced "speech at the core of the First Amendment." "The PACs in this case, of course, are not lone pamphleteers or street corner orators.... But for purposes of presenting political views in connection with a nationwide Presidential election, allowing the presentation of views while forbidding the expenditure of more than $1,000 to express them is much like allowing a speaker in a public hall to express his views while denying him the use of an amplifying system." Furthermore, there was no issue of corruption in the case, according to Rehnquist, because there was no connection to the candidate. "The hallmark of corruption is the financial quid pro quo: dollars for political favors. But here the conduct proscribed is not contributions to the candidate, but independent expenditures in support of the candidate."

The ruling in *Federal Election Comm'n. v. NCPAC* seems to make campaign financing a unique category of speech. Ordinarily, after all, restrictions on the use of amplifying devices are the classic example of a content neutral time, place, and manner restriction that is permitted even in a traditional public forum. The focus on PACs as uniquely independent entities, moreover, was dropped from the analysis in 1996. Ten years earlier, the Colorado Republican Federal Campaign Committee had exceeded spending limits in purchasing radio ads attacking a Democratic candidate for Congress. Unlike NCPAC, the Colorado committee was an operation of the Republican Party. In another sharply divided opinion, Justice Breyer wrote: "We do not see how a Constitution that grants to individuals, candidates, and ordinary political committees the right to make unlimited independent expenditures could deny the same right to political parties." Breyer's opinion was joined only by Justices O'Connor and Souter; Justice Kennedy wrote separately, dissenting in part, joined by Chief Justice Rehnquist and Justice Scalia. Justice Thomas similarly wrote separately, dissenting in part, joined by Justices Rehnquist and Scalia.

Justice Stevens, joined by Justice Ginsburg, dissented outright. Justices Stevens and Ginsburg would have upheld the restriction on expenditures by political parties. Justice Kennedy would have treated political parties as outside the *Buckley* analytical framework, while Justices Thomas, Rehnquist, and Scalia would have abandoned *Buckley* altogether and struck down all restrictions on campaign financing.

Nonetheless, the *Buckley* distinction between expenditures and contributions has survived. In 2000, by a vote of 6 to 3 (Justices Scalia, Thomas, and Kennedy dissenting), the Court upheld the authority of state governments to establish limits on contributions to candidates in state political races, and reaffirmed the validity of *Buckley*. *Nixon v. Shrink Missouri Government PAC*, 120 S. Ct. 897 (2000). Writing for the majority, Justice Souter wryly noted that the analysis of campaign financing did not fit easily into established standards for First Amendment review. "Precision about the relative rigor of the standard to review contribution limits," he observed, "was not a pretense of the *Buckley* per curiam opinion."

Notes

1. Thomas Jefferson, letter to Thomas McKean (February 19, 1803), in Paul Leicester Ford, ed., *The Works of Thomas Jefferson* (New York: G.P. Putnam and Sons, 1905), pp. 449–52.

2. Saul Cornell, *The Other Founders: Anti-Federalism and the Dissenting Tradition in America, 1788–1828* (Chapel Hill, NC: University of North Carolina Press, 1999), p. 103.

3. Lowell H. Harrison, *Kentucky's Road to Statehood* (Louisville, KY: University of Kentucky Press, 1992), p. 28.

IV. Speech-Plus and Expressive Conduct; Compelled Speech and the Right of Association

A. *Speech-Plus and Expressive Conduct*

In 1969, in *Brandenburg*, Justice Douglas spoke of the special case of government's authority to act where "speech is brigaded with action." To take an easy case, a man who runs down the street yelling political slogans while breaking windows cannot expect that the First Amendment will protect him from the legal consequences of breaking windows, regardless of the level of protection that it affords to his yelling political slogans. This is a situation of expression combined with conduct, or "speech-plus." The cases in which this concept was most thoroughly explored involved picketing, boycotts, and parades. In 1939, for example, the Court ruled that a city could not ban leafleting in public places. In dicta, however, Justice Roberts suggested the limit of the principle he was expressing:

> Municipal authorities...may lawfully regulate the conduct of those using the streets. For example, a person could not exercise this liberty by taking his stand in the middle of a crowded street, contrary to traffic regulations, and maintain his position to the stoppage of all traffic; a group of distributors could not insist upon ...a constitutional right to form a cordon across the street and to allow no pedestrian to pass who did not accept a tendered leaflet; nor does the guarantee of freedom of speech or of the press deprive a municipality of power to enact regulations against throwing literature broadcast in the streets. Prohibition of such conduct would not abridge the constitutional liberty since such activity bears no necessary relationship to the freedom to speak, write, print or distribute information or opinion. *Schneider v. New Jersey*, 308 U.S. 147 (1939).

Two years later, the Court upheld the convictions of a group of Jehovah's Witnesses for parading through a public street without a permit. *Cox v. New Hampshire*, 312 U.S. 569 (1941). The law requiring a permit was found to be one enacted "with regard only to consideration of time, place and manner so as to conserve the public convenience" by permitting "proper policing" and securing "convenient use of the streets by other travelers." Such laws are considered neutral time, place, and manner restrictions because they focus on the conduct element of a speech-plus situation. Courts, moreover, may issue injunctions prohibiting particular parades or marches, and impose penalties for contempt on anyone who violates their order. *Walker v. City of Birmingham*, 388 U.S. 307 (1967).

It is critical, however, that such orders be based on existing neutral laws. Where a court finds that government is using a facially neutral regulation to suppress parades or demonstrations by a particular group, then strict scrutiny will be applied. In *Walker*, an Alabama judge found Martin Luther King Jr. to be in contempt of court for holding a march in Birmingham in violation of an injunction. In retrospect, that outcome may be thought of as questionable. By contrast, in *Forsyth County v. The Nationalist Movement*, 505 U.S. 123 (1992), a five-member majority struck down an ordinance, enacted in the aftermath of fighting between Ku Klux Klan members and participants in a pro-civil rights demonstration, that created a fee system for parades. The size of the fee would depend on a city administrator's determination of the likelihood that there would be extra costs to the city in the form of added police protection. Justice Blackmun, writing for the majority, found the facially neutral statute to be a pretext for silencing the Klan, and struck down the law (Chief Justice Rehnquist and Justices White, Scalia, and Thomas dissented).

The difficulty with defining a category of "speech-plus" is that it requires a sharp distinction between speech and conduct. Since "speech" extends beyond the act of talking to include other forms of expression, what is the dividing line between "conduct" that is expression, and conduct that is merely associated *with* expression? The difficulty of drawing this distinction is one reason that even neutral time, place, and manner restrictions are required to serve "substantial" government interests. In many cases, moreover, the distinction appears nearly invisible. These are cases that involve attempts by government to regulate "expressive conduct," behavior that is, itself, the expression of a message.

Early cases discussing expressive conduct focused on government's attempts to prevent citizens from displaying their political convictions. In *Stromberg v. California*, 283 U.S. 359 (1931), a state law prohibiting display of a red flag was struck down. In 1943, in *West Virginia State Bd. of Ed. v. Barnette*, 319 U.S. 624 (1943), the Court held that a rule requiring students to stand at attention with their right arms outstretched in the manner of a Facist salute involved compelled speech, and was consequently unconstitutional (see discussion, below.) And in *Brown v. Louisiana*, 383 U.S. 131 (1966), the Court held that black students holding a sit-in at a whites-only library were engaging in protected expression. It was not until 1968, however, that the Court formalized a test for the constitutionality of laws regulating expressive conduct.

In March, 1966, David O'Brien burned his draft card on the steps of a Boston courthouse. He was convicted of violating an amendment to the

Selective Service Act, passed the year before (referred to in the case as "the 1965 Amendment"). In reviewing his conviction, Chief Justice Warren defined a four-part test for cases involving expressive conduct: "a government regulation is sufficiently justified if it is within the constitutional power of the Government; if it furthers an important or substantial governmental interest; if the governmental interest is unrelated to the suppression of free expression; and if the incidental restriction on alleged First Amendment freedoms is no greater than is essential to the furtherance of that interest." The emphasis on a "substantial" government interest marks this as a form of intermediate scrutiny, similar to that applied to content-based restrictions on expression in a limited public forum.

UNITED STATES v. O'BRIEN

SUPREME COURT OF THE UNITED STATES

391 U.S. 367 (1968)

CHIEF JUSTICE WARREN delivered the opinion of the Court.

...We note at the outset that the 1965 Amendment plainly does not abridge free speech on its face, and we do not understand O'Brien to argue otherwise. Amended § 12 (b)(3) on its face deals with conduct having no connection with speech. It prohibits the knowing destruction of certificates issued by the Selective Service System, and there is nothing necessarily expressive about such conduct. The Amendment does not distinguish between public and private destruction, and it does not punish only destruction engaged in for the purpose of expressing views. Compare *Stromberg v. California*, 283 U.S. 359 (1931). A law prohibiting destruction of Selective Service certificates no more abridges free speech on its face than a motor vehicle law prohibiting the destruction of drivers' licenses, or a tax law prohibiting the destruction of books and records. O'Brien nonetheless argues that the 1965 Amendment is unconstitutional in its application to him, and is unconstitutional as enacted because what he calls the "purpose" of Congress was "to suppress freedom of speech." We consider these arguments separately.

O'Brien first argues that the 1965 Amendment is unconstitutional as applied to him because his act of burning his registration certificate was protected "symbolic speech" within the First Amendment. His argument is that the freedom of expression which the First Amendment guarantees includes all modes of "communication of ideas by conduct," and that his conduct is within this definition because he did it in "demonstration against the war and against the draft."

We cannot accept the view that an apparently limitless variety of conduct can be labeled "speech" whenever the person engaging in the conduct intends thereby to express an idea. However, even on the assumption that the alleged communicative element in O'Brien's conduct is sufficient to bring into play the First

Amendment, it does not necessarily follow that the destruction of a registration certificate is constitutionally protected activity. This Court has held that when "speech" and "nonspeech" elements are combined in the same course of conduct, a sufficiently important governmental interest in regulating the nonspeech element can justify incidental limitations on First Amendment freedoms. To characterize the quality of the governmental interest which must appear, the Court has employed a variety of descriptive terms: compelling; substantial; subordinating; paramount; cogent; strong. Whatever imprecision inheres in these terms, we think it clear that a government regulation is sufficiently justified if it is within the constitutional power of the Government; if it furthers an important or substantial governmental interest; if the governmental interest is unrelated to the suppression of free expression; and if the incidental restriction on alleged First Amendment freedoms is no greater than is essential to the furtherance of that interest. We find that the 1965 Amendment to § 12 (b)(3) of the Universal Military Training and Service Act meets all of these requirements, and consequently that O'Brien can be constitutionally convicted for violating it.

Early protests against American involvement in Vietnam also provided the context for the second important case defining the constitutional issues involved in the regulation of expressive conduct. In December 1965, John and Mary Beth Tinker, ages fifteen and thirteen, wore black armbands to school in protest of the Vietnam War, and were suspended. The case made its way through the courts, arriving at the Supreme Court in 1969. *Tinker v. Des Moines Independent Community School District*, 393 U.S. 503 (1969). By a vote of 7 to 2, the Court held that the school district did not have the authority to punish the Tinker children because their "symbolic act" of wearing armbands was expressive conduct protected by the First Amendment. "It is closely akin to 'pure speech,'" wrote Justice Fortas, "which, we have repeatedly held, is entitled to comprehensive protection under the First Amendment." The school argued that its interest in maintaining discipline was a sufficiently compelling interest to justify its disciplinary action. In response, Justice Fortas reiterated his "pure speech" formulation, and in addition challenged the adequacy of the state's interest:

The problem presented by the present case does not relate to regulation of the length of skirts or the type of clothing, to hair style, or deportment. It does not concern aggressive, disruptive action or even group demonstrations. Our problem involves direct, primary First Amendment rights akin to "pure speech." The school officials banned and sought to punish petitioners for a silent, passive expression of opinion, unaccompanied by any disorder or disturbance. There is here no evidence whatever of petitioners' interference, actual or nascent, with the school's work or of collision with the rights of other students to be secure and to be let alone.

The majority also focused on the idea that the school had singled out a particular idea for suppression. Students were allowed to wear campaign buttons and other political symbols. "[A] particular symbol—black armbands worn to exhibit opposition to this Nation's involvement in Vietnam—was singled out for prohibition. Clearly, the prohibition of expression of one particular opinion, at least without evidence that is necessary to avoid material and substantial interference with schoolwork or discipline, is not constitutionally permissible." Fortas implied that in another case, with a greater showing of disruption as a result of expressive conduct, the outcome might be different. Justice Black, dissenting, argued that the courts should not interfere with school officials' efforts to maintain discipline. "[I]f the time has come when pupils of state-supported schools, kindergartens, grammar schools, or high schools, can defy and flout orders of school officials to keep their minds on their own schoolwork, it is the beginning of a new era of revolutionary permissiveness in this country fostered by the judiciary." *Tinker v. Des Moines Independent Community School District*, 393 U.S. 503 (1969). In fact, while the Supreme Court has had few occasions to review specific school policies, lower courts have generally deferred to school officials' determinations of the level of conformity in dress or behavior that is required to maintain school discipline. (See, for example, the discussion of *Bethel School District No. 403 v. Fraser*, 478 U.S. 675 [1986] in the previous chapter).

Tinker did not involve a significant examination of the *O'Brien* factors because, in the eyes of the majority at least, it was an easy case. In other cases, however, the principles that govern courts' review of government's attempts to limit expressive conduct have included some of the most controversial issues that arise in the free speech context. In 1978, the Seventh Circuit Court of Appeals applied the *O'Brien* test to invalidate the decision of Skokie, Illinois, to grant a parade permit to the National Socialist (Nazi) Party of America. *Collin v. Smith*, 578 F.2d 1197 (7th Cir., 1978). The case involved a plan by the American Nazi Party to conduct a silent, peaceful march through the Village of Skokie, Illinois, a venue which contained a large population of elderly Jewish people, including a significant number of Holocaust survivors. In order to justify refusing the application for a parade permit, the Village of Skokie enacted several statutes, which prohibited marches in uniform, required demonstration of insurance coverage, and prohibited assemblies which would "portray criminality, depravity or lack of virtue in, or incite violence, hatred, abuse or hostility toward a person or group of persons by reason of reference to religious, racial, ethnic, national or regional affiliation." The Seventh

Circuit's treatment of the case involved a review of nearly all the free speech doctrines that have been mentioned thus far. Judge Pell, for example, questioned whether *Beauharnais* remained good law in light of *Cohen* and *Brandenburg*, but also found that *Beauharnais* did not apply because Skokie had not argued that it feared violence as a result of the march. The regulations were found not to be neutral time, place, and manner regulations appropriate to a public forum because they were found to be content-specific. The residents of Skokie were found not to be a captive audience, nor would the march invade the privacy of their homes.

Finally, concerning the "facially neutral" requirement of insurance, the court applied the *O'Brien* test:

> The *O'Brien* test, then, deals only with situations where such nonspeech conduct is entwined with speech elements and a restriction on that conduct creates merely "incidental limitations" on protected activity. The limitations here totally and directly prohibit the First Amendment activity; calling them "incidental" manner restrictions does not make them so. Moreover, *O'Brien* did not involve a prior restraint, nor does the dissent's analysis give more than cursory recognition to the increased burden of justifying such restraints. Even if *O'Brien's* test could somehow be applied here, the use of the insurance requirement to prohibit the proposed demonstration would fail it. First, it is difficult, following even a casual examination of the chronological exegesis of the ordinances, particularly in light of the religious complexion of the Village, to think other than that the governmental interest here was directly related to the suppression of these plaintiffs' First Amendment rights. Second, the governmental interest advanced by the dissent could more narrowly be served by criminalizing, as has no doubt already been done, the conduct (by appellees or others) directly producing any feared injury to persons or property and by marshaling local, county, and state police to prevent violations. Instead, the Village has flatly prohibited First Amendment activity, not itself directly productive of the feared injury, by those too controversial to obtain commercial insurance.... *Collin v. Smith*, 578 F.2d 1197 (7th Cir., 1978).

Based on this reasoning, the Seventh Circuit ordered the Village of Skokie to allow the march. The public outcry was intense, and perhaps as a result the American Nazi Party decided to call off its march.

The Supreme Court took on a case much harder than *Tinker* in 1990. A group of protesters marched, chanted slogans, and burned a flag outside the 1984 Republican National Convention in Dallas, Texas. Gregory Johnson was arrested and convicted of violating a Texas statute prohibiting "desecration of a venerated object" (defined as public monuments, places of worship or burial, and flags). In 1990 the case reached the Supreme Court. In an opinion written for a five-member majority, Justice Brennan first applied the *O'Brien* criteria to determine that the statute at issue was aimed at the suppression of expression and hence subject to strict scrutiny. Applying that level of review, he concluded that Texas could not criminalize flag-burning. Justice Rehnquist, in a dissenting opinion notable for its lengthy quotations from poetry and historical imagery, argued that the Court should have recognized a unique "mystical" importance for the flag and made its destruction an exception from generally applicable First Amendment principles.

TEXAS v. JOHNSON

SUPREME COURT OF THE UNITED STATES

491 U.S. 397 (1989)

JUSTICE BRENNAN delivered the opinion of the Court, in which MARSHALL, BLACKMUN, SCALIA, and KENNEDY joined. JUSTICE KENNEDY filed a concurring opinion. CHIEF JUSTICE REHNQUIST filed a dissenting opinion, in which WHITE and O'CONNOR. joined. JUSTICE STEVENS filed a dissenting opinion.

...Johnson was convicted of flag desecration for burning the flag rather than for uttering insulting words. This fact somewhat complicates our consideration of his conviction under the First Amendment. We must first determine whether Johnson's burning of the flag constituted expressive conduct, permitting him to invoke the First Amendment in challenging his conviction. If his conduct was expressive, we next decide whether the State's regulation is related to the suppression of free expression. See, e.g., *United States v. O'Brien*, 391 U.S. 367 (1968). If the State's regulation is not related to expression, then the less stringent standard we announced in *United States v. O'Brien* for regulations of noncommunicative conduct controls. If it is, then we are outside of *O'Brien*'s test, and we must ask whether this interest justifies Johnson's conviction under a more demanding standard. A third possibility is that the State's asserted interest is simply not implicated on these facts, and in that event the interest drops out of the picture....

The State of Texas conceded for purposes of its oral argument in this case that Johnson's conduct was expressive conduct, and this concession seems to us as prudent.... Johnson burned an American flag as part—indeed, as the culmination—of a political demonstration that coincided with the convening of the Republican Party and its renomination of Ronald Reagan for President. The expressive, overtly political nature of this conduct was both intentional and overwhelmingly apparent. At his trial, Johnson explained his reasons for burning the flag as follows: "The American Flag was burned as Ronald Reagan was being renominated as President. And a more powerful statement of symbolic speech, whether you agree with it or not, couldn't have been made at that time. It's quite a just position [juxtaposition]. We had new patriotism and no patriotism." In these circumstances, Johnson's burning of the flag was conduct sufficiently imbued with elements of communication, to implicate the First Amendment.

The government generally has a freer hand in restricting expressive conduct than it has in restricting the written or spoken word. It may not, however, proscribe particular conduct because it has expressive elements. What might be termed the more generalized guarantee of freedom of expression makes the communicative nature of conduct an inadequate basis for singling out that conduct for proscription. A law directed at the communicative nature of conduct must, like a law directed at speech itself, be justified by the substantial showing of need that the First Amendment requires. It is, in short, not simply the verbal or nonverbal nature of the expression, but the governmental interest at stake, that helps to determine whether a restriction on that expression is valid.

Thus, although we have recognized that where speech and nonspeech elements are combined in the same course of conduct, a sufficiently important governmental interest in regulating the nonspeech element can justify incidental limitations on First Amendment freedoms, we have limited the applicability of *O'Brien*'s relatively lenient standard to those cases in which the governmental interest is unrelated to the suppression of free expression. In stating, moreover, that *O'Brien*'s test in the last analysis is little, if any, different from the standard applied to time, place, or manner restrictions, we have highlighted the requirement that the governmental interest in question be unconnected to expression in order to come under *O'Brien*'s less demanding rule.

In order to decide whether *O'Brien*'s test applies here, therefore, we must decide whether Texas has asserted an interest in support of Johnson's conviction that is unrelated to the suppression of expression. If we find that an interest asserted by the State is simply not implicated on the facts before us, we need not ask whether *O'Brien*'s test applies. The State offers two separate interests to justify this conviction: preventing breaches of the peace and preserving the flag as a symbol of nationhood and national unity. We hold that the first interest is not implicated on this record and that the second is related to the suppression of expression.

Texas claims that its interest in preventing breaches of the peace justifies Johnson's conviction for flag desecration. However, no disturbance of the peace actually occurred or threatened to occur because of Johnson's burning of the flag.... The State's position, therefore, amounts to a claim that an audience that takes serious offense at particular expression is necessarily likely to disturb the peace and that the expression may be prohibited on this basis. Our precedents do not countenance such a presumption. On the contrary, they recognize that a principal function of free speech under our system of government is to invite dispute. It may indeed best serve its high purpose when it induces a condition of unrest, creates dissatisfaction with conditions as they are, or even stirs people to anger. It would be odd indeed to conclude both that if it is the speaker's opinion that gives offense, that consequence is a reason for according it constitutional protection, and that the government may ban the expression of certain disagreeable ideas on the unsupported presumption that their very disagreeableness will provoke violence.

Thus, we have not permitted the government to assume that every expression of a provocative idea will incite a riot, but have instead required careful consideration of the actual circumstances surrounding such expression, asking whether the expression "is directed to inciting or producing imminent lawless action and is likely to incite or produce such action." *Brandenburg v. Ohio*, 395 U.S. 444, 447 (1969) (reviewing circumstances surrounding rally and speeches by Ku Klux Klan). To accept Texas' arguments that it need only demonstrate "the potential for a breach of the peace," and that every flag burning necessarily possesses that potential, would be to eviscerate our holding in *Brandenburg*. This we decline to do.

Nor does Johnson's expressive conduct fall within that small class of "fighting words" that are "likely to provoke the average person to retaliation, and thereby cause a breach of the peace." No reasonable onlooker would have regarded Johnson's generalized expression of dissatisfaction with the policies of the Federal Government as a direct personal insult or an invitation to exchange fisticuffs....

The State also asserts an interest in preserving the flag as a symbol of nationhood and national unity.... The State, apparently, is concerned that such conduct will lead people to believe either that the flag does not stand for nationhood and national unity, but instead reflects other, less positive concepts, or that the concepts reflected in the flag do not in fact exist, that is, that we do not enjoy unity as a Nation. These concerns blossom only when a person's treatment of the flag communicates some message, and thus are related "to the suppression of free expression" within the meaning of *O'Brien*. We are thus outside of *O'Brien*'s test altogether.

It remains to consider whether the State's interest in preserving the flag as a symbol of nationhood and national unity justifies Johnson's conviction....

Johnson's political expression was restricted because of the content of the message he conveyed. We must therefore subject the State's asserted interest in preserving the special symbolic character of the flag to "the most exacting scrutiny."

Texas argues that its interest in preserving the flag as a symbol of nationhood and national unity survives this close analysis. Quoting extensively from the writings of this Court chronicling the flag's historic and symbolic role in our society, the State emphasizes the "special place" reserved for the flag in our Nation. The State's argument is not that it has an interest simply in maintaining the flag as a symbol of something, no matter what it symbolizes; indeed, if that were the State's position, it would be difficult to see how that interest is endangered by highly symbolic conduct such as Johnson's. Rather, the State's claim is that it has an interest in preserving the flag as a symbol of nationhood and national unity, a symbol with a determinate range of meanings. According to Texas, if one physically treats the flag in a way that would tend to cast doubt on either the idea that nationhood and national unity are the flag's referents or that national unity actually exists, the message conveyed thereby is a harmful one and therefore may be prohibited.

If there is a bedrock principle underlying the First Amendment, it is that the government may not prohibit the expression of an idea simply because society finds the idea itself offensive or disagreeable. We have not recognized an exception to this principle even where our flag has been involved....

CHIEF JUSTICE REHNQUIST, with whom JUSTICE WHITE and JUSTICE O'CONNOR join, dissenting.

In holding this Texas statute unconstitutional, the Court ignores Justice Holmes' familiar aphorism that "a page of history is worth a volume of logic." For more than 200 years, the American flag has occupied a unique position as the symbol of our Nation, a uniqueness that justifies a governmental prohibition against flag burning in the way respondent Johnson did here....

The American flag, then, throughout more than 200 years of our history, has come to be the visible symbol embodying our Nation. It does not represent the views of any particular political party, and it does not represent any particular political philosophy. The flag is not simply another "idea" or "point of view" competing for recognition in the marketplace of ideas. Millions and millions of Americans regard it with an almost mystical reverence regardless of what sort of social, political, or philosophical beliefs they may have. I cannot agree that the First Amendment invalidates the Act of Congress, and the laws of 48 of the 50 States, which make criminal the public burning of the flag....

But the Court insists that the Texas statute prohibiting the public burning of the American flag infringes on respondent Johnson's freedom of expression. Such freedom, of course, is not absolute. See *Schenck v. United States*, 249 U.S. 47 (1919). In *Chaplinsky v. New Hampshire*, 315 U.S. 568 (1942), a unanimous Court said: "Allowing the broadest scope to the language and purpose of the Fourteenth Amendment, it is well understood that the right of free speech is not absolute at all times and under all circumstances. There are certain well-defined and narrowly limited classes of speech, the prevention and punishment of which have never been thought to raise any Constitutional problem. These include the lewd and obscene, the profane, the libelous, and the insulting or 'fighting' words—those which by their very utterance inflict injury or tend to incite an immediate breach of the peace. It has been well observed that such utterances are no essential part of any exposition of ideas, and are of such slight social value as a step to truth that any benefit that may be derived from them is clearly outweighed by the social interest in order and morality."

The Court upheld Chaplinsky's conviction under a state statute that made it unlawful to "address any offensive, derisive or annoying word to any person who is lawfully in any street or other public place...." Here it may equally well be said that the public burning of the American flag by Johnson was no essential part of any exposition of ideas, and at the same time it had a tendency to incite a breach of the peace. Johnson was free to make any verbal denunciation of the flag that he wished; indeed, he was free to burn the flag in private. He could publicly burn other symbols of the Government or effigies of political leaders. He did lead a march through the streets of Dallas, and conducted a rally in front of the Dallas City Hall. He engaged in a "die-in" to protest nuclear weapons. He shouted out various slogans during the march, including: "Reagan, Mondale which will it be? Either one means World War III"; "Ronald Reagan, killer of the hour, Perfect example of U. S. power"; and "red, white and blue, we spit on you, you stand for plunder, you will go under." For none of these acts was he arrested or prosecuted; it was only when he proceeded to burn publicly an American flag stolen from its rightful owner that he violated the Texas statute.

The Court could not, and did not, say that Chaplinsky's utterances were not expressive phrases—they clearly and succinctly conveyed an extremely low opinion of the addressee. The same may be said of Johnson's public burning of the flag in this case; it obviously did convey Johnson's bitter dislike of his country. But his act, like Chaplinsky's provocative words, conveyed nothing that could not have been conveyed and was not conveyed just as forcefully in a dozen different ways. As with "fighting words," so with flag burning, for purposes of the First Amendment: It is "no essential part of any exposition of ideas, and [is] of such slight social value as a step to truth that any benefit that may be derived from [it] is clearly outweighed" by the public interest in avoiding a probable breach of the peace. The highest courts of several States have upheld state statutes prohibiting the public burning of the flag on the grounds that it is so inherently inflammatory that it may cause a breach of public order.

The result of the Texas statute is obviously to deny one in Johnson's frame of mind one of many means of "symbolic speech." Far from being a case of "one picture being worth a thousand words," flag burning is the equivalent of an inarticulate grunt or roar that, it seems fair to say, is most likely to be indulged in not to express any particular idea, but to antagonize others.... [T]he First Amendment does not guarantee the right to employ every conceivable method of communication at all times and in all places." The Texas statute deprived Johnson of only one rather inarticulate symbolic form of protest—a form of protest that was profoundly offensive to many—and left him with a full panoply of other symbols and every conceivable form of verbal expression to express his deep disapproval of national policy. Thus, in no way can it be said that Texas is punishing him because his hearers—or any other group of people—were profoundly opposed to the message that he sought to convey. Such opposition is no proper basis for restricting speech or expression under the First Amendment. It was Johnson's use of this particular symbol, and not the idea that he sought to convey by it or by his many other expressions, for which he was punished....

JUSTICE STEVENS, dissenting.

...Had [Johnson] chosen to spray paint—or perhaps convey with a motion picture projector—his message of dissatisfaction on the facade of the Lincoln Memorial, there would be no question about the power of the Government to prohibit his means of expression. The prohibition would be supported by the legitimate interest in preserving the quality of an important national asset. Though the asset at stake in this case is intangible, given its unique value, the same interest supports a prohibition on the desecration of the American flag.

In the aftermath of *Texas v. Johnson*, President Bush called for a constitutional amendment to ban flag-burning, a proposal that has been renewed in the House of Representatives as an annual ritual ever since. Congress did pass the Federal Flag Protection Act of 1989, criminalizing "desecration" of an American flag, which was signed into law. That law was struck down, however, in *United States v. Eichman*, 496 U.S. 310 (1990).

Cases like *O'Brien, Tinker, Collin,* and *Texas v. Johnson* all deal with political expression, that which is given the highest or most "core" position in the hierarchy of First Amendment values by those who reject the strict categorical approach. The tendency to distinguish between categories (or subcategories) of protected speech becomes more evident, and plays a more important role, in cases in which states seek to regulate expressive conduct that itself conveys a message that courts do not value highly. This was most clear in two cases involving laws prohibiting nude dancing.

BARNES, PROSECUTING ATTORNEY OF ST. JOSEPH COUNTY v. GLEN THEATRE, INC.

SUPREME COURT OF THE UNITED STATES

501 U.S. 560 (1991)

CHIEF JUSTICE Rehnquist delivered the opinion of the Court, in which O'CONNOR and KENNEDY joined. SCALIA and SOUTER filed opinions concurring in the judgment. JUSTICE WHITE filed a dissenting opinion, in which MARSHALL, BLACKMUN, AND STEVENS joined.

...Several of our cases contain language suggesting that nude dancing of the kind involved here is expressive conduct protected by the First Amendment. "Although the customary 'barroom' type of nude dancing may involve only the barest minimum of protected expression, we recognized in *California v. LaRue*, 409 U.S. 109, 118, (1972), that this form of entertainment might be entitled to First and Fourteenth Amendment protection under some circumstances.... [F]urthermore, as the state courts in this case recognized, nude dancing is not without its First Amendment protections from official regulation." These statements support the conclusion of the Court of Appeals that nude dancing of the kind sought to be performed here is expressive conduct within the outer perimeters of the First Amendment, though we view it as only marginally so. This, of course, does not end our inquiry. We must determine the level of protection to be afforded to the expressive conduct at issue, and must determine whether the Indiana statute is an impermissible infringement of that protected activity.

Indiana, of course, has not banned nude dancing as such, but has proscribed public nudity across the board. The Supreme Court of Indiana has construed the Indiana statute to preclude nudity in what are essentially places of public accommodation such as the Glen Theatre and the Kitty Kat Lounge. In such places, respondents point out, minors are excluded and there are no nonconsenting viewers. Respondents contend that while the State may license establishments such as the ones involved here, and limit the geographical area in which they do business, it may not in any way limit the performance of the dances within them without violating the First Amendment. The petitioners contend, on the other hand, that Indiana's restriction on nude dancing is a valid "time, place, or manner" restriction under cases such as *Clark v. Community for Creative Non-Violence*, 468 U.S. 288, (1984).

The "time, place, or manner" test was developed for evaluating restrictions on expression taking place on public property which had been dedicated as a "public forum," although we have on at least one occasion applied it to conduct occurring on private property. See *Renton v. Playtime Theatres*, Inc., 475 U.S. 41 (1986). In Clark we observed that this test has been interpreted to embody much the same standards as those set forth in *United States v. O'Brien*, 391 U.S. 367 (1968), and we turn, therefore, to the rule enunciated in *O'Brien*....

Applying the four-part *O'Brien* test...we find that Indiana's public indecency statute is justified despite its incidental limitations on some expressive activity. The public indecency statute is clearly within the constitutional power of the State and furthers substantial governmental interests. It is impossible to discern, other than from the text of the statute, exactly what governmental interest the Indiana legislators had in mind when they enacted this statute, for Indiana does not record legislative history, and the State's highest court has not shed additional light on the statute's purpose. Nonetheless, the statute's purpose of protecting societal order and morality is clear from its text and history. Public indecency statutes of this sort are of ancient origin and presently exist in at least 47 States.... This public indecency statute follows a long line of earlier Indiana statutes banning all public nudity. The history of Indiana's public indecency statute shows that it predates barroom nude dancing and was enacted as a general prohibition. At least as early as 1831, Indiana had a statute punishing "open and notorious lewdness, or...any grossly scandalous and public indecency." A gap during which no statute was in effect was filled by the Indiana Supreme Court in *Ardery v. State*, 56 Ind. 328 (1877), which held that the court could sustain a conviction for exhibition of "privates" in the presence of others. The court traced the offense to the Bible story of Adam and Eve....

This and other public indecency statutes were designed to protect morals and public order. The traditional police power of the States is defined as the authority to provide for the public health, safety, and morals, and we have upheld such a basis for legislation. In *Paris Adult Theatre I v. Slaton*, 413 U.S. 49 (1973), we said: "In deciding *Roth v. United States*, 354 U.S. 476 (1957), this Court implicitly accepted that a legislature could legitimately act on such a conclusion to protect the social interest in order and morality." And in *Bowers v. Hardwick*, 478 U.S. 186, 196 (1986), we said: "The law, however, is constantly based on notions of morality, and if all laws representing essentially moral choices are to be invalidated under the Due Process Clause, the courts will be very busy indeed." Thus, the public indecency statute furthers a substantial government interest in protecting order and morality.

This interest is unrelated to the suppression of free expression. Some may view restricting nudity on moral grounds as necessarily related to expression. We disagree.... It is possible to find some kernel of expression in almost every activity a person undertakes—for example, walking down the street or meeting one's friends at a shopping mall—but such a kernel is not sufficient to bring the activity within the protection of the First Amendment. We think the activity of these dance-hall patrons—coming together to engage in recreational dancing—is not protected by the First Amendment.

Respondents contend that even though prohibiting nudity in public generally may not be related to suppressing expression, prohibiting the performance of nude dancing is related to expression because the State seeks to prevent its erotic message. Therefore, they reason that the application of the Indiana statute to the nude dancing in this case violates the First Amendment, because it fails the third part of the *O'Brien* test, viz: the governmental interest must be unrelated to the suppression of free expression.

But we do not think that when Indiana applies its statute to the nude dancing in these nightclubs it is proscribing nudity because of the erotic message conveyed by the dancers. Presumably numerous other erotic performances are presented at these establishments and similar clubs without any interference from the State, so long as the performers wear a scant amount of clothing. Likewise, the requirement that the dancers don pasties and G-strings does not deprive the dance of whatever erotic message it conveys; it simply makes the message slightly less graphic. The perceived evil that Indiana seeks to address is not erotic dancing, but public nudity. The appearance of people of all shapes, sizes and ages in the nude at a beach, for example, would convey little if any erotic message, yet the State still seeks to prevent it. Public nudity is the evil the State seeks to prevent, whether or not it is combined with expressive activity....

The fourth part of the *O'Brien* test requires that the incidental restriction on First Amendment freedom be no greater than is essential to the furtherance of the governmental interest. As indicated in the discussion above, the governmental interest served by the text of the prohibition is societal disapproval of nudity in public places and among strangers. The statutory prohibition is not a means to some greater end, but an end in itself. It is without cavil that the public indecency statute is "narrowly tailored"; Indiana's requirement that the dancers wear at least pasties and G-strings is modest, and the bare minimum necessary to achieve the State's purpose.

The key point of the majority's analysis was the application of the third *O'Brien* test: "We do not think that when Indiana applies its statute to the nude dancing in these nightclubs it is proscribing nudity because of the erotic message conveyed by the dancers." Only four justices accepted this position. Justice Scalia, concurring in the outcome, concluded that the law was being applied to suppress expression, but argued that that fact should not matter. "The plurality purports to apply to this general law, insofar as it regulates this allegedly expressive conduct, an intermediate level of First Amendment scrutiny.... As I have indicated, I do not believe such a heightened standard exists. I think we should avoid wherever possible, moreover, a method of analysis that requires judicial assessment of the "importance" of government interests—and especially of government interests in various aspects of morality." Instead of the *O'Brien* test's intermediate scrutiny, Scalia proposed a neutrality principle: where a law was not enacted for the purpose of suppressing expression, courts should give no consideration to the incidental burdens that the law might impose on protected speech in practice. Strikingly, Scalia cited his own earlier opinion from *Employment Division, Dept. of Human Resources of Oregon v. Smith*, 494 U.S. 872 (1990) to explain his approach. *Smith* was a case about the free exercise of religion, which suggests that Justice Scalia was reaching for a version of "neutrality" that would cut across the different categories of First Amendment jurisprudence, a proposition that received extensive discussion later in *Mitchell v. Helms*, 530 U.S. 793 (2000) (*Smith* and *Mitchell* are discussed in chapter 6). As far as Justice Scalia was concerned, the moral preferences of the majority were a sufficient basis for any law that did not specifically target protected expression. *Barnes v. Glen Theatre*, 501 U.S. 560 (1991).

Justice Souter also concurred in the outcome, but he based his agreement on the conclusion that the purpose of the statute was not the suppression of communication but only control of the "secondary effects" of expression, making the law a form of content neutral time, place, and manner restriction (see discussion, chapter 3). Justices White, Marshall, Blackmun, and Stevens dissented outright. Thus, while there was a 5 to 4 majority in support of the outcome of the case in *Barnes*, only three justices joined in the opinion that expressed the explanation for that outcome.

Unsurprisingly, perhaps, local governments were left unsure of their prerogatives following *Barnes*. Citing the case by name, the City of Erie, Pennsylvania, adopted a law in which was nearly identical to the one at issue in *Barnes*, with one crucial difference; the Erie city council identified the suppression of nude dancing as the point of their ordinance. "Council specifically wishes to adopt the concept of Public Indecency prohibited by the laws...approved by the U.S. Supreme Court in *Barnes v. Glen Theatre, Inc*...for the purpose of limiting a recent increase in nude live entertainment within the City." *City of Erie v. Pap's A.M., dba "Kandyland,"* 529 U.S. 277 (2000).

Justice O'Connor, writing for the majority, began by citing the conclusions of *Barnes*. "Being in a state of nudity is not an inherently expressive condition. As we explained in *Barnes*, however, nude dancing of the type at issue here is expressive conduct, although we think that it falls only within the outer ambit of the First Amendment's protection." The question, therefore, was framed as a choice between *O'Brien* and *Texas v. Johnson.*

> To determine what level of scrutiny applies to the ordinance at issue here, we must decide "whether the State's regulation is related to the suppression of expression. If the governmental purpose in enacting the regulation is unrelated to the suppression of expression, then the regulation need only satisfy the 'less stringent' standard from *O'Brien* for evaluating restrictions on symbolic speech. If the government interest is related to the content of the expression, however, then the regulation falls outside the scope of the *O'Brien* test and must be justified under a more demanding standard. *Texas v. Johnson.*

O'Connor found that the statute was not intended to suppress expression. First, she observed that "on its face" the law was content neutral in that it banned all public nudity, not only nude dancing. Regarding the language adopted by the city council that expressly targeted nude dancing, Justice O'Connor found that the law was not aimed at suppressing the message of nude dancing but only its secondary effects: "[T]the ordinance does not attempt to regulate the primary effects of the expression, i.e., the effect on the audience of watching nude erotic dancing, but rather the secondary effects, such as the impacts on public health, safety, and welfare, which we have previously recognized are caused by the presence of even one such establishment." As a result, the statute was held to be constitutional since its restrictions on expression were incidental, and no greater than necessary to pursue substantial state interests:

> [E]ven if Erie's public nudity ban has some minimal effect on the erotic message by muting that portion of the expression that occurs when the last stitch is dropped, the dancers at Kandyland and other such establishments are free to perform wearing pasties and G-strings. Any effect on the overall expression is de minimis. And as JUSTICE STEVENS eloquently stated for the plurality in *Young v. American Mini Theatres, Inc.*, "even though we recognize that the First Amendment will not tolerate the total suppression of erotic materials that have some arguably artistic value, it is manifest that society's interest in protecting this type of expression is of a wholly different, and lesser, magnitude than the interest in untrammeled political debate," and "few of us would march our sons or daughters off to war to preserve the citizen's right to see" specified anatomical areas exhibited at establishments like Kandyland. *City of Erie v. Pap's A.M., dba "Kandyland,"* 529 U.S. 277 (2000).

The last sentence explains the significance of Justice O'Connor's reference to "the outer ambit of First Amendment protection." When it comes to expressive conduct, at least, all protected expression is not protected equally.

Justice Scalia, in a concurrence in which he was joined by Justice Thomas, proposed adding a different distinction to the analysis. Instead of asking to what degree the expression at issue is deserving of First Amendment protection, Scalia proposed a second level of analysis of the reach of the statutes at issue. In this proposed approach, in addition to distinguishing between laws regulating pure expression and those regulating expressive conduct, courts would further distinguish between laws regulating the expression element of expressive conduct and those regulating the conduct element of such activities:

> When conduct other than speech itself is regulated, it is my view that the First Amendment is violated only where the government prohibits conduct precisely because of its communicative attributes. Here, even if one hypothesizes that the city's object was to suppress only nude dancing, that would not establish an intent to suppress what (if anything) nude dancing communicates. I do not feel the need, as the Court does, to identify some "secondary effects" associated with nude dancing that the city could properly seek to eliminate.... The traditional power of government to foster good morals (bonos mores), and the acceptability of the traditional judgment (if Erie wishes to endorse it) that nude public dancing itself is immoral, have not been repealed by the First Amendment.

Justices Stevens and Ginsburg dissented, on the grounds that the City of Erie had, in their view, targeted a particular expressive activity because of its content. Furthermore, Stevens argued that the law at issue was quite different from zoning regulations or other forms of restriction since it barred the activity at issue from the city entirely. "[N]ude dancing still receives First Amendment protection, even if that protection lies only in the 'outer ambit' of that Amendment.... If one assumes that the same erotic message is conveyed by nude dancers as by those wearing minuscule costumes, one means of expressing that message is banned; if one assumes that the messages are different, one of those messages is banned. In either event, the ordinance is a total ban. *City of Erie v. Pap's A.M., dba "Kandyland,"* 529 U.S. 277 (2000).

Justice Souter acknowledged the legitimacy of a secondary effects rationale but questioned whether the city had made an adequate evidentiary showing—either of the harms associated with the presence of adult establishments or the efficacy of a rule banning total nudity—to justify the burden that was placed on protected expression. Souter acknowledged that this view represented a shift from his opinion in *Barnes*. In a comment unusual for its candor, he wrote, "I may not be less ignorant of nude dancing than I was nine years ago, but after many subsequent occasions to think further about the needs of the First Amendment, I have come to believe that a government must toe the mark more carefully than I first insisted. I hope it is enlightenment on my part, and acceptable even if a little late."

City of Erie demonstrates the unsettled state of First Amendment doctrine as it relates to expressive conduct. As Justice Stevens pointed out in his dissent, the use of secondary effects to justify a ban on a means of expression is something quite different from traditional zoning ordinances. It is noteworthy that in the context of the Internet the analogy to zoning was rejected by the Court in *Reno v. ACLU*, (see discussion, chapter 3), precisely on the grounds that the practical effect of the Communications Decency Act would be to ban protected expression entirely. By the same logic, the City of Erie should not have been able to use a secondary effects argument to justify its ban on nude dancing.

Justice Scalia's concurring opinion refined the sharp distinction between expression and conduct that he emphasized in *Barnes*. Having previously distinguished between laws designed to suppress expression and laws that only had the effect of doing so, Justice Scalia now added another twist. It should be perfectly permissible, he argued, for government to enact laws directed at suppressing expression so long as those laws are not directed at suppressing the expressive part *of* that expression. So it was perfectly acceptable for a city to ban nude dancing on the grounds that it involved nudity, because nudity was not the expressive element in nude dancing. The expressive part of nude dancing would only be incidentally banned, and the incidental suppression of expression did not require constitutional scrutiny. This analysis, which restores the sharp distinction between expression and behavior that most of the justices have found difficult to ascertain, connects with Justice Scalia's argument in *Barnes* that a single standard should apply across speech and religion cases: in both situations, only direct (intended) burdens on expression are grounds for finding a law unconstitutional.

Justice Souter, whose emphasis on secondary effects has become the majority's new doctrine, raises the question of the sufficiency of evidence. How much investigation, if any, is a legislature required to undertake before determining that disfavored forms of expressive conduct are associated with negative secondary effects? In addition, is there a requirement that there be any basis to believe that the statute in question will ameliorate those effects? In the absence of a requirement of supporting evidence, Justice Souter suggests, legislatures will be free to suppress expression by reciting the magic words "secondary effects." The question of the extent to which courts should scrutinize a legislature's explanation of the motivation behind their actions is one that arises throughout First Amendment jurisprudence. It is precisely the question, for example, that is left open by Justice Scalia's arguments in *City of Erie*. How closely should a court look to determine whether a burden imposed on expression is "direct" or "incidental" to the purpose of the statute?

B. Compelled Speech and the Right of Association

Compelled speech and the right of association may at first glance seem to be quite separate concepts. In recent years, however, the two have become closely connected. The basic principle of compelled speech is simple; just as government may not prevent someone from expressing themselves, government cannot compel a person to declare adherence to any doctrine or creed. The roots of this principle lie in the separation of church and state exemplified in the constitutional rule against religious tests for office, which is based on the fundamental belief that government has no authority over conscience (see discussion, chapter 5). In modern times, that principle has extended to political and even commercial speech. Yet, as we have noted in this chapter, expression inheres in many more acts than speaking. Does associating with a person or group express a message of support for their views? If so, would not compelling people to associate with one another not be to compel them to engage in expressive conduct, and thus constitute a form of compelled speech? In the 1990s, the question arises whether the rule against compelled speech extends also to compelled association.

1. Compelled Speech

In 1914, at the height of the patriotic fervor of the First World War, a Pennsylvania town enacted a law requiring every student in its schools to salute the flag in the manner of a Fascist salute (right arm raised stiffly, palm forward) while reciting the Pledge of Allegiance. That law was upheld by the Supreme Court in 1940. *Minersville School District v. Gobitis*, 310 U.S. 586 (1940). Following that case, the state legislature enacted a law requiring the flag salute statewide, on punishment of expulsion and a fine to be imposed on the parents of noncomplying children. That law was challenged by a Jehovah's Witness named Walter Barnette. Barnette's objections to the law were based on his religion, but the principle that emerges from the case extends to a wide array of speech. Justice Jackson, writing for the majority, insisted that the case stood for the proposition that government has no authority to compel speech under any circumstances: "While religion supplies appellees' motive for enduring the discomforts of making the issue in this case, many citizens who do not share these religious views hold such a compulsory rite to infringe constitutional liberty of the individual. It is not necessary to inquire whether nonconformist beliefs will exempt from the duty to salute unless we first find power to make the salute a legal duty." Dicta in the case, however, suggest that the Court might have been willing to balance school administrators' interests in preserving order or achieving the educational missions of schools, had the justices felt that these interests were threatened by Barnette's actions (see *Tinker v. Des Moines Independent Community School District*, above).

The case was decided in 1943, by which time two things had changed since *Gobitis*: Justices Hughes and McReynolds had retired, and World War II was well under way. The historical context of the case may help explain the fact that three justices who had concurred in *Gobitis*, Black, Douglas, and Murphy, changed their position. Strikingly, Felix Frankfurter, the only Jewish justice on the Court, dissented from the 6-to-3 majority decision which was based on the conclusion that the flag salute was expressive conduct.

WEST VIRGINIA STATE BD. OF EDUCATION v. BARNETTE

SUPREME COURT OF THE UNITED STATES

319 U.S. 624 (1943)

JUSTICE BLACK delivered the opinion of the Court.

The freedom asserted by these appellees does not bring them into collision with the rights asserted by any other individual. It is such conflicts which most frequently require intervention of the State to determine where the rights of one end and those of another begin. But the refusal of these persons to participate in the ceremony does not interfere or deny rights of others to do so. Nor is there any question in this case that their behavior is peaceable and orderly. The sole conflict is between authority and rights of the individual. The State asserts power to condition access to public education on making a prescribed sign and profession and at the same time to coerce attendance by punishing both parent and child. The latter stand on a right of self-determination in matters that touch individual opinion and personal attitude. As the present Chief Justice [Stone] said in dissent in the *Gobitis* case, the State may "require teaching by instruction and study in all our history and in the structure and organization of our government, including the guaranties of civil liberty which tend to inspire patriotism and love of country." Here, however, we are dealing with a compulsion of students to declare a belief....

There is no doubt that, in connection with the pledges, the flag salute is a form of utterance. Symbolism is a primitive but effective way of communicating ideas. The use of an emblem or flag to symbolize some system, idea, institution, or personality is a shortcut from mind to mind. Causes and nations, political parties, lodges and ecclesiastical groups seek to knit the loyalty of their followings to a flag or banner, a color or design.... Associated with many of these symbols are appropriate gestures of acceptance or respect: a salute, a bowed or bared head, a bended knee. A person gets from a symbol the meaning he puts into it, and what is one man's comfort and inspiration is another's jest and scorn. Over a decade ago Chief Justice Hughes led this Court in holding that the display of a red flag as a symbol of opposition by peaceful and legal means to organized government was protected by the free speech guarantees of the constitution. *Stromberg v. California*, 283 U.S. 359 (1931). Here it is the State that employs a flag as a symbol of adherence to government as presently organized. It requires the individual to communicate by word and sign his acceptance of the political ideas it thus bespeaks.... To sustain the compulsory flag salute we are required to say that a Bill of Rights which guards the individual's right to speak his own mind, left it open to public authorities to compel him to utter what is not in his mind....

The very purpose of a Bill of Rights was to withdraw certain subjects from the vicissitudes of political controversy, to lace them beyond the reach of majorities and officials and to establish them as legal principles to be applied by the courts. One's right to life, liberty, and property, to free speech, a free press, freedom of worship and assembly, and other fundamental rights may not be submitted [to political decision-making]....

Struggles to coerce uniformity of sentiment in support of some end thought essential to their time and country have been waged by many good as well as by evil men. Nationalism is a relatively recent phenomenon but at other times and places the ends have been racial or territorial security, support of a dynasty or regime, and particular plans for saving souls. As first and moderate methods to attain unity have failed, those bent on its accomplishment must resort to an ever-increasing severity. As governmental pressure toward unity becomes greater, so strife becomes more bitter as to whose unity it shall be. Probably no deeper division of our people could proceed from any provocation than from finding it necessary to choose what doctrine and whose program public educational officials shall compel youth to unite in embracing.... There is no mysticism in the American concept of the State or of the nature or origin of its authority. We set up government by consent of the governed, and the Bill of rights denies those in power any legal opportunity to coerce that consent. Authority here is to be controlled by public opinion, not public opinion by authority....

If there is any fixed star in our constitutional constellation, it is that no official, high or petty, can prescribe what shall be orthodox in politics, nationalism, religion, or other matters of opinion or force citizens to confess by word or act their faith therein. If there are any circumstances which permit an exception, they do not now occur to us.

JUSTICE FRANKFURTER, dissenting.

> One who belongs to the most vilified and persecuted minority in history is not likely to be insensible to the freedoms guaranteed by our Constitution. Were my purely personal attitude relevant I should wholeheartedly associate myself with the general libertarian views in the Court's opinion, representing as they do the thought and action of a lifetime. But as judges we are neither Jew nor Gentile, neither Catholic nor agnostic. We owe equal attachment to the Constitution and are equally bound by our judicial obligations whether we derive our citizenship from the earliest or the latest immigrants to these shores.... Most unwillingly, therefore, I must differ from my brethren with regard to legislation like this. I cannot bring my mind to believe that the "liberty" secured by the Due Process Clause gives this Court authority to deny to the State of West Virginia the attainment of that which we all recognize as a legitimate legislative end, namely, the promotion of good citizenship, by employment of the means here chosen.

In 1977, the idea of compelled speech was extended to compelled expenditures of money. *Abood v. Detroit Bd. of Educ.*, 431 U.S. 209 (1977) involved a Michigan law that gave unions that represented government employees the right to collect "service charges" from nonmembers employed by local government, equal in amount to union dues. These fees were used, in part, to conduct political activities intended to promote the interests of the employees and the union. The law was challenged by public school teachers who were not members of the teachers' union on the grounds that the mandatory contributions constituted compelled speech. The teachers also challenged the collective bargaining agreement itself. The Court, in an opinion by Justice Stewart, refused to strike down the law that authorized the teachers' union to negotiate conditions of employment for all teachers as the exclusive bargaining agent, but the political activities of the union were a different matter. These activities, said the Court, were unrelated to the union's purpose as a collective bargaining agent, which was the only role in the context of which the union could be authorized to speak for nonmembers:

> The fact that the appellants are compelled to make, rather than prohibited from making, contributions for political purposes works no less an infringement of their constitutional rights. For at the heart of the First Amendment is the notion that an individual should be free to believe as he will, and that in a free society one's beliefs should be shaped by his mind and his conscience rather than coerced by the State.... These principles prohibit a State from compelling any individual to affirm his belief in God, *Torcaso v. Watkins*, or to associate with a political party, as a condition of retaining public employment. They are no less applicable to the case at bar, and they thus prohibit the appellees from requiring any of the appellants to contribute to the support of an ideological cause he may oppose as

a condition of holding a job as a public school teacher. We do not hold that a union cannot constitutionally spend funds for the expression of political views, on behalf of political candidates, or towards the advancement of other ideological causes not germane to its duties as collective bargaining representative. Rather, the Constitution requires only that expenditures be financed from [charges] paid by employees who do not object to advancing those ideas and who are not coerced into doing so against their will by the threat of loss of government employment. *Abood v. Detroit Bd. of Educ.*, 431 U.S. 209 (1977).

Justice Powell, joined by Chief Justice Burger and Justice Blackmun, wrote a concurring opinion in which he went further than the majority. Powell argued that the distinction between public and private employers was fundamental. "[C]ompelling a government employee to give financial support to a union in the public sector—regardless of the use to which the union puts the contribution—impinges seriously upon interests in free speech and association protected by the First Amendment." Justice Stewart had refused to go as far as Powell and his fellows would have liked in part because of the "free rider" problem, whereby nonunion members would reap the benefits of collectively bargained contracts without contributing to the process. The unions had argued, and the majority agreed, that this would create incentives to avoid joining a union that would undermine the collective bargaining provisions of federal labor statutes that had previously been upheld in the context of private employment. "The desirability of labor peace is no less important in the public sector," wrote Stewart, "nor is the risk of 'free riders' any smaller."

The *Abood* rule was reiterated in a unanimous 1990 decision that limited the use of state bar dues to expenses relating to the proper function of a bar association. Chief Justice Rehnquist argued that political advocacy was not germane to the purpose of the bar. "Compulsory dues may not be expended to endorse or advance a gun control or nuclear weapons freeze initiative; at the other end of the spectrum petitioners have no valid constitutional objection to their compulsory dues being spent for activities connected with disciplining members of the bar or proposing ethical codes for the profession." *Keller v. State Bar of California*, 496 U.S. 1 (1990).

In *Barnette*, the Court drew on the idea that the issue involved expressive conduct. In *Abood* and *Keller*, the same parallel might have been drawn, but the decision in *Buckley v. Valeo* seemed to imply that spending money was something closer to "pure speech." The focus on the purpose for which contributions are compelled suggests a similarity between the ability of government to require contributions and the ability of government to restrict speech in a limited forum. In fact, the latter is precisely the analogy toward which the Court was working, a development that received its clearest articulations in a series of cases concerning the authority of government to restrict or promote access to a limited forum. (These "access" cases are discussed in chapter 7.) The basic principle that emerges from *Barnette, Abood,* and *Keller,* however, is that government may not compel speech, nor compel financial support for speech except to the extent that such contributions are necessary to serve a legitimate public purpose such as labor negotiation or the regulation of a public profession. It appears, moreover, that the public purpose at issue need only be substantial rather than compelling; this is the same standard by which courts review regulations of expressive conduct (*O'Brien*) and regulation of expression in a limited forum (*Lee*).

One interesting pair of cases concerns the question of whether commercial enterprises may be required to contribute to the cost of generic advertising for their products. In *Glickman v. Wileman Bros. & Elliott, Inc.,* 521 U.S. 457 (1997), Justice Stevens concluded that the First Amendment did not preclude such compelled contributions. "Three characteristics of the regulatory scheme at issue distinguish it from laws that we have found to abridge the freedom of speech protected by the First Amendment. First, the marketing orders impose no restraint on the freedom of any producer to communicate any message to any audience. Second, they do not compel any person to engage in any actual or symbolic speech. Third, they do not compel the producers to endorse or to finance any political or ideological views." Stevens' analysis echoes the treatments of commercial speech, generally, as a less protected category of expression. In 2001, however, the Court revisited the issue. *USDA v. United Foods, Inc.,* 121 S. Ct. 2334 (2001) involved a challenge to a law requiring mushroom growers to contribute to a fund for the promotion of mushrooms. By a 7 to 2 majority, the Court upheld this law. The distinction between the mushroom promotion law and the fruit promotion law at issue in *Glickman*, according to the majority, was the extent of the legitimate state interest at stake. This was precisely the balancing that the Court eschewed in *Barnette*, indicating again the difference in the level of protection accorded commercial and political or religious speech.

2. *Association and Compelled Association*

The idea that the First Amendment contains a right of association as an outgrowth of its guarantee of free speech was first clearly articulated in *NAACP v. Alabama*, 357 U.S. 449 (1958). In that case, the Supreme Court struck down an Alabama statute that would have required the NAACP to produce its membership lists, which in the past had led to "economic reprisal, loss of employment, threat of physical coercion, and other manifestations of public hostility" toward the organization's members. Justice Harlan, writing for a unanimous Court, declared that "[i]t is beyond debate that freedom to engage in association for the advancement of beliefs and ideas is an inseparable aspect of...freedom of speech."

The constitutional right of association is limited, however. There is no right to associate in a purely social sense of the word: rather the First Amendment only protects the right to associate "for the purpose of engaging in those activities protected by the First Amendment—speech, assembly, petition for the redress of grievances, and the exercise of religion. The [First Amendment] guarantees freedom of association of this kind as an indispensable means of preserving other individual liberties." The words quoted are from Justice Brennan's opinion for a unanimous Court in *Roberts v. United States Jaycees*, 468 U.S. 609 (1984), which held that the Jaycee's did not have a right of association that permitted them to exclude women. (It is important to recognize that constitutional guarantees apply to a private organization such as the Jaycees only when such organizations receive state support.)

The Court found that the exclusion of women was not essential to any First Amendment purpose involved in the Jaycees' activities. The majority applied a test that sounds very much like the *O'Brien* test for regulation of expressive conduct, but that requires a compelling, rather than a merely substantial, state interest. In applying the test, the Court focused on the characterization of the purpose underlying the association and the impact that the intrusion of female members would have on that purpose. The Court balanced those factors against the state's interest, making it clear—again, unlike *Barnette*—that in an appropriate case government may have the authority to compel unwilling association.

Brennan began by observing that in an appropriate case, government interference with membership constitutes an infringement on an organization's ability to express its message:

> There can be no clearer example of an intrusion into the internal structure or affairs of an association than a regulation that forces the group to accept members it does not desire. Such regulation may impair the ability of the original members to express only those views that brought them together. Freedom of association therefore plainly presupposes a freedom not to associate. See *Abood*. The right to associate for expressive purposes is not, however, absolute. Infringements on that right may be justified by regulations adopted to serve compelling state interests,

unrelated to the suppression of ideas, that cannot be achieved through means significantly less restrictive of associational freedoms.

Abood, of course, had not involved membership in an organization, but rather compelled support for speech undertaken by the organization. The question of whether, and when, membership and expression were coextensional was thus at the heart of the *Roberts* analysis:

> [T]he Jaycees have failed to demonstrate that the Act imposes any serious burdens on the male members' freedom of expressive association.... The Act requires no change in the Jaycees' creed of promoting the interests of young men, and it imposes no restrictions on the organization's ability to exclude individuals with ideologies or philosophies different from those of its existing members.... [C]laiming that women might have a different attitude about such issues as the federal budget, school prayer, voting rights, and foreign relations, or that the organization's public positions would have a different effect if the group were not "a purely young men's association," the Jaycees rely solely on unsupported generalizations about the relative interests and perspectives of men and women.... In the absence of a showing far more substantial than that attempted by the Jaycees, we decline to indulge in the sexual stereotyping that underlies appellee's contention that, by allowing women to vote, application of the Minnesota Act will change the content or impact of the organization's speech. *Roberts v. United States Jaycees*, 468 U.S. 609 (1984).

Justice O'Connor concurred in the outcome, but took serious issue with the standard that the Court had used in reviewing the case. O'Connor described the Court's approach as "both over-protective of activities undeserving of constitutional shelter and under-protective of important First Amendment concerns." She criticized the majority for its "membership-message connection" as "objectionable." "[C]ertain commercial associations, by engaging occasionally in certain kinds of expressive activities, might improperly gain protection for discrimination...would the Court's analysis of this case be different if, for example, the Jaycees' membership had a steady history of opposing public issues thought (by the Court) to be favored by women?" Instead of the majority's attempt to balance the interests of government against those of a private association, O'Connor proposed a sharp division between associations that are or are not formed for expressive purposes:

> On the one hand, an association engaged exclusively in protected expression enjoys First Amendment protection of both the content of its message and the choice of its members. Protection of the message itself is judged by the same standards as protection of speech by an individual. Protection of the association's right to define its membership derives from the recognition that the formation of

an expressive association is the creation of a voice, and the selection of members is the definition of that voice.... On the other hand, there is only minimal constitutional protection of the freedom of *commercial* association.... [A]n association should be characterized as commercial, and therefore subject to rationally related state regulation of its membership and other associational activities, when, and only when, the association's activities are not predominately of the type protected by the First Amendment. *Roberts v. United States Jaycees,* 468 U.S. 609 (1984).

Two important rules emerge from *Roberts*. First, association is protected by the First Amendment only to the extent that such association is "expressive." Second, the negative right not to associate—that is, the right to exclude persons from membership—is protected against the operation of otherwise valid laws only if there is a showing that such exclusion is necessary to preserve the message that provided the expressive purpose for the group's association. The first rule was repeated in two other important cases: *New York State Club Ass'n v. New York*, 487 U.S. 1 (1988) (clubs that act as public restaurants have to comply with state anti-discrimination laws); and *Dallas v. Stanglin*, 490 U.S. 19 (1989) (age restrictions on dance halls do not interfere with any constitutionally protected right of association).

The right not to associate was initially conceived of narrowly. In 1976, for instance, the Court upheld a federal statute that prohibited racial discrimination by private schools (under Congress' authority to regulate commerce). One of the arguments raised by the operators of a whites-only school was that compelling their association with African-Americans would violate their right of nonassociation:

In *NAACP v. Alabama* and similar decisions, the Court has recognized a First Amendment right "to engage in association for the advancement of beliefs and ideas...." That right is protected because it promotes and may well be essential to the "[effective] advocacy of both public and private points of view, particularly controversial ones" that the First Amendment is designed to foster. From this principle it may be assumed that parents have a First Amendment right to send their children to educational institutions that promote the belief that racial segregation is desirable, and that the children have an equal right to attend such institutions. But it does not follow that the practice of excluding racial minorities from such institutions is also protected by the same principle. "[T]he Constitution ...places no value on discrimination," and while "[invidious] private discrimination may be characterized as a form of exercising freedom of association protected by the First Amendment...it has never been accorded affirmative constitutional protections.... In any event, as the Court of Appeals noted, "there is no showing that discontinuance of [the] discriminatory admission practices would inhibit in any way the teaching in these schools of any ideas or dogma." *Runyon v. McCrary*, 427 U.S. 160 (1976).

The proposition that a school dedicated to promoting racial segregation would not find its message contradicted by the presence of African-American students is an interesting one. Can it truly be maintained that teaching the desirability of racial separation can be accomplished as easily in a racially mixed classroom as in one that is segregated? The basic point, "the Constitution places no value on discrimination," seems to have been that the limiting principle on the right of non-association was that preservation of a message could not be used as an excuse to exclude persons on the basis of race.

The right not to associate has been understood to mean that a political party can hold closed primaries. In *California Democratic Party v. Jones*, 530 U.S. 567 (2000), the Court considered a challenge to a California law requiring "blanket" primaries (i.e., those in which any registered voter could participate) and found it to be unconstitutional. Writing for a seven-vote majority, Justice Scalia articulated the connection between a right not to associate and the positive rights of expression:

> The First Amendment protects the freedom to join together to further common political beliefs, which presupposes the freedom to identify those who constitute the association, and to limit the association to those people. In no area is the political association's right to exclude more important than in its candidate-selection process. That process often determines the party's positions on significant public policy issues, and it is the nominee who is the party's ambassador charged with winning the general electorate over to its views. The First Amendment reserves a special place, and accords a special protection, for that process, because the moment of choosing the party's nominee is the crucial juncture at which the appeal to common principles may be translated into concerted action, and hence to political power. California's blanket primary violates these principles.

In other cases, moreover, the connection between preserving expression and preventing association has been drawn in ways that pushed closer to the conflation of message and speaker that Justice O'Connor warned against in *Roberts*. *Runyon* may establish the principle that preservation of a message cannot justify the exclusion of persons on the basis of race, but in two recent cases, *Hurley v. Irish-American Gay, Lesbian and Bisexual Group of Boston*, and more clearly in *Dale v. Boy Scouts of America*, that same limitation has been found not to apply to prevent the exclusion of homosexuals. In both cases, the question was not whether homosexuals have a First Amendment right of association that requires private organizations to admit them; the question, rather, was whether Massachusetts and New Jersey could enforce nondiscrimination statutes that prohibited the exclusions of homosexuals without violating the organizations' right of nonassociation.

March 17 is celebrated in Boston both as St. Patrick's Day and as Evacuation Day (commemorating the withdrawal of British troops during the American Revolution), and has traditionally been marked by a parade. In 1947, sponsorship of the parade was transferred from the city to a private organization, the South Boston Allied War Veterans Council. Every year the Council applied for and received a permit to conduct a large St. Patrick's–Evacuation Day parade, and in fact no other organization had ever applied for such a permit. Until 1992, moreover, the Council was permitted to use the city seal, and public funds were used to help cover the cost of the parade. In 1992, a group of gay, lesbian, and bisexual persons of Irish descent ("GLIB") applied to march in the parade, and was turned down. The group obtained a court order compelling the Council to allow them to march, and participated in the parade without incident. The next year GLIB again applied to join the parade and were again turned down, and this time the organization sued. The Court's decision was unanimous.

HURLEY v. IRISH-AMERICAN GAY, LESBIAN AND BISEXUAL GROUP OF BOSTON

SUPREME COURT OF THE UNITED STATES

515 U.S. 557 (1995)

JUSTICE SOUTER delivered the opinion of the Court.

The issue in this case is whether Massachusetts may require private citizens who organize a parade to include among the marchers a group imparting a message the organizers do not wish to convey. We hold that such a mandate violates the First Amendment....

If there were no reason for a group of people to march from here to there except to reach a destination, they could make the trip without expressing any message beyond the fact of the march itself. Some people might call such a procession a parade, but it would not be much of one. Real "parades are public dramas of social relations, and in them performers define who can be a social actor and what subjects and ideas are available for communication and consideration...."

The protected expression that inheres in a parade is not limited to its banners and songs...for the Constitution looks beyond written or spoken words as mediums of expression. Noting that "symbolism is a primitive but effective way of communicating ideas," *West Virginia Bd. of Ed. v. Barnette*, 319 U.S. 624 (1943), our cases have recognized that the First Amendment shields such acts as saluting a flag (and refusing to do so), wearing an armband to protest a war, *Tinker v. Des Moines Independent Community School Dist.*, 393 U.S. 503 (1969), displaying a red flag, *Stromberg v. California*, 283 U.S. 359 (1931), and even "marching, walking or parading" in uniforms displaying the swastika, *National Socialist Party of America v. Skokie*, 432 U.S. 43 (1977). As some of these examples show, a narrow, succinctly articulable message is not a condition of constitutional protection, which if confined to expressions conveying a "particularized message" would never reach the unquestionably shielded painting of Jackson Pollock, music of Arnold Schoenberg, or Jabberwocky verse of Lewis Carroll.

Not many marches, then, are beyond the realm of expressive parades, and the South Boston celebration is not one of them. Spectators line the streets; people march in costumes and uniforms, carrying flags and banners with all sorts of messages (e.g., "England get out of Ireland," "Say no to drugs"); marching bands and pipers play; floats are pulled along; and the whole show is broadcast over Boston television. To be sure, we agree with the state courts that in spite of excluding some applicants, the Council is rather lenient in admitting participants. But a private speaker does not forfeit constitutional protection simply by combining multifarious voices, or by failing to edit their themes to isolate an exact message as the exclusive subject matter of the speech. Nor, under our precedent, does First Amendment protection require a speaker to generate, as an original matter, each item featured in the communication. Cable operators, for example, are engaged in protected speech activities even when they only select programming originally produced by others. For that matter, the presentation of an edited compilation of speech generated by other persons is a staple of most newspapers' opinion pages, which, of course, fall squarely within the core of First Amendment security, as does even the simple selection of a paid noncommercial advertisement for inclusion in a daily paper. The selection of contingents to make a parade is entitled to similar protection.

Respondents' participation as a unit in the parade was equally expressive. GLIB was formed for the very purpose of marching in it, as the trial court found, in order to celebrate its members' identity as openly gay, lesbian, and bisexual descendants of the Irish immigrants, to show that there are such individuals in the community, and to support the like men and women who sought to march in the New York parade. The organization distributed a fact sheet describing the members' intentions, and the record otherwise corroborates the expressive nature of GLIB's participation. In 1993, members of GLIB marched behind a shamrock-strewn banner with the simple inscription "Irish-American Gay, Lesbian and Bisexual Group of Boston." GLIB understandably seeks to communicate its ideas as part of the existing parade, rather than staging one of its own.

The Massachusetts public accommodations law under which respondents brought suit has a venerable history. At common law, innkeepers, smiths, and others who "made profession of a public employment," were prohibited from refusing, without good reason, to serve a customer. As one of the 19th-century English judges put it, the rule was that "the innkeeper is not to select his guests[;] he has no right to say to one, you shall come into my inn, and to another you shall not, as every one coming and conducting himself in a proper manner has a right to be received; and for this purpose innkeepers are a sort of public servants." After the Civil War, the Commonwealth of Massachusetts was the first State to codify this principle to ensure access to public accommodations regardless of race....

In the case before us, however, the Massachusetts law has been applied in a peculiar way. Its enforcement does not address any dispute about the participation of openly gay, lesbian, or bisexual individuals in various units admitted to the parade. Petitioners disclaim any intent to exclude homosexuals as such, and no individual member of GLIB claims to have been excluded from parading as a member of any group that the Council has approved to march. Instead, the disagreement goes to the admission of GLIB as its own parade unit carrying its own banner. Since every participating unit affects the message conveyed by the private organizers, the state courts' application of the statute produced an order essentially requiring petitioners to alter the expressive content of their parade. Although the state courts spoke of the parade as a place of public accommodation, once the expressive character of both the parade and the marching GLIB contingent is understood, it becomes apparent that the state courts' application of the statute had the effect of declaring the sponsors' speech itself to be the public accommodation. Under this approach any contingent of protected individuals with a message would have the right to participate in petitioners' speech, so that the communication produced by the private organizers would be shaped by all those protected by the law who wished to join in with some expressive demonstration of their own. But this use of the State's power violates the fundamental rule of protection under the First Amendment, that a speaker has the autonomy to choose the content of his own message.

"Since all speech inherently involves choices of what to say and what to leave unsaid," one important manifestation of the principle of free speech is that one who chooses to speak may also decide "what not to say." Although the State may at times "prescribe what shall be orthodox in commercial advertising" by requiring the dissemination of "purely factual and uncontroversial information..." outside that context it may not compel affirmance of a belief with which the speaker disagrees. Indeed this general rule, that the speaker has the right to tailor the speech, applies not only to expressions of value, opinion, or endorsement, but equally to statements of fact the speaker would rather avoid...subject, perhaps, to the permissive law of defamation.... Nor is the rule's benefit restricted to the press, being enjoyed by business corporations generally and by ordinary people engaged in unsophisticated expression as well as by professional publishers. Its point is simply the point of all speech protection, which is to shield just those choices of content that in someone's eyes are misguided, or even hurtful.

Petitioners' claim to the benefit of this principle of autonomy to control one's own speech is as sound as the South Boston parade is expressive. Rather like a composer, the Council selects the expressive units of the parade from potential participants, and though the score may not produce a particularized message, each contingent's expression in the Council's eyes comports with what merits celebration on that day. Even if this view gives the Council credit for a more considered judgment than it actively made, the Council clearly decided to exclude a message it did not like from the communication it chose to make, and that is enough to invoke its right as a private speaker to shape its expression by speaking on one subject while remaining silent on another. The message it disfavored is not difficult to identify. Although GLIB's point (like the Council's) is not wholly articulate, a contingent marching behind the organization's banner would at least bear witness to the fact that some Irish are gay, lesbian, or bisexual, and the presence of the organized marchers would suggest their view that people of their sexual orientations have as much claim to unqualified social acceptance as heterosexuals and indeed as members of parade units organized around other identifying characteristics. The parade's organizers may not believe these facts about Irish sexuality to be so, or they may object to unqualified social acceptance of gays and lesbians or have some other reason for wishing to keep GLIB's message out of the parade. But whatever the reason, it boils down to the choice of a speaker not to propound a particular point of view, and that choice is presumed to lie beyond the government's power to control....

[In] *New York State Club Assn*...we turned back a facial challenge to a state antidiscrimination statute on the assumption that the expressive associational character of a dining club with over 400 members could be sufficiently attenuated to permit application of the law even to such a private organization, but we also recognized that the State did not prohibit exclusion of those whose views were at odds with positions espoused by the general club memberships. In other words, although the association provided public benefits to which a State could ensure equal access, it was also engaged in expressive activity; compelled access to the benefit, which was upheld, did not trespass on the organization's message itself. If we were to analyze this case strictly along those lines, GLIB would lose. Assuming the parade to be large enough and a source of benefits (apart from its expression) that would generally justify a mandated access provision, GLIB could nonetheless be refused admission as an expressive contingent with its own message just as readily as a private club could exclude an applicant whose manifest views were at odds with a position taken by the club's existing members.

Our holding today rests not on any particular view about the Council's message but on the Nation's commitment to protect freedom of speech. Disapproval of a private speaker's statement does not legitimize use of the Commonwealth's power to compel the speaker to alter the message by including one more acceptable to others. Accordingly, the judgment of the Supreme Judicial Court is reversed and the case remanded for proceedings not inconsistent with this opinion.

In *Hurley*, the Court noted that the parade organizers were not seeking to exclude participation by all gay individuals, only by a gay organization. The message of that organization, in turn, was taken to be "to celebrate its members' identity as openly gay, lesbian, and bisexual descendants of the Irish immigrants, to show that there are such individuals in the community, and to support the like men and women who sought to march in the New York parade." The second message—the fact of the existence of the category of person—most nearly dissolves the difference between message and person. In dicta, furthermore, Justice Souter implied that in an appropriate case the distinction could be blurred still further. "A private club could exclude an applicant whose manifest views were at odds with a position taken by the club's existing members." On the one hand, it is easy to imagine cases where this principle would be obviously appropriate, such as the ability of the NAACP to exclude Ku Klux Klan members, or the American National Socialist Party to preserve itself against the sudden enrollment of 500,000 Jewish members. On the other hand, the issues of when a view is "manifest," and under what circumstances compelling association interferes with a message, are much more difficult.

In 2000, the Court heard the case of James Dale. A Boy Scout since the age of eight, and an Eagle Scout in 1988, Dale applied for adult membership in 1989 and became a scoutmaster. Thereafter, however, while a student at Rutgers University, "Dale first acknowledged to himself and others that he is gay," becoming the copresident of the Rutgers University Lesbian/Gay Alliance. In 1990, a New Jersey newspaper published an interview with Dale about the need for role models for gay teens. After the interview appeared, the Boy Scouts revoked Dale's membership, and in response he sued under a New Jersey "public accommodations" statute (similar to the one at issue in *Hurley*). Writing for a five-member majority, Chief Justice Rehnquist concluded that the Boy Scouts' right of nonassociation would be violated by the application of the New Jersey law on the grounds that Dale's presence would interfere with the organization's message.

BOY SCOUTS OF AMERICA AND MONMOUTH COUNCIL v. JAMES DALE

SUPREME COURT OF THE UNITED STATES

530 U.S. 640 (2000)

CHIEF JUSTICE REHNQUIST delivered the opinion of the Court, in which O'CONNOR, SCALIA, KENNEDY, and THOMAS joined. JUSTICE STEVENS filed a dissenting opinion, in which SOUTER, GINSBURG, and BREYER joined. JUSTICE SOUTER filed a dissenting opinion, in which GINSBURG and BREYER, joined.

...In *Roberts v. United States Jaycees*, 468 U.S. 609 (1984), we observed that "implicit in the right to engage in activities protected by the First Amendment" is "a corresponding right to associate with others in pursuit of a wide variety of political, social, economic, educational, religious, and cultural ends." This right is crucial in preventing the majority from imposing its views on groups that would rather express other, perhaps unpopular, ideas. Government actions that may unconstitutionally burden this freedom may take many forms, one of which is "intrusion into the internal structure or affairs of an association" like a "regulation that forces the group to accept members it does not desire." Forcing a group to accept certain members may impair the ability of the group to express those views, and only those views, that it intends to express. Thus, "[f]reedom of association...plainly presupposes a freedom not to associate."

The forced inclusion of an unwanted person in a group infringes the group's freedom of expressive association if the presence of that person affects in a significant way the group's ability to advocate public or private viewpoints. But the freedom of expressive association, like many freedoms, is not absolute. We have held that the freedom could be overridden "by regulations adopted to serve compelling state interests, unrelated to the suppression of ideas, that cannot be achieved through means significantly less restrictive of associational freedoms."

To determine whether a group is protected by the First Amendment's expressive associational right, we must determine whether the group engages in "expressive association." The First Amendment's protection of expressive association is not reserved for advocacy groups. But to come within its ambit, a group must engage in some form of expression, whether it be public or private.

Because this is a First Amendment case where the ultimate conclusions of law are virtually inseparable from findings of fact, we are obligated to independently review the factual record to ensure that the state court's judgment does not unlawfully intrude on free expression. The record reveals the following. The Boy Scouts is a private, nonprofit organization. According to its mission statement: "It is the mission of the Boy Scouts of America to serve others by helping to instill values in young people and, in other ways, to prepare them to make ethical choices over their lifetime in achieving their full potential." "The values we strive to instill are based on those found in the Scout Oath and Law...." Thus, the general mission of the Boy Scouts is clear: "To instill values in young people...." It seems indisputable that an association that seeks to transmit such a system of values engages in expressive activity.

Given that the Boy Scouts engages in expressive activity, we must determine whether the forced inclusion of Dale as an assistant scoutmaster would significantly affect the Boy Scouts' ability to advocate public or private viewpoints. This inquiry necessarily requires us first to explore, to a limited extent, the nature of the Boy Scouts' view of homosexuality.

The values the Boy Scouts seeks to instill are "based on" those listed in the Scout Oath and Law. The Boy Scouts explains that the Scout Oath and Law provide "a positive moral code for living; they are a list of 'do's' rather than 'don'ts.'" The Boy Scouts asserts that homosexual conduct is inconsistent with the values embodied in the Scout Oath and Law, particularly with the values represented by the terms "morally straight" and "clean."

Obviously, the Scout Oath and Law do not expressly mention sexuality or sexual orientation. And the terms "morally straight" and "clean" are by no means self-defining. Different people would attribute to those terms very different meanings. For example, some people may believe that engaging in homosexual conduct is not at odds with being "morally straight" and "clean." And others may believe that engaging in homosexual conduct is contrary to being "morally straight" and "clean." The Boy Scouts says it falls within the latter category.... The Boy Scouts asserts that it "teaches that homosexual conduct is not morally straight," and that it does "not want to promote homosexual conduct as a legitimate form of behavior." We accept the Boy Scouts' assertion....

We must then determine whether Dale's presence as an assistant scoutmaster would significantly burden the Boy Scouts' desire to not "promote homosexual conduct as a legitimate form of behavior." As we give deference to an association's assertions regarding the nature of its expression, we must also give deference to an association's view of what would impair its expression. That is not to say that an expressive association can erect a shield against antidiscrimination laws simply by asserting that mere acceptance of a member from a particular group would impair its message. But here Dale, by his own admission, is one of a group of gay Scouts who have "become leaders in their community and are open and honest about their sexual orientation." Dale was the copresident of a gay and lesbian organization at college and remains a gay rights activist. Dale's presence in the Boy Scouts would, at the very least, force the organization to send a message, both to the youth members and the world, that the Boy Scouts accepts homosexual conduct as a legitimate form of behavior.

Hurley is illustrative on this point. There we considered whether the application of Massachusetts' public accommodations law to require the organizers of a private St. Patrick's Day parade to include among the marchers an Irish-American gay, lesbian, and bisexual group, GLIB, violated the parade organizers' First Amendment rights. We noted that the parade organizers did not wish to exclude the GLIB members because of their sexual orientations, but because they wanted to march behind a GLIB banner....

Here, we have found that the Boy Scouts believes that homosexual conduct is inconsistent with the values it seeks to instill in its youth members; it will not "promote homosexual conduct as a legitimate form of behavior." As the presence of GLIB in Boston's St. Patrick's Day parade would have interfered with the parade organizers' choice not to propound a particular point of view, the presence of Dale as an assistant scoutmaster would just as surely interfere with the Boy Scouts' choice not to propound a point of view contrary to its beliefs....

[A]ssociations do not have to associate for the "purpose" of disseminating a certain message in order to be entitled to the protections of the First Amendment. An association must merely engage in expressive activity that could be impaired in order to be entitled to protection. For example, the purpose of the St. Patrick's Day parade in *Hurley* was not to espouse any views about sexual orientation, but we held that the parade organizers had a right to exclude certain participants nonetheless.

Second, even if the Boy Scouts discourages Scout leaders from disseminating views on sexual issues—a fact that the Boy Scouts disputes with contrary evidence—the First Amendment protects the Boy Scouts' method of expression. If the Boy Scouts wishes Scout leaders to avoid questions of sexuality and teach only by example, this fact does not negate the sincerity of its belief discussed above.

Third, the First Amendment simply does not require that every member of a group agree on every issue in order for the group's policy to be "expressive association." The Boy Scouts takes an official position with respect to homosexual conduct, and that is sufficient for First Amendment purposes. In this same vein,

Dale makes much of the claim that the Boy Scouts does not revoke the membership of heterosexual Scout leaders that openly disagree with the Boy Scouts' policy on sexual orientation. But if this is true, it is irrelevant. The presence of an avowed homosexual and gay rights activist in an assistant scoutmaster's uniform sends a distinctly different message from the presence of a heterosexual assistant scoutmaster who is on record as disagreeing with Boy Scouts policy. The Boy Scouts has a First Amendment right to choose to send one message but not the other. The fact that the organization does not trumpet its views from the housetops, or that it tolerates dissent within its ranks, does not mean that its views receive no First Amendment protection....

JUSTICE STEVENS, with whom JUSTICE SOUTER, JUSTICE GINSBURG and JUSTICE BREYER join, dissenting

...Surely there are instances in which an organization that truly aims to foster a belief at odds with the purposes of a State's antidiscrimination laws will have a First Amendment right to association that precludes forced compliance with those laws. But that right is not a freedom to discriminate at will....

BSA has not contended, nor does the record support, that Dale had ever advocated a view on homosexuality to his troop before his membership was revoked. Accordingly, BSA's revocation could only have been based on an assumption that he would do so in the future.... The majority, though, does not rest its conclusion on the claim that Dale will use his position as a bully pulpit. Rather, it contends that Dale's mere presence among the Boy Scouts will itself force the group to convey a message about homosexuality—even if Dale has no intention of doing so. The majority holds that "the presence of an avowed homosexual and gay rights activist in an assistant scoutmaster's uniform sends a distinct...message," and, accordingly, BSA is entitled to exclude that message. In particular, "Dale's presence in the Boy Scouts would, at the very least, force the organization to send a message, both to the youth members and the world, that the Boy Scouts accepts homosexual conduct as a legitimate form of behavior."

The majority's argument relies exclusively on *Hurley v. Irish-American Gay, Lesbian and Bisexual Group of Boston, Inc....* Though Hurley has a superficial similarity to the present case, a close inspection reveals a wide gulf between that case and the one before us today.

First, it was critical to our analysis that GLIB was actually conveying a message by participating in the parade—otherwise, the parade organizers could hardly claim that they were being forced to include any unwanted message at all.... Second, we found it relevant that GLIB's message "would likely be perceived" as the parade organizers' own speech.... Dale's inclusion in the Boy Scouts is nothing like the case in Hurley. His participation sends no cognizable message to the Scouts or to the world. Unlike GLIB, Dale did not carry a banner or a sign; he did not distribute any fact sheet; and he expressed no intent to send any message. If there is any kind of message being sent, then, it is by the mere act of joining the Boy Scouts. Such an act does not constitute an instance of symbolic speech under the First Amendment.

It is true, of course, that some acts are so imbued with symbolic meaning that they qualify as "speech" under the First Amendment. At the same time, however, "we cannot accept the view that an apparently limitless variety of conduct can be labeled 'speech' whenever the person engaging in the conduct intends thereby to express an idea." Though participating in the Scouts could itself conceivably send a message on some level, it is not the kind of act that we have recognized as speech. Indeed, if merely joining a group did constitute symbolic speech; and such speech were attributable to the group being joined; and that group has the right to exclude that speech (and hence, the right to exclude that person from joining), then the right of free speech effectively becomes a limitless right to exclude for every organization, whether or not it engages in any expressive activities. That cannot be, and never has been, the law.

The only apparent explanation for the majority's holding, then, is that homosexuals are simply so different from the rest of society that their presence alone—unlike any other individual's—should be singled out for special First Amendment treatment. Under the majority's reasoning, an openly gay male is irreversibly affixed with the label "homosexual." That label, even though unseen, communicates a message that permits his exclusion wherever he goes. His openness is the sole and sufficient justification for his ostracism. Though unintended, reliance on such a justification is tantamount to a constitutionally prescribed symbol of inferiority. As counsel for the Boy Scouts remarked, Dale "put a banner around his neck when he...got himself into the newspaper.... He created a reputation.... He can't take that banner off. He put it on himself and, indeed, he has continued to put it on himself...."

Furthermore, it is not likely that BSA would be understood to send any message, either to Scouts or to the world, simply by admitting someone as a member. Over the years, BSA has generously welcomed over 87 million young Americans into its ranks. In 1992 over one million adults were active BSA members. The notion that an organization of that size and enormous prestige implicitly endorses the views that each of those adults may express in a non-Scouting context is simply mind boggling....

It is obviously difficult to square the outcome and reasoning in *Dale* with those in *Runyon* (Justice Rehnquist dissented in *Runyon* on grounds unrelated to the First Amendment). Arguably, *Roberts* might also come out differently if that case were heard today. The precise contours of the right of nonassociation are not clear, but it is evident that it is an aspect of the First Amendment that the Rehnquist Court takes very seriously, and at least five members of the Court are prepared to apply that principle broadly to limit the power of the state and federal governments.

V. "Congress Shall Make No Law Respecting an Establishment of Religion..."

Read together, the two religion clauses appear to establish the limiting principles for one another; government may not favor religion too much (a law respecting establishment) nor impede its exercise. As a result, as Chief Justice Burger famously put the matter in 1970, "if expanded to a logical extreme, [each] would tend to clash with the other." *Walz v. Tax Comm'n*, 397 U.S. 664 (1970). There is no other place in the Constitution where two countervailing principles are presented in this way, nor is there any other part of the First Amendment that limits what the government may say, rather than protecting speech against government interference. Thus religion appears simultaneously as specially valuable and specially dangerous, as the religion clauses appear to both protect politics from religion and religion from politics. One way to describe this would be to say that the Constitution defines religion as a private area, one neither subject to government control nor appropriate for government support. The latter question—the limits on government action that are imposed by the prohibition on laws "respecting an establishment of religion"—is the subject of this chapter, while the limits of free exercise will be taken up in chapter 6.

The term "establishment," in the late eighteenth-century context, referred to the model of the Church of England, in which the King of England was also the leader of the national church, which claimed sole legitimacy in the nation and had special authority and privileges (e.g., the right to maintain ecclesiastical courts, immunity from civil prosecutions, vast landholdings granted from the Crown). From the seventeenth century forward, dissenters had argued that an established national church was anathema to the Calvinist tradition. Their Anglican opponents were the Antidisestablishmentarianists, a word beloved of elementary school spelling champions everywhere. As noted in the Introduction, the Anglican Church and the English government, together, repressed dissenting movements with considerable harshness, prompting some dissenters to become separationists and ultimately to settle in New England.

Given this historical background, it is unsurprising that the Free Exercise Clause defines religion as something especially valuable. Religion, after all, fits essentially all of Emerson's criteria for protected speech (in chapter 1): It is a search for truth, an important part of many people's self-actualization, and so on. As for the idea that free speech is a prerequisite for political freedom (or, in Emerson's terms, a necessary element of political participation), surely the religious dissenters of early America would have had a clear negative model in the oppression of the established Anglican Church as well as those of the Catholic Inquisition of the fifteenth and sixteenth centuries. Thus, it is not too surprising, perhaps, that the freedom to exercise their religion should be considered a crucial political freedom.

But the dissenting Protestants of early America chafed at the restrictions of the established Anglican Church in part because they were firmly convinced that their own was the one true faith. Thus it may be obvious that the heirs of their religious tradition would want to prevent the establishment of a "wrong" church, but why did they want to preclude the establishment of the right church (whatever that happened to be)? One answer might be that by the late 1700s America was a country of considerable religious diversity. Along with a history of religious oppression, England had a history of civil wars in which religion was often an issue, such as the conflict between Elizabeth I and Mary, Queen of Scots, or the English Civil War between Cromwell's Roundheads and the forces of Charles I. Thus, one problem with permitting the possibility of an established church was that the competition for the position of supremacy among religious groups could have torn the nation apart. Madison, for one, was keenly aware of the dangers of permitting religion to become the basis of political factions. An important argument for the separation of church and state, then, was that the state needed protection against the divisive influence of religion.

A different objection to the admixture of church and state was an argument that state support for churches degraded their purpose. If the state established an official church, then people might join that church not out of genuine religious conviction but in order to secure a position of political security. Even government support for a church risked diminishing the authenticity and commitment of its members in the eyes of those whose conception of a congregation involved deeply shared commitments, sacrifice, and above all, complete independence from an hierarchical church polity. This is not the model for all forms of Protestantism, but it was the hallmark of Congregationalism, Baptism, and many of the less well-defined local churches that arose during the Great Awakening of the 1740s. By the time of the Constitution, America was home to a great number of churches that, despite diverse points of disagreements on other matters, were generally committed to independence from state authority.

Finally, there was the matter that was closest to Jefferson's heart, the effect that establishment might have on those who were not members of the "official" faith. Just as there were those who feared that even government support—let alone actual establishment—could corrupt the purpose of a congregation, Jefferson and others like him feared that government support for one religion necessarily infringed on the freedom of those who followed another or, like himself, none at all. (Although Jefferson was not an atheist, he was emphatically not a follower of Christianity in any form. Among other things, he denied both the divinity of Jesus and the authority of scripture.) Above all, Jefferson was opposed to the idea of using monies collected in taxes to support churches.

The First Amendment reflects some version of Jefferson's position in the way it goes beyond prohibiting state establishment to prohibit any law "respecting" an establishment. The text of the Constitution already contained prohibitions on religious tests for office, one of the basic elements of the Church of England's established position in English government. Yet the First Amendment went further; the word "respecting" has been understood to include laws tending toward state establishment, not merely those that can be argued to actually accomplish such an outcome. In the words of Justice Frankfurter, "the First and Fourteenth Amendments have a secular reach far more penetrating in the conduct of Government than merely to forbid an 'established church'...we have staked the very existence of our country on the faith that complete separation between the state and religion is best for the state and best for religion." *McCollum v. Bd. of Ed.*, 333 U.S. 203 (1948) (Frankfurter, J., concurring). So it goes without saying that the government not only cannot require everyone to belong to the "First Church of the United States" (nor, since the incorporation of the religion clauses in 1931, of the "First Church of the State of California"), but also cannot declare an official preference for one faith over another, nor use public funds to promote a particular church. Beyond that, however, there are considerable areas of disagreement over the meaning of the Establishment Clause. There are three basic categories of government action that have been the basis of Establishment Clause jurisprudence: direct material support for religious institutions; "endorsement," or official government expressions of support for religion; and "accommodation," or special exemptions from otherwise applicable laws that the government grants to members of religious groups.

Many of the cases addressing these questions have arisen in the contexts of schools. Upon reflection, this is not surprising; educating children is one of the few areas in which the government and religious institutions both conceive of themselves as having a mandate for action. Furthermore, both governmental and religious authorities have a great deal at stake in the education of future citizens and congregants. So, under the category of direct support there is a long line of cases concerning the limits of the power of government to give money, materials, or services to parochial schools. The question of endorsement is central to issues of whether schools may require prayer or prayerlike activities. The issue of accommodation is raised when parents refuse, for religious reasons, to send their children to school or otherwise claim exemptions from the legal requirements that all other parents are required to accept.

Across each of these categories, arguments have been arrayed around two conceptual divisions. First, there is the division between what is sometimes called the "high wall of separation theory" and the "neutrality" theory. The "high wall of separation" refers to the idea that government and religion ought to be kept completely separate. In practice, this means that government must not only refrain from favoring one religion over another, but also may not favor religion over irreligion generally, on the theory that what people believe is simply none of the government's business. The "neutrality" approach, on the other hand, suggests that it is perfectly appropriate for government to favor religion in general, so long as it does not identify a specific favored sect. (The word "neutrality," however, appears in a number of different guises in the discussion that follows.) The second division has to do with whether one thinks courts should focus on the actions of the government, or on the effects of those actions for citizens. That is, does the First Amendment mean that government may not act in ways that have the *effect* of favoring one religion over another (or, if one adopts the "high wall" model, religion over irreligion), or only that government may not act in ways *intended* to show such favoritism? These arguments have been carried out across each of the three major areas described above (direct support, endorsement, and accommodation).

It should be noted that, throughout, there have been certain principles that have been universally accepted by the Court. In 1982, the Court had no trouble finding that Massachusetts had violated the Establishment Clause when it gave the local Catholic archdiocese the power to allocate liquor licenses in Cambridge. *Larkin v. Grendel's Den, Inc.*, 459 U.S. 116 (1982). Nor did the Justices have any trouble dispensing with a ruling by a federal judge in Alabama that said that the Establishment Clause did not apply to the states. *Wallace v. Jaffree*, 472 U.S. 38 (1967).

Finally, there is one particular inquiry that has been reserved for the next chapter (discussing the Free Exercise Clause). That is the question of what constitutes a "religion"? At various times, courts have given different answers. In 1961, in a footnote, Justice Black observed that some "religions" do not involve theism. "Among religions in this country which do not teach what would generally be considered a belief in the existence of God are Buddhism, Taoism, Ethical Culture, Secular Humanism and others." *Torcaso v. Watkins* 367 U.S. 488 (1961). For purposes of the Establishment Clause, the definition of "religion" has generally been treated very broadly. This is to some extent overdetermined, since hostility toward religion is as suspect as favoritism, and in addition the government is independently prohibited from discriminating on the basis of viewpoint under the Free Speech Clause.

The discussion that follows is divided into three parts: cases considering problems of direct support, cases concerned with endorsement, and cases addressing the limits of permissible accommodation. It is important to keep track of the chronology of these cases, however, and to realize that, for example, *Walz* and *Lemon* were decided only one year apart and reflect a common understanding.

A. Subsidies for Religious Activities

The interpretation of the Establishment Clause begins in 1947 in *Everson v. Bd. of Educ. of the Township of Ewing*, 330 U.S. 1 (1947). As Justice Rutledge noted in his dissenting opinion, "This case forces us to determine squarely for the first time what was 'an establishment of religion' in the First Amendment's conception." Prior to that time, a century and a half after the adoption of the First Amendment, there was essentially no body of law interpreting the meaning of this obviously crucial element of the Constitution. The case concerned a challenge to a New Jersey statute that permitted the use of public funds to pay for bus transportation to parochial schools.

In the most quoted passage of this majority opinion, Justice Black expressed the principle of high wall separationism in ringing terms. "In the words of Jefferson," he wrote, "the clause against establishment of religion by law was intended to erect 'a wall of separation between church and State.'" The rhetoric of the majority opinion in *Everson* is curiously matched with its outcome, however, as the Court in fact *upheld* the challenged law by a vote of 5 to 4. The majority's conclusion that the law was constitutional turned to a great extent on the conclusion that the government had a secular, public purpose, an argument to which the dissenting justices took great exception. Justices Jackson, Frankfurter, Rutledge, and Burton argued that the separation of church and state could not be reconciled with any use of public funds to support parochial schools.

EVERSON v. BOARD OF EDUCATION OF THE TOWNSHIP OF EWING ET AL.

SUPREME COURT OF THE UNITED STATES

330 U.S. 1 (1947)

JUSTICE BLACK delivered the opinion of the Court.

...A large proportion of the early settlers of this country came here from Europe to escape the bondage of laws which compelled them to support and attend government-favored churches. The centuries immediately before and contemporaneous with the colonization of America had been filled with turmoil, civil strife, and persecutions, generated in large part by established sects determined to maintain their absolute political and religious supremacy. With the power of government supporting them, at various times and places, Catholics had persecuted Protestants, Protestants had persecuted Catholics, Protestant sects had persecuted other Protestant sects, Catholics of one shade of belief had persecuted Catholics of another shade of belief, and all of these had from time to time persecuted Jews. In efforts to force loyalty to whatever religious group happened to be on top and in league with the government of a particular time and place, men and women had been fined, cast in jail, cruelly tortured, and killed. Among the offenses for which these punishments had been inflicted were such things as speaking disrespectfully of the views of ministers of government-established churches, non-attendance at those churches, expressions of non-belief in their doctrines, and failure to pay taxes and tithes to support them.

These practices of the old world were transplanted to and began to thrive in the soil of the new America.... Catholics found themselves hounded and proscribed because of their faith; Quakers who followed their conscience went to jail; Baptists were peculiarly obnoxious to certain dominant Protestant sects; men and women of varied faiths who happened to be in a minority in a particular locality were persecuted because they steadfastly persisted in worshiping God only as their own consciences dictated. And all of these dissenters were compelled to pay tithes and taxes to support government-sponsored churches whose ministers preached inflammatory sermons designed to strengthen and consolidate the established faith by generating a burning hatred against dissenters.

These practices became so commonplace as to shock the freedom-loving colonials into a feeling of abhorrence. The imposition of taxes to pay ministers' salaries and to build and maintain churches and church property aroused their indignation. It was these feelings which found expression in the First Amendment....

The "establishment of religion" clause of the First Amendment means at least this: Neither a state nor the Federal Government can set up a church. Neither can pass laws which aid one religion, aid all religions, or prefer one religion over another. Neither can force nor influence a person to go to or to remain away from church against his will or force him to profess a belief or disbelief in any religion. No person can be punished for entertaining or professing religious beliefs or disbeliefs, for church attendance or non-attendance. No tax in any amount, large or small, can be levied to support any religious activities or institutions, whatever they may be called, or whatever form they may adopt to teach or practice religion. Neither a state nor the Federal Government can, openly or secretly, participate in the affairs of any religious organizations or groups and vice versa. In the words of Jefferson, the clause against establishment of religion by law was intended to erect "a wall of separation between church and State."

We must consider the New Jersey statute in accordance with the foregoing limitations imposed by the First Amendment. But we must not strike that state statute down if it is within the State's constitutional power even though it approaches the verge of that power. New Jersey cannot consistently with the "establishment of religion" clause of the First Amendment contribute tax-raised funds to the support of an institution which teaches the tenets and faith of any church. On the other hand, other language of the amendment commands that New Jersey cannot hamper its citizens in the free exercise of their own religion.... While we do not mean to intimate that a state could not provide transportation only to children attending public schools, we must be careful, in protecting the citizens of New Jersey against state-established churches, to be sure that we do not inadvertently prohibit New Jersey from extending its general state law benefits to all its citizens without regard to their religious belief.

Measured by these standards, we cannot say that the First Amendment prohibits New Jersey from spending tax-raised funds to pay the bus fares of parochial school pupils as a part of a general program under which it pays the fares of pupils attending public and other schools. It is undoubtedly true that children are helped to get to church schools. There is even a possibility that some of the children might not be sent to the church schools if the parents were compelled to pay their children's bus fares out of their own pockets when transportation to a public school would have been paid for by the State. The same possibility exists where the state requires a local transit company to provide reduced fares to school children including those attending parochial schools, or where a municipally owned transportation system undertakes to carry all school children free of charge. Moreover, state-paid policemen, detailed to protect children going to and from church schools from the very real hazards of traffic, would serve much the same purpose and accomplish much the same result as state provisions intended to guarantee free transportation of a kind which the state deems to be best for the school children's welfare. And parents might refuse to risk their children to the serious danger of traffic accidents going to and from parochial schools, the approaches to which were not protected by policemen. Similarly, parents might be reluctant to permit their children to attend schools which the state had cut off from such general government services as ordinary police and fire protection, connections for sewage disposal, public highways and sidewalks. Of course, cutting off church schools from these services, so separate and so indisputably marked off from the religious function, would make it far more difficult for the schools to operate. But such is obviously not the purpose of the First Amendment. That Amendment requires the state to be neutral in its relations with groups of religious believers and non-believers; it does not require the state to be their adversary. State power is no more to be used so as to handicap religions than it is to favor them....

MR. JUSTICE JACKSON, dissenting.

> I find myself, contrary to first impressions, unable to join in this decision.... The Court's opinion marshals every argument in favor of state aid and puts the case in its most favorable light, but much of its reasoning confirms my conclusions that there are no good grounds upon which to support the present legislation. In fact, the undertones of the opinion, advocating complete and uncompromising separation of Church from State, seem utterly discordant with its conclusion yielding support to their commingling in educational matters. The case which irresistibly comes to mind as the most fitting precedent is that of Julia who, according to Byron's reports, "whispering 'I will ne'er consent,' consented...."

MR. JUSTICE RUTLEDGE, with whom MR. JUSTICE FRANKFURTER, MR. JUSTICE JACKSON and MR. JUSTICE BURTON agree, dissenting.

> ...The Amendment's purpose was not to strike merely at the official establishment of a single sect, creed or religion, outlawing only a formal relation such as had prevailed in England and some of the colonies. Necessarily it was to uproot all such relationships. But the object was broader than separating church and state in this narrow sense. It was to create a complete and permanent separation of the spheres of religious activity and civil authority by comprehensively forbidding every form of public aid or support for religion....

Despite the arguable inconsistencies between its rhetoric and its rule, it is striking that in *Everson* all of the justices were united in their commitment to "high wall separationism" of a particularly strict form. In the years that followed, the Court tried on a number of occasions to work out exactly what kinds of support for religion were and were not permitted. Sunday closing laws were upheld in *McGowan v. Maryland*, 366 U.S. 420 (1961) on the grounds that they served a secular purpose. "[S]ecular justifications have been advanced for making Sunday a day of rest, a day when people may recover from the labors of the week just passed." The fact that the choice of Sunday facilitated religious worship was considered only an incidental benefit to religion, and one that itself served a secular purpose. "It would seem unrealistic for enforcement purposes and perhaps detrimental to the general welfare to require a State to choose a common day of rest other than that which most persons would select of their own accord." In *Board of Educ. v. Allen* (1968), the Court found no violation of the Establishment Clause in a law that required local school boards to make textbooks available to all children in grades 7 through 12, including those enrolled in parochial schools. Writing for the majority in that case, Justice White returned to the theme of a secular "public purpose," and added a distinction between direct and indirect support:

> The express purpose...was stated by the New York Legislature to be furtherance of the educational opportunities available to the young. Appellants have shown us nothing about the necessary effects of the statute that is contrary to its stated purpose. The law merely makes available to all children the benefits of a general program to lend school books free of charge.... [N]o funds or books are furnished to parochial schools, and the financial benefit is to parents and children, not to schools. Perhaps free books make it more likely that some children choose to attend a sectarian school, but that was true of the state-paid bus fares in *Everson* and does not alone demonstrate an unconstitutional degree of support for a religious institution.

Thus the private schools, in using the publicly provided secular texts, were acting as instruments of public policy. "[T]his Court has long recognized that religious schools pursue two goals, religious instruction and secular education." *Board of Educ. v. Allen*, 392 U.S. 236 (1968).

Justice Harlan, concurring, proposed adding an additional element to the formula. "I would hold that where the contested governmental activity is calculated to achieve nonreligious purposes otherwise within the competence of the State, and where the activity does not involve the State so significantly and directly in the realm of the sectarian as to give rise to...divisive influences and inhibitions of freedom, it is not forbidden by the religion clauses of the First Amendment." In dissent, Justice Black declared that this case was different from *Everson* because books are different from bus rides. "Books are the most essential tool of education since they contain the resources of knowledge which the educational process is designed to exploit. In this sense it is not difficult to distinguish books, which are the heart of any school, from bus fares, which provide a convenient and helpful general public transportation service." *Board of Educ. v. Allen*, 392 U.S. 236 (1968).

The issues of secular public purpose, direct versus indirect support, and above all, Justice Harlan's comment about the degree of involvement of the state "in the realm of the sectarian" were at the heart of the next key case in the development of the Establishment Clause, *Walz v. Tax Comm'n*, 397 U.S. 664 (1970). *Walz* was a challenge to a New York state tax exemption for "property used exclusively for religious, educational or charitable purpose." By allowing churches to be free from property taxes, argued the petitioners, the state was indirectly using taxpayer monies to subsidize their operation in the form of the shared benefit that churches derived—in common with everyone else—from publicly provided services.

Writing for the majority, Chief Justice Burger made two basic arguments. First, he found that the tax exemption only incidentally benefited religion in the process of pursuing a legitimate public purpose.

"The legislative purpose of a property tax exemption is neither the advancement nor the inhibition of religion; it is neither sponsorship nor hostility. New York, in common with other states, has determined that certain entities that exist in a harmonious relationship to the community at large, and that foster its moral or mental improvement, should not be inhibited in their activities by property taxation...." In addition, Burger picked up on the theme that Harlan had introduced in his concurring opinion in *Allen*. "We must also be sure that the end result—the effect—is not an excessive government entanglement with religion.... Elimination of exemption would tend to expand the involvement of government by giving rise to tax valuation of church property, tax liens, tax foreclosures." The issue of "entanglement," for Burger, was what distinguished direct provision of monies to religious organizations from the kind of indirect subsidies involved in *Walz* and *Allen*. "Obviously," he wrote, "a direct money subsidy would be a relationship pregnant with involvement and, as with most governmental grant programs, could encompass sustained and detailed administrative relationships." Justice Douglas dissented, on the grounds that exempting churches from taxation was a remnant of "the early days when the church was an agency of the state." He also rejected the majority's reliance on the distinction between direct and indirect support, stating that "a tax exemption is a subsidy."

The next year, in 1971, the Court decided *Lemon v. Kurtzman*, 403 U.S. 602 (1971). In a unanimous opinion (Justice Marshall did not participate), Chief Justice Burger used the case to establish an approach that synthesized the tests that emerged from *Everson*, *Allen*, and *Walz*. The *Lemon* test would be used to determine the constitutionality of government subsidies for religious activities for more than twenty years. Justice Black's *Allen* argument that books were different from buses also makes an appearance in *Lemon*, this time in the form of a distinction between teachers and books. The case involved state programs in Rhode Island and Pennsylvania that provided salary supplements for teachers of secular subjects in private schools. The laws referred only to "non-public" schools, but as the majority noted, "about 95% of these pupils attended schools affiliated with the Roman Catholic church. To date some 250 teachers have applied for benefits under the Act. All of them are employed by the Roman Catholic church." In his analysis of the case, Burger formulated a three-part test: "First, the statute must have a secular legislative purpose; second, its principal or primary effect must be one that neither advances nor inhibits religion; finally, the statute must not foster an excessive government entanglement with religion." The excerpt that follows is Chief Justice

Burger's explanation and application of the entanglement test, the most complex and the most controversial element of the case.

LEMON v. KURTZMAN, SUPERINTENDENT OF PUBLIC INSTRUCTION OF PENNSYLVANIA

SUPREME COURT OF THE UNITED STATES

403 U.S. 602 (1971)

CHIEF JUSTICE BURGER delivered the opinion of the Court.

...The language of the Religion Clauses of the First Amendment is at best opaque, particularly when compared with other portions of the Amendment. Its authors did not simply prohibit the establishment of a state church or a state religion, an area history shows they regarded as very important and fraught with great dangers. Instead they commanded that there should be "no law respecting an establishment of religion." A law may be one "respecting" the forbidden objective while falling short of its total realization. A law "respecting" the proscribed result, that is, the establishment of religion, is not always easily identifiable as one violative of the Clause. A given law might not establish a state religion but nevertheless be one "respecting" that end in the sense of being a step that could lead to such establishment and hence offend the First Amendment.

In the absence of precisely stated constitutional prohibitions, we must draw lines with reference to the three main evils against which the Establishment Clause was intended to afford protection: "sponsorship, financial support, and active involvement of the sovereign in religious activity."

Every analysis in this area must begin with consideration of the cumulative criteria developed by the Court over many years. Three such tests may be gleaned from our cases. First, the statute must have a secular legislative purpose; second, its principal or primary effect must be one that neither advances nor inhibits religion; finally, the statute must not foster "an excessive government entanglement with religion."

In order to determine whether the government entanglement with religion is excessive, we must examine the character and purposes of the institutions that are benefited, the nature of the aid that the State provides, and the resulting relationship between the government and the religious authority. MR. JUSTICE HARLAN, in a separate opinion in *Walz*, supra, echoed the classic warning as to "programs, whose very nature is apt to entangle the state in details of administration." Here we find that both statutes foster an impermissible degree of entanglement.

(a) Rhode Island program

...The church schools involved in the program are located close to parish churches. This understandably permits convenient access for religious exercises since instruction in faith and morals is part of the total educational process. The school buildings contain identifying religious symbols such as crosses on the exterior and crucifixes, and religious paintings and statues either in the classrooms or hallways. Although only approximately 30 minutes a day are devoted to direct religious instruction, there are religiously oriented extracurricular activities. Approximately two-thirds of the teachers in these schools are nuns of various religious orders. Their dedicated efforts provide an atmosphere in which religious instruction and religious vocations are natural and proper parts of life in such schools.... On the basis of these findings the District Court concluded that the parochial schools constituted "an integral part of the religious mission of the Catholic Church." The various characteristics of the schools make them "a powerful vehicle for transmitting the Catholic faith to the next generation." This process of inculcating religious doctrine is, of course, enhanced by the impressionable age of the pupils, in primary schools particularly. In short, parochial schools involve substantial religious activity and purpose.

The substantial religious character of these church-related schools gives rise to entangling church-state relationships of the kind the Religion Clauses sought to avoid. Although the District Court found that concern for religious values did not inevitably or necessarily intrude into the content of secular subjects, the considerable religious activities of these schools led the legislature to provide for careful governmental controls and surveillance by state authorities in order to ensure that state aid supports only secular education.

The dangers and corresponding entanglements are enhanced by the particular form of aid that the Rhode Island Act provides. Our decisions from *Everson* to *Allen* have permitted the States to provide church-related schools with secular, neutral, or nonideological services, facilities, or materials. Bus transportation, school lunches, public health services, and secular textbooks supplied in common to all students were not thought to offend the Establishment Clause. We note that the dissenters in *Allen* seemed chiefly concerned with the pragmatic difficulties involved in ensuring the truly secular content of the textbooks provided at state expense.

In *Allen* the Court refused to make assumptions, on a meager record, about the religious content of the textbooks that the State would be asked to provide. We cannot, however, refuse here to recognize that teachers have a substantially different ideological character from books. In terms of potential for involving some aspect of faith or morals in secular subjects, a textbook's content is ascertainable, but a teacher's handling of a subject is not. We cannot ignore the danger that a teacher under religious control and discipline poses to the separation of the religious from the purely secular aspects of pre-college education. The conflict of functions inheres in the situation....

The Rhode Island Legislature has not, and could not, provide state aid on the basis of a mere assumption that secular teachers under religious discipline can avoid conflicts. The State must be certain, given the Religion Clauses, that subsidized teachers do not inculcate religion—indeed the State here has undertaken to do so. To ensure that no trespass occurs, the State has therefore carefully conditioned its aid with pervasive restrictions. An eligible recipient must teach only those courses that are offered in the public schools and use only those texts and materials that are found in the public schools. In addition the teacher must not engage in teaching any course in religion.

A comprehensive, discriminating, and continuing state surveillance will inevitably be required to ensure that these restrictions are obeyed and the First Amendment otherwise respected. Unlike a book, a teacher cannot be inspected once so as to determine the extent and intent of his or her personal beliefs and subjective acceptance of the limitations imposed by the First Amendment. These prophylactic contacts will involve excessive and enduring entanglement between state and church....

(b) Pennsylvania program

The Pennsylvania statute also provides state aid to church-related schools for teachers' salaries.... The Pennsylvania statute, moreover, has the further defect of providing state financial aid directly to the church-related school. This factor distinguishes both *Everson* and *Allen*, for in both those cases the Court was careful to point out that state aid was provided to the student and his parents—not to the church-related school. In *Walz v. Tax Commission*, supra, at 675, the Court warned of the dangers of direct payments to religious organizations: "Obviously a direct money subsidy would be a relationship pregnant with involvement and, as with most governmental grant programs, could encompass sustained and detailed administrative relationships for enforcement of statutory or administrative standards...."

A broader base of entanglement of yet a different character is presented by the divisive political potential of these state programs. In a community where such a large number of pupils are served by church-related schools, it can be assumed that state assistance will entail considerable political activity. Partisans of parochial schools, understandably concerned with rising costs and sincerely dedicated to both the religious and secular educational missions of their schools, will inevitably champion this cause and promote political action to achieve their goals. Those who oppose state aid, whether for constitutional, religious, or fiscal reasons, will inevitably respond and employ all of the usual political campaign techniques to prevail. Candidates will be forced to declare and voters to choose. It would be unrealistic to ignore the fact that many people confronted with issues of this kind will find their votes aligned with their faith.

Ordinarily political debate and division, however vigorous or even partisan, are normal and healthy manifestations of our democratic system of government, but political division along religious lines was one of the principal evils against which the First Amendment was intended to protect.... The potential for political divisiveness related to religious belief and practice is aggravated in these two statutory programs by the need for continuing annual appropriations and the likelihood of larger and larger demands as costs and populations grow....

Although *Lemon* is remembered primarily for its three-part test, the opinion in fact goes into extensive discussions of a number of important issues in the context of defining "excessive entanglement," including the dangers to the political system of divisiveness, and the problems for religions that are engendered by any program that requires extensive government supervision. In addition, although the ruling of the Court in *Lemon* was unanimous regarding the Pennsylvania program, Justice White dissented from the decision as it affected the Rhode Island program on the grounds that any support for religion was only "indirect." Furthermore, there were conflicting explanatory theories concerning even the unanimous part of the holding. Chief Justice Burger had emphasized the need for continuing surveillance (thus protecting the church from the state) and the danger of political divisiveness (protecting the state from the church). Justices Douglas, Black, and Marshall rejected the distinction between direct and indirect aid on the grounds that use of public funds for one purpose freed up other funds to be used for others, an argument that would later come to be called "divertability" (discussed in *Mitchell v. Helms*, below). They also emphasized the Jeffersonian principle that money collected from a person of one faith, or none, should not be used to support another. Justice Brennan agreed, and added the principle that the state ought not to be allowed to pursue secular ends through religious means. Thus, from the beginning there was disagreement about the key principle at work behind the "entanglement" element of the *Lemon* test.

From 1971 until 1997, the three-part *Lemon* test defined the scope of the Establishment Clause in cases involving government subsidies to religious institutions. The meaning of that test for particular fact patterns, however, was a matter of considerable disagreement, and cases turned—as Chief Justice Burger had said that they would—on the facts of each case. The Court upheld federal funding for the construction of buildings to be used by religious colleges, (*Tilton v. Richardson*, 403 U.S. 672 [1971]) and the provision of funds to such colleges to be used for nonsectarian purposes (*Roemer v. Maryland Public Works Bd.*, 426 U.S. 736 [1976]). The Court also approved programs that loaned secular textbooks and provided diagnostic and testing services to students in parochial schools (*Meek v. Pittenger*, 413 U.S. 349 [1973]; *Wolman v. Walter*, 433 U.S. 229 [1977]). The Court similarly upheld tax deductions for the cost of private schools, including parochial schools (*Mueller v. Allen*, 463 U.S. 388 [1983]), upheld tuition grants that could be used to attend a religiously affiliated college (*Witters v. Washington Dept. of Services for the Blind*, 474 U.S. 481 [1986]), and approved public funding to provide sign-language interpreters for deaf children in parochial schools (*Zobrest v. Catalina Foothills School District*, 509 U.S. 1 [1993]). In 1990, the Court upheld the Equal Access Law of 1984, which prohibited public schools from excluding religious student groups from holding meetings on school grounds. (*Board of Educ. of the Westside Community Schools v. Mergens*, 496 U.S. 226 [1990]) (see discussion of Equal Access, below).

The same practices that would be upheld where they applied generally, and only incidentally benefited religious schools, would be struck down when they were specifically aimed at promoting religious education. During the same period the Court struck down a tuition rebate for children attending religious schools (*Essex v. Wolman*, 409 U.S. 808 [1972]), programs providing financial aid to parochial schools (*Committee for Public Education and Religious Liberty v. Nyquist*, 413 U.S. 756 [1973]), public provision of remedial classes and counseling services to students in religious schools (*Meek v. Pittenger*, 413 U.S. 349 [1973], see above), the provision of funds for field trips and class materials (*Wolman v. Walter*, 433 U.S. 229 [1977]), the provision of remedial instruction by publicly employed special education teachers where such instruction took place on the grounds of religious schools (*Aguilar v. Felton*, 473 U.S. 402 [1985]), and a program of subsidies for private school where it was found that forty of forty-one recipient institutions were parochial schools (*School Dist. of Grand Rapids v. Ball*, 473 U.S. 373, 381 [1985]). Revisiting the question that had been raised in *Walz*, in 1988 the Court found a Texas law that provided a tax exemption specifically for religious publications to be unconstitutional (*Texas Monthly, Inc. v. Bullock*, 489 U.S. 1 [1988]).

Justice Brennan, writing for the Court in *Bullock*, observed that there was no problem with a law that only incidentally benefited religion. "The nonsectarian aims of government and the interests of religious groups often overlap, and this Court has never required that public authorities refrain from implementing reasonable measures to advance legitimate secular goals merely because they would thereby relieve religious groups of costs they would otherwise incur." What set the case apart from those in which programs were upheld was the fact that the Texas exemption was specifically directed at religious publications. "In all of these cases, however, we emphasized that the benefits derived by religious organizations flowed to a large number of nonreligious groups as well. Indeed, were those benefits confined to religious organizations, they could not have appeared other than as state sponsorship of religion; if that were so, we would not have hesitated to strike them down for lacking a secular purpose and effect." In practice, then, the effect of the *Lemon* test was primarily to strike down programs that specifically targeted religious institutions as their beneficiaries, while leaving in place programs that incidentally benefited religion in the course of pursuing some legitimate secular goal.

By the 1990s, the *Lemon* test had begun to be seriously questioned by members of the Court. In 1991, Justice Scalia described *Lemon* as an example of "formulaic abstractions that are not derived from, but positively conflict with, our long-accepted constitutional traditions." *Lee v. Weisman*, 505 U.S. 577 (1992) (Scalia, dissenting). In 1997, Justice O'Connor authored an opinion for a majority of the Court that reevaluated the meaning of the "effects" and "entanglement" elements of the *Lemon* test. The case reached the Court on the basis of a highly unusual argument. A New York City program that put special education teachers into classrooms in private schools, including parochial schools, had been declared unconstitutional in *Aguilar v. Felton* in 1985. In *Agostini*, the Board of Education argued that the very same program should be found to be constitutional on the ground that in the intervening twelve years the meaning of the Establishment Clause had been changed by decisions upholding programs in *Zobrest* (1993, upholding the provision of sign-language interpreters to deaf children in parochial schools) and *Witters* (1986, upholding tuition grants that could be used to pursue religious education). Justice O'Connor compared the logic of those cases with the reasoning in *Aguilar* and other cases like it, and concluded that the two sets of cases were in conflict and that *Aguilar* was no longer accurate as expressions of the prevailing understanding of the Establishment Clause. In the process of reviewing the line of past cases, O'Connor also announced substantial revisions in the reading of *Lemon*. The excerpt from her opinion that is provided below quite justly ends with the statement "our Establishment Clause law has 'significantly changed' since we decided *Aguilar*."

AGOSTINI v. FELTON

SUPREME COURT OF THE UNITED STATES

521 U.S. 203 (1997)

JUSTICE O'CONNOR delivered the opinion of the Court.

In *Aguilar v. Felton*, 473 U.S. 402 (1985), this Court held that the Establishment Clause of the First Amendment barred the city of New York from sending public school teachers into parochial schools to provide remedial education to disadvantaged children pursuant to a congressionally mandated program. On remand, the District Court for the Eastern District of New York entered a permanent injunction reflecting our ruling. Twelve years later, petitioners—the parties bound by that injunction—seek relief from its operation. Petitioners maintain that *Aguilar* cannot be squared with our intervening Establishment

Clause jurisprudence and ask that we explicitly recognize what our more recent cases already dictate: *Aguilar* is no longer good law. We agree....

As we have repeatedly recognized, government inculcation of religious beliefs has the impermissible effect of advancing religion. Our cases subsequent to *Aguilar* have, however, modified in two significant respects the approach we use to assess indoctrination. First, we have abandoned the presumption...that the placement of public employees on parochial school grounds inevitably results in the impermissible effect of state-sponsored indoctrination or constitutes a symbolic union between government and religion. In *Zobrest v. Catalina Foothills School Dist.*, 509 U.S. 1 (1993)...[w]e refused to presume that a publicly employed interpreter would be pressured by the pervasively sectarian surroundings to inculcate religion by "adding to [or] subtracting from" the lectures translated. In the absence of evidence to the contrary, we assumed instead that the interpreter would dutifully discharge her responsibilities as a full-time public employee and comply with the ethical guidelines of her profession by accurately translating what was said. Because the only government aid in *Zobrest* was the interpreter, who was herself not inculcating any religious messages, no government indoctrination took place and we were able to conclude that "the provision of such assistance [was] not barred by the Establishment Clause." *Zobrest* therefore expressly rejected the notion...that, solely because of her presence on private school property, a public employee will be presumed to inculcate religion in the students. *Zobrest* also implicitly repudiated another assumption...that the presence of a public employee on private school property creates an impermissible "symbolic link" between government and religion....

Second, we have departed from the rule relied on in *Ball* that all government aid that directly aids the educational function of religious schools is invalid. In *Witters v. Washington Dept. of Servs. for Blind*, 474 U.S. 481 (1986), we held that the Establishment Clause did not bar a State from issuing a vocational tuition grant to a blind person who wished to use the grant to attend a Christian college and become a pastor, missionary, or youth director. Even though the grant recipient clearly would use the money to obtain religious education, we observed that the tuition grants were made available generally without regard to the sectarian-nonsectarian, or public-nonpublic nature of the institution benefited. The grants were disbursed directly to students, who then used the money to pay for tuition at the educational institution of their choice. In our view, this transaction was no different from a State's issuing a paycheck to one of its employees, knowing that the employee would donate part or all of the check to a religious institution. In both situations, any money that ultimately went to religious institutions did so "only as a result of the genuinely independent and private choices...."

Nor under current law can we conclude that a program placing full-time public employees on parochial campuses to provide Title I instruction would impermissibly finance religious indoctrination. In all relevant respects, the provision of instructional services under Title I is indistinguishable from the provision of sign-language interpreters.... Both programs make aid available only to eligible recipients. That aid is provided to students at whatever school they choose to attend. Although Title I instruction is provided to several students at once, whereas an interpreter provides translation to a single student, this distinction is not constitutionally significant. Moreover, as in *Zobrest*, Title I services are by law supplemental to the regular curricula. These services do not, therefore, "relieve sectarian schools of costs they otherwise would have borne in educating their students."

We turn now to *Aguilar*'s conclusion that New York City's Title I program resulted in an excessive entanglement between church and state. Whether a government aid program results in such an entanglement has consistently been an aspect of our Establishment Clause analysis. We have considered entanglement both in the course of assessing whether an aid program has an impermissible effect of advancing religion, and as a factor separate and apart from "effect." Regardless of how we have characterized the issue, however, the factors we use to assess whether an entanglement is "excessive" are similar to the factors we use to examine "effect." That is, to assess entanglement, we have looked to "the character and purposes of the institutions that are benefited, the nature of the aid that the State provides, and the resulting relationship between the government and religious authority." Similarly, we have assessed a law's "effect" by examining the character of the institutions benefited (e.g., whether the religious institutions were "predominantly religious"), and the nature of the aid that the State provided (e.g., whether it was neutral and nonideological). Indeed, in *Lemon* itself, the entanglement that the Court found "independently" to necessitate the program's invalidation also was found to have the effect of inhibiting religion. ("We cannot ignore here the danger that pervasive modern governmental power will ultimately intrude on religion....") Thus, it is simplest to recognize why entanglement is significant and treat it—as we did in *Walz*—as an aspect of the inquiry into a statute's effect.

Not all entanglements, of course, have the effect of advancing or inhibiting religion. Interaction between church and state is inevitable, and we have always tolerated some level of involvement between the two. Entanglement must be "excessive" before it runs afoul of the Establishment Clause.

The pre-*Aguilar* Title I program does not result in an "excessive" entanglement that advances or inhibits religion. As discussed previously, the Court's finding of "excessive" entanglement in *Aguilar* rested on three grounds: (i) the program would require "pervasive monitoring by public authorities" to ensure that Title I employees did not inculcate religion; (ii) the program required "administrative cooperation" between the Board and parochial schools; and (iii) the program might increase the dangers of "political divisiveness." Under our current understanding of the Establishment Clause, the last two considerations are insufficient by themselves to create an "excessive" entanglement. They are present no matter where Title I services are offered, and no court has held that Title I services cannot be offered off-campus.... Further, the assumption underlying the first consideration has been undermined. In *Aguilar*, the Court presumed that full-time public employees on parochial school grounds would be tempted to inculcate religion, despite the ethical standards they were required to uphold. Because of this risk pervasive monitoring would be required. But after *Zobrest* we no longer presume that public employees will inculcate religion simply because they happen to be in a sectarian environment. Since we have abandoned the assumption that properly instructed public employees will fail to discharge their duties faithfully, we must also discard the assumption that pervasive monitoring of Title I teachers is required.... We therefore conclude that our Establishment Clause law has "significantly changed" since we decided *Aguilar*....

The revision of Establishment Clause jurisprudence by the Rehnquist Court did not end with *Agostini*. In 2000, in *Mitchell v. Helms* (excerpted below), the Court disposed of a whole series of traditional arguments that had appeared in earlier cases. The case concerned a federal program of funding used by local authorities to provide educational materials and equipment to public and private schools. Among the earlier tests considered and rejected in Justice Thomas's majority opinion were the divertability of funds from secular to religious purposes, the distinction between direct and indirect aid, the idea that the government may not pursue secular goals through religious means, a focus on incidental—as opposed to intended—benefits to religion, the Jeffersonian objection to funds collected from a person of one faith going to support institutions of another, and the *Everson* principle of separation between government and religious institutions *per se*. The reconsideration of *Lemon* was also extended, resulting in its near-complete replacement. Where *Agostini* had retained the purpose and effects tests from *Lemon*, *Mitchell* essentially did away with consideration of effects altogether. In place of this complicated set of principles and ideas, the Rehnquist Court has articulated a single test for formal neutrality: So long as a government program is not directly intended to benefit religious groups or institutions exclusively, it will not be found to violate the Establishment Clause by virtue of its effects.

In the context of government aid to schools, *Mitchell* makes it clear that the fact that money is spent by parents and students, on the basis of private choices, is the critical criterion for determining "neutrality." In fact, the program at issue in the case provided financial assistance to private schools based on their enrollment; thus the monies in fact went directly to the schools, but the amount of money received by each school depended on the prior choices of parents and students. Justice O'Connor, for one, found the majority's equation of aid to students with per capita aid delivered directly to religious schools to be a troubling extension of her own reasoning in *Agostini*. The majority's approach, moreover, marks the sharp distinction between the current state of the law and the pre-*Agostini* meaning of the Establishment Clause in cases like *School Dist. Of Grand Rapids v. Ball*, 473 U.S. 373 (1985), in which the fact that forty out of forty-one private schools receiving state aid were parochial schools was considered dispositive of the outcome. As we shall see in the next section, the emphasis on a single test of formal neutrality is also characteristic of the current Court's treatment of many Free Exercise issues, and indeed of the First Amendment generally. (In the chapters dealing with the Free Speech Clause, consider *R.A.V. v. City of St. Paul, Minnesota* in the section on hate speech, and Justice Scalia's discussion in *City of Erie* in the section dealing with pornography.)

MITCHELL. v. HELMS

SUPREME COURT OF THE UNITED STATES

530 U.S. 793 (2000)

JUSTICE THOMAS announced the judgment of the Court and delivered an opinion, in which CHIEF JUSTICE REHNQUIST, SCALIA, and KENNEDY joined.

...The Establishment Clause of the First Amendment dictates that "Congress shall make no law respecting an establishment of religion." In the over 50 years since *Everson*, we have consistently struggled to apply these simple words in the context of governmental aid to religious schools. As we admitted in *Tilton v. Richardson*, 403 U.S. 672 (1971), "candor compels the acknowledgment that we can only dimly perceive the boundaries of permissible government activity in this sensitive area."

In *Agostini*, however, we brought some clarity to our case law, by overruling two anomalous precedents (one in whole, the other in part) and by consolidating some of our previously disparate considerations under a revised test. Whereas in *Lemon* we had considered whether a statute (1) has a secular purpose, (2) has a primary effect of advancing or inhibiting religion, or (3) creates an excessive entanglement between government and religion, in *Agostini* we modified *Lemon* for purposes of evaluating aid to schools and examined only the first and second factors. We acknowledged that our cases discussing excessive entanglement had applied many of the same considerations as had our cases discussing primary effect, and we therefore recast *Lemon*'s entanglement inquiry as simply one criterion relevant to determining a statute's effect. We also acknowledged that our cases had pared somewhat the factors that could justify a finding of excessive entanglement. We then set out revised criteria for determining the effect of a statute....

As we indicated in *Agostini*, and have indicated elsewhere, the question whether governmental aid to religious schools results in governmental indoctrination is ultimately a question whether any religious indoctrination that occurs in those schools could reasonably be attributed to governmental action. We have also indicated that the answer to the question of indoctrination will resolve the question whether a program of educational aid "subsidizes" religion, as our religion cases use that term.

In distinguishing between indoctrination that is attributable to the State and indoctrination that is not, we have consistently turned to the principle of neutrality, upholding aid that is offered to a broad range of groups or persons without regard to their religion. If the religious, irreligious, and areligious are all alike eligible for governmental aid, no one would conclude that any indoctrination that any particular recipient conducts has been done at the behest of the government. For attribution of indoctrination is a relative question. If the government is offering assistance to recipients who provide, so to speak, a broad range of indoctrination, the government itself is not thought responsible for any particular indoctrination. To put the point differently, if the government, seeking to further some legitimate secular purpose, offers aid on the same terms, without regard to religion, to all who adequately further that purpose, then it is fair to say that any aid going to a religious recipient only has the effect of furthering that secular purpose. The government, in crafting such an aid program, has had to conclude that a given level of aid is necessary to further that purpose among secular recipients and has provided no more than that same level to religious recipients.

As a way of assuring neutrality, we have repeatedly considered whether any governmental aid that goes to a religious institution does so "only as a result of the genuinely independent and private choices of individuals." We have viewed as significant whether the "private choices of individual parents," as opposed to the "unmediated" will of government, determine what schools ultimately benefit from the governmental aid, and how much. For if numerous private choices, rather than the single choice of a government, determine the distribution of aid pursuant to neutral eligibility criteria, then a government cannot, or at least cannot easily, grant special favors that might lead to a religious establishment. Private choice also helps guarantee neutrality by mitigating the preference for pre-existing recipients that is arguably inherent in any governmental aid program, and that could lead to a program inadvertently favoring one religion or favoring religious private schools in general over nonreligious ones....

Respondents...offer two rules that they contend should govern our determination of whether [the funding program] has the effect of advancing religion. They argue first, and chiefly, that "direct, nonincidental" aid to the primary educational mission of religious schools is always impermissible. Second, they argue that provision to religious schools of aid that is divertible to religious use is similarly impermissible. Respondents' arguments are inconsistent with our more recent case law, in particular *Agostini* and *Zobrest*, and we therefore reject them....

Respondents...contend that the Establishment Clause requires that aid to religious schools not be impermissibly religious in nature or be divertible to religious use. We agree with the first part of this argument but not the second. Respondents' "no divertibility" rule is inconsistent with our more recent case law and is unworkable. So long as the governmental aid is not itself "unsuitable for use in the public schools because of religious content," and eligibility for aid is determined in a constitutionally permissible manner, any use of that aid to indoctrinate cannot be attributed to the government and is thus not of constitutional concern. And, of course, the use to which the aid is put does not affect the criteria governing the aid's allocation and thus does not create any impermissible incentive under *Agostini*'s second criterion....

A concern for divertibility, as opposed to improper content, is misplaced not only because it fails to explain why the sort of aid that we have allowed is permissible, but also because it is boundless—enveloping all aid, no matter how trivial—and thus has only the most attenuated (if any) link to any realistic concern for preventing an "establishment of religion." Presumably, for example, government-provided lecterns, chalk, crayons, pens, paper, and paintbrushes would have to be excluded from religious schools under respondents' proposed rule. But we fail to see how indoctrination by means of (i.e., diversion of) such aid could be attributed to the government. In fact, the risk of improper attribution is less when the aid lacks content, for there is no risk (as there is with books) of the government inadvertently providing improper content....

[T]he religious nature of a recipient should not matter to the constitutional analysis, so long as the recipient adequately furthers the government's secular purpose. If a program offers permissible aid to the religious (including the pervasively sectarian), the areligious, and the irreligious, it is a mystery which view of religion the government has established, and thus a mystery what the constitutional violation would be. The pervasively sectarian recipient has not received any special favor, and it is most bizarre that the Court would, as the dissent seemingly does, reserve special hostility for those who take their religion seriously, who think that their religion should affect the whole of their lives, or who make the mistake of being effective in transmitting their views to children.

[T]he inquiry into the recipient's religious views required by a focus on whether a school is pervasively sectarian is not only unnecessary but also offensive. It is well established, in numerous other contexts, that courts should refrain from trolling through a person's or institution's religious beliefs....

Finally, hostility to aid to pervasively sectarian schools has a shameful pedigree that we do not hesitate to disavow. Although the dissent professes concern for "the implied exclusion of the less favored," the exclusion of pervasively sectarian schools from government-aid programs is just that, particularly given the history of such exclusion. Opposition to aid to "sectarian" schools acquired prominence in the 1870's with Congress's consideration (and near passage) of the Blaine Amendment, which would have amended the Constitution to bar any aid to sectarian institutions. Consideration of the amendment arose at a time of pervasive hostility to the Catholic Church and to Catholics in general, and it was an open secret that "sectarian" was code for "Catholic".... In short, nothing in the Establishment Clause requires the exclusion of pervasively sectarian schools from otherwise permissible aid programs, and other doctrines of this Court bar it. This doctrine, born of bigotry, should be buried now.

JUSTICE O'CONNOR, with whom JUSTICE BREYER joins, concurring in the judgment.

...Reduced to its essentials, the plurality's rule states that government aid to religious schools does not have the effect of advancing religion so long as the aid is offered on a neutral basis and the aid is secular in content. The plurality also rejects the distinction between direct and indirect aid, and holds that the actual diversion of secular aid by a religious school to the advancement of its religious mission is permissible. Although the expansive scope of the plurality's rule is troubling, two specific aspects of the opinion compel me to write separately. First, the plurality's treatment of neutrality comes close to assigning that factor singular importance in the future adjudication of Establishment Clause challenges to government school-aid programs. Second, the plurality's approval of actual diversion of government aid to religious indoctrination is in tension with our precedents and, in any event, unnecessary to decide the instant case.... *Agostini* represents our most recent attempt to devise a general framework for approaching questions concerning neutral school-aid programs. *Agostini* also concerned an Establishment Clause challenge to a school-aid program closely related to the one at issue here. For these reasons, as well as my disagreement with the plurality's approach, I would decide today's case by applying the criteria set forth in *Agostini*....

JUSTICE SOUTER, with whom JUSTICE STEVENS and JUSTICE GINSBURG join, dissenting.

...The Court's decisions demonstrate its repeated attempts to isolate considerations relevant in classifying particular benefits as between those that do not discernibly support or threaten support of a school's religious mission, and those that cross or threaten to cross the line into support for religion.

The most deceptively familiar of those considerations is "neutrality," the presence or absence of which, in some sense, we have addressed from the moment of *Everson* itself. I say "some sense," for we have used the term in at least three ways in our cases, and an understanding of the term's evolution will help to explain the concept as it is understood today, as well as the limits of its significance in Establishment Clause analysis. "Neutrality" has been employed as a term to describe the requisite state of government equipoise between the forbidden encouragement and discouragement of religion; to characterize a benefit or aid as secular; and to indicate evenhandedness in distributing it.

As already mentioned, the Court first referred to neutrality in *Everson*, simply stating that government is required "to be a neutral" among religions and between religion and nonreligion. Although "neutral" may have carried a hint of inaction when we indicated that the First Amendment "does not require the state to be [the] adversary" of religious believers, ibid., or to cut off general government services from religious organizations, *Everson* provided no explicit definition of the term or further indication of what the government was required to do or not do to be a "neutral" toward religion. In practical terms, "neutral" in *Everson* was simply a term for government in its required median position between aiding and handicapping religion....

The Court began to employ "neutrality" in a sense different from equipoise, however, as it explicated the distinction between "religious" and "secular" benefits to religious schools, the latter being in some circumstances permissible.... Such was the Court's premise in *Lemon* for shifting the use of the word "neutral" from labeling the required position of the government to describing a benefit that was nonreligious. We spoke of "our decisions from *Everson* to *Allen* [as] permitting the States to provide church-related schools with secular, neutral, or nonideological services, facilities, or materials," and thereafter, we regularly used "neutral" in this second sense of "secular" or "nonreligious...."

The shift from equipoise to secular was not, however, our last redefinition, for the Court again transformed the sense of "neutrality" in the 1980s. Reexamining and reinterpreting *Everson* and *Allen*, we began to use the word "neutral" to mean "evenhanded," in the sense of allocating aid on some common basis to religious and secular recipients....

In the days when "neutral" was used in *Everson*'s sense of equipoise, neutrality was tantamount to constitutionality; the term was conclusory, but when it applied it meant that the government's position was constitutional under the Establishment Clause. This is not so at all, however, under the most recent use of "neutrality" to refer to generality or evenhandedness of distribution. This kind of neutrality is relevant in judging whether a benefit scheme so characterized should be seen as aiding a sectarian school's religious mission, but this neutrality is not alone sufficient to qualify the aid as constitutional.... [I]f we looked no further than evenhandedness, and failed to ask what activities the aid might support, or in fact did support, religious schools could be blessed with government funding as massive as expenditures made for the benefit of their public school counterparts, and religious missions would thrive on public money. This is why the consideration of less than universal neutrality has never been recognized as dispositive and has always been teamed with attention to other facts bearing on the substantive prohibition of support for a school's religious objective....

As Justice Souter observes, the language of "neutrality" has been an element of discussions of government subsidies to religious schools since *Everson*. In *Mitchell*, Souter is one of five justices—a majority of the Court—who conclude that Justice Thomas's opinion gives too much weight to neutrality, and employs a version of the concept different from that used in earlier cases. (Note that Justices O'Connor and Breyer disagreed with Justice Thomas' interpretation of "neutrality," but nonetheless joined in voting for the outcome favored by Justices Thomas, Rehnquist, and Scalia.)

In the most recent school funding case, *Zelman v. Simmons-Harris*, 122 S. Ct. 2460 (2002), the Court by a 5-to-4 vote upheld an Ohio program that provided vouchers to parents of schoolchildren in Cleveland to pay for the cost of private schools. Writing for the majority, Chief Justice Rehnquist treated the question as an exploration of the "primary effects" prong of the *Lemon* test, as restated in *Agostini*:

> The Establishment Clause of the First Amendment, applied to the States through the Fourteenth Amendment, prevents a State from enacting laws that have the "purpose" or "effect" of advancing or inhibiting religion. *Agostini v. Felton*, 521 U.S. 203 (1997). There is no dispute that the program challenged here was enacted

for the valid secular purpose of providing educational assistance to poor children in a demonstrably failing public school system. Thus, the question presented is whether the Ohio program nonetheless has the forbidden effect of advancing or inhibiting religion. *Zelman v. Simmons-Harris*, 122 S. Ct. 2460 (2002).

Rehnquist found that the program did not involve any direct aid to religion because the money went to parents rather than directly to schools, as was the case in *Witters*:

> Any aid that ultimately flows to religious institutions does so only as a result of the genuinely independent and private choices of aid recipients.... [W]here a government aid program is neutral with respect to religion, and provides assistance directly to a broad class of citizens who, in turn, direct government aid to religious schools wholly as a result of their own genuine and independent private choice, the program is not readily subject to challenge under the Establishment Clause.... The incidental advancement of a religious mission...is reasonably attributable to the individual recipient, not to the government, whose role ends with the disbursement of benefits. *Zelman v. Simmons-Harris*, 122 S. Ct. 2460 (2002).

In reaching this conclusion, Rehnquist was not impressed by statistics that showed that during the years of the program's operation 96 percent of all voucher funds had gone to parochial schools. "The constitutionality of a neutral educational aid program simply does not turn on whether and why, in a particular area, at a particular time, most private schools are run by religious organizations, or most recipients choose to use the aid at a religious school." Interestingly, Rehnquist left open the possibility that in another case the Court might find that a program did not provide a "genuine" choice to parents, if there was a particular incentive to choose parochial over secular private schools. "The only preference stated anywhere in the program is a preference for low-income families, who receive greater assistance and are given priority for admission at participating schools. There are no financial incentives that skew the program toward religious schools." Thus, the majority found the Ohio voucher program to be "entirely neutral with respect to religion," supporting "true private choice."

The outcome in *Zelman v. Simmons-Harris* certainly secures the current Court's view of the constitutionality of "neutral" funding programs. The references to endorsement, the continued invocation of the *Lemon-Agostini* analysis, and the repeated reference to "genuine" private choice leave room for ambiguity in future cases, however. The four dissenting justices, furthermore, used the case to reiterate their objections to the neutrality approach of the majority, which they find pays insufficient attention to the effects of a program in practice. Future challenges, or future changes in the personnel of the Court, thus leave open the possibility of further doctrinal development in this area.

B. *Endorsement*

One of the arguments that Justice O'Connor raised in her concurring opinion in *Mitchell* concerned the possibility that certain forms of government support are more likely than others to create a public impression of official favoritism:

> In terms of public perception, a government program of direct aid to religious schools based on the number of students attending each school differs meaningfully from the government distributing aid directly to individual students who, in turn, decide to use the aid at the same religious schools. In the former example, if the religious school uses the aid to inculcate religion in its students, it is reasonable to say that the government has communicated a message of endorsement. Because the religious indoctrination is supported by government assistance, the reasonable observer would naturally perceive the aid program as government support for the advancement of religion. *Mitchell v. Helms*, 530 U.S. 793 (2000).

This is the essence of the "endorsement" test, which says that government action that sends a message of favor or disfavor to a religion, or to religion generally (depending on which version of the theory one accepts), violates the Establishment Clause.

One immediate question is whether it is the best approach to think of the endorsement test as separate from the *Lemon* or *Mitchell* tests that apply in cases involving direct government subsidies. The development of the endorsement test was often undertaken in the name of giving substance to the test prescribed in *Lemon*. As a result, justices opposed to *Lemon* may also be expected to oppose the idea that the First Amendment prohibits endorsement. In the cases that are excerpted below, we will see that Justices Rehnquist, Scalia, and Thomas have usually opposed the endorsement principle. (Although in *Zelman-Harris* Chief Justice Rehnquist took pains to argue that there was no risk of a perception of endorsement because the decision to spend the voucher funds rested with the parents.) On this issue, however, these three justices are in the minority, as Justices O'Connor and Kennedy have thus far declined to join them. Although a majority of the Court has moved away from the *Lemon* approach in *Agostini* and *Mitchell*, since a (different) majority nonetheless continues to apply some version of the endorsement test it seems reasonable to conclude that the two should be thought of separately.

The idea that the government should not endorse religion may sound strange to students of modern American politics. Since the 1980s, in particular, evocation of religious themes has been a staple of American political rhetoric. In 1999, George W. Bush was one of nine governors who signed bills into law that proclaimed "Jesus Day," and during the 2000 election both he and Al Gore declared themselves to be "born-again Christians" and asserted that this was part of their qualification to govern. This seems to suggest acceptance for some level of public and more or less official approval of religion and religious activities. The question, then, is what is too much, or impermissible, government endorsement?

Primarily, the question of what constitutes impermissible government endorsement of religion has come before the Court in the context of three issues: public prayer, especially prayer taking place in a school context; religious displays on public property during the Christmas season; and attempts to either prohibit the teaching of the theory of evolution or to mandate the teaching of an explanation that accords with one or both of the biblical creation stories. Each of these lines of cases has developed a different emphasis. Cases involving prayers have come to be determined primarily on the basis of whether attendance at those prayers is thought to be coerced. Whether public religious displays are permitted turns on whether the Court finds that a reasonable observer would interpret the presence of the displays as a statement of favoritism toward religion, and hence as an implicit official devaluation of persons who do not share that religion. Cases involving school curriculum have come to be decided primarily on the basis of the first element of the *Lemon* test: whether, in the Court's opinion, the legislature's primary purpose was actually to further a religious agenda rather than to enhance secular education. These are not three unrelated concepts. Instead, they represent three points at which government endorsement is found to go too far under the Establishment Clause. As we will see, like the test for permissible government subsidies, the tests for permissible or prohibited endorsement are a matter of sharp disagreement among the justices.

1. *Public Prayers*

The first important case concerning public prayers was *Engel v. Vitale* in 1962. The case concerned a New York law that required teachers to recite a prayer, composed by the legislature, at the beginning of each school day. Students could join in the prayer but were not required to do so. In the excerpt from that case that follows, we can see the basic arguments about the relationship between endorsement and coercion that will inform this line of analysis to the present day. The majority finds that the teachers' recitation of the prayers creates an endorsement of religion, and a de facto element of coercion to participate as well. In dissent, Justice Stewart argues that in the absence of a law that specifically requires students to recite a prayer there is no coercion, and hence no impermissible endorsement. In reading this excerpt, note that the majority takes great pains to express their recognition of the historical importance of religion. Both the majority and dissent agree that a complete separation between government and religion is impossible; their disagreement is over the place to draw the line that limits permissible endorsement, and the basis on which that place should be determined. (Justice Douglas, in a concurring opinion that is not presented here, found no coercion on the students and hence no impermissible endorsement, but found that the fraction of the teachers' salary that covered the minutes spent reciting the required prayer constituted financial support for religious expression.)

ENGEL v. VITALE

SUPREME COURT OF THE UNITED STATES

370 U.S. 421 (1962)

JUSTICE BLACK delivered the opinion of the Court.

...The petitioners contend among other things that the state laws requiring or permitting use of the Regents' prayer must be struck down as a violation of the Establishment Clause because that prayer was composed by governmental officials as a part of a governmental program to further religious beliefs. For this reason, petitioners argue, the State's use of the Regents' prayer in its public school system breaches the constitutional wall of separation between Church and State. We agree with that contention since we think that the constitutional prohibition against laws respecting an establishment of religion must at least mean that in this country it is no part of the business of government to compose official prayers for any group of the American people to recite as a part of a religious program carried on by government....

By the time of the adoption of the Constitution, our history shows that there was a widespread awareness among many Americans of the dangers of a union of Church and State. These people knew, some of them from bitter personal experience, that one of the greatest dangers to the freedom of the individual to worship in his own way lay in the Government's placing its official stamp of approval upon one particular kind of prayer or one particular form of religious services....

There can be no doubt that New York's state prayer program officially establishes the religious beliefs embodied in the Regents' prayer. The respondents' argument to the contrary, which is largely based upon the contention that the Regents' prayer is "non-denominational" and the fact that the program, as modified and approved by state courts, does not require all pupils to recite the prayer but permits those who wish to do so to remain silent or be excused from the room, ignores the essential nature of the program's constitutional defects. Neither the fact that the prayer may be denominationally neutral nor the fact that its observance on the part of the students is voluntary can serve to free it from the limitations of the Establishment Clause....

The Establishment Clause, unlike the Free Exercise Clause, does not depend upon any showing of direct governmental compulsion and is violated by the enactment of laws which establish an official religion whether those laws operate directly to coerce nonobserving individuals or not. This is not to say, of course, that laws officially prescribing a particular form of religious worship do not involve coercion of such individuals. When the power, prestige and financial support of government is placed behind a particular religious belief, the indirect coercive pressure upon religious minorities to conform to the prevailing officially approved religion is plain. But the purposes underlying the Establishment Clause go much further than that. Its first and most immediate purpose rested on the belief that a union of government and religion tends to destroy government and to degrade religion. The history of governmentally established religion, both in England and in this country, showed that whenever government had allied itself with one particular form of religion, the inevitable result had been that it had incurred the hatred, disrespect and even contempt of those who held contrary beliefs. That same history showed that many people had lost their respect for any religion that had relied upon the support of government to spread its faith. The Establishment Clause thus stands as an expression of principle on the part of the Founders of our Constitution that religion is too personal, too sacred, too holy, to permit its "unhallowed perversion" by a civil magistrate. Another purpose of the Establishment Clause rested upon an awareness of the historical fact that governmentally established religions and religious persecutions go hand in hand....

MR. JUSTICE STEWART, dissenting.

...With all respect, I think the Court has misapplied a great constitutional principle. I cannot see how an "official religion" is established by letting those who want to say a prayer say it. On the contrary, I think that to deny the wish of these school children to join in reciting this prayer is to deny them the opportunity of sharing in the spiritual heritage of our Nation.... I think that the Court's task, in this as in all areas of constitutional adjudication, is not responsibly aided by the uncritical invocation of metaphors like the "wall of separation," a phrase nowhere to be found in the Constitution. What is relevant to the issue here is not the history of an established church in sixteenth century England or in eighteenth century

America, but the history of the religious traditions of our people, reflected in countless practices of the institutions and officials of our government....

Following *Engel*, in *Abington School District v. Schempp*, 374 U.S. 203, 237 (1963) the Court had little difficulty in striking down a Pennsylvania law that required students to recite the Lord's Prayer at the beginning of each school day, following readings from the Bible. The practice, according to a majority opinion written by Justice Clark, violated the principle of "wholesome neutrality" toward religion that the Establishment Clause required:

> The wholesome "neutrality" of which this Court's cases speak...stems from a recognition of the teachings of history that powerful sects or groups might bring about a fusion of governmental and religious functions or a concert or dependency of one upon the other to the end that official support of the State or Federal Government would be placed behind the tenets of one or of all orthodoxies. This the Establishment Clause prohibits.... The test may be stated as follows: what are the purpose and the primary effect of the enactment? If either is the advancement or inhibition of religion then the enactment exceeds the scope of legislative power as circumscribed by the Constitution. That is to say that to withstand the strictures of the Establishment Clause there must be a secular legislative purpose and a primary effect that neither advances nor inhibits religion.

Given that test, the outcome was determined by the combination of the Court's findings that the purpose of the laws in question was to advance religion, and that their effect was coercive. "[T]he States are requiring the selection and reading at the opening of the school day of verses from the Holy Bible and the recitation of the Lord's Prayer by the students in unison. These exercises are prescribed as part of the curricular activities of students who are required by law to attend school."

Three particular arguments in *Abington* should be noted. First, the argument had been made that the prayer and Bible-reading were nondenominational, since teachers were free to choose the translation of the Bible that they would employ. This argument was rejected on the basis of the "high wall of separation" theory of *Everson*, that read the Establishment Clause as prohibiting the government not only from favoring a particular religious sect but also from favoring religion over irreligion (or, of course, the converse). Second, Justice Clark rejected the argument that the majority's ruling was establishing a "religion of secularism." "Nothing we have said here indicates that such study of the Bible or of religion, when presented objectively as part of a secular program of education, may not be effected consistently with the First Amendment. But the exercises here do not fall into those categories." Finally, Clark also addressed an argument that prohibiting prayers in school violated the majority's freedom to exercise its religious beliefs. "While the Free Exercise Clause clearly prohibits the use of state action to deny the rights of free exercise to anyone, it has never meant that a majority could use the machinery of the State to practice its beliefs."

In 1983, however, the Court had little trouble in deciding, by a vote of 6 to 3, to uphold as constitutional the practice of beginning each session of the Nebraska state legislature with a prayer delivered by an appointed chaplain. Chief Justice Burger's majority opinion consisted of a discussion of the long historical practice of opening legislative sessions with prayers by chaplains. *Engel* is never mentioned in the majority opinion, and *Abington* is mentioned only once:

> Here, the individual claiming injury by the practice is an adult, presumably not readily susceptible to "religious indoctrination," or peer pressure. In light of the unambiguous and unbroken history of more than 200 years, there can be no doubt that the practice of opening legislative sessions with prayer has become part of the fabric of our society. To invoke Divine guidance on a public body entrusted with making the laws is not, in these circumstances, an "establishment" of religion or a step toward establishment; it is simply a tolerable acknowledgment of beliefs widely held among the people of this country.

Turning to three specific features of Nebraska's legislative chaplaincy, the majority concluded that there were no constitutional problems in the fact that "a clergyman of only one denomination—Presbyterian—has been selected for 16 years"; second, that the chaplain was paid at public expense; and third, nor that the prayers were in the Judeo-Christian tradition. "Weighed against the historical background, these factors do not serve to invalidate Nebraska's practice." *Marsh v. Chambers*, 463 U.S. 783 (1983).

Read together, *Abington* and *Marsh* suggest the central role that the idea of coercion, and the special vulnerability of children compelled by law to attend school, play in the formulation of the endorsement concept. Adult legislators were free to get up and leave, and were presumed strong enough to resist any attempts at majoritarian influence, but the same was not true of schoolchildren. *Wallace v. Jaffree*, 472 U.S. 38 (1985), confirmed that this was the correct interpretation of the Court's thinking:

> [When] the power, prestige and financial support of government is placed behind a particular religious belief, the indirect coercive pressure upon religious minorities to conform to the prevailing officially approved religion is plain. This comment has special force in the public-school context where attendance is mandatory. That a child is offered an alternative may reduce the constraint; it does not eliminate the operation of influence by the school in matters sacred to

conscience and outside the school's domain. The law of imitation operates, and non-conformity is not an outstanding characteristic of children.

Thus the implication was that *Engel-Abington-Wallace* defined one line of cases, governing the introduction of prayers into the schoolroom, and that *Marsh* defined a separate rule for public events involving adults.

In 1992 the Court confronted a case that mixed these categories together by asking whether it was constitutionally permissible to have a prayer read aloud at a high school graduation. The case, *Lee v. Weisman*, had some of the characterizing elements of both of the earlier lines of cases: it involved schools, and school students, but it was a public event at which attendance was not legally required, and the students were graduating high school seniors. School officials chose a local member of the clergy to deliver an "invocation" and a "benediction," providing the selected speaker with a set of written guidelines prepared by the National Conference of Christians and Jews designed to ensure that the prayers that were offered would be "nonsectarian." As the excerpt below indicates, the majority in this case—over the vigorous and colorful objections of Justice Scalia—based their decision on a coercive effect, rather than on formal coercion by legal sanction.

LEE v. WEISMAN

SUPREME COURT OF THE UNITED STATES

505 U.S. 577 (1992)

JUSTICE KENNEDY delivered the opinion of the Court.

...It is beyond dispute that, at a minimum, the Constitution guarantees that government may not coerce anyone to support or participate in religion or its exercise, or otherwise act in a way which "establishes a [state] religion or religious faith, or tends to do so." The State's involvement in the school prayers challenged today violates these central principles.

That involvement is as troubling as it is undenied. A school official, the principal, decided that an invocation and a benediction should be given; this is a choice attributable to the State, and from a constitutional perspective it is as if a state statute decreed that the prayers must occur. The principal chose the religious participant, here a rabbi, and that choice is also attributable to the State. The reason for the choice of a rabbi is not disclosed by the record, but the potential for divisiveness over the choice of a particular member of the clergy to conduct the ceremony is apparent.

Divisiveness, of course, can attend any state decision respecting religions, and neither its existence nor its potential necessarily invalidates the State's attempts to accommodate religion in all cases. The potential for divisiveness is of particular relevance here though, because it centers around an overt religious exercise in a secondary school environment where, as we discuss below, subtle coercive pressures exist and where the student had no real alternative which would have allowed her to avoid the fact or appearance of participation.

The State's role did not end with the decision to include a prayer and with the choice of a clergyman. Principal Lee provided Rabbi Gutterman with a copy of the "Guidelines for Civic Occasions," and advised him that his prayers should be nonsectarian. Through these means the principal directed and controlled the content of the prayers.... It is a cornerstone principle of our Establishment Clause jurisprudence that "it is no part of the business of government to compose official prayers for any group of the American people to recite as a part of a religious program carried on by government," and that is what the school officials attempted to do.

Petitioners argue, and we find nothing in the case to refute it, that the directions for the content of the prayers were a good-faith attempt by the school to ensure that the sectarianism which is so often the flashpoint for religious animosity be removed from the graduation ceremony. The concern is understandable, as a prayer which uses ideas or images identified with a particular religion may foster a different sort of sectarian rivalry than an invocation or benediction in terms more neutral. The school's explanation, however, does not resolve the dilemma caused by its participation. The question is not the good faith of the school in attempting to make the prayer acceptable to most persons, but the legitimacy of its undertaking that enterprise at all when the object is to produce a prayer to be used in a formal religious exercise which students, for all practical purposes, are obliged to attend....

The First Amendment's Religion Clauses mean that religious beliefs and religious expression are too precious to be either proscribed or prescribed by the State. The design of the Constitution is that preservation and transmission of religious beliefs and worship is a responsibility and a choice committed to the private sphere, which itself is promised freedom to pursue that mission. It must not be forgotten then, that while concern must be given to define the protection granted to an objector or a dissenting nonbeliever, these same Clauses exist to protect religion from government interference. James Madison, the principal author of the Bill of Rights, did not rest his opposition to a religious establishment on the sole ground of its effect on the minority. A principal ground for his view was: "Experience witnesseth that ecclesiastical establishments, instead of maintaining the purity and efficacy of Religion, have had a contrary operation." These concerns have particular application in the case of school officials, whose effort to monitor prayer will be perceived by the students as inducing a participation they might otherwise reject....

We turn our attention now to consider the position of the students, both those who desired the prayer and she who did not. To endure the speech of false ideas or offensive content and then to counter it is part of learning how to live in a pluralistic society, a society which insists upon open discourse towards the end of a tolerant citizenry. And tolerance presupposes some mutuality of obligation. It is argued that our constitutional vision of a free society requires confidence in our own ability to accept or reject ideas of which we do not approve, and that prayer at a high school graduation does nothing more than offer a choice. By the time they are seniors, high school students no doubt have been required to attend classes and assemblies and to complete assignments exposing them to ideas they find distasteful or immoral or absurd or all of these. Against this background, students may consider it an odd measure of justice to be subjected during the course of their educations to ideas deemed offensive and irreligious, but to be denied a brief, formal prayer ceremony that the school offers in return. This argument cannot prevail, however. It overlooks a fundamental dynamic of the Constitution.

The First Amendment protects speech and religion by quite different mechanisms. Speech is protected by ensuring its full expression even when the government participates, for the very object of some of our most important speech is to persuade the government to adopt an idea as its own.... The method for protecting freedom of worship and freedom of conscience in religious matters is quite the reverse. In religious debate or expression the government is not a prime participant, for the Framers deemed religious establishment antithetical to the freedom of all. The Free Exercise Clause embraces a freedom of conscience and worship that has close parallels in the speech provisions of the First Amendment, but the Establishment Clause is a specific prohibition on forms of state intervention in religious affairs with no precise counterpart in the speech provisions. The explanation lies in the lesson of history that was and is the inspiration for the Establishment Clause, the lesson that in the hands of government what might begin as a tolerant expression of religious views may end in a policy to indoctrinate and coerce. A state-created orthodoxy puts at grave risk that freedom of belief and conscience which are the sole assurance that religious faith is real, not imposed....

Our decisions in *Engel v. Vitale* and *School Dist. of Abington v. Schempp* recognize, among other things, that prayer exercises in public schools carry a particular risk of indirect coercion. The concern may not be limited to the context of schools, but it is most pronounced there. What to most believers may seem nothing more than a reasonable request that the nonbeliever respect their religious practices, in a school context may appear to the nonbeliever or dissenter to be an attempt to employ the machinery of the State to enforce a religious orthodoxy.

We need not look beyond the circumstances of this case to see the phenomenon at work. The undeniable fact is that the school district's supervision and control of a high school graduation ceremony places public pressure, as well as peer pressure, on attending students to stand as a group or, at least, maintain respectful silence during the invocation and benediction. This pressure, though subtle and indirect, can be as real as any overt compulsion. Of course, in our culture standing or remaining silent can signify adherence to a view or simple respect for the views of others. And no doubt some persons who have no desire to join a prayer have little objection to standing as a sign of respect for those who do. But for the dissenter of high school age, who has a reasonable perception that she is being forced by the State to pray in a manner her conscience will not allow, the injury is no less real. There can be no doubt that for many, if not most, of the students at the graduation, the act of standing or remaining silent was an expression of participation in the rabbi's prayer. That was the very point of the religious exercise. It is of little comfort to a dissenter, then, to be told that for her the act of standing or remaining in silence signifies mere respect, rather than participation. What matters is that, given our social conventions, a reasonable dissenter in this milieu could believe that the group exercise signified her own participation or approval of it.

Finding no violation under these circumstances would place objectors in the dilemma of participating, with all that implies, or protesting. We do not address whether that choice is acceptable if the affected citizens are mature adults, but we think the State may not, consistent with the Establishment Clause, place primary and secondary school children in this position. Research in psychology supports the common assumption that adolescents are often susceptible to pressure from their peers towards conformity, and that the influence is strongest in matters of social convention.... To recognize that the choice imposed by the State constitutes an unacceptable constraint only acknowledges that the government may no more use social pressure to enforce orthodoxy than it may use more direct means....

Our society would be less than true to its heritage if it lacked abiding concern for the values of its young people, and we acknowledge the profound belief of adherents to many faiths that there must be a place in the student's life for precepts of a morality higher even than the law we today enforce. We express no hostility to those aspirations, nor would our oath permit us to do so. A relentless and all-pervasive attempt to exclude religion from every aspect of public life could itself become inconsistent with the Constitution. We recognize that, at graduation time and throughout the course of the educational process, there will be instances when religious values, religious practices, and religious persons will have some interaction with the public schools and their students. But these matters, often questions of accommodation of religion, are not before us. The sole question presented is whether a religious exercise may be conducted at a graduation ceremony in circumstances where, as we have found, young graduates who object are induced to conform. No holding by this Court suggests that a school can persuade or compel a student to participate in a religious exercise. That is being done here, and it is forbidden by the Establishment Clause of the First Amendment....

JUSTICE SCALIA, with whom THE CHIEF JUSTICE, JUSTICE WHITE, and JUSTICE THOMAS join, dissenting.

...In holding that the Establishment Clause prohibits invocations and benedictions at public school graduation ceremonies, the Court—with nary a mention that it is doing so—lays waste a tradition that is as old as public school graduation ceremonies themselves, and that is a component of an even more longstanding American tradition of nonsectarian prayer to God at public celebrations generally. As its instrument of destruction, the bulldozer of its social engineering, the Court invents a boundless, and boundlessly manipulable, test of psychological coercion.... Today's opinion shows more forcefully than volumes of argumentation why our Nation's protection, that fortress which is our Constitution, cannot possibly rest upon the changeable philosophical predilections of the Justices of this Court, but must have deep foundations in the historic practices of our people....

The Court presumably would separate graduation invocations and benedictions from other instances of public "preservation and transmission of religious beliefs" on the ground that they involve "psychological coercion." I find it a sufficient embarrassment that our Establishment Clause jurisprudence regarding holiday displays...has come to "require scrutiny more commonly associated with interior decorators than with the judiciary." But interior decorating is a rock-hard science compared to psychology practiced by amateurs. A few citations of "research in psychology" that have no particular bearing upon the precise issue here, cannot disguise the fact that the Court has gone beyond the realm where judges know what they are doing. The Court's argument that state officials have "coerced" students to take part in the invocation and benediction at graduation ceremonies is, not to put too fine a point on it, incoherent....

[W]hile I have no quarrel with the Court's general proposition that the Establishment Clause "guarantees that government may not coerce anyone to support or participate in religion or its exercise," I see no warrant for expanding the concept of coercion beyond acts backed by threat of penalty—a brand of coercion that, happily, is readily discernible to those of us who have made a career of reading the disciples of Blackstone rather than of Freud. The Framers were indeed opposed to coercion of religious worship by the National Government; but, as their own sponsorship of nonsectarian prayer in public events demonstrates, they understood that "speech is not coercive; the listener may do as he likes."

The Court relies on our "school prayer" cases, *Engel v. Vitale* and *School Dist. of Abington v. Schempp*. But whatever the merit of those cases, they do not support, much less compel, the Court's psycho-journey. In the first place, *Engel* and *Schempp* do not constitute an exception to the rule, distilled from historical practice, that public ceremonies may include prayer, rather, they simply do not fall within the scope of the rule (for the obvious reason that school instruction is not a public ceremony). Second, we have made clear our understanding that school prayer occurs within a framework in which legal coercion to attend school (i.e., coercion under threat of penalty) provides the ultimate backdrop.... And finally, our school prayer cases turn in part on the fact that the classroom is inherently an instructional setting, and daily prayer there—where parents are not present to counter "the students' emulation of teachers as role models and the children's susceptibility to peer pressure"—might be thought to raise special concerns regarding state interference with the liberty of parents to direct the religious upbringing of their children.... Voluntary prayer at graduation—a one-time ceremony at which parents, friends, and relatives are present—can hardly be thought to raise the same concerns....

The reader has been told much in this case about the personal interest of Mr. Weisman and his daughter, and very little about the personal interests on the other side. They are not inconsequential. Church and state would not be such a difficult subject if religion were, as the Court apparently thinks it to be, some purely personal avocation that can be indulged entirely in secret, like pornography, in the privacy of one's room. For most believers it is not that, and has never been. Religious men and women of almost all denominations have felt it necessary to acknowledge and beseech the blessing of God as a people, and not just as individuals, because they believe in the "protection of divine Providence," as the Declaration of Independence put it, not just for individuals but for societies; because they believe God to be, as Washington's first Thanksgiving Proclamation put it, the "Great Lord and Ruler of Nations." One can believe in the effectiveness of such public worship, or one can deprecate and deride it. But the longstanding American tradition of prayer at official ceremonies displays with unmistakable clarity that the Establishment Clause does not forbid the government to accommodate it....

The majority opinion classified the situation in *Lee* as similar to that in the school prayer cases on the basis of two notions: that informal as well as legal coercion raises Establishment Clause concerns, and that the case involved schoolchildren. Justice Scalia, in his dissent, argued that only formal, de jure coercion should be a cognizable basis for an Establishment Clause claim, and further that prayer at a high school graduation is more like prayers at solemn public occasions than prayers in a classroom. Underlying this dispute over how to characterize the situation at issue in *Lee* were two broader claims: the majority arguing that members of religious or irreligious minorities should not be forced to participate in religious activities, and the dissent arguing that the majority of a community has the historically recognized right to insert religion into its public life. What was at stake in this exchange was the tension that arises between the Establishment and Free Exercise Clauses with the inclusion of the concept of "endorsement." In essence, Justice Scalia was raising the possibility that the majority's right of free exercise might *require* governmental endorsement of religion, while the Establishment Clause should only be read to prohibit forcible compulsion, not mere endorsement. The majority, in response, took pains to insist that it was not hostile to religion or religious expression, but rather was only reiterating the position that had been expressed in *Abington*: "While the Free Exercise Clause clearly prohibits the use of state action to deny the rights of free exercise to anyone, it has never meant that a majority could use the machinery of the State to practice its beliefs."

These underlying points of disagreement were reiterated three years later in *Santa Fe School District v. Doe* (2000). The case involved a challenge to the practice of having students read prayers of their own choosing or composition at the beginning of high school football games. The policy called for two student elections; one to determine whether there would be "invocations" at school games, and a second to select the student to compose and deliver them. The policy also required that the invocations be "nonsectarian and nonproselytizing." Here there was nothing of state authorities composing prayers, as there had been in *Lee*; instead, the issue was entirely one of coercion and the issue of whether the majority's desire to hear prayers read aloud had to be sacrificed to the interests of religious or irreligious minorities in being able to attend high school football games in ideological comfort. Justice Stevens began by quoting the key passage from *Lee*: "It is beyond dispute that, at a minimum, the Constitution guarantees that government may not coerce anyone to support or participate in religion or its exercise, or otherwise act in a way which establishes a [state] religion or religious faith, or tends to do so." In this case, a policy that called for "invocations" was found to involve religion, and the context of the presentation established endorsement:

> The actual or perceived endorsement of the message, moreover, is established by factors beyond just the text of the policy. Once the student speaker is selected and the message composed, the invocation is then delivered to a large audience assembled as part of a regularly scheduled, school-sponsored function conducted on school property. The message is broadcast over the school's public address system, which remains subject to the control of school officials. It is fair to assume that the pregame ceremony is clothed in the traditional indicia of school sporting events.... In this context the members of the listening audience must perceive the pregame message as a public expression of the views of the majority of the student body delivered with the approval of the school administration.

The election procedures, far from preventing a perception of endorsement, exacerbated the expression of majoritarian preference. The reliance on student elections "guarantees, by definition, that minority candidates will never prevail and that their views will be effectively silenced.... [W]hile Santa Fe's majoritarian election might ensure that most of the students are represented, it does nothing to protect the minority; indeed, it likely serves to intensify their offense." *Santa Fe School District v. Doe*, 530 U.S. 290 (2000).

Stevens also argued that the student election procedures pointed to the risk of divisiveness. "The election mechanism, when considered in light of the history in which the policy in question evolved, reflects a device the District put in place that determines whether religious messages will be delivered at home football games. The mechanism encourages divisiveness along religious lines in a public school setting, a result at odds with the Establishment Clause." Finally, Stevens extended the coercion analysis of *Lee*, finding that for players and cheerleaders, and to a lesser extent for the student body as a whole, there was a significant level of coercion to attend football games:

> There are some students, however, such as cheerleaders, members of the band, and, of course, the team members themselves, for whom seasonal commitments mandate their attendance, sometimes for class credit. The District also minimizes the importance to many students of attending and participating in extracurricular activities as part of a complete educational experience.... To assert that high school students do not feel immense social pressure, or have a truly genuine desire, to be involved in the extracurricular event that is American high school football is formalistic in the extreme.... [T]he choice between whether to attend these games or to risk facing a personally offensive religious ritual is in no practical sense an easy one. The Constitution, moreover, demands that the school may not force this difficult choice upon these students.... *Santa Fe School District v. Doe*, 530 U.S. 290 (2000).

That being the case, said the majority, the inclusion of prayers at a state-sponsored function ran afoul of the *Lee* principle.

The dissenting justices, predictably, were those who had dissented in *Lee*: Rehnquist, Scalia, and Thomas. Chief Justice Rehnquist's dissent, however, raised somewhat different arguments from those that Justice Scalia had raised earlier. Rather than complaining of an undue reliance on fuzzy psychological concepts, Rehnquist accused the majority of actively seeking to suppress the religious sensibilities of the majority, in effect accusing them of violating the principle that the Establishment Clause prohibits either official favoritism *or hostility* toward religion. "[E]ven more disturbing than its holding is the tone of the Court's opinion; it bristles with hostility to all things religious in public life. Neither the holding nor the tone of the opinion is faithful to the meaning of the Establishment Clause, when it is recalled that George Washington himself, at the request of the very Congress which passed the Bill of Rights, proclaimed a day of "public thanksgiving and prayer, to be observed by acknowledging with grateful hearts the many and signal favors of Almighty God." Like Scalia, Rehnquist would look to historical experience to determine what was permissible under the Establishment Clause, while the majority would employ current understandings of the meaning of "coercion" and "endorsement."

Lee and *Santa Fe* define the state of the law concerning public prayers as of the end of the 2000–2001 term. To summarize, where a public prayer carries the implication of state endorsement for religion, it will be permitted only if the setting is one that involves voluntary participation by adults. After these two cases, it seems clearly correct to describe the analysis of cases involving public prayers as quite distinct from that in cases involving subsidies to religious institutions. The disagreement between the majority and the minorities in the endorsement cases turns on a single question:

Where shall the balance be drawn between the majority's desire to express its religious preferences and the burden that is imposed on religious or irreligious minorities as a result of such expression? The majority in *Lee* was very concerned that nonconforming religious minorities ought not be forced to bear the burden of avoiding offense, while the dissent felt equally strongly that the majority ought not to be forced to bear the burden of abandoning its cherished religious rituals in order to avoid offending. That same pair of competing principles, and the same disagreements over the proper balance between them, is the driving force behind the discussions of public displays of religious symbols.

2. *Public Displays*

The rules developed by the Court in the context of public displays of religious symbols follow the logic of the endorsement principle. In practice, however, there are a few factors that make these cases different from cases such as *Marsh* and *Lee*. Those cases involved events, one-time occurrences which adults were free to attend or not attend, and in which children were thought to feel coerced to participate. Returning to the case of adults, however, what is the impact of a religious symbol that occupies a prominent public place for a period of days or weeks? On the one hand, it may not be meaningfully possible for an adult who is offended by such a display to simply avoid seeing it. (See the discussion of the "avert their eyes" principle as it relates to public displays of indecency in *Cohen v. California* in chapter 5, below.) Moreover, if it is the case that such displays convert public spaces into vehicles for endorsement of religion, then the burden of avoiding offense is unfairly placed on nonconformists who are in a place where they have a right to be.

One of the first important cases of this type was *Stone v. Graham*, 449 U.S. 39 (1980), striking down a law requiring that the Ten Commandments be posted on the walls in public schools. Supporters of the policy argued that it served a secular purpose and reminded students of the nation's historical heritage. The Court had little trouble disposing of this argument, however, in light of the fact that among the Commandments were, "I am the Lord thy God, Thou shalt have no other gods before me," a sentiment hardly susceptible of secular interpretation, particularly in the sensitive setting of a schoolroom. In a per curiam (unsigned by any one justice) opinion, the majority declared that "[p]osting of religious texts on the wall serves [no] educational function." Justice Rehnquist, dissenting, argued that the Court should have shown deference to the legislature's claim of a secular purpose, quoting *Schempp* for the proposition that "religion has been closely identified with our history and government."

In light of the school prayer cases reviewed above, the outcome in *Stone* is unsurprising. The Court had rather more difficulty, however, in analyzing public displays of religious symbols in the context of holiday celebrations. The first important case of this type was *Lynch v. Donnelly*, 465 U.S. 668 (1984). The majority in that case upheld the display of a Christmas crèche in Pawtucket, Rhode Island, using a narrow definition of "establishment." Chief Justice Burger began by disclaiming the "wall" metaphor of separation. "Total separation is not possible in an absolute sense.... The Court has sometimes described the Religion Clauses as erecting a 'wall' between church and state. The concept of a 'wall' of separation is a useful figure of speech.... But the metaphor itself is not a wholly accurate description of the practical aspects of the relationship that in fact exists between church and state." Furthermore, Burger proposed that the exclusion of religion from public life might, itself, run afoul of the Free Exercise Clause. "Nor does the Constitution require complete separation of church and state; it affirmatively mandates accommodation, not merely tolerance, of all religions, and forbids hostility toward any. Anything less would require the 'callous indifference' we have said was never intended by the Establishment Clause. Indeed, we have observed, such hostility would bring us into 'war with our national tradition as embodied in the First Amendment's guaranty of the free exercise of religion.'"

Turning to the case at hand, Burger found that the crèche served a secular government purpose. "The display is sponsored by the city to celebrate the Holiday and to depict the origins of that Holiday. These are legitimate secular purposes." The primary effect of the display, too, was deemed to be secular. To rule otherwise, wrote Burger, would require conceiving of the crèche as a greater endorsement than any of the other forms of government support that had been previously upheld:

> [M]ore an endorsement of religion...than expenditure of large sums of public money for textbooks supplied throughout the country to students attending church-sponsored schools; expenditure of public funds for transportation of students to church-sponsored schools; federal grants for college buildings of church-sponsored institutions of higher education combining secular and religious education, noncategorical grants to church-sponsored colleges and universities, and the tax exemptions for church properties sanctioned in *Walz v. Tax Comm'n*.

As for the claim that the display constituted a public endorsement of religion, Burger did not find this to be a sufficient benefit to religion to offend the Establishment Clause. "The Court has made it abundantly clear...that not every law that confers an indirect, remote, or incidental benefit upon [religion] is, for that reason alone, constitutionally invalid. Here, whatever benefit there is to one faith or religion or to all religions, is indirect, remote, and incidental...." *Lynch v. Donnelly*, 465 U.S. 668 (1984).

Lynch v. Donnelly is more often remembered because of Justice O'Connor's concurring opinion than for the majority's holding. Justice O'Connor agreed with the outcome of the case, but she proposed a way of thinking about endorsement that completely separated it from the *Lemon* tests for direct government subsidies:

> The Establishment Clause prohibits government from making adherence to a religion relevant in any way to a person's standing in the political community.... Endorsement sends a message to nonadherents that they are outsiders, not full members of the political community, and an accompanying message to adherents that they are insiders, favored members of the political community. Disapproval sends the opposite message.... What is crucial is that a government practice not have the effect of communicating a message of government endorsement or disapproval of religion. It is only practices having that effect, whether intentionally or unintentionally, that make religion relevant, in reality or public perception, to status in the political community.

By implication, Justice O'Connor's argument provides the answer to the majority's concern that finding the display of a crèche unconstitutional would require finding a host of other programs unconstitutional. This was precisely the argument, in fact, that Justice Brennan raised in his dissenting opinion when he described the crèche as a "re-creation of an event that lies at the heart of Christian faith." *Lynch v. Donnelly*, 465 U.S. 668 (1984). Justices Blackmun and Stevens also dissented.

Five years after the decision in *Lynch*, the Court visited the question of holiday displays again in *County of Allegheny v. ACLU*, 492 U.S. 573 (1989). The case concerned the city of Pittsburgh's tradition of allowing a Catholic group to set up a crèche in front of the Grand Staircase of the Allegheny County Courthouse, and a separate display sponsored by the city itself outside the City-County Building (housing various municipal offices) that consisted of a Chanukah menorah, Christmas tree, and sign that read: "During this holiday season, the city of Pittsburgh salutes liberty. Let these festive lights remind us that we are the keepers of the flame of liberty and our legacy of freedom." This time, a majority found that the City of Pittsburgh's crèche was in violation of the Establishment Clause, but that the display outside the City-County Building was not.

Writing for a five-member majority, Justice Blackmun adopted Justice O'Connor's *Lynch* concurrence in its entirety:

> First and foremost, the [O'Connor] concurrence squarely rejects any notion that this Court will tolerate some government endorsement of religion. Rather, the concurrence recognizes any endorsement of religion as "invalid," because it "sends a message to nonadherents that they are outsiders, not full members of the political community, and an accompanying message to adherents that they are insiders, favored members of the political community," Second, the concurrence articulates a method for determining whether the government's use of an object with religious meaning has the effect of endorsing religion. The effect of the display depends upon the message that the government's practice communicates: the question is "what viewers may fairly understand to be the purpose of the display." That inquiry, of necessity, turns upon the context in which the contested object appears: "[A] typical museum setting, though not neutralizing the religious content of a religious painting, negates any message of endorsement of that content." The concurrence thus emphasizes that the constitutionality of the crèche in that case depended upon its "particular physical setting," and further observes: "Every government practice must be judged in its unique circumstances to determine whether it [endorses] religion." *County of Allegheny v. ACLU*, 492 U.S. 573 (1989).

Applying the endorsement analysis to the case before him, Blackmun explained that the situation was different from that in *Lynch* primarily because Pittsburgh's crèche was on public ground (Pawtucket's crèche was in a private park in a shopping district), which conveyed a message of endorsement. In addition, the Pawtucket display had included a number of secular items in addition to the crèche, whereas in the Pittsburgh situation the religiously significant crèche stood alone, its message undiluted by its setting. As a general principle, Blackmun argued that every display must be considered on its particular facts, and evaluated in light of the likely effect that it would have on a reasonable viewer:

> [T]he relevant question for Establishment Clause purposes is whether the combined display of the tree, the sign, and the menorah has the effect of endorsing both Christian and Jewish faiths, or rather simply recognizes that both Christmas and Chanukah are part of the same winter-holiday season, which has attained a secular status in our society. Of the two interpretations of this particular display, the latter seems far more plausible and is also in line with *Lynch*. *County of Allegheny v. ACLU*, 492 U.S. 573 (1989).

Justice Kennedy, who had authored the opinion in *Lee v. Weisman*, wrote a lengthy and furious dissenting opinion in which he was joined by Justices Rehnquist, White, and Scalia. Kennedy accused the majority of hostility to religion and argued that the endorsement standard was incoherent and ought to be abandoned. Instead, he argued that the coercion standard that was applied in cases involving public prayers ought to apply also to cases involving public displays. Specifically, Justice Kennedy wanted the Court to focus on the question of whether the government was involved in intentional proselytization, rather than (as he saw it) getting bogged down in the questions that arise when one tries to determine the effects of a display. He also accused the majority of precisely the "callous indifference" and "hostility" toward religion that Chief Justice Burger had warned against in *Lynch*, arguing that if the government only articulates a secular holiday message it endorses secularism. It is important to recognize that his argument was not that the government should, instead, endorse religion, but rather that the focus on "endorsement" ought not to be part of Establishment Clause jurisprudence at all. The dispute between Justices Blackmun and Kennedy provides a clear illustration of the stark divide that persists to this day over the role of the endorsement test in Establishment Clause jurisprudence.

COUNTY OF ALLEGHENY v. AMERICAN CIVIL LIBERTIES UNION, GREATER PITTSBURGH CHAPTER

SUPREME COURT OF THE UNITED STATES

492 U.S. 573 (1989)

JUSTICE BLACKMUN announced the judgment of the Court and delivered the opinion of the Court with respect to Parts III-A, IV, and V, an opinion with respect to Parts I and II, in which STEVENS and O'CONNOR joined, an opinion with respect to Part III-B, in which STEVENS joined, an opinion with respect to Part VII, in which O'CONNOR joined, and an opinion with respect to Part VI.

...Justice Kennedy's reading...would gut the core of the Establishment Clause, as this Court understands it. The history of this Nation, it is perhaps sad to say, contains numerous examples of official acts that endorsed Christianity specifically. Some of these examples date back to the Founding of the Republic, but this heritage of official discrimination against non-Christians has no place in the jurisprudence of the Establishment Clause. Whatever else the Establishment Clause may mean (and we have held it to mean no official preference even for religion over nonreligion, see, e.g., *Texas Monthly, Inc. v. Bullock*), it certainly means at the very least that government may not demonstrate a preference for one particular sect or creed (including a preference for Christianity over other religions). "The clearest command of the Establishment Clause is that one religious denomination cannot be officially preferred over another." There have been breaches of this command throughout this Nation's history, but they cannot diminish in any way the force of the command....

The Justice would substitute the term "proselytization" for "endorsement," but his "proselytization" test suffers from the same "defect," if one must call it that, of requiring close factual analysis. Justice Kennedy has no doubt, "for example, that the [Establishment] Clause forbids a city to permit the permanent erection of a large Latin cross on the roof of city hall...because such an obtrusive year-round religious display would place the government's weight behind an obvious effort to proselytize on behalf of a particular religion." He also suggests that a city would demonstrate an unconstitutional preference for Christianity if it displayed a Christian symbol during every major Christian holiday but did not display the religious symbols of other faiths during other religious holidays. But, for Justice Kennedy, would it be enough of a preference for Christianity if that city each year displayed a crèche for 40 days during the Christmas season and a cross for 40 days during Lent (and never the symbols of other religions)? If so, then what if there were no cross but the 40-day crèche display contained a sign exhorting the city's citizens "to offer up their devotions to God their Creator, and his Son Jesus Christ, the Redeemer of the world?..."

The government does not discriminate against any citizen on the basis of the citizen's religious faith if the government is secular in its functions and operations. On the contrary, the Constitution mandates that the government remain secular, rather than affiliate itself with religious beliefs or institutions, precisely in order to avoid discriminating among citizens on the basis of their religious faiths.

A secular state, it must be remembered, is not the same as an atheistic or antireligious state. A secular state establishes neither atheism nor religion as its official creed. Justice Kennedy thus has it exactly backwards when he says that enforcing the Constitution's requirement that government remain secular is a prescription of orthodoxy. It follows directly from the Constitution's proscription against government affiliation with religious beliefs or institutions that there is no orthodoxy on religious matters in the secular state. Although Justice Kennedy accuses the Court of "an Orwellian rewriting of history," perhaps it is Justice Kennedy himself who has slipped into a form of Orwellian newspeak when he equates the constitutional command of secular government with a prescribed orthodoxy....

JUSTICE KENNEDY, with whom THE CHIEF JUSTICE, JUSTICE WHITE, and JUSTICE SCALIA join, concurring in the judgment in part and dissenting in part.

This view of the Establishment Clause reflects an unjustified hostility toward religion, a hostility inconsistent with our history and our precedents, and I dissent from this holding.... Neither government nor this Court can or should ignore the significance of the fact that a vast portion of our people believe in and worship God and that many of our legal, political and personal values derive historically from religious teachings. Government must inevitably take cognizance of the existence of religion. The ability of the organized community to recognize and accommodate religion in a society with a pervasive public sector requires diligent observance of the border between accommodation and establishment. Our cases disclose two limiting principles: government may not coerce anyone to support or participate in any religion or its exercise; and it may not, in the guise of avoiding hostility or callous indifference, give direct benefits to religion in such a degree that it in fact "establishes a [state] religion or religious faith, or tends to do so." These two principles, while distinct, are not unrelated, for it would be difficult indeed to establish a religion without some measure of more or less subtle coercion, be it in the form of taxation to supply the substantial benefits that would sustain a state-established faith, direct compulsion to observance, or governmental exhortation to religiosity that amounts in fact to proselytizing.

It is no surprise that without exception we have invalidated actions that further the interests of religion through the coercive power of government.... [C]oercion need not be a direct tax in aid of religion or a test oath. Symbolic recognition or accommodation of religious faith may violate the Clause in an extreme case. I doubt not, for example, that the Clause forbids a city to permit the permanent erection of a large Latin cross on the roof of city hall. This is not because government speech about religion is per se suspect, as the majority would have it, but because such an obtrusive year-round religious display would place the government's weight behind an obvious effort to proselytize on behalf of a particular religion....

If government is to participate in its citizens' celebration of a holiday that contains both a secular and a religious component, enforced recognition of only the secular aspect would signify the callous indifference toward religious faith that our cases and traditions do not require; for by commemorating the holiday only as it is celebrated by nonadherents, the government would be refusing to acknowledge the plain fact, and the historical reality, that many of its citizens celebrate its religious aspects as well. Judicial invalidation of government's attempts to recognize the religious underpinnings of the holiday would signal not neutrality but a pervasive intent to insulate government from all things religious. The Religion Clauses do not require government to acknowledge these holidays or their religious component; but our strong tradition of government accommodation and acknowledgment permits government to do so.

There is no suggestion here that the government's power to coerce has been used to further the interests of Christianity or Judaism in any way. No one was compelled to observe or participate in any religious ceremony or activity. Neither the city nor the county contributed significant amounts of tax money to serve the cause of one religious faith. The crèche and the menorah are purely passive symbols of religious holidays. Passersby who disagree with the message conveyed by these displays are free to ignore them, or even to turn their backs, just as they are free to do when they disagree with any other form of government speech....

The notion that cases arising under the Establishment Clause should be decided by an inquiry into whether a "reasonable observer" may "fairly understand" government action to "sen[d] a message to nonadherents that they are outsiders, not full members of the political community," is a recent, and in my view most unwelcome, addition to our tangled Establishment Clause jurisprudence....

I take it as settled law that, whatever standard the Court applies to Establishment Clause claims, it must at least suggest results consistent with our precedents and the historical practices that, by tradition, have informed our First Amendment jurisprudence. It is true that, for reasons quite unrelated to the First Amendment, displays commemorating religious holidays were not commonplace in 1791. But the relevance of history is not confined to the inquiry into whether the challenged practice itself is a part of our accepted traditions dating back to the Founding.... Whatever test we choose to apply must permit not only legitimate practices two centuries old but also any other practices with no greater potential for an establishment of religion. The First Amendment is a rule, not a digest or compendium. A test for implementing the protections of the Establishment Clause that, if applied with consistency, would invalidate longstanding traditions cannot be a proper reading of the Clause....

Justice Kennedy's statement that "[a] test for implementing the protections of the Establishment Clause that, if applied with consistency, would invalidate longstanding traditions cannot be a proper reading of the Clause" places *Allegheny County* and the public display cases, generally, in context with *Lee v. Weisman* and *Santa Fe*. In both sets of cases, the deep division within the Court is between those justices who consider the Establishment Clause a mandate to prevent certain consequences, and those who consider the clause to be a prohibition on certain specific practices: that is, those that were understood to constitute impermissible "establishment" in the late eighteenth century. Beyond that question, the dispute between Kennedy and Blackmun points to the basic question of the proper relationship between the state and religion. Kennedy argues that the endorsement test should be abandoned, so that the majority is simply free to endorse whatever it likes so long as other tests (coercion, proselytization) are satisfied. Blackmun, in essence, argues that the Constitution requires the government to preserve a secular public sphere, just as it is required to protect a private sphere of religious liberty. The five to four decision in *County of Allegheny*, like the five to four decision in *Lee*, represented the close division in the Court between these two fundamentally opposing views of the Establishment Clause. *Santa Fe*, by contrast, was decided six to three; the difference between *Santa Fe* and *County of Allegheny* was that in one case Justice Kennedy perceived coercion, and in the other he did not.

3. *Revisiting the Question of Legislative Intent: Endorsement and School Curricula*

On three separate occasions in modern times the Supreme Court has reviewed laws aimed at altering the way in which theories of biological evolution and cosmology (i.e., the Big Bang theory) are taught in public schools. The idea of evolution is troubling for those who read the creation stories of the Old Testament literally, because it posits that variations in biological forms are the result of a gradual process of change and differentiation, whereas the Bible posits that each kind of plant and creature was created with its separate identity complete. In addition, evolutionary theory—like geology and the other earth sciences—concludes that the Earth is approximately 4.5 billion years old, whereas some biblical literalists insist that the Creation occurred within the last 6,000 years. Finally, evolution and cosmology do not require an intelligent being who willed the universe into existence, although they do not require that there be no such Creator, either. In other words, these are theories that are equally compatible with atheism, irreligion, or a variety of religious doctrines, but not with biblical literalism. The teaching of these theories is therefore viewed as threats to some parents' efforts to inculcate religious beliefs in their children.

As a result of these concerns, various states have made efforts to either ban the teaching of evolution or to require the concomitant teaching of "creationist" theories. The latter are theories that assert some version of a "creator" and a specific "act of creation." Unlike evolution and cosmology, creationist theories are therefore not merely compatible with Judeo-Christian religious teachings, but are also incompatible with atheism, irreligious theism (which would deny the authority of sacred texts), and various non-Western religious traditions. Supporters of the inclusion of creationism in school curricula argue that they reflect a diversity of views about important scientific questions, and insist that creationist theories have as good a claim to inclusion in the curriculum as evolution or cosmology. This argument can be characterized either as one that asserts a secular purpose and no more than an incidental benefit to religion, or, alternatively, as an argument for using religious means to achieve secular ends (the education of children). Those who oppose including creationism in the public school curriculum argue that these theories lack the basic characteristics of "science" in that they were not derived from empirical observations and were not "defeasible," i.e., subject to being disproved on the basis of evidence. As a result, they argued, the inclusion of such theories served no secular purpose and instead represented a thinly veiled attempt to introduce religious teachings into the public schools in violation of the Establishment Clause.

EDWARDS, GOVERNOR OF LOUISIANA. v. AGUILLARD

SUPREME COURT OF THE UNITED STATES

482 U.S. 578 (1987)

JUSTICE BRENNAN delivered the opinion of the Court, in which MARSHALL, BLACKMUN, POWELL, and STEVENS joined, and in all but Part II of which O'CONNOR joined. POWELL filed a concurring opinion, in which O'CONNOR joined. WHITE filed an opinion concurring in the judgment. SCALIA filed a dissenting opinion, in which REHNQUIST, C. J., joined.

The question for decision is whether Louisiana's "Balanced Treatment for Creation-Science and Evolution-Science in Public School Instruction" Act (Creationism Act) is facially invalid as violative of the Establishment Clause of the First Amendment.

The Creationism Act forbids the teaching of the theory of evolution in public schools unless accompanied by instruction in "creation science." No school is required to teach evolution or creation science. If either is taught, however, the other must also be taught. The theories of evolution and creation science are statutorily defined as "the scientific evidences for [the two theories] and inferences from those scientific evidences...."

The Court has been particularly vigilant in monitoring compliance with the Establishment Clause in elementary and secondary schools. n5 Families entrust public schools with the education of their children, but condition their trust on the understanding that the classroom will not purposely be used to advance religious views that may conflict with the private beliefs of the student and his or her family. Students in such institutions are impressionable and their attendance is involuntary. The State exerts great authority and coercive power through mandatory attendance requirements, and because of the students' emulation of teachers as role models and the children's susceptibility to peer pressure. Furthermore, "the public school is at once the symbol of our democracy and the most pervasive means for promoting our common destiny. In no activity of the State is it more vital to keep out divisive forces than in its schools...."

---

n5 The potential for undue influence is far less significant with regard to college students who voluntarily enroll in courses. "This distinction warrants a difference in constitutional results." *Abington School Dist. v. Schempp*, supra, at 253 (BRENNAN, J., concurring). Thus, for instance, the Court has not questioned the authority of state colleges and universities to offer courses on religion or theology.

...Therefore, in employing the three-pronged *Lemon* test, we must do so mindful of the particular concerns that arise in the context of public elementary and secondary schools. We now turn to the evaluation of the Act under the *Lemon* test.

Lemon's first prong focuses on the purpose that animated adoption of the Act. "The purpose prong of the *Lemon* test asks whether government's actual purpose is to endorse or disapprove of religion." A governmental intention to promote religion is clear when the State enacts a law to serve a religious purpose. This intention may be evidenced by promotion of religion in general, or by advancement of a particular religious belief. If the law was enacted for the purpose of endorsing religion, "no consideration of the second or third criteria [of *Lemon*] is necessary." In this case, appellants have identified no clear secular purpose for the Louisiana Act.

True, the Act's stated purpose is to protect academic freedom. This phrase might, in common parlance, be understood as referring to enhancing the freedom of teachers to teach what they will. The Court of Appeals, however, correctly concluded that the Act was not designed to further that goal. We find no merit in the State's argument that the "legislature may not [have] used the terms 'academic freedom' in the correct legal sense. They might have [had] in mind, instead, a basic concept of fairness; teaching all of the evidence." Even if "academic freedom" is read to mean "teaching all of the evidence" with respect to the origin of human beings, the Act does not further this purpose. The goal of providing a more comprehensive science curriculum is not furthered either by outlawing the teaching of evolution or by requiring the teaching of creation science.

While the Court is normally deferential to a State's articulation of a secular purpose, it is required that the statement of such purpose be sincere and not a sham....

It is clear from the legislative history that the purpose of the legislative sponsor, Senator Bill Keith, was to narrow the science curriculum. During the legislative hearings, Senator Keith stated: "My preference would be that neither [creationism nor evolution] be taught." Such a ban on teaching does not promote—indeed, it undermines—the provision of a comprehensive scientific education.

It is equally clear that requiring schools to teach creation science with evolution does not advance academic freedom. The Act does not grant teachers a flexibility that they did not already possess to supplant the present science curriculum with the presentation of theories, besides evolution, about the origin of life. Indeed, the Court of Appeals found that no law prohibited Louisiana public school teachers from teaching any scientific theory. As the president of the Louisiana Science Teachers Association testified, "any scientific concept that's based on established fact can be included in our curriculum already, and no legislation allowing this is necessary." The Act provides Louisiana schoolteachers with no new authority. Thus the stated purpose is not furthered by it....

Furthermore, the goal of basic "fairness" is hardly furthered by the Act's discriminatory preference for the teaching of creation science and against the teaching of evolution. While requiring that curriculum guides be developed for creation science, the Act says nothing of comparable guides for evolution. Similarly, resource services are supplied for creation science but not for evolution. Only "creation scientists" can serve on the panel that supplies the resource services. The Act forbids school boards to discriminate against anyone who "chooses to be a creation-scientist" or to teach "creationism," but fails to protect those who choose to teach evolution or any other noncreation science theory, or who refuse to teach creation science....

[W]e need not be blind in this case to the legislature's preeminent religious purpose in enacting this statute. There is a historic and contemporaneous link between the teachings of certain religious denominations and the teaching of evolution. It was this link that concerned the Court in *Epperson v. Arkansas* (1968), which also involved a facial challenge to a statute regulating the teaching of evolution. In that case, the Court reviewed an Arkansas statute that made it unlawful for an instructor to teach evolution or to use a textbook that referred to this scientific theory. Although the Arkansas antie-volution law did not explicitly state its predominate religious purpose, the Court could not ignore that "the statute was a product of the upsurge of 'fundamentalist' religious fervor" that has long viewed this particular scientific theory as contradicting the literal interpretation of the Bible. After reviewing the history of antievolution statutes, the Court determined that "there can be no doubt that the motivation for the [Arkansas] law was the same [as other anti-evolution statutes]: to suppress the teaching of a theory which, it was thought, 'denied' the divine creation of man." The Court found that there can be no legitimate state interest in protecting particular religions from scientific views "distasteful to them," and concluded "that the First Amendment does not permit the State to require that teaching and learning must be tailored to the principles or prohibitions of any religious sect or dogma."

These same historic and contemporaneous antagonisms between the teachings of certain religious denominations and the teaching of evolution are present in this case.... Furthermore, it is not happenstance that the legislature required the teaching of a theory that coincided with this religious view. The legislative history documents that the Act's primary purpose was to change the science curriculum of public schools in order to provide persuasive advantage to a particular religious doctrine that rejects the factual basis of evolution in its entirety. The sponsor of the Creationism Act...explained during the legislative hearings that his disdain for the theory of evolution resulted from the support that evolution supplied to views contrary to his own religious beliefs....

We do not imply that a legislature could never require that scientific critiques of prevailing scientific theories be taught. Indeed, the Court acknowledged in *Stone* that its decision forbidding the posting of the Ten Commandments did not mean that no use could ever be made of the Ten Commandments, or that the Ten Commandments played an exclusively religious role in the history of Western Civilization. In a similar way, teaching a variety of scientific theories about the origins of humankind to schoolchildren might be validly done with the clear secular intent of enhancing the effectiveness of science instruction. But because the primary purpose of the Creationism Act is to endorse a particular religious doctrine, the Act furthers religion in violation of the Establishment Clause.

Justice Scalia, joined by Chief Justice Rehnquist, made three arguments in his lengthy dissenting opinion. First, he insisted that the Louisiana legislature had articulated an adequate secular purpose in the form of their desire to promote academic freedom. Unlike the majority, however, Justice

Scalia defined "academic freedom" not as the freedom of teachers to choose what to teach, but rather "students' freedom from indoctrination." "The legislature wanted to ensure that students would be free to decide for themselves how life began, based upon a fair and balanced presentation of the scientific evidence—that is, to protect the right of each [student] voluntarily to determine what to believe (and what not to believe) free of any coercive pressures from the State." Justice Scalia did not indicate his own conception of the contours of such a student "right," but his point was that if the state legislature conceived of academic freedom in that way, their assertion of a secular interest could be justified. This was, in fact, the central point of disagreement between Scalia and the majority, his unwillingness to find a "sham" in the state's explanation of its motives. The same issue arose in connection with the assertion that the state considered creationism to be a valid form of "science." "[T]he parties are sharply divided over what creation science consists of. Appellants insist that it is a collection of educationally valuable scientific data that has been censored from classrooms by an embarrassed scientific establishment. Appellees insist it is not science at all but thinly veiled religious doctrine. Both interpretations of the intended meaning of that phrase find considerable support in the legislative history." Justice Scalia argued that the Court could not be sure that the Louisiana legislature was not acting at least partly from secular motives. "We have no way of knowing, of course, how many legislators believed the testimony of Senator Keith and his witnesses. But in the absence of evidence to the contrary, we have to assume that many of them did. Given that assumption, the Court today plainly errs in holding that the Louisiana legislature passed the Balanced Treatment Act for exclusively religious purposes." *Edwards v. Aguillard*, 482 U.S. 578 (1987).

In fact, however, Justice Scalia's real objection was not so much to the application of the "intent" prong of the *Lemon* test to the particular facts of the case. Instead, Scalia contested the legitimacy of inquiring into a legislator's subjective "intent"—as opposed to the "objective intent" of a statute—at all. "[W]hile it is possible to discern the objective 'purpose' of a statute (i.e., the public good at which its provisions appear to be directed), or even the formal motivation for a statute where that is explicitly set forth (as it was, to no avail, here), discerning the subjective motivation of those enacting the statute is, to be honest, almost always an impossible task." *Edwards v. Aguillard*, 482 U.S. 578 (1987). Thus, the majority's scrutiny of the actions of the Louisiana legislature, and its finding of a "sham" justification, appeared to Justice Scalia to be an impossible and unwise project. Instead, the basis for determining the purpose of a statute should be "objective," i.e., the words of the law or the statements made in its support by legislators. Despite the ruling in *Mitchell v. Helms*, however, it appears unlikely that a majority of the Court is willing to follow Justice Scalia in abandoning the examination of legislative motives.

C. *The Establishment Clause and the Problem of Accommodation*

Reviewing the Establishment Clause rulings above, three distinct approaches become evident: Justice O'Connor's endorsement approach, Justice Kennedy's coercion approach, and Justice Scalia's neutrality approach. Across the differences between these three approaches there cut disagreements about the relative importance of the effects of a statute versus its purpose, the related question of the extent to which judges should question the motives of legislators, and the extent to which the Establishment Clause calls for preservation of, or departure from, historical practice.

One of the points that appeared repeatedly in the discussions of these different approaches was the idea that government might be obliged to accommodate religious preferences in order to avoid "hostility" or "callous indifference" toward religion. Thus, in *County of Allegheny*, Justice Kennedy wrote, "The ability of the organized community to recognize and accommodate religion in a society with a pervasive public sector requires diligent observance of the border between accommodation and establishment." This was part of Kennedy's argument, in which he was joined by Justices Rehnquist, Scalia, and Thomas, that the endorsement approach went too far in constraining the government's ability to sponsor religious messages. Conversely, in *Lee v. Weisman*, Justice Kennedy wrote, "The principle that government may accommodate the free exercise of religion does not supersede the fundamental limitations imposed by the Establishment Clause."

The balance that Justice Kennedy is seeking is the balance between avoiding actions that put the force of government behind the promotion of religion (or of a particular religion), and avoiding actions that infringe on the space necessary to permit individuals the freedom to make religious choices. "The design of the Constitution," wrote Justice Kennedy in *Lee*, "is that preservation and transmission of religious beliefs and worship is a responsibility and a choice committed to the private sphere, which itself is promised freedom to pursue that mission." Kennedy's statement describes the dual function of the Establishment and Free Exercise Clauses; the protection of politics from religion, and religion from politics. Chief Justice Burger stated this understanding clearly in *Lemon*: "Under our system the choice has been made that government is to be entirely excluded from the area of religious instruction and churches excluded from the affairs of government. The Constitution decrees that religion must be a private matter for the individual, the family, and the institutions of private choice, and that while some involvement and entanglement are inevitable, lines must be drawn."

The next chapter, discussing the Free Exercise Clause, is primarily devoted to an analysis of a single question: How far ought (must/may/should) government go in making special arrangements to ensure freedom to religious minorities? "Accommodation," in this context, refers to a rule written in order to protect the private sphere of religious freedom from the intrusions of government power. The difficulty arises in that too much accommodation approaches establishment. As we shall see in the next chapter, the current approaches to establishment are paralleled by differing approaches to the question of accommodation. The remaining question is whether the two Religion Clauses can be interpreted in a way that harmonizes them with each other, or whether they are necessarily in conflict.

VI. "...Or Prohibiting the Free Exercise Thereof"

The wording of the Free Exercise Clause makes the issue immediately evident. Government may not outlaw a religion...but what does it mean to say that the "exercise" of religion may not be outlawed? The word "exercise" seems to reach beyond belief into conduct. But of course, governments exist in order to regulate conduct. What is the limiting principle on the prohibition against regulation of religious conduct? Do only certain recognized religions count? Alternatively, is the limit found in the nature of the conduct in question? Does the Free Exercise Clause require "accommodation"—i.e., exceptions to general rules governing conduct where those rules limit religious activities—or only prohibit laws that *uniquely* target religious conduct? No one doubts that the Free Exercise Clause prohibits a law making it a crime to conduct a Catholic Mass or Jewish service, but what other kinds of conduct are protected?

There have been two basic approaches to answering these questions. The first is the "accommodationist" approach, which starts from the premise that the Constitution requires the government to treat religious conduct differently from other kinds of conduct. Therefore, according to this argument, the government has to make allowances for persons who are acting out of religious motivations to a greater extent than for persons who are acting for other reasons. At a minimum, the accommodationist approach requires that government make a stronger showing to justify the application of its laws in situations where they have the effect of burdening religious practice than in other situations.

The second approach is one that has come to the fore in recent years. This is the "neutrality" approach (a concept that plays a key role in current Establishment Clause jurisprudence as well). Under this approach, the Free Exercise Clause requires only that the government refrain from making laws that specifically target religions or religious practices. So long as a law has a secular purpose, and applies to everyone equally, there is no constitutional requirement that government make any special accommodations for persons whose conduct is religiously motivated. That does not mean, of course, that government *may not* choose to make such an accommodation—during Prohibition, for example, there was an exception that allowed the use of wine for sacramental purposes—but under the neutrality approach "generally applicable laws" can be applied to religious and secular conduct equally without offending the Free Exercise Clause.

One of the first cases to consider these questions arose shortly after Utah became a state. Congress required that Utah outlaw bigamy, a practice encouraged by the Mormon religion. In 1878, Reynolds was convicted of the crime of bigamy. He appealed the conviction on the grounds that the law was in conflict with his religious beliefs; in other words, he argued that he was entitled to an accommodation under the Free Exercise Clause. Chief Justice Waite, writing for a unanimous Court, established the basic arguments against accommodation: that permitting a religious exception to generally applicable law would make "each man a law unto himself," and that where the government acts in pursuit of legitimate secular goals it must have the power to regulate conduct.

REYNOLDS v. UNITED STATES

SUPREME COURT OF THE UNITED STATES

98 U.S. 145 (1878)

CHIEF JUSTICE WAITE delivered the opinion of the Court.

...Marriage, while from its very nature a sacred obligation, is nevertheless, in most civilized nations, a civil contract, and usually regulated by law.... Upon it society may be said to be built, and out of its fruits spring social relations and social obligations and duties, with which government is necessarily required to deal. There cannot be a doubt that, unless restricted by some form of constitution, it is within the legitimate scope of the power of every civil government to determine whether polygamy or monogamy shall be the law of social life under its dominion.

In our opinion, the statute immediately under consideration is within the legislative power of Congress. It is constitutional and valid as prescribing a rule of action for all those residing in the Territories, and in places over which the United States have exclusive control. This being so, the only question which remains is, whether those who make polygamy a part of their religion are excepted from the operation of the statute. If they are, then those who do not make polygamy a part of their religious belief may be found guilty and punished, while those who do, must be acquitted and go free. This would be introducing a new element into criminal law. Laws are made for the government of actions, and while they cannot interfere with mere religious belief and opinions, they may with practices. Suppose one believed that human sacrifices were a necessary part of religious worship, would it be seriously contended that the civil government under which he lived could not interfere to prevent a sacrifice? Or if a wife religiously believed it was her duty to burn herself upon the funeral pile of her dead husband, would it be beyond the power of the civil government to prevent her carrying her belief into practice?

So here, as a law of the organization of society under the exclusive dominion of the United States, it is provided that plural marriages shall not be allowed. Can a man excuse his practices to the contrary because of his religious belief? To

> permit this would be to make the professed doctrines of religious belief superior to the law of the land, and in effect to permit every citizen to become a law unto himself. Government could exist only in name under such circumstances.... In *Regina v. Wagstaff*, the parents of a sick child, who omitted to call in medical attendance because of their religious belief that what they did for its cure would be effective, were held not to be guilty of manslaughter, while it was said the contrary would have been the result if the child had actually been starved to death by the parents, under the notion that it was their religious duty to abstain from giving it food. But when the offence consists of a positive act which is knowingly done, it would be dangerous to hold that the offender might escape punishment because he religiously believed the law which he had broken ought never to have been made. No case, we believe, can be found that has gone so far. *Cantwell v. Connecticut*, 310 U.S. 296 (1940).

The counter argument, in favor of accommodation, received its most profound early articulation in *Cantwell v. Connecticut*, 310 U.S. 296 (1940). Newton Cantwell, along with his sons Jesse and Russell Cantwell, were arrested while distributing literature and soliciting donations on behalf of the Jehovah's Witnesses. The Cantwells were going door-to-door in a heavily Catholic neighborhood and asking people for permission to play a recording of a book on a portable phonograph. The recording contained an attack on organized religion, generally, and on the Catholic Church, in particular. The Cantwells were convicted of two crimes; inciting breach of the peace, and violation of a law that required anyone soliciting donations from the public to first obtain a permit. Justice Roberts began by reviewing the issue that was raised by the issue of accommodation:

> The Amendment embraces two concepts, freedom to believe and freedom to act. The first is absolute but, in the nature of things, the second cannot be. Conduct remains subject to regulation for the protection of society. The freedom to act must have appropriate definition to preserve the enforcement of that protection. In every case the power to regulate must be so exercised as not, in attaining a permissible end, unduly to infringe the protected freedom. No one would contest the proposition that a State may not, by statute, wholly deny the right to preach or to disseminate religious views. Plainly such a previous and absolute restraint would violate the terms of the guarantee. It is equally clear that a State may by general and non-discriminatory legislation regulate the times, the places, and the manner of soliciting upon its streets, and of holding meetings thereon; and may in other respects safeguard the peace, good order and comfort of the community. *Cantwell v. Connecticut*, 310 U.S. 296 (1940).

(For a discussion of "time, place, and manner" regulations, see chapter 2.)

Like Justice Waite in *Reynolds*, Justice Roberts recognized the proposition that the state may not regulate belief, but retains at all times the authority to regulate conduct. The question, then, was the limit of that authority in cases where the conduct in question had religious significance. In this context, freedom to exercise religious beliefs appeared as an instance of a broader freedom of expression:

> The fundamental law declares the interest of the United States that the free exercise of religion be not prohibited and that freedom to communicate information and opinion be not abridged. The State of Connecticut has an obvious interest in the preservation and protection of peace and good order within her borders. We must determine whether the alleged protection of the State's interest, means to which end would, in the absence of limitation by the Federal Constitution, lie wholly within the State's discretion, has been pressed, in this instance, to a point where it has come into fatal collision with the overriding interest protected by the federal compact.

Under Connecticut's permitting statute, a state official would review an application for a solicitation permit, and determine whether the cause for which funds were being solicited was a "religion":

> If he finds that the cause is not that of religion, to solicit for it becomes a crime. He is not to issue a certificate as a matter of course. His decision to issue or refuse it involves appraisal of facts, the exercise of judgment, and the formation of an opinion. He is authorized to withhold his approval if he determines that the cause is not a religious one. Such a censorship of religion as the means of determining its right to survive is a denial of liberty protected by the First Amendment and included in the liberty which is within the protection of the Fourteenth. *Cantwell v. Connecticut*, 310 U.S. 296 (1940).

In other words, the first principle of the *Cantwell* decision was that the troublesome question of determining what constitutes a "religion" for purposes of the Free Exercise Clause could not be a matter for the government to decide.

In overturning the Cantwells' conviction for inciting a breach of the peace, the Court established a second important principle, one that was directly in tension with the underlying logic of *Reynolds*. The theory behind the conviction had been that the Cantwells were offending members of the community to the point that they might be inspired to violence (see discussion of "fighting words" in chapter 5). It was in this context that *Cantwell* most clearly drew a connection between the Free Exercise and Free Speech Clauses, and in the process provided the first description of the principle that limited the government's authority to prevent disorder.

CANTWELL v. CONNECTICUT

SUPREME COURT OF THE UNITED STATES

310 U.S. 296 (1940)

JUSTICE ROBERTS delivered the opinion of the Court.

...No one would have the hardihood to suggest that the principle of freedom of speech sanctions incitement to riot or that religious liberty connotes the privilege to exhort others to physical attack upon those belonging to another sect. When clear and present danger of riot, disorder, interference with traffic upon the public streets, or other immediate threat to public safety, peace, or order, appears, the power of the State to prevent or punish is obvious. Equally obvious is it that a State may not unduly suppress free communication of views, religious or other, under the guise of conserving desirable conditions. Here we have a situation analogous to a conviction under a statute sweeping in a great variety of conduct under a general and indefinite characterization, and leaving to the executive and judicial branches too wide a discretion in its application.

Having these considerations in mind, we note that Jesse Cantwell, on April 26, 1938, was upon a public street, where he had a right to be, and where he had a right peacefully to impart his views to others. There is no showing that his deportment was noisy, truculent, overbearing or offensive. He requested of two pedestrians permission to play to them a phonograph record. The permission was granted. It is not claimed that he intended to insult or affront the hearers by playing the record. It is plain that he wished only to interest them in his propaganda. The sound of the phonograph is not shown to have disturbed residents of the street, to have drawn a crowd, or to have impeded traffic. Thus far he had invaded no right or interest of the public or of the men accosted.

The record played by Cantwell embodies a general attack on all organized religious systems as instruments of Satan and injurious to man; it then singles out the Roman Catholic Church for strictures couched in terms which naturally would offend not only persons of that persuasion, but all others who respect the honestly held religious faith of their fellows. The hearers were in fact highly offended. One of them said he felt like hitting Cantwell and the other that he was tempted to throw Cantwell off the street. The one who testified he felt like hitting Cantwell said, in answer to the question "Did you do anything else or have any other reaction?" "No, sir, because he said he would take the victrola and he went." The other witness testified that he told Cantwell he had better get off the street before something happened to him and that was the end of the matter as Cantwell picked up his books and walked up the street.

Cantwell's conduct, in the view of the court below, considered apart from the effect of his communication upon his hearers, did not amount to a breach of the peace. One may, however, be guilty of the offense if he commit acts or make statements likely to provoke violence and disturbance of good order, even though no such eventuality be intended. Decisions to this effect are many, but examination discloses that, in practically all, the provocative language which was held to amount to a breach of the peace consisted of profane, indecent, or abusive remarks directed to the person of the hearer. Resort to epithets or personal abuse is not in any proper sense communication of information or opinion safeguarded by the Constitution, and its punishment as a criminal act would raise no question under that instrument.

We find in the instant case no assault or threatening of bodily harm, no truculent bearing, no intentional discourtesy, no personal abuse. On the contrary, we find only an effort to persuade a willing listener to buy a book or to contribute money in the interest of what Cantwell, however misguided others may think him, conceived to be true religion.

In the realm of religious faith, and in that of political belief, sharp differences arise. In both fields the tenets of one man may seem the rankest error to his neighbor. To persuade others to his own point of view, the pleader, as we know, at times, resorts to exaggeration, to vilification of men who have been, or are, prominent in church or state, and even to false statement. But the people of this nation have ordained in the light of history, that, in spite of the probability of excesses and abuses, these liberties are, in the long view, essential to enlightened opinion and right conduct on the part of the citizens of a democracy.

The essential characteristic of these liberties is, that under their shield many types of life, character, opinion and belief can develop unmolested and unobstructed. Nowhere is this shield more necessary than in our own country for a people composed of many races and of many creeds. There are limits to the exercise of these liberties. The danger in these times from the coercive activities of those who in the delusion of racial or religious conceit would incite violence and breaches of the peace in order to deprive others of their equal right to the exercise of their liberties, is emphasized by events familiar to all. These and other transgressions of those limits the States appropriately may punish.

Although the contents of the record not unnaturally aroused animosity, we think that, in the absence of a statute narrowly drawn to define and punish specific conduct as constituting a clear and present danger to a substantial interest of the State, the petitioner's communication, considered in the light of the constitutional guarantees, raised no such clear and present menace to public peace and order as to render him liable to conviction....

The free speech issues raised in *Cantwell* were discussed in chapter 5. For purposes of this discussion, what is important to recognize is that the freedom to express and promulgate competing systems of belief was declared to be the backbone for a more specific freedom of religion. This principle, in turn, explains the defect of the permitting scheme, which left it up to the discretion of a government agent to determine which belief systems were entitled to this special level of protection. Four years later the Court issued the second opinion that would become the basis for the pro-accommodation position. Like *Cantwell*, *Pierce v. Society of Sisters*, decided in 1925, was not decided exclusively on the basis of a right to religious freedom, but rather on the idea that free exercise rights were implicated in another, broader category of freedom. The case involved an Oregon statute requiring children between the ages of eight and sixteen to attend public schools. The law was challenged by a religious order that operated for-profit private schools on the basis that it impermissibly interfered with their business. In addition, the Society of Sisters argued that while the state had full authority to regulate the content of their teaching to prevent the inculcation of "teaching of disloyalty, sedition, or pacifism," there was no justification for prohibiting the operation of their schools outright, which would interfere with the parents' freedom to "give to their children such education and religious training as the parents may see fit, subject to the valid regulations of the State."

The Court's decision, written by Justice McReynolds, was evenly divided between affirming the Society of Sisters' right to make money in a wholesome business enterprise and affirming the right of parents to have the choice of how their children should be educated, with no specific mention of religion:

> The inevitable practical result of enforcing the Act under consideration would be destruction of appellees' primary schools, and perhaps all other private primary schools for normal children within the State of Oregon. These parties are engaged in a kind of undertaking not inherently harmful, but long regarded as useful and meritorious. Certainly there is nothing in the present records to indicate that they have failed to discharge their obligations to patrons, students or the State. And there are no peculiar circumstances or present emergencies which demand extraordinary measures relative to primary education. [W]e think it entirely plain that the Act of 1922 unreasonably interferes with the liberty of parents and guardians to direct the upbringing and education of children under their control. As often heretofore pointed out, rights guaranteed by the Constitution may not be abridged by legislation which has no reasonable relation to some purpose within the competency of the State. The fundamental theory of liberty upon which all governments in this Union repose excludes any general power of the State to standardize its children by forcing them to accept instruction from public teachers only. The child is not the mere creature of the State; those who nurture him and direct his destiny have the right, coupled with the high duty, to recognize and prepare him for additional obligations. *Pierce v. Society of Sisters*, 268 U.S. 510 (1925).

Despite the absence of a single explicit reference to free exercise principles, *Pierce v. Society of Sisters* has been one of the most often-quoted cases in discussions of issues involving parochial schools. The reason is that the case clearly stands for the propositions that religious schooling serves a positive societal function, and that a choice of religious education is an important element of parental control over the upbringing of children—more important, for example, than education in dissenting political traditions. It is particularly noteworthy, in this latter context, that the preservation of the right to private education is presented as security for the right of nonconformity with state orthodoxy.

Out of these two cases, neither of which explicitly declares a doctrine specific to the Free Exercise Clause, and building on other cases from the 1940s, the Warren and Burger Courts of the 1960s and 1970s fashioned the modern accommodationist interpretation of the Free Exercise Clause. The Rehnquist Court has to a great extent replaced that approach by an alternative understanding in the 1990s. Throughout both periods, two distinct questions provided the basis for discussion: What is a "religion," and what is a law "burdening the free exercise" thereof?

A.   *What is a "Religion"?*

While the definition of a "religion" obviously has as much importance for the Establishment Clause as for the Free Exercise Clause, in fact it has most often been considered in the latter context. In the first case considered in this chapter, *Reynolds v. United States*, Chief Justice Waite described protected religious practices as those sanctified by long historical recognition. "The word 'religion' is not defined in the Constitution. We must go elsewhere, therefore, to ascertain its meaning, and nowhere more appropriately, we think, than to the history of the times in the midst of which the provision was adopted." Reviewing that history, Waite found that "[p]olygamy has always been odious among the northern and western nations of Europe, and, until the establishment of the Mormon Church, was almost exclusively a feature of the life of Asiatic and of African people." *Reynolds v. United States*, 98 U.S. 145 (1878). By contrast, a very different analysis resulted in 1944 when the Court considered the criminal conviction for fraud of the widow and son of Guy Ballard. Ballard had been the founder of the "I Am" religion, part of which included his claim to be able to effect miraculous cures. The Ballards were prosecuted for repeating these claims knowing them to be false. Justice Douglas, reviewing the conviction, determined that it was improper to permit the jury to decide whether the miraculous powers claimed by the Ballards in their solicitations were true or false. "Men may believe what they cannot prove. They may not be put to the proof of their religious doctrines or beliefs." *United States v. Ballard*, 322 U.S. 78 (1944). The *Ballard* principle that religion should be defined broadly was extended in 1961 in *Torcaso v. Watkins*, 367 U.S. 488 (1961), a case that challenged a Maryland requirement that a state officer declare his or her belief in God before taking office. Torcaso was appointed to the position of notary public, but was then denied his commission when he refused to swear the required oath.

TORCASO v. WATKINS

SUPREME COURT OF THE UNITED STATES

367 U.S. 488 (1961)

JUSTICE BLACK delivered the opinion of the Court.

Article 37 of the Declaration of Rights of the Maryland Constitution provides: "No religious test ought ever to be required as a qualification for any office of profit or trust in this State, other than a declaration of belief in the existence of God"....

There is, and can be, no dispute about the purpose or effect of the Maryland Declaration of Rights requirement before us—it sets up a religious test which was designed to and, if valid, does bar every person who refuses to declare a belief in God from holding a public "office of profit or trust" in Maryland. The power and authority of the State of Maryland thus is put on the side of one particular sort of believers—those who are willing to say they believe in "the existence of God." It is true that there is much historical precedent for such laws. Indeed, it was largely to escape religious test oaths and declarations that a great many of the early colonists left Europe and came here hoping to worship in their own way. It soon developed, however, that many of those who had fled to escape religious test oaths turned out to be perfectly willing, when they had the power to do so, to force dissenters from their faith to take test oaths in conformity with that faith. This brought on a host of laws in the new Colonies imposing burdens and disabilities of various kinds upon varied beliefs depending largely upon what group happened to be politically strong enough to legislate in favor of its own beliefs. The effect of all this was the formal or practical "establishment" of particular religious faiths in most of the Colonies, with consequent burdens imposed on the free exercise of the faiths of nonfavored believers.

There were, however, wise and far-seeing men in the Colonies—too many to mention—who spoke out against test oaths and all the philosophy of intolerance behind them....

[The First] Amendment broke new constitutional ground in the protection it sought to afford to freedom of religion, speech, press, petition and assembly. Since prior cases in this Court have thoroughly explored and documented the history behind the First Amendment, the reasons for it, and the scope of the religious freedom it protects, we need not cover that ground again. What was said in our prior cases we think controls our decision here....

We repeat and again reaffirm that neither a State nor the Federal Government can constitutionally force a person "to profess a belief or disbelief in any religion."

> Neither can constitutionally pass laws or impose requirements which aid all religions as against nonbelievers, and neither can aid those religions based on a belief in the existence of God as against those religions founded on different beliefs. n11

> n11 Among religions in this country which do not teach what would generally be considered a belief in the existence of God are Buddhism, Taoism, Ethical Culture, Secular Humanism and others.

> In upholding the State's religious test for public office the highest court of Maryland said: "The petitioner is not compelled to believe or disbelieve, under threat of punishment or other compulsion. True, unless he makes the declaration of belief he cannot hold public office in Maryland, but he is not compelled to hold office." The fact, however, that a person is not compelled to hold public office cannot possibly be an excuse for barring him from office by state-imposed criteria forbidden by the Constitution.... This Maryland religious test for public office unconstitutionally invades the appellant's freedom of belief and religion and therefore cannot be enforced against him.

The list of nontheistic religions in footnote 11 raises some intriguing and potentially problematic possibilities. "Secular Humanism," for example, is the name of a specific philosophy which posits man as the "measure of all things" and has its roots in the humanist writers of the sixteenth century. The phrase "secular humanism," however, is frequently used in debates as though it simply meant secularism, a belief that religion ought to be kept out of political discussions. It has been argued that secularism is itself a "religion" for purposes of the Free Exercise and Establishment Clauses, so that the First Amendment prohibits government from excluding religion from the public sphere. Taken to its extreme, this interpretation of the First Amendment ends up as a prohibition on the government favoring any philosophy, including the philosophy of the Constitution itself, over any other. This leads to a paradox, as attempts to enforce the Establishment Clause by limiting the role of religion in state action appear to violate the Free Exercise Clause by promoting the philosophy that the role of religion in state action ought to be limited. On the one hand, "high wall separation" becomes impossible because the absence of religion is itself an expression of a religion, but on the other hand the neutrality approach (government may not favor one religion over another but may favor religion generally) doesn't work either, since irreligion is itself a religion. Ultimately, it is not possible to escape the problem of defining what is and is not a religion if the Religion Clauses are to be taken seriously.

Torcaso was followed by two cases that questioned the authority of Congress to limit conscientious objector status (i.e., exemption from service in the military during a period of draft) to those whose objections were grounded in beliefs "in relation to a Supreme Being." In 1965, the Court unanimously found that the test for conscientious objector status had to be "whether a given belief that is sincere and meaningful occupies a place in the life of its possessor parallel to that filled by the orthodox belief in God of one who clearly qualifies for the exemption." *United States v. Seeger*, 380 U.S. 163 (1965).

Five years later, at the height of America's involvement in the conflict in Vietnam, the Court explained that the application of *Seeger* did not depend on an objector's invocation of the word "religion." "[I]f an individual deeply and sincerely holds beliefs which are purely ethical or moral in source and content but that nevertheless impose upon him a duty of conscience to refrain from participating in any war at any time, those beliefs certainly occupy in the life of that individual 'a place parallel to that filled [by] God' in traditionally religious persons." Such persons, wrote Justice Black, must be included in the provision allowing a conscientious objector to avoid military service. Black went so far as to include those whose "conscientious objection to participation in all wars is founded to a substantial extent upon considerations of public policy." *Welsh v. United States*, 398 U.S. 333 (1970). The key phrase was "to all wars"; the next year the Court held that the Free Exercise Clause did not prohibit the conscription of "persons who oppose *a particular war* on grounds of conscience and religion." The draft served a legitimate secular function, wrote Justice Marshall, and the government's interests were sufficiently compelling to justify the incidental burdens that were placed on those who had specific objections to the Viet Nam war rather than to participation in wars generally. *Gillette v. United States*, 401 U.S. 437 (1971).

More recent cases have pointed in inconsistent directions. In 1982, the Unification Church challenged a Minnesota statute that imposed registration and reporting requirements on "religious organzations that solicit more than fifty percent of their funds from nonmembers." Justice Brennan and the majority found that the state's secular interest in "protecting its citizens from abusive practices in the solicitation of funds for charity" was not sufficiently compelling to overcome the burden that the neutral law imposed on the religious activities of the followers of the Rev. Sun Myung Moon. (Justices White and Rehnquist dissented from the decision.) In 1989, however, the Court confronted a tax regulation that did not permit deductions to be taken for "charitable contributions" to the Church of Scientology that took the form of payments for training sessions. The sessions required the payment of "fixed donations," and the Internal Revenue Service therefore concluded that the payments were in return for goods or services, and hence not tax deductible. The Church of Scientology argued that declining to grant the exemption burdened the practice of their religion in violation of the Free Exercise Clause. Specifically, the church argued that "the deduction disallowance...[would] deter adherents from engaging in auditing and training sessions." Second, the church argued that paying the tax on the fixed donations required for the sessions would violate the "doctrine of exchange, which mandates equality of an adherent's 'outflow' and 'inflow.'"

Justice Marshall was not swayed by these arguments:

> It is not within the judicial ken to question the centrality of particular beliefs or practices to a faith, or the validity of particular litigants' interpretations of those creeds. We do, however, have doubts whether the alleged burden imposed by the deduction disallowance on the Scientologists' practices is a substantial one. Neither the payment nor the receipt of taxes is forbidden by the Scientology faith generally, and Scientology does not proscribe the payment of taxes in connection with auditing or training sessions specifically. Any burden imposed on auditing or training therefore derives solely from the fact that, as a result of the deduction denial, adherents have less money available to gain access to such sessions. This burden is no different from that imposed by any public tax or fee.... Likewise, it is unclear why the doctrine of exchange would be violated by a deduction disallowance so long as an adherent is free to equalize "outflow" with "inflow" by paying for as many auditing and training sessions as he wishes.... In [an earlier case], we rejected an Amish taxpayer's claim that the Free Exercise Clause commanded his exemption from Social Security tax obligations, noting that "[t]he tax system could not function if denominations were allowed to challenge the tax system" on the ground that it operated "in a manner that violates their religious belief...."
> *Hernandez v. Commissioner*, 490 U.S. 680 (1989).

Justices O'Connor and Scalia dissented, noting that donations to Christian churches and Jewish synagogues were often rewarded with reserved seats at services and rewarded with religious honors. The case was not explicitly decided on the question of what constitutes a "religion," but the implication raised by the dissenters—that more established and recognized religions might have been treated more generously—cannot be easily avoided. The discussion in *Hernandez* points to the other side of the problematic coin that was presented in *Torcaso*. If it is the case that courts will inevitably be required to consider what constitutes a religion—or a protected religious practice—for purposes of the Free Exercise Clause, how can judges avoid being put in the position of deciding questions of religious doctrine? In the quotation above, is the first sentence consonant with the rest? The Supreme Court has never established a clearly defined test for a "religion." The *Reynolds* approach of granting religious status only to those groups and practices that were known and approved of in the late 18th century has obvious problems in a modern, pluralistic society. Nonetheless, long historical tradition is often accorded great weight by courts in determining whether a particular practice is entitled to the protections of the Free Exercise Clause.

One other case that is noteworthy in this context never made it to the Supreme Court. In *Peyote Way Church of God v. Thornburgh*, the Fifth Circuit Court of Appeals considered an exemption in a Texas law criminalizing the use and possession of peyote for the Native American Church of North America ("NAC"). The Peyote Way Church of God, formed by a breakaway faction of the NAC, and asserted that under the Free Exercise and Establishment Clauses they were entitled to the same accommodation. The court emphasized the history of the two churches in denying the Peyote Way Church's claim. "The NAC was established in Oklahoma in 1918 as the corporate form of a centuries-old Native American peyotist religion without changing the ancient religion's practices or beliefs. The NAC currently has approximately 250,000 Native American members, most of whom live on reservations in the western half of this country." By contrast, the Peyote Way Church was incorporated in 1979. "Peyote Way's single place of worship is a ranch in southern Arizona. Its principals and resident members are Trujillo, Ann Zapf, and Matthew Kent. Zapf, Kent, and the majority of Peyote Way's approximately 150 non-resident members are not of Native American descent." As a result, the Fifth Circuit concluded that the Peyote Way Church was not entitled to the accommodation that had previously been assured to the NAC. *Peyote Way Church of God v. Thornburgh*, 922 F.2d 1210 (5th Cir., 1991)

B. What is a "Law Prohibiting the Free Exercise" of Religion?

As noted earlier, even in the case of a well-recognized religion, the Free Exercise Clause has never been understood to absolutely prevent the government from regulating conduct motivated by religion. Instead, the question has always been one of balancing the government's proper, secular interests against the burden that its laws impose on religious practices. One area in which the government's interest is often found to be sufficient to justify burdening religious practices is the treatment of children. In *Prince v. Massachusetts*, the Court upheld a Massachusetts child labor law against a challenge by Jehovah's Witnesses whose children sold literature on the street. The parents of the children involved were prosecuted under a statute that prohibited children under specified ages (eighteen for girls, twelve for boys) from selling "newspapers, magazines, periodicals or any other articles of merchandise of any description...in any street or public place." The parents argued that where the sales were of religious literature, and were undertaken for religious rather than commercial purposes, the state should be required to make an accommodation. The Supreme Court disagreed. The crucial element, in Justice Rutledge's majority opinion, was the involvement of children:

> The state's authority over children's activities is broader than over like actions of adults. This is peculiarly true of public activities and in matters of employment. A democratic society rests, for its continuance, upon the healthy, well-rounded growth of young people into full maturity as citizens, with all that implies. It may secure this against impeding restraints and dangers within a broad range of selection. Among evils most appropriate for such action are the crippling effects of child employment, more especially in public places, and the possible harms arising from other activities subject to all the diverse influences of the street.... What may be wholly permissible for adults therefore may not be so for children, either with or without their parents' presence. *Prince v. Massachusetts*, 321 U.S. 158 (1944).

In addition, the majority noted that the particular activity at issue carried risks by virtue of the fact that it involved the promulgation of unpopular religious views:

> The zealous though lawful exercise of the right to engage in propagandizing the community, whether in religious, political or other matters, may and at times does create situations difficult enough for adults to cope with and wholly inappropriate for children, especially of tender years, to face. Other harmful possibilities could be stated, of emotional excitement and psychological or physical injury. Parents may be free to become martyrs themselves. But it does not follow they are free, in identical circumstances, to make martyrs of their children before they have reached the age of full and legal discretion when they can make that choice for themselves. *Prince v. Massachusetts*, 321 U.S. 158 (1944).

Justice Murphy dissented. The case, he wrote, presented a clear example of an "indirect restraint" on religious practice. "This indirect restraint is no less effective than a direct one. A square conflict between the constitutional guarantee of religious freedom and the state's legitimate interest in protecting the welfare of its children is thus presented." To justify its actions, the state should be required to show that its expression of concern for the welfare of the children was based on real and immediate dangers:

> [T]he bare possibility that such harms might emanate from distribution of religious literature is not, standing alone, sufficient justification for restricting freedom of conscience and religion.... The evils must be grave, immediate, substantial. Yet there is not the slightest indication in this record, or in sources subject to judicial notice, that children engaged in distributing literature pursuant to their religious beliefs have been or are likely to be subject to any of the harmful diverse influences of the street.

Jehovah's Witnesses, he observed, were a minority that had suffered a long history of persecution. Turning the *Reynolds* formulation on its head, he argued that recognition of the historical fact of majoritarian suppression should be at the heart of the analysis of the Free Exercise Clause. "To... religious minorities, befalls the burden of testing our devotion to the ideals and constitutional guarantees of religious freedom. We should therefore hesitate before approving the application of a statute that might be used as another instrument of oppression. Religious freedom is too sacred a right to be restricted or prohibited in any degree without convincing proof that a legitimate interest of the state is in grave danger." *Prince v. Massachusetts*, 321 U.S. 158 (1944).

Where children were not involved, the Court was more willing to find that accommodation was required in cases where there was a negative burden imposed on religious practices, particularly where the law in question appeared to have been enacted in order to discourage those activities in the first place. In that situation, the question is not one of a neutral law imposing an incidental burden on religious practice. This was the reasoning in a series of cases in which the Court overruled statutes that either by design or effect discouraged Jehovah's Witnesses from engaging in door-to-door proselytizing, including one case (*Murdock*) in which citizens had complained that such visits on Sundays were offensive to their own religious feelings. *Murdock v. Commonwealth of Pennsylvania*, 319 U.S. 105 (1943); *Martin v. Struthers*, 319 U.S. 141 (1943); *Douglas v. City of Jeanette*, 319 U.S. 157 (1943). Those cases obviously involved elements of free speech as well as religious practice, and indeed that connection was often at the forefront of early cases.

One particularly important pair of cases that demonstrates the connection was *Minersville School Dist. v. Gobitis*, 310 U.S. 587 (1940) and *West Virginia State Bd. of Educ. v. Barnette*, 319 U.S. 624 (1943). In

Gobitis, the court held that children who were Jehovah's Witnesses could be compelled to recite the Pledge of Allegiance despite their religious objections. In *Barnette*, the Court reversed this ruling, establishing a category of compelled speech that is prohibited by the Free Speech Clause. These two cases are discussed in chapter 4, but for the purposes of this discussion it is important to recognize that in its early incarnation, free exercise often overlapped to a considerable degree with free speech. The reason was that the Free Speech Clause, itself, had not yet been given sufficient weight to prevent broadly phrased restrictions on expression that had the incidental effect of limiting religious practices. As a result, free exercise cases in those early years frequently turned on the question of whether religious speech was a special case of expression protected by the Constitution. As principles of free speech were developed that limited the government's power to limit expression generally, the focus of free exercise cases turned to the question of when religious conduct, rather than speech, represented the kind of special case that the Religion Clauses are designed to identify. In response to this question, the Warren Court of the 1960s began to develop an accommodationist jurisprudence that was expanded upon by the Burger Court in the 1970s.

In a pair of cases in 1961—*McGowan v. Maryland*, 366 U.S. 420 (1961), and *Braunfeld v. Brown*, 366 U.S. 599 (1961)—the Court upheld laws requiring businesses to be closed on Sunday. The argument was that such laws gave a competitive advantage to those whose religion happened to treat Sunday as the Sabbath, and conversely imposed costs on business owners whose religious beliefs required them to be closed on Saturdays ("Sabbatarians," primarily Jews and Seventh-Day Adventists), since such businesses would be closed for two days, rather than only one. Writing for the majority in *Braunfeld*, Chief Justice Warren rejected the argument, noting that the laws in question did not directly burden any religious practice, they only had the effect of creating an incidental economic disincentive. "To strike down...legislation which imposes only an indirect burden on the exercise of religion...would radically restrict the operating latitude of the legislature." Establishment Clause concerns were dispensed with by the observation that the state had an important secular interest in ensuring a day of rest for employees each week, and that it was only practical to make that day the one that most people would prefer.

It is important to note that the laws at issue in *McGowan* and *Braunfeld* did not impose a disadvantage on anyone because of their religion; it granted an advantage to others, who happened to be in the majority. One of the arguments of the majority, in that case, was that to require an accommodation for Sabbatarian merchants—i.e., to require that they be exempt from the application of the Sunday closing law—would give them too great a competitive advantage vis-à-vis adherents to the majority religions. In other words, if the legislature has a valid secular purpose, and its pursuit of that purpose could not avoid giving an advantage to *somebody*, there was no constitutional objection to the legislature's choice of the majority as the class who should be the beneficiaries of its actions.

The first key opinion that defined the accommodationist position was *Sherbert v. Verner*, 374 U.S. 398 (1963). The case involved a Seventh-Day Adventist who was fired for refusing to work on Saturday. Her court action was not brought to challenge her dismissal, however, but rather the decision of the South Carolina Employment Security Commission to deny her application for unemployment benefits. The Commission's position was that her refusal to work on Saturdays disqualified her for benefits on grounds of failure to accept suitable work, noting that since her dismissal she had been turned down for several other jobs on that basis. The Supreme Court ruled that the Commission's actions had been unconstitutional. The denial of unemployment compensation, said Justice Brennan, restricted Sherbert's free exercise of her religion. That being the case, the state had to show a compelling interest in achieving a legitimate secular aim to justify its actions. South Carolina's asserted interests were avoiding fraudulent unemployment claims and preserving employers' ability to schedule work on weekends. These interests, said Brennan, were not sufficient to justify a rule whose effect was to burden the exercise of religion. In a dissenting opinion, Justice Harlan (joined by Justice White) argued that the Court's opinion had the effect of requiring religious accommodation.

SHERBERT v. VERNER

SUPREME COURT OF THE UNITED STATES

374 U.S. 398 (1963)

JUSTICE BRENNAN delivered the opinion of the Court.

The door of the Free Exercise Clause stands tightly closed against any governmental regulation of religious beliefs as such, *Cantwell v. Connecticut*, 310 U.S. 296, 303. Government may neither compel affirmation of a repugnant belief; nor penalize or discriminate against individuals or groups because they hold religious views abhorrent to the authorities; nor employ the taxing power to inhibit the dissemination of particular religious views. On the other hand, the Court has rejected challenges under the Free Exercise Clause to governmental regulation of certain overt acts prompted by religious beliefs or principles, for "even when the action is in accord with one's religious convictions, [it] is not totally free from legislative restrictions." The conduct or actions so regulated have invariably posed some substantial threat to public safety, peace or order.

Plainly enough, appellant's conscientious objection to Saturday work constitutes no conduct prompted by religious principles of a kind within the reach of state legislation. If, therefore, the decision of the South Carolina Supreme Court is to withstand appellant's constitutional challenge, it must be either because her disqualification as a beneficiary represents no infringement by the State of her constitutional rights of free exercise, or because any incidental burden on the free exercise of appellant's religion may be justified by a compelling state interest in the regulation of a subject within the State's constitutional power to regulate.

JUSTICE HARLAN, whom JUSTICE WHITE joins, dissenting.

In no proper sense can it be said that the State discriminated against the appellant on the basis of her religious beliefs or that she was denied benefits because she was a Seventh-day Adventist. She was denied benefits just as any other claimant would be denied benefits who was not "available for work" for personal reasons. With this background, this Court's decision comes into clearer focus. What the Court is holding is that if the State chooses to condition unemployment compensation on the applicant's availability for work, it is constitutionally compelled to carve out an exception—and to provide benefits—for those whose unavailability is due to their religious convictions. n2 Such a holding has particular significance in two respects.

---

n2 The Court does suggest, in a rather startling disclaimer, that its holding is limited in applicability to those whose religious convictions do not make them "nonproductive" members of society, noting that most of the Seventh-day Adventists in the Spartanburg area are employed. But surely this disclaimer cannot be taken seriously, for the Court cannot mean that the case would have come out differently if none of the Seventh-day Adventists in Spartanburg had been gainfully employed, or if the appellant's religion had prevented her from working on Tuesdays instead of Saturdays. Nor can the Court be suggesting that it will make a value judgment in each case as to whether a particular individual's religious convictions prevent him from being "productive." I can think of no more inappropriate function for this Court to perform.

First, despite the Court's protestations to the contrary, the decision necessarily overrules *Braunfeld v. Brown*, 366 U.S. 599, which held that it did not offend the "Free Exercise" Clause of the Constitution for a State to forbid a Sabbatarian to do business on Sunday. The secular purpose of the statute before us today is even clearer than that involved in *Braunfeld*. And just as in *Braunfeld*—where exceptions to the Sunday closing laws for Sabbatarians would have been inconsistent with the purpose to achieve a uniform day of rest and would have required case-by-case inquiry into religious beliefs—so here, an exception to the rules of eligibility based on religious convictions would necessitate judicial examination of those convictions and would be at odds with the limited purpose of the statute to smooth out the economy during periods of industrial instability. Finally, the indirect financial burden of the present law is far less than that involved in Braunfeld. Forcing a store owner to close his business on Sunday may well have the effect of depriving him of a satisfactory livelihood if his religious convictions require him to close on Saturday as well. Here we are dealing only with temporary benefits, amounting to a fraction of regular weekly wages and running for not more than 22 weeks. Clearly, any differences between this case and *Braunfeld* cut against the present appellant.

Second, the implications of the present decision are far more troublesome than its apparently narrow dimensions would indicate at first glance. The meaning of today's holding, as already noted, is that the State must furnish unemployment benefits to one who is unavailable for work if the unavailability stems from the exercise of religious convictions. The State, in other words, must single out for financial assistance those whose behavior is religiously motivated, even though it denies such assistance to others whose identical behavior (in this case, inability to work on Saturdays) is not religiously motivated.

It has been suggested that such singling out of religious conduct for special treatment may violate the constitutional limitations on state action. My own view, however, is that at least under the circumstances of this case it would be a permissible accommodation of religion for the State, if it chose to do so, to create an exception to its eligibility requirements for persons like the appellant. The constitutional obligation of "neutrality" is not so narrow a channel that the slightest deviation from an absolutely straight course leads to condemnation. There are too many instances in which no such course can be charted, too many areas in which the pervasive activities of the State justify some special provision for religion to prevent it from being submerged by an all-embracing secularism. The State violates its obligation of neutrality when, for example, it mandates a daily religious exercise in its public schools, with all the attendant pressures on the school children that such an exercise entails. See *Engel v. Vitale*; *School District of Abington Township v. Schempp*. But there is, I believe, enough flexibility in the Constitution to permit a legislative judgment accommodating an unemployment compensation law to the exercise of religious beliefs such as appellant's.

For very much the same reasons, however, I cannot subscribe to the conclusion that the State is constitutionally compelled to carve out an exception to its general rule of eligibility in the present case. Those situations in which the Constitution may require special treatment on account of religion are, in my view, few and far between, and this view is amply supported by the course of constitutional litigation in this area. Such compulsion in the present case is particularly inappropriate in light of the indirect, remote, and insubstantial effect of the decision below on the exercise of appellant's religion and in light of the direct financial assistance to religion that today's decision requires.

Like the *Lemon* test for establishment, the *Sherbert* test for free exercise established a broad principle that would have to be applied to a myriad situations. In *Garber v. Kansas*, 389 U.S. 51 (1967), the Court refused to review a decision by the State Supreme Court of Kansas compelling children of Amish families to attend public schools on the ground that the Court lacked jurisdiction, which suggests a conclusion that no federal constitutional issue was raised in the case. This outcome would be revisited, in 1972, with drastically different results, in *Wisconsin v. Yoder*, the most important interpretation of the *Sherbert* standard. *Yoder* involved elements of nearly all of the cases that have been mentioned so far. Revisiting the issue that it had declined to review in *Garber*, the Supreme Court considered the argument of an Amish community that its children should be exempted from a state law requiring attendance at a public or publicly certified private high school. The case mixed together the issues of protecting the welfare of children (*Prince*) and the claim that religious attitudes toward the education of children are doubly protected as an aspect of privacy as well as religious freedom (*Pierce*). In addition, the case involved a religious minority with a long history of persecution contesting the application of a law whose general legitimacy was not in question.

Writing for the majority, Chief Justice Burger relied on two basic arguments: that the Amish religiously grounded way of life was one that deserved constitutional protection; and that requiring Amish children to attend high school would destroy the Amish religion, apparently because such children would grow into adults who would not be satisfied with life in an Amish community. Thus, the "religious conduct" that was directly burdened by the statute was all-encompassing and negatively defined; it comprised the avoidance of contact with the rest of the world, preservation of ignorance about events and ideas external to the community, and isolation from exposure to ways of life other than those favored by the parents. In applying the *Sherbert* test to these facts, the majority seemed to embrace the *Reynolds* idea that some religious practices—those that are sanctified by historical longevity—are more deserving of protection than others. The Amish, it appeared, were a deserving case because their community was sufficiently wealthy to be self-sufficient: "Whatever their idiosyncrasies as seen by the majority, this record strongly shows that the Amish community has been a highly successful social unit within our society.... Its members are productive and very law-abiding members of society; they reject public welfare in any of its usual modern forms." (Compare Justice Harlan's footnote 2 in *Sherbert*, above.) In addition, the

Court seemed to be impressed by the fact that the material lifestyle that was produced by the Amish community's practices harkened back to an earlier, presumably virtuous age, exemplifying "the simple life of the early Christian era that continued in America during much of our early national life." *Wisconsin v. Yoder*, 406 U.S. 205 (1972). These were the majority's answers to the State of Wisconsin's assertion that it had a compelling interest in requiring high school education in order to ensure that future adults would be self-sufficient and independent.

Wisconsin also argued that Amish children were not receiving the education necessary for participation in a modern democracy. In response, the majority simply observed that Amish adults do not participate in democracy, as it is against their religion, and hence needed no additional education for political purposes. "The Amish alternative to formal secondary school education has enabled them to function effectively in their day-to-day life under self-imposed limitations on relations with the world, and to survive and prosper in contemporary society as a separate, sharply identifiable and highly self-sufficient community for more than 200 years in this country." This observation should be compared with the statement of the state's compelling interest in preventing child labor in *Prince*: "A democratic society rests, for its continuance, upon the healthy, well-rounded growth of young people into full maturity as citizens, with all that implies." The conclusion in *Yoder*, presumably, was that where a community guarantees that its members will not vote or engage in political discourse, they cannot constitutionally be compelled to prepare themselves for activities of that sort. Chief Justice Burger also observed that in Thomas Jefferson's day, many farmers had no more than an eighth grade education, which was taken as evidence that further formal schooling is not a requirement for effective citizenship. As for the issue of child labor, the majority in *Yoder* pointed once again to a lengthy historical record as evidence of the benign nature of the practice in question.

There are several additional striking aspects of the *Yoder* opinion. Just as it later would in *Hernandez*, the Court undertook an examination of the centrality and importance that the religiously motivated practice held for the community in question. (The standard of evaluation, however, was noticeably more deferential to the Amish community in 1972 than it would be to the Church of Scientology in 1989.) The second striking element about the case is the lengths to which Chief Justice Burger was willing to go to avoid considering the question of whether the children in the case were being deprived of constitutionally protected rights by virtue of their parents' refusal to allow them to receive any academic training beyond the eighth grade. Finally, it is important to note that Chief Justice Burger recognized the possibility that the majority's interpretation of *Sherbert* was pushing the Free Exercise Clause toward the point at which it might come into conflict with the Establishment Clause. "The Court must not ignore the danger that an exception from a general obligation of citizenship on religious grounds may run afoul of the Establishment Clause, but that danger cannot be allowed to prevent any exception no matter how vital it may be to the protection of values promoted by the right of free exercise."

WISCONSIN v. YODER

SUPREME COURT OF THE UNITED STATES

406 U.S. 205 (1972)

CHIEF JUSTICE BURGER delivered the opinion of the Court.

...The trial testimony showed that respondents believed, in accordance with the tenets of Old Order Amish communities generally, that their children's attendance at high school, public or private, was contrary to the Amish religion and way of life. They believed that by sending their children to high school, they would not only expose themselves to the danger of the censure of the church community, but, as found by the county court, also endanger their own salvation and that of their children. The State stipulated that respondents' religious beliefs were sincere....

Formal high school education beyond the eighth grade is contrary to Amish beliefs, not only because it places Amish children in an environment hostile to Amish beliefs with increasing emphasis on competition in class work and sports and with pressure to conform to the styles, manners, and ways of the peer group, but also because it takes them away from their community, physically and emotionally, during the crucial and formative adolescent period of life. During this period, the children must acquire Amish attitudes favoring manual work and self-reliance and the specific skills needed to perform the adult role of an Amish farmer or housewife. They must learn to enjoy physical labor.

Once a child has learned basic reading, writing, and elementary mathematics, these traits, skills, and attitudes admittedly fall within the category of those best learned through example and "doing" rather than in a classroom. And, at this time in life, the Amish child must also grow in his faith and his relationship to the Amish community if he is to be prepared to accept the heavy obligations imposed by adult baptism. In short, high school attendance with teachers who are not of the Amish faith—and may even be hostile to it—interposes a serious barrier to the integration of the Amish child into the Amish religious community. Dr. John Hostetler, one of the experts on Amish society, testified that the modern high school is not equipped, in curriculum or social environment, to impart the values promoted by Amish society....

On the basis of such considerations, Dr. Hostetler testified that compulsory high school attendance could not only result in great psychological harm to Amish children, because of the conflicts it would produce, but would also, in his opinion, ultimately result in the destruction of the Old Order Amish church community as it exists in the United States today. The testimony of Dr. Donald A. Erickson, an expert witness on education, also showed that the Amish succeed in preparing their high school age children to be productive members of the Amish community. He described their system of learning through doing the skills directly relevant to their adult roles in the Amish community as "ideal" and perhaps superior to ordinary high school education. The evidence also showed that the Amish have an excellent record as law-abiding and generally self-sufficient members of society.

Although the trial court in its careful findings determined that the Wisconsin compulsory school-attendance law "does interfere with the freedom of the Defendants to act in accordance with their sincere religious belief," it also concluded that the requirement of high school attendance until age 16 was a "reasonable and constitutional" exercise of governmental power, and therefore denied the motion to dismiss the charges....

There is no doubt as to the power of a State, having a high responsibility for education of its citizens, to impose reasonable regulations for the control and duration of basic education. Providing public schools ranks at the very apex of the function of a State. Yet even this paramount responsibility was, in *Pierce*, made to yield to the right of parents to provide an equivalent education in a privately operated system.... Thus, a State's interest in universal education, however highly we rank it, is not totally free from a balancing process when it impinges on fundamental rights and interests, such as those specifically protected by the Free Exercise Clause of the First Amendment, and the traditional interest of parents with respect to the religious upbringing of their children so long as they, in the words of *Pierce*, "prepare [them] for additional obligations."

It follows that in order for Wisconsin to compel school attendance beyond the eighth grade against a claim that such attendance interferes with the practice of a legitimate religious belief, it must appear either that the State does not deny the free exercise of religious belief by its requirement, or that there is a state interest of sufficient magnitude to override the interest claiming protection under the Free Exercise Clause....

We come then to the quality of the claims of the respondents concerning the alleged encroachment of Wisconsin's compulsory school-attendance statute on their rights and the rights of their children to the free exercise of the religious beliefs they and their forebears have adhered to for almost three centuries. In evaluating those claims we must be careful to determine whether the Amish religious faith and their mode of life are, as they claim, inseparable and interdependent. A way of life, however virtuous and admirable, may not be interposed as a barrier to reasonable state regulation of education if it is based on purely secular considerations; to have the protection of the Religion Clauses, the claims must be rooted in religious belief. Although a determination of what is a "religious" belief or practice entitled to constitutional protection may present a most delicate question, the very concept of ordered liberty precludes allowing every person to make his own standards on matters of conduct in which society as a whole has important interests. Thus, if the Amish asserted their claims because of their subjective evaluation and rejection of the contemporary secular values accepted by the majority, much as Thoreau rejected the social values of his time and isolated himself at Walden Pond, their claims would not rest on a religious basis. Thoreau's choice was philosophical and personal rather than religious, and such belief does not rise to the demands of the Religion Clauses.

Giving no weight to such secular considerations, however, we see that the record in this case abundantly supports the claim that the traditional way of life of the Amish is not merely a matter of personal preference, but one of deep religious conviction, shared by an organized group, and intimately related to daily living.... Nor is the impact of the compulsory attendance law confined to grave interference with important Amish religious tenets from a subjective point of view. It carries with it precisely the kind of objective danger to the free exercise of religion that the First Amendment was designed to prevent. As the record shows, compulsory school attendance to age 16 for Amish children carries with it a very real threat of undermining the Amish community and religious practice as they exist today; they must either abandon belief and be assimilated into society at large, or be forced to migrate to some other and more tolerant region.

In sum, the unchallenged testimony of acknowledged experts in education and religious history, almost 300 years of consistent practice, and strong evidence of a sustained faith pervading and regulating respondents' entire mode of life support the claim that enforcement of the State's requirement of compulsory formal education after the eighth grade would gravely endanger if not destroy the free exercise of respondents' religious beliefs....

Nor can this case be disposed of on the grounds that Wisconsin's requirement for school attendance to age 16 applies uniformly to all citizens of the State and does not, on its face, discriminate against religions or a particular religion, or that it is motivated by legitimate secular concerns. A regulation neutral on its face may, in its application, nonetheless offend the constitutional requirement for governmental neutrality if it unduly burdens the free exercise of religion. *Sherbert v. Verner*, supra. The Court must not ignore the danger that an exception from a general obligation of citizenship on religious grounds may run afoul of the Establishment Clause, but that danger cannot be allowed to prevent any exception no matter how vital it may be to the protection of values promoted by the right of free exercise. By preserving doctrinal flexibility and recognizing the need for a sensible and realistic application of the Religion Clauses "we have been able to chart a course that preserved the autonomy and freedom of religious bodies while avoiding any semblance of established religion." This is a "tight rope" and one we have successfully traversed.

We turn, then, to the State's broader contention that its interest in its system of compulsory education is so compelling that even the established religious practices of the Amish must give way. Where fundamental claims of religious freedom are at stake, however, we cannot accept such a sweeping claim; despite its admitted validity in the generality of cases, we must searchingly examine the interests that the State seeks to promote by its requirement for compulsory education to age 16, and the impediment to those objectives that would flow from recognizing the claimed Amish exemption....

The State advances two primary arguments in support of its system of compulsory education. It notes, as Thomas Jefferson pointed out early in our history, that some degree of education is necessary to prepare citizens to participate effectively and intelligently in our open political system if we are to preserve freedom and independence. Further, education prepares individuals to be self-reliant and self-sufficient participants in society. We accept these propositions.

However, the evidence adduced by the Amish in this case is persuasively to the effect that an additional one or two years of formal high school for Amish children in place of their long-established program of informal vocational education would do little to serve those interests. Respondents' experts testified at trial, without challenge, that the value of all education must be assessed in terms of its capacity to prepare the child for life. It is one thing to say that compulsory education for a year or two beyond the eighth grade may be necessary when its goal is the preparation of the child for life in modern society as the majority live, but it is quite another if the goal of education be viewed as the preparation of the child for life in the separated agrarian community that is the keystone of the Amish faith.

The State attacks respondents' position as one fostering "ignorance" from which the child must be protected by the State. No one can question the State's duty to protect children from ignorance but this argument does not square with the facts disclosed in the record. Whatever their idiosyncrasies as seen by the majority, this record strongly shows that the Amish community has been a highly successful social unit within our society, even if apart from the conventional "mainstream." Its members are productive and very law-abiding members of society; they reject public welfare in any of its usual modern forms. The Congress itself recognized their self-sufficiency by authorizing exemption of such groups as the Amish from the obligation to pay social security taxes....

The State, however, supports its interest in providing an additional one or two years of compulsory high school education to Amish children because of the possibility that some such children will choose to leave the Amish community, and that if this occurs they will be ill-equipped for life. The State argues that if Amish children leave their church they should not be in the position of making their way in the world without the education available in the one or two additional years the State requires. However, on this record, that argument is highly speculative. There is no specific evidence of the loss of Amish adherents by attrition, nor is there any showing that upon leaving the Amish community Amish children, with their practical agricultural training and habits of industry and self-reliance, would become burdens on society because of educational shortcomings. Indeed, this argument of the State appears to rest primarily on the State's mistaken assumption, already noted, that the Amish do not provide any education for their children beyond the eighth grade, but allow them to grow in "ignorance." To the contrary, not only do the Amish accept the necessity for formal schooling through the eighth grade level, but continue to provide what has been characterized by the undisputed testimony of expert educators as an "ideal" vocational education for their children in the adolescent years.

There is nothing in this record to suggest that the Amish qualities of reliability, self-reliance, and dedication to work would fail to find ready markets in today's society. Absent some contrary evidence supporting the State's position, we are unwilling to assume that persons possessing such valuable vocational skills and habits are doomed to become burdens on society should they determine to leave the Amish faith, nor is there any basis in the record to warrant a finding that an additional one or two years of formal school education beyond the eighth grade would serve to eliminate any such problem that might exist.

Insofar as the State's claim rests on the view that a brief additional period of formal education is imperative to enable the Amish to participate effectively and intelligently in our democratic process, it must fall. The Amish alternative to formal secondary school education has enabled them to function effectively in their day-to-day life under self-imposed limitations on relations with the world, and to survive and prosper in contemporary society as a separate, sharply identifiable and highly self-sufficient community for more than 200 years in this country. In itself this is strong evidence that they are capable of fulfilling the social and political responsibilities of citizenship without compelled attendance beyond the eighth grade at the price of jeopardizing their free exercise of religious belief. When Thomas Jefferson emphasized the need for education as a bulwark of a free people against tyranny, there is nothing to indicate he had in mind compulsory education through any fixed age beyond a basic education. Indeed, the Amish communities singularly parallel and reflect many of the virtues of Jefferson's ideal of the "sturdy yeoman" who would form the basis of what he considered as the ideal of a democratic society. Even their idiosyncratic separateness exemplifies the diversity we profess to admire and encourage....

However read, the Court's holding in *Pierce* stands as a charter of the rights of parents to direct the religious upbringing of their children. And, when the interests of parenthood are combined with a free exercise claim of the nature revealed by this record, more than merely a "reasonable relation to some purpose within the competency of the State" is required to sustain the validity of the State's requirement under the First Amendment. To be sure, the power of the parent, even when linked to a free exercise claim, may be subject to limitation under *Prince* if it appears that parental decisions will jeopardize the health or safety of the child, or have a potential for significant social burdens. But in this case, the Amish have introduced persuasive evidence undermining the arguments the State has advanced to support its claims in terms of the welfare of the child and society as a whole....

In the 1970s and 1980s the Court made it clear just how exceptional a case *Yoder* really was. In 1982, another Amish community fared less well in its argument that it ought to be exempted from paying social security taxes. *United States v. Lee*, 455 U.S. 252 (1982). And in 1990, the Court held that the Amish were not entitled to an exemption from Minnesota's highway safety laws in the operation of their horse-drawn vehicles. *Minnesota v. Hershberger*, 495 U.S. 901 (1990).

In 1986, the Court ruled that the United States Air Force was not required to accommodate an Orthodox Jewish officer's desire to wear a yarmulke, as required by Jewish law. The facts of the case were fascinating. Simcha Goldman was an ordained Jewish rabbi and an Orthodox Jew. In return for a government fellowship to support his graduate studies in clinical psychology, he accepted a one-year post in the medical services division of an Air Force base. During the year, he appeared as a witness in a court martial wearing his yarmulke. The opposing lawyer filed a complaint about Lt. Goldman's unorthodox headgear. Goldman was sanctioned, and challenged the rule forbidding him to wear his yarmulke in federal court. The result was a 5-to-4 decision featuring stinging dissents by Justices Brennan, Marshall, Blackmun, and O'Connor.

GOLDMAN v. WEINBERGER

SUPREME COURT OF THE UNITED STATES

475 U.S. 503 (1986)

JUSTICE REHNQUIST delivered the opinion of the Court, in which CHIEF JUSTICE BURGER and WHITE, POWELL, and STEVENS joined. STEVENS filed a concurring opinion, in which WHITE and POWELL joined. BRENNAN filed a dissenting opinion, in which MARSHALL joined. BLACKMUN filed a dissenting opinion. O'CONNOR, J., filed a dissenting opinion, in which MARSHALL joined.

JUSTICE REHNQUIST delivered the opinion of the Court.

...Our review of military regulations challenged on First Amendment grounds is far more deferential than constitutional review of similar laws or regulations designed for civilian society. The military need not encourage debate or tolerate protest to the extent that such tolerance is required of the civilian state by the First Amendment; to accomplish its mission the military must foster instinctive obedience, unity, commitment, and esprit de corps. The essence of military service "is the subordination of the desires and interests of the individual to the needs of the service."

These aspects of military life do not, of course, render entirely nugatory in the military context the guarantees of the First Amendment. But "within the military community there is simply not the same [individual] autonomy as there is in the larger civilian community." In the context of the present case, when evaluating whether military needs justify a particular restriction on religiously motivated conduct, courts must give great deference to the professional judgment of military authorities concerning the relative importance of a particular military interest. Not only are courts "ill-equipped to determine the impact upon discipline that any particular intrusion upon military authority might have," but the military authorities have been charged by the Executive and Legislative Branches with carrying out our Nation's military policy. "[Judicial] deference...is at its apogee when legislative action under the congressional authority to raise and support armies and make rules and regulations for their governance is challenged."

The considered professional judgment of the Air Force is that the traditional outfitting of personnel in standardized uniforms encourages the subordination of personal preferences and identities in favor of the overall group mission. Uniforms encourage a sense of hierarchical unity by tending to eliminate outward individual distinctions except for those of rank. The Air Force considers them as vital during peacetime as during war because its personnel must be ready to provide an effective defense on a moment's notice; the necessary habits of discipline and unity must be developed in advance of trouble. We have acknowledged that "[the] inescapable demands of military discipline and obedience to orders cannot be taught on battlefields; the habit of immediate compliance with military procedures and orders must be virtually reflex with no time for debate or reflection...."

Petitioner Goldman contends that the Free Exercise Clause of the First Amendment requires the Air Force to make an exception to its uniform dress requirements for religious apparel unless the accouterments create a "clear danger" of undermining discipline and esprit de corps. He asserts that in general, visible but "unobtrusive" apparel will not create such a danger and must therefore be accommodated. He argues that the Air Force failed to prove that a specific exception for his practice of wearing an unobtrusive yarmulke would threaten discipline. He contends that the Air Force's assertion to the contrary is mere ipse dixit, with no support from actual experience or a scientific study in the record, and is contradicted by expert testimony that religious exceptions to AFR 35-10 [the rule in question] are in fact desirable and will increase morale by making the Air Force a more humane place.

But whether or not expert witnesses may feel that religious exceptions to AFR 35-10 are desirable is quite beside the point. The desirability of dress regulations in the military is decided by the appropriate military officials, and they are under no constitutional mandate to abandon their considered professional judgment. Quite obviously, to the extent the regulations do not permit the wearing of religious apparel such as a yarmulke, a practice described by petitioner as silent devotion akin to prayer, military life may be more objectionable for petitioner and probably others. But the First Amendment does not require the military to accommodate such practices in the face of its view that they would detract from the uniformity sought by the dress regulations. The Air Force has drawn the line essentially between religious apparel that is visible and that which is not, and we hold that those portions of the regulations challenged here reasonably and evenhandedly regulate dress in the interest of the military's perceived need for uniformity. The First Amendment therefore does not prohibit them from being applied to petitioner even though their effect is to restrict the wearing of the headgear required by his religious beliefs.

The judgment of the Court of Appeals is
Affirmed.

JUSTICE STEVENS, with whom JUSTICE WHITE and JUSTICE POWELL join, concurring.

...I believe we must test the validity of the Air Force's rule not merely as it applies to Captain Goldman but also as it applies to all service personnel who have sincere religious beliefs that may conflict with one or more military commands.

JUSTICE BRENNAN is unmoved by the Government's concern that "while a yarmulke might not seem obtrusive to a Jew, neither does a turban to a Sikh, a saffron robe to a Satchidananda Ashram-Integral Yogi, nor do dreadlocks to a Rastafarian." He correctly points out that "turbans, saffron robes, and dreadlocks are not before us in this case," and then suggests that other cases may be fairly decided by reference to a reasonable standard based on "functional utility, health and safety considerations, and the goal of a polished, professional appearance." As the Court has explained, this approach attaches no weight to the separate interest in uniformity itself. Because professionals in the military service attach great importance to that plausible interest, it is one that we must recognize as legitimate and rational even though personal experience or admiration for the performance of the "rag-tag band of soldiers" that won us our freedom in the Revolutionary War might persuade us that the Government has exaggerated the importance of that interest.

The interest in uniformity, however, has a dimension that is of still greater importance for me. It is the interest in uniform treatment for the members of all religious faiths. The very strength of Captain Goldman's claim creates the danger that a similar claim on behalf of a Sikh or a Rastafarian might readily be dismissed as "so extreme, so unusual, or so faddish an image that public confidence in his ability to perform his duties will be destroyed".... [T]he difference between a turban or a dreadlock on the one hand, and a yarmulke on the other, is not merely a difference in "appearance"—it is also the difference between a Sikh or a Rastafarian, on the one hand, and an Orthodox Jew on the other. The Air Force has no business drawing distinctions between such persons when it is enforcing commands of universal application. As the Court demonstrates, the rule that is challenged in this case is based on a neutral, completely objective standard—visibility. It was not motivated by hostility against, or any special respect for, any religious faith. An exception for yarmulkes would represent a fundamental departure from the true principle of uniformity that supports that rule. For that reason, I join the Court's opinion and its judgment.

JUSTICE BRENNAN, with whom JUSTICE MARSHALL joins, dissenting.

...The Government dangles before the Court a classic parade of horribles, the specter of a brightly-colored, "rag-tag band of soldiers." Although turbans, saffron robes, and dreadlocks are not before us in this case and must each be evaluated against the reasons a service branch offers for prohibiting personnel from wearing them while in uniform, a reviewing court could legitimately give deference to dress and grooming rules that have a reasoned basis in, for example, functional utility, health and safety considerations, and the goal of a polished, professional appearance. It is the lack of any reasoned basis for prohibiting yarmulkes that is so striking here.... Implicit in JUSTICE STEVENS' concurrence, and in the Government's arguments, is what might be characterized as a fairness concern. It would be unfair to allow Orthodox Jews to wear yarmulkes, while prohibiting members of other minority faiths with visible dress and grooming requirements from wearing their saffron robes, dreadlocks, turbans, and so forth. While I appreciate and share this concern for the feelings and the free exercise rights of members of these other faiths, I am baffled by this formulation of the problem. What puzzles me is the implication that a neutral standard that could result in the disparate treatment of Orthodox Jews and, for example, Sikhs is more troublesome or unfair than the existing neutral standard that does result in the different treatment of Christians, on the one hand, and Orthodox Jews and Sikhs on the other. Both standards are constitutionally suspect; before either can be sustained, it must be shown to be a narrowly tailored means of promoting important military interests....

In the year following *Goldman*, Congress amended military law so that the dress code would accommodate religious dress, an outcome which points again to the fact that the absence of a constitutional right to an accommodation does nothing to preclude a legislature from reaching a political decision on the question. In another 5-4 decision in 1987, the Court held that Muslim prisoners could be prevented from attending religious services based on asserted security concerns. *O'Lone v. Shabazz*, 482 U.S. 342 (1987). And in *Lying v. Northwest Indian Cemetery Protective Association*, 485 U.S. 439 (1988), by a vote of five to three (Justice Scalia did not participate), the Court upheld a forest service plan to construct roads and harvest timber in areas of national parks that had been used for religious purposes by Indian tribes for centuries.

Other decisions in the same period were less contentious. In 1983, the Court ruled 8 to 1 that the IRS could deny tax-exempt status to Bob Jones University because of that institution's racially restrictive policies. *Bob Jones University v. United States* (heard with *Goldboro Christian School v. United States*). In that case, the IRS had promulgated a rule stating as follows: "Based on the "national policy to discourage racial discrimination in education," the IRS ruled that "a [private] school not having a racially nondiscriminatory policy as to students is not 'charitable' within the common law concepts reflected."

The concept of "charitable" in question, drawn from the common law, was the idea that, to be charitable, "[a]n institution...must serve a public purpose and not be contrary to established public policy." At its establishment in 1963, Bob Jones University, a fundamentalist but nondenominational Christian school, had excluded African-Americans from admission. From 1971 until 1975, the university accepted applications from married African-Americans so long as they were "married within their race." In 1975, following a Court decision that held that private schools could not discriminate on the basis of race, the university permitted unmarried African-Americans to enroll, but maintained a disciplinary rule that prohibited interracial dating by students. The other school involved in the case was Goldsboro Christian School, a K-12 private Christian school. "Since its incorporation in 1963, Goldsboro Christian Schools has maintained a racially discriminatory admissions policy based upon its interpretation of the Bible. Goldsboro has for the most part accepted only Caucasians. On occasion, however, the school has accepted children from racially mixed marriages in which one of the parents is Caucasian." *Bob Jones University v. United States*, 461 U.S. 574 (1983). The IRS concluded that these policies precluded the two schools from being considered charitable institutions.

In challenging the actions of the IRS, the schools argued that racial discrimination motivated by religious beliefs was entitled to accommodation (in addition, Bob Jones University argued that its dating policy was not, in fact, racially discriminatory, an argument the Court rejected out of hand based on earlier decisions):

> This Court has long held the Free Exercise Clause of the First Amendment to be an absolute prohibition against governmental regulation of religious beliefs. As interpreted by this Court, moreover, the Free Exercise Clause provides substantial protection for lawful conduct grounded in religious belief. However, "[not] all burdens on religion are unconstitutional".... [T]he Government has a fundamental, overriding interest in eradicating racial discrimination in education— discrimination that prevailed, with official approval, for the first 165 years of this Nation's constitutional history. That governmental interest substantially outweighs whatever burden denial of tax benefits places on petitioners' exercise of their religious beliefs. *Bob Jones University v. United States*, 461 U.S. 574 (1983).

Justice Rehnquist dissented on the grounds that Congress had not made its intentions clear regarding the relevant provisions of the tax code.

Also in the 1980s, the Court also ruled 9 to 0 that religious organizations are not entitled to exemptions from federal minimum wage laws, and 8 to 1 that government may use social security numbers for purposes of identification even for persons who had religious objections to the system with which those numbers were associated. *Tony and Susan Alamo Foundation v. Sec'y of Labor*, 471 U.S. 290 (1985); *Bowen v. Roy*, 476 U.S. 693 (1986). Further, in 1990, the Court ruled unanimously that Jimmy

Swaggart Ministries was not entitled to an exemption from California's sales tax; *Swaggart v. Bd. of Equalization*, 493 U.S. 378 (1990). In *Bowen*, the case involving social security numbers, Chief Justice Burger urged the adoption of a standard that would uphold a requirement for government benefits that was shown to be "neutral and uniform in its application" and "a reasonable means of promoting a legitimate public interest," a standard that would be much more permissive of government action than the one first announced in *Sherbert v. Verner*.

In addition to these cases, however, the 1980s saw a trio of cases concerning unemployment compensation that echoed and built upon the logic that had been announced in *Sherbert*. All three cases involved employees who had been terminated for refusing to work in ways that contradicted their religious principles (two involved objections to working on Saturdays, and one involved objections to working in a plant that manufactured arms). In all three cases, the Court applied the *Sherbert* test, requiring the state to demonstrate a compelling interest that would be served by the denial of benefits, and found no such sufficient interest. *Thomas v. Review Board of Indiana Employment Security Division*, 450 U.S. 707 (1981); *Hobbie v. Unemployment Appeals Comm'n. of Fla.*, 480 U.S. 136 (1987); *Frazee v. Illinois Dept. of Employment Security*, 489 U.S. 829 (1989). In *Thomas*, Chief Justice Burger proposed a standard less demanding than the one that had been established in *Sherbert*. "[T]he Government meets its burden when it demonstrates that a challenged requirement for governmental benefits, neutral and uniform in its application, is a reasonable means of promoting a legitimate public interest." Under this approach, government would not be required to demonstrate a "compelling" interest, only a legitimate purpose and a neutral rule served by that purpose. Justice Brennan, writing for the majority, rejected Burger's proposed standard:

> Where the state conditions receipt of an important benefit upon conduct proscribed by a religious faith, or where it denies such a benefit because of conduct mandated by religious belief, thereby putting substantial pressure on an adherent to modify his behavior and to violate his beliefs, a burden upon religion exists. While the compulsion may be indirect, the infringement upon free exercise is nonetheless substantial. *Thomas v. Review Board of Indiana Employment Security Division*, 450 U.S. 707 (1981).

The decisions in *Hobbie* and *Frazee* reiterated the Court's commitment to protecting religious convictions against the demands of employers by ensuring the availability of unemployment benefits to employees. The three decisions were decided by votes of 8 to 1, 8 to 1, and 9 to 0, respectively.

At the end of the 1980s, cases like *Goldman* appeared to be exceptions to a general rule that said that the *Sherbert-Yoder* analysis was the proper approach to reviewing statutes under the Free Exercise Clause. In 1990 however, *Sherbert* was abruptly overruled outright in *Employment Division, Dept. of Human Resources of Oregon v. Smith*, 494 U.S. 872 (1990). The case involved two employees who were denied unemployment compensation after being terminated from their jobs at a drug rehabilitation center for using peyote. The two employees were members of the Native American Church, and had taken the drug as part of a religious ritual. Nonetheless, the Employment Division of Oregon's Department of Human Resources ruled that they had been terminated for misconduct, and were therefore not entitled to benefits. The case thus presented a more extreme instance of exactly the kind of questions that had been considered in *Thomas, Hobbie*, and *Frazee*. The analysis, however, was entirely different. Writing for a six-justice majority, Justice Scalia revisited the development of the law since *Sherbert* and concluded that *Reynolds*, the 1878 case concerning polygamy, provided a better model. *Sherbert*, he wrote, established a rule that had only been clearly applied in the specific context of unemployment benefits, and that rule was wrong. Reviewing nonemployment cases that had applied strict scrutiny, Scalia concluded that these had involved "hybrid" claims in which the free exercise of religion was connected with the freedom of speech (*Cantwell*) or the rights of parents to raise their children as they saw fit (*Pierce, Yoder*). But where a case presents a facially neutral law that only incidentally burdened religious practices, the rule after *Smith* is essentially that proposed by Chief Justice Burger in *Bowen v. Roy*: such laws are constitutional so long as they are generally applicable and serve a legitimate state purpose. "Generally applicable," in this context, appears very much like "neutrality" as that idea would later appear in the Rehnquist Court's interpretations of the Establishment Clause in *Agostini* (1997) and *Mitchell* (2000).

As for the accommodation of religious minorities, in the most controversial passage of the opinion, Justice Scalia observed that this could be left to the political process. "It may fairly be said that leaving accommodation to the political process will place at a relative disadvantage those religious practices that are not widely engaged in; but that unavoidable consequence of democratic government must be preferred to a system in which each conscience is a law unto itself or in which judges weigh the social importance of all laws against the centrality of religious beliefs." Justice O'Connor concurred in the outcome (i.e., agreed that Oregon was justified in denying unemployment benefits in the case) but angrily disputed the validity of Justice Scalia's reliance on politics to secure the rights of minorities. "In my view...the First Amendment was enacted precisely to protect the rights of those whose religious practices are not shared by the majority and may be viewed with hostility." Justices Blackmun, Brennan, and Marshall dissented outright. Thus while the outcome of the case was 6 to 3, the new approach to the evaluation of free exercise claims was adopted by a narrow 5-to-4 vote.

EMPLOYMENT DIVISION, DEPARTMENT OF HUMAN RESOURCES OF OREGON v. SMITH

SUPREME COURT OF THE UNITED STATES

494 U.S. 872 (1990)

JUSTICE SCALIA delivered the opinion of the Court.

...The free exercise of religion means, first and foremost, the right to believe and profess whatever religious doctrine one desires. Thus, the First Amendment obviously excludes all "governmental regulation of religious beliefs as such." The government may not compel affirmation of religious belief, punish the expression of religious doctrines it believes to be false, impose special disabilities on the basis of religious views or religious status, or lend its power to one or the other side in controversies over religious authority or dogma.

But the "exercise of religion" often involves not only belief and profession but the performance of (or abstention from) physical acts: assembling with others for a worship service, participating in sacramental use of bread and wine, proselytizing, abstaining from certain foods or certain modes of transportation. It would be true, we think (though no case of ours has involved the point), that a State would be "prohibiting the free exercise [of religion]" if it sought to ban such acts or abstentions only when they are engaged in for religious reasons, or only because of the religious belief that they display. It would doubtless be unconstitutional, for example, to ban the casting of "statues that are to be used for worship purposes," or to prohibit bowing down before a golden calf.

Respondents in the present case, however, seek to carry the meaning of "prohibiting the free exercise [of religion]" one large step further. They contend that their religious motivation for using peyote places them beyond the reach of a criminal law that is not specifically directed at their religious practice, and that is concededly constitutional as applied to those who use the drug for other reasons. They assert, in other words, that "prohibiting the free exercise [of religion]" includes requiring any individual to observe a generally applicable law that requires (or forbids) the performance of an act that his religious belief forbids (or requires). As a textual matter, we do not think the words must be given that meaning....

We have never held that an individual's religious beliefs excuse him from compliance with an otherwise valid law prohibiting conduct that the State is free to regulate. On the contrary, the record of more than a century of our free exercise jurisprudence contradicts that proposition. "Conscientious scruples have not, in the course of the long struggle for religious toleration, relieved the individual from obedience to a general law not aimed at the promotion or restriction of religious beliefs. The mere possession of religious convictions which contradict the relevant concerns of a political society does not relieve the citizen from the discharge of political responsibilities." We first had occasion to assert that principle in *Reynolds v. United States*, 98 U.S. 145 (1879), where we rejected the claim that criminal laws against polygamy could not be constitutionally applied to those whose religion commanded the practice. "Laws," we said, "are made for the government of actions, and while they cannot interfere with mere religious belief and opinions, they may with practices.... Can a man excuse his practices to the contrary because of his religious belief? To permit this would be to make the professed doctrines of religious belief superior to the law of the land, and in effect to permit every citizen to become a law unto himself."

Subsequent decisions have consistently held that the right of free exercise does not relieve an individual of the obligation to comply with a "valid and neutral law of general applicability on the ground that the law proscribes (or prescribes) conduct that his religion prescribes (or proscribes)".... In *Prince v. Massachusetts*, 321 U.S. 158 (1944), we held that a mother could be prosecuted under the child labor laws for using her children to dispense literature in the streets, her religious motivation notwithstanding. We found no constitutional infirmity in "excluding [these children] from doing there what no other children may do." In *Braunfeld v. Brown*, 366 U.S. 599 (1961) (plurality opinion), we upheld Sunday-closing laws against the claim that they burdened the religious practices of persons whose religions compelled them to refrain from work on other days....

The only decisions in which we have held that the First Amendment bars application of a neutral, generally applicable law to religiously motivated action have involved not the Free Exercise Clause alone, but the Free Exercise Clause in conjunction with other constitutional protections, such as freedom of speech and of the press, see *Cantwell v. Connecticut*, 310 U.S., at 304-307 (invalidating a licensing system for religious and charitable solicitations under which the administrator had discretion to deny a license to any cause he deemed nonreligious); *Murdock v. Pennsylvania*, 319 U.S. 105 (1943) (invalidating a flat tax on solicitation as applied to the dissemination of religious ideas)...or the right of parents, acknowledged in *Pierce v. Society of Sisters*, 268 U.S. 510 (1925), to direct the education of their children, see *Wisconsin v. Yoder*, 406 U.S. 205 (1972) (invalidating compulsory school-attendance laws as applied to Amish parents who refused on religious grounds to send their children to school). Some of our cases prohibiting compelled expression, decided exclusively upon free speech grounds, have also involved freedom of religion. And it is easy to envision a case in which a challenge on freedom of association grounds would likewise be reinforced by Free Exercise Clause concerns.

The present case does not present such a hybrid situation, but a free exercise claim unconnected with any communicative activity or parental right. Respondents urge us to hold, quite simply, that when otherwise prohibitable conduct is accompanied by religious convictions, not only the convictions but the conduct itself must be free from governmental regulation. We have never held that, and decline to do so now....

Respondents argue that even though exemption from generally applicable criminal laws need not automatically be extended to religiously motivated actors, at least the claim for a religious exemption must be evaluated under the balancing test set forth in *Sherbert v. Verner*, 374 U.S. 398 (1963). Under the *Sherbert* test, governmental actions that substantially burden a religious practice must be justified by a compelling governmental interest. Applying that test we have, on three occasions, invalidated state unemployment compensation rules that conditioned the availability of benefits upon an applicant's willingness to work under conditions forbidden by his religion. We have never invalidated any governmental action on the basis of the *Sherbert* test except the denial of unemployment compensation. Although we have sometimes purported to apply the *Sherbert* test in contexts other than that, we have always found the test satisfied. In recent years we have abstained from applying the *Sherbert* test (outside the unemployment compensation field) at all....

We conclude today that the sounder approach, and the approach in accord with the vast majority of our precedents, is to hold the test inapplicable to such challenges. The government's ability to enforce generally applicable prohibitions of socially harmful conduct, like its ability to carry out other aspects of public policy, cannot depend on measuring the effects of a governmental action on a religious objector's spiritual development. To make an individual's obligation to obey such a law contingent upon the law's coincidence with his religious beliefs, except where the State's interest is "compelling"—permitting him, by virtue of his beliefs, "to become a law unto himself,"—contradicts both constitutional tradition and common sense.

The "compelling government interest" requirement seems benign, because it is familiar from other fields. But using it as the standard that must be met before the government may accord different treatment on the basis of race, or before the government may regulate the content of speech, is not remotely comparable to using it for the purpose asserted here. What it produces in those other fields—equality of treatment and an unrestricted flow of contending speech—are constitutional norms; what it would produce here—a private right to ignore generally applicable laws—is a constitutional anomaly.... Precisely because "we are a cosmopolitan nation made up of people of almost every conceivable religious preference," and precisely because we value and protect that religious divergence, we cannot afford the luxury of deeming presumptively invalid, as applied to the religious objector, every regulation of conduct that does not protect an interest of the highest order. The rule respondents favor would open the prospect of constitutionally required religious exemptions from civic obligations of almost every conceivable kind—ranging from compulsory military service, to the payment of taxes, to health and safety regulation such as manslaughter and child neglect laws, compulsory vaccination laws, drug laws, and traffic laws; to social welfare legislation such as minimum wage laws, child labor laws, animal cruelty laws, environmental protection laws, and laws providing for equality of opportunity for the races. The First Amendment's protection of religious liberty does not require this.

Values that are protected against government interference through enshrinement in the Bill of Rights are not thereby banished from the political process. Just as a society that believes in the negative protection accorded to the press by the First Amendment is likely to enact laws that affirmatively foster the dissemination of the printed word, so also a society that believes in the negative protection accorded to religious belief can be expected to be solicitous of that value in its legislation as well. It is therefore not surprising that a number of States have made an exception to their drug laws for sacramental peyote use. But to say that a nondiscriminatory religious-practice exemption is permitted, or even that it is desirable, is not to say that it is constitutionally required, and that the appropriate occasions for its creation can be discerned by the courts. It may fairly be said that leaving accommodation to the political process will place at a relative disadvantage those religious practices that are not widely engaged in; but that unavoidable consequence of democratic government must be preferred to a system in which each conscience is a law unto itself or in which judges weigh the social importance of all laws against the centrality of all religious beliefs....

CONCUR: JUSTICE O'CONNOR, with whom JUSTICE BRENNAN, JUSTICE MARSHALL, and JUSTICE BLACKMUN join as to Parts I and II, concurring in the judgment.

...The Court today...interprets the Clause to permit the government to prohibit, without justification, conduct mandated by an individual's religious beliefs, so long as that prohibition is generally applicable. But a law that prohibits certain conduct—conduct that happens to be an act of worship for someone—manifestly does prohibit that person's free exercise of his religion. A person who is barred from engaging in religiously motivated conduct is barred from freely exercising his religion. Moreover, that person is barred from freely exercising his religion regardless of whether the law prohibits the conduct only when engaged in for religious reasons, only by members of that religion, or by all persons. It is difficult to deny that a law that prohibits religiously motivated conduct, even if the law is generally applicable, does not at least implicate First Amendment concerns.

The Court responds that generally applicable laws are "one large step" removed from laws aimed at specific religious practices. The First Amendment, however, does not distinguish between laws that are generally applicable and laws that target particular religious practices. Indeed, few States would be so naive as to enact a law directly prohibiting or burdening a religious practice as such. Our free exercise cases have all concerned generally applicable laws that had the effect of significantly burdening a religious practice. If the First Amendment is to have any vitality, it ought not be construed to cover only the extreme and hypothetical situation in which a State directly targets a religious practice....

The Court today gives no convincing reason to depart from settled First Amendment jurisprudence. There is nothing talismanic about neutral laws of general applicability or general criminal prohibitions, for laws neutral toward religion can coerce a person to violate his religious conscience or intrude upon his religious duties just as effectively as laws aimed at religion. Although the Court suggests that the compelling interest test, as applied to generally applicable laws, would result in a "constitutional anomaly," the First Amendment unequivocally makes freedom of religion, like freedom from race discrimination and freedom of speech, a "constitutional norm," not an "anomaly...."

Finally, the Court today suggests that the disfavoring of minority religions is an "unavoidable consequence" under our system of government and that accommodation of such religions must be left to the political process. In my view, however, the First Amendment was enacted precisely to protect the rights of those whose religious practices are not shared by the majority and may be viewed with hostility. The history of our free exercise doctrine amply demonstrates the harsh impact majoritarian rule has had on unpopular or emerging religious groups such as the Jehovah's Witnesses and the Amish. Indeed, the words of Justice Jackson in *West Virginia State Bd. of Ed. v. Barnette* are apt: "The very purpose of a Bill of Rights was to withdraw certain subjects from the vicissitudes of political controversy, to place them beyond the reach of majorities and officials and to establish them as legal principles to be applied by the courts. One's right to life, liberty, and property, to free speech, a free press, freedom of worship and assembly, and other fundamental rights may not be submitted to vote; they depend on the outcome of no elections".... The Court's holding today not only misreads settled First Amendment precedent; it appears to be unnecessary to this case. I would reach the same result applying our established free exercise jurisprudence....

Few recent Supreme Court decisions have provoked as much controversy as *Smith*. One of the first bills submitted to Congress by the Clinton Administration was the Religious Freedom Restoration Act ("RFRA"), a law aimed explicitly at overturning the decision in *Smith* and restoring the compelling interest test of *Sherbert* to all cases involving Free Exercise claims. RFRA was passed overwhelmingly by both Houses of Congress in a rare show of bipartisanship, and was signed into law in 1993. In 1997, the Supreme Court reviewed RFRA and found it unconstitutional by a vote of 6 to 3 (Justices O'Connor, Souter, and Breyer dissenting); it was not the business of Congress, said the majority, to determine the constitutional standards for judicial review. In his majority opinion Justice Kennedy explained that Congress only had power under the Fourteenth Amendment to enact laws "enforcing" constitutional rights. "Legislation which alters the meaning of the Free Exercise Clause cannot be said to be enforcing the Clause.... [Congress] has been given the power 'to enforce,' not the power to determine what constitutes a constitutional violation." *City of Boerne v. Flores*, 521 U.S. 507 (1997).

In the aftermath of *Smith* (and *City of Boerne*), the crucial remaining question concerned the level of deference that courts would show to legislative statements of purpose. How hard should judges lean on legislative histories or past practices in order to detect instances where apparently "neutral" or "generally applicable" laws were really political pretexts for suppression of religious practices? As in the case of the Establishment Clause, on this score a solid majority of the Court continued to insist that a mere review of the text of a statute would not suffice.

In 1987, the Church of the Lukumi Babalu Aye announced its intention to open a Santerian church in the city of Hialeah, Florida. The practices of Santeria include the ritual sacrifice of animals, a fact which gave rise to immediate and vociferous public opposition to the opening of the church. Responding to public pressure, the City Council of Hialeah enacted a number of new ordinances prohibiting "the sacrifice of animals," and killing animals "unnecessarily." The term "sacrifice" was defined as "to unnecessarily kill...an animal in a...ritual." The statutes were accompanied by a Resolution which expressed "concern" over "religious practices inconsistent with public morals, peace, or safety." The case came to the Supreme Court in *Church of the Lukumi Babalu Aye v. City of Hialeah*, 508 U.S. 520 (1993). Justice Kennedy, writing for a unanimous Court, found that the statute was not a neutral law that only incidentally burdened religious practice, but rather an attempt to target a particular religion. In that situation, wrote Kennedy, the compelling interest test of *Sherbert* should apply. "[I]f the object of a law is to infringe upon or restrict practices because of their religious motivation, the law is not neutral, and it is invalid unless it is justified by a compelling interest and is narrowly tailored to advance that interest."

The question, then, became how a court might go about determining the "object of a law." On this point, Justice Kennedy insisted on the prerogative of a reviewing court to question the truthfulness of a legislature's proclaimed intentions:

> To determine the object of a law, we must begin with its text, for the minimum requirement of neutrality is that a law not discriminate on its face. A law lacks facial neutrality if it refers to a religious practice without a secular meaning discernable from the language or context.... [But] facial neutrality is not determinative. The Free Exercise Clause, like the Establishment Clause, extends beyond facial discrimination. The Clause forbids subtle departures from neutrality, and covert suppression of particular religious beliefs. Official action that targets religious conduct for distinctive treatment cannot be shielded by mere compliance with the requirement of facial neutrality.... The record in this case compels the conclusion that suppression of the central element of the Santeria worship service was the object of the ordinance. *Church of the Lukumi Babalu Aye v. City of Hialeah*, 508 U.S. 520 (1993).

Justice Scalia concurred in the outcome of the case, but wrote separately to emphasize his disapproval of the Court's attempt to determine the subjective intent of legislators. "As I have noted elsewhere, it is virtually impossible to determine the singular 'motive' of a collective legislative body, and this Court has a long tradition of refraining from such inquiries...." Justices Souter, O'Connor, and Blackmun concurred in the outcome, but wrote separately to reiterate their opposition to the adoption of the *Smith* standard.

Smith and *Hialeah* define the jurisprudence of the Free Exercise Clause as of this writing. Like the Establishment Clause, the Free Exercise Clause has increasingly come to be interpreted in terms of an overarching principle of neutrality, which holds that government may not single out a religion for favor or ill-treatment, but that general laws that incidentally burden or benefit religious practice are not constitutionally suspect. In both situations, the neutrality standard has been recently adopted over vociferous protests, a pattern that demonstrates the extent to which the Religion Clauses are very much the subjects of ongoing debates. In the late 1990s, however, the Court considered another series of cases that combined both religion clauses (and some free speech issues, as well). These are the access cases, in which the question has been to what extent government is obliged by the Free Exercise and Free Speech Clauses, or prevented by the Free Exercise Clause, from permitting private speakers to use public resources to promulgate religious messages or to engage in religious practices. In *Abington School Dist. v. Schempp* (1963), a key conclusion had been that "the Free Exercise Clause...has never meant that a majority could use the machinery of the State to practice its beliefs." The access cases challenged that proposition, leading to the conclusion that religious groups and speakers must have the same access to "the machinery of the State" as everyone else. Those cases are as much about free speech as the free exercise of religion, however, so they will be discussed in a later chapter. The question that remains with us at the end of the discussion of the Religion Clauses is whether the two clauses in fact conflict with each other. The neutrality principle is one effort to read the Establishment and Free Exercise Clauses as harmonious, but dissenting justices continue to argue that something fundamental has been lost in the process.

VII. Government as Speaker; Access Cases

The subject matter of this chapter comprises some of the most controversial and most difficult cases in recent years, involving nearly every aspect of the First Amendment that has been discussed thus far. Forum analysis, the Free Speech Clause, and the Free Exercise and Establishment Clauses all meet when the question is whether the government may choose to promote one message over another or whether a religious group may have access to public facilities on the same basis as a secular group. For forum analysis purposes, it is important to recall that the cases established a "tripartite" system in which traditional public forums and forums created for the purpose of public discussion required the greatest protection for free speech rights (strict scrutiny of any content-based restriction on speech), while limited forums required less protection (intermediate scrutiny). In either case, content-neutral time, place, and manner restrictions are presumed to be valid (*Clark v. Committee for Creative Non-Violence, Ward v. Rock Against Racism*), and laws restricting unprotected speech require lesser scrutiny (*Chaplinsky v. New Hampshire, Miller v. California*). Even in limited forums, however, and even where the subject matter of regulation is so-called "unprotected speech," content-specific restrictions must be viewpoint neutral (*R.A.V. v. St. Paul*). Concerning the Free Exercise Clause, in *Agostini v. Felton* and *Mitchell v. Helms* the Court, led by Justice Scalia, has devised a general neutrality approach. That approach, however, has never commanded a majority of justices, and coexists—somewhat uneasily, perhaps—with Justice Kennedy's preference for a coercion test (*Lee v. Weisman*) and Justice O'Connor's focus on endorsement. It is well established, however, that where benefits are generally distributed to students or their parents, the fact that those benefits have the effect of supporting religious schools does not, in itself, indicate that there has been any violation of the Establishment Clause. Finally, in the context of the Free Exercise Clause, we again see a hotly contested "neutrality" approach, again authored by Justice Scalia (*Employment Division, Dept. of Human Resources of Oregon v. Smith*), which says that incidental burdens that are imposed on religious practice do not give rise to constitutional challenges to generally applicable laws. With that background in mind, in this chapter we will consider two special cases: what limits does the First Amendment place on the government's expression, and does the First Amendment grant to private speakers a right of access to public facilities or support?

A. Government as Speaker

As a basic principle, when the government itself is the speaker, there are no restrictions on its expression except for those imposed by the Establishment Clause. The government is free to fund antismoking campaigns without similarly funding advertisements in favor of smoking, for example, or to promote the use of seatbelts. Moving beyond safety concerns, the government can, and does, underwrite the cost of commercial advertising on behalf of private companies, declare "National Broccoli Day," or define cheesemaking as the favored traditional industry of Wisconsin if it so chooses. The fact that government pays to fund prodemocracy radio broadcasts does not mean that it must equally fund procommunism radio broadcasts. When the government itself speaks, then, it stands as a private speaker with free speech rights of its own. This raises a series of questions that have never been fully explored by the Court. Presidents often exhort voters to support candidates from their party. From a First Amendment perspective, can a government agency spend money to promote candidates of a particular party in an election? (Note that federal election laws of various types impose independent barriers to this type of activity.)

The right to speak, however, includes not only the right not to speak but also the right not to be spoken for. That principle arises only ambiguously in the case of private speakers (review Justice Kennedy's discussion of the concern that standing in silence might be construed as endorsement of a message in *Lee v. Weisman*, for example), but in the case of the government it is central to the issue. When the government is the speaker, it is free not only to tailor its message but also to prevent its distortion. This principle has been used to justify restrictions on the speech of government employees and recipients of government funds. How far can the government go in conditioning receipt of funds on suppression of nonconforming speech? Consider the wide range of institutions that receive government funds, from universities and public schools to museums, news media, commercial enterprises, and public works. Would the First Amendment really permit a law that said that no employee of any institution receiving such funds—which includes a significant portion of the American population—can criticize the Republican Party, or that every government employee must praise a Democratic President? The answer to the last question was "no" in *Abood v. Detroit Bd. of Educ.*, 431 U.S. 209 (1977) (see discussion, chapter 4), and in *Rankin v. McPherson*, 483 U.S. 378 (1987), the Court held that a public employee's statement that he hoped an attempt to assassinate President Reagan would succeed was protected speech when uttered privately to a fellow government employee. In 1983, furthermore, the Court suggested that where government provides subsidies to selected speech, it must do so in a way that does not suggest that disfavored viewpoints are being suppressed. In *Regan v. Taxation with Representation of Washington*, 461 U.S. 540 (1983), the Court upheld a law permitting tax deductions for contributions to veterans organizations but denying deductions for contributions to other organizations that engaged in lobbying. The law was upheld as a viewpoint-neutral subsidy, with the observation that "the case would be different if Congress were to discriminate invidiously in its subsidies in such a way as to aim at the suppression of dangerous ideas."

In 1991 the Court considered a case that presented the *Regan* question directly. But in *Rust v. Sullivan*, 500 U.S. 173 (1991), by a 5-to-4 decision, the Court upheld a "gag rule" that said that doctors who worked at family planning clinics funded in part by federal money (Title X) could not "provide counseling concerning the use of abortion as a method of family planning or provide referral for abortion as a method of family planning." The regulations thus went beyond restricting the use of government money, to impose restrictions on the speech of employees of recipients of public funds even though only some of the organizations' money came from that source. Doctors employed at Title X clinics sued, claiming that the law would impose "viewpoint-discriminatory conditions on government subsidies and thus penalize speech funded with non-Title X monies."

Chief Justice Rehnquist's majority opinion turned on two important analytical moves. First, he described the statutory restrictions as limitations on "conduct" rather than on "speech":

> Government can, without violating the Constitution, selectively fund a program to encourage certain activities it believes to be in the public interest, without at the same time funding an alternate program which seeks to deal with the problem in another way. In so doing, the Government has not discriminated on the basis of viewpoint; it has merely chosen to fund one activity to the exclusion of the other.... The Title X program is designed not for prenatal care, but to encourage family planning. A doctor who wished to offer prenatal care to a project patient who became pregnant could properly be prohibited from doing so because such service is outside the scope of the federally funded program. The regulations prohibiting abortion counseling and referral are of the same ilk.... This is not a case of the Government "suppressing a dangerous idea," but of a prohibition on a project grantee or its employees from engaging in activities outside of its scope. *Rust v. Sullivan*, 500 U.S. 173 (1991).

The second analytical move was to equate the rule prohibiting referral and counseling with a decision not to *fund* such activities:

> When Congress established a National Endowment for Democracy to encourage other countries to adopt democratic principles, it was not constitutionally required to fund a program to encourage competing lines of political philosophy such as Communism or Fascism. Petitioners' assertions ultimately boiled down to the position that if the government chooses to subsidize one protected right, it must subsidize analogous counterpart rights. But the Court has soundly rejected that proposition. Within far broader limits than petitioners are willing to concede, when the government appropriates public funds to establish a program it is entitled to define the limits of that program. *Rust v. Sullivan*, 500 U.S. 173 (1991).

Since Congress was not required to provide funds to support abortion counseling, reasoned Chief Justice Rehnquist, it followed that Congress is permitted to prohibit persons receiving federal funds for other purposes from providing such counseling. The limits of the principle announced by Rehnquist were not clear. By the same logic, could the government deny drivers' licenses, revoke veterans' benefits, or withdraw subsidies for student loans to persons critical of its policies, on the theory that criticizing the government is not the "activity" that federal funding is intended to support? Or is government funding used to hire employment the only form of "subsidy" that can be conditioned on a surrender of the right of free speech? Is there another context in which the threat of loss of employment is not considered "coercion"?

One possible limit to the *Rust* principle was described in dicta. In some part, paralleling the forum analysis that we saw earlier, the *Rust* approach depended on the character of the particular institution or setting in which government support was disbursed:

> The existence of a Government "subsidy," in the form of Government-owned property, does not justify the restriction of speech in areas that have been traditionally open to the public for expressive activity, or have been expressly dedicated to speech activity. Similarly, we have recognized that the university is a traditional sphere of free expression so fundamental to the functioning of our society that the Government's ability to control speech within that sphere by means of conditions attached to the expenditure of Government funds is restricted by the vagueness and overbreadth doctrines of the First Amendment. *Rust v. Sullivan*, 500 U.S. 173 (1991).

What was required, then, was some amount of case-by-case analysis of the particular setting in which government support was being provided, and the effects of the restrictions on expression that were a condition of receipt of those funds. In the particular case before the Court, for example, Rehnquist found that there was no need to consider whether the doctor-patient relationship was one in which free expression deserved protection. "[T]he Title X program regulations do not significantly impinge upon the doctor-patient relationship.... The program does not provide post-conception medical advice, and therefore a doctor's silence with regard to abortion cannot reasonably be thought to mislead a client into thinking that the doctor does not consider abortion an appropriate option for her." This conclusion, of course, depended on the equation of the government's funding program with the scope of the doctor-patient relationship, which otherwise would include "post-conception medical advice." Under the *Rust* analysis, it seems, when a doctor accepts employment in a facility that receives any government funds, the scope of the government's funding program becomes the definition of the doctor's employment, medical responsibilities, and professional duties.

Dissenting in *Rust*, Justice Blackmun (joined by Justices Marshall, Stevens, and O'Connor) took issue with the majority's characterization of the case. "It cannot seriously be disputed that the counseling and referral provisions at issue in the present cases constitute content-based regulation of speech. Title X grantees may provide counseling and referral regarding any of a wide range of family planning and other topics, save abortion. The Regulations are also clearly viewpoint-based. While suppressing speech favorable to abortion with one hand, the Secretary compels anti-abortion speech with the other...." (The latter observation refers to the requirement that Title X recipients "facilitate access to...social services, including adoption services, that might be needed by the pregnant client to promote her well-being and that of her child.") Disputing Rehnquist's argument concerning "a doctor's silence," Blackmun argued that the mandate to refer patients to one form of care implicitly precluded others. "[T]he Regulations command that a project refer for prenatal care each woman diagnosed as pregnant, irrespective of the woman's expressed desire to continue or terminate her pregnancy. If a client asks directly about abortion, a Title X physician or counselor is required to say, in essence, that the project does not consider abortion to be an appropriate method of family planning." Most importantly, the dissenters challenged the proposition that government funding decisions could properly be made on the basis of viewpoint. "By refusing to fund those family-planning projects that advocate abortion *because* they advocate abortion, the Government plainly has targeted a particular viewpoint.... [I]t has never been sufficient to justify an otherwise unconstitutional condition upon public employment that the employee may escape the condition by relinquishing his or her job." Finally, Blackmun compared the treatment of abortion counseling with other forms of speech: "[T]he speech the Secretary would suppress is truthful information regarding constitutionally protected conduct of vital importance to the listener. One can imagine no legitimate governmental interest that might be served by suppressing such information." *Rust v. Sullivan*, 500 U.S. 173 (1991).

In dicta, Chief Justice Rehnquist had suggested that the permissible scope of restrictions imposed on speech by the recipients of government funds would depend on the context, invoking the familiar categories of forum analysis. In addition, the status of health workers as quasi-government employees was implicit in the majority's discussion of the proposition that those who did not agree with the statutory restrictions could seek employment elsewhere. Both of these factors were arguably pushed further in 1998 in *NEA v. Finley*, 524 U.S. 569 (1998). The case involved the distribution of federal grants to support the arts, an area traditionally conceived of as close to the core of free speech values. The actual basis for denying funding was "indecency," a classic free speech category. The grants, moreover, were made on a one-time basis, which could have differentiated the situation from that of the health care providers in *Rust*. The analysis in the case, however, did not turn on an application of the factors that Rehnquist had described as relevant to determining the nature of the funding, but rather drew from *Rust* the proposition that where government support can be classified as government speech—rather than as government support for others' private speech—the government is free to "tailor its message."

As the Court noted, the vast majority of NEA grants went to "state arts agencies...symphony orchestras, fine arts museums, dance theater foundations, and opera associations." In the late 1980s, however, two particular grants, totaling less than $50,000, had gone to controversial projects featuring the work of Robert Mapplethorpe and Andrew Serrano. In response, Congress had enacted new regulations including § 954(d)(1), which required the NEA to "take into consideration general standards of decency and respect for the diverse beliefs and values of the American public." The question, then, was whether government was free to restrict its support for "the arts" to those efforts that comport with prevalent standards of "decency." Justice O'Connor, writing for the majority, concluded that so long as "decency" was merely one factor among many, and the mandate to consider factors was "merely hortatory" (advisory) rather than an outright ban on funding indecent art, there was no risk that the government was using its subsidy powers to suppress ideas. Justice Scalia (joined by Justice Thomas) concurred in the outcome, but would have gone much further. Scalia insisted that the regulations in question were, indeed, viewpoint restrictions, but drew from *Rust* a rule that said, quite simply, that the First Amendment simply does not apply when the government is engaged in distributing support rather than punishing expression. Justice Souter, dissenting, agreed with Justice Scalia that what was at stake was regulation based on viewpoint, but insisted that this fact was relevant to the evaluation of government spending programs. Returning to the consideration of factors that Chief Justice Rehnquist had identified in *Rust*, Souter argued that the purpose and nature of the NEA was such that, like a university, it could not be compelled to limit its support of otherwise protected expression on the basis of viewpoint.

NATIONAL ENDOWMENT FOR THE ARTS v. FINLEY

SUPREME COURT OF THE UNITED STATES

524 U.S. 569 (1998)

JUSTICE O'CONNOR delivered the opinion of the Court. JUSTICE SCALIA filed an opinion concurring in the judgment, in which THOMAS joined. JUSTICE SOUTER, filed a dissenting opinion.

JUSTICE O'CONNOR delivered the opinion of the Court.

...Respondents argue that the provision is a paradigmatic example of viewpoint discrimination because it rejects any artistic speech that either fails to respect mainstream values or offends standards of decency. The premise of respondents' claim is that § 954(d)(1) constrains the agency's ability to fund certain categories of artistic expression. The NEA, however, reads the provision as merely hortatory, and contends that it stops well short of an absolute restriction.... It is clear...that the text of § 954(d)(1) imposes no categorical requirement. The advisory language stands in sharp contrast to congressional efforts to prohibit the funding of certain classes of speech. When Congress has in fact intended to affirmatively constrain the NEA's grant-making authority, it has done so in no uncertain terms. See § 954(d)(2) ("Obscenity is without artistic merit, is not protected speech, and shall not be funded")....

That § 954(d)(1) admonishes the NEA merely to take "decency and respect" into consideration, and that the legislation was aimed at reforming procedures rather than precluding speech, undercut respondents' argument that the provision inevitably will be utilized as a tool for invidious viewpoint discrimination. In cases where we have struck down legislation as facially unconstitutional, the dangers were both more evident and more substantial. In *R.A.V. v. St. Paul*, 505

U.S. 377 (1992), for example, we invalidated on its face a municipal ordinance that defined as a criminal offense the placement of a symbol on public or private property "which one knows or has reasonable grounds to know arouses anger, alarm, or resentment in others on the basis of race, color, creed, religion, or gender." That provision set forth a clear penalty, proscribed views on particular disfavored subjects, and suppressed distinctive ideas, conveyed by a distinctive message. In contrast, the "decency and respect" criteria do not silence speakers by expressly "threatening censorship of ideas." Thus, we do not perceive a realistic danger that § 954(d)(1) will compromise First Amendment values....

Respondents' claim that the provision is facially unconstitutional may be reduced to the argument that the criteria in § 954(d)(1) are sufficiently subjective that the agency could utilize them to engage in viewpoint discrimination. Given the varied interpretations of the criteria and the vague exhortation to "take them into consideration," it seems unlikely that this provision will introduce any greater element of selectivity than the determination of "artistic excellence" itself....

Finally, although the First Amendment certainly has application in the subsidy context, we note that the Government may allocate competitive funding according to criteria that would be impermissible were direct regulation of speech or a criminal penalty at stake. So long as legislation does not infringe on other constitutionally protected rights, Congress has wide latitude to set spending priorities. In the 1990 Amendments that incorporated § 954(d)(1), Congress modified the declaration of purpose in the NEA's enabling act to provide that arts funding should "contribute to public support and confidence in the use of taxpayer funds," and that "public funds...must ultimately serve public purposes the Congress defines." § 951(5). And as we held in *Rust*, Congress may "selectively fund a program to encourage certain activities it believes to be in the public interest, without at the same time funding an alternative program which seeks to deal with the problem in another way." In doing so, "the Government has not discriminated on the basis of viewpoint; it has merely chosen to fund one activity to the exclusion of the other...."

JUSTICE SCALIA, with whom JUSTICE THOMAS joins, concurring in the judgment.

"The operation was a success, but the patient died." What such a procedure is to medicine, the Court's opinion in this case is to law. It sustains the constitutionality of 20 U.S.C. § 954(d)(1) by gutting it. The most avid congressional opponents of the provision could not have asked for more. I write separately because, unlike the Court, I think that § 954(d)(1) must be evaluated as written, rather than as distorted by the agency it was meant to control. By its terms, it establishes content- and viewpoint-based criteria upon which grant applications are to be evaluated. And that is perfectly constitutional....

The First Amendment reads: "Congress shall make no law...abridging the freedom of speech." To abridge is "to contract, to diminish; to deprive of." With the enactment of § 954(d)(1), Congress did not abridge the speech of those who disdain the beliefs and values of the American public, nor did it abridge indecent speech. Those who wish to create indecent and disrespectful art are as unconstrained now as they were before the enactment of this statute. Avant-garde artistes such as respondents remain entirely free to epater les bourgeois; they are merely deprived of the additional satisfaction of having the bourgeoisie taxed to pay for it. It is preposterous to equate the denial of taxpayer subsidy with measures aimed at the suppression of dangerous ideas. The reason that denial of participation in a tax exemption or other subsidy scheme does not necessarily "infringe" a fundamental right is that—unlike direct restriction or prohibition— such a denial does not, as a general rule, have any significant coercive effect...The nub of the difference between me and the Court is that I regard the distinction between "abridging" speech and funding it as a fundamental divide, on this side of which the First Amendment is inapplicable....

JUSTICE SOUTER, dissenting.

...The Government calls attention to the roles of government-as-speaker and government-as-buyer, in which the government is of course entitled to engage in viewpoint discrimination: if the Food and Drug Administration launches an advertising campaign on the subject of smoking, it may condemn the habit without also having to show a cowboy taking a puff on the opposite page; and if the Secretary of Defense wishes to buy a portrait to decorate the Pentagon, he is free to prefer George Washington over George the Third.

The Government freely admits, however, that it neither speaks through the expression subsidized by the NEA, nor buys anything for itself with its NEA grants. On the contrary, believing that "the arts...reflect the high place accorded by the American people to the nation's rich cultural heritage," § 951(6), and that "it is vital to a democracy...to provide financial assistance to its artists and the organizations that support their work," § 951(10), the Government acts as a patron, financially underwriting the production of art by private artists and impresarios for independent consumption. Accordingly, the Government would have us liberate government-as-patron from First Amendment strictures not by placing it squarely within the categories of government-as-buyer or government-as-speaker, but by recognizing a new category by analogy to those accepted ones. The analogy is, however, a very poor fit, and this patronage falls embarrassingly on the wrong side of the line between government-as-buyer or -speaker and government-as-regulator-of-private-speech....

Congress brought the NEA into being to help all Americans "achieve a better understanding of the past, a better analysis of the present, and a better view of the future." The NEA's purpose is to "support new ideas" and "to help create and sustain...a climate encouraging freedom of thought, imagination, and inquiry." Given this congressional choice to sustain freedom of expression...the First Amendment forbids decisions based on viewpoint popularity. So long as Congress chooses to subsidize expressive endeavors at large, it has no business requiring the NEA to turn down funding applications of artists and exhibitors who devote their "freedom of thought, imagination, and inquiry" to defying our tastes, our beliefs, or our values. It may not use the NEA's purse to "suppress...dangerous ideas."

Following *Rust* and *NEA v. Finley*, there was considerable ambiguity about the position of the majority of the Court with regard to government-supported speech, or speech by persons receiving government support for other purposes. Seven of the justices (all except for Scalia and Thomas) continued to declare their commitment to some version of the pre-*Rust* rule of *Regan v. Taxation with Representation of Washington*, that government was free to decide how to distribute its resources so long as it did not "discriminate invidiously in its subsidies in such a way as to aim at the suppression of dangerous ideas." While restrictions on expression by recipients of government funding had been upheld in both *Rust* and *Finley*, in both cases the majorities had left open the possibility that in another case they might find a limit to the principle that the government as speaker is free to tailor its message.

That case arrived in 2001. The federal government operates the Legal Services Corporation ("LSC"), a program that among other things provides counsel to indigent persons challenging denial of welfare benefits. In 1997 the LSC program was changed by the addition of §504(a)(16). Under the new rule, an LSC-funded lawyer could challenge a denial of benefits on the facts of the case, but was prohibited from challenging the statutory or constitutional validity of the rule under which benefits had been denied. "Even in cases where constitutional or statutory challenges became apparent after representation was well under way, LSC advised that its attorneys must withdraw." Writing for a narrow five member majority, in *Legal Services Corporation v. Velazquez* Justice Kennedy argued that this went too far. Government did not have to pay for legal services, he wrote, but if it did so it could not condition its assistance on the acceptance of limitations that "distorted" the basic function of legal representation. In his opinion, Kennedy argued that both the function of a lawyer and the function of the judiciary, as the branch entrusted with the task of reviewing statutes, were placed at risk by the new rule. Thus, Kennedy and the other justices in the majority (Stevens, Souter, Ginsburg, and Breyer) arguably found that legal representation constituted a government program "expressly dedicated to speech activity," similar to that of the university, which had been discussed in *Rust*. Alternatively, it may be concluded that the justices of the Court were more readily willing to accept an argument that lawyers, as opposed to doctors, are bound by professional duties with which the government may not interfere as a condition of their employment. "The advice from the attorney to the client," wrote Justice Kennedy, "and the advocacy by the attorney to the courts cannot be classified as governmental speech even under a generous understanding of the concept."

LEGAL SERVICES CORPORATION v. VELAZQUEZ

SUPREME COURT OF THE UNITED STATES

531 U.S. 533 (2001)

JUSTICE KENNEDY delivered the opinion of the Court. JUSTICE SCALIA filed a dissenting opinion in which REHNQUIST, C. J., and O'CONNOR and THOMAS joined.

...We have said that viewpoint-based funding decisions can be sustained in instances in which the government is itself the speaker, or instances, like *Rust*, in which the government "used private speakers to transmit information pertaining to its own program...." The latitude which may exist for restrictions on speech where the government's own message is being delivered flows in part from our observation that, "when the government speaks, for instance to promote its own policies or to advance a particular idea, it is, in the end, accountable to the electorate and the political process for its advocacy...." Neither the latitude for government speech nor its rationale applies to subsidies for private speech in every instance, however. As we have pointed out, "it does not follow...that viewpoint-based restrictions are proper when the [government] does not itself speak or subsidize transmittal of a message it favors but instead expends funds to encourage a diversity of views from private speakers." *Rosenberger*.

Although the LSC program differs from the program at issue in *Rosenberger* in that its purpose is not to "encourage a diversity of views," the salient point is that...the LSC program was designed to facilitate private speech, not to promote a governmental message. Congress funded LSC grantees to provide attorneys to represent the interests of indigent clients. In the specific context of § 504(a)(16) suits for benefits, an LSC-funded attorney speaks on the behalf of the client in a claim against the government for welfare benefits. The lawyer is not the government's speaker. The attorney defending the decision to deny benefits will deliver the government's message in the litigation. The LSC lawyer, however, speaks on the behalf of his or her private, indigent client.

The Government has designed this program to use the legal profession and the established Judiciary of the States and the Federal Government to accomplish its end of assisting welfare claimants in determination or receipt of their benefits. The advice from the attorney to the client and the advocacy by the attorney to the courts cannot be classified as governmental speech even under a generous understanding of the concept. In this vital respect this suit is distinguishable from *Rust*....

By providing subsidies to LSC, the Government seeks to facilitate suits for benefits by using the State and Federal courts and the independent bar on which those courts depend for the proper performance of their duties and responsibilities. Restricting LSC attorneys in advising their clients and in presenting arguments and analyses to the courts distorts the legal system by altering the traditional role of the attorneys.... LSC has advised us, furthermore, that upon determining a question of statutory validity is present in any anticipated or pending case or controversy, the LSC-funded attorney must cease the representation at once. This is true whether the validity issue becomes apparent during initial attorney-client consultations or in the midst of litigation proceedings. A disturbing example of the restriction was discussed during oral argument before the Court. It is well understood that when there are two reasonable constructions for a statute, yet one raises a constitutional question, the Court should prefer the interpretation which avoids the constitutional issue. Yet, as the LSC advised the Court, if, during litigation, a judge were to ask an LSC attorney whether there was a constitutional concern, the LSC attorney simply could not answer.

Interpretation of the law and the Constitution is the primary mission of the judiciary when it acts within the sphere of its authority to resolve a case or controversy. An informed, independent judiciary presumes an informed, independent bar. Under § 504(a)(16), however, cases would be presented by LSC attorneys who could not advise the courts of serious questions of statutory validity. The disability is inconsistent with the proposition that attorneys should present all the reasonable and well-grounded arguments necessary for proper resolution of the case. By seeking to prohibit the analysis of certain legal issues and to truncate presentation to the courts, the enactment under review prohibits speech and expression upon which courts must depend for the proper exercise of the judicial power.... The statute is an attempt to draw lines around the LSC program to exclude from litigation those arguments and theories Congress finds unacceptable but which by their nature are within the province of the courts to consider....

Congress cannot recast a condition on funding as a mere definition of its program in every case, lest the First Amendment be reduced to a simple semantic exercise. Here, notwithstanding Congress' purpose to confine and limit its program, the restriction operates to insulate current welfare laws from constitutional scrutiny and certain other legal challenges, a condition implicating central First Amendment concerns.... It is fundamental that the First Amendment was fashioned to assure unfettered interchange of ideas for the bringing about of political and social changes desired by the people. There can be little doubt that the LSC Act funds constitutionally protected expression; and in the context of this statute there is no programmatic message of the kind recognized in *Rust* and which sufficed there to allow the Government to specify the advice deemed necessary for its legitimate objectives....

Congress was not required to fund an LSC attorney to represent indigent clients; and when it did so, it was not required to fund the whole range of legal representations or relationships. The LSC and the United States, however, in effect ask us to permit Congress to define the scope of the litigation it funds to exclude certain vital theories and ideas. The attempted restriction is designed to insulate the Government's interpretation of the Constitution from judicial challenge. The Constitution does not permit the Government to confine litigants and their attorneys in this manner....

JUSTICE SCALIA, with whom THE CHIEF JUSTICE, JUSTICE O'CONNOR, and JUSTICE THOMAS join, dissenting.

...The LSC Act is a federal subsidy program, not a federal regulatory program, and "there is a basic difference between [the two]." Regulations directly restrict speech; subsidies do not. Subsidies, it is true, may indirectly abridge speech, but only if the funding scheme is "manipulated" to have a "coercive effect" on those who do not hold the subsidized position. Proving unconstitutional coercion is difficult enough when the spending program has universal coverage and excludes only certain speech—such as a tax exemption scheme excluding lobbying expenses. The Court has found such programs unconstitutional only when the exclusion was "aimed at the suppression of dangerous ideas...." When the limited spending program does not create a public forum, proving coercion is virtually impossible, because simply denying a subsidy "does not 'coerce' belief," and because the criterion of unconstitutionality is whether denial of the subsidy threatens "to drive certain ideas or viewpoints from the marketplace...." The LSC Act, like the scheme in *Rust*, does not create a public forum.... Nor does §504(a)(16) discriminate on the basis of viewpoint, since it funds neither challenges to nor defenses of existing welfare law.... It may well be that the bar of §504(a)(16) will cause LSC-funded attorneys to decline or to withdraw from cases that involve statutory validity. But that means at most that fewer statutory challenges to welfare laws will be presented to the courts because of the unavailability of free legal services for that purpose. So what? The same result would ensue from excluding LSC-funded lawyers from welfare litigation entirely....

The statement that the LSC Act was viewpoint neutral because "it funds neither challenges to nor defenses of existing welfare law" is simply bizarre. As Justice Scalia was aware, by definition the party in a suit who could be in the position of defending an existing law would be the government, which is hardly dependent upon LSC for its representation. Similarly, a welfare agency can never be in the position of challenging the constitutionality of a statute under which it acts: That role is limited to lawyers representing welfare recipients. (If one adds the further observation that a significant number of welfare recipients are likely to be unable to afford private counsel, one begins to understand how the majority concluded that the law was "designed to insulate the Government's interpretation of the Constitution from judicial challenge.") Justice Scalia's comment, therefore, must be taken as an indication of the extent to which he simply does not consider the question of viewpoint discrimination to be relevant in the case, as he wrote in *NEA v. Finley*. Justice Thomas joined in Justice Scalia's *Finley* concurrence; Chief Justice Rehnquist and Justice O'Connor, however, by joining Scalia in dissenting in *Velazquez*, leave open the question of whether they continue to believe that the government's freedom to selectively support messages is limited by the principle that it may not seek to suppress ideas.

The majority's concern in *Velazquez*, and Justice Scalia's challenge to their analysis, both center on the question of whether there are circumstances under which government's decision not to extend its support to expression constitutes the suppression of ideas. During the same period that the Court was developing the *Rust-Finley-Velazquez* doctrine, it was also hearing a series of cases that revisited the definition of public and limited forums in ways that tested the limits of "government speech" as well as the relationship between the Free Speech, Free Exercise, and Establishment Clauses. These were cases concerning private parties' access to government facilities or support.

The most important of the access cases, cited in *Velazquez*, was *Rosenberger v. Rector and Visitors of the University of Virginia*, 515 U.S. 819 (1995). *Rosenberger* had established a crucial proposition between the time of *NEA v. Finley* and *Velazquez*. The case involved a university funding program, and the basic ruling was that the university could not exclude religious activities from eligibility for such funds because doing so would constitute viewpoint discrimination. The details of the case are discussed and an excerpt is provided below, but there are two basic propositions that it is important to recognize before going further. First, *Rosenberger* had drawn an analogy between the availability of government funds and the access to government property; both, according to Justice Kennedy's majority opinion, were forms of public forums. In addition, *Rosenberger* also included a single sentence of dictum that pointed to the arc of development in the understanding of the *Rust* principle among the majority of the Court. Describing the earlier ruling in *Rust*, Justice Kennedy in *Rosenberger* wrote, "There, the government did not create a program to encourage private speech but instead used private speakers to transmit specific information *pertaining to its own program*" (emphasis added).

Thus one way to read both *Velazquez* and *Finley* is to imply that the *Rust* principle gives the government the authority to withhold its support from those who fail to express its message only when the expression of that government message was the purpose of the funding in the first instance. This reading, of course, denies the absolute distinction between "abridging" and funding expression that Justice Scalia insisted upon in his *Finley* concurrence. Furthermore, it is difficult to square this interpretation of *Velazquez* with the actual facts of *Rust*, since the stated purpose of Title X funding in that case was the provision of health and family planning services, not the promulgation of any government message. Another way to understand *Velazquez*, therefore, is as an implicit overruling of key portions of *Rust*, achieved by a shift from one 5-4 majority to another over the space of a decade.

B. Access to Public Facilities

In Chief Justice Rehnquist's *Rust* opinion, he noted that one limiting factor in government's ability to limit access to its resources would be the extent to which a party could argue that the intent of the government program was to create a forum dedicated to free expression. To review, in a traditional public forum or in a forum dedicated to open discussion, any regulation that is specific as to content is subject to strict scrutiny, and viewpoint discrimination is never permitted. In a limited forum, content restrictions are permitted to preserve the purpose of the forum, subject only to intermediate scrutiny for "reasonableness," but, again, viewpoint discrimination is prohibited.

In *Widmar v. Vincent*, 454 U.S. 263 (1981), the Court ruled that a state could not prohibit the use of university facilities "for religious worship" on free exercise and free speech grounds. *Widmar* involved a rule adopted by the University of Missouri that banned the use of university property for religious worship, while allowing uses of the property by registered student groups. An evangelical student organization called Cornerstone sued. Writing for an eight member majority, Justice Powell observed that it was "the stated policy of the University of Missouri at Kansas City to encourage the activities of student organizations" and that use of university facilities was "routinely" granted to more than one hundred diverse groups. Based on these facts, Powell concluded that the university had thus created a public forum. Considering the Establishment Clause, the Court found that university students were less impressionable than younger students and that there was no realistic danger of a public perception of endorsement in permitting religious use of campus facilities.

WIDMAR v. VINCENT

SUPREME COURT OF THE UNITED STATES

454 U.S. 263 (1981)

JUSTICE POWELL delivered the opinion of the Court. JUSTICE WHITE filed a dissenting opinion.

...Through its policy of accommodating their meetings, the University has created a forum generally open for use by student groups. Having done so, the University has assumed an obligation to justify its discriminations and exclusions under applicable constitutional norms. The Constitution forbids a State to enforce certain exclusions from a forum generally open to the public, even if it was not required to create the forum in the first place....

Here UMKC has discriminated against student groups and speakers based on their desire to use a generally open forum to engage in religious worship and discussion. These are forms of speech and association protected by the First Amendment. In order to justify discriminatory exclusion from a public forum based on the religious content of a group's intended speech, the University must therefore satisfy the standard of review appropriate to content-based exclusions. It must show that its regulation is necessary to serve a compelling state interest and that it is narrowly drawn to achieve that end. In this case the University claims a compelling interest in maintaining strict separation of church and State. It derives this interest from the "Establishment Clauses" of both the Federal and Missouri Constitutions.

The University first argues that it cannot offer its facilities to religious groups and speakers on the terms available to other groups without violating the Establishment Clause of the Constitution of the United States. We agree that the interest of the University in complying with its constitutional obligations may be characterized as compelling. It does not follow, however, that an "equal access" policy would be incompatible with this Court's Establishment Clause cases. Those cases hold that a policy will not offend the Establishment Clause if it can pass a three-pronged test.... In this case two prongs of the test are clearly met. Both the District Court and the Court of Appeals held that an open-forum policy, including nondiscrimination against religious speech, would have a secular purpose and would avoid entanglement with religion. But the District Court concluded, and the University argues here, that allowing religious groups to share the limited public forum would have the "primary effect" of advancing religion.

The University's argument misconceives the nature of this case. The question is not whether the creation of a religious forum would violate the Establishment Clause. The University has opened its facilities for use by student groups, and the question is whether it can now exclude groups because of the content of their speech. In this context we are unpersuaded that the primary effect of the public forum, open to all forms of discourse, would be to advance religion.... We are satisfied that any religious benefits of an open forum at UMKC would be "incidental" within the meaning of our cases. Two factors are especially relevant.

First, an open forum in a public university does not confer any imprimatur of state approval on religious sects or practices. n14 As the Court of Appeals quite aptly stated, such a policy "would no more commit the University...to religious goals" than it is "now committed to the goals of the Students for a Democratic Society, the Young Socialist Alliance," or any other group eligible to use its facilities.

> n14 University students are, of course, young adults. They are less impressionable than younger students and should be able to appreciate that the University's policy is one of neutrality toward religion....

> Having created a forum generally open to student groups, the University seeks to enforce a content-based exclusion of religious speech. Its exclusionary policy violates the fundamental principle that a state regulation of speech should be content-neutral, and the University is unable to justify this violation under applicable constitutional standards....

Justice White, dissenting, argued that the case ought to have been understood as one involving only incidental burdens on religion, since the only prohibition was on a certain set of activities rather than on religious groups per se:

> I have long argued that Establishment Clause limits on state action which incidentally aids religion are not as strict as the Court has held. The step from the permissible to the necessary, however, is a long one. In my view, just as there is room under the Religion Clauses for state policies that may have some beneficial effect on religion, there is also room for state policies that may incidentally burden religion. In other words, I believe the States to be a good deal freer to formulate policies that affect religion in divergent ways than does the majority. The majority's position will inevitably lead to those contradictions and tensions between the Establishment and Free Exercise Clauses warned against by Justice Stewart in *Sherbert v. Verner. Widmar v. Vincent*, 454 U.S. 263 (1981).

In 1984, Congress extended this principle with the Equal Access Act of 1984, which prohibits public schools from limiting groups' access to facilities on the basis of "religious, political, philosophical or other content of the speech" that might occur during their meetings. That law was upheld in *Bd. of Educ. of the Westside Community Schools v. Mergens*, 496 U.S. 226 (1990), in part on the grounds that the use of school facilities did not constitute government endorsement of religion.

In 1993, the forum analysis that had been introduced in *Widmar* was tested when the Court heard a challenge to the practices of a school district that made its buildings available after hours to nonstudent community groups under a local ordinance called "Rule 10," for the purpose of presenting lectures and/or films relating to child-rearing. Rule 10 contained a restriction that barred use of the facilities to religious groups. The Court considered the case as one involving a limited forum, asking first whether the religious groups' proposed activities were consistent with the purpose of the forum, and, second, whether excluding religious groups from the forum constituted viewpoint discrimination. Because the groups at issue were religious, however, there was a third level of analysis that was required: What is the relationship between preserving viewpoint neutrality and the Establishment Clause? The judgment of the Court was unanimous.

LAMB'S CHAPEL v. CENTER MORICHES UNION FREE SCHOOL DISTRICT

SUPREME COURT OF THE UNITED STATES

508 U.S. 384 (1993)

JUSTICE WHITE delivered the opinion of the Court.

...There is no question that the District, like the private owner of property, may legally preserve the property under its control for the use to which it is dedicated.... With respect to public property that is not a designated public forum open for indiscriminate public use for communicative purposes, we have said that "control over access to a nonpublic forum can be based on subject matter and speaker identity so long as the distinctions drawn are reasonable in light of the purpose served by the forum and are viewpoint neutral...."

There is no suggestion from the courts below or from the District or the State that a lecture or film about child rearing and family values would not be a use for social or civic purposes otherwise permitted by Rule 10. That subject matter is not one that the District has placed off limits to any and all speakers. Nor is there any indication in the record before us that the application to exhibit the particular film series involved here was, or would have been, denied for any reason other than the fact that the presentation would have been from a religious perspective. In our view, denial on that basis was plainly invalid.... [A]lthough a speaker may be excluded from a nonpublic forum if he wishes to address a topic not encompassed within the purpose of the forum, or if he is not a member of the class of speakers for whose especial benefit the forum was created, the government violates the First Amendment when it denies access to a speaker solely to suppress the point of view he espouses on an otherwise includable subject.

The film series involved here no doubt dealt with a subject otherwise permissible under Rule 10, and its exhibition was denied solely because the series dealt with the subject from a religious standpoint. The principle that has emerged from our cases "is that the First Amendment forbids the government to regulate speech in ways that favor some viewpoints or ideas at the expense of others."

The District, as a respondent, would save its judgment below on the ground that to permit its property to be used for religious purposes would be an establishment of religion forbidden by the First Amendment. This Court suggested in *Widmar v. Vincent*, 454 U.S. 263 (1981), that the interest of the State in avoiding an Establishment Clause violation "may be [a] compelling" one justifying an abridgment of free speech otherwise protected by the First Amendment; but the Court went on to hold that permitting use of university property for religious purposes under the open access policy involved there would not be incompatible with the Court's Establishment Clause cases.

We have no more trouble than did the *Widmar* Court in disposing of the claimed defense on the ground that the posited fears of an Establishment Clause violation are unfounded. The showing of this film series would not have been during school hours, would not have been sponsored by the school, and would have been open to the public, not just to church members. The District property had repeatedly been used by a wide variety of private organizations. Under these circumstances, as in *Widmar*, there would have been no realistic danger that the community would think that the District was endorsing religion or any particular creed, and any benefit to religion or to the Church would have been no more than incidental. As in *Widmar*, permitting District property to be used to exhibit the film series involved in this case would not have been an establishment of religion under the three-part test articulated in *Lemon v. Kurtzman*, 403 U.S. 602 (1971): The challenged governmental action has a secular purpose, does not have the principal or primary effect of advancing or inhibiting religion, and does not foster an excessive entanglement with religion....

Lamb's Chapel was followed by *Capitol Square Review and Advisory Bd. v. Pinette* (1995). The Ku Klux Klan had filed an application to erect a plain cross in a small park adjacent to the state capitol building in Cleveland. Other groups were allowed to erect symbols of various kinds in the park, but the City of Cleveland argued that the cross could be excluded on the grounds that permitting its presence would violate the Establishment Clause. Cleveland argued that the case was different from *Lamb's Chapel* because the proximity of the park to government buildings increased the risk of a perception of government endorsement of religion. In the majority opinion, Justice Scalia used the case to develop the Establishment Clause side of the forum argument that had emerged in *Lamb's Chapel*. In a concurring opinion joined by Justices Souter and Breyer, Justice O'Connor found that on the facts of the case the danger of perceived endorsement was insufficient to justify exclusion of the cross. Justice Scalia, however, went farther, creating a blanket rule limiting the applicability of "endorsement" as a test for constitutionality in the context of access to a public or dedicated forum:

> Petitioners argue that absence of perceived endorsement was material in *Lamb's Chapel* and *Widmar*. We did state in *Lamb's Chapel* that there was "no realistic danger that the community would think that the District was endorsing religion or any particular creed." But that conclusion was not the result of empirical investigation; it followed directly, we thought, from the fact that the forum was open and the religious activity privately sponsored. It is significant that we referred only to what would be thought by "the community"—not by outsiders or individual members of the community uninformed about the school's practice.

> Surely some of the latter, hearing of religious ceremonies on school premises, and not knowing of the premises' availability and use for all sorts of other private activities, might leap to the erroneous conclusion of state endorsement. But, we in effect said, given an open forum and private sponsorship, erroneous conclusions do not count.... Religious expression cannot violate the Establishment Clause where it (1) is purely private and (2) occurs in a traditional or designated public forum, publicly announced and open to all on equal terms. Those conditions are satisfied here, and therefore the State may not bar respondents' cross from Capitol Square. *Capitol Square Review and Advisory Bd. v. Pinette*, 515 U.S. 753 (1995).

The two-part rule announced in *Capitol Square* thus essentially made the Establishment Clause irrelevant in any case in which the Court found there to be a public or dedicated forum. Not only could government be permitted to allow access to such fora to religious symbols and expressions, it would be required to do so. Secular governments who did not want to see religious expressions in their public spaces would have to refrain from opening those spaces to the community, a parallel, of sorts, to the situation of religious organizations that refuse government funding in order to avoid secular obligations such as nondiscrimination in employment or maintenance of public records.

Widmar, *Lamb's Chapel*, and *Capitol Square* altered the balance of considerations between the Free Speech and Establishment Clauses in the context of a public or dedicated forum, but at the same time they did not fundamentally alter the conception of the forum itself. A park or public building that has been opened to a particular set of uses is a classic example of a forum, whether public, dedicated to expression, or limited to a purpose. Similarly, *Lamb's Chapel*, in particular, concluded that a religious viewpoint could not be treated differently from other viewpoints, but nothing in the analysis required reconceptualizing the categories of "content" and "viewpoint." There was nothing wrong with the school district making its facilities open solely for purposes of discussing child-rearing, to the exclusion of other topics, it was only that the school district was not permitted to discriminate among different viewpoints concerning the stated topic of discussion. In this sense, the *Lamb's Chapel* analysis fit perfectly into the traditional analysis of a limited forum (content-based regulations are permitted so long as they are viewpoint neutral and related to the purpose for which the forum was created.) The analysis becomes somewhat more complex, however, when the forum in question takes the form of a pool of government funds rather than access to public property.

C. Access to Public Support

The case that introduced the idea that money could constitute a forum was *Rosenberger v. Rector and Visitors of the University of Virginia*, 515 U.S. 819 (1995). The University of Virginia funded a wide array of student organizations out of mandatory student fees, using a somewhat complicated two-step funding process. First, a student group would apply to be declared eligible for funding ("CIO status"). After having received CIO status, a group could then, separately, apply for funds collected out of student activity fees ("SAF" funding). Not all student groups could become CIOs; among other restrictions, CIO status was not available to "religious organizations." A "religious organization" was defined in the university's funding guidelines as "an organization whose purpose is to practice a devotion to an acknowledged ultimate reality or deity." Furthermore, according to the rules, not all CIO activities were eligible for SAF funding. Among activities ineligible for funding were "religious activities, philanthropic contributions and activities, political activities, activities that would jeopardize the University's tax-exempt status, those which involve payment of honoraria or similar fees, or social entertainment or related expenses."

An evangelical Christian student group called Wide Awake Productions (WAP) was denied funds to cover third-party costs (primarily the cost of printing its newsletter), on the grounds that the publication of the newsletter constituted a religious activity. The group sued on the theory that *Lamb's Chapel* required the university to grant equal access to money in the same way that it required equal access to buildings. The ability of the university to define its forum to exclude "religious groups" was not at issue, only the refusal to fund "religious activities" by (presumptively) nonreligious organizations. The exclusion of religious groups from CIO status would have been permissible if such a restriction was found to be "reasonable in light of the purpose served by the forum," an issue that the Court did not undertake to analyze.

The Court, in a majority opinion written by Justice Kennedy, agreed that in a proper case, making funding available for student organizations constituted the creation of a forum. In addition, the distinction between content and viewpoint, which had been central to *Lamb's Chapel*, was reconsidered in novel ways. The University had argued that it was drawing a reasonable content distinction between expression about religion and speech that constituted religious expression. Justice Kennedy rejected the distinction:

[D]iscrimination against one set of views or ideas is but a subset or particular instance of the more general phenomenon of content discrimination. And, it must be acknowledged, the distinction is not a precise one. It is, in a sense, something of an understatement to speak of religious thought and discussion as just a viewpoint, as distinct from a comprehensive body of thought.... Religion may be a vast area of inquiry, but it also provides, as it did here, a specific premise, a perspective, a standpoint from which a variety of subjects may be discussed and considered. *Rosenberger v. Rector and Visitors of the University of Virginia*, 515 U.S. 819 (1995).

The significance of this statement is not entirely clear; is religion a unique case, or is the division between content and viewpoint "not a precise one" in all cases? Note that in the past the Court has been quite willing to distinguish between teaching about communism and communist political speech; after *Rosenberger*, is that distinction still valid? How does the blurring of the distinction between religious expression and speech about religion relate to the determination of whether a content restriction is reasonably related to the purpose of a forum?

Regardless of these ambiguities, the majority opinion in *Rosenberger* stands clearly for the propositions that money can be a forum, and that religious expression cannot be excluded from access to money any more than it could be excluded from a public park in *Capitol Square* or the use of facilities in *Widmar* and *Lamb's Chapel*. Those conclusions were far from unanimous, however. The decision was 5 to 4, with Justices Souter, Stevens, Ginsburg, and Breyer dissenting. Justice O'Connor wrote a separate concurring opinion, in which she was joined by Justice Thomas, that focused heavily on the particular facts of the case rather than adopting Justice Kennedy's sweeping statement of principle.

ROSENBERGER v. RECTOR AND VISITORS OF THE
UNIVERSITY OF VIRGINIA

SUPREME COURT OF THE UNITED STATES

515 U.S. 819 (1995)

JUSTICE KENNEDY, delivered the opinion of the Court, in which REHNQUIST, C. J., and O'CONNOR, SCALIA, and THOMAS joined. JUSTICE O'CONNOR and THOMAS filed concurring opinions. JUSTICE SOUTER filed a dissenting opinion, in which STEVENS, GINSBURG, and BREYER joined.

...It is axiomatic that the government may not regulate speech based on its substantive content or the message it conveys. Other principles follow from this precept. In the realm of private speech or expression, government regulation may not favor one speaker over another. Discrimination against speech because of its message is presumed to be unconstitutional. These rules informed our determination that the government offends the First Amendment when it imposes financial burdens on certain speakers based on the content of their expression. When the government targets not subject matter, but particular views taken by speakers on a subject, the violation of the First Amendment is all the more blatant. Viewpoint discrimination is thus an egregious form of content discrimination. The government must abstain from regulating speech when the specific motivating ideology or the opinion or perspective of the speaker is the rationale for the restriction.

These principles provide the framework forbidding the State from exercising viewpoint discrimination, even when the limited public forum is one of its own creation.... The necessities of confining a forum to the limited and legitimate purposes for which it was created may justify the State in reserving it for certain groups or for the discussion of certain topics. Once it has opened a limited forum, however, the State must respect the lawful boundaries it has itself set. The State may not exclude speech where its distinction is not "reasonable in light of the purpose served by the forum," nor may it discriminate against speech on the basis of its viewpoint. Thus, in determining whether the State is acting to preserve the limits of the forum it has created so that the exclusion of a class of speech is legitimate, we have observed a distinction between, on the one hand, content discrimination, which may be permissible if it preserves the purposes of that limited forum, and, on the other hand, viewpoint discrimination, which is presumed impermissible when directed against speech otherwise within the forum's limitations.

The SAF is a forum more in a metaphysical than in a spatial or geographic sense, but the same principles are applicable. The most recent and most apposite case is our decision in *Lamb's Chapel*....

The University does acknowledge (as it must in light of our precedents) that "ideologically driven attempts to suppress a particular point of view are presumptively unconstitutional in funding, as in other contexts," but insists that this case does not present that issue because the Guidelines draw lines based on content, not viewpoint. As we have noted, discrimination against one set of views or ideas is but a subset or particular instance of the more general phenomenon of content discrimination. And, it must be acknowledged, the distinction is not a precise one. It is, in a sense, something of an understatement to speak of religious thought and discussion as just a viewpoint, as distinct from a comprehensive body of thought. The nature of our origins and destiny and their dependence upon the existence of a divine being have been subjects of philosophic inquiry throughout human history. We conclude, nonetheless, that here, as in *Lamb's Chapel*, viewpoint discrimination is the proper way to interpret the University's objections to Wide Awake. By the very terms of the SAF prohibition, the University does not exclude religion as a subject matter but selects for disfavored treatment those student journalistic efforts with religious editorial viewpoints. Religion may be a vast area of inquiry, but it also provides, as it did here, a specific premise, a perspective, a standpoint from which a variety of subjects may be discussed and considered. The prohibited perspective, not the general subject matter, resulted in the refusal to make third-party payments, for the subjects discussed were otherwise within the approved category of publications....

The University tries to escape the consequences of our holding in *Lamb's Chapel* by urging that this case involves the provision of funds rather than access to facilities. The University begins with the unremarkable proposition that the State must have substantial discretion in determining how to allocate scarce resources to accomplish its educational mission. Citing our [decision] in *Rust v. Sullivan*...the University argues that content-based funding decisions are both inevitable and lawful. Were the reasoning of *Lamb's Chapel* to apply to funding decisions as well as to those involving access to facilities, it is urged, its holding "would become a judicial juggernaut, constitutionalizing the ubiquitous content-based decisions that schools, colleges, and other government entities routinely make in the allocation of public funds."

To this end the University relies on our assurance in *Widmar v. Vincent*. There, in the course of striking down a public university's exclusion of religious groups from use of school facilities made available to all other student groups, we stated: "Nor do we question the right of the University to make academic judgments as to how best to allocate scarce resources." The quoted language in *Widmar* was but a proper recognition of the principle that when the State is the speaker, it may make content-based choices.... It does not follow, however, and we did not suggest in *Widmar*, that viewpoint-based restrictions are proper when the University does not itself speak or subsidize transmittal of a message it favors but instead expends funds to encourage a diversity of views from private speakers. A holding that the University may not discriminate based on the viewpoint of private persons whose speech it facilitates does not restrict the University's own speech, which is controlled by different principles....

The distinction between the University's own favored message and the private speech of students is evident in the case before us. The University itself has taken steps to ensure the distinction in the agreement each CIO must sign. The University declares that the student groups eligible for SAF support are not the University's agents, are not subject to its control, and are not its responsibility. Having offered to pay the third-party contractors on behalf of private speakers who convey their own messages, the University may not silence the expression of selected viewpoints....

Based on the principles we have discussed, we hold that the regulation invoked to deny SAF support, both in its terms and in its application to these petitioners, is a denial of their right of free speech guaranteed by the First Amendment. It remains to be considered whether the violation following from the University's action is excused by the necessity of complying with the Constitution's prohibition against state establishment of religion....

If there is to be assurance that the Establishment Clause retains its force in guarding against those governmental actions it was intended to prohibit, we must in each case inquire first into the purpose and object of the governmental action in question and then into the practical details of the program's operation.... The governmental program here is neutral toward religion. There is no suggestion that the University created it to advance religion or adopted some ingenious device with the purpose of aiding a religious cause. The object of the SAF is to open a forum for speech and to support various student enterprises, including the publication of newspapers, in recognition of the diversity and creativity of student life. The University's SAF Guidelines have a separate classification for, and do not make third-party payments on behalf of, "religious organizations," which are those "whose purpose is to practice a devotion to an acknowledged ultimate reality or deity." The category of support here is for "student news, information, opinion, entertainment, or academic communications media groups," of which Wide Awake was 1 of 15 in the 1990 school year. WAP did not seek a subsidy because of its Christian editorial viewpoint; it sought funding as a student journal, which it was.

The neutrality of the program distinguishes the student fees from a tax levied for the direct support of a church or group of churches. A tax of that sort, of course, would run contrary to Establishment Clause concerns dating from the earliest days of the Republic.... But the $14 paid each semester by the students is not a general tax designed to raise revenue for the University. The SAF cannot be used for unlimited purposes, much less the illegitimate purpose of supporting one religion. Much like the arrangement in *Widmar*, the money goes to a special fund from which any group of students with CIO status can draw for purposes consistent with the University's educational mission; and to the extent the student is interested in speech, withdrawal is permitted to cover the whole spectrum of speech, whether it manifests a religious view, an antireligious view, or neither. Our decision, then, cannot be read as addressing an expenditure from a general tax fund. Here, the disbursements from the fund go to private contractors for the cost of printing that which is protected under the Speech Clause of the First Amendment. This is a far cry from a general public assessment designed and effected to provide financial support for a church.

Government neutrality is apparent in the State's overall scheme in a further meaningful respect. The program respects the critical difference "between government speech endorsing religion, which the Establishment Clause forbids, and private speech endorsing religion, which the Free Speech and Free Exercise Clauses protect." In this case, "the government has not fostered or encouraged" any mistaken impression that the student newspapers speak for the University....

Were the dissent's view to become law, it would require the University, in order to avoid a constitutional violation, to scrutinize the content of student speech, lest the expression in question—speech otherwise protected by the Constitution—contain too great a religious content. The dissent, in fact, anticipates such censorship as "crucial" in distinguishing between "works characterized by the evangelism of Wide Awake and writing that merely happens to express views that a given religion might approve." That eventuality raises the specter of governmental censorship, to ensure that all student writings and publications meet some baseline standard of secular orthodoxy. To impose that standard on student speech at a university is to imperil the very sources of free speech and expression. As we recognized in *Widmar*, official censorship would be far more inconsistent with the Establishment Clause's dictates than would governmental provision of secular printing services on a religion-blind basis....

JUSTICE O'CONNOR, with whom THOMAS joins, concurring.

When two bedrock principles so conflict, understandably neither can provide the definitive answer. Reliance on categorical platitudes is unavailing. Resolution instead depends on the hard task of judging—sifting through the details and determining whether the challenged program offends the Establishment Clause. Such judgment requires courts to draw lines, sometimes quite fine, based on the particular facts of each case....

First, the student organizations, at the University's insistence, remain strictly independent of the University.... Second, financial assistance is distributed in a manner that ensures its use only for permissible purposes.... Third, assistance is provided to the religious publication in a context that makes improbable any perception of government endorsement of the religious message.... When bedrock principles collide, they test the limits of categorical obstinacy and expose the flaws and dangers of a Grand Unified Theory that may turn out to be neither grand nor unified. The Court today does only what courts must do in many Establishment Clause cases—focus on specific features of a particular government action to ensure that it does not violate the Constitution....

JUSTICE SOUTER, with whom STEVENS, GINSBURG, and BREYER join, dissenting.

The Court today, for the first time, approves direct funding of core religious activities by an arm of the State. It does so, however, only after erroneous treatment of some familiar principles of law implementing the First Amendment's Establishment and Speech Clauses, and by viewing the very funds in question as beyond the reach of the Establishment Clause's funding restrictions as such. Because there is no warrant for distinguishing among public funding sources for purposes of applying the First Amendment's prohibition of religious establishment, I would hold that the University's refusal to support petitioners' religious activities is compelled by the Establishment Clause....

The Court's difficulties will be all the more clear after a closer look at Wide Awake than the majority opinion affords. The character of the magazine is candidly disclosed on the opening page of the first issue, where the editor-in-chief announces Wide Awake's mission in a letter to the readership signed, "Love in Christ": it is "to challenge Christians to live, in word and deed, according to the faith they proclaim and to encourage students to consider what a personal relationship with Jesus Christ means." The masthead of every issue bears St. Paul's exhortation, that "the hour has come for you to awake from your slumber, because our salvation is nearer now than when we first believed. Romans 13:11." Each issue of Wide Awake contained in the record makes good on the editor's promise and echoes the Apostle's call to accept salvation: "The only way to salvation through Him is by confessing and repenting of sin. It is the Christian's duty to make sinners aware of their need for salvation. Thus, Christians must confront and condemn sin, or else they fail in their duty of love...."

> Using public funds for the direct subsidization of preaching the word is categorically forbidden under the Establishment Clause, and if the Clause was meant to accomplish nothing else, it was meant to bar this use of public money....

Read literally, the rules announced in *Rosenberger* seem to invite implausible conclusions. One way of interpreting the decision is that a public entity can exclude any expression that it wants to, including religious expression, merely by defining the purpose of its forum in an appropriately limited way. On this reading, the University of Virginia could avoid the effects of this case merely by reformulating the statement of purpose; instead of providing support for "extracurricular student activities that 'are related to the educational purpose of the University,'" it could propose to provide support for "*secular* extracurricular student activities that 'are related to the educational purpose of the University.'" The whole tenor of the majority opinion, however, suggests that this would not be acceptable. But if such a restriction in the definition of a forum is not acceptable, or if the issue involves anything more than the use of magic words, then how can *Rosenberger* be reconciled with *NEA v. Finley*?

In addition, Justice Kennedy's apparent acceptance of the exclusion of "religious organizations" from funding eligibility, combined with his aversion to university scrutiny of funded activities, points to a conclusion that discrimination against persons based on their religious viewpoint is permissible while discrimination against religious conduct is not, with the peculiar consequence that a state could refuse to fund a religious group's efforts to engage in secular activities but would be required to simultaneously fund a (putatively) secular group's program of religious or anti-religious proselytization, thus effectively rewarding dishonesty. Alternatively, if religion is literally never a content but always a viewpoint, religious proselytizing cannot be excluded from any forum regardless of its stated purpose, whether an association of gardening clubs, or an academic medical conference. None of these extreme interpretations, of course, were likely what Justice Kennedy had in mind. Furthermore, only a plurality of three justices clearly adopted Kennedy's reasoning. Therefore, while the meaning of *Rosenberger* was clear in its essential points—government funding programs may create limited public forums from which religious viewpoints may not be excluded—the results of applying these principles in a particular case continued to be a matter of speculation.

In 2001, the Court considered yet another twist on the fact patterns of access cases in *Good News Club v. Milford Central School*, 533 U.S. 98 (2001). In the town of Milford, Connecticut, the school board allowed classrooms to be used by community groups for discussions of matters "pertaining to the welfare of the community." Cognizant of the ruling in *Lamb's Chapel*, the school board established a rule that explicitly permitted "discussions of subjects such as child rearing, and 'the development of character and morals from a religious perspective.'" At the same time, the school board attempted to draw a content-based limit on the use of its classrooms by excluding religious activities, as opposed to discussions of approved topics from a religious perspective. The Good News Club's activities included religious services and discussions of Christian teachings.

By a 5-to-4 decision, the Court ruled that Milford's attempt at a distinction between content and viewpoint failed because religious activities include moral messages. "[I]t is clear," wrote Justice Thomas for the majority, "that the Club teaches morals and character development to children."

> For example, no one disputes that the Club instructs children to overcome feelings of jealousy, to treat others well regardless of how they treat the children, and to be obedient, even if it does so in a nonsecular way. We disagree that something that is "quintessentially religious" or "decidedly religious in nature" cannot also be characterized properly as the teaching of morals and character development from a particular viewpoint. What matters for purposes of the Free Speech Clause is that we can see no logical difference in kind between the invocation of Christianity by the Club and the invocation of teamwork, loyalty, or patriotism by other associations to provide a foundation for their lessons.... [W]e reaffirm our holdings in *Lamb's Chapel* and *Rosenberger* that speech discussing otherwise permissible subjects cannot be excluded from a limited public forum on the ground that the subject is discussed from a religious viewpoint. Thus, we conclude that Milford's exclusion of the Club from use of the school, pursuant to its community use policy, constitutes impermissible viewpoint discrimination. *Good News Club v. Milford Central School*, 2001 Lexis 4312 (2001).

To some extent, then, Justice Kennedy's dissolution of the distinction between content and viewpoint in the context of religion was bearing fruit. Religious services, according to *Good News Club*, are not different from religious organizations' discussions of moral issues, nor from academic discussions of how religious teachings might treat such issues. Once again, the question is whether the school board might have described the purpose of its limited forum in a way that would have accomplished its goals (to permit participation by religious groups while excluding religious services, or proselytizing) in a constitutionally permissible fashion.

The answer to the question of the limits of permissible forum design may lie in the second key element that *Good News Club* brought to *Lamb's Chapel* and *Rosenberger*. Justice Thomas's treatment of the Establishment Clause differed markedly from the way that clause had appeared in earlier access cases, reflecting current, recent trends in the development of the Court's understanding of the religion clauses. In *Agostini* and *Mitchell v. Helms*, the Court—by narrow 5-to-4 majorities—interpreted the Establishment Clause to require "neutrality" in the context of school funding. In his opinion in *Good News Club*, Justice Thomas applied the neutrality principle of the Establishment Clause in a way that came close to *requiring*, rather than permitting, the inclusion of religious expression in a wide range of limited forums:

> Milford's implication that granting access to the Club would do damage to the neutrality principle defies logic. For the "guarantee of neutrality is respected, not offended, when the government, following neutral criteria and evenhanded policies, extends benefits to recipients whose ideologies and viewpoints, including religious ones, are broad and diverse." The Good News Club seeks nothing more than to be treated neutrally and given access to speak about the same topics as are other groups. Because allowing the Club to speak on school grounds would ensure neutrality, not threaten it, Milford faces an uphill battle in arguing that the Establishment Clause compels it to exclude the Good News Club. *Good News Club v. Milford Central School*, 2001 Lexis 4312 (2001).

Since Justice Thomas had previously declared that a "religious viewpoint" included teaching religious doctrine as it applied to the subject matter, the implication was that Establishment Clause neutrality would preclude defining a limited forum in a way that distinguished religious practice from a religious perspective.

Milford also attempted to invoke the endorsement/coercion approach of *Lee v. Weisman* and *Santa Fe School District v. Doe*. "According to Milford, children will perceive that the school is endorsing the Club and will feel coercive pressure to participate, because the Club's activities take place on school grounds, even though they occur during nonschool hours." Justice Thomas, however, found this argument "unpersuasive" on its facts:

> [T]o the extent we consider whether the community would feel coercive pressure to engage in the Club's activities, the relevant community would be the parents, not the elementary school children.... Because the children cannot attend without their parents' permission, they cannot be coerced into engaging in the Good News Club's religious activities. Milford does not suggest that the parents of elementary school children would be confused about whether the school was endorsing religion. Nor do we believe that such an argument could be reasonably advanced. *Good News Club v. Milford Central School*, 2001 Lexis 4312 (2001).

The fact that the children in question were of elementary school age rather than college students, as in *Widmar*, was not dispositive. "[W]e have never extended our Establishment Clause jurisprudence to foreclose private religious conduct during nonschool hours merely because it takes place on school premises where elementary school children may be present. None of the cases discussed by Milford persuades us that our Establishment Clause jurisprudence has gone this far."

Justice Thomas also concluded that there was no reasonable risk of a perception of endorsement on the particular facts of the case. It was in the context of this argument that Thomas crafted what is potentially the most far-reaching application of the neutrality principle, when he insisted that the absence of religious expression was as significant as its presence. "Finally, even if we were to inquire into the minds of schoolchildren in this case, we cannot say the danger that children would misperceive the endorsement of religion is any greater than the danger that they would perceive a hostility toward the religious viewpoint if the Club were excluded from the public forum." *Good News Club v. Milford Central School*, 2001 Lexis 4312 (2001). Once again, the effect of Justice Thomas's neutrality analysis appears to be that the Establishment Clause requires, rather than merely permits, state support for religious expression if support is provided for expression generally, since the absence of such support might be perceived as "hostility toward the religious viewpoint." If the state does not visibly provide access to school property for religious activities, by this argument, school-children will perceive that it has cast its lot with religion's enemies (presumably either atheists or adherents of a different, incommensurate faith).

Justice Scalia, concurring, wrote separately to emphasize his view that the "coercion" approach of *Lee v. Weisman* was wrongheaded. He wrote that he agreed with the majority's treatment of the endorsement and coercion issues because the outcome reached by the majority "to the extent that the law makes such factors relevant, is consistent with the belief (which I hold) that in this case that extent is zero." Scalia argued that the only "coercion" at work was the persuasiveness of the ideas that the Good News Club promulgated. "A priest," he wrote, "has as much liberty to proselytize as a patriot." Justice Breyer also concurred, but on procedural grounds; he thought the case should have been sent back to the trial court for a further development of the factual record.

Justices Stevens, Souter, and Ginsburg dissented, finding enough in the facts before them to reach a conclusion different from that of the majority. Justice Souter argued that the Good News Club had been engaged in holding religious services, an activity distinguishable in its content—rather than its viewpoint—from the purpose of the forum. In addition, Souter observed that unlike *Widmar* or *Lamb's Chapel*, the Good News Club was open only to elementary students, and of the four groups that held meetings in the school, only the Good News Club held its meetings immediately at the close of school:

> Although school is out at 2:56 p.m., Good News apparently requested use of the school beginning at 2:30 on Tuesdays during the school year, so that instruction could begin promptly at 3:00, at which time children who are compelled by law to attend school surely remain in the building. Good News's religious meeting follows regular school activities so closely that the Good News instructor must wait to begin until "the room is clear," and "people are out of the room" before starting proceedings in the classroom located next to the regular third- and fourth-grade rooms. *Good News Club v. Milford Central School*, 2001 Lexis 4312 (2001).

Based on these facts, and his general acceptance of the endorsement test, Souter would have found the activities of the Good News Club to create an impermissible impression of government endorsement of religion.

Between *Rosenberger* and *Good News Club*, the Court considered one other question concerning the right of access to government support for expression. The access cases had already provided a platform for a reexamination of the public forum doctrine, the reach of the Establishment Clause, and the content-viewpoint distinction. Did they also require a reconsideration of the meaning of compelled speech? That was the question in *Bd. of Regents of the University of Wisconsin System v. Southworth*, 529 U.S. 217 (2000). Like the University of Virginia, the University of Wisconsin had a system of mandatory student fees that it used, in part, to fund student groups engaged in various kinds of expression. Scott Southworth and a group of fellow students objected to the fact that their money was being used to support speech which they found offensive. Southworth argued that this constituted compelled speech and was therefore unconstitutional under *Abood* and *Keller*. Unlike the case in *Rosenberger*, there was no issue of viewpoint discrimination in the case, as the parties stipulated to the fact that the funding system was viewpoint-neutral. (A separate part of the funding system, used exclusively to fund the Wisconsin Public Interest Research Group, was run on the basis of a referendum. The Court concluded that this element of the system was not viewpoint-neutral and ruled it unconstitutional under *Rosenberger*.) *Southworth*, therefore, presented the Court with the question of whether the principle against compelled speech created a right to opt out of a forum. Unlike the other access cases, this time the opinion was 9 to 0. The other access cases had stood for the proposition that once a university created a forum, it could not impose restrictions on the expression that entered into that forum. *Southworth* stood for the proposition that the university had the authority to create a forum in the first place, and that participants in a forum had no authority to demand that the university distinguish between different kinds of expression in the distribution of funds.

BOARD OF REGENTS OF THE UNIVERSITY OF WISCONSIN SYSTEM v. SOUTHWORTH

SUPREME COURT OF THE UNITED STATES

529 U.S. 217 (2000)

JUSTICE KENNEDY delivered the opinion of the Court, in which REHNQUIST, C. J., and O'CONNOR, SCALIA, THOMAS, and GINSBURG joined. JUSTICE SOUTER filed an opinion concurring in the judgment, in which STEVENS and BREYER joined.

...It is inevitable that government will adopt and pursue programs and policies within its constitutional powers but which nevertheless are contrary to the profound beliefs and sincere convictions of some of its citizens. The government, as a general rule, may support valid programs and policies by taxes or other exactions binding on protesting parties. Within this broader principle it seems inevitable that funds raised by the government will be spent for speech and other expression to advocate and defend its own policies. See, e.g., *Rust v. Sullivan*, 500 U.S. 173 (1991). The case we decide here, however, does not raise the issue of the government's right, or, to be more specific, the state-controlled University's right, to use its own funds to advance a particular message. The University's whole justification for fostering the challenged expression is that it springs from the initiative of the students, who alone give it purpose and content in the course of their extracurricular endeavors.

The University having disclaimed that the speech is its own, we do not reach the question whether traditional political controls to ensure responsible government action would be sufficient to overcome First Amendment objections and to allow the challenged program under the principle that the government can speak for itself. If the challenged speech here were financed by tuition dollars and the University and its officials were responsible for its content, the case might be evaluated on the premise that the government itself is the speaker. That is not the case before us.

The University of Wisconsin exacts the fee at issue for the sole purpose of facilitating the free and open exchange of ideas by, and among, its students. We conclude the objecting students may insist upon certain safeguards with respect to the expressive activities which they are required to support. Our public forum cases are instructive here by close analogy. This is true even though the student activities fund is not a public forum in the traditional sense of the term and despite the circumstance that those cases most often involve a demand for access, not a claim to be exempt from supporting speech. The standard of viewpoint neutrality found in the public forum cases provides the standard we find controlling. We decide that the viewpoint neutrality requirement of the University program is in general sufficient to protect the rights of the objecting students. The student referendum aspect of the program for funding speech and expressive activities, however, appears to be inconsistent with the viewpoint neutrality requirement....

The proposition that students who attend the University cannot be required to pay subsidies for the speech of other students without some First Amendment protection follows from the *Abood* and *Keller* cases. Students enroll in public universities to seek fulfillment of their personal aspirations and of their own potential. If the University conditions the opportunity to receive a college education, an opportunity comparable in importance to joining a labor union or bar association, on an agreement to support objectionable, extracurricular expression by other students, the rights acknowledged in *Abood* and *Keller* become implicated. It infringes on the speech and beliefs of the individual to be required, by this mandatory student activity fee program, to pay subsidies for the objectionable speech of others without any recognition of the State's corresponding duty to him or her. Yet recognition must be given as well to the important and substantial purposes of the University, which seeks to facilitate a wide range of speech.

In *Abood* and *Keller* the constitutional rule took the form of limiting the required subsidy to speech germane to the purposes of the union or bar association. The standard of germane speech as applied to student speech at a university is unworkable, however, and gives insufficient protection both to the objecting students and to the University program itself. Even in the context of a labor union, whose functions are, or so we might have thought, well known and understood by the law and the courts after a long history of government regulation and judicial involvement, we have encountered difficulties in deciding what is germane and what is not.... If it is difficult to define germane speech with ease or precision where a union or bar association is the party, the standard becomes all the more unmanageable in the public university setting, particularly where the State undertakes to stimulate the whole universe of speech and ideas.

The speech the University seeks to encourage in the program before us is distinguished not by discernable limits but by its vast, unexplored bounds. To insist upon asking what speech is germane would be contrary to the very goal the University seeks to pursue....

The University must provide some protection to its students' First Amendment interests, however. The proper measure, and the principal standard of protection for objecting students, we conclude, is the requirement of viewpoint neutrality in the allocation of funding support. Viewpoint neutrality was the obligation to which we gave substance in *Rosenberger v. Rector and Visitors of Univ. of Va.*... While *Rosenberger* was concerned with the rights a student has to use an extracurricular speech program already in place, today's case considers the antecedent question, acknowledged but unresolved in *Rosenberger*: whether a public university may require its students to pay a fee which creates the mechanism for the extracurricular speech in the first instance. When a university requires its students to pay fees to support the extracurricular speech of other students, all in the interest of open discussion, it may not prefer some viewpoints to others. There is symmetry then in our holding here and in *Rosenberger*: Viewpoint neutrality is the justification for requiring the student to pay the fee in the first instance and for ensuring the integrity of the program's operation once the funds have been collected. We conclude that the University of Wisconsin may sustain the extracurricular dimensions of its programs by using mandatory student fees....

For those who suspected (or feared) that *Lamb's Chapel* and *Rosenberger* meant only that the majority of the Court had special solicitude for religion, *Southworth* came as a reminder that constitutional principles extend beyond the case and litigants at hand. *Rosenberger* had left open the question of the authority of a university or other public authority to create and tailor a forum; *Southworth* partly answered the question. Even after both *Southworth* and *Good News Club*, however, the question of whether it is possible for a public authority to create a forum in such a way as to permit the exclusion of religious services remains open. Furthermore, Justice Kennedy noted in *Southworth* that the case might have been different if the university had been using tuition dollars rather than a separate fee. The distinction between the two situations is, presumably, intended to illuminate a line that divides *Rosenberger* from *NEA v. Finley*, but the substantive basis for that distinction remains unclear. Is the question one of formal semantics, such that a university that describes its program as "a forum for secular discussions," or describes its student activities fees as "ancillary tuition payments," thereby avoids the viewpoint-neutrality requirements developed in the access cases? If not, what factors should courts consider in distinguishing between government-funded expression and government-funding-as-forum? Is religion a unique case, or is the viewpoint-content distinction vulnerable to challenge across a spectrum of perspectives? These questions remain unanswered, and will undoubtedly be the subject of considerable analysis in future access cases. What is clear is that the First Amendment doctrines that have emerged from cases involving access to public resources are among the most significant, as well as the most controversial, areas of development in the current Court.

VIII. Freedom of the Press

None of the rights mentioned in the First Amendment were more central to the eighteenth-century American conception of a free political system than the freedom of the press. The rights of a free press have to a great extent been discussed in the course of various aspects of our examination of free speech. The *Zenger* case, for example, that announced the principle (if not the legal rule) that truth is a defense to suits for libel, was based on a publication. The "clear and present danger test" was most often applied to review of laws designed and applied to suppress printed expression. Similarly, the cases that defined the scope and constitutional status of "obscenity" involved attempts to criminalize publications. All of these involved the products of the press, but all of them were dealt with primarily on the basis of general principles of free speech. In this chapter, then, we will look at the development of First Amendment principles that are specific to the operation of a free press, taking it as given that the press is covered by the general protections of free speech.

A. *Prior Restraints*

In the English Common Law tradition, as noted earlier, there was no generalized understanding of a freedom of speech or the press, only a principle of opposition to "prior restraint." The difference between prior restraint and subsequent punishment may seem unclear to modern ears. "Prior restraint" referred to an order banning the publication of materials, or only permitting the publication of specific materials in the tradition of the Church imprimatur. An edict from the King saying that no pamphlet, journal, or book containing criticism of the Church of England could be printed or sold in England would be an example of prior restraint. (The alternative way to deal with problematic publications is to punish the author or publisher after they appear.)

The special importance attached to the press as an element of American democracy has led to a deep suspicion of prior restraints. The Supreme Court issued its first important treatment of prior restraints on the press in 1931. A Minnesota paper had published a series of articles which combined antisemitic rantings with accusations that named public officials were involved in organized crime. "There have been too many men in this city and especially those in official life, who HAVE been taking orders and suggestions from JEW GANGSTERS, therefore we HAVE Jew Gangsters, practically ruling Minneapolis" was a typical statement in one of the articles. The state government sued, and obtained an injunction prohibiting the publisher from producing anything "which is a malicious, scandalous or defamatory newspaper" under a state law authorizing the "abatement" of such publications. By a 5-to-4 vote, the Supreme Court struck down the ordinance in *Near v. Minnesota*.

NEAR v. MINNESOTA

SUPREME COURT OF THE UNITED STATES

283 U.S. 697 (1931)

CHIEF JUSTICE HUGHES delivered the opinion of the Court.

...The question is whether a statute authorizing such proceedings in restraint of publication is consistent with the conception of the liberty of the press as historically conceived and guaranteed. In determining the extent of the constitutional protection, it has been generally, if not universally, considered that it is the chief purpose of the guaranty to prevent previous restraints upon publication. The struggle in England, directed against the legislative power of the licenser, resulted in renunciation of the censorship of the press. The liberty deemed to be established was thus described by Blackstone: "The liberty of the press is indeed essential to the nature of a free state; but this consists in laying no previous restraints upon publications, and not in freedom from censure for criminal matter when published. Every freeman has an undoubted right to lay what sentiments he pleases before the public; to forbid this, is to destroy the freedom of the press; but if he publishes what is improper, mischievous or illegal, he must take the consequence of his own temerity." The distinction was early pointed out between the extent of the freedom with respect to censorship under our constitutional system and that enjoyed in England. Here, as Madison said, "the great and essential rights of the people are secured against legislative as well as against executive ambition. They are secured, not by laws paramount to prerogative, but by constitutions paramount to laws. This security of the freedom of the press requires that it should be exempt not only from previous restraint by the Executive, as in Great Britain, but from legislative restraint also." *Report on the Virginia Resolutions*....

[I]t is recognized that punishment for the abuse of the liberty accorded to the press is essential to the protection of the public, and that the common law rules that subject the libeler to responsibility for the public offense, as well as for the private injury, are not abolished by the protection extended in our constitutions. The law of criminal libel rests upon that secure foundation. There is also the conceded authority of courts to punish for contempt when publications directly tend to prevent the proper discharge of judicial functions. In the present case, we have no occasion to inquire as to the permissible scope of subsequent punishment. For whatever wrong the appellant has committed or may commit, by his publications, the State appropriately affords both public and private redress by its libel laws. As has been noted, the statute in question does not deal with punishments; it provides for no punishment, except in case of contempt for violation of the court's order, but for suppression and injunction, that is, for restraint upon publication.

The objection has also been made that the principle as to immunity from previous restraint is stated too broadly, if every such restraint is deemed to be prohibited. That is undoubtedly true; the protection even as to previous restraint is not absolutely unlimited. But the limitation has been recognized only in exceptional cases.... No one would question but that a government might prevent actual obstruction to its recruiting service or the publication of the sailing dates of transports or the number and location of troops. On similar grounds, the primary requirements of decency may be enforced against obscene publications. The security of the community life may be protected against incitements to acts of violence and the overthrow by force of orderly government. The constitutional guaranty of free speech does not protect a man from an injunction against uttering words that may have all the effect of force. These limitations are not applicable here....

The conception of the liberty of the press in this country had broadened with the exigencies of the colonial period and with the efforts to secure freedom from oppressive administration. That liberty was especially cherished for the immunity it afforded from previous restraint of the publication of censure of public officers and charges of official misconduct.... Madison, who was the leading spirit in the preparation of the First Amendment of the Federal Constitution, thus described the practice and sentiment which led to the guaranties of liberty of the press in state constitutions: "In every State, probably, in the Union, the press has exerted a freedom in canvassing the merits and measures of public men of every description which has not been confined to the strict limits of the common law. On this footing the freedom of the press has stood; on this footing it yet stands.... Some degree of abuse is inseparable from the proper use of everything, and in no instance is this more true than in that of the press. It has accordingly been decided by the practice of the States, that it is better to leave a few of its noxious branches to their luxuriant growth, than, by pruning them away, to injure the vigour of those yielding the proper fruits" *Report on the Virginia Resolutions*....

The importance of this immunity has not lessened. While reckless assaults upon public men, and efforts to bring obloquy upon those who are endeavoring faithfully to discharge official duties, exert a baleful influence and deserve the severest condemnation in public opinion, it cannot be said that this abuse is greater, and it is believed to be less, than that which characterized the period in which our institutions took shape. Meanwhile, the administration of government has become more complex, the opportunities for malfeasance and corruption have multiplied, crime has grown to most serious proportions, and the danger of its protection by unfaithful officials and of the impairment of the fundamental security of life and property by criminal alliances and official neglect, emphasizes the primary need of a vigilant and courageous press, especially in great cities. The fact that the liberty of the press may be abused by miscreant purveyors of scandal does not make any the less necessary the immunity of the press from previous restraint in dealing with official misconduct. Subsequent punishment for such abuses as may exist is the appropriate remedy, consistent with constitutional privilege....

The statute in question cannot be justified by reason of the fact that the publisher is permitted to show, before injunction issues, that the matter published is true and is published with good motives and for justifiable ends. If such a statute, authorizing suppression and injunction on such a basis, is constitutionally valid, it would be equally permissible for the legislature to provide that at any time the publisher of any newspaper could be brought before a court, or even an administrative officer (as the constitutional protection may not be regarded as resting on mere procedural details) and required to produce proof of the truth of his publication, or of what he intended to publish, and of his motives, or stand enjoined. If this can be done, the legislature may provide machinery for determining in the complete exercise of its discretion what are justifiable ends and restrain publication accordingly. And it would be but a step to a complete system of censorship. The recognition of authority to impose previous restraint upon publication in order to protect the community against the circulation of charges of misconduct, and especially of official misconduct, necessarily would carry with it the admission of the authority of the censor against which the constitutional barrier was erected. The preliminary freedom, by virtue of the very reason for its existence, does not depend, as this Court has said, on proof of truth.

Equally unavailing is the insistence that the statute is designed to prevent the circulation of scandal which tends to disturb the public peace and to provoke assaults and the commission of crime. Charges of reprehensible conduct, and in particular of official malfeasance, unquestionably create a public scandal, but the theory of the constitutional guaranty is that even a more serious public evil would be caused by authority to prevent publication.... The danger of violent reactions becomes greater with effective organization of defiant groups resenting exposure, and if this consideration warranted legislative interference with the initial freedom of publication, the constitutional protection would be reduced to a mere form of words.

For these reasons we hold the statute...to be an infringement of the liberty of the press guaranteed by the Fourteenth Amendment....

JUSTICE BUTLER, dissenting, joined by JUSTICE VAN DEVANTER, JUSTICE McREYNOLDS, and JUSTICE SUTHERLAND.

The decision of the Court in this case declares Minnesota and every other State powerless to restrain by injunction the business of publishing and circulating among the people malicious, scandalous and defamatory periodicals that in due course of judicial procedure has been adjudged to be a public nuisance. It gives to freedom of the press a meaning and a scope not heretofore recognized and construes "liberty" in the due process clause of the Fourteenth Amendment to put upon the States a federal restriction that is without precedent....

The record shows, and it is conceded, that defendants' regular business was the publication of malicious, scandalous and defamatory articles concerning the principal public officers, leading newspapers of the city, many private persons and the Jewish race. It also shows that it was their purpose at all hazards to continue to carry on the business. In every edition slanderous and defamatory matter predominates to the practical exclusion of all else. Many of the statements are so highly improbable as to compel a finding that they are false. The articles themselves show malice....

The dissenting justices drew a connection between the general principle against prior restraints and the categorical approach that defines "libel" as an unprotected category of expression. By this argument, the scope of the freedom of the press is no greater than the scope of the freedom of expression generally; hence libelous statements are outside the scope of press freedoms. The issue of libel, in particular, has been one of the most contentious areas of constitutional development in the area of press freedoms. To be sure, the press must be free to fulfill its appointed political purpose, but when does it go too far? Recall that Jefferson, who wrote so eloquently against the Alien and Sedition Acts, had no hesitation about recommending "a few salutary prosecutions" under state law—e.g., the law of libel—to restrain the excesses of a partisan Federalist press critical of his own administration. When does political criticism cross the line into actionable libel, and are the standards different for the press than for anyone else, and does it matter whether the target of the alleged libel is a public official?

Libel was not the only basis on which government has attempted to seek prior restraints on the press in modern times. Probably no case in modern history (until, perhaps, *Bush v. Gore* in 2000) thrust the Court into the political debates of the times more than *New York Times Co. v. United States*, 403 U.S. 713 (1971). The case involved a forty-seven-volume secret Pentagon report tracing the history of American involvement in Viet Nam through 1968 known as "the Pentagon Papers." The contents of the secret report were immensely embarrassing to the United States government, casting doubt on the veracity of two administrations and the Defense Department in their presentation of the conflicts to the American public and to Congress. A Defense Department analyst named Daniel Ellsberg leaked the report to the *New York Times* and the *Washington Post*, both of whom planned to publish excerpts. The United States went to court and secured an injunction preventing the publication of the materials, claiming that their publication would damage national security.

The case produced a per curiam opinion for the Court barely two paragraphs long, and nine separate opinions—six concurring, three dissenting—from the individual justices. In general, however, the nine opinions centered around two competing arguments. The majority (Black, Douglas, Brennan, Stewart, White, and Marshall) argued that prior restraints on publication were automatically suspect, and that the Executive branch should not be able to use the courts to create what Justice Marshall called "government by injunction." Black and Douglas argued that the press must be left unrestrained to publish matters of public concern, and that "the guarding of military and diplomatic secrets at the expense of informed representative government was not justified." Brennan took a less absolutist attitude toward the issue of what might be published, but declared an absolute opposition to prior restraints in the form of injunctions. Brennan also remarked on the extraordinary circumstances of the case. "So far as I can determine," he wrote "never before has the United States sought to enjoin a newspaper from publishing information in its possession." Stewart, White, and Marshall focused on the doctrine of separation of powers, concluding that the Executive had gone to the Judiciary to obtain an order that would have the effect of determining a question (the secrecy of the materials involved) that ought properly to be decided by the Legislature. White, in particular, took pains to observe that his objections to the use of a court-ordered injunction did not imply that there could not be criminal penalties imposed on the two papers in a later court proceeding under laws properly enacted by Congress.

The dissenters, Burger, Harlan, and Blackmun, all focused on the same thing: the case had been decided too quickly, under too much pressure, without adequate review of either the record or the law. In addition, all three expressed concerns that an unduly absolutist interpretation of the free press clause was creating a situation in which the courts were interfering with the Executive's exercise of its authority over foreign affairs under Article II. Burger, finally, additionally argued that a newspaper, like any other citizen, had a responsibility to voluntarily submit classified materials that came into its possession to the government for review and permission before publishing them.

NEW YORK TIMES CO. v. UNITED STATES

SUPREME COURT OF THE UNITED STATES

403 U.S. 713 (1971)

Per Curiam

Any system of prior restraints of expression comes to this Court bearing a heavy presumption against its constitutional validity. The Government thus carries a heavy burden of showing justification for the imposition of such a restraint. The District Court for the Southern District of New York in the *New York Times* case and the District Court for the District of Columbia and the Court of Appeals for the District of Columbia Circuit in the *Washington Post* case held that the Government had not met that burden. We agree....

JUSTICE BLACK, with whom JUSTICE DOUGLAS joins, concurring.

...In the First Amendment the Founding Fathers gave the free press the protection it must have to fulfill its essential role in our democracy. The press was to serve the governed, not the governors. The Government's power to censor the press was abolished so that the press would remain forever free to censure the Government. The press was protected so that it could bare the secrets of government and inform the people. Only a free and unrestrained press can effectively expose deception in government. And paramount among the responsibilities of a free press is the duty to prevent any part of the government from deceiving the people and sending them off to distant lands to die of foreign fevers and foreign shot and shell. In my view, far from deserving condemnation for their courageous reporting, the *New York Times*, the *Washington Post*, and other newspapers should be commended for serving the purpose that the Founding Fathers saw so clearly. In revealing the workings of government that led to the Vietnam war, the newspapers nobly did precisely that which the Founders hoped and trusted they would do.

The Government's case here is based on premises entirely different from those that guided the Framers of the First Amendment.... [W]e are asked to hold that despite the First Amendment's emphatic command, the Executive Branch, the Congress, and the Judiciary can make laws enjoining publication of current news and abridging freedom of the press in the name of "national security." The Government does not even attempt to rely on any act of Congress. Instead it makes the bold and dangerously far-reaching contention that the courts should take it upon themselves to "make" a law abridging freedom of the press in the name of equity, presidential power and national security, even when the representatives of the people in Congress have adhered to the command of the First Amendment and refused to make such a law. To find that the President has "inherent power" to halt the publication of news by resort to the courts would wipe out the First Amendment and destroy the fundamental liberty and security of the very people the Government hopes to make "secure." No one can read the history of the adoption of the First Amendment without being convinced beyond any doubt that it was injunctions like those sought here that Madison and his collaborators intended to outlaw in this Nation for all time....

JUSTICE DOUGLAS, with whom JUSTICE BLACK joins, concurring.

...[T]he First Amendment provides that "Congress shall make no law... abridging the freedom of speech, or of the press." That leaves, in my view, no room for governmental restraint on the press. There is, moreover, no statute barring the publication by the press of the material which the *Times* and the *Post* seek to use.... Thus Congress has been faithful to the command of the First Amendment in this area. So any power that the Government possesses must come from its "inherent power." The power to wage war is "the power to wage war successfully." But the war power stems from a declaration of war. The Constitution by Art. I, § 8, gives Congress, not the President, power "to declare War." Nowhere are presidential wars authorized. We need not decide therefore what leveling effect the war power of Congress might have.... The Government says that it has inherent powers to go into court and obtain an injunction to protect the national interest, which in this case is alleged to be national security. *Near v. Minnesota*, 283 U.S. 697, repudiated that expansive doctrine in no uncertain terms. The dominant purpose of the First Amendment was to prohibit the widespread practice of governmental suppression of embarrassing information. It is common knowledge that the First Amendment was adopted against the widespread use of the common law of seditious libel to punish the dissemination of material that is embarrassing to the powers-that-be. The present cases will, I think, go down in history as the most dramatic illustration of that principle. A debate of large proportions goes on in the Nation over our posture in Vietnam. That debate antedated the disclosure of the contents of the present documents. The latter are highly relevant to the debate in progress....

JUSTICE WHITE, with whom JUSTICE STEWART joins, concurring.

...The Government's position is simply stated: The responsibility of the Executive for the conduct of the foreign affairs and for the security of the Nation is so basic that the President is entitled to an injunction against publication of a newspaper story whenever he can convince a court that the information to be revealed threatens "grave and irreparable" injury to the public interest; and the injunction should issue whether or not the material to be published is classified, whether or not publication would be lawful under relevant criminal statutes enacted by Congress, and regardless of the circumstances by which the newspaper came into possession of the information.

At least in the absence of legislation by Congress, based on its own investigations and findings, I am quite unable to agree that the inherent powers of the Executive and the courts reach so far as to authorize remedies having such sweeping potential for inhibiting publications by the press.... The Criminal Code contains numerous provisions potentially relevant to these cases. Section 797 makes it a crime to publish certain photographs or drawings of military installations. Section 798, also in precise language, proscribes knowing and willful publication of any classified information concerning the cryptographic systems or communication intelligence activities of the United States as well as any information obtained from communication intelligence operations. If any of the material here at issue is of this nature, the newspapers are presumably now on full notice of the position of the United States and must face the consequences if they publish. I would have no difficulty in sustaining convictions under these sections on facts that would not justify the intervention of equity and the imposition of a prior restraint.

JUSTICE MARSHALL, concurring.

...It would...be utterly inconsistent with the concept of separation of powers for this Court to use its power of contempt to prevent behavior that Congress has specifically declined to prohibit. There would be a similar damage to the basic concept of these co-equal branches of Government if when the Executive Branch has adequate authority granted by Congress to protect "national security" it can choose instead to invoke the contempt power of a court to enjoin the threatened conduct. The Constitution provides that Congress shall make laws, the President execute laws, and courts interpret laws. It did not provide for government by injunction in which the courts and the Executive Branch can "make law" without regard to the action of Congress. It may be more convenient for the Executive Branch if it need only convince a judge to prohibit conduct rather than ask the Congress to pass a law, and it may be more convenient to enforce a contempt order than to seek a criminal conviction in a jury trial. Moreover, it may be considered politically wise to get a court to share the responsibility for arresting those who the Executive Branch has probable cause to believe are violating the law. But convenience and political considerations of the moment do not justify a basic departure from the principles of our system of government....

CHIEF JUSTICE BURGER, dissenting.

...In these cases, the imperative of a free and unfettered press comes into collision with another imperative, the effective functioning of a complex modern government and specifically the effective exercise of certain constitutional powers of the Executive. Only those who view the First Amendment as an absolute in all circumstances—a view I respect, but reject—can find such cases as these to be simple or easy.

These cases are not simple for another and more immediate reason. We do not know the facts of the cases. No District Judge knew all the facts. No Court of Appeals judge knew all the facts. No member of this Court knows all the facts. Why are we in this posture, in which only those judges to whom the First Amendment is absolute and permits of no restraint in any circumstances or for any reason, are really in a position to act? I suggest we are in this posture because these cases have been conducted in unseemly haste.... It is not disputed that the *Times* has had unauthorized possession of the documents for three to four months, during which it has had its expert analysts studying them, presumably digesting them and preparing the material for publication. During all of this time, the *Times*, presumably in its capacity as trustee of the public's "right to know," has held up publication for purposes it considered proper and thus public knowledge was delayed.... Would it have been unreasonable, since the newspaper could anticipate the Government's objections to release of secret material, to give the Government an opportunity to review the entire collection and determine whether agreement could be reached on publication? Stolen or not, if security was not in fact jeopardized, much of the material could no doubt have been declassified, since it spans a period ending in 1968. With such an approach—one that great newspapers have in the past practiced and stated editorially to be the duty of an honorable press—the newspapers and Government might well have narrowed the area of disagreement as to what was and was not publishable, leaving the remainder to be resolved in orderly litigation, if necessary. To me it is hardly believable that a newspaper long regarded as a great institution in American life would fail to perform one of the basic and simple duties of every citizen with respect to the discovery or possession of stolen property or secret government documents. That duty, I had thought—perhaps naively—was to report forthwith, to responsible public officers. This duty rests on taxi drivers, Justices, and the *New York Times*. The course followed by the *Times*, whether so calculated or not, removed any possibility of orderly litigation of the issues. If the action of the judges up to now has been correct, that result is sheer happenstance....

Reading the opinions, it is difficult to escape the impression that many of the justices simply disbelieved the government's claims. As Chief Justice Burger pointed out, the events in the classified reports were all at least three years old. The dissenting justices objected to the procedures that had been followed, but they, too, gave notice that on a more thorough review they were prepared to rule against the government in reference to some significant portion of the Pentagon Papers. The government had not come forward and identified particular secrets that were essential to national security; instead it had sought a permanent injunction on publication of the entire forty-seven volumes. And both the concurring and dissenting justices observed that under the laws enacted by Congress, much of the material contained in the reports could not properly be classified as "secret" in the first place. It seems likely that in a different case, one in which a government whose credibility is less tarnished identifies specific items and makes a plausible case for preventing their publication, a future Court might be more willing to consider permitting an injunction to remain in place.

B. *Libel and Invasion of Privacy*

The Pentagon Papers case, in 1971, was not the first time the *New York Times* found itself before the Court in a First Amendment case. In 1964, the *New York Times* was sued by one of the City Commissioners of Montgomery, Alabama. The basis for the libel suit was a paid advertisement, signed by sixty-four prominent civil rights leaders, which decried the violence against civil rights marchers that had taken place in Montgomery. Two allegations, in particular, were the basis for the libel claim:

> In Montgomery, Alabama, after students sang "My Country, 'Tis of Thee" on the State Capitol steps, their leaders were expelled from school, and truckloads of police armed with shotguns and tear-gas ringed the Alabama State College Campus...Again and again the Southern violators have answered Dr. King's peaceful protests with intimidation and violence. They have bombed his home almost killing his wife and child. They have assaulted his person. They have arrested him seven times—for "speeding," "loitering" and similar "offenses." And now they have charged him with "perjury"—a felony under which they could imprison him for ten years."

Although Commissioner Sullivan was never named in the advertisement, he claimed that the references to "police" and "arrested" would suggest to readers that he was personally responsible for the acts alleged in the ad. The majority noted, first, that the allegations in the ad were not correct: the song that had been sung was the national anthem, not "My Country 'Tis of Thee," Dr. King had only been arrested four times, and there was no evidence that the police were implicated in the bombing of his home (assuming that the paragraph complained of could be read to imply the contrary). Commissioner Sullivan did not present evidence to show that he had suffered any monetary damages, but Alabama law permitted an action for "libel per se," which would permit the recovery of punitive damages. The case reached the Court on the basis of the *New York Times'* argument that Alabama's libel law violated the First Amendment, but the opinion went much farther than that.

NEW YORK TIMES CO. v. SULLIVAN

SUPREME COURT OF THE UNITED STATES

376 U.S. 254 (1964)

JUSTICE BRENNAN delivered the opinion of the Court.

...The question before us is whether this rule of liability, as applied to an action brought by a public official against critics of his official conduct, abridges the freedom of speech and of the press that is guaranteed by the First and Fourteenth Amendments.

Respondent relies heavily, as did the Alabama courts, on statements of this Court to the effect that the Constitution does not protect libelous publications. Those statements do not foreclose our inquiry here. None of the cases sustained the use of libel laws to impose sanctions upon expression critical of the official conduct of public officials.... In *Beauharnais v. Illinois*, 343 U.S. 250, the Court sustained an Illinois criminal libel statute as applied to a publication held to be both defamatory of a racial group and "liable to cause violence and disorder." But the Court was careful to note that it "retains and exercises authority to nullify action which encroaches on freedom of utterance under the guise of punishing libel"; for "public men, are, as it were, public property, and "discussion cannot be denied and the right, as well as the duty, of criticism must not be stifled...." Like insurrection, contempt, advocacy of unlawful acts, breach of the peace, obscenity, solicitation of legal business, and the various other formulae for the repression of expression that have been challenged in this Court, libel can claim no talismanic immunity from constitutional limitations. It must be measured by standards that satisfy the First Amendment.

The general proposition that freedom of expression upon public questions is secured by the First Amendment has long been settled by our decisions. The constitutional safeguard, we have said, "was fashioned to assure unfettered interchange of ideas for the bringing about of political and social changes desired by the people...." Thus we consider this case against the background of a profound national commitment to the principle that debate on public issues should be uninhibited, robust, and wide-open, and that it may well include vehement, caustic, and sometimes unpleasantly sharp attacks on government and public officials. The present advertisement, as an expression of grievance and protest on one of the major public issues of our time, would seem clearly to qualify for the constitutional protection. The question is whether it forfeits that protection by the falsity of some of its factual statements and by its alleged defamation of respondent.

Authoritative interpretations of the First Amendment guarantees have consistently refused to recognize an exception for any test of truth—whether administered by judges, juries, or administrative officials—and especially one that puts the burden of proving truth on the speaker. The constitutional protection does not turn upon "the truth, popularity, or social utility of the ideas and beliefs which are offered." As Madison said, "Some degree of abuse is inseparable from the proper use of every thing; and in no instance is this more true than in that of the press...." Injury to official reputation affords no more warrant for repressing speech that would otherwise be free than does factual error....

If neither factual error nor defamatory content suffices to remove the constitutional shield from criticism of official conduct, the combination of the two elements is no less inadequate. This is the lesson to be drawn from the great controversy over the Sedition Act of 1798, 1 Stat. 596, which first crystallized a national awareness of the central meaning of the First Amendment.... What a State may not constitutionally bring about by means of a criminal statute is likewise beyond the reach of its civil law of libel. The fear of damage awards under a rule such as that invoked by the Alabama courts here may be markedly more inhibiting than the fear of prosecution under a criminal statute....

The state rule of law is not saved by its allowance of the defense of truth. A defense for erroneous statements honestly made is no less essential here than was the requirement of proof of guilty knowledge which, in *Smith v. California*, 361 U.S. 147, we held indispensable to a valid conviction of a bookseller for possessing obscene writings for sale. We said: "For if the bookseller is criminally liable without knowledge of the contents...he will tend to restrict the books he sells to those he has inspected; and thus the State will have imposed a restriction upon the distribution of constitutionally protected as well as obscene literature.... And the bookseller's burden would become the public's burden, for by restricting him the public's access to reading matter would be restricted.... [His] timidity in the face of his absolute criminal liability, thus would tend to restrict the public's access to forms of the printed word which the State could not constitutionally suppress directly. The bookseller's self-censorship, compelled by the State, would be a censorship affecting the whole public, hardly less virulent for being privately administered. Through it, the distribution of all books, both obscene and not obscene, would be impeded."

A rule compelling the critic of official conduct to guarantee the truth of all his factual assertions—and to do so on pain of libel judgments virtually unlimited in amount—leads to a comparable "self-censorship." Allowance of the defense of truth, with the burden of proving it on the defendant, does not mean that only false speech will be deterred. Even courts accepting this defense as an adequate safeguard have recognized the difficulties of adducing legal proofs that the alleged libel was true in all its factual particulars. Under such a rule, would-be critics of official conduct may be deterred from voicing their criticism, even though it is believed to be true and even though it is in fact true, because of doubt whether it can be proved in court or fear of the expense of having to do so. They tend to make only statements which "steer far wider of the unlawful zone." The rule thus dampens the vigor and limits the variety of public debate. It is inconsistent with the First and Fourteenth Amendments.

The constitutional guarantees require, we think, a federal rule that prohibits a public official from recovering damages for a defamatory falsehood relating to his official conduct unless he proves that the statement was made with "actual malice"—that is, with knowledge that it was false or with reckless disregard of whether it was false or not....

Since respondent may seek a new trial, we deem that considerations of effective judicial administration require us to review the evidence in the present record to determine whether it could constitutionally support a judgment for respondent. This Court's duty is not limited to the elaboration of constitutional principles; we must also in proper cases review the evidence to make certain that those principles have been constitutionally applied. This is such a case.... [W]e consider that the proof presented to show actual malice lacks the convincing clarity which the constitutional standard demands, and hence that it would not constitutionally sustain the judgment for respondent under the proper rule of law. The case of the individual petitioners requires little discussion. Even assuming that they could constitutionally be found to have authorized the use of their names on the advertisement, there was no evidence whatever that they were aware of any erroneous statements or were in any way reckless in that regard. The judgment against them is thus without constitutional support.

As to the *Times*, we similarly conclude that the facts do not support a finding of actual malice.... We think the evidence against the *Times* supports at most a finding of negligence in failing to discover the misstatements, and is constitutionally insufficient to show the recklessness that is required for a finding of actual malice....

New York Times v. Sullivan is one of the most influential cases for First Amendment doctrine. At a minimum, the case stands for the proposition that there is a special privilege of criticizing public figures. Read more broadly, however, the commitment that "debate on public issues should be uninhibited, robust, and wide-open" has been cited as the justifying principle for enforcement of viewpoint neutrality in cases like *R. A. V. v. St. Paul*, and to argue that cases like *Beauharnais* are no longer good law. In subsequent cases, the Court had to consider the question of whether the *New York Times v. Sullivan* principle restricted the ability of public figures to sue the press for libel. In *Gertz v. Robert Welch, Inc.*, 418 U.S. 323 (1974) (previously discussed in chapter 3), writing for a 5 to 4 majority, Justice Powell concluded that the distinction between public and private figures requires that fundamentally different considerations be taken into account.

GERTZ v. ROBERT WELCH, INC.

SUPREME COURT OF THE UNITED STATES

418 U.S. 323 (1974)

JUSTICE POWELL delivered the opinion of the Court.

...The *New York Times* standard defines the level of constitutional protection appropriate to the context of defamation of a public person. Those who, by reason of the notoriety of their achievements or the vigor and success with which they seek the public's attention, are properly classed as public figures and those who hold governmental office may recover for injury to reputation only on clear and convincing proof that the defamatory falsehood was made with knowledge of its falsity or with reckless disregard for the truth. This standard administers an extremely powerful antidote to the inducement to media self-censorship of the common-law rule of strict liability for libel and slander.... For the reasons stated below, we conclude that the state interest in compensating injury to the reputation of private individuals requires that a different rule should obtain with respect to them....

The first remedy of any victim of defamation is self-help—using available opportunities to contradict the lie or correct the error and thereby to minimize its adverse impact on reputation. Public officials and public figures usually enjoy significantly greater access to the channels of effective communication and hence have a more realistic opportunity to counteract false statements than private individuals normally enjoy. n9 Private individuals are therefore more vulnerable to injury, and the state interest in protecting them is correspondingly greater.

n9 Of course, an opportunity for rebuttal seldom suffices to undo harm of defamatory falsehood. Indeed, the law of defamation is rooted in our experience that the truth rarely catches up with a lie. But the fact that the self-help remedy of rebuttal, standing alone, is inadequate to its task does not mean that it is irrelevant to our inquiry.

More important than the likelihood that private individuals will lack effective opportunities for rebuttal, there is a compelling normative consideration underlying the distinction between public and private defamation plaintiffs. An individual who decides to seek governmental office must accept certain necessary consequences of that involvement in public affairs. He runs the risk of closer public scrutiny than might otherwise be the case.... Those classed as public figures stand in a similar position. Hypothetically, it may be possible for someone to become a public figure through no purposeful action of his own, but the instances of truly involuntary public figures must be exceedingly rare. For the most part those who attain this status have assumed roles of special prominence in the affairs of society. Some occupy positions of such persuasive power and influence that they are deemed public figures for all purposes. More commonly, those classed as public figures have thrust themselves to the forefront of particular public controversies in order to influence the resolution of the issues involved. In either event, they invite attention and comment.

Even if the foregoing generalities do not obtain in every instance, the communications media are entitled to act on the assumption that public officials and public figures have voluntarily exposed themselves to increased risk of injury from defamatory falsehood concerning them. No such assumption is justified with respect to a private individual. He has not accepted public office or assumed an "influential role in ordering society." He has relinquished no part of his interest in the protection of his own good name, and consequently he has a more compelling call on the courts for redress of injury inflicted by defamatory falsehood. Thus, private individuals are not only more vulnerable to injury than public officials and public figures; they are also more deserving of recovery.

For these reasons we conclude that the States should retain substantial latitude in their efforts to enforce a legal remedy for defamatory falsehood injurious to the reputation of a private individual.... We hold that, so long as they do not impose liability without fault, the States may define for themselves the appropriate standard of liability for a publisher or broadcaster of defamatory falsehood injurious to a private individual. This approach provides a more equitable boundary between the competing concerns involved here. It recognizes the strength of the legitimate state interest in compensating private individuals for wrongful injury to reputation, yet shields the press and broadcast media from the rigors of strict liability for defamation. At least this conclusion obtains where, as here, the substance of the defamatory statement "makes substantial danger to reputation apparent...." [W]e endorse this approach in recognition of the strong and legitimate state interest in compensating private individuals for injury to reputation. But this countervailing state interest extends no further than compensation for actual injury. For the reasons stated below, we hold that the States may not permit recovery of presumed or punitive damages, at least when liability is not based on a showing of knowledge of falsity or reckless disregard for the truth....

The most controversial element in *Gertz* was Powell's sharp distinction between "public" and "private" figures. Powell found that Gertz himself, for example, was a private figure, despite his law practice, authorship of several books and numerous articles, and active involvement in a wide range of community affairs. "Although petitioner was consequently well known in some circles, he had achieved no general fame or notoriety in the community. None of the prospective jurors called at the trial had ever heard of petitioner prior to this litigation, and respondent offered no proof that this response was atypical of the local population. We would not lightly assume that a citizen's participation in community and professional affairs rendered him a public figure for all purposes. Absent clear evidence of general fame or notoriety in the community, and pervasive involvement in the affairs of society, an individual should not be deemed a public personality for all aspects of his life."

But persons who fit the description of private figures in *Gertz* play important roles in influencing public debates, by running PACs, creating newsletters and disseminating information, offering expert opinions, or pursuing public interest litigation which critics sometimes describe as thinly veiled attempts to use the courts for partisan political purposes. Imagine a published Report by a Committee of Scientists that proposes that smoking is healthy for children, and another Report by a Different Committee of Scientists that states that smoking is more unhealthy than injecting heroin. Might it be a matter of public interest if a journalist discovers that the authors of one report or the other are widely considered dishonest, and have past records of falsifying data on behalf of paying clients? Dissenting Justices Burger, Douglas, Brennan, and White all argued variations on this theme, that the *Gertz* standard gave states too much authority to silence discussions of matters of genuine public interest when they involved persons who did not fit the definition of public figures.

In 1985, the court considered a case that tested the *Gertz* standard. Dun & Bradstreet, a well-known financial services company, published a newsletter in which they falsely reported that a company called Greenmoss was going bankrupt. Greenmoss sued for libel, and Dun & Bradstreet challenged the verdict against them on the grounds that their publication should be covered by the "actual malice" rule of *Sullivan*. The Supreme Court upheld the verdict, finding that, under *Gertz*, Greenmoss was not a "public figure." There were two interesting things about the case, however, that (presumably) caused the Court to grant certiorari in the first place. First, the plaintiff was not an individual but a corporation. Under what circumstances would a corporation fit the category of "public figure"? Conversely, in what sense can a corporation be described as a "private" individual? The focus of Justice Powell's opinion, however, was on the state court's decision to grant punitive and "presumptive" (i.e., damages awarded in the absence of proof of actual pecuniary loss) damages. These were the sorts of damages that had not been allowed in *Gertz* without a showing of actual malice, but in *Dun & Bradstreet* a majority of the Court voted to permit them. The distinction was that the speech at issue in *Gertz* had been on a matter of public interest:

> We have never considered whether the *Gertz* balance obtains when the defamatory statements involve no issue of public concern. To make this determination, we must employ the approach approved in *Gertz* and balance the State's interest in compensating private individuals for injury to their reputation against the First Amendment interest in protecting this type of expression. This state interest is identical to the one weighed in *Gertz*. There we found that it was "strong and legitimate." A State should not lightly be required to abandon it.... In contrast, speech on matters of purely private concern is of less First Amendment concern.... While such speech is not totally unprotected by the First Amendment, its protections are less stringent. In *Gertz*, we found that the state interest in awarding presumed and punitive damages was not "substantial" in view of their effect on speech at the core of First Amendment concern. This interest, however, is "substantial" relative to the incidental effect these remedies may have on speech of significantly less constitutional interest. The rationale of the common-law rules has been the experience and judgment of history that "proof of actual damage will be impossible in a great many cases where, from the character of the defamatory words and the circumstances of publication, it is all but certain that serious harm has resulted in fact." As a result, courts for centuries have allowed juries to presume that some damage occurred from many defamatory utterances and publications. This rule furthers the state interest in providing remedies for defamation by ensuring that those remedies are effective. In light of the reduced constitutional value of speech involving no matters of public concern, we hold that the state interest adequately supports awards of presumed and punitive damages—even absent a showing of "actual malice." *Dun & Bradstreet v. Greenmoss Builders, Inc.*, 472 U.S. 749 (1985).

Justice Powell's opinion was joined by two other justices (Rehnquist and O'Connor). Justices Burger and White wrote a concurring opinion in which they agreed with the outcome but took issue with the new "private figure/public interest" standard. Justices Brennan, Marshall, Blackmun, and Stevens all dissented, taking the position that punitive and presumptive damages should never be allowed in the absence of a showing of actual malice, as the threat of such damages would have a chilling effect on speech.

The emphasis on "public interest" in speech concerning private figures became the formal basis for a separate level of press protection between *Sullivan* and *Dun & Bradstreet* in 1986 in *Philadelphia Newspapers v. Hepps*, 475 U.S. 767 (1986). The issue was not about damages, however, but about the more fundamental question of the burden of proof in a libel suit against a newspaper. Hepps was the owner of a series of franchised stores in the Philadelphia area. A newspaper had run a series of stories linking Hepps to organized crime, and he had sued for libel in state court. Under Pennsylvania law, in a defamation suit the statements at issue would be presumed to be false, with the defendant carrying the burden of demonstrating truth as a defense. The reason for the rule, as noted in *Dun & Bradstreet*, was that in many cases it is difficult or impossible to prove the falsity of defamatory statements (the problem of "proving a negative,") whereas if the publisher has a good basis for making an accusation, he or she should presumably be able to present the evidence of its truth.

Reviewing the case, however, the Supreme Court declared that when a private figure sues a newspaper for libel, and the allegedly libelous statement is a matter of "public interest," then the plaintiff has the burden of proving that the statements are false. This is a standard that fills in the details of the scheme that was implied in *Dun & Bradstreet*. Where a public figure sues the press for libel, such a person must show actual malice to recover damages (*Sullivan*). Where the plaintiff is a private figure, states are free to set up whatever standards of liability they want except for strict liability (*Gertz*). When the plaintiff is a private figure, but the subject-matter of the statements at issue is of public interest, then the plaintiff bears the burden of proving that the statements were false (*Hepps*), and punitive and exemplary damages can only be allowed on a showing of actual malice (*Dun & Bradstreet*). Justice O'Connor wrote the opinion in *Hepps* for a five-member majority, with Justices Stevens, Burger, Rehnquist, and White dissenting on the grounds that the "public interest" rule put private citizens at the mercy of negligent publishers who, under this rule, need not bother to check the veracity of their stories in order to avoid the threat of liability.

PHILADELPHIA NEWSPAPERS, INC. v. HEPPS

SUPREME COURT OF THE UNITED STATES

475 U.S. 767 (1986)

JUSTICE O'CONNOR delivered the opinion of the Court, in which BRENNAN, MARSHALL, BLACKMUN, and POWELL joined. JUSTICE STEVENS filed a dissenting opinion, in which BURGER, C. J., and WHITE and REHNQUIST joined.

This case requires us once more to "[struggle]...to define the proper accommodation between the law of defamation and the freedoms of speech and press protected by the First Amendment." In *Gertz*, the Court held that a private figure who brings a suit for defamation cannot recover without some showing that the media defendant was at fault in publishing the statements at issue. Here, we hold that, at least where a newspaper publishes speech of public concern, a private-figure plaintiff cannot recover damages without also showing that the statements at issue are false....

The Court most recently considered the constitutional limits on suits for defamation in *Dun & Bradstreet, Inc. v. Greenmoss Builders, Inc.*, 472 U.S. 749 (1985). In sharp contrast to *New York Times*, *Dun & Bradstreet* involved not only a private-figure plaintiff, but also speech of purely private concern. A plurality of the Court in *Dun & Bradstreet* was convinced that, in a case with such a configuration of speech and plaintiff, the showing of actual malice needed to recover punitive damages under either *New York Times* or *Gertz* was unnecessary: "In light of the reduced constitutional value of speech involving no matters of public concern, we hold that the state interest [in preserving private reputation] adequately supports awards of presumed and punitive damages—even absent a showing of actual malice."

One can discern in these decisions two forces that may reshape the common-law landscape to conform to the First Amendment. The first is whether the plaintiff is a public official or figure, or is instead a private figure. The second is whether the speech at issue is of public concern. When the speech is of public concern and the plaintiff is a public official or public figure, the Constitution clearly requires the plaintiff to surmount a much higher barrier before recovering damages from a media defendant than is raised by the common law. When the speech is of public concern but the plaintiff is a private figure, as in *Gertz*, the Constitution still supplants the standards of the common law, but the constitutional requirements are, in at least some of their range, less forbidding than when the plaintiff is a public figure and the speech is of public concern. When the speech is of exclusively private concern and the plaintiff is a private figure, as in *Dun & Bradstreet*, the constitutional requirements do not necessarily force any change in at least some of the features of the common-law landscape.

Here, as in *Gertz*, the plaintiff is a private figure and the newspaper articles are of public concern. In *Gertz*, as in *New York Times*, the common-law rule was superseded by a constitutional rule. We believe that the common law's rule on falsity—that the defendant must bear the burden of proving truth—must similarly fall here to a constitutional requirement that the plaintiff bear the burden of showing falsity, as well as fault, before recovering damages.

There will always be instances when the fact finding process will be unable to resolve conclusively whether the speech is true or false; it is in those cases that the burden of proof is dispositive. Under a rule forcing the plaintiff to bear the burden of showing falsity, there will be some cases in which plaintiffs cannot meet their burden despite the fact that the speech is in fact false. The plaintiff's suit will fail despite the fact that, in some abstract sense, the suit is meritorious. Similarly, under an alternative rule placing the burden of showing truth on defendants, there would be some cases in which defendants could not bear their burden despite the fact that the speech is in fact true. Those suits would succeed despite the fact that, in some abstract sense, those suits are unmeritorious. Under either rule, then, the outcome of the suit will sometimes be at variance with the outcome that we would desire if all speech were either demonstrably true or demonstrably false.

This dilemma stems from the fact that the allocation of the burden of proof will determine liability for some speech that is true and some that is false, but all of such speech is unknowably true or false. Because the burden of proof is the deciding factor only when the evidence is ambiguous, we cannot know how much of the speech affected by the allocation of the burden of proof is true and how much is false. In a case presenting a configuration of speech and plaintiff like the one we face here, and where the scales are in such an uncertain balance, we believe that the Constitution requires us to tip them in favor of protecting true speech. To ensure that true speech on matters of public concern is not deterred, we hold that the common-law presumption that defamatory speech is false cannot stand when a plaintiff seeks damages against a media defendant for speech of public concern.

In the context of governmental restriction of speech, it has long been established that the government cannot limit speech protected by the First Amendment without bearing the burden of showing that its restriction is justified. It is not immediately apparent from the text of the First Amendment, which by its terms applies only to governmental action, that a similar result should obtain here: a suit by a private party is obviously quite different from the government's direct enforcement of its own laws. Nonetheless, the need to encourage debate on public issues that concerned the Court in the governmental restriction cases is of concern in a similar manner in this case involving a private suit for damages: placement by state law of the burden of proving truth upon media defendants who publish speech of public concern deters such speech because of the fear that liability will unjustifiably result. Because such a "chilling" effect would be antithetical to the First Amendment's protection of true speech on matters of public concern, we believe that a private-figure plaintiff must bear the burden of showing that the speech at issue is false before recovering damages for defamation from a media defendant. To do otherwise could "only result in a deterrence of speech which the Constitution makes free."

We recognize that requiring the plaintiff to show falsity will insulate from liability some speech that is false, but unprovably so. Nonetheless, the Court's previous decisions on the restrictions that the First Amendment places upon the common law of defamation firmly support our conclusion here with respect to the allocation of the burden of proof. In attempting to resolve related issues in the defamation context, the Court has affirmed that "[the] First Amendment requires that we protect some falsehood in order to protect speech that matters...."

We recognize that the plaintiff's burden in this case is weightier because of Pennsylvania's "shield" law, which allows employees of the media to refuse to divulge their sources. But we do not have before us the question of the permissible reach of such laws....

In 1988, the Court added one more gloss to their treatment of libel and the press in the context of public figures. The movie *The People v. Larry Flint* is a portrayal of the events leading up to the 1988 case *Hustler v. Falwell*. *Hustler Magazine* had published a short parody that pretended to be Jerry Falwell's recollections of his first sexual experiences. Falwell sued for intentional infliction of emotional distress (in this context, a close cousin to libel), arguing that under the *Sullivan* standards there was little question that *Hustler* had quite deliberately printed false allegations about him in a way designed to embarrass him personally. *Hustler Magazine*, in response, argued that the parody did not contain false statements of fact, but rather was an expression of an opinion. Chief Justice Rehnquist, writing for a unanimous Court, chose instead to recognize a privilege for parody of public officials:

> Respondent would have us find that a State's interest in protecting public figures from emotional distress is sufficient to deny First Amendment protection to speech that is patently offensive and is intended to inflict emotional injury, even when that speech could not reasonably have been interpreted as stating actual facts about the public figure involved. This we decline to do.... Of course, this does not mean that any speech about a public figure is immune from sanction in the form of damages.... False statements of fact are particularly valueless; they interfere with the truth-seeking function of the marketplace of ideas, and they cause damage to an individual's reputation that cannot easily be repaired by counterspeech, however persuasive or effective. But even though falsehoods have little value in and of themselves, they are "nevertheless inevitable in free debate," and a rule that would impose strict liability on a publisher for false factual assertions would have an undoubted "chilling" effect on speech relating to public figures that does have constitutional value. "Freedoms of expression require 'breathing space.'" This breathing space is provided by a constitutional rule that allows public figures to recover for libel or defamation only when they can prove both that the statement was false and that the statement was made with the requisite level of culpability. *Hustler v. Falwell*, 485 U.S. 46 (1988).

The plaintiffs in the case had argued that the rule for claims of emotional distress should be different from the rules for libel, on the grounds that their claims involved the assertion of a "bad motive" on the part of the speaker. Rehnquist, while expressing sympathy for the victims of insult, refused to separate the categories:

> [I]n the world of debate about public affairs, many things done with motives that are less than admirable are protected by the First Amendment.... Thus while such

a bad motive may be deemed controlling for purposes of tort liability in other areas of the law, we think the First Amendment prohibits such a result in the area of public debate about public figures. Were we to hold otherwise, there can be little doubt that political cartoonists and satirists would be subjected to damages awards without any showing that their work falsely defamed its subject. *Hustler v. Falwell*, 485 U.S. 46 (1988).

Rehnquist's focus on the "world of debate about public affairs" points to the fact that the line that runs through the constitutional principles governing libel actions against the press is the line that divides public from private. The *Gertz* distinction between public and private figures becomes, in cases like *Hepps*, a distinction between public and private stories. Falwell, of course, was a public figure by any definition, but would the *Hustler* ruling apply equally to the plaintiff in *Hepps*, a private figure who was exposed to public accusations of wrongdoing by virtue of the public interest in his activities? In *Cohen v. California*, the Court powerfully declared that when persons venture forth in public they are required to endure the indecency that they find there. The press cases concerning libel go further, effectively giving the press the power to pull a person into that public sphere, and *Hustler* explains the thick-skinned resistance to offense that one is required, in the name of values of free expression, to display thereafter. That issue, of the power of the press to pull a person into the public eye, has been at the heart of the efforts of states to protect their people against invasions of privacy. What are the limits on the right of the press to investigate and make public matters of private concern?

Although the issues involved in the invasion of privacy by the press are profound, the early cases established a simple rule: The press cannot be prevented from obtaining and publishing information contained in public records. In 1975, Georgia had a law that made it a misdemeanor to publish the name of a rape victim. A reporter obtained the name of such a victim from a police record and included it in a story. In reviewing a prosecution of the reporter under the Georgia law, the Court reached the conclusion that the press's publication of truthful information, obtained lawfully from public records, cannot be made a crime. The facts of a crime, and its subsequent investigation and prosecution, were deemed to be matters of public interest, and the press's ability to report such matters was therefore conceived of as central to its political function. In addition, the fact that the information had appeared in a public record was central to the holding; access to public records, argued Justice White for the majority, was central to the investigative role of the press. If the government wanted to restrict publication of such matters, he reasoned, it could amend its public record-keeping statutes accordingly. Once a matter was made "public," however, it was fair game. The ruling was 8 to 1, and the sole dissenter, Justice Rehnquist, took issue with the Court's handling of a procedural issue relating to jurisdiction, not with the outcome. *Cox Broadcasting Corp. v. Cohn*, 420 U.S. 469 (1974).

Fifteen years later, the Court considered the same issue again, but with important variations. In 1983, a Florida woman known to the Court by her initials "B. J. F.," was raped and robbed at knifepoint. She reported the crime to the police department, which prepared an incident report that was placed in the department press room in accordance with department policy so that reporters could track the incidence of crimes in the area. The press room contained a sign which stated that reports found there were not public records. A novice ("cub") reporter for the *Florida Star* either did not see or ignored the sign, and recorded the details of a crime—including the full name of the victim—in a story. That story, in turn, was published in the paper despite an internal policy against the publication of the names of rape victims.

The *Florida Star* asserted, and the trial court accepted, that the violation of both their internal policy and the police department's policy had been inadvertent on the part of the publisher. Nonetheless, the trial court upheld a verdict in favor of B. J. F. for negligent infliction of emotional distress by violation of the privacy statute. "[B. J. F.] stated that she had heard about the article from fellow workers and acquaintances; that her mother had received several threatening phone calls from a man who stated that he would rape B. J. F. again; and that these events had forced B. J. F. to change her phone number and residence, to seek police protection, and to obtain mental health counseling." Reviewing the case, the Court concluded that the law in question violated the First Amendment by an application of the reasoning in *Cox Broadcasting*. This time, however, the issue was more contentious, and three justices dissented from the ruling.

THE FLORIDA STAR v. B. J. F.

SUPREME COURT OF THE UNITED STATES

491 U.S. 524 (1989)

JUSTICE MARSHALL delivered the opinion of the Court.

...The tension between the right which the First Amendment accords to a free press, on the one hand, and the protections which various statutes and common-law doctrines accord to personal privacy against the publication of truthful information, on the other, is a subject we have addressed several times in recent years. Our decisions in cases involving government attempts to sanction the accurate dissemination of information as invasive of privacy, have not, however, exhaustively considered this conflict. On the contrary, although our decisions have without exception upheld the press' right to publish, we have emphasized each time that we were resolving this conflict only as it arose in a discrete factual context. n5

---

n5 The somewhat uncharted state of the law in this area thus contrasts markedly with the well-mapped area of defamatory falsehoods, where a long line of decisions has produced relatively detailed legal standards governing the multifarious situations in which individuals aggrieved by the dissemination of damaging untruths seek redress.

Appellant takes the position that this case is indistinguishable from *Cox Broadcasting*. Alternatively, it urges that our decisions in the above trilogy, and in other cases in which we have held that the right of the press to publish truth overcame asserted interests other than personal privacy, can be distilled to yield a broader First Amendment principle that the press may never be punished, civilly or criminally, for publishing the truth. Appellee counters that the privacy trilogy is inapposite, because in each case the private information already appeared on a "public record," and because the privacy interests at stake were far less profound than in the present case. In the alternative, appellee urges that *Cox Broadcasting* be overruled and replaced with a categorical rule that publication of the name of a rape victim never enjoys constitutional protection.

We conclude that imposing damages on appellant for publishing B. J. F.'s name violates the First Amendment, although not for either of the reasons appellant urges. Despite the strong resemblance this case bears to *Cox Broadcasting*, that case cannot fairly be read as controlling here. The name of the rape victim in that case was obtained from courthouse records that were open to public inspection, a fact which Justice White's opinion for the Court repeatedly noted. Significantly, one of the reasons we gave in *Cox Broadcasting* for invalidating the challenged damages award was the important role the press plays in subjecting trials to public scrutiny and thereby helping guarantee their fairness. That role is not directly compromised where, as here, the information in question comes from a police report prepared and disseminated at a time at which not only had no adversarial criminal proceedings begun, but no suspect had been identified.

Nor need we accept appellant's invitation to hold broadly that truthful publication may never be punished consistent with the First Amendment. Our cases have carefully eschewed reaching this ultimate question, mindful that the future may bring scenarios which prudence counsels our not resolving anticipatorily. Indeed, in *Cox Broadcasting*, we pointedly refused to answer even the less sweeping question "whether truthful publications may ever be subjected to civil or criminal liability" for invading "an area of privacy" defined by the State.

Respecting the fact that press freedom and privacy rights are both "plainly rooted in the traditions and significant concerns of our society," we instead focused on the less sweeping issue "whether the State may impose sanctions on the accurate publication of the name of a rape victim obtained from public records—more specifically, from judicial records which are maintained in connection with a public prosecution and which themselves are open to public inspection." We continue to believe that the sensitivity and significance of the interests presented in clashes between First Amendment and privacy rights counsel relying on limited principles that sweep no more broadly than...the instant case.

In our view, this case is appropriately analyzed with reference to such a limited First Amendment principle. It is the one, in fact, which we articulated in *Smith v. Daily Mail Pub. Co.*, 443 U.S. 97 (1979).... n8 If a newspaper lawfully obtains truthful information about a matter of public significance then state officials may not constitutionally punish publication of the information, absent a need to further a state interest of the highest order....

[T]he government retains ample means of safeguarding significant interests upon which publication may impinge, including protecting a rape victim's anonymity. To the extent sensitive information rests in private hands, the government may under some circumstances forbid its nonconsensual acquisition.... To the extent sensitive information is in the government's custody, it has even greater power to forestall or mitigate the injury caused by its release. The government may classify certain information, establish and enforce procedures ensuring its redacted release, and extend a damages remedy against the government or its officials where the government's mishandling of sensitive information leads to its dissemination. Where information is entrusted to the government, a less drastic means than punishing truthful publication almost always exists for guarding against the dissemination of private facts.

---

n8 The *Daily Mail* principle does not settle the issue whether, in cases where information has been acquired unlawfully by a newspaper or by a source, government may ever punish not only the unlawful acquisition, but the ensuing publication as well. This issue was raised but not definitively resolved in *New York Times Co. v. United States*, 403 U.S. 713 (1971).... We have no occasion to address it here.

A second consideration undergirding the *Daily Mail* principle is the fact that punishing the press for its dissemination of information which is already publicly available is relatively unlikely to advance the interests in the service of which the State seeks to act. It is not, of course, always the case that information lawfully acquired by the press is known, or accessible, to others. But where the government has made certain information publicly available, it is highly anomalous to sanction persons other than the source of its release. We noted this anomaly in *Cox Broadcasting*: "By placing the information in the public domain on official court records, the State must be presumed to have concluded that the public interest was thereby being served."

A third and final consideration is the "timidity and self-censorship" which may result from allowing the media to be punished for publishing certain truthful information. *Cox Broadcasting* noted this concern with overdeterrence in the context of information made public through official court records, but the fear of excessive media self-suppression is applicable as well to other information released, without qualification, by the government. A contrary rule, depriving protection to those who rely on the government's implied representations of the lawfulness of dissemination, would force upon the media the onerous obligation of sifting through government press releases, reports, and pronouncements to prune out material arguably unlawful for publication. This situation could inhere even where the newspaper's sole object was to reproduce, with no substantial change, the government's rendition of the event in question....

Our holding today is limited. We do not hold that truthful publication is automatically constitutionally protected, or that there is no zone of personal privacy within which the State may protect the individual from intrusion by the press, or even that a State may never punish publication of the name of a victim of a sexual offense. We hold only that where a newspaper publishes truthful information which it has lawfully obtained, punishment may lawfully be imposed, if at all, only when narrowly tailored to a state interest of the highest order, and that no such interest is satisfactorily served by imposing liability under § 794.03 to appellant under the facts of this case.

JUSTICE WHITE, with whom THE CHIEF JUSTICE and JUSTICE O'CONNOR join, dissenting.

Florida has done precisely what we suggested, in *Cox Broadcasting*, that States wishing to protect the privacy rights of rape victims might do: respond [to the challenge] by means which avoid public documentation or other exposure of private information. By amending its public records statute to exempt rape victims names from disclosure, and forbidding its officials to release such information, the State has taken virtually every step imaginable to prevent what happened here.... Unfortunately, as this case illustrates, mistakes happen: even when States take measures to "avoid" disclosure, sometimes rape victims' names are found out. As I see it, it is not too much to ask the press, in instances such as this, to respect simple standards of decency and refrain from publishing a victim's name, address, and/or phone number.

In a footnote to his opinion in *B. J. F.*, Justice White suggested that there were particular grounds for concern "when one considers the extensive powers of the State to collect information," referring to a Pennsylvania case involving a reporter who obtained a transcript of a police wiretap that had been accidentally filed as part of a court document by a prosecutor. It was a prescient hypothetical question, both in terms of the possibilities of reporters obtaining information from the police and in terms of the concern for the effects of technological advances in the field of eavesdropping. In 1999, the Court confronted the first of those two issues in *Wilson v. Layne*, 526 U.S. 603 (1999). Unlike most of the cases discussed here, *Layne* involved a situation in which reporters and the government were cooperating. The police department of Rockville, Maryland, working in a special operation in conjunction with federal marshals, invited reporters for "ride-alongs" which included accompanying officers during searches of private residences. Reviewing the policy, the Court unanimously agreed that the presence of such reporters was a violation of the Fourth Amendment:

> There is certainly language in our opinions interpreting the First Amendment which points to the importance of "the press" in informing the general public about the administration of criminal justice. In *Cox Broadcasting Corp. v. Cohn*, 420 U.S. 469 (1975), for example, we said "in a society in which each individual has but limited time and resources with which to observe at first hand the operations of his government, he relies necessarily upon the press to bring to him in convenient form the facts of those operations." No one could gainsay the truth of these observations, or the importance of the First Amendment in protecting press freedom from abridgement by the government. But the Fourth Amendment also protects a very important right, and in the present case it is in terms of that right that the media ride-alongs must be judged. Surely the possibility of good public relations for the police is simply not enough, standing alone, to justify the ride-along intrusion into a private home. And even the need for accurate reporting on police issues in general bears no direct relation to the constitutional justification for the police intrusion into a home in order to execute a felony arrest. *Wilson v. Layne*, 526 U.S. 603 (1999).

By implication, then, the Court in *Layne* suggested that the mere fact that a person comes into contact with the police does not, by itself, make them fair game for the news media. When government and the press are adversaries, the rules are that reporters may use anything the government lets slip, but that principle does not extend to relations between the press and private citizens.

In 2001, the court for the first time squarely confronted an issue that had been raised but avoided in *New York Times* (the Pentagon Papers case). Can reporters be punished for making use of information which was improperly obtained by third parties? *New York Times* had been decided on the basis of the Court's disapproval of prior restraints on publication, and in the context of a heated political debate. A number of the justices in that case had taken pains to explain that nothing in their opinions implies any reluctance to see reporters and publishers subjected to criminal penalties for misusing information in a proper case. In *Bartnicki v. Vopper*, the Court confronted a situation in which a Pennsylvania radio station and a newspaper had published a private cell phone conversation relating to a teachers' strike. The conversation had been illegally intercepted and taped by an unnamed third party and given to the radio station, which played the tape on the air. The participants in the conversation sued under both federal and state law for invasion of privacy. The Court's decision was 6-3, with Justices Rehnquist, Scalia, and Thomas dissenting.

BARTNICKI v. VOPPER

SUPREME COURT OF THE UNITED STATES

121 S. Ct. 1753 (2001)

JUSTICE STEVENS delivered the opinion of the Court, in which O'CONNOR, KENNEDY, SOUTER, GINSBURG, and BREYER joined. CHIEF JUSTICE REHNQUIST, filed a dissenting opinion, in which SCALIA and THOMAS joined.

...As a general matter, state action to punish the publication of truthful information seldom can satisfy constitutional standards. More specifically, this Court has repeatedly held that if a newspaper lawfully obtains truthful information about a matter of public significance then state officials may not constitutionally punish publication of the information, absent a need...of the highest order.... Simply put, the issue here is this: Where the punished publisher of information has obtained the information in question in a manner lawful in itself but from a source who has obtained it unlawfully, may the government punish the ensuing publication of that information based on the defect in a chain?

Our refusal to construe the issue presented more broadly is consistent with this Court's repeated refusal to answer categorically whether truthful publication may ever be punished consistent with the First Amendment. Rather, "our cases have carefully eschewed reaching this ultimate question, mindful that the future may bring scenarios which prudence counsels our not resolving anticipatorily.... We continue to believe that the sensitivity and significance of the interests presented in clashes between [the] First Amendment and privacy rights counsel relying on limited principles that sweep no more broadly than the appropriate context of the instant case."

Accordingly, we consider whether, given the facts of this case, the interests served by § 2511(1)(c) can justify its restrictions on speech.

The Government identifies two interests served by the statute—first, the interest in removing an incentive for parties to intercept private conversations, and second, the interest in minimizing the harm to persons whose conversations have been illegally intercepted. We assume that those interests adequately justify the prohibition...against the interceptor's own use of information that he or she acquired by violating § 2511(1)(a), but it by no means follows that punishing disclosures of lawfully obtained information of public interest by one not involved in the initial illegality is an acceptable means of serving those ends.

The normal method of deterring unlawful conduct is to impose an appropriate punishment on the person who engages in it. If the sanctions that presently attach to a violation of § 2511(1)(a) do not provide sufficient deterrence, perhaps those sanctions should be made more severe. But it would be quite remarkable to hold that speech by a law-abiding possessor of information can be suppressed in order to deter conduct by a non-law-abiding third party. Although there are some rare occasions in which a law suppressing one party's speech may be justified by an interest in deterring criminal conduct by another, this is not such a case....

Privacy of communication is an important interest, and Title III's restrictions are intended to protect that interest, thereby "encouraging the uninhibited exchange of ideas and information among private parties...." Moreover, the fear of public disclosure of private conversations might well have a chilling effect on private speech.... Accordingly, it seems to us that there are important interests to be considered on both sides of the constitutional calculus. In considering that balance, we acknowledge that some intrusions on privacy are more offensive than others, and that the disclosure of the contents of a private conversation can be an even greater intrusion on privacy than the interception itself. As a result, there is a valid independent justification for prohibiting such disclosures by persons who lawfully obtained access to the contents of an illegally intercepted message, even if that prohibition does not play a significant role in preventing such interceptions from occurring in the first place.

We need not decide whether that interest is strong enough to justify the application of § 2511(c) to disclosures of trade secrets or domestic gossip or other information of purely private concern. In other words, the outcome of the case does not turn on whether § 2511(1)(c) may be enforced with respect to most violations of the statute without offending the First Amendment. The enforcement of that provision in this case, however, implicates the core purposes of the First Amendment because it imposes sanctions on the publication of truthful information of public concern. In this case, privacy concerns give way when balanced against the interest in publishing matters of public importance. As Warren and Brandeis stated in their classic law review article: "The right of privacy does not prohibit any publication of matter which is of public or general interest." The Right to Privacy, 4 *Harv. L. Rev.* 193, 214 (1890). One of the costs associated with participation in public affairs is an attendant loss of privacy.

Our opinion in *New York Times Co. v. Sullivan*, 376 U.S. 254 (1964), reviewed many of the decisions that settled the "general proposition that freedom of expression upon public questions is secured by the First Amendment." Those cases all relied on our "profound national commitment to the principle that debate on public issues should be uninhibited, robust and wide-open." It was the overriding importance of that commitment that supported our holding that neither factual error nor defamatory content, nor a combination of the two, sufficed to remove the First Amendment shield from criticism of official conduct.

We think it clear that parallel reasoning requires the conclusion that a stranger's illegal conduct does not suffice to remove the First Amendment shield from speech about a matter of public concern. The months of negotiations over the proper level of compensation for teachers at the Wyoming Valley West High School were unquestionably a matter of public concern, and respondents were clearly engaged in debate about that concern. That debate may be more mundane than the Communist rhetoric that inspired Justice Brandeis' classic opinion in *Whitney v. California*, 274 U.S. at 372, but it is no less worthy of constitutional protection....

CHIEF JUSTICE REHNQUIST, with whom SCALIA and THOMAS join, dissenting.

Technology now permits millions of important and confidential conversations to occur through a vast system of electronic networks. These advances, however, raise significant privacy concerns. We are placed in the uncomfortable position of not knowing who might have access to our personal and business e-mails, our medical and financial records, or our cordless and cellular telephone conversations. In an attempt to prevent some of the most egregious violations of privacy, the United States, the District of Columbia, and 40 States have enacted laws prohibiting the intentional interception and knowing disclosure of electronic communications. The Court holds that all of these statutes violate the First Amendment insofar as the illegally intercepted conversation touches upon a matter of "public concern," an amorphous concept that the Court does not even attempt to define. But the Court's decision diminishes, rather than enhances, the purposes of the First Amendment: chilling the speech of the millions of Americans who rely upon electronic technology to communicate each day....

The Constitution should not protect the involuntary broadcast of personal conversations. Even where the communications involve public figures or concern public matters, the conversations are nonetheless private and worthy of protection. Although public persons may have forgone the right to live their lives screened from public scrutiny in some areas, it does not and should not follow that they also have abandoned their right to have a private conversation without fear of it being intentionally intercepted and knowingly disclosed.... Surely "the interest in individual privacy," at its narrowest must embrace the right to be free from surreptitious eavesdropping on, and involuntary broadcast of, our cellular telephone conversations. The Court subordinates that right, not to the claims of those who themselves wish to speak, but to the claims of those who wish to publish the intercepted conversations of others. Congress' effort to balance the above claim to privacy against a marginal claim to speak freely is thereby set at naught....

C. *Limits on Newsgathering*

In the cases discussing the attempts of governments to protect citizens' privacy, the Court seemed to emphasize the desirability of a kind of adversarial relationship between the press and the government. If the government slips, the press is entitled to take advantage of its opportunities, but, conversely, the government gets to exercise control over the information that it releases in the first place. In other words, there are rules to this relationship, and both government and the press are bound to obey them. The Court, for example, repeatedly emphasized that it was speaking of information that had been lawfully obtained. That caveat raises an obvious question: what are the limits that government, or the courts, can place on the efforts of the press to gather news?

The Court first considered these issues in its consideration of whether the press, by virtue of its special constitutional function, has any special rights of access to information beyond those possessed by members of the general public. Somewhat surprisingly, perhaps, the answer was "no."

Pell v. Procunier (1974) concerned a prison regulation prohibiting face-to-face interviews by journalists with specifically named inmates. The Court found that the prison system had neutral, valid reasons for the regulation, and that both the inmates' freedom of speech and the reporters' access to information could be pursued through other channels. The ruling concerning the inmates' rights was 6-3. Justice Stewart, writing for the majority, found that the prison regulations did not cut inmates off from communication with the outside world, nor even from the press, since inmates had access to the mails and were free to have visits from family, attorneys, and clergy. Concerning the press, the opinion was 5-4, with Justices Powell, Douglas, Brennan, and Marshall dissenting. Stewart proceeded from the argument that "[t]he First Amendment does not guarantee the press a...right of special access to information not available to the public generally." But Stewart was also careful to note that the press did, in fact, have exceptional access to California prisons:

> We note at the outset that this regulation is not part of an attempt by the State to conceal the conditions in its prisons or to frustrate the press' investigation and reporting of those conditions. Indeed, the record demonstrates that, under current corrections policy, both the press and the general public are accorded full opportunities to observe prison conditions. The Department of Corrections regularly conducts public tours through the prisons for the benefit of interested citizens. In addition, newsmen are permitted to visit both the maximum security and minimum security sections of the institutions and to stop and speak about any subject to any inmates whom they might encounter. If security considerations permit, corrections personnel will step aside to permit such interviews to be confidential. Apart from general access to all parts of the institutions, newsmen are also permitted to enter the prisons to interview inmates selected at random by the corrections officials. By the same token, if a newsman wishes to write a story on a particular prison program, he is permitted to sit in on group meetings and to interview the inmate participants. In short, members of the press enjoy access to California prisons that is not available to other members of the public. *Pell v. Procunier*, 417 U.S. 817 (1974).

Noting that conditions inside prisons are "a matter that is both newsworthy and of great public importance, Stewart concluded that the regulations at issue did not unduly interfere with "the paramount public interest in a free flow of information to the people concerning public officials."

Powell, dissenting, argued that "California's absolute ban against prisoner-press interviews impermissibly restrains the ability of the press to perform its constitutionally established function of informing the people on the conduct of their government," and the other dissenters made similar assertions. Douglas observed that "the interest [the Free Press Clause] protects is not possessed by the media themselves...but rather [is] the right of the people, the true sovereign under our constitutional scheme, to govern in an informed manner." *Pell v. Procunier*, 417 U.S. 817 (1974). Later the same year, the Court considered an almost identical prison policy from the District of Columbia. Again, Justice Stewart wrote for a five-member majority, and again Douglas, Powell, Brennan, and Marshall dissented. *Saxbe v. Washington Post*, 417 U.S. 843 (1974).

In 1977, the Court revisited the question of whether the press had any right of access to information greater than those of members of the public in *Houchins v. KQED*, 438 U.S. 1 (1977). The case involved a television station's attempt to investigate conditions at a California jail in which there had been reports of violence and mistreatment of prisoners. The Alameda County sheriff refused to allow reporters to come into the jail to take pictures, and the television station went to court. A District Court ordered the sheriff to permit the reporters into the jail, but on appeal the Supreme Court reversed that ruling. Only seven justices participated in the decision, however, and this time only three of them, Burger, Rehnquist, and White, agreed to the proposition that the press has no special right of access to information. Chief Justice Burger, writing for the majority in a plurality opinion joined by only two other justices, acknowledged that prison conditions were a matter of public concern, but concluded that while the press had an undoubted right to publish information, that did not imply a concomitant right to obtain that information in the first place. "[A]n analysis of [earlier] cases reveals that the Court was concerned with the freedom of the media to communicate information once it is obtained; neither case intimated that the Constitution compels the government to provide the media with information or access to it on demand." If the government wanted to make prisons open to public or press inspection, it could, but the Constitution did not require any such access. "Whether the government should open penal institutions in the manner sought by respondents is a question of policy which a legislative body might appropriately resolve one way or the other."

Justice Stewart concurred in the outcome, but argued that restrictions on access appropriate to the general public might, in a different case, be impermissible as applied to the press. In the process, he appeared to back off somewhat from the position he had staked out in *Pell* and *Saxbe*:

> I agree substantially with what the opinion of THE CHIEF JUSTICE has to say on that score. We part company, however, in applying these abstractions to the facts of this case. Whereas he appears to view "equal access" as meaning access that is identical in all respects, I believe that the concept of equal access must be accorded more flexibility in order to accommodate the practical distinctions between the press and the general public.... That the First Amendment speaks separately of freedom of speech and freedom of the press is no constitutional accident, but an acknowledgment of the critical role played by the press in American society. The Constitution requires sensitivity to that role, and to the special needs of the press in performing it effectively. A person touring Santa Rita jail can grasp its reality with his own eyes and ears. But if a television reporter is to convey the jail's sights and sounds to those who cannot personally visit the place, he must use cameras and sound equipment. In short, terms of access that are reasonably imposed on individual members of the public may, if they impede effective reporting without sufficient justification, be unreasonable as applied to journalists who are there to convey to the general public what the visitors see. *Houchins v. KQED*, 438 U.S. 1 (1977).

Thus Chief Justice Burger's argument in *Houchins* in fact had the support of only three votes on the Court, and the outcome was supported by a plurality of only four. Nonetheless, by adding his vote to those of the justices who joined in the plurality opinion, Stewart gave his support to a continuation of the rule that the press has no special right of access.

Dissenting, Justice Stevens (joined by Justices Powell and Brennan) focused on the fact that in *Houchins*, "equal access" was being used to prevent the public from seeing the conditions in the jail. Stevens reviewed some of the history of the jail in question, including a federal judge's 1972 conclusion that its operation constituted "cruel and unusual punishment" and steps taken by the jail administration to prevent investigations, including the firing of a staff psychologist who publicly commented on jail conditions and "public tours" that consisted of scripted visits to limited areas of the prison that had been specially cleaned and prepared for the purpose. In *Pell v. Procunier* (1974), the Court had found "that the policy of prohibiting interviews with inmates specifically designated by the press was 'not part of an attempt by the State to conceal the conditions in its prisons.'" The situation in the Santa Rita jail, said Stevens, was different:

> [T]he restrictions on access to the inner portions of the Santa Rita jail that existed on the date this litigation commenced concealed from the general public the conditions of confinement within the facility. The question is whether petitioner's policies, which cut off the flow of information at its source, abridged the public's right to be informed about those conditions. The answer to that question does not depend upon the degree of public disclosure which should attend the operation of most governmental activity. Such matters involve questions of policy which generally must be resolved by the political branches of government. Moreover, there are unquestionably occasions when governmental activity may properly be carried on in complete secrecy. For example, the public and the press are commonly excluded from grand jury proceedings, our own conferences, [and] the meetings of other official bodies gathered in executive session.... In such situations the reasons for withholding information from the public are both apparent and legitimate. In this case, however, respondents do not assert a right to force disclosure of confidential information or to invade in any way the decisionmaking processes of governmental officials. They simply seek an end to petitioner's policy of concealing prison conditions from the public. Those conditions are wholly without claim to confidentiality. While prison officials have an interest in the time and manner of public acquisition of information about the institutions they administer, there is no legitimate penological justification for concealing from citizens the conditions in which their fellow citizens are being confined. *Houchins v. KQED*, 438 U.S. 1 (1977).

The two justices who did not participate, Marshall and Blackmun, both had tended in the past to support broad rights of press access, so it is plausible that if the entire Court had been sitting the outcome might have been different.

In 1980 the Court altered its longstanding position concerning public access to criminal proceedings. In two earlier cases, *Nebraska Press Ass'n. v. Stewart*, 427 U.S. 539 (1976), and *Gannett Co. v. DePasquale*, 443 U.S. 368 (1979), the Court had ruled that defendants' Sixth Amendment rights included the right to ask a judge to exclude the public and the press from pretrial criminal proceedings. Focusing on the specific history of trials as public events, Chief Justice Burger ruled in *Richmond Newspapers Inc. v. Virginia*, 448 U.S. 555 (1980), that the public's right to know included a right to attend and observe trials as an "unenumerated right," "implicit in the guarantees of the First Amendment." The verdict in that case was 8 to 1, and several justices who had written dissenting opinions in earlier cases expressed their sense that the Court had come around to their way of thinking to at least some degree.

Justice Stevens, concurring, wrote, "This is a watershed case. Until today the Court has accorded virtually absolute protection to the dissemination of information or ideas, but never before has it squarely held that the acquisition of newsworthy matter is entitled to any constitutional protection whatsoever." Justice Blackmun called the majority opinion "gratifying," for two reasons: first, that the Court had come to take the historical traditions of public proceedings seriously; and, second, because of the reversal of the ruling in *Gannett* from which he had dissented. Unlike Chief Justice Burger, however, Justice Blackmun would not have treated the case as one that involved the First Amendment at all: "I remain convinced that the right to a public trial is to be found where the Constitution explicitly placed it—in the Sixth Amendment." *Richmond Newspapers Inc. v. Virginia*, 448 U.S. 555 (1980).

Justice Rehnquist dissented, arguing that in the context of judicial administration the First Amendment should be read narrowly out of concern for federalist principles:

> The proper administration of justice in any nation is bound to be a matter of the highest concern to all thinking citizens. But to gradually rein in, as this Court has done over the past generation, all of the ultimate decisionmaking power over how justice shall be administered, not merely in the federal system but in each of the 50 States, is a task that no Court consisting of nine persons, however gifted, is equal to. Nor is it desirable that such authority be exercised by such a tiny numerical fragment of the 220 million people who compose the population of this country.... However high-minded the impulses which originally spawned this trend may have been...it is basically unhealthy to have so much authority concentrated in a small group of lawyers who have been appointed to the Supreme Court and enjoy virtual life tenure.... *Richmond Newspapers Inc. v. Virginia*, 448 U.S. 555 (1980).

Richmond Newspapers, however, did not establish any particular rule applicable to the press. Although that case, like *Gannett Co.* and *Nebraska Press Ass'n.*, involved newspapers as plaintiffs, the ruling concerned a general right of public access. Thus the *Houchins* rule of no special rights of access for the press, established by the thinnest of pluralities, remains the starting premise for adjudications in this area of constitutional law.

One question that has never been authoritatively resolved by the Supreme Court is when the press can be punished for its conduct in newsgathering, and whether suppression of the information that was improperly obtained can be an element of that punishment. The presumption against suppressing the publication of truthful information of public interest is usually, if not always, accompanied by the caveat "lawfully obtained." What if the press acts unlawfully, or merely improperly, in obtaining its information? In one famous case, ABC reporters took jobs at different Food Lion stores, and while there used hidden cameras to record employees redating meat, putting barbecue sauce on expired chicken to hide its smell, grinding expired meat in with fresh meat, and engaging in a variety of other criminal practices designed to pass unwholesome meat and fish products to consumers. The videos thus obtained were shown on the television show *Prime Time Live*. Food Lion sued for fraud and trespass, and asked for damages to cover the harm to their reputation. At trial, Food Lion won an award of $1,400 in compensatory damages on its fraud claim, $1.00 each on its duty of loyalty and trespass claims, and $1,500 on a claim of unfair trade practices. The major award was for punitive damages, based on harm done to Food Lion's reputation. The jury awarded $5,545,750 in punitive damages, which was lowered in posttrial proceedings to $315,000. ABC appealed the case to the Fourth Circuit, which heard the case in 1999. *Food Lion v. Capital Cities/ABC*, 194 F.3d 505 (4th Cir. 1999).

Judge Michael, writing for a three-judge panel, found that the tort claims against the reporters for fraud and trespass were valid. He refused to accept ABC's argument that the business of reporting the news conferred any immunity from generally applicable tort law. "It is true that there are First Amendment interests in newsgathering. However, the Supreme Court has said in no uncertain terms that 'generally applicable laws do not offend the First Amendment simply because their enforcement against the press has incidental effects on its ability to gather and report the news.'" The reporters' acts, said Judge Michael, constituted "breach of the duty of loyalty and trespass."

> Neither tort targets or singles out the press. Each applies to the daily transactions of the citizens of North and South Carolina. If, for example, an employee of a competing grocery chain hired on with Food Lion and videotaped damaging information in Food Lion's non-public areas for later disclosure to the public, these tort laws would apply with the same force.... Nor do we believe that applying these laws against the media will have more than an 'incidental effect' on newsgathering. We are convinced that the media can do its important job effectively without resort to the commission of run-of-the-mill torts. *Food Lion v. Capital Cities/ABC*, 194 F.3d 505 (4th Cir. 1999).

On the other hand, the judge reduced the award of damages on those tort claims to $2.00, since Food Lion could not show any damages; the reporters had shown up for work and, by all accounts, had done a good job while surreptitiously videotaping the conduct of their fellow employees.

As for the major damage award for harms to Food Lion's reputation, that judgment was overturned because Food Lion had made no attempt to prove that the representations were false and made with actual malice. The fact that Food Lion had not sued for defamation, ruled Judge Michael, did not change the fact that they were seeking to recover damages for harm to their reputation based on the publication of materials of public interest. As such, they would be required to meet the *Sullivan* standard of actual malice (which, at a minimum, requires that the facts alleged be false) in order to recover damages. The reporters' fraudulent job applications were irrelevant to the First Amendment issues involved in permitting the press to act as a vehicle for public information and debate. "In *Hustler*," Judge Michael pointed out, "the magazine's conduct would have been sufficient to constitute an unlawful act, the intentional infliction of emotional distress.... Notwithstanding the nature of the underlying act, the Court held that satisfying *New York Times* [*v. Sullivan*] was a prerequisite to the recovery of publication damages. That result was 'necessary,' the Court concluded, in order 'to give adequate breathing space to the freedoms protected by the First Amendment.'" *Food Lion v. Capital Cities/ABC*, 194 F.3d 505 (4th Cir. 1999).

The Fourth Circuit's analysis in *Food Lion*, building on *Sullivan* and *Hustler*, suggests that while reporters may be subject to ordinary liability for any wrongful acts they commit in the course of newsgathering, there is no parallel to the "exclusionary rule" of criminal procedure that says that information wrongfully obtained may not thereafter be published, nor that the First Amendment issues involved in such a case will be analyzed differently based on disapproval of the reporters' conduct. In addition, the Fourth Circuit's opinion appears to answer a question left open in *Gertz*: By the Fourth Circuit's reasoning, a business corporation is a public figure. Whether that was based on public interest in the conduct of the corporation or the nature of its business (operating stores open to the public) was unclear; it remains possible that, in the future, courts will find some corporations to be private figures and others to be public figures for purposes of a *Sullivan/Gertz* analysis.

D.   *Reporter's Privilege*

One of the great traditions in journalism is the protection of a reporter's sources. To be sent to jail for contempt of court rather than reveal the identity of a source is considered by many journalists to be a mark of integrity and distinction. Yet the legal status of such a claim of privilege is uncertain; unlike traditional privileges such as those between a doctor and patient or a clergyman and a member of a congregation, the "reporter's privilege" has no ancient common law tradition behind it. A number of states have "shield laws" that permit a reporter to withhold the identity of his or her sources, but that is a matter of a political choice by the legislature. Given the important role that a free press plays in the system of First Amendment rights, does the Constitution require government to recognize a reporter's privilege?

In 1972 the Supreme Court confronted that question directly, and answered "no." The outcome, however, was not unambiguous. The case involved three reporters who had been summoned to testify before grand juries about the sources for stories they had written on, respectively, the drug trade and the Black Panther movement. The reporters argued that they should not be forced to appear before a grand jury to answer questions about their sources "until and unless sufficient grounds are shown for believing that the reporter possesses information relevant to a crime the grand jury is investigating, that the information the reporter has is unavailable from other sources, and that the need for the information is sufficiently compelling to override the claimed invasion of First Amendment interests occasioned by the disclosure." Thus, what the reporters were claiming was not an absolute privilege against disclosure, but the equivalent of a constitutional right which, they argued, had to be balanced against the government's interest in their information. In a 5-to-4 decision, the majority ruled that reporters had no special constitutional rights of nondisclosure that the government is required to overcome.

BRANZBURG v. HAYES

SUPREME COURT OF THE UNITED STATES

408 U.S. 665 (1972)

JUSTICE WHITE wrote the opinion of the Court, in which BURGER, C. J., and BLACKMUN, POWELL, and REHNQUIST joined. JUSTICE POWELL filed a concurring opinion. JUSTICE DOUGLAS filed a dissenting opinion. JUSTICE STEWART filed a dissenting opinion, in which BRENNAN and MARSHALL joined.

...The heart of the claim is that the burden on news gathering resulting from compelling reporters to disclose confidential information outweighs any public interest in obtaining the information.... We do not question the significance of free speech, press, or assembly to the country's welfare. Nor is it suggested that news gathering does not qualify for First Amendment protection; without some protection for seeking out the news, freedom of the press could be eviscerated. But these cases involve no intrusions upon speech or assembly, no prior restraint or restriction on what the press may publish, and no express or implied command that the press publish what it prefers to withhold. No exaction or tax for the privilege of publishing, and no penalty, civil or criminal, related to the content of published material is at issue here. The use of confidential sources by the press is not forbidden or restricted; reporters remain free to seek news from any source by means within the law. No attempt is made to require the press to publish its sources of information or indiscriminately to disclose them on request.

The sole issue before us is the obligation of reporters to respond to grand jury subpoenas as other citizens do and to answer questions relevant to an investigation into the commission of crime. Citizens generally are not constitutionally immune from grand jury subpoenas; and neither the First Amendment nor any other constitutional provision protects the average citizen from disclosing to a grand jury information that he has received in confidence. The claim is, however, that reporters are exempt from these obligations because if forced to respond to subpoenas and identify their sources or disclose other confidences, their informants will refuse or be reluctant to furnish newsworthy information in the future. This asserted burden on news gathering is said to make compelled testimony from newsmen constitutionally suspect and to require a privileged position for them.

It is clear that the First Amendment does not invalidate every incidental burdening of the press that may result from the enforcement of civil or criminal statutes of general applicability. Under prior cases, otherwise valid laws serving substantial public interests may be enforced against the press as against others, despite the possible burden that may be imposed. The Court has emphasized that the publisher of a newspaper has no special immunity from the application of general laws. He has no special privilege to invade the rights and liberties of others....

It has generally been held that the First Amendment does not guarantee the press a constitutional right of special access to information not available to the public generally. Despite the fact that news gathering may be hampered, the press is regularly excluded from grand jury proceedings, our own conferences, the meetings of other official bodies gathered in executive session, and the meetings of private organizations. Newsmen have no constitutional right of access to the scenes of crime or disaster when the general public is excluded, and they may be prohibited from attending or publishing information about trials if such restrictions are necessary to assure a defendant a fair trial before an impartial tribunal.... It is thus not surprising that the great weight of authority is that newsmen are not exempt from the normal duty of appearing before a grand jury and answering questions relevant to a criminal investigation....

The prevailing constitutional view of the newsman's privilege is very much rooted in the ancient role of the grand jury that has the dual function of determining if there is probable cause to believe that a crime has been committed and of protecting citizens against unfounded criminal prosecutions. Grand jury proceedings are constitutionally mandated for the institution of federal criminal prosecutions for capital or other serious crimes, and "its constitutional prerogatives are rooted in long centuries of Anglo-American history...." [T]he grand jury's authority to subpoena witnesses is not only historic, but essential to its task. Although the powers of the grand jury are not unlimited and are subject to the supervision of a judge, the longstanding principle that "the public...has a right to every man's evidence," except for those persons protected by a constitutional, common-law, or statutory privilege, is particularly applicable to grand jury proceedings.

A number of States have provided newsmen a statutory privilege of varying breadth, but the majority have not done so, and none has been provided by federal statute. Until now the only testimonial privilege for unofficial witnesses that is rooted in the Federal Constitution is the Fifth Amendment privilege against compelled self-incrimination. We are asked to create another by interpreting the First Amendment to grant newsmen a testimonial privilege that other citizens do not enjoy. This we decline to do. Fair and effective law enforcement aimed at providing security for the person and property of the individual is a fundamental function of government, and the grand jury plays an important, constitutionally mandated role in this process. On the records now before us, we perceive no basis for holding that the public interest in law enforcement and in ensuring effective grand jury proceedings is insufficient to override the consequential, but uncertain, burden on news gathering that is said to result from insisting that reporters, like other citizens, respond to relevant questions put to them in the course of a valid grand jury investigation or criminal trial.

This conclusion itself involves no restraint on what newspapers may publish or on the type or quality of information reporters may seek to acquire, nor does it threaten the vast bulk of confidential relationships between reporters and their sources. Grand juries address themselves to the issues of whether crimes have been committed and who committed them. Only where news sources themselves are implicated in crime or possess information relevant to the grand jury's task need they or the reporter be concerned about grand jury subpoenas. Nothing before us indicates that a large number or percentage of all confidential news sources falls into either category and would in any way be deterred by our holding that the Constitution does not, as it never has, exempt the newsman from performing the citizen's normal duty of appearing and furnishing information relevant to the grand jury's task....

[A]s we have earlier indicated, news gathering is not without its First Amendment protections, and grand jury investigations if instituted or conducted other than in good faith, would pose wholly different issues for resolution under the First Amendment. Official harassment of the press undertaken not for purposes of law enforcement but to disrupt a reporter's relationship with his news sources would have no justification. Grand juries are subject to judicial control and subpoenas to motions to quash. We do not expect courts will forget that grand juries must operate within the limits of the First Amendment as well as the Fifth....

JUSTICE DOUGLAS, dissenting.

...The press has a preferred position in our constitutional scheme, not to enable it to make money, not to set newsmen apart as a favored class, but to bring fulfillment to the public's right to know. The right to know is crucial to the governing powers of the people, to paraphrase Alexander Meiklejohn. Knowledge is essential to informed decisions....

A reporter is no better than his source of information. Unless he has a privilege to withhold the identity of his source, he will be the victim of governmental intrigue or aggression. If he can be summoned to testify in secret before a grand jury, his sources will dry up and the attempted exposure, the effort to enlighten the public, will be ended. If what the Court sanctions today becomes settled law, then the reporter's main function in American society will be to pass on to the public the press releases which the various departments of government issue.... The record in this case is replete with weighty affidavits from responsible newsmen, telling how important is the sanctity of their sources of information. When we deny newsmen that protection, we deprive the people of the information needed to run the affairs of the Nation in an intelligent way....

JUSTICE STEWART, with whom BRENNAN and MARSHALL join, dissenting.

The Court's crabbed view of the First Amendment reflects a disturbing insensitivity to the critical role of an independent press in our society. The question whether a reporter has a constitutional right to a confidential relationship with his source is of first impression here, but the principles that should guide our decision are as basic as any to be found in the Constitution....

Enlightened choice by an informed citizenry is the basic ideal upon which an open society is premised, and a free press is thus indispensable to a free society. Not only does the press enhance personal self-fulfillment by providing the people with the widest possible range of fact and opinion, but it also is an incontestable precondition of self-government.... In keeping with this tradition, we have held that the right to publish is central to the First Amendment and basic to the existence of constitutional democracy. A corollary of the right to publish must be the right to gather news. The full flow of information to the public protected by the free-press guarantee would be severely curtailed if no protection whatever were afforded to the process by which news is assembled and disseminated.... News must not be unnecessarily cut off at its source, for without freedom to acquire information the right to publish would be impermissibly compromised. Accordingly, a right to gather news, of some dimensions, must exist. As Madison wrote: "A popular Government, without popular information, or the means of acquiring it, is but a Prologue to a Farce or a Tragedy; or, perhaps both."

The right to gather news implies, in turn, a right to a confidential relationship between a reporter and his source. This proposition follows as a matter of simple logic once three factual predicates are recognized: (1) newsmen require informants to gather news; (2) confidentiality—the promise or understanding that names or certain aspects of communications will be kept off the record—is essential to the creation and maintenance of a news-gathering relationship with informants; and (3) an unbridled subpoena power—the absence of a constitutional right protecting, in any way, a confidential relationship from compulsory process—will either deter sources from divulging information or deter reporters from gathering and publishing information....

In addition to the closeness of the outcome, the ambiguity in the ruling in *Branzburg* derives from two aspects of the opinion. First, although the outcome is adverse to the newsmen involved in the case, the majority opinion contains strong statements to the effect that the act of newsgathering is constitutionally protected. Second, Justice White focused heavily, in his opinion, on the historical and political significance of the grand jury. By implication, it is possible that in a different situation, the government's interest in forcing a reporter to disclose confidential information or the names of sources might not be sufficient to justify a contempt citation. In other words, the very balancing test that the reporters sought at the outset of the case, and which the majority rejects, arguably reappears in the form of Justice White's emphasis on the strength of the government's interest in the particular setting of the case. This has been the interpretation of some of the circuit courts. The Fourth Circuit, for example, has turned the mandate of *Branzburg* into a three part test: "(1) whether the information is relevant, (2) whether the information can be obtained by alternative means, and (3) whether there is a compelling interest in the information." *Ashcraft v. Conoco, Inc.* 218 F.3d 282 (4th Cir. 2000). Other issues in this area similarly remain to be worked out by the courts, and will undoubtedly require resolution by the Supreme Court in the future.

E. *The Special Case of Broadcast Media:*
   The Rise and Fall of the Equal Time Doctrine

The Federal Communications Commission was created in the 1920s to regulate the burgeoning and chaotic field of broadcasting. The impetus for the commission's creation came from within the industry. Radio stations were discovering that their signals could be interfered with or blocked by rival stations using the same frequencies. As a result, they demanded that the federal government institute a system of licensing which would grant monopolies within regions to the use of certain bandwidths on the radio (and, later, television) spectrum. In return, the FCC demanded that these monopolies be operated in a way that served the public interest. Thus the heavy regulation of broadcast media, from its outset, was justified not as a regulation on otherwise free expression, but as a condition of receipt of an immensely valuable government benefit. Under what became known as "the fairness doctrine," broadcasters were required, as a condition of their license, "to cover vitally important controversial issues of interest in their communities," and second, "to provide a reasonable opportunity for the presentation of contrasting viewpoints." In 1967, the fairness doctrine was formally codified in regulations that required broadcasters who offered editorial opinions to provide equal time for opposing views. The fear was that without such regulations, media outlets controlled by companies with virtual monopolies over a given area could subvert the political function of a free press by making themselves vehicles for propaganda.

The rules that comprised the "fairness doctrine" were controversial from the outset. Broadcasters challenged their constitutionality as an infringement on free expression, while supporters of the rules argued that they were a fair exchange for the benefits that broadcasters received from the government, and necessary to ensure that the media would play a constructive role in covering political matters.

RED LION BROADCASTING CO., INC. v. FEDERAL COMMUNICATIONS COMMISSION

SUPREME COURT OF THE UNITED STATES

395 U.S. 367 (1969)

JUSTICE WHITE delivered the opinion of the Court

...The broadcasters challenge the fairness doctrine and its specific manifestations in the personal attack and political editorial rules on conventional First Amendment grounds, alleging that the rules abridge their freedom of speech and press. Their contention is that the First Amendment protects their desire to use their allotted frequencies continuously to broadcast whatever they choose, and to exclude whomever they choose from ever using that frequency. No man may be prevented from saying or publishing what he thinks, or from refusing in his speech or other utterances to give equal weight to the views of his opponents. This right, they say, applies equally to broadcasters.

Although broadcasting is clearly a medium affected by a First Amendment interest, differences in the characteristics of new media justify differences in the First Amendment standards applied to them. For example, the ability of new technology to produce sounds more raucous than those of the human voice justifies restrictions on the sound level, and on the hours and places of use, of sound trucks so long as the restrictions are reasonable and applied without discrimination.

Just as the Government may limit the use of sound-amplifying equipment potentially so noisy that it drowns out civilized private speech, so may the Government limit the use of broadcast equipment. The right of free speech of a broadcaster, the user of a sound truck, or any other individual does not embrace a right to snuff out the free speech of others.

When two people converse face to face, both should not speak at once if either is to be clearly understood. But the range of the human voice is so limited that there could be meaningful communications if half the people in the United States were talking and the other half listening. Just as clearly, half the people might publish and the other half read. But the reach of radio signals is incomparably greater than the range of the human voice and the problem of interference is a massive reality. The lack of know-how and equipment may keep many from the air, but only a tiny fraction of those with resources and intelligence can hope to communicate by radio at the same time if intelligible communication is to be had, even if the entire radio spectrum is utilized in the present state of commercially acceptable technology.

It was this fact, and the chaos which ensued from permitting anyone to use any frequency at whatever power level he wished, which made necessary the enactment of the Radio Act of 1927 and the Communications Act of 1934.... It was this reality which at the very least necessitated first the division of the radio spectrum into portions reserved respectively for public broadcasting and for other important radio uses such as amateur operation, aircraft, police, defense, and navigation; and then the subdivision of each portion, and assignment of specific frequencies to individual users or groups of users. Beyond this, however, because the frequencies reserved for public broadcasting were limited in number, it was essential for the Government to tell some applicants that they could not broadcast at all because there was room for only a few.

Where there are substantially more individuals who want to broadcast than there are frequencies to allocate, it is idle to posit an unabridgeable First Amendment right to broadcast comparable to the right of every individual to speak, write, or publish. If 100 persons want broadcast licenses but there are only 10 frequencies to allocate, all of them may have the same "right" to a license; but if there is to be any effective communication by radio, only a few can be licensed and the rest must be barred from the airwaves. It would be strange if the First Amendment, aimed at protecting and furthering communications, prevented the Government from making radio communication possible by requiring licenses to broadcast and by limiting the number of licenses so as not to overcrowd the spectrum.

This has been the consistent view of the Court. Congress unquestionably has the power to grant and deny licenses and to eliminate existing stations. No one has a First Amendment right to a license or to monopolize a radio frequency; to deny a station license because "the public interest" requires it "is not a denial of free speech."

By the same token, as far as the First Amendment is concerned those who are licensed stand no better than those to whom licenses are refused. A license permits broadcasting, but the licensee has no constitutional right to be the one who holds the license or to monopolize a radio frequency to the exclusion of his fellow citizens. There is nothing in the First Amendment which prevents the Government from requiring a licensee to share his frequency with others and to conduct himself as a proxy or fiduciary with obligations to present those views and voices which are representative of his community and which would otherwise, by necessity, be barred from the airwaves.

This is not to say that the First Amendment is irrelevant to public broadcasting. On the contrary, it has a major role to play as the Congress itself recognized in § 326, which forbids FCC interference with "the right of free speech by means of radio communication." Because of the scarcity of radio frequencies, the Government is permitted to put restraints on licensees in favor of others whose views should be expressed on this unique medium. But the people as a whole retain their interest in free speech by radio and their collective right to have the medium function consistently with the ends and purposes of the First Amendment. It is the right of the viewers and listeners, not the right of the broadcasters, which is paramount. It is the purpose of the First Amendment to preserve an uninhibited marketplace of ideas in which truth will ultimately prevail, rather than to countenance monopolization of that market, whether it be by the Government itself or a private licensee. "Speech concerning public affairs is more than self-expression; it is the essence of self-government." It is the right of the public to receive suitable access to social, political, esthetic, moral, and other ideas and experiences which is crucial here. That right may not constitutionally be abridged either by Congress or by the FCC.

Rather than confer frequency monopolies on a relatively small number of licensees, in a Nation of 200,000,000, the Government could surely have decreed that each frequency should be shared among all or some of those who wish to use it, each being assigned a portion of the broadcast day or the broadcast week. The ruling and regulations at issue here do not go quite so far. They assert that under specified circumstances, a licensee must offer to make available a reasonable amount of broadcast time to those who have a view different from that which has already been expressed on his station. The expression of a political endorsement, or of a personal attack while dealing with a controversial public issue, simply triggers this time sharing. As we have said, the First Amendment confers no right on licensees to prevent others from broadcasting on "their" frequencies and no right to an unconditional monopoly of a scarce resource which the Government has denied others the right to use.

In terms of constitutional principle, and as enforced sharing of a scarce resource, the personal attack and political editorial rules are indistinguishable from the equal-time provision of § 315, a specific enactment of Congress requiring stations to set aside reply time under specified circumstances and to which the fairness doctrine and these constituent regulations are important complements. That provision, which has been part of the law since 1927, has been held valid by this Court as an obligation of the licensee relieving him of any power in any way to prevent or censor the broadcast, and thus insulating him from liability for defamation. The constitutionality of the statute under the First Amendment was unquestioned.

Nor can we say that it is inconsistent with the First Amendment goal of producing an informed public capable of conducting its own affairs to require a broadcaster to permit answers to personal attacks occurring in the course of discussing controversial issues, or to require that the political opponents of those endorsed by the station be given a chance to communicate with the public. Otherwise, station owners and a few networks would have unfettered power to make time available only to the highest bidders, to communicate only their own views on public issues, people and candidates, and to permit on the air only those with whom they agreed. There is no sanctuary in the First Amendment for unlimited private censorship operating in a medium not open to all. Freedom of the press from governmental interference under the First Amendment does not sanction repression of that freedom by private interests.

It is strenuously argued, however, that if political editorials or personal attacks will trigger an obligation in broadcasters to afford the opportunity for expression to speakers who need not pay for time and whose views are unpalatable to the licensees, then broadcasters will be irresistibly forced to self-censorship and their coverage of controversial public issues will be eliminated or at least rendered wholly ineffective. Such a result would indeed be a serious matter, for should licensees actually eliminate their coverage of controversial issues, the purposes of the doctrine would be stifled.

At this point, however, as the Federal Communications Commission has indicated, that possibility is at best speculative.... [I]f present licensees should suddenly prove timorous, the Commission is not powerless to insist that they give adequate and fair attention to public issues. It does not violate the First Amendment to treat licensees given the privilege of using scarce radio frequencies as proxies for the entire community, obligated to give suitable time and attention to matters of great public concern. To condition the granting or renewal of licenses on a willingness to present representative community views on controversial issues is consistent with the ends and purposes of those constitutional provisions forbidding the abridgment of freedom of speech and freedom of the press. Congress need not stand idly by and permit those with licenses to ignore the problems which beset the people or to exclude from the airways anything but their own views of fundamental questions. The statute, long administrative practice, and cases are to this effect.

Licenses to broadcast do not confer ownership of designated frequencies, but only the temporary privilege of using them. Unless renewed, they expire within three years. The statute mandates the issuance of licenses if the "public convenience, interest, or necessity will be served thereby." In applying this standard the Commission for 40 years has been choosing licensees based in part on their program proposals....

It is argued that even if at one time the lack of available frequencies for all who wished to use them justified the Government's choice of those who would best serve the public interest by acting as proxy for those who would present differing views, or by giving the latter access directly to broadcast facilities, this condition no longer prevails so that continuing control is not justified. To this there are several answers.

Scarcity is not entirely a thing of the past. Advances in technology, such as microwave transmission, have led to more efficient utilization of the frequency spectrum, but uses for that spectrum have also grown apace....

The rapidity with which technological advances succeed one another to create more efficient use of spectrum space on the one hand, and to create new uses for that space by ever growing numbers of people on the other, makes it unwise to speculate on the future allocation of that space. It is enough to say that the resource is one of considerable and growing importance whose scarcity impelled its regulation by an agency authorized by Congress. Nothing in this record, or in our own researches, convinces us that the resource is no longer one for which there are more immediate and potential uses than can be accommodated, and for which wise planning is essential. This does not mean, of course, that every possible wavelength must be occupied at every hour by some vital use in order to sustain the congressional judgment. The substantial capital investment required for many uses, in addition to the potentiality for confusion and interference inherent in any scheme for continuous kaleidoscopic reallocation of all available space may make this unfeasible. The allocation need not be made at such a breakneck pace that the objectives of the allocation are themselves imperiled.

Even where there are gaps in spectrum utilization, the fact remains that existing broadcasters have often attained their present position because of their initial government selection in competition with others before new technological advances opened new opportunities for further uses. Long experience in broadcasting, confirmed habits of listeners and viewers, network affiliation, and other advantages in program procurement give existing broadcasters a substantial advantage over new entrants, even where new entry is technologically possible. These advantages are the fruit of a preferred position conferred by the Government. Some present possibility for new entry by competing stations is not enough, in itself, to render unconstitutional the Government's effort to assure that a broadcaster's programming ranges widely enough to serve the public interest.

In view of the scarcity of broadcast frequencies, the Government's role in allocating those frequencies, and the legitimate claims of those unable without governmental assistance to gain access to those frequencies for expression of their views, we hold the regulations and ruling at issue here are both authorized by statute and constitutional....

While *Red Lion* established the constitutionality of the fairness doctrine in general, specific rules continued to be challenged, both in court and politically. In 1985, under the Reagan administration, the FCC issued a "Fairness Report" that announced the effective end of the fairness doctrine in its broad form, on the grounds that new media technologies and outlets ensured dissemination of diverse viewpoints without need for federal regulation. In addition, the Report found that the fairness doctrine chilled speech on controversial subjects, and that the doctrine interfered too greatly with journalistic freedom. In 1987, in the course of court proceedings, the FCC announced that it would no longer enforce the fairness doctrine. Two specific rules, however, continued in force. One was a rule that required stations to provide free reply time for opponents of political candidates endorsed by the stations, and another that required the provision of free air time for candidates and other public figures whose personal integrity had been called into question during broadcasts.

While that order was still in effect, a federal appeals court considered the issue and struck down the last elements of the fairness doctrine. In

1999, a federal appeals court ruled that the FCC had failed to meet its burden of demonstrating adequate grounds for the continuation of the rules and had been dilatory in responding to challenges to its authority. *Radio-Television News Directors Ass'n. and National Ass'n. of Broadcasters v. Federal Communications Commission*, 184 F.3d 872 (D.C. Cir. 1999). In 2000, the debate over the remaining elements of the fairness doctrine became an issue in the presidential campaign, as the Republican Party called for abolition of the rules while the Democratic Party made their retention an element of its national platform. A closely divided (three Democrats, two Republicans) FCC decided to suspend the rules for sixty days as an "experiment" during the presidential election, and subsequently abandoned them altogether.

It remains the case that broadcast media are subject to a greater degree of regulation than print media concerning matters such as indecency, allowable amounts of advertising per hour of broadcast, child-friendly programming, and so on. In principle, moreover, *Red Lion* remains good law, so that a future FCC might attempt to reinstate some version of the fairness doctrine based on a more detailed showing of public need. In the meantime, however, the negative limitations on press activities are not accompanied by an affirmative political duty to present issues to the public in any particular way.

IX. Rights of Assembly and Petition

A. *Assembly*

The right of free assembly has for the most part already been dealt with in the discussions of freedom of speech, speech-plus, and expressive conduct. Like the right of association, the right of assembly has never been understood to refer to any gathering of persons, but only to gatherings motivated by some political purpose. As a result, in the few cases where government is found to have violated the right of assembly, what is involved is a none-too-subtle attempt to silence political speech in the form of peaceful protests in public forums. A classic example, excerpted below, is *Edwards v. South Carolina*, 372 U.S. 229 (1963), a civil rights–era case involving an attempt by police to prevent a peaceful political protest on the steps of the state Capitol.

EDWARDS v. SOUTH CAROLINA

SUPREME COURT OF THE UNITED STATES

372 U.S. 229 (1963)

JUSTICE STEWART delivered the opinion of the Court.

...Late in the morning of March 2, 1961, the petitioners, high school and college students of the Negro race, met at the Zion Baptist Church in Columbia. From there, at about noon, they walked in separate groups of about 15 to the South Carolina State House grounds, an area of two city blocks open to the general public. Their purpose was "to submit a protest to the citizens of South Carolina, along with the Legislative Bodies of South Carolina, our feelings and our dissatisfaction with the present condition of discriminatory actions against Negroes, in general, and to let them know that we were dissatisfied and that we would like for the laws which prohibited Negro privileges in this State to be removed."

Already on the State House grounds when the petitioners arrived were 30 or more law enforcement officers, who had advance knowledge that the petitioners were coming. Each group of petitioners entered the grounds through a driveway and parking area known in the record as the "horseshoe." As they entered, they were told by the law enforcement officials that "they had a right, as a citizen, to go through the State House grounds, as any other citizen has, as long as they were peaceful." During the next half hour or 45 minutes, the petitioners, in the same small groups, walked single file or two abreast in an orderly way through the grounds, each group carrying placards bearing such messages as "I am proud to be a Negro" and "Down with segregation."

During this time a crowd of some 200 to 300 onlookers had collected in the horseshoe area and on the adjacent sidewalks. There was no evidence to suggest that these onlookers were anything but curious, and no evidence at all of any threatening remarks, hostile gestures, or offensive language on the part of any member of the crowd. The City Manager testified that he recognized some of the onlookers, whom he did not identify, as "possible trouble makers," but his subsequent testimony made clear that nobody among the crowd actually caused or threatened any trouble. There was no obstruction of pedestrian or vehicular traffic within the State House grounds. No vehicle was prevented from entering or leaving the horseshoe area.... Police protection at the scene was at all times sufficient to meet any foreseeable possibility of disorder.

In the situation and under the circumstances thus described, the police authorities advised the petitioners that they would be arrested if they did not disperse within 15 minutes. Instead of dispersing, the petitioners engaged in what the City Manager described as "boisterous," "loud," and "flamboyant" conduct, which, as his later testimony made clear, consisted of listening to a "religious harangue" by one of their leaders, and loudly singing "The Star Spangled Banner" and other patriotic and religious songs, while stamping their feet and clapping their hands. After 15 minutes had passed, the police arrested the petitioners and marched them off to jail. Upon this evidence the state trial court convicted the petitioners of breach of the peace....

It has long been established that these First Amendment freedoms are protected by the Fourteenth Amendment from invasion by the States. The circumstances in this case reflect an exercise of these basic constitutional rights in their most pristine and classic form. The petitioners felt aggrieved by laws of South Carolina which allegedly "prohibited Negro privileges in this State." They peaceably assembled at the site of the State Government and there peaceably expressed their grievances "to the citizens of South Carolina, along with the Legislative Bodies of South Carolina." Not until they were told by police officials that they must disperse on pain of arrest did they do more. Even then, they but sang patriotic and religious songs after one of their leaders had delivered a "religious harangue." There was no violence or threat of violence on their part, or on the part of any member of the crowd watching them. Police protection was "ample."

This, therefore, was a far cry from the situation in *Feiner v. New York*, 340 U.S. 315, where two policemen were faced with a crowd which was "pushing, shoving and milling around," where at least one member of the crowd "threatened violence if the police did not act," where "the crowd was pressing closer around petitioner and the officer," and where "the speaker passes the bounds of argument or persuasion and undertakes incitement to riot." And the record is barren of any evidence of "fighting words." See *Chaplinsky v. New Hampshire*, 315 U.S. 568....

The Fourteenth Amendment does not permit a State to make criminal the peaceful expression of unpopular views.... As in *Terminiello v. Chicago*, 337 U.S. 1, the courts of South Carolina have defined a criminal offense so as to permit conviction of the petitioners if their speech "stirred people to anger, invited public dispute, or brought about a condition of unrest. A conviction resting on any of those grounds may not stand"....

JUSTICE CLARK, dissenting.

...In *Cantwell v. Connecticut*, supra, at 308, this Court recognized that "when clear and present danger of riot, disorder, interference with traffic upon the public streets, or other immediate threat to public safety, peace, or order, appears, the power of the State to prevent or punish is obvious." And in *Feiner v. New York*, 340 U.S. 315 (1951), we upheld a conviction for breach of the peace in a situation no more dangerous than that found here. There the demonstration was conducted by only one person and the crowd was limited to approximately 80, as compared with the present lineup of some 200 demonstrators and 300 onlookers. There the petitioner was "endeavoring to arouse the Negro people against the whites, urging that they rise up in arms and fight for equal rights." Only one person—in a city having an entirely different historical background—was exhorting adults. Here 200 youthful Negro demonstrators were being aroused to a "fever pitch" before a crowd of some 300 people who undoubtedly were hostile. Perhaps their speech was not so animated but in this setting their actions, their placards reading "You may jail our bodies but not our souls" and their chanting of "I Shall Not Be Moved," accompanied by stamping feet and clapping hands, created a much greater danger of riot and disorder. It is my belief that anyone conversant with the almost spontaneous combustion in some Southern communities in such a situation will agree that the City Manager's action may well have averted a major catastrophe.

The gravity of the danger here surely needs no further explication. The imminence of that danger has been emphasized at every stage of this proceeding, from the complaints charging that the demonstrations "tended directly to immediate violence" to the State Supreme Court's affirmance on the authority of *Feiner*, supra. This record, then, shows no steps backward from a standard of "clear and present danger." But to say that the police may not intervene until the riot has occurred is like keeping out the doctor until the patient dies. I cannot subscribe to such a doctrine....

While *Edwards* represents the situation in which the right of assembly is the clearest (along with *Thornhill v. Alabama*, 310 U.S. 102 [1940], a case with similar facts), *City of Chicago v. Morales* demonstrates the limits of the right guaranteed by the First Amendment. In 1992, the Chicago City Council enacted the Gang Congregation Ordinance, which made loitering by gang members a crime. The offense was defined by four elements:

First, the police officer must reasonably believe that at least one of the two or more persons present in a "public place" is a "criminal street gang member." Second, the persons must be "loitering," which the ordinance defines as "remaining in any one place with no apparent purpose." Third, the officer must then order "all" of the persons to disperse and remove themselves "from the area."

Fourth, a person must disobey the officer's order. If any person, whether a gang member or not, disobeys the officer's order, that person is guilty of violating the ordinance.

During three years in which the law was enforced, the police issued over 89,000 dispersal orders and arrested over 42,000 people for violating the ordinance. Reviewing the statute, Justice Stevens explicitly found that no First Amendment rights of association were involved. Leaving open the possibility that other protected rights might be at issue, he ultimately decided the case for a 6-to-3 majority on the grounds that the statute was void for vagueness under the Due Process Clause of the Fourteenth Amendment. Thus the closest thing to a clear right of assembly case to be considered by the Court in modern times ended with a no-decision on the First Amendment questions.

CITY OF CHICAGO v. MORALES

SUPREME COURT OF THE UNITED STATES

527 U.S. 41 (1998)

JUSTICE STEVENS announced the judgment of the Court and delivered the opinion of the Court with respect to Parts I, II, and V, and an opinion with respect to Parts III, IV, and VI, in which JUSTICE SOUTER and JUSTICE GINSBURG join.

...The basic factual predicate for the city's ordinance is not in dispute. As the city argues in its brief, "the very presence of a large collection of obviously brazen, insistent, and lawless gang members and hangers-on on the public ways intimidates residents, who become afraid even to leave their homes and go about their business. That, in turn, imperils community residents' sense of safety and security, detracts from property values, and can ultimately destabilize entire neighborhoods." The findings in the ordinance explain that it was motivated by these concerns. We have no doubt that a law that directly prohibited such intimidating conduct would be constitutional, but this ordinance broadly covers a significant amount of additional activity. Uncertainty about the scope of that additional coverage provides the basis for respondents' claim that the ordinance is too vague.

We are confronted at the outset with the city's claim that it was improper for the state courts to conclude that the ordinance is invalid on its face. The city correctly points out that imprecise laws can be attacked on their face under two different doctrines. First, the overbreadth doctrine permits the facial invalidation of laws that inhibit the exercise of First Amendment rights if the impermissible applications of the law are substantial when "judged in relation to the statute's plainly legitimate sweep." *Broadrick v. Oklahoma*, 413 U.S. 601 (1973). Second, even if an enactment does not reach a substantial amount of constitutionally protected conduct, it may be impermissibly vague because it fails to establish standards for the police and public that are sufficient to guard against the arbitrary deprivation of liberty interests.

While we, like the Illinois courts, conclude that the ordinance is invalid on its face, we do not rely on the overbreadth doctrine. We agree with the city's submission that the law does not have a sufficiently substantial impact on conduct protected by the First Amendment to render it unconstitutional. The ordinance does not prohibit speech. Because the term "loiter" is defined as remaining in one place "with no apparent purpose," it is also clear that it does not prohibit any form of conduct that is apparently intended to convey a message. By its terms, the ordinance is inapplicable to assemblies that are designed to demonstrate a group's support of, or opposition to, a particular point of view. Its impact on the social contact between gang members and others does not impair the First Amendment "right of association" that our cases have recognized.

On the other hand, as the United States recognizes, the freedom to loiter for innocent purposes is part of the "liberty" protected by the Due Process Clause of the Fourteenth Amendment. We have expressly identified this "right to remove from one place to another according to inclination" as "an attribute of personal liberty" protected by the Constitution....

There is no need, however, to decide whether the impact of the Chicago ordinance on constitutionally protected liberty alone would suffice to support a facial challenge under the overbreadth doctrine. For it is clear that the vagueness of this enactment makes a facial challenge appropriate. This is not an ordinance that "simply regulates business behavior and contains a scienter requirement." It is a criminal law that contains no mens rea requirement, and infringes on constitutionally protected rights. When vagueness permeates the text of such a law, it is subject to facial attack....

B. *Petition*

The two cases excerpted above, *Edwards* and *Morales*, demonstrate that, in practice, the right of peaceful assembly adds few if any prerogatives to those already guaranteed by the Free Speech clause. To an extent, the same kind of redundancy appears in many of the cases concerning the right "to petition for the redress of grievances." One of the most commonly litigated scenarios, for example, involves claims by prisoners that their jailors have denied them the right of petition by restricting their access to legal materials or advice. These claims, however, have arisen in the context of prisoners' desires to submit writs of habeas corpus. Since the right of habeas corpus appeals is separately guaranteed (Article I, § 9), the treatment of the issue falls only incidentally under the Petition Clause of the First Amendment. The cases are nonetheless interesting, however, as they constitute the only extended line of jurisprudential development in the general area of a right to petition courts (one version of a petition to the government for redress of grievances.)

In *Ex parte Hull*, 312 U.S. 546 (1941), the Court struck down a regulation that required prisoners' habeas petitions to be reviewed by state officers, who would only permit them to be delivered to a court if they decided that the prisoners' claims had "merit." The principle that prison officials could not interfere with prisoners' exercise of their right to submit habeas petitions was further developed in *Avery v. Johnson*, 393 U.S. 483 (1968). That case involved an appeal by a prisoner transferred to maximum security for violating a rule against giving assistance to other prisoners in preparing writs of habeas corpus. The rule under which the prisoner was disciplined was ruled unconstitutional in a 7-to-2 opinion written by Justice Fortas. "There can be no doubt that Tennessee could not constitutionally adopt and enforce a rule forbidding illiterate or poorly educated prisoners to file habeas corpus petitions. Here Tennessee has adopted a rule which, in the absence of any other source of assistance for such prisoners, effectively does just that...." *Avery*, however, was decided without any reference to the First Amendment or a right of petition generally.

In *Bounds v. Smith* (1977), by a vote of 6 to 3, the Court found that the obligations of prison officials went beyond refraining from interference with prisoners' attempts to file writs. Justice Marshall, writing for the majority, concluded that "prisoners have a constitutional right of access to the courts," and that this implied that prisoners be affirmatively provided with the resources necessary to exercise that right:

> Thus, in order to prevent "effectively foreclosed access," indigent prisoners must be allowed to file appeals and habeas corpus petitions without payment of docket fees. Because we recognized that "adequate and effective appellate review" is impossible without a trial transcript or adequate substitute, we held that States must provide trial records to inmates unable to buy them. Similarly, counsel must be appointed to give indigent inmates "a meaningful appeal" from their convictions.... It is indisputable that indigent inmates must be provided at state expense with paper and pen to draft legal documents, with notarial services to authenticate them, and with stamps to mail them. States must forgo collection of docket fees otherwise payable to the treasury and expend funds for transcripts. State expenditures are necessary to pay lawyers for indigent defendants at trial, and in appeals as of right. This is not to say that economic factors may not be considered, for example, in choosing the methods used to provide meaningful access. But the cost of protecting a constitutional right cannot justify its total denial. Thus, neither the availability of jailhouse lawyers nor the necessity for affirmative state action is dispositive of respondents' claims. The inquiry is rather whether law libraries or other forms of legal assistance are needed to give prisoners a reasonably

adequate opportunity to present claimed violations of fundamental constitutional rights to the courts. *Bounds v. Smith*, 430 U.S. 817 (1977).

Specifically, Marshall ruled that prisoners were entitled to have access to "adequate law libraries or adequate assistance from persons trained in the law."

Bounds seemed to suggest an affirmative right of access to courts, one that government would be obliged to satisfy. In 1996, however, the extent of that ruling was sharply curtailed, when the Court ruled that in order to challenge the adequacy of resources provided by a prison, a prisoner had to demonstrate that they had suffered a particular harm in the form of a legal pleading that they were unable to prepare adequately on their own behalf. In *Lewis v. Casey* (1996), inmates filed a claim seeking a court order requiring a prison to provide better legal materials. When their claim reached the Supreme Court, Justice Scalia, writing for a five-member majority (Justice Stevens dissenting, Justices Souter, Ginsburg, and Breyer dissenting in part), found that the prisoners lacked standing by virtue of the nature of the right that *Bounds* had created:

> [R]espondents seem to assume [that] the right at issue…[is] the right to a law library or to legal assistance. But *Bounds* established no such right…. The right that *Bounds* acknowledged was the (already well-established) right of access to the courts…. Although it affirmed a court order requiring North Carolina to make law library facilities available to inmates, it stressed that that was merely "one constitutionally acceptable method to assure meaningful access to the courts," and that "our decision here…does not foreclose alternative means to achieve that goal." In other words, prison law libraries and legal assistance programs are not ends in themselves, but only the means for ensuring "a reasonably adequate opportunity to present claimed violations of fundamental constitutional rights to the courts…." It must be acknowledged that several statements in *Bounds* went beyond the right of access recognized in the earlier cases on which it relied, which was a right to bring to court a grievance that the inmate wished to present. These statements appear to suggest that the State must enable the prisoner to discover grievances, and to litigate effectively once in court. These elaborations upon the right of access to the courts have no antecedent in our pre-*Bounds* cases, and we now disclaim them. To demand the conferral of such sophisticated legal capabilities upon a mostly uneducated and indeed largely illiterate prison population is effectively to demand permanent provision of counsel, which we do not believe the Constitution requires. *Lewis v. Casey*, 518 U.S. 343 (1996).

The reference to "permanent provision of counsel" points to the heart of the opinion, which holds that the right of access to the courts does not translate into a right of *effective* access to the courts, nor to a right to investigate the possibility that the courts might be able to provide redress. Justice Stevens, dissenting, appealed directly to the First Amendment as a more general supplement to the specific right of habeas corpus:

> Within the residuum of liberty retained by prisoners are freedoms identified in the First Amendment to the Constitution: freedom to worship according to the dictates of their own conscience, freedom to communicate with the outside world, and the freedom to petition their government for a redress of grievances.... The "well-established" right of access to the courts is one of these aspects of liberty that States must affirmatively protect. *Lewis v. Casey*, 518 U.S. 343 (1996).

The idea of a right of access to courts could be taken much further than cases involving prisoners' petitions for habeas corpus. The right to petition for redress of grievances could be thought of as directly related to the Sixth Amendment right to counsel in criminal trials, or even to extend to a right to publicly supplied counsel in civil cases and administrative proceedings independent of the Due Process Clause (traditionally thought of as the source for whatever generalizable right to counsel exists outside the criminal context). Such an expansive interpretation was presumably what Justice Scalia was warning against when he suggested that *Bounds* pointed toward a requirement of "permanent provision of counsel."

While the prisoner cases point to a specific right of access to courts to appeal criminal punishments, the First Amendment's Petition Clause can be understood much more broadly to refer to access to the political system generally. There are two important cases in which the Court has considered that possibility, in both instances declining to find any such broadly defined right. In the first case, *Minnesota State Board of Community Colleges v. Knight*, the Court ruled that a collective bargaining agreement that limited formal communications between faculty and university administrators did not violate the right of petition, in part because informal channels of communication remained open. In the second, *Romer v. Evans*, the Court considered an amendment to the Colorado state constitution that prohibited the state, cities, or localities from enacting laws prohibiting discrimination on the basis of sexual orientation. There is a difficult double, or even triple, negative inherent in this formulation; government may not pass a law saying that someone may not decide that someone will not be given a job or an apartment because they are homosexual. The amendment was declared unconstitutional, but not on the basis of a fundamental right of political access grounded in the First Amendment. Instead, the Court treated the case as one that involved questions of equal protection. In addition, however, both the majority of the Court and the Colorado Supreme Court spoke of a fundamental right of political access; a concept that is most clearly expressed in the Petition Clause of the First Amendment (particularly if the substantive protections of the Due Process Clause are understood as incorporations of rights named elsewhere in the Bill of Rights). As a result, the principles articulated in *Romer* have the effect of defining a limit on the ability of government to restrict the right of petition. The First Amendment was also involved in the arguments made by proponents of Amendment 2, who argued that the free exercise of their religious faiths required that they be allowed to limit the ability of homosexuals to use the legislature to gain protections against private acts of discrimination. Together, *Knight* and *Romer* define the current understanding of the right to seek the attention of the government.

Knight involved a challenge to a statute adopted by the Minnesota legislature in 1971 called the Public Employment Labor Relations Act (PELRA). As amended, PELRA divided public employees into appropriate bargaining units and established collective bargaining procedures that required the designation of an exclusive bargaining agent for each unit. Public employers were required to "meet and negotiate" in good faith with these exclusive representatives concerning the terms and conditions of employment. PELRA also granted professional employees, such as college faculty, the right to "meet and confer" with their employers on matters related to employment that are outside the scope of mandatory negotiations. This provision rested on the recognition that "professional employees possess knowledge, expertise, and dedication which is helpful and necessary to the operation and quality of public services and which may assist public employers in developing their policies." There was no statutory requirement, however, that the state employers demonstrate "good faith" in such meet-and-confer sessions. The exclusive unit representative selected for purposes of collective bargaining was also the exclusive unit representative, where appropriate, for meet-and-confer sessions with employers. State employers, in fact, were affirmatively prohibited from having either meet-and-negotiate or meet-and-confer meetings with any members of that bargaining unit except through their exclusive representative. The challenge to the statute was brought by community college teachers whose views were not being presented by their exclusive representative, and who wanted separate access to meet-and-confer sessions with their employers. Justice O'Connor, writing for a 6-to-3 majority, upheld the statute on the grounds that there is no generalized right of petition.

MINNESOTA STATE BOARD FOR COMMUNITY COLLEGES v. KNIGHT

SUPREME COURT OF THE UNITED STATES

465 U.S. 271 (1984)

JUSTICE O'CONNOR delivered the opinion of the Court, in which BURGER, C. J., and WHITE, BLACKMUN, and REHNQUIST joined. JUSTICE MARSHALL filed an opinion concurring in the judgment. JUSTICE BRENNAN filed a dissenting opinion. JUSTICE STEVENS filed a dissenting opinion, in all but Part III of which BRENNAN joined, and in all but Part II of which POWELL joined.

...The Constitution does not grant to members of the public generally a right to be heard by public bodies making decisions of policy. In (1915), this Court rejected a claim to such a right founded on the Due Process Clause of the Fourteenth Amendment. Speaking for the Court, Justice Holmes explained: "Where a rule of conduct applies to more than a few people it is impracticable that every one should have a direct voice in its adoption. The Constitution does not require all public acts to be done in town meeting or an assembly of the whole. General statutes within the state power are passed that affect the person or property of individuals, sometimes to the point of ruin, without giving them a chance to be heard. Their rights are protected...by their power, immediate or remote, over those who make the rule...."

Policymaking organs in our system of government have never operated under a constitutional constraint requiring them to afford every interested member of the public an opportunity to present testimony before any policy is adopted. Legislatures throughout the Nation, including Congress, frequently enact bills on which no hearings have been held or on which testimony has been received from only a select group. Executive agencies likewise make policy decisions of widespread application without permitting unrestricted public testimony. Public officials at all levels of government daily make policy decisions based only on the advice they decide they need and choose to hear. To recognize a constitutional right to participate directly in government policymaking would work a revolution in existing government practices.

Not least among the reasons for refusing to recognize such a right is the impossibility of its judicial definition and enforcement. Both federalism and separation-of-powers concerns would be implicated in the massive intrusion into state and federal policymaking that recognition of the claimed right would entail.... Government makes so many policy decisions affecting so many people that it would likely grind to a halt were policymaking constrained by constitutional requirements on whose voices must be heard. There must be a limit to individual argument in such matters if government is to go on. Absent statutory restrictions, the State must be free to consult or not to consult whomever it pleases. However wise or practicable various levels of public participation in various kinds of policy decisions may be, this Court has never held, and nothing in the Constitution suggests it should hold, that government must provide for such participation....

Appellees thus have no constitutional right as members of the public to a government audience for their policy views. As public employees, of course, they have a special interest in public policies relating to their employment. Minnesota's statutory scheme for public-employment labor relations recognizes as much. Appellees' status as public employees, however, gives them no special constitutional right to a voice in the making of policy by their government employer.

In *Smith v. Arkansas State Highway Employees*, 441 U.S. 463 (1979), a public employees' union argued that its First Amendment rights were abridged because the public employer required employees' grievances to be filed directly with the employer and refused to recognize the union's communications concerning its members' grievances. The Court rejected the argument. "The public employee surely can associate, and speak freely and petition openly, and he is protected by the First Amendment from retaliation for doing so. But the First Amendment does not impose any affirmative obligation on the government to listen, to respond or, in this context, to recognize the association and bargain with it." The Court acknowledged that "[the] First Amendment protects the right of an individual to speak freely, to advocate ideas, to associate with others, and to petition his government for redress of grievances." The government had not infringed any of those rights, the Court concluded. "[All] that the [government] has done in its challenged conduct is simply to ignore the union. That it is free to do."

The conduct challenged here is the converse of that challenged in *Smith*. There the government listened only to individual employees and not to the union. Here the government "meets and confers" with the union and not with individual employees. The applicable constitutional principles are identical to those that controlled in *Smith*. When government makes general policy, it is under no greater constitutional obligation to listen to any specially affected class than it is to listen to the public at large.

The academic setting of the policymaking at issue in these cases does not alter this conclusion. To be sure, there is a strong, if not universal or uniform, tradition of faculty participation in school governance, and there are numerous policy arguments to support such participation. But this Court has never recognized a constitutional right of faculty to participate in policymaking in academic institutions....

JUSTICE STEVENS, with whom BRENNAN joins in all but Part III, and with whom POWELL joins in all but Part II, dissenting.

...There can be no question but that the First Amendment secures the right of individuals to communicate with their government. And the First Amendment was intended to secure something more than an exercise in futility—it guarantees a meaningful opportunity to express one's views. For example, this Court has recognized that the right to forward views might become a practical nullity if government prohibited persons from banding together to make their voices heard. Thus, the First Amendment protects freedom of association because it makes the right to express one's views meaningful. Because of the importance of this right to play a meaningful part in the "uninhibited, robust, and wide-open" debate envisioned by the First Amendment, *New York Times Co. v. Sullivan*, 376 U.S. 254, 270 (1964), the Court has not permitted government to deny associational rights critical to this opportunity unless the abridgment is no broader than necessary to serve a vital state purpose....

[B]y prohibiting the administration from listening to appellees, the PELRA ensures that appellees' speech can have no meaningful impact upon the administration. Appellees do not rely on the government's "obligation" to hear them; they rely only on their right to have a meaningful opportunity to speak. If a public employer does not wish to listen to appellees, that is its privilege, but the First Amendment at least requires that that decision be made in an open marketplace of ideas, rather than under a statutory scheme that does not permit appellees' speech to be considered, no matter how much merit it may contain....

The First Amendment favors unabridged communication among members of a free society—including communication between employer and employee. The process of collective bargaining requires that a limited exception to that general principle be recognized, but until today we have not tolerated any broadening of that exception beyond the collective-bargaining process. The effect of the Minnesota statute is to make the union the only authorized spokesman for all employees on political matters as well as contractual matters. In my opinion, such state-sponsored orthodoxy is plainly impermissible. The Court, however, relies on a newly found state interest in promoting conformity—the "interest in ensuring that its public employers hear one, and only one, voice presenting the majority view of its professional employees on employment-related policy questions, whatever other advice they may receive on those questions." The notion that there is a state interest in fostering a private monopoly on any form of communication is at war with the principle that "the desire to favor one form of speech over all others" is not merely trivial; it "is illegitimate." *Carey v. Brown*, 447 U.S. 455, 468 (1980)....

Justice Stevens's invocation of a "private monopoly on...[a] form of communication" is essentially an argument that restricting communication between government and the governed to formal channels is inimical to the spirit of the First Amendment. By contrast, Justice O'Connor's majority opinion essentially argued that the Petition Clause of the First Amendment goes no further than assuring the existence of procedures by means of which individuals are able to participate in the political process. By implication, then, the Petition Clause might have teeth if there were a case in which access to political participation itself were diminished by government.

Precisely such a case came to the Supreme Court in 1995 in *Romer v. Evans*. Disappointingly for the purposes of this discussion, the case was decided on the basis of an equal protection analysis, without reference to the First Amendment. Nonetheless, it spells out the thinking of the current Court on the question of a right to political participation, and would undoubtedly provide the key precedent for any future argument that attempts to find a substantive guarantee of rights in the Petition Clause. In this roundabout way, the Court came as close as it has come to engaging the question of whether there is any substantive meaning to the Petition Clause.

In 1992, an amendment to the state constitution of Colorado appeared as an item in a statewide referendum vote. Amendment 2 had been drafted by a conservative Christian organization called Colorado for Family Values, assisted by national organizations such as the Family Research Council and the National Legal Foundation, which filed amicus briefs in the case (other ballot measures sponsored by these organizations and the Moral Majority appeared in the same year in Oregon and Maine). The purpose of the amendment was to undo a series of laws adopted by Aspen, Denver, and Boulder to protect homosexuals against discrimination in employment and housing. Amendment 2 provided that no such laws could be enacted either by the state government or by any subunit of the state government such as a municipality, and that any statute having such an effect could not be enforced:

> Neither the State of Colorado, through any of its branches or departments, nor any of its agencies, political subdivisions, municipalities or school districts, shall enact, adopt or enforce any statute, regulation, ordinance or policy whereby homosexual, lesbian or bisexual orientation, conduct, practices or relationships shall constitute or otherwise be the basis of or entitle any person or class of persons to have or claim any minority status quota preferences, protected status or claim of discrimination. *Romer v. Evans*, 517 U.S. 620 (1996).

Amendment 2 was adopted as a result of the 1992 Colorado state referendum, but before it could go into effect it was challenged in court, resulting in an injunction preventing it from taking effect.

The case reached the Colorado Supreme Court in 1993 on an appeal from the injunction that had been issued by the trial court. The state supreme court reasoned that the amendment infringed on "the fundamental right to participate equally in the political process":

> The right to participate equally in the political process is clearly affected by Amendment 2, because it bars gay men, lesbians, and bisexuals from having an effective voice in governmental affairs.... Amendment 2 alters the political process so that a targeted class is prohibited from obtaining legislative, executive, and judicial protection or redress from discrimination absent the consent of a majority of the electorate through the adoption of a constitutional amendment.

The use of the term "redress," in particular, points to a connection to the Petition Clause. The state court also appealed for its reasoning to voting rights cases from the 1960s which had been decided under the Due Process and Equal Protection Clauses of the Fourteenth Amendment. The case was remanded, to give the State of Colorado an opportunity to demonstrate its compelling interests, and returned to the Colorado Supreme Court in 1994. The state had asserted six interests on remand:

> (1) deterring factionalism; (2) preserving the integrity of the state's political functions; (3) preserving the ability of the state to remedy discrimination against suspect classes; (4) preventing the government from interfering with personal, familial, and religious privacy; (5) preventing government from subsidizing the political objectives of a special interest group; and (6) promoting the physical and psychological well-being of Colorado children. *Romer v. Evans*, 517 U.S. 620 (1996).

Several of these arguments—especially number 4—were grounded in the Religion Clauses of the First Amendment. On appeal in 1994, the Colorado Supreme Court, by a vote of 6 to 1, found all of the reasons either insufficiently compelling or else insufficiently closely related to the measure that was adopted to survive constitutional scrutiny. That opinion, in turn, was appealed to the U.S. Supreme Court.

The Supreme Court affirmed the ruling of the Colorado Supreme Court, but in doing so found it unnecessary to assert a fundamental right to access to the political process. Instead, Justice Kennedy, writing for a six-member majority, focused on an equal protection claim. Kennedy did not find it necessary to reach the question of what level of constitutional scrutiny was required, however, because he found that Amendment 2 failed even rational basis review as a mere pretext for discrimination. As a result, the status of the right in question—access to government—was not explored. In dissent, Justice Scalia, joined by Justices Rehnquist and Thomas, argued that the majority's argument implicitly granted that there is no fundamental right to participation in the political process, and that a law that classifies persons by sexual orientation requires only rational basis scrutiny. Applying rational basis scrutiny, in turn, Justice Scalia found that the adoption of Amendment 2 was justified by the state's legitimate interest in preventing a politically powerful homosexual minority from seizing control through local political processes. In Scalia's analogy, the prevention of such takeovers by powerful minorities is similar to the prevention of corruption by rules preventing the award of city contracts to relatives of officials. As for the proposition that there was something constitutionally suspect about a law making it harder for a "disfavored group" to gain access to normal political processes, Justice Scalia characterized this as "terminal silliness."

In other words, the very prevention of access to local political processes that had triggered strict scrutiny in the state court appeared to Justice Scalia and his fellow dissenters to be a legitimate state purpose, while the majority deemed it unnecessary to take a strong position on the question. Neither the majority nor the dissent explicitly considered the possibility that a right of political access might be inherent in the Petition Clause. In reading the excerpt below, consider the analogy that Justice Scalia makes to rules limiting the awarding of government contracts. Does the Petition Clause provide a basis for distinguishing that situation from the one at issue in this case? Conversely, can the majority's analysis stand without invoking a version of the right to participate in the political process that the state supreme court relied upon?

ROMER v. EVANS

SUPREME COURT OF THE UNITED STATES

517 U.S. 620 (1996)

JUSTICE KENNEDY delivered the opinion of the Court, in which STEVENS, O'CONNOR, SOUTER, GINSBURG, and BREYER joined. JUSTICE SCALIA filed a dissenting opinion, in which REHNQUIST, C. J., and THOMAS joined.

...[T]he State Supreme Court held that Amendment 2 was subject to strict scrutiny under the Fourteenth Amendment because it infringed the fundamental right of gays and lesbians to participate in the political process. To reach this conclusion, the state court relied on our voting rights cases, and on our precedents involving discriminatory restructuring of governmental decisionmaking. On remand, the State advanced various arguments in an effort to show that Amendment 2 was narrowly tailored to serve compelling interests, but the trial court found none sufficient. It enjoined enforcement of Amendment 2, and the Supreme Court of Colorado, in a second opinion, affirmed the ruling. We granted certiorari, and now affirm the judgment, but on a rationale different from that adopted by the State Supreme Court.

The State's principal argument in defense of Amendment 2 is that it puts gays and lesbians in the same position as all other persons. So, the State says, the measure does no more than deny homosexuals special rights. This reading of the amendment's language is implausible. We rely not upon our own interpretation of the amendment but upon the authoritative construction of Colorado's Supreme Court. The state court, deeming it unnecessary to determine the full extent of the amendment's reach, found it invalid even on a modest reading of its implications. The critical discussion of the amendment...is as follows: "The immediate objective of Amendment 2 is, at a minimum, to repeal existing statutes, regulations, ordinances, and policies of state and local entities that barred discrimination based on sexual orientation.... The 'ultimate effect' of Amendment 2 is to prohibit any governmental entity from adopting similar, or more protective statutes, regulations, ordinances, or policies in the future unless the state constitution is first amended to permit such measures."

Sweeping and comprehensive is the change in legal status effected by this law. So much is evident from the ordinances that the Colorado Supreme Court declared would be void by operation of Amendment 2. Homosexuals, by state decree, are put in a solitary class with respect to transactions and relations in both the private and governmental spheres. The amendment withdraws from homosexuals, but no others, specific legal protection from the injuries caused by discrimination, and it forbids reinstatement of these laws and policies....

[E]ven if, as we doubt, homosexuals could find some safe harbor in laws of general application, we cannot accept the view that Amendment 2's prohibition on specific legal protections does no more than deprive homosexuals of special rights. To the contrary, the amendment imposes a special disability upon those persons alone. Homosexuals are forbidden the safeguards that others enjoy or may seek without constraint. They can obtain specific protection against discrimination only by enlisting the citizenry of Colorado to amend the state constitution or perhaps, on the State's view, by trying to pass helpful laws of general applicability. This is so no matter how local or discrete the harm, no matter how public and widespread the injury. We find nothing special in the protections Amendment 2 withholds. These are protections taken for granted by most people either because they already have them or do not need them; these are protections against exclusion from an almost limitless number of transactions and endeavors that constitute ordinary civic life in a free society.

The Fourteenth Amendment's promise that no person shall be denied the equal protection of the laws must co-exist with the practical necessity that most legislation classifies for one purpose or another, with resulting disadvantage to various groups or persons. We have attempted to reconcile the principle with the reality by stating that, if a law neither burdens a fundamental right nor targets a suspect class, we will uphold the legislative classification so long as it bears a rational relation to some legitimate end.

Amendment 2 fails, indeed defies, even this conventional inquiry. First, the amendment has the peculiar property of imposing a broad and undifferentiated disability on a single named group, an exceptional and, as we shall explain, invalid form of legislation. Second, its sheer breadth is so discontinuous with the reasons offered for it that the amendment seems inexplicable by anything but animus toward the class that it affects; it lacks a rational relationship to legitimate state interests.

Taking the first point, even in the ordinary equal protection case calling for the most deferential of standards, we insist on knowing the relation between the classification adopted and the object to be attained. The search for the link between classification and objective gives substance to the Equal Protection Clause; it provides guidance and discipline for the legislature, which is entitled to know what sorts of laws it can pass; and it marks the limits of our own authority. In the ordinary case, a law will be sustained if it can be said to advance a legitimate government interest, even if the law seems unwise or works to the disadvantage of a particular group, or if the rationale for it seems tenuous. The laws challenged in the cases just cited were narrow enough in scope and grounded in a sufficient factual context for us to ascertain that there existed some relation between the classification and the purpose it served. By requiring that the classification bear a rational relationship to an independent and legitimate legislative end, we ensure that classifications are not drawn for the purpose of disadvantaging the group burdened by the law.

Amendment 2 confounds this normal process of judicial review. It is at once too narrow and too broad. It identifies persons by a single trait and then denies them protection across the board. The resulting disqualification of a class of persons from the right to seek specific protection from the law is unprecedented in our jurisprudence. The absence of precedent for Amendment 2 is itself instructive; "discriminations of an unusual character especially suggest careful consideration to determine whether they are obnoxious to the constitutional provision."

It is not within our constitutional tradition to enact laws of this sort. Central both to the idea of the rule of law and to our own Constitution's guarantee of equal protection is the principle that government and each of its parts remain open on impartial terms to all who seek its assistance. Equal protection of the laws is not achieved through indiscriminate imposition of inequalities. Respect for this principle explains why laws singling out a certain class of citizens for disfavored legal status or general hardships are rare. A law declaring that in general it shall be more difficult for one group of citizens than for all others to seek aid from the government is itself a denial of equal protection of the laws in the most literal sense. The guaranty of "equal protection of the laws" is a pledge of the protection of equal laws....

A second and related point is that laws of the kind now before us raise the inevitable inference that the disadvantage imposed is born of animosity toward the class of persons affected. "If the constitutional conception of 'equal protection of the laws' means anything, it must at the very least mean that a bare...desire to harm a politically unpopular group cannot constitute a legitimate governmental interest." Even laws enacted for broad and ambitious purposes often can be explained by reference to legitimate public policies which justify the incidental disadvantages they impose on certain persons. Amendment 2, however, in making a general announcement that gays and lesbians shall not have any particular protections from the law, inflicts on them immediate, continuing, and real injuries that outrun and belie any legitimate justifications that may be claimed for it. We conclude that, in addition to the far-reaching deficiencies of Amendment 2 that we have noted, the principles it offends, in another sense, are conventional and venerable; a law must bear a rational relationship to a legitimate governmental purpose, and Amendment 2 does not.

The primary rationale the State offers for Amendment 2 is respect for other citizens' freedom of association, and in particular the liberties of landlords or employers who have personal or religious objections to homosexuality. Colorado also cites its interest in conserving resources to fight discrimination against other groups. The breadth of the Amendment is so far removed from these particular justifications that we find it impossible to credit them. We cannot say that Amendment 2 is directed to any identifiable legitimate purpose or discrete objective. It is a status-based enactment divorced from any factual context from which we could discern a relationship to legitimate state interests; it is a classification of persons undertaken for its own sake, something the Equal Protection Clause does not permit. "Class legislation...[is] obnoxious to the prohibitions of the Fourteenth Amendment...."

We must conclude that Amendment 2 classifies homosexuals not to further a proper legislative end but to make them unequal to everyone else. This Colorado cannot do. A State cannot so deem a class of persons a stranger to its laws. Amendment 2 violates the Equal Protection Clause, and the judgment of the Supreme Court of Colorado is affirmed.

JUSTICE SCALIA, with whom REHNQUIST, C.J. and THOMAS join, dissenting.

...The only denial of equal treatment it contends homosexuals have suffered is this: They may not obtain preferential treatment without amending the state constitution. That is to say, the principle underlying the Court's opinion is that one who is accorded equal treatment under the laws, but cannot as readily as others obtain preferential treatment under the laws, has been denied equal protection of the laws. If merely stating this alleged "equal protection" violation does not suffice to refute it, our constitutional jurisprudence has achieved terminal silliness.

The central thesis of the Court's reasoning is that any group is denied equal protection when, to obtain advantage (or, presumably, to avoid disadvantage), it must have recourse to a more general and hence more difficult level of political decisionmaking than others. The world has never heard of such a principle, which is why the Court's opinion is so long on emotive utterance and so short on relevant legal citation. And it seems to me most unlikely that any multilevel democracy can function under such a principle. For whenever a disadvantage is imposed, or conferral of a benefit is prohibited, at one of the higher levels of democratic decisionmaking (i.e., by the state legislature rather than local government, or by the people at large in the state constitution rather than the legislature), the affected group has (under this theory) been denied equal protection. To take the simplest of examples, consider a state law prohibiting the award of municipal contracts to relatives of mayors or city councilmen. Once such a law is passed, the group composed of such relatives must, in order to get the benefit of city contracts, persuade the state legislature—unlike all other citizens, who need only persuade the municipality. It is ridiculous to consider this a denial of equal protection, which is why the Court's theory is unheard-of.

The Court might reply that the example I have given is not a denial of equal protection only because the same "rational basis" (avoidance of corruption) which renders constitutional the substantive discrimination against relatives (i.e., the fact that they alone cannot obtain city contracts) also automatically suffices to sustain what might be called the electoral-procedural discrimination against them (i.e., the fact that they must go to the state level to get this changed). This is of course a perfectly reasonable response, and would explain why "electoral-procedural discrimination" has not hitherto been heard of: a law that is valid in its substance is automatically valid in its level of enactment. But the Court cannot afford to make this argument, for as I shall discuss next, there is no doubt of a rational basis for the substance of the prohibition at issue here. The Court's entire novel theory rests upon the proposition that there is something special—something that cannot be justified by normal "rational basis" analysis—in making a disadvantaged group (or a nonpreferred group) resort to a higher decisionmaking level. That proposition finds no support in law or logic.

I turn next to whether there was a legitimate rational basis for the substance of the constitutional amendment—for the prohibition of special protection for homosexuals. n1 It is unsurprising that the Court avoids discussion of this question, since the answer is so obviously yes. The case most relevant to the issue before us today is not even mentioned in the Court's opinion: In *Bowers v. Hardwick*, 478 U.S. 186 (1986), we held that the Constitution does not prohibit what virtually all States had done from the founding of the Republic until very recent years—making homosexual conduct a crime. That holding is unassailable, except by those who think that the Constitution changes to suit current fashions.... If it is constitutionally permissible for a State to make homosexual conduct criminal, surely it is constitutionally permissible for a State to enact other laws merely disfavoring homosexual conduct.... And a fortiori it is constitutionally permissible for a State to adopt a provision not even disfavoring homosexual conduct, but merely prohibiting all levels of state government from bestowing special protections upon homosexual conduct.

---

n1 The Court evidently agrees that "rational basis"—the normal test for compliance with the Equal Protection Clause—is the governing standard. The trial court rejected respondents' argument that homosexuals constitute a "suspect" or "quasi-suspect" class, and respondents elected not to appeal that ruling to the Supreme Court of Colorado. And the Court implicitly rejects the Supreme Court of Colorado's holding that Amendment 2 infringes upon a "fundamental right" of "independently identifiable classes" to "participate equally in the political process."

But assuming that, in Amendment 2, a person of homosexual "orientation" is someone who does not engage in homosexual conduct but merely has a tendency or desire to do so, *Bowers* still suffices to establish a rational basis for the provision. If it is rational to criminalize the conduct, surely it is rational to deny special favor and protection to those with a self-avowed tendency or desire to engage in the conduct....

The foregoing suffices to establish what the Court's failure to cite any case remotely in point would lead one to suspect: No principle set forth in the Constitution, nor even any imagined by this Court in the past 200 years, prohibits what Colorado has done here. But the case for Colorado is much stronger than that. What it has done is not only unprohibited, but eminently reasonable....

First, as to its eminent reasonableness. The Court's opinion contains grim, disapproving hints that Coloradans have been guilty of "animus" or "animosity" toward homosexuality, as though that has been established as unAmerican. Of course it is our moral heritage that one should not hate any human being or class of human beings. But I had thought that one could consider certain conduct reprehensible—murder, for example, or polygamy, or cruelty to animals—and could exhibit even "animus" toward such conduct. Surely that is the only sort of "animus" at issue here: moral disapproval of homosexual conduct, the same sort of moral disapproval that produced the centuries-old criminal laws that we held constitutional in *Bowers*. The Colorado amendment does not, to speak entirely precisely, prohibit giving favored status to people who are homosexuals; they can be favored for many reasons—for example, because they are senior citizens or members of racial minorities. But it prohibits giving them favored status because of their homosexual conduct—that is, it prohibits favored status for homosexuality.

But though Coloradans are, as I say, entitled to be hostile toward homosexual conduct, the fact is that the degree of hostility reflected by Amendment 2 is the smallest conceivable. The Court's portrayal of Coloradans as a society fallen victim to pointless, hate-filled "gay-bashing" is so false as to be comical. Colorado not only is one of the 25 States that have repealed their antisodomy laws, but was among the first to do so. But the society that eliminates criminal punishment for homosexual acts does not necessarily abandon the view that homosexuality is morally wrong and socially harmful; often, abolition simply reflects the view that enforcement of such criminal laws involves unseemly intrusion into the intimate lives of citizens.

There is a problem, however, which arises when criminal sanction of homosexuality is eliminated but moral and social disapprobation of homosexuality is meant to be retained. The Court cannot be unaware of that problem; it is evident in many cities of the country, and occasionally bubbles to the surface of the news, in heated political disputes over such matters as the introduction into local schools of books teaching that homosexuality is an optional and fully acceptable "alternate life style." The problem (a problem, that is, for those who wish to retain social disapprobation of homosexuality) is that, because those who engage in homosexual conduct tend to reside in disproportionate numbers in certain communities, have high disposable income, and of course care about homosexual-rights issues much more ardently than the public at large, they possess political power much greater than their numbers, both locally and statewide. Quite understandably, they devote this political power to achieving not merely a grudging social toleration, but full social acceptance, of homosexuality.

By the time Coloradans were asked to vote on Amendment 2, their exposure to homosexuals' quest for social endorsement was not limited to newspaper accounts of happenings in places such as New York, Los Angeles, San Francisco, and Key West. Three Colorado cities—Aspen, Boulder, and Denver—had enacted ordinances that listed "sexual orientation" as an impermissible ground for discrimination, equating the moral disapproval of homosexual conduct with racial and religious bigotry. The phenomenon had even appeared statewide: the Governor of Colorado had signed an executive order pronouncing that "in the State of Colorado we recognize the diversity in our pluralistic society and strive to bring an end to discrimination in any form," and directing state agency-heads to "ensure non-discrimination" in hiring and promotion based on, among other things, "sexual orientation." I do not mean to be critical of these legislative successes; homosexuals are as entitled to use the legal system for reinforcement of their moral sentiments as are the rest of society. But they are subject to being countered by lawful, democratic countermeasures as well.

That is where Amendment 2 came in. It sought to counter both the geographic concentration and the disproportionate political power of homosexuals by (1) resolving the controversy at the statewide level, and (2) making the election a single-issue contest for both sides. It put directly, to all the citizens of the State, the question: Should homosexuality be given special protection? They answered no....

Romer v. Evans is a fascinating case because it contains elements of so many different First Amendment arguments even though it was not decided on that basis. The Equal Protection argument of the majority is reminiscent of the arguments in *Carey v. Brown* that struck down laws prohibiting pickets except on specified topics on the grounds that such laws treated different subject matters unequally. The arguments that landlords and employers should not be compelled to extend opportunities to persons whose conduct offends the tenets of their religions was rejected by the Colorado Supreme Court by an invocation of *Employment Division, Dept. of Human Resources of Oregon v. Smith*, 494 U.S. 872 (1990). And both sides in the cases insisted in their briefs that their position was justified by the First Amendment's prohibition against government coercion in matters of conscience. Neither the majority nor the dissent seems to have attached any significance to the fact that Amendment 2, on its face, was directed at a content-specific class of expression. (Note that Amendment 2 did not restrict the ability of homosexuals to propose legislation, it restricted the ability of *anyone* to propose legislation whose purpose was to prevent discrimination against homosexuals.)

Among the thorniest issues raised in *Romer*, as Justice Scalia observed, are those concerning the relationship between the state and local governments. Scalia took it as given that a state may remove an issue from local control, but in the ordinary case that is an issue that arises when the state decides to prohibit conduct that a locality might wish to permit (e.g., possession of marijuana, or driving at speeds of eighty miles per hour). In *Romer*, the issue was one of the state preventing the locality from declaring conduct illegal within its own borders. Does this raise special First Amendment concerns? Consider the fact that the only conduct being regulated by Amendment 2 was the conduct of legislators peaceably assembling to express the will of their constituents. Could the City of Denver have argued that its citizens were being denied their right to express themselves through the acts of their legislators?

It is particularly interesting, in this context, to consider the consequences of the absence of any substantive analysis of the right to petition the government. Since there is no such independent guarantee, questions concerning government's authority to regulate the political process are addressed by the application of analogies to other more-or-less politically significant activities. In *Buckley v. Valeo*, the analogy was between money and speech, and the Free Speech Clause was found to guarantee an effective voice in influencing elections. Compare that analysis with the analysis of either the majority or the dissent in *Romer*. Is access to influencing elections on a par with access to influencing the policies of governments once they are elected? Are either or both of those issues analogous to the question of access to government contracts? How might both cases have looked if the Court had analyzed them under the Petition Clause of the First Amendment? This kind of speculation is only an intellectual exercise, of course. For the moment, it remains the case that the Petition Clause is the least developed, and consequently least substantive, section of the First Amendment.

X. Three Views of the First Amendment; the First Amendment and the Problem of Equality; the Future of the First Amendment

A. *Approaches to Understanding the First Amendment*

At the beginning of this book, we considered an essay by Thomas Emerson that asked whether there is a unifying set of concepts that binds the provisions of the First Amendment together in a coherent whole. We might ask the same question about the body of jurisprudence that has grown up in each of the different areas—speech, religion, press—in which the First Amendment is brought to bear. Are there unifying principles, or trends, that connect these many different lines of cases over the eighty or so years in which the First Amendment jurisprudence has developed?

In this chapter, I will suggest that the answer is "yes." This answer is not a given. There have been numerous instances in which justices seem to adopt a kind of constitutional nihilism, throwing their hands up in despair at the immensity of the task involved in trying to derive general principles from the First Amendment. Potter Stewart's famous characterization of "obscenity" in *Jacobellis v. Ohio*, 378 U.S. 184, 195 (1964), is one example: "I shall not today attempt further to define the kinds of material I understand to be embraced within that short-hand description; and perhaps I could never succeed in intelligibly doing so. But I know it when I see it, and the motion picture involved in this case is not that." Other justices, however, have clearly attempted to draw connections between different parts of the First Amendment, as when Justice Scalia appealed to *Employment Division, Dept. of Human Resources of Oregon v. Smith*, 494 U.S. 872 (1990), a free exercise case, to explain his opinion in *Barnes v. Glen Theatre*, 501 U.S. 560 (1991), a case about indecent expressive conduct. It is therefore well worth the while of any student of the First Amendment to take up Emerson's challenge and look for unifying themes that connect different strands of jurisprudence in this area.

Throughout the discussions in the preceding chapters, we have repeatedly seen the First Amendment presented as occupying a central place in competing visions of American democracy. Two competing versions of this vision, in particular, have informed broad swaths of jurisprudential development. These can be broadly categorized as an affirmative and a negative conception of First Amendment rights. A negative right is one that is expressed simply as a limit on government action; "I have a right, therefore government may not do X." An affirmative right, by contrast, takes the form "I have a right, therefore government must do Y," or "the government must create conditions Z."

The distinction is between avoiding undesirable government actions and achieving desirable outcomes. In the context of the Free Speech Clause, a negative rights approach reads the First Amendment as a proscription against certain specific government actions, such as censorship, while an affirmative rights approach understands the First Amendment to require government to protected unpopular expression in order to maintain the marketplace of ideas. In the context of the Free Exercise Clause, the distinction is captured in the difference between the statement that government may neither suppress nor specifically prohibit religious practices, and the statement that government is obliged to create an exception in otherwise generally applicable laws to accommodate religious practices. In the context of the Establishment Clause, the negative rights approach finds that government is precluded from declaring a state religion, while the affirmative rights approach conceives of an obligation to create an environment in which everyone feels equally free to practice their religion or none at all, by avoiding endorsement. In practice, the distinction between the two may sometimes become blurred, and it is by no means the case that the two different approaches always yield different outcomes in First Amendment cases. It may, indeed, be equally useful to characterize these two approaches simply as a narrow versus a broad interpretation. Nonetheless, it is useful to think about the broadly defined themes that have characterized the interpretation of the First Amendment in the lines of cases that were presented in the earlier chapters.

A third approach to understanding the First Amendment is what I will call the "activist" approach. This is an understanding that treats the First Amendment, and by extent the Constitution generally, as neither a blueprint for an ideal political society nor as a set of formal limits on government authority, but rather as a tool for the pursuit of political ideals whose source is found elsewhere. This last conception is one that has appeared only occasionally in court cases, but is at the center of current debates among constitutional critics and theorists.

1. *The Affirmative Approach*

The affirmative view of the First Amendment describes the clauses less in terms of specific limitations on government actions than as a guarantor of equality for minority groups, especially minorities whose viewpoints are unpopular. From this view, the First Amendment is understood as a description of the conditions required for a certain democratic ideal, and government actions are tested against that model. Not only particular government actions but more generally the range of goals that the majority may legitimately pursue through the democratic process is limited by the First Amendment.

In particular, the affirmative conception of the First Amendment is at the heart of the application of the idea of equal protection to ideas. In *Carey v. Brown*, 447 U.S. 455 (1980), and *Chicago Police Dept. v. Mosley*, 408 U.S. 92 (1972), different Courts ruled that government could not restrict the subject matter of picketing on the grounds that doing so would mean treating different messages unequally. The same principle is at work in arguments that government may not choose between protected forms of speech. According to this understanding, unless expression can be shown to be so dangerous or so utterly without value that it does not warrant First Amendment protection at all, government is obliged to protect all speech equally. One version of this argument is expressed in the famous quotation from *Roth v. United States*, heard with a companion case, *Alberts v. California*, 354 U.S. 476 (1957): "All ideas having even the slightest redeeming importance—unorthodox ideas, controversial ideas, even ideas hateful to the prevailing climate of opinion—have the full protection of the guaranties, unless excludable because they encroach upon the limited area of more important interests." Another version of the same argument, based on an ideal of achieving the original intent of the Constitution's framers, appears in Brandeis's dissenting opinion in *Olmstead v. United States*, 277 U.S. 438 (1928), for First Amendment arguments: "The makers of our Constitution undertook to secure conditions favorable to the pursuit of happiness.... They sought to protect Americans in their beliefs, their thoughts, their emotions and their sensations. They conferred, as against the Government, the right to be let alone—the most comprehensive of rights and the right most valued by civilized man." Thus, entertainment is as "core" a form of First Amendment expression as political argumentation, as both are equally entitled to the protection of the First Amendment.

One of the important elements in this understanding is a tacit commitment to a kind of agnosticism. Justice Holmes provides the most famous articulation of this principle:

> If you have no doubt of your premises or your power and want a certain result with all your heart you naturally express your wishes in law and sweep away all opposition.... But when men have realized that time has upset many fighting faiths,

they may come to believe even more than they believe the very foundations of their own conduct that the ultimate good desired is better reached by free trade in ideas—that the best test of truth is the power of the thought to get itself accepted in the competition of the market.... That at any rate is the theory of our Constitution. It is an experiment, as all life is an experiment. Every year if not every day we have to wager our salvation upon some prophecy based upon imperfect knowledge. *Abrams v. United States*, 250 U.S. 616 (1919).

The observation that "time has upset many fighting faiths" and the reference to "imperfect knowledge" point out the aspect of the marketplace of ideas metaphor that is most troubling to many of its critics. To assert that we must permit Nazis to march in Skokie to preserve the free market in ideas seems to imply the possibility that *they might be right*, a disturbing conclusion to find embedded in the First Amendment. Applied to other kinds of cases, however, the insistence that government protect the expression of all viewpoints stands as the guarantor of equal protection for minority beliefs.

Applied to the Establishment Clause, Holmes's enforced agnosticism supports the rule that government must avoid endorsement of religion, lest an implicit message of inferiority be transmitted to members of a religious or irreligious minority. *County of Allegheny v. ACLU*, 492 U.S. 573 (1989). Applied to the Free Exercise Clause, the same argument emphasizes the necessity of securing space for religious minorities to engage in those practices that are important to them. *Sherbert v. Verner*, 374 U.S. 398 (1963), *Wisconsin v. Yoder*, 406 U.S. 205 (1972). In the regulation of public forums, this view insists that it is more important that persons wishing to express themselves "indecently" be free to do so than that passers-by be spared the necessity of looking away. *Cohen v. California*, 403 U.S. 15 (1971). In the press, this affirmative vision calls for avoiding chilling effects so that "debate on public issues" is "uninhibited, robust, and wide-open." *New York Times v. Sullivan*, 376 U.S. 254 (1964). The uncertainty about questions of value leads to the unsettling conclusion that government must protect the expression of the message "sex is good," but may not, itself, express the message "God loves you." The justification for this outcome cannot be articulated in terms of negative rights; instead, it must be understood as the obligation of government to ensure an environment in which unpopular viewpoints are protected against majoritarian pressure.

Put another way, Holmes's position and the tradition that it expresses can be described as the proposition that "courts are certain, so government must not be." That is, it is courts' certainty about constitutional meaning that justifies them in requiring government to act as though it were agnostic on questions of faith and ideology. In practice, the insistence that government avoid choosing sides in debates over values leads to a greater willingness on the part of judges to question legislative motives, the adequacy of proffered justifications, and the adequacy of alternative means of achieving social goals.

The insistence on uncertainty also has implications for constitutional interpretation. If one takes as a starting point the proposition that what we believe today we may not believe tomorrow, then the First Amendment becomes a mandate for openness to change, a blueprint for societal development in new and unpredicted directions. Those who take this view are likely to be sympathetic to an argument that the Constitution itself must be read in the context of present historical conditions. Since the premise of the First Amendment is that the Constitution requires us to accept the possibility that our values are neither those of past generations nor those of future generations to come, it would be inconsistent to simultaneously argue that the Constitution itself must be read as an expression of a fixed set of values which may be alien to those of the country at the moment of discussion. This is not a necessary conclusion. One can argue that the amendment process is the guarantor of flexibility, or that openness to change is, itself, the primary fixed value that the Constitution secures against the tides of history. But Holmes's agnostic attitude lends itself well to the view that the Constitution is a living document whose meaning evolves to reflect the understanding of the time. In Benjamin Cardozo's words, "we can never see...with any eyes except our own."[1]

2. *The Negative Approach*

The idea that the First Amendment requires us to assume a lack of certainty about what ideas might someday be accepted as true is deeply troubling to those who conceive of the First Amendment as a narrow, purely negative description of the limits of government action. This view leaves the greatest possible range for popular majorities to exercise their democratic will precisely so that communities *can* express their values. Put another way, this position can be expressed as the proposition that courts cannot be certain that the First Amendment affirmatively requires government to act in any particular way, so government must be left free—through the democratic process—to reach conclusions on questions of value. Vague balancing tests are eschewed in favor of formal, categorical rules intended to give legislators clear notice of the limits of their powers without influencing their choice of actions within those bounds. Furthermore, in this conception the First Amendment bestows only "negative rights," in the sense that while certain government actions may be proscribed, none are constitutionally required. In Justice Rehnquist's words, "the Due Process Clause generally confers no affirmative right to governmental aid, even where such aid may be necessary to secure life, liberty, or property interests of which the government itself may not deprive the individual." *Rust v. Sullivan*, 500 U.S. 173 (1991).

It follows logically that from this view certain forms of "protected" speech will, in practice, be more valued than others. Furthermore, this is an approach that supports an argument for finding unequal value in different kinds of expression to be a premise of the First Amendment. This view does not define the scope of the First Amendment in terms of the conditions for ongoing societal development, but rather in terms of preserving a set of values embedded in the constitutional system, a version of originalism that reserves the highest levels of protection for the kinds of speech most Americans "would march our sons or daughters off to war to preserve." *City of Erie v. Pap's A.M.*, 120 S.Ct. 1382 (2000). The government, from this perspective, may not silence political criticism of its policies—but that does not mean that it is required to tolerate nude dancing.

Unlike Holmes' uncertainty, those who argue from this perspective insist that the First Amendment takes as given, even requires for its coherence, a recognition that in fact we know perfectly well what kinds of speech are most valuable, that the answer to that question is the same as it has always been. The certainty of these eternal verities appears in both the valorization of tradition and the refusal to extend protection to lesser orders of expression. The flag is a "sacred symbol" (*Texas v. Johnson*, 491 U.S. 397 [1989], Rehnquist dissenting), so government is free to protect it against desecration. Similarly, from this perspective, the First Amendment leaves government free to regulate less valued expression as part of the expression of the majority's moral preferences (*Barnes v. Glen Theatre*, 501 U.S. 560 [1991]). Applied to the Establishment Clause, this view rejects the logic of the endorsement test, preferring to read the clause as precluding only the formal, legal establishment of a mandatory religion (*Lee v. Weisman*, 505 U.S. 577 [1992], Scalia dissenting; *Santa Fe Ind. School District v. Doe*, 530 U.S. 290 [2000], Rehnquist dissenting). Applied to the Free Exercise Clause, this perspective is one that yields no requirements that legislatures accommodate the desires of unpopular minorities to engage in conduct of which the majority disapproves, although if such accommodation is the majority's will, that, too, is constitutionally permissible. *Employment Division, Dept. of Human Resources of Oregon v. Smith*, 494 U.S. 872 (1990).

Justices who hold this view do not find the First Amendment to provide a mandate to judge the worthiness of the majority's goals, only to ask whether in pursuit of those goals government has crossed a strictly defined boundary that protects a narrowly drawn area of traditional political activities. As a result, justices who take this view are less likely to look deeply into legislative motives. Conversely, from this perspective, where a legislature oversteps the limits of the First Amendment it makes no difference that its goals were consistent with some vision of democratic governance. So, from this perspective, in some settings the Free Speech Clause does not limit government's ability to favor some messages over others at all, (*NEA v. Finley*, 524 U.S. 569 [1998]; *Rust v. Sullivan*, 500 U.S. 173 [1991]), while in others the requirement of viewpoint neutrality precludes a legislature from attempting to value some messages over others. *R. A. V. v. St. Paul*, 505 U.S. 377 (1992). The certainty that political expression is valuable but entertainment is not leads to the conclusion that communities are required to protect the expression of Nazi propaganda but may limit the expression of the message "sex is good."

3. Test Cases: Access and Association

Two of the most interesting sets of cases, from the perspective of these broadly defined conceptions of the First Amendment, are access cases and association cases. Association cases initially involved efforts by government to prevent unpopular groups from associating, and in these situations courts had no difficulty in finding a violation of the First Amendment. In more recent cases, the issue has become the extent of the ability of quasi-public organizations to exclude individuals and groups from participation, an inquiry that is the reverse of the earlier one. Those who favor a broad, affirmative view of the First Amendment as a tool for the creation of conditions of political participation are likely to support the authority of government to require groups to admit minority members as part of their public duties. *Runyon v. McCrary*, 427 U.S. 160 (1976); *Boy Scouts of America v. Dale*, 530 U.S. 640 (2000) (dissenting opinions). Those who view the First Amendment as solely a negative check on government authority are unlikely to find it a mandate for the creation of public duties to be imposed on private organizations, and are therefore likely to be more willing to strike down laws as violative of the right of non-association just as they are likely to strike down laws that infringe on individual conscience by requiring participation in expression, *Abood v. Detroit Bd. of Ed.*, 431 U.S. 209 (1977); *Keller v. State Bar of California*, 496 U.S. 1 (1990); *Boy Scouts of America v. Dale*, 530 U.S. 640 (2000) (majority opinion).

Access cases, too, turn traditional First Amendment issues on their heads, by asking whether the government may choose to refrain from extending support to religion in its efforts to pursue a constitutional vision of a secular public sphere. Those who take the broad, affirmative, view of the First Amendment may likely to approve of such government choices as part of the broader effort to create a certain set of political conditions. By contrast, those who view the role of the Constitution as describing strict negative checks on government action argue that while the government, speaking in its own voice, is free to endorse a religious message, it is required to be "neutral" in providing access to a public forum. (Compare majority and dissenting opinions in *Rosenberger v. Rector and Visitors of the University of Virginia*, 515 U.S. 819 [1995]; *Capitol Square Review and Advisory Bd. v. Pinette*, 515 U.S. 753 [1995].) If one thinks of access to the political process as a parallel issue, the broad view would hold that government is prohibited from limiting such access lest First Amendment values of "free exchange of ideas" be inhibited, while the narrow view would find no mandate in the First Amendment for interfering in the ways in which the majority chooses to structure its lines of political communication so long as specifically defined limits ("suspect classes") are observed. (Compare majority and dissenting opinions, *Minnesota State Board of Community Colleges v. Knight*, 465 U.S. 271 (1984); *Romer v. Evans*, 517 U.S. 620 [1996].)

Yet, both camps agree that government may not exclude religious groups from access to facilities where there is no risk of a perception of endorsement (*Lamb's Chapel v. Center Moriches Union Free School District*, 508 U.S. 384 [1993, unanimous], and that one group of private citizens may not undertake to limit the support of government to another group (*Board of Regents of the University of Wisconsin System v. Southworth*, 529 U.S. 217 [2000, unanimous]). The Court was similarly unanimous in ruling that government may not compel a group to allow participation where doing so would require it to adopt as its own a message with which it disagreed (*Hurley v. Irish-American Gay, Lesbian and Bisexual Group of Boston*, 515 U.S. 557 [1995, unanimous]). These points of difference and agreement point to the central importance of the definitions of "public" and "private" in the debates over the proper understanding of the First Amendment, and to the difficult distinction between a speaker and his speech.

The distinction between public and private spheres defines the limits of legitimate government action. The two basic perspectives on First Amendment jurisprudence described above, however, do not map neatly onto a parallel division between a broad and narrow view of the public sphere. Those who adopt the broad view of the First Amendment tend to find that it requires putting a wide range of what might be thought of as "personal" activities off limits as private, an attitude exemplified in the declaration that government has no business regulating men's minds. *Stanley v. Georgia*, 394 U.S. 557 (1969). The view of the Free Exercise Clause that requires protection of minority practices embodies a similar attitude, as does the position that entertainment is as valid a goal as political education when it comes to limiting government's ability to restrict expression. The justification for such strict limitations on government authority is that they serve the affirmative goal of furthering a particular political vision. In a case where the same vision is furthered by permitting government action, that is an equally acceptable outcome. So government should, according to this view, be free to declare certain private expressions intolerable, and to impose public duties on private citizens and organizations to serve a positive political function. *Red Lion Broadcasting Co. v. Federal Communications Commission*, 395 U.S. 367 (1969).

The narrow, negative conception of the First Amendment similarly leads to different definitions of the scope of the public sphere in different situations. From this perspective, conduct and expression are not shielded from regulation merely because the unwilling public is shielded from exposure, and it is perfectly within the majority's legitimate purview to articulate its moral preferences and to limit the ability of minorities to ignore those preferences. Yet the government is not free to limit expression of which it disapproves if the basis for the disapproval is political, rather than moral. From this perspective, the public-private distinction follows the level of First Amendment protection that is extended to the expression at issue. The First Amendment requires viewpoint neutrality in political matters, lest the individual's political conscience be invaded, but permits the exercise of moral preference in nonpolitical ("noncore," or "less protected") areas of expression because the preservation of moral standards is a proper matter of community concern.

Concerning the distinction between a speaker and his or her speech in the context of association cases, compare *Runyon* and *Hurley*. Is it really plausible, after all, that the admission of African-American children into a private school would not diminish the ability of that school to promulgate a message of white racial superiority? Is it really the case that excluding all known homosexuals from the Boy Scouts only affects a particular message, rather than excluding an unpopular class of persons? Or consider the same issue in relation to access cases. If government may—or even must—deny access to religious or antireligious messages, does this not limit the ability of certain classes of people from being heard? But then, too, compare the treatment of money as a form of public access in *Rosenberger* and *Finley*. Is it really the case that funding for the arts is so fundamentally different from funding student activities that in one case the First Amendment has nothing to say while in the other it imposes an absolute requirement of "neutrality" (however defined)? A careful review of these issues suggests a tacit dimension to both the broad, affirmative view and the narrow, negative view of the First Amendment.

This returns us to the question of equality and liberty. Implicit in the broad, affirmative view of the First Amendment is an idea that it is a design for the further development of American democracy toward a greater degree of political equality. The affirmative view is unwilling to permit communities to express their certain moral convictions, but in doing so articulates its own certain preference for equality as a constitutional norm.

4. Another View: The Activist Approach

There is a third voice in the debate over the meaning of the First Amendment, particularly the Free Speech Clause, although it is one that is heard more in law journals than from the bench of the Supreme Court. The view of the First Amendment that is informed by Homes's uncertainty principle leaves us in the uncomfortable position of implying that we may someday decide that the Nazis are right (although it is difficult to see how any elements of that philosophy could be made into government policy consistent with other provisions of the Constitution). The view of the First Amendment as a narrowly defined negative check on government leaves us in the uncomfortable position of implying that we are certain that permitting Nazis to march through Jewish neighborhoods is the best possible outcome. The third view is in some ways a combination of the first two; it argues that the function of the First Amendment is, indeed, to affirmatively create conditions of broadly conceived equality, and that doing so requires declaring our collective certainty that some ideas are simply wrong. Both courts and the other branches of government, in this view, are equally capable of reaching conclusions, and in fact there is a shared consensus in favor of equality whose expression is inhibited only by formalistic First Amendment jurisprudence that ignores the reality of human experience.

This is a different sense in which the First Amendment is conceived as an instrument for achieving political equality. Among the cases that have been discussed here, this approach is most clearly seen in the argument in *Beauharnais v. Illinois*, 343 U.S. 250 (1951), that group libel is unworthy of First Amendment protection because it causes harm to the reputations of whole populations and thus renders them unequal. From this perspective, the insistence on the constitutional equality of all ideas gives the protection of the law to the perpetuation or creation of inequalities among groups of people. Far from a value neutral set of rules for an intellectual marketplace, from this view the First Amendment is understood as a statement about the kind of citizens and the kind of environment that are considered necessary for the realization of America's democratic vision.

Like the affirmative approach exemplified in Holmes's evocation of a marketplace, the activist interpretation sees the various clauses of the First Amendment as obligations for government action to achieve a certain kind of political environment. A little thought, however, will demonstrate that these two versions of the First Amendment will yield nearly opposite conclusions in many cases. Whereas the affirmative approach seeks an environment in which unpopular viewpoints will be freely expressed, the activist approach seeks a mandate for the government to protect people against the effects of hearing unwholesome messages.

From the activist perspective, for example, the American Nazi Party ought not to be allowed to march in Skokie, Illinois. This is a perspective that embraces the principle that the First Amendment is fundamentally about equality, but argues that Holmes's agnosticism substitutes the formal equality of ideas for the real, lived equality of persons. Skokie was a community whose population was uniquely vulnerable to understanding the presence of the marchers as a message of inequality and a threat. Thus, according to the activist argument, the speech in question should have been unprotected by virtue of the social harms that it would cause, like libel, fraud, or fighting words. This is yet another illustration of the point that the approach that one takes to reading the First Amendment cannot be reduced to a mere preference in outcomes. It is often easy to declare a preference for one party or another in a case; the hard work is in articulating constitutional principles that will apply equally validly in a future case as they do in the one before us.

B. *The First Amendment and the Problem of Equality*

It should be noted that all of the approaches above share certain characteristics. The affirmative, negative, and activist views of the First Amendment all accept the basic premises of the categorical approach, although the activist view comes the closest to restoring a system in which the degree to which expression is protected depends on circumstances rather than content. All three, moreover, share a commitment to some version of "equality"; the trouble lies in the definition of the term. In particular, there is often tension between those who argue that the rights of persons must be understood in a way that promotes the equality of speech, and those who argue that the rights of speech and expression must be understood in a way that promotes the equality of persons.

In 1985, in *American Booksellers Ass'n. v. Hudnut*, the Seventh Circuit Court of Appeals heard a challenge to a city ordinance that combined elements of the theory of hate speech with the theory of obscenity. The ordinance had been originally proposed by two prominent feminist legal theorists, Catharine MacKinnon and Andrea Dworkin, and a version of their proposal had been adopted by the City of Indianapolis. MacKinnon's and Dworkin's proposal was grounded in the idea that pornography is a category of expression that should be viewed as beyond the protection of the First Amendment for reasons independent of its characterization as "obscene." Instead, the argument ran, pornography of a certain type should be understood in the same terms that hate speech is understood, as "words that wound" the listener, the onlooker, and society at large. The logic is straightforward: Pornography is low-value speech that causes harm, and should therefore be subject to regulation either as a category of unprotected speech, or as conduct rather than as speech at all.

On review, the Seventh Circuit disagreed, and their decision was subsequently affirmed, without comment, by the Supreme Court. The court's opinion, however, raises the same kinds of important and difficult questions that were raised by *Beauharnais* and *R. A. V.* If libeling a commercial product is not protected against regulation, on what theory is the degradation of women properly considered a protected category? Since the Seventh Circuit seemed willing to accept the empirical proposition that pornography is causally connected to social harms, why was that finding not a sufficient basis for defining a category of unprotected speech?

AMERICAN BOOKSELLERS ASSOCIATION, INC., et al., v. WILLIAM H. HUDNUT, III, Mayor, City of Indianapolis

UNITED STATES COURT OF APPEALS FOR THE SEVENTH CIRCUIT

771 F.2d 323 (1985)

JUDGES: Cudahy and Easterbrook, Circuit Judges, and Swygert, Senior Circuit Judge. Swygert, Senior Circuit Judge, concurring.

JUDGE EASTERBROOK delivered the opinion of the court.

Indianapolis enacted an ordinance defining "pornography" as a practice that discriminates against women. "Pornography" is to be redressed through the administrative and judicial methods used for other discrimination. The City's definition of "pornography" is considerably different from "obscenity," which the Supreme Court has held is not protected by the First Amendment....

"Pornography" under the ordinance is "the graphic sexually explicit subordination of women, whether in pictures or in words, that also includes one or more of the following:

(1) Women are presented as sexual objects who enjoy pain or humiliation; or

(2) Women are presented as sexual objects who experience sexual pleasure in being raped; or

(3) Women are presented as sexual objects tied up or cut up or mutilated or bruised or physically hurt, or as dismembered or truncated or fragmented or severed into body parts; or

(4) Women are presented as being penetrated by objects or animals; or

(5) Women are presented in scenarios of degradation, injury abasement, torture, shown as filthy or inferior, bleeding, bruised, or hurt in a context that makes these conditions sexual; or

(6) Women are presented as sexual objects for domination, conquest, violation, exploitation, possession, or use, or through postures or positions of servility or submission or display." Indianapolis Code § 16-3(q).

The statute provides that the "use of men, children, or transsexuals in the place of women in paragraphs (1) through (6) above shall also constitute pornography under this section." The ordinance as passed in April 1984 defined "sexually explicit" to mean actual or simulated intercourse or the uncovered exhibition of the genitals, buttocks or anus. An amendment in June 1984 deleted this provision, leaving the term undefined.

The Indianapolis ordinance does not refer to the prurient interest, to offensiveness, or to the standards of the community. It demands attention to particular depictions, not to the work judged as a whole. It is irrelevant under the ordinance whether the work has literary, artistic, political, or scientific value. The City and many amici point to these omissions as virtues. They maintain that pornography influences attitudes, and the statute is a way to alter the socialization of men and women rather than to vindicate community standards of offensiveness. And as one of the principal drafters of the ordinance has asserted, "if a woman is subjected, why should it matter that the work has other value?" Catharine A. MacKinnon, "Pornography, Civil Rights, and Speech," 20 *Harv. Civ. Rts-Civ. Lib. L. Rev.* 1, 21 (1985).

Civil rights groups and feminists have entered this case as amici on both sides. Those supporting the ordinance say that it will play an important role in reducing the tendency of men to view women as sexual objects, a tendency that leads to both unacceptable attitudes and discrimination in the workplace and violence away from it. Those opposing the ordinance point out that much radical feminist literature is explicit and depicts women in ways forbidden by the ordinance and that the ordinance would reopen old battles. It is unclear how Indianapolis would treat works from James Joyce's *Ulysses* to Homer's *Iliad*; both depict women as submissive objects for conquest and domination.

We do not try to balance the arguments for and against an ordinance such as this. The ordinance discriminates on the ground of the content of the speech. Speech treating women in the approved way—in sexual encounters "premised on equality" (MacKinnon, supra, at 22)—is lawful no matter how sexually explicit. Speech treating women in the disapproved way—as submissive in matters sexual or as enjoying humiliation—is unlawful no matter how significant the literary, artistic, or political qualities of the work taken as a whole. The state may not ordain preferred viewpoints in this way. The Constitution forbids the state to declare one perspective right and silence opponents....

"If there is any fixed star in our constitutional constellation, it is that no official, high or petty, can prescribe what shall be orthodox in politics, nationalism, religion, or other matters of opinion or force citizens to confess by word or act their faith therein." *West Virginia State Board of Education v. Barnette*, 319 U.S. 624 (1943). Under the First Amendment the government must leave to the people the evaluation of ideas. Bald or subtle, an idea is as powerful as the audience allows it to be. A belief may be pernicious—the beliefs of Nazis led to the death of millions, those of the Klan to the repression of millions. A pernicious belief may prevail. Totalitarian governments today rule much of the planet, practicing suppression of billions and spreading dogma that may enslave others. One of the things that separates our society from theirs is our absolute right to propagate opinions that the government finds wrong or even hateful.

The ideas of the Klan may be propagated. *Brandenburg v. Ohio*, 395 U.S. 444 (1969). Communists may speak freely and run for office. *DeJonge v. Oregon*, 299 U.S. 353 (1937). The Nazi Party may march through a city with a large Jewish population. *Collin v. Smith*, 578 F.2d 1197 (7th Cir.), cert. denied, 439 U.S. 916 (1978). People may criticize the President by misrepresenting his positions, and they have a right to post their misrepresentations on public property. People may seek to repeal laws guaranteeing equal opportunity in employment or to revoke the constitutional amendments granting the vote to blacks and women. They may do this because "above all else, the First Amendment means that government has no power to restrict expression because of its message [or] its ideas...." *Police Department v. Mosley*, 408 U.S. 92 2286 (1972).

Under the ordinance graphic sexually explicit speech is "pornography" or not depending on the perspective the author adopts. Speech that "subordinates" women and also, for example, presents women as enjoying pain, humiliation, or rape, or even simply presents women in "positions of servility or submission or display" is forbidden, no matter how great the literary or political value of the work taken as a whole. Speech that portrays women in positions of equality is lawful, no matter how graphic the sexual content. This is thought control. It establishes an "approved" view of women, of how they may react to sexual encounters, of how the sexes may relate to each other. Those who espouse the approved view may use sexual images; those who do not, may not.

Indianapolis justifies the ordinance on the ground that pornography affects thoughts. Men who see women depicted as subordinate are more likely to treat them so. Pornography is an aspect of dominance. n1 It does not persuade people so much as change them. It works by socializing, by establishing the expected and the permissible. In this view pornography is not an idea; pornography is the injury.

---

n1 "Pornography constructs what a woman is in terms of its view of what men want sexually.... What pornography does goes beyond its content: It eroticizes hierarchy, it sexualizes inequality. It makes dominance and submission sex. Inequality is its central dynamic; the illusion of freedom coming together with the reality of force is central to its working.... Pornography is neither harmless fantasy nor a corrupt and confused misrepresentation of an otherwise neutral and healthy sexual situation. It institutionalizes the sexuality of male supremacy, fusing the erotization of dominance and submission with the social construction of male and female...." MacKinnon, supra, at 17–18 (note omitted, emphasis in original). See also Andrea Dworkin, *Pornography: Men Possessing Women* (1981). A national commission in Canada recently adopted a similar rationale for controlling pornography. *Special Commission on Pornography and Prostitution, 1 Pornography and Prostitution* in Canada 49-59 (Canadian Government Publishing Centre 1985).

There is much to this perspective. Beliefs are also facts. People often act in accordance with the images and patterns they find around them. People raised in a religion tend to accept the tenets of that religion, often without independent examination. People taught from birth that black people are fit only for slavery rarely rebelled against that creed; beliefs coupled with the self-interest of the masters established a social structure that inflicted great harm while enduring for centuries. Words and images act at the level of the subconscious before they persuade at the level of the conscious. Even the truth has little chance unless a statement fits within the framework of beliefs that may never have been subjected to rational study.

Therefore we accept the premises of this legislation. Depictions of subordination tend to perpetuate subordination. The subordinate status of women in turn leads to affront and lower pay at work, insult and injury at home, battery and rape on the streets. n2 In the language of the legislature, "pornography is central in creating and maintaining sex as a basis of discrimination. Pornography is a systematic practice of exploitation and subordination based on sex which differentially harms women. The bigotry and contempt it produces, with the acts of aggression it fosters, harm women's opportunities for equality and rights [of all kinds]." Indianapolis Code § 16-1(a)(2).

n2 MacKinnon's article collects empirical work that supports this proposition. The social science studies are very difficult to interpret, however, and they conflict. Because much of the effect of speech comes through a process of socialization, it is difficult to measure incremental benefits and injuries caused by particular speech. Several psychologists have found, for example, that those who see violent, sexually explicit films tend to have more violent thoughts. But how often does this lead to actual violence? National commissions on obscenity here, in the United Kingdom, and in Canada have found that it is not possible to demonstrate a direct link between obscenity and rape or exhibitionism....

Yet this simply demonstrates the power of pornography as speech. All of these unhappy effects depend on mental intermediation. Pornography affects how people see the world, their fellows, and social relations. If pornography is what pornography does, so is other speech. Hitler's orations affected how some Germans saw Jews. Communism is a world view, not simply a Manifesto by Marx and Engels or a set of speeches. Efforts to suppress communist speech in the United States were based on the belief that the public acceptability of such ideas would increase the likelihood of totalitarian government. Religions affect socialization in the most pervasive way. The opinion in *Wisconsin v. Yoder*, 406 U.S. 205 (1972), shows how a religion can dominate an entire approach to life, governing much more than the relation between the sexes. Many people believe that the existence of television, apart from the content of specific programs, leads to intellectual laziness, to a penchant for violence, to many other ills. The Alien and Sedition Acts passed during the administration of John Adams rested on a sincerely held belief that disrespect for the government leads to social collapse and revolution—a belief with support in the history of many nations. Most governments of the world act on this empirical regularity, suppressing critical speech. In the United States, however, the strength of the support for this belief is irrelevant. Seditious libel is protected speech unless the danger is not only grave but also imminent. See *New York Times Co. v. Sullivan*, 376 U.S. 254 (1964); cf. *Brandenburg v. Ohio*, supra; *New York Times Co. v. United States*, 403 U.S. 713 (1971).

Racial bigotry, anti-semitism, violence on television, reporters' biases—these and many more influence the culture and shape our socialization. None is directly answerable by more speech, unless that speech too finds its place in the popular culture. Yet all is protected as speech, however insidious. Any other answer leaves the government in control of all of the institutions of culture, the great censor and director of which thoughts are good for us.

Sexual responses often are unthinking responses, and the association of sexual arousal with the subordination of women therefore may have a substantial effect. But almost all cultural stimuli provoke unconscious responses. Religious ceremonies condition their participants. Teachers convey messages by selecting what not to cover; the implicit message about what is off limits or unthinkable may be more powerful than the messages for which they present rational argument. Television scripts contain unarticulated assumptions. People may be conditioned in subtle ways. If the fact that speech plays a role in a process of conditioning were enough to permit governmental regulation, that would be the end of freedom of speech....

Much of Indianapolis's argument rests on the belief that when speech is "unanswerable," and the metaphor that there is a "marketplace of ideas" does not apply, the First Amendment does not apply either. The metaphor is honored; Milton's *Aeropagitica* and John Stewart Mill's *On Liberty* defend freedom of speech on the ground that the truth will prevail, and many of the most important cases under the First Amendment recite this position. The Framers undoubtedly believed it. As a general matter it is true. But the Constitution does not make the dominance of truth a necessary condition of freedom of speech. To say that it does would be to confuse an outcome of free speech with a necessary condition for the application of the amendment.

A power to limit speech on the ground that truth has not yet prevailed and is not likely to prevail implies the power to declare truth. At some point the government must be able to say (as Indianapolis has said): "We know what the truth is, yet a free exchange of speech has not driven out falsity, so that we must now prohibit falsity." If the government may declare the truth, why wait for the failure of speech? Under the First Amendment, however, there is no such thing as a false idea, *Gertz v. Robert Welch, Inc.*, 418 U.S. 323 (1974), so the government may not restrict speech on the ground that in a free exchange truth is not yet dominant.

At any time, some speech is ahead in the game; the more numerous speakers prevail. Supporters of minority candidates may be forever "excluded" from the political process because their candidates never win, because few people believe their positions. This does not mean that freedom of speech has failed....

We come, finally, to the argument that pornography is "low value" speech, that it is enough like obscenity that Indianapolis may prohibit it. Some cases hold that speech far removed from politics and other subjects at the core of the Framers' concerns may be subjected to special regulation. These cases do not sustain statutes that select among viewpoints, however. In *Pacifica* the FCC sought to keep vile language off the air during certain times. The Court held that it may; but the Court would not have sustained a regulation prohibiting scatological descriptions of Republicans but not scatological descriptions of Democrats, or any other form of selection among viewpoints.

At all events, "pornography" is not low value speech within the meaning of these cases. Indianapolis seeks to prohibit certain speech because it believes this speech influences social relations and politics on a grand scale, that it controls attitudes at home and in the legislature. This precludes a characterization of the speech as low value. True, pornography and obscenity have sex in common. But Indianapolis left out of its definition any reference to literary, artistic, political, or scientific value. The ordinance applies to graphic sexually explicit subordination in works great and small. The Court sometimes balances the value of speech against the costs of its restriction, but it does this by category of speech and not by the content of particular works. Indianapolis has created an approved point of view and so loses the support of these cases.... The definition of "pornography" is unconstitutional. No construction or excision of particular terms could save it.

The *Hudnut* case raises the most profound possible challenges to the concept of a fixed set of unprotected categories of speech. How are those categories justified? If it is on the basis of some characteristic or consequences of the speech in question, then a showing that an additional category of expression meets those criteria ought to justify the recognition of a new unprotected category of expression. If the justification is not based on the characteristics of the expression at issue, what is the justification for determining that obscenity is not protected expression? Judge Easterbrook, writing for the Seventh Circuit, relied primarily on the argument that the ordinance did not define an area of unprotected content, but rather restricted speech on the basis of viewpoint. He also seemed to imply, however, that there was an element of overbreadth at work, i.e., that the ordinance might not have been so problematic if its scope had been narrowed to exclude speech considered to be of value. Each of these arguments is easier to assert than to explain.

One critical point to observe is that Easterbrook appears to have accepted as given the proposition that the Indianapolis ordinance regulated "speech" rather than "expressive conduct." If an actress portrays a woman deriving sexual enjoyment from pain, is that more like the words "Fuck the Draft" (pure speech, *Cohen v. California*, 403 U.S. 15 [1971]) or a nude dancer performing for an audience (expressive conduct, *Barnes v. Glen Theatre*, 501 U.S. 560 [1991])? On the one hand, if one concludes that the movie is expressive conduct rather than pure speech, then according to the logic of *Barnes*, particularly the argument of Justice Scalia's concurring opinion, Indianapolis ought to have been permitted to ban such a movie if its actions passed the four-part test established in *United States v. O'Brien*, 391 U.S. 367 (1968) (see discussion in chapter 4). On the other hand, to the extent that the ordinance might have reached both expressive conduct and pure speech, then surviving the *O'Brien* test should not save it from a charge of unconstitutional overbreadth. As noted above, Judge Easterbrook seemed to be pointing in that direction in parts of his discussion. Undoubtedly, Catharine MacKinnon's quoted comment, "if a woman is subjected, why should it matter that the work has other value?" invited a challenge on overbreadth grounds to the extent that the ordinance was to be applied to speech rather than expressive conduct, but in the final analysis Judge Easterbrook rejected the entire concept of the statute, not merely the form in which it was drafted.

Assuming that the ordinance reached only "pure speech," what is the strength of the suggestion that the definition of pornography turned on viewpoint rather than content? The distinction between viewpoint and content, as Justice Kennedy acknowledged in another context, is far from clear. "As we have noted, discrimination against one set of views or ideas is but a subset or particular instance of the more general phenomenon of content discrimination. And, it must be acknowledged, the distinction is not a precise one." *Rosenberger v. Rector and Visitors of the Univ. of Virginia,* 515 U.S. 819 (1995). In *Rosenberger,* Justice Kennedy went on to argue that religion is always a viewpoint as well as a content area, and hence could not be excluded from a limited public forum on the basis of a content restriction. Other, long-recognized content areas are similarly problematic. Libel, for example, is always derogatory; it makes no sense to speak of "complimentary libel." Why is it permissible to distinguish false derogatory speech from false complimentary speech, but not to identify speech portraying women in a certain way as an unprotected category of speech? "Fighting words," too, is a problematic category from this perspective (they do not include words that an average person would expect to provoke a kiss on the cheek), as are blackmail (which applies only to the threat of revealing harmful information), false advertising (can a person be prosecuted for knowingly understating the virtues of his own product?), and most other allegedly viewpoint neutral categories. We may presume, returning to the case of expressive conduct, that the dancers at the Kitty Kat Lounge, (in *Barnes v. Glen Theatre*) and Kandyland (in *City of Erie v. Pap's A.M.*) wanted to produce a fairly specific set of impressions on the part of the viewers.

In the absence of a formal recognition of a new category of unprotected speech, there is little question but that *Hudnut* was correctly decided according to traditional First Amendment jurisprudence. Under either the strict scrutiny required by *Brandenburg v. Ohio* (for cases involving speech) or the intermediate scrutiny of *United States v. O'Brien* (for cases involving expressive conduct), a law must be narrowly tailored to the goals that it proposes to serve, and there is little question but that the Indianapolis ordinance failed that test. It is conceivable that at some time in the future, in an appropriate case, the Supreme Court might someday recognize "violent pornography" as an unprotected class of speech, perhaps employing some of the same elements that have traditionally been applied to the definition of obscenity in order to avoid reaching valuable works of art or literature in the process. In the absence of such a definition, however, it is unsurprising that the Indianapolis ordinance was unable to survive judicial scrutiny conducted in accordance with traditional free speech analysis.

But there is another argument that was raised in *Hudnut*. This is the argument that the First Amendment should be understood as an affirmative instrument of equality as well as a source of negative liberties. Catharine MacKinnon and Andrea Dworkin have been quoted as describing the argument for equality in this way:

> The First Amendment mainly prohibits state acts that interfere with speech. But there is an affirmative, if less prominent side, to the First Amendment that would allow the silence of women because of discrimination to be taken into the balance. The fairness doctrine in broadcasting, for example, recognizes that government sometimes has an obligation to help make access to speech available on an equal basis. The First Amendment's goals are furthered by restricting the speech of some so that others might have access to it.... Equal access to the means of speech, which pornography discriminately denies to women sexually and socially, is a First Amendment goal that is furthered by this law.[2]

The idea that furthering a state of equality is couched, here, as a right of equal access to the means of self-expression. This idea has been at the heart of a number of attempts to articulate a theory of the First Amendment based on equality. Critical race theorists have argued that hate speech should be recognized as an unprotected category of speech on the grounds that it is "speech that silences other speech"; these writers, like MacKinnon, urge us to consider the necessity of silencing some speech to make room for other speech. For example, Mari Matsuda, a leading writer among critical race theorists, has proposed the following as a test for defining an unprotected category of "racial hate speech":

1. The message is of racial inferiority.
2. The message is directed against a historically oppressed group.
3. The message is persecutory, hateful, and degrading.[3]

It is not difficult to see parallels between these three standards and the elements of the *Miller v. California*, 415 U.S. 15 (1973), test for obscenity (see discussion, chapter 3): The first defines the content, the second appeals to an historical understanding, and the third characterizes the particular instance of expression, taken as a whole, as without serious value.

Elsewhere, feminist legal writers, in the First Amendment context as elsewhere, have urged abandonment of the liberal focus on limiting state power in the name of privacy in favor of a set of principles that would recognize the fundamental function of the law to be to require the state to provide the conditions necessary for everyone to have an opportunity for autonomy and self-expression. These are complex ideas, and there are differences between them, but they share a basic presumption that "free speech" can and should be understood as an ideal of equal opportunity, not merely as a formal limitation on state authority.

In response, defenders of traditional First Amendment principles often argue that in practice it is impossible to define the proposed categories of unprotected speech, with the result that any attempt to regulate such speech results in statutes that are fatally overbroad, as was (arguably) the case with the Indianapolis statute at issue in *Hudnut* or the St. Paul statute at issue in *R. A. V. v. City of St. Paul, Minnesota*, 505 U.S. 377 (1992). Responding to Mari Matsuda's argument, Henry Louis Gates Jr. proposes that the application of the categorical approach to defining unprotected speech cannot work in the context of racial hate speech or pornography by virtue of the nature of the expression that is at issue. "Curiously," he writes, "what trips up the content-specific approach is that it can never be content-specific enough."

> [T]he test of membership in a "historically oppressed" group is in danger of being either too narrow (just blacks?) Or too broad (just about everybody). Are poor Appalachians—a group I know well from growing up in a West Virginia mill town—"historically oppressed" or "dominant group members"? Once we had adopted the "historically oppressed" proviso, I suspect it would just be a matter of time before a group of black women in Chicago are arraigned for calling a policeman a "dumb Polack."[4]

Gates is not entirely speculating here. He notes that in the early 1990s, the Canada Supreme Court adopted something very much like the definition of "pornography" in the Indianapolis statute and defined such expression as a criminal offense. That decision was immediately put to use: The first target was a gay and lesbian bookstore in Toronto, and later targets of prosecutions under the law included works by feminist scholar bell hooks...and the works of Catharine MacKinnon herself.

Ironies of prosecutorial discretion aside—the Toronto prosecutor, after all, may have been grandstanding to make a point—the argument that the First Amendment's guarantee of free speech should be understood as a promise of equality has considerable weight behind it. In a 1994 essay that appeared in a collection along with the Gates essay quoted above, William Rubenstein, then the director of the ACLU's Lesbian and Gay Rights Project, argued that for homosexuals the freedom of expression was the first condition of political equality. "The oppression of silence is possible because sexual orientation is not, like race or gender, visually identifiable....

Because taking on a lesbian/gay identity involves coming out, society can oppress gay people most directly simply by ensuring that such expressions are silenced." Rubenstein joins with MacKinnon, Matsuda, and others in finding that "the First Amendment...includes within it a narrative of equal rights." Far from joining in a call to interpret the First Amendment to permit government to suppress homophobic speech, however, Rubenstein concluded that the most important consequence of interpreting the First Amendment as a promise of equality was the reinforcement of the traditional suspicion of government power. "[H]ate speech regulation can yield more power to the government, to the majority, to the oppressors—power I am very hesitant to yield because I feel it is inevitable that the power will ultimately and inevitably be used against oppressed minorities."[5]

Political and social conservatives, too, are divided over the interpretation of the First Amendment. To a considerable extent, conservative arguments have shaped the Supreme Court's recent First Amendment jurisprudence concerning the regulation of obscene materials, restrictions on expressive conduct, the government's power to control the speech of those who receive use public funds, and, conversely, government's inability to exclude religious expression from the range of voices receiving government support. In general, the conservative position has been one that emphasizes the virtues of neutrality, thus emphasizing the equal treatment of different kinds of speech as opposed to the equality of different kinds of speakers or listeners. This, too, is an approach that looks for coherence among the different elements of the First Amendment in a theory of equality, albeit a different theory of equality from that championed by critical race theorists, feminists, and others.

The essay excerpt that follows comes from a symposium that was held to discuss the actions of the Court in *Employment Division, Dept. of Human Resources of Oregon v. Smith*, 494 U.S. 872 (1990), and subsequent cases. As you will see from the initial comments, many of the participants at the symposium took a dim view of the Court's adoption of a neutrality test in these cases. Professor William Marshall, however, proposes that we should applaud the decision in *Smith* and others like it as expressions of a commitment to equality, understood as a purely negative check on government action. The latitude that is given to majoritarian preference, by this view, is only the freedom to enact generally prohibitions that treat minority and majority populations equally.

William P. Marshall, "What Is the Matter with Equality?: An Assessment of the Equal Treatment of Religion and Nonreligion in First Amendment Jurisprudence"

The one point on which all the participants in this Symposium agree is that current Supreme Court decisions interpreting the religion clause are heavily influenced by equality considerations. The Court, with limited exception, has indicated that, for constitutional purposes, religion should be treated equally with nonreligion. This means that religion will generally not be constitutionally entitled to benefits unavailable to nonreligion, nor will it be denied benefits that are generally available to nonreligion.

There has also been remarkable consensus, thus far, about the wisdom of the Court's approach. It has pleased absolutely no one. To some, the equality approach does not sufficiently protect religion, to others it is too deferential to religion, and to still others it assumes its own conclusions by facilely positing that religion and nonreligion can be meaningfully equated. Daniel Conkle's remarks may also reflect a general consensus when he argues that the equality approach is deficient because it devalues religion by not according it with the recognition that it is both "distinct and distinctly important."

The Court's approach, accordingly, is in dire need of a defender, and it is in precisely that role that I intend to fill in this Article. I do so for two reasons. First, although I do not necessarily ascribe to every aspect of an equality approach, I believe that, at least in its current form, it sensibly furthers religious liberty interests. Second, and relatedly, I also believe that the Court's reliance on this approach has promoted a stability in the case law that itself furthers religion clause goals....

Before proceeding further, however, three points need to be introduced to place the equality approach in perspective. One, the Supreme Court's tack in pursuing an equality approach is not new. Rather, as shall be discussed, it has pervaded modern religion clause jurisprudence virtually from its inception. The only new development, if any, is that in some cases the role of equality has become more explicit. Two, the role of equality is not absolute. There are numerous areas within the religion clause jurisprudence where religion/nonreligion equality has no part at all. Three, the role of equality in religion clause cases should not be exaggerated even in situations where it is in play. In some of these circumstances, for example, the use of equality as a rule of decision has been either explicitly or implicitly rejected. The role of equality in religion clause cases, accordingly, is more accurately described as a vehicle that works as a center of gravity, assuring that the constitutional status of religion does not veer too far in any one direction.

THE ROLE OF EQUALITY IN RELIGION CLAUSE DECISIONS

A superficial review of current religion clause jurisprudence would likely lead to the conclusion that the area is in tumult. There is no underlying theory of religious freedom that has captured a majority of the Court, and the Court's commitment to its announced doctrines is tenuous at best. Every new case accepted for argument presents the very real possibility that the Court might totally abandon its previous efforts and start over.

As Kent Greenawalt observes, the tests applied by the United States Supreme Court in religion clause cases are "in nearly total disarray." The compelling interest test that the Court initially set forth in *Sherbert v. Verner* as applicable to free exercise challenges was overturned in *Employment Division v. Smith*, at least in so far as that test was to be applied in assessing First Amendment attacks on neutrally applicable laws. *Smith*, in turn, has generated its own confusion as lower courts have struggled to determine the bounds of the various exceptions that the Court announced would still warrant compelling interest.

Meanwhile, the Court's Establishment Clause test, while not suffering the indignity of being directly overruled, has not fared much better. The Court's test, originally set forth in *Lemon v. Kurtzman*, has been weakened, recharacterized, or simply not applied in recent decisions. Indeed, the test is so unpredictable that in a recent case the Court took the unprecedented step of overruling a decision that it had reached under *Lemon* based on the grounds that its original holding had been undercut by later cases. The Court took this step, moreover, while adhering to *Lemon* as still providing the applicable law.

Even amidst this doctrinal tumult, however, scholars have noted that there is more consistency in religion clause jurisprudence than meets the eye. For example, while virtually everybody agrees that *Smith*'s abandonment of the compelling interest test in free exercise cases was a major event in religion clause jurisprudence, nobody argues that *Smith* signaled a major change in the results of free exercise cases. *Sherbert*'s compelling interest test had never been given much vitality by the Court, and its doctrinal abandonment in *Smith* simply echoed the actual results in the cases.

Similarly, the Establishment Clause may yield more consistency than is popular to admit.... This is not to say that religion clause cases are models of clarity. Free exercise jurisprudence, after all, is the area that gave us the rather unique and impenetrable notion of "hybrid rights." Establishment jurisprudence, meanwhile, has been frustrating. The Court's establishment decisions, for example, have maintained that there is a constitutional difference between the state providing textbooks to parochial school children and the state providing maps to them and that the constitutionality of nativity scenes at city hall depends on whether the display is accompanied by secular symbols or is freestanding. But, even if the religion clause cases have provided problematic and, at times, comical distinctions, the central observation is correct. There is a general, discernible pattern that emerges from the case law. This pattern suggests the Court has implicitly been guided by a general notion of equality—both equality between religions and between religion and nonreligion. The equality principle is straight-forward. On one side, the Court has been reluctant to grant (or to allow) religion greater benefit than that provided to nonreligion. On the other, the Court has been reluctant to disfavor religion vis-à-vis its secular counterparts....

The Court's commitment to the equality approach is not absolute. This is most apparent in the simple fact that equality has not been used as an explicit rule of decision in religion clause cases (excepting the religious speech cases noted above). Indeed, in many circumstances the Court has explicitly rejected the notion that religion and nonreligion are to be equated for the purposes of constitutional analysis.

In fact, there are settled areas of religion clause jurisprudence in which there is no equivalency. Some have already been alluded to. The Establishment Clause's prohibition of state funding of institutions or organizations is unique to religion. There is no comparable limitation on government funding of nonreligious groups and activities. Similarly, the Establishment Clause's nonendorsement principle recognized in the nativity scene cases is also a religion-only limitation. The state may endorse nonreligious institutions or ideologies if it so chooses.

Third, the nonentanglement principle recognized in *Larkin v. Grendel's Den* and other cases is also religion-specific. In *Larkin*, the Court invalidated a provision which gave a church the right to veto the grant of a liquor license to an establishment within a five-hundred-foot radius on the grounds that the relationship between church and state generated by the statute amounted to impermissible entanglement. There would be little constitutional objection, however, if a similar right was granted to a secular institution.

Fourth, religion is the unique beneficiary of the rule which limits how far the state may intrude into internal church doctrinal disputes. Although the Court has not made clear whether the specific constitutional provision underlying the rule is the Free Exercise Clause, the Establishment Clause, or some combination of both, the Court has held that the state is not empowered to decide matters of church doctrine. No similar rule bars the state intervention into the internal doctrine of nonreligious groups.

Finally, there are constitutional restrictions that inhibit the state's ability to determine the bona fides of particular religious claims that do not apply to nonreligious claims. In *United States v. Ballard*, the Court held that in a mail fraud prosecution in which the defendants had represented themselves as divine messengers, the jury could not decide that a fraud occurred based upon its own disbelief of the defendants' religious claims. The determination of whether the defendants' claims were true was held to be beyond the competence of the Court, because allowing judicial fact finders to engage in the determination of religious bona fides would threaten the abilities of persons to believe what they choose—no matter how incredulous those beliefs may be to others.

WHEN ARE RELIGION AND NONRELIGION EQUAL?

The conclusion that religion should be treated equally with nonreligion is neither inevitably correct nor inevitably false.... There are enough similarities between religion and nonreligion to support their equation, in certain circumstances, and there are enough dissimilarities to justify differential treatment in other situations. As with other equality claims the question of whether religion should be treated as equal to nonreligion depends upon the existence (or nonexistence) of sound reason for doing so. This Part will offer some of those reasons.

The policy considerations underlying the equality principle are most convincing in the context of free exercise claims; so with that in mind, let us review the facts in a pre-*Smith* free exercise case—*Thomas v. Review Board*. In *Thomas*, the Court was faced with the claim of a Jehovah's Witness that he should be entitled to receive unemployment compensation benefits because his religious conviction made him unable to work in an armaments factory. The Court granted him relief under the Free Exercise Clause. The Court made clear in the course of its holding, however, that the state could have justifiably withheld unemployment compensation benefits if Thomas's refusal to work in the armaments factory was based on philosophical or moral beliefs rather than on religious beliefs. According to the *Thomas* Court, it was appropriate to treat the religious claimant and nonreligious claimant differently.

Does such a holding violate religion/nonreligion equality or does it simply stand for the proposition that religious and nonreligious claimants are not so similarly situated as to implicate equality concerns? The answer, of course, depends on how one views the underlying interests.

Arguments could be made (and I have made them frequently) that a religious objection to working in an armaments factory and a philosophical or moral objection to working in an armaments factory are essentially indistinguishable. Religion and nonreligion simply present two alternative modes of ideology. The soundness of the position that it is wrong to work in factories that produce war machines does not depend upon whether the basis of that position is religious or secular. There is nothing in the substance of the beliefs that suggests that the religious and the secular objections should be treated differently.

If the premise that religious and nonreligious objections to working in an armaments factory are equivalent is accepted, then a fair amount follows. First, from a First Amendment (speech) perspective, granting the religious believer exclusive benefit violates the equality of ideas principle that lies at the heart of the Free Speech Clause. The equality of ideas principle posits that every idea has equal dignity in the competition for acceptance in the marketplace of ideas. Protecting only some ideas (those based on religion) is inappropriate because it improperly skews the marketplace of ideas in his favor by, in effect, shielding the religious beliefs from antagonistic social forces. The effect of religion, after all, is not confined to the mind of the believer. Rather, religion is a powerful social force that frames, shapes, and influences political responses to a wide range of issues. Specially protecting religious beliefs, therefore, could have real political consequence. Thomas's pacifism, if accepted by a wide range of people, would have as dramatic an effect on the political landscape as would the religious beliefs of groups such as those who claim their religious beliefs forbid their children from being exposed to humanistic material or the claim that traditional tribal lands should not be developed.

Second, from an Establishment Clause perspective, protecting only the religious objection places an official imprimatur on the religious belief that may violate establishment concerns against impermissible government endorsement of religion. The conclusion that a particular belief is entitled to unique constitutional protection, after all, would bestow upon that belief a Supreme Court sanctioned credibility and legitimacy.

The equivalence of the workplace objections of Thomas and his nonreligious counterpart, moreover, extends beyond their similarity as articulated ideas. Free exercise exemptions of the kind granted by the Court in *Thomas*, for example, have been justified on such grounds as promoting pluralism, protecting conscience, preserving the self-identity of the adherent, or saving the believer from the purported special hardship that occurs when one is forced to violate religious principles. All of these rationales, however, would also serve to equate Thomas with his secular counterpart rather than distinguish him....

Conscience...is not a uniquely religious concern. The objections to war of a moral opponent and a religious opponent can not be distinguished on the grounds that the latter is based on conscience while the former is not. Similarly, religion is not a unique aspect of self-identity. Social affiliations, personal relationships, and family also play critical roles in the individual's development of her sense of self. Finally, the conclusion that violations of religious precepts cause special suffering is both overinclusive and underinclusive. A secular belief that it is immoral to kill in war may be far more deeply felt than the belief of a religious adherent that she should not work on Saturdays—and the violation of the moral belief may be far more excruciating to the secular believer than a violation of the sectarian principle is to the religious devotee....

Note that to this point, I have not made the argument that religious and nonreligious claims for exemption are equal...[and] claiming that two matters are equal does not make it so. My claim to this point is only that, in the free exercise area, religion and nonreligion are arguably functionally equivalent, and not treating religion and nonreligion equally in certain circumstances also raises its own set of policy and constitutional concerns. On this basis, I conclude that there are sensible reasons for treating religion and nonreligion alike—at least in free exercise exemption cases such as *Thomas*.

Others disagree. Indeed, there is a growing body of scholarship that, while conceding that religion and nonreligion can be equated based upon the secular, functional arguments offered above, strenuously argues that religion and nonreligion are different nonetheless. The position taken in this scholarship, straightforwardly enough, is that religion must be understood as being different because of distinctly religious concerns—specifically that humanity's relationship with God should be understood to transcend all other allegiances or activities. For the rest of this discussion, I shall refer to this argument as the "sectarian claim."

On one hand, it is difficult to dispute the logic of the sectarian claim. If God does exist and is knowable, then presumably humanity's obligation and allegiance to him would be primary. This, as Søren Kierkegaard teaches us, is the lesson of the story of Abraham and Isaac. Because Abraham was ordered by God to kill Isaac, he was compelled to suspend the secular strictures against murder. Abraham's religious obligation, in short, transcended his temporal duties. Translated into constitutional law, this means that the state's interest in preventing murder, no matter how compelling, would be obligated to give way to the divine command.

Closely examined, however, the applicability of the sectarian claim is an extraordinarily limited assertion. It directly applies only upon a showing that the religious belief in question is True. The importance of the state's accommodating

Abraham is not because Abraham believes he must kill Isaac; it is because of the Truth of the command (that he must kill Isaac). If Abraham is misguided, there is no value in protecting his belief.... [T]he essence of the sectarian claim is not that religion is good—it is that "True religion is good." But how is one to know what is True? More importantly, how is the state to accept that one has found True religion? In this respect, the sectarian claim runs up against the first amendment prohibition against the states declaring what is religiously True. Given these concerns, it would seem that the sectarian claim has simply led us down a blind alley.

There is a response. Defenders of the sectarian claim might argue that it is unnecessary to show that a particular religious claim is True. All they need to show is that a religious claim might be True. As Michael McConnell has argued, "the liberal state...cannot reject in principle the possibility that a religion may be true...." But the problem with this approach is that a jurisprudence which must act on the basis that any sincere, religious belief is True would quickly prove unworkable. The claim that a matter is compelled by Divine Law admits no possibility of an overriding secular interest. The state, however, cannot suspend the operations of its laws any time an adherent asserts her religious beliefs are True. Such an approach truly would create a rule which, as Justice Scalia warned, would allow every person to be a law unto herself.

Undoubtedly, the effects of such an approach could be watered down by a jurisprudential device such as the compelling interest test (Abraham could still be arrested for murder); but would this meet the concerns of the sectarian claim?.... [W]hy should a compelling secular (state) interest ever override the interest in satisfying God's commands? From the believer's perspective, God's commands trump those of the state, however "compelling" the latter might seem to nonbelievers.

There is a final argument that could be made on behalf of the sectarian claim. Religion might be distinguished from nonreligion on the conclusory assertion that religion is different because religion is different. This is not a facetious argument, nor is it a straw man. Nothing requires that matters that are at times functional equivalents always be treated as equals. Accordingly, those who believe in the primacy of religion for its own sake may equally believe that no further justification of religion's distinctiveness is required. That being so, the position that granting religious exemptions offends the principle of the equality of ideas would necessarily fail because, to those who believe in the primacy of religion, there is no equality of ideas in the first place. To those who assert the innate distinctiveness of religion, the result of the previous analysis equating religion and nonreligion is unlikely to be persuasive.

THE INEQUALITY PREMISE UNDERLYING EQUALITY

There is, however, another line of argument. As noted previously, there are some areas in which religion and nonreligion are not treated equally. The state is precluded, for example, from resolving intrachurch theological disputes and/or determining religious sincerity (by reference to the believability of the religious claim). As shall be discussed, the religion-specific policies underlying these limitations may also support treating religious claims as equal to nonreligious claims. It is the distinctiveness of religion that arguably counsels that it be treated as equal with nonreligion. This Part will investigate this position.

Both the limitation on civil court adjudication of intrachurch disputes and upon the determination of religious sincerity reflect the special sensitivity that is required whenever the state adjudicates matters involving religion. Some of these concerns are constitutionally based. Adjudicating religious sincerity on the basis of whether the asserted religious belief is True, for example, would place the state in the position of declaring what is religious Truth—a power that both inserts the state in the quintessential religious role, in violation of Establishment Clause principles, and that usurps the church's own essential function, in derogation of free exercise concerns.

Concern about the competency of civil courts to resolve issues with religious implications is also a factor. In the intrachurch dispute context, for example, the Court as early as 1871 expressed the concern that civil courts resolving religious matters would in effect permit an appeal "from the more learned tribunal in the law which should decide the case, to one which is less so." But the competency concern is not simply with getting a doctrinal issue right. After all, civil courts are frequently called upon to decide matters of foreign law with which they have no particular expertise. Rather the competing concern is that adjudicating religious matters, unlike foreign law, involves a series of interpretive decisions that are generally beyond the ken, or at least beyond the common experience, of the civil tribunals....

Consider, for example, what a free exercise regime that treated religion distinctively would require of adjudicating courts. The court would need to determine (1) whether the alleged belief was religious; (2) whether the believer was sincere in her religious claim (an inquiry which we have seen must be limited by constitutional concerns); (3) what role the particular religious belief has in the believer's religious order; (4) whether the religious exercise was burdened by the state enactment; and (5) what the religious effect that violating the religious norm will have on the believer. These are extraordinarily difficult questions with no easily ascertainable standards available for application. Indeed, the notion that such inquiries could be standardized across religious traditions may itself offend religious liberty concerns by placing religious belief and practice into cookie-cutter modes. There is, after all, no religion archetype. The importance of doctrine, the sources of religious obligation, and the consequence of violating religious norms, to name but some indicia of belief, all vary among religions and religious traditions. Addressing religious claims on religious terms, in short, would ultimately require developing a separate set of standards with respect to each religion. Indeed if the Supreme Court is to be taken at its word, that it is the personal beliefs of the individual that trigger free exercise protection and not the formal doctrine of the religion to which the believer adheres, then a separate set of standards would need to be applied to each believer.

Moreover, it is not only that the judicial task is so difficult, it is also that the implications of error are so great. Defining religion incorrectly, for example, can raise its own establishment and free exercise concerns. It is therefore no wonder that Justice Scalia in *Smith* relied upon judicial competency concerns in holding that the Free Exercise Clause did not demand constitutionally compelled exemptions from neutral laws for religious believers.

Additionally, even if the courts are in some sense competent to address religion related issues, there is considerable doubt as to whether they are likely to do so in a way that serves (or at least fairly serves) religious liberty values. First, minority belief systems will undoubtedly be the worse for wear. A court is far more likely to be sympathetic to claims that are consistent with dominant cultural norms than with religious claims that seem bizarre or incredulous. Second, as the pre-*Smith* free exercise and the Religious Freedom and Restoration Act ("RFRA") cases attest, courts will be likely to under-enforce religious exemption claims because of the difficult interpretive steps that religion claims require.

Finally, even if the courts do all in their power to factor away cultural preferences and guard against under-enforcement the resulting jurisprudence will likely still appear jumbled. This is because of the range of differences among and between religions and religious beliefs. Let me offer an illustration.

Assume for the moment that there are five different religious landlords all of whom object to having to rent to unmarried couples under an equal housing ordinance. Claimant A's objection is central to her religion and has doctrinal support; Claimant B's objection is based upon a principle in her faith that unmarried people should not live together, but the religion is silent on the question of whether renting to such couples is a religious violation; Claimant C's objection is based upon an idiosyncratic belief that the claimant adopted at the time the unmarried couple applied for an apartment; Claimant D's objection is based upon religious tenet, but her religion does not indicate that there are any adverse religious consequences for violating the belief; and Claimant E's objection is based upon discussions she has had with other members of her religious community. Assume that the state's interest is found to be significant but not so "compelling" that it would outweigh all challenges. In this circumstance, courts evaluating the factors of religiosity, sincerity, centrality, burden, and effect could, and likely should, come out differently in these cases. But how the cases would result is not predictable. As we have seen, the nature of religious belief and conviction is not easily universalized and there is no common (or at least readily apparent) baseline from which courts could promote a consistent approach that accounts for the myriad forms of religious belief and attachment. Moreover, as if this were not enough, the inconsistency created by the inherent variability within religious belief would be compounded by litigation factors such as the nature of the evidence proffered and the identity of the trier of fact.

But even if all variables were eliminated to the fullest extent possible, imagine the resulting case law, in which some of the religious landlord claimants win while others fail. Should the same religious belief (or what appears to be the same religious belief) be treated differently? And if so, would not the resulting appearance of sect preference create its own set of concerns?

Treating religion as distinct, at least in the context of free exercise claims for exemption, in short, is a recipe for instability. It demands inquiries that are fraught with constitutional peril, it places extraordinary demands on civil tribunals, it leads to a jurisprudence that would likely favor mainstream beliefs, and it would create the appearance of sect favoritism. The equality approach, on the other hand, avoids these pitfalls....

Institutional concerns play a more limited role in supporting the use of the equality approach in establishment cases. After all, establishment cases only rarely raise the need for defining religion and virtually never require investigations into sincerity, centrality, burden, and effect. Nevertheless, the interest in avoiding sensitive religious determinations can, and has, had some role in establishment cases.

The best example of this may be found in *Widmar v. Vincent*. In *Widmar* a religious group was denied permission to engage in prayer meetings in university buildings, although nonreligious organizations were allowed access to the university facilities. The university defended its actions on anti-establishment grounds, contending that its decision to exclude the prayer meetings was compelled by the Establishment Clause. The Court found for the religious organization holding that the university restriction was a classic form of content discrimination and therefore prohibited by the Free Speech Clause. But it is the Court's particular treatment of prayer that, for our purposes, is most interesting. In a dramatic example of the equality approach, the Court refused to accept the argument that prayer was different than any other form of speech.

From a religious perspective, however, worship is different than speech. To believers, worship is less a verbal activity than it is a most sacred and profound religious act...a "means by which believers affirm to each other and to their god their participation in a community set apart from others." As such, worship is not as much an act of communication to the outside world as it is an act of "commitment to a community."

Worship thus "captures something deeply important about religion" that the *Widmar* Court chose to ignore. But how could the Court do otherwise coherently? As the Court explained, the question of whether a particular action, such as reading from the Bible, should be characterized as speech or worship was not a determination that could be made intelligibly. Accordingly, the Court faced the alternative of either reflexively treating worship as speech or inserting itself (and the lower courts to follow) in the task of providing secular interpretation and secular appraisals of religious significance to a fundamentally religious act. As in the free exercise area, the equality approach allowed the Court to avoid the type of perilous inquiry for which it was ill-equipped....

As has been noted by others, the problems inherent in achieving a coherent religion clause jurisprudence are extraordinarily difficult and pervasive. The problems, moreover, extend beyond the juridical concerns with adjudicating religion as a distinct phenomenon noted in the previous Part (although those certainly play a part). They also include, for example, the fact that constitutional law is individualistic while religion is often communitarian, thus raising the square peg/round hole dilemma. And there is the inescapable dilemma of the religion clauses: that complete neutrality towards religion is impossible. The act of deciding religion clause cases necessarily requires the adoption of a posture towards religion that will itself hold inherent religious implication.

In these circumstances, some connection to less problematic inquiries may be both desirable and appropriate. Enter equality. The advantage of the equality approach is that it provides a baseline from which the constitutionality of the treatment of religion can be adjudged—the baseline of nonreligion. Although the treatment of religion and nonreligion may vary when policies demand, the equality approach provides a center of gravity, assuring that the inherent vagaries in religion clause jurisprudence do not take the case law beyond accessible standards.

CONCLUSION—RELIGIOUS LIBERTY AT THE DAWN OF A NEW MILLENNIUM

If the purpose of entitling this Symposium "Religious Liberty at the Dawn of a New Millennium" was to prod the participants into evaluating the current state of religious liberty in the United States, then the consensus among us should be that the state of religious liberty is strong.... [R]eligion in the United States is thriving. The United States remains one of the most religious countries in the world and there is little of the sectarian strife that plagues much of the rest of the world. Diverse religions are flourishing and...the pace of this religious flourishing is accelerating.

Interestingly, most of this religious prospering has occurred under a jurisprudential regime that has tended to minimize religion's distinctiveness and importance. As we have seen, the Court has only weakly recognized religion as distinctive under the Establishment Clause and has virtually eliminated a distinctive accord for religion under the Free Exercise Clause. Accordingly, there may yet be one remaining argument in defense of the equality approach—it works. Causal relationships should not be too easily claimed; but given the robust state of religion at the dawn of the new millennium, the question posed by this Article, deserves some consideration. What is the matter with equality?

The answer to this last question is, of course, that there is nothing "the matter with equality"; it may even be a concept that provides the basis for a unified conception of the First Amendment. The question is, what kind of equality does the First Amendment guarantee? Note that Marshall's arguments ultimately rest on institutional concerns; keeping courts out of questions which they are ill-equipped to handle, and promoting doctrinal stability. Are there other approaches that equally achieve these desirable institutional outcomes while employing a different understanding of the Religion Clauses? Is it clearly the case that a court is incapable of distinguishing worship from the expression of a religious viewpoint?

It is also not necessarily the case that Marshall's description of the equality approach to the Religion Clauses accords with the approach being taken by the current Court (note, for example, that Marshall includes nonendorsement as an element of current jurisprudence). Do the outcomes in recent cases comport with Marshall's conception of "equality"? Marshall was writing to defend the Rehnquist Court, but might one accept Marshall's argument without necessarily joining him in lauding the conclusions of the Court?

The kinds of questions that Marshall raises, and that can be raised in response to his arguments, apply beyond the Religion Clauses. Defining "speech" is no less problematic than defining "religion," and determining the kinds of questions that are best left to legislatures rather than courts is an essential part of deciding the scope of judicial review. In other cases, where First Amendment questions appear as conflicts between government and individuals, the range of questions that courts are free to ask defines the scope of the First Amendment itself.

C. The Future of the First Amendment

As this book was being written, events were occurring that have the potential to shape the debates over the First Amendment as they are likely to shape the contours of American political and legal thought generally. The attacks of September 11, 2001, created conditions of crisis in the United States that have not been seen in many years. Justice O'Connor expressed her concerns in this regard after a visit to the site of the World Trade Center in October:

> We're likely to experience more restrictions on our personal freedom than has ever been the case in our country.... First, can a society that prides itself on equality before the law treat terrorists differently than ordinary criminals? And where do we draw the line between them? Second, at what point does the cost to civil liberties from legislation designed to prevent terrorism outweigh the added security that that legislation provides?.... These are tough questions, and they're going to require a great deal of study, goodwill and expertise to resolve them. And in the years to come, it will become clear that the need for lawyers does not diminish in times of crisis; it only increases.[6]

The issues of equality that were raised in the last chapter have resonance here, as well, as one can ask whether the future of the First Amendment looks different for members of certain groups, or proponents of certain viewpoints, than for the rest of Americans.

In large part, the legislative responses to September 11 did not directly affect First Amendment rights, as they were primarily oriented toward the creation of new procedures for the investigation and prosecution of terror-related crimes. New laws also gave the government new powers to investigate, detain, and deport aliens, primarily by the enactment of the Uniting and Strengthening America by Providing Appropriate Tools

Required to Intercept and Obstruct Terrorism Act of 2001 (the "USA PATRIOT Act," P.L. 107–56). Some of these provisions, however, struck directly at First Amendment concerns. For example, provisions permitting trials to be held outside the view of the public pose a challenge to the principle that members of the public have a First Amendment right to view criminal proceedings. *Richmond Newspapers Inc. v. Virginia*, 448 U.S. 555 (1980) (discussed in chapter 8). In *United States v. Zacarias Moussaoui*, 2002 U.S. Dist. LEXIS 1608 (E.D. Vir. 2002), a group of television stations argued that the special public interest in the trial required that they be permitted to broadcast the proceedings. Relying in part on the fact that there were security concerns involved, the federal district court ruled that physical access to the courtroom was sufficient to meet the requirements of *Richmond Newspapers*. The same question may arise again in the future, however, if the government attempts to hold closed, "secret" proceedings, possibly involving secret evidence (not shared with the defense), which are allowed under the USA PATRIOT law.

In addition to official actions by the United States government, in the weeks following September 11 there were a number of incidents in which persons expressing unpopular viewpoints found themselves subject to reactions ranging from criticism to official sanction. These events were most prominently featured on college campuses. To mention only a few instances, an Orange Coast College professor was suspended for eleven weeks for various comments including the statement "silence in the face of Islamic terror is akin to complicity,"[7] while a professor at the University of New Mexico was banned from teaching freshmen and subjected to post-tenure review for telling a class that "anyone who can blow up the Pentagon has my vote."[8] At UCLA, a library assistant was suspended for five days without pay after sending an e-mail criticizing U.S. support for Israel in response to a coworker's mass e-mail praising U.S. policy.[9] In Canada, a University of British Columbia professor was charged with committing a hate crime, "publicly inciting hatred against Americans," for criticizing the United States following September 11.[10] All of these statements, clearly, were examples of pure protected speech.

The high point of this kind of hysterical reaction was arguably reached in a report published by the American Council of Trustees and Alumni, an organization whose governing board counts among its members Lynne Cheney (wife of the Vice President and herself a past government official), Senator Joseph Lieberman, former Colorado Governor Richard Lamm, former Cabinet Secretary William Bennett, and Nobel laureate Saul Bellow. The report, issued October 5, 2001 and sent to three thousand college and university trustees, was titled "Defending Civilization: How Our Universities Are Failing America and What Can Be Done About It." The report asserted that the continued vitality of Western civilization is threatened by the failure of professors to articulate clear and unanimous moral messages, and in response called on American universities to require courses in American history.[11] The claim that university faculty have the power to threaten Western civilization, and the implicit equation of Western civilization and the United States, are both questionable. From a First Amendment perspective, what is important is the possible consequences of this kind of action for free expression, particularly in the special setting of public universities.

One thing that is striking about the reactions described above is that they came from both ends of the political spectrum. In addition, the kind of more or less hysterical reaction exemplified above faded from view fairly quickly, for the most part, although a few controversies continue. The more substantial effect of the post–September 11 atmosphere is likely to be found in the potential chilling effects of other kinds of government action. When the federal government is empowered to investigate and prosecute organizations alleged to be connected to Muslim terrorist organizations, will Muslim Americans feel discouraged from joining or contributing money to such organizations out of fear of attracting unwanted government attention? In the summer of 2002, the Justice Department announced a program called the "Terrorism Information and Prevention System," a program to enable "millions of American truckers, letter carriers, train conductors, ship captains, utility employees, and others" a way to "report suspicious activity" by calling a toll-free hotline number.[12] An additional "Citizens' Preparedness Guide," prepared and distributed by the Department of Justice, instructs all Americans to "contact the FBI immediately" if they "observe a pattern of suspicious activity, such as someone unfamiliar to you loitering in a parking lot, government building, or around a school or playground."[13] The TIPS program aroused immediate political opposition, from both parties, and its future is uncertain. Nor is there any reason to assume that any of the millions of eventual designated TIPS informers would misuse the system. From a First Amendment perspective, however, the question is whether programs like these are likely to create an atmosphere in which people are afraid to speak freely.

There do not appear to be court cases on the horizon that directly raise these concerns. Instead, the Religion Clauses—which produced several important decisions in the 2001–2002 term—continue to be the focus of First Amendment activity, especially where religion and free speech are conjoined in a single case. That, arguably, was the situation in a case that was heard recently by a Ninth Circuit court, *American Family Association v. City and County of San Francisco*, 277 F.3d 1114 (9th Cir. 2001). The case involved a newspaper ad that was taken out by a group of conservative Christian organizations in San Francisco newspapers. The ad stated that "God abhors any form of sexual sin," that everyone "makes a choice in yielding to temptation," and that homosexuals have "walked out of homosexuality into sexual celibacy or even marriage through the help of Jesus Christ." The ad also quoted statistics that homosexual behavior "accounts for a disproportionate number of sexually transmitted diseases," that "65% of all reported AIDS cases among males since 1981 have been men engaged in homosexual behavior," and that "homosexual youth are twenty-three times more likely to contract STD's than heterosexuals."

Responding to the advertisement, the San Francisco Board of Supervisors sent a letter to the sponsors of the letter, which said "[w]hat happened to Matthew Shepard is in part due to the message being espoused by your groups that gays and lesbians are not worthy of the most basic equal rights and treatment." The City and County of San Francisco also adopted two resolutions calling on "the Religious Right to take accountability for the impact of their long-standing rhetoric denouncing gays and lesbians," and decrying "anti-gay" advertisements. The latter resolution named one of the plaintiffs and asserted that such ads sought to "promote an agenda which denies basic equal rights for gays and lesbians and routinely state their opposition to toleration of gay and lesbian citizens." *American Family Association v. City and County of San Francisco*, 277 F.3d 1114 (9th Cir. 2001).

The plaintiffs sued, claiming violations of the Free Exercise and Free Speech rights, and a violation of the Establishment Clause. In an opinion written by Judge Michael Daly Hawkins, with a dissent by Judge John Noonan, the Ninth Circuit rejected the Free Exercise claim on the grounds that neither the letter nor the two resolutions constituted government action:

> There is no actual "law" at issue.... [T]here does not appear to be any case in this circuit applying *Smith* or *Lukumi* to some non-regulatory or non-compulsory governmental action—in other words, to something other than an actual law.... Plaintiffs allege in the complaint that the Defendants' actions violated their free exercise rights and chilled the exercise of their free speech rights. We have previously explained, however, that when the challenged government action is neither regulatory, proscriptive or compulsory, alleging a subjective chilling effect on free exercise rights is not sufficient to constitute a substantial burden. The complaint does not otherwise allege any specific religious conduct that was

affected by the Defendants' actions. The Plaintiffs have therefore failed to state a viable constitutional claim under the Free Exercise Clause....

The "hybrid" free speech claim was dispensed with on a similar theory. "[T]he Defendants have not imposed or even threatened any prohibitions or sanctions for the Plaintiffs' viewpoint. The district court properly determined that the Plaintiffs had failed to allege a colorable viewpoint discrimination claim and properly dismissed this portion of the hybrid claim as well." *American Family Association v. City and County of San Francisco*, 277 F.3d 1114 (9th Cir. 2001).

The Establishment Clause argument received a lengthier analysis. The Ninth Circuit applied all three elements of the *Lemon v. Kurtzman* test, on the theory that hostility to religion is as offensive to the Establishment Clause as favoritism. Concerning the first *Lemon* test, requiring that a law have a secular purpose, the court declared that "a practice will stumble on the purpose prong only if it is motivated wholly by an impermissible purpose.... [A]lthough the letter and resolutions may appear to contain attacks on the Plaintiffs' religious views, in particular that homosexuality is sinful, there is also a plausible secular purpose in the Defendants' actions—protecting gays and lesbians from violence...." The second *Lemon* test asks whether the primary effect of a government action is to promote or discourage religion. Calling this "a closer question," the court nonetheless found that the actions of the City of San Francisco passed the test. "Certainly, the letter and resolution may contain over-generalizations about the Religious Right, at times misconstrue the Plaintiffs' message, and may be based on a tenuous perceived connection between the Plaintiffs' advertisements and the increase in violence against gays and lesbians. This does not, however, make religious hostility the primary effect of the Defendants' actions."

This was the argument that aroused the greatest opposition from Judge Noonan in his dissenting opinion. Drawing a direct connection to the political environment after September 11, 2001, Noonan took the majority to task for ignoring what he took to be the real impact of the city's actions:

> The city is saved as to its purpose by its plausible purpose of seeking to reduce violence against gays and lesbians; but this plausible purpose does not neutralize the effect of the means chosen by the city.... To reach the plaintiffs, to strike at what the city perceived as a danger, the city had to strike at the heart of the plaintiffs' religious belief, to focus on their belief that the conduct they were trying to change was an offense to God and to make that belief responsible for murder. Suppose a city council today, in the year 2002, adopted a resolution condemning Islam because its teachings embraced the concept of a holy war and so, the

resolution said, were "directly correlated" with the bombing of the World Trade Center. Plausibly the purpose might be to discourage terror bombings. Would any reasonable, informed observer doubt that the primary effect of such an action by a city could be the expression of official hostility to the religion practiced by a billion people?

The case thus presents a clash over the significance of the idea of endorsement. Where a government action does not involve coercion, to what extent is the Establishment Clause offended by the fact that it carries an endorsement—or, in this instance, a criticism—of religious beliefs? In earlier cases, conservative justices have tended to view endorsement as a nonissue, while more liberal justices have shared Justice O'Connor's concern with the possibility that government action might convey a message of inferiority to members of a nonfavored group. Those arguments, however, took place in the context of government actions that proclaimed favor for a particular religion, or for religion generally, rather than disapproval of a particular religious philosophy. This case, or one like it, may at some point provide an opportunity for the Court to consider the significance of endorsement in Establishment Clause jurisprudence in a different context.

The case is also interesting for the way it illustrates the ways in which lower federal courts apply Supreme Court decisions. Confronted by claims brought under the Establishment and Free Exercise Clauses, the Ninth Circuit applied versions of the *Lemon* and *Sherbert* tests, both of which have arguably been called into question—if not outright overruled—by subsequent opinions in *Agostini v. Felton*, 521 U.S. 203 (1997), and *Smith* (see discussions, chapters 5 and 6).

The principles of First Amendment jurisprudence are never permanently fixed. They are always the subject of debate, and the resolutions that are reached by one Court, or in one generation, are not likely to remain the same in another. Across time, then, the First Amendment appears as the center of an ongoing discussion that is of the utmost importance to the system of American constitutional ideas but which can never reach a final resolution. The contents of this book are a portrait of a moment in that ongoing discussion, presented in the hope of contributing to its vigorous continuation.

Notes

1. Benjamin Cardozo, *The Nature of the Judicial Process* (Boston: Little, Brown, 1921) p. 13.

2. David Bryden, "Between Two Constitutions: Feminism and Pornography," 2 *Constitutional Commentary* 147 (1985), pp. 171–72.

3. Mari Matsuda, Charles R. Lawrence III, Richard Delgado, Kimberle Williams Crenshaw, *Words That Wound: Critical Race Theory, Assaultive Speech, and the First Amendment* (Boulder, CO: Westview Press, 1993), p. 36.

4. Henry Louis Gates Jr., "Critical Race Theory and the First Amendment," in Gates, Henry Louis Jr., Anthony P. Griffin, Donald E. Lively, Robert C. Post, William B. Rubenstein, Nadine Strossen, and Ira Glasser, *Speaking of Race, Speaking of Sex* (New York: NYU Press, 1993), p. 33.

5. William Rubenstein, "Since When Is the Fourteenth Amendment Our Route to Equality? Some Reflections on the Construction of the 'Hate-Speech' Debate from a Lesbian/Gay Perspective," in *Speaking of Sex, Speaking of Race*, pp. 283, 290, 292.

6. Linda Greenhouse, "A Nation Challenged: The Supreme Court," *New York Times*, September 29, 2001, p. B5.

7. William Lobdell, "Response to Terror," *Los Angeles Times*, Dec. 11, 2001, p. A1.

8. Michael A. Fletcher, "Dissenters Find Colleges Less Tolerant of Discord Following Attacks," *Washington Post*, Oct. 30, 2001, p. A6.

9. Diana Jean Schemo, "A Nation Challenged: The Campuses," *New York Times*, Nov. 25, 2001, p. B1.

10. Editorial, *Montreal Gazette*, Oct. 10, 2001, p. C12.

11. Jerry Martin and Anne Neal, "Defending Civilization: How Our Universities are Failing America and What Can Be Done About It," *Report of the Defense of Civilization Fund, American Council of Trustees and Alumni* (Washington, DC: 2001), available at http://www.goacta.org/Reports/ defciv.pdf.

12. Available at http://www.citizencorps.gov/tips.html

13. Available at http://www.citizencorps.gov/guidebook.html.

Table of Cases

44 Liquormart, Inc. v. Rhode Island, 517 U.S. 484 (1996) 120–22

Abington School District v. Schempp, 374 U.S. 203 (1963) 193–94, 257

Abood v. Detroit Bd. of Educ., 431 U.S. 209 (1977) 148–49, 259, 369

Abrams v. United States, 250 U.S. 616 (1919) 39–40, 364–65

Agostini v. Felton, 521 U.S. 203 (1997) 179–82, 258, 399

Aguilar v. Felton, 473 U.S. 402 (1985) 178

Alberts v. California, 354 U.S. 476 (1957) 51, 74

Amalgamated Food Employees Union v. Logan Valley Plaza,
391 U.S. 308 (1968) 67

American Booksellers Ass'n. v. Hudnut, 771 F.2d 323 (1985) 373–78

American Communications Ass'n. v. Douds, 339 U.S. 382 (1950) 42

American Family Association v. City and County of San Francisco,
277 F.3d 1114 (9th Cir. 2001) 396–98

Ardery v. State, 56 Ind. 328 (1877) 139

Ashcraft v. Conoco, Inc. 218 F.3d 282 (4th Cir. 2000) 333

Ashcroft v. Free Speech Coalition, 122 S.Ct. 1389 (2002) 89

Avery v. Johnson, 393 U.S. 483 (1968) 345

Avis Rent A Care System v. Aguilar, 529 U.S. 1138 (2000) 118

Barnes v. Glen Theatre, 501 U.S. 560 (1991) 79, 96, 138–41, 362, 367, 379–80

Bartnicki v. Vopper, 121 S. Ct. 1753 (2001) 319–21

Bates v. State Bar of Ariz., 433 U.S. 350 (1977) 119

Bd. of Educ. v. Allen, 392 U.S. 236 (1968) 171–72

Bd. of Educ. of the Westside Community Schools v. Mergens,
    496 U.S. 226 (1990) 178, 274

*Bd. of Regents of the University of Wisconsin System v.
    Southworth*, 529 U.S. 217 (2000) 288–91, 369

Beauharnais v. Illinois, 343 U.S. 250 (1951) 52–5, 372

Bethel School District No. 403 v. Fraser, 478 U.S. 675 (1986) 96–97, 131

Bigelow v. Virginia, 421 U.S. 809 (1975) 118–19

*Bob Jones University and Goldboro Christian School v.
    United States*, 461 U.S. 574 (1983) 247–48

Bounds v. Smith, 430 U.S. 817 (1977) 345–46

Bowen v. Roy, 476 U.S. 693 (1986) 248

Bowers v. Hardwick, 478 U.S. 186 (1986) 139, 358–59

Boy Scouts of America v. Dale, 530 U.S. 640 (2000) 154, 159–63, 368, 369

Brandenburg v. Ohio, 395 U.S. 444 (1969) 44, 45–46

Branzburg v. Hayes, 408 U.S. 665 (1972) 329–32

Braunfeld v. Brown, 366 U.S. 599 (1961) 233

Breard v. Alexandria, 341 U.S. 622 (1951) 58

Broadrick v. Oklahoma, 413 U.S. 601 (1973) 72

Brown v. Louisiana, 383 U.S. 131 (1966) 128

Buckley v. Valeo, 424 U.S. 1 (1976) 122–23

Burson v. Freeman, 504 U.S. 191 (1992) 69

Butler v. Michigan, 352 U.S. 380 (1957) 85–86

California v. LaRue, 409 U.S. 109 (1972) 138

California Democratic Party v. Jones, 530 U.S. 567 (2000) 154

Camfield v. City of Oklahoma, 248 F.3d 1214 (2001) 88

Cantwell v. Connecticut, 310 U.S. 296 (1940) 41, 48, 220–23

Capitol Square Review and Advisory Bd. v. Pinette,
515 U.S. 753 (1995) 276–77, 369

Carey v. Brown, 447 U.S. 455 (1980) 60, 364

Carey v. Population Services Int'l, 431 U.S. 678 (1977) 119

Central Hudson Gas & Elec. Corp. v. Public Serv. Comm'n of N.Y.,
447 U.S. 557 (1980) 120

Chaplinsky v. State of New Hampshire, 315 U.S. 568 (1942) 48–50, 258

Chicago Police Dept. v. Mosley, 408 U.S. 92 (1972) 60, 364

Church of the Lukumi Babalu Aye v. City of Hialeah,
508 U.S. 520 (1993) 256–57

City of Boerne v. Flores, 521 U.S. 507 (1997) 255

City of Chicago v. Morales, 527 U.S. 41 (1998) 342–44

City of Erie v. Pap's A.M., dba "Kandyland,"
529 U.S. 277 (2000) 141–43, 367, 380

*City of Madison Joint School District v. Wisconsin Employment
Relations Comm'n.*, 429 U.S. 167 (1976) 69

Clark v. Community for Creative Non-Violence, 468 U.S. 288 (1984) 59, 258

Cohen v. California, 403 U.S. 15 (1971) 56, 90–94, 313, 365, 379

Collin v. Smith, 578 F.2d 1197 (7th Cir., 1978) 131–32

Committee for Public Education and Religious Liberty v. Nyquist,
413 U.S. 756 (1973) 178

*Communist Party of the United States v. Subversive Activities
Control Board*, 367 U.S. 1 (1961) 44

Cornelius v. NAACP Defense and Education Fund, 473 U.S. 788 (1985) 69

County of Allegheny v. ACLU, 492 U.S. 573 (1989) 205–10, 365

Cox v. Louisiana, 379 U.S. 536 (1965) 59

Cox v. Louisiana, 379 U.S. 559 (1965) 59

Cox v. New Hampshire, 312 U.S. 569 (1941) 127

Cox Broadcasting Corp. v. Cohn, 420 U.S. 469 (1974) 314

Dallas v. Stanglin, 490 U.S. 19 (1989) 153

Debs v. United States, 249 U.S. 211 (1919) 39

Democratic Party of the United States v. NCPAC, 470 U.S. 480 (1985) 125

Dennis v. United States, 341 U.S. 494 (1951) 43–44

Deutch v. United States, 367 U.S. 456 (1961) 44

Douglas v. City of Jeanette, 319 U.S. 157 (1943) 232

Dun & Bradstreet v. Greenmoss Builders, Inc., 472 U.S. 749 (1985) 307–9

Edwards v. Agiullard, 482 U.S. 578 (1987) 212–15

Edwards v. South Carolina, 372 U.S. 229 (1963) 59, 340–42

Employment Division, Dept. of Human Resources of Oregon
  v. Smith, 494 U.S. 872 (1990) 141, 250–55, 258, 362, 367, 383

Engel v. Vitale, 370 U.S. 421 (1962) 191–93

Epperson v. Arkansas, 393 U.S. 97 (1968) 213

Erzoznik v. City of Jacksonville, 422 U.S. 205 (1975) 94

Essex v. Wolman, 409 U.S. 808 (1972) 178

Everson v. Bd. of Educ. of the Township of Ewing, 330 U.S. 1 (1947) 169–71

Ex parte Hull, 312 U.S. 546 (1941) 345

Federal Communications Comm'n. v. Pacifica, 438 U.S. 726 (1978) 97–99

Federal Election Comm'n. v. NCPAC 470 U.S. 480 (1985) 125–26

Feiner v. New York, 340 U.S. 315 (1951) 341–42

Florida Star v. B. J. F., 491 U.S. 524 (1989) 314–17

Food Lion v. Capital Cities/ABC, 194 F.3d 505 (4th Cir. 1999) 326–28

Forsyth County v. The Nationalist Movement, 505 U.S. 123 (1992) 128

Frazee v. Illinois Dept. of Employment Security, 489 U.S. 829 (1989) 249

Free Speech Coalition v. Reno, 198 F.3d 1083 (9th Cir. 1999) 88

Frisby v. Schultz, 487 U.S. 474 (1988) 61, 68, 89

Frohwerk v. United States, 249 U.S. 204 (1919) 39

Gannett Co. v. DePasquale, 443 U.S. 368 (1979) 325

Garber v. Kansas, 389 U.S. 51 (1967) 237

Gertz v. Robert Welch, Inc., 418 U.S. 323 (1974) 72, 74, 305–7

Gillette v. United States, 401 U.S. 437 (1971) 228

Ginsberg v. New York, 390 U.S. 629 (1968) 78, 102, 105

Gitlow v. New York, 268 U.S. 652 (1925) 14, 40

Glickman v. Wileman Bros. & Elliott, Inc., 521 U.S. 457 (1997) 150

Goldboro Christian School v. United States, 461 U.S. 574 (1983) 247–48

Goldman v. Weinberger, 475 U.S. 503 (1986) 244–47

Good News Club v. Milford Central School, 533 U.S. 98 (2001) 284–88

Greer v. Spock, 424 U.S. 828 (1976) 68

Gresham v. Peterson, 225 F.3d 899 (7th Cir. 2000) 65

Griswold v. Connecticut, 391 U.S. 145 (1965) 6, 24

Hague v. CIO, 307 U.S. 496 (1939) 59

Harris v. Forklift Systems, 510 U.S. 17 (1993) 107–8

Hernandez v. Commissioner, 490 U.S. 680 (1989) 229

Hill v. Colorado, 530 U.S. 703 (2000) 63–66

Hobbie v. Unemployment Appeals Comm'n. of Fla., 480 U.S. 136 (1987) 249

Houchins v. KQED, 438 U.S. 1 (1977) 323–25

Hudgens v. NLRB, 424 U.S. 507 (1976) 67

Hurley v. Irish-American Gay, Lesbian and Bisexual Group of Boston,
515 U.S. 557 (1995) 154, 155–58, 369

Hustler v. Falwell, 485 U.S. 46 (1988) 312–13

International Society for Krishna Consciousness v. Lee, 505 U.S. 672 (1992) 69, 70

Jacobellis v. Ohio, 378 U.S. 184, 195 (1964) 75, 362

Jones v. Opelika, 316 U.S. 584, 608 (1942) 5, 41

Keller v. State Bar of California, 496 U.S. 1 (1990) 149, 369

Kovacs v. Cooper, 336 U.S. 77 (1949) 58, 59

Lamb's Chapel v. Center Moriches Union Free School Dist.,
    508 U.S. 384 (1993) 275–76, 369

Larkin v. Grendel's Den, Inc., 459 U.S. 116 (1982) 167

Lee v. International Society for Krishna Consciousness, 505 U.S. 830 (1992) 70

Lee v. Weisman, 505 U.S. 577 (1992) 179, 195–200, 258, 367

Legal Services Corp. v. Velasquez, 531 U.S. 533 (2001) 268–70

Lehman v. City of Shaker Heights, 418 U.S. 298 (1974) 66–67

Lemon v. Kurtzman, 403 U.S. 602 (1971) 173–77, 398

Lewis v. Casey, 518 U.S. 343 (1996) 346–47

Linmark Associates, Inc. v. Willingboro, 431 U.S. 85 (1977) 119

Lloyd Corp. v. Tanner, 407 U.S. 551 (1972) 67

Loper v. New York City Police Dept., 999 F.2d 699 (1993) 65

Lying v. Northwest Indian Cemetery Protective Association, 485 U.S. 439 (1988) ... 247

Lynch v. Donnelly, 465 U.S. 668 (1984) 204–5

Madsen v. Women's Health Center, 512 U.S. 753 (1994) 61–63

Marsh v. Chambers, 463 U.S. 783 (1983) 194

Martin v. Struthers, 319 U.S. 141 (1943) 232

Massachusetts v. Davis, 162 Mass. 510 (1895) 58

Massachusetts v. Davis, 167 U.S. 43 (1897) 58

Massachusetts v. Oakes, 491 U.S. 576 (1989) 87

McCollum v. Bd. of Ed., 333 U.S. 203 (1948) 166

McGowan v. Maryland, 366 U.S. 420 (1961) 171, 233

Meek v. Pittenger, 413 U.S. 349 (1973) 177, 178

Memoirs v. Massachusetts, 383 U.S. 413 (1966) 75

Meritor Savings Bank v. Vinson, 477 U.S. 57 (1986) 107

Miller v. California, 415 U.S. 15 (1973) 76–78, 79, 258, 381

Minersville School District v. Gobitis, 310 U.S. 586 (1940) 145, 232–33

Minnesota v. Hershberger, 495 U.S. 901 (1990) 244

Minnesota St. Bd. of Comm'ty. Colleges v. Knight, 465 U.S. 271 (1984) ... 347–51, 369

Mishkin v. New York, 383 U.S. 502 (1966) 78

Mitchell v. Helms, 530 U.S. 793 (2000) 141, 182–87, 189, 258

Mueller v. Allen, 463 U.S. 388 (1983) 177

Murdock v. Pennsylvania, 319 U.S. 105 (1943) 41, 232

NAACP v. Alabama, 357 U.S. 449 (1958) 24, 150–51

National Socialist Party of America v. Skokie, 432 U.S. 43 (1977) 156

NEA v. Finley, 524 U.S. 569 (1998) 263–66, 368

Near v. Minnesota, 283 U.S. 697 (1931) 292–96

Nebraska Press Ass'n. v. Stewart, 427 U.S. 539 (1976) 325

New York v. Ferber, 458 U.S. 747 (1982) 73, 86–87

New York State Club Ass'n v. New York, 487 U.S. 1 (1988) 153

New York Times Co. v. Sullivan, 376 U.S. 254 (1964) 301–4, 365

New York Times Co. v. United States, 403 U.S. 713 (1971) 297–301

Nixon v. Shrink Missouri Government PAC, 528 U.S. 377 (2000) 126

Noto v. California, 367 U.S. 290 (1961) 45

Olmstead v. United States, 277 U.S. 438, 478 (1928) 5, 364

O'Lone v. Shabazz, 482 U.S. 342 (1987) 247

Oncale v. Sundowner Offshore, 523 U.S. 75 (1998) 109

Osborne v. Ohio, 495 U.S. 103 (1990) 87

Palko v. Connecticut, 302 U.S. 319 (1937) 5

Paris Adult Theatre I v. Slaton, 413 U.S. 49 (1973) 82

Pell v. Procunier, 417 U.S. 817 (1974) 322–23

People v. Croswell, 3 Johns. Cas. 337 (N.Y. 1804) 34

Perry Education Assn. v. Perry Local Educators' Assn., 460 U.S. 37 (1983) 68

Peyote Way Church of God v. Thornburgh, 922 F.2d 1210 (5th Cir., 1991) 230

Philadelphia Newspapers v. Hepps, 475 U.S. 767 (1986) 309–12

Pierce v. Society of Sisters, 268 U.S. 510 (1925) 223–25

Pierce v. United States, 252 U.S. 239 (1919) 39

Pinkus v. United States, 436 U.S. 293 (1978) 78

Pope v. Illinois, 481 U.S. 497 (1987) 78–79, 82

Prince v. Massachusetts, 321 U.S. 158 (1944) 231–32

Pruneyard Shopping Center v. Robins, 447 U.S. 74 (1980) 67

Radio-Television News Directors Ass'n. and National Ass'n. of Broadcasters v. FCC, 184 F.3d 872 (D.C. Cir. 1999) 339

Rankin v. McPherson, 483 U.S. 378 (1987) 259

R. A. V. v. City of St. Paul, Minnesota,
505 U.S. 377 (1992) 50, 55, 111–15, 258, 368, 381–82

Red Lion Broadcasting Co. v. FCC, 395 U.S. 367 (1969) 97, 334–38, 370

Regan v. Taxation with Representation of Washington, 461 U.S. 540 (1983) ... 260, 267

Regina v. Hicklin, L. R. 3, Q. B. 360 (1868) 36, 47, 74

Regina v. Wagstaff, 10 Cox Crim. Cases 531 (1868) 220

Reno v. ACLU, 521 U.S. 844 (1997) 102–6, 144

Renton v. Playtime Theatres, Inc., 475 U.S. 41 (1986) 96, 102, 139

Reynolds v. United States, 98 U.S. 145 (1878) 219–20, 225

Richmond Newspapers Inc. v. Virginia, 448 U.S. 555 (1980) 325–26, 394–95

Roberts v. United States Jaycees, 468 U.S. 609 (1984) 151–53

Roemer v. Maryland Public Works Bd., 426 U.S. 736 (1976) 177

Romer v. Evans, 517 U.S. 620 (1996) 351–60, 369

Rosenberger v. Rector and Visitors of the University of Virginia,
515 U.S. 819 (1995) 271, 278–84, 369, 379–80

Roth v. United States, 354 U.S. 476 (1957) 51, 74–75, 364

Rowan v. Post Office Dept., 397 U.S. 728 (1970) 58, 89

Runyon v. McCrary, 427 U.S. 160 (1976) 153–54, 368

Rust v. Sullivan, 500 U.S. 173 (1991) 260–63, 367, 368

Sable Communications of California v. Federal Communications Commission, 492 U.S. 115 (1989) 83

Santa Fe Independent School District v. Doe, 530 U.S. 290 (2000) 200–2, 367

Saxbe v. Washington Post, 417 U.S. 843 (1974) 323

Scales v. United States, 367 U.S. 203 (1961) 44

Schaefer v. United States, 251 U.S. 466 (1919) 39

Schenck v. United States, 249 U.S. 47 (1919) 38

Schneider v. New Jersey, 308 U.S. 147 (1939) 59, 127

School Dist. of Abington Township v. Schempp, 374 U.S. 203 (1963) 193, 197, 204, 212, 257

School Dist. of Grand Rapids v. Ball, 473 U.S. 373 (1985) 178, 182

Sherbert v. Verner, 374 U.S. 398 (1963) 234–36, 365

Smith v. Arkansas State Highway Employees, 441 U.S. 463 (1979) 350

Smith v. California, 361 U.S. 147 (1959) 7, 303

Smith v. City of Ft. Lauderdale, 177 F.3d 954 (11th Cir. 1999) 65

Smith v. Daily Mail Publishing Co., 433 U.S. 97 (1979) 316

Smith v. United States, 431 U.S. 291 (1977) 83

Stanley v. Georgia, 394 U.S. 557 (1969) 80–81, 370

Stone v. Graham, 449 U.S. 39 (1980) 203–04

Stromberg v. California, 283 U.S. 359 (1931) 128

Swaggart v. Bd. of Equalization, 493 U.S. 378 (1990) 248

Terminiello v. Chicago, 337 U.S. 1 (1949) 56

Texas v. Johnson, 491 U.S. 397 (1989) 55, 56, 133–37, 367

Texas Monthly, Inc. v. Bullock, 489 U.S. 1 (1988) 178

Thomas v. Review Board of Indiana Employment Security Division,
450 U.S. 707 (1981) 249

Thornhill v. Alabama, 310 U.S. 102 (1940) 342

Tilton v. Richardson, 403 U.S. 672 (1971) 177

Tinker v. Des Moines Independent Community School District,
393 U.S. 503 (1969) 130–31, 146

Tony and Susan Alamo Foundation v. Sec'y of Labor, 471 U.S. 290 (1985) 248

Torcaso v. Watkins 367 U.S. 488 (1961) 168, 225–27

United States v. 12,200 Ft. Reels, 413 U.S. 123 (1973) 85

United States v. Ballard, 322 U.S. 78 (1944) 225

United States v. Eichman, 496 U.S. 310 (1990) 138

United States v. Fox, 248 F.3d 394 (5th Cir. 2001) 88

United States v. Grace, 461 U.S. 171 (1983) 68

United States v. Hamling, 418 U.S. 87 (1974) 82

United States v. J. H. H., 22 F.3d 821 (8th Cir. 1994) 116

United States v. Kokinda, 497 U.S. 720 (1990) 68

United States v. Lee, 455 U.S. 252 (1982) 243

United States v. O'Brien, 391 U.S. 367 (1968) 129–30, 379

United States v. Playboy Entertainment Group, 529 U.S. 803 (2000) 100–1, 118

United States v. Seeger, 380 U.S. 163 (1965) 228

United States v. Stewart, 65 F.3d 918 (11th Cir. 1996) 117

United States v. Thomas, 74 F.3d 701 (6th Cir. 1996) 84–85

United States v. Zacarias Moussaoui, 2002 U.S. Dist. LEXIS 1608
    (E.D. Vir. 2002) 395

USDA v. United Foods, Inc., 533 U.S. 405 (2001) 150

Virginia v. American Booksellers Association, 484 U.S. 383 (1988) 96

Virginia Bd. of Pharmacy v. Virginia Citizens Consumer Council, Inc.,
    425 U.S. 748 (1976) 119

Walker v. City of Birmingham, 388 U.S. 307 (1967) 127

Wallace v. Jaffree, 472 U.S. 38 (1985) 167, 194–95

Walz v. Tax Comm'n, 397 U.S. 664 (1970) 164, 172–73

Ward v. Rock Against Racism, 491 U.S. 781 (1989) 59, 64, 258

Welsh v. United States, 398 U.S. 333 (1970) 228

West Virginia State Bd. of Ed. v. Barnette,
    319 U.S. 624 (1943) 41, 128, 146–48, 232–33

Whitney v. California, 274 U.S. 357 (1927) 40–41

Widmar v. Vincent, 454 U.S. 263 (1981) 69, 272–74

Wilson v. Layne, 526 U.S. 603 (1999) 318

Wisconsin v. Mitchell, 508 U.S. 476 (1993) 116–17

Wisconsin v. Yoder, 406 U.S. 205 (1972) 237–43, 365

Witters v. Washington Dept. of Services for the Blind, 474 U.S. 481 (1986) 177

Wolman v. Walter, 433 U.S. 229 (1977) 177, 178

Yates v. United States, 354 U.S. 178 (1957) 44

Young v. American Mini-Theatres, Inc., 427 U.S. 50 (1976) 94–96

Zelman v. Simmons-Harris, 122 S.Ct. 2460 (2002) 187–88

Zobrest v. Catalina Foothills School District, 509 U.S. 1 (1993) 177

Sources

Adams, Arlin M., and Charles J. Emmerich. *A Nation Dedicated to Religious Liberty: The Constitutional Heritage of the Religion Clauses.* Philadelphia: University of Pennsylvania Press, 1990.

Berns, Walter. *The First Amendment and the Future of American Democracy.* New York: Basic Books, 1976.

Blackstone, William. *Commentaries on the Laws of England: A Facsimile of the First Edition.* 4 vols., Chicago: University of Chicago Press, 1979.

Boyd, Julian P., ed. *The Papers of Thomas Jefferson.* Princeton: Princeton University Press, 1950.

Bryden, David. "Between Two Constitutions: Feminism and Pornography." 2 *Constitutional Commentary* 147, 1985.

Caldwell, Samuel L. *Complete Writings of Roger Williams.* Providence, RI: Narragansett Club.

Cardozo, Benjamin. *The Nature of the Judicial Process.* Boston: Little, Brown, 1921.

Carter, T. Barton, Marc A. Franklin, and Jay B. Wright. *The First Amendment and the Fourth Estate: The Law of Mass Media.* Westbury, NY: Foundation Press, 1991.

Cogan, Neil H. *Contexts of the Constitution.* New York: Foundation Press, 1999.

Coquillette, Daniel R., ed. *Law in Colonial Massachusetts 1630–1800.* Boston: Publications of the Colonial Society of Massachusetts, 1984.

Cornell, Saul. *The Other Founders: Anti-Federalists and the Dissenting Tradition in America, 1788–1828.* Chapel Hill, NC: University of North Carolina Press, 1999.

Curry, Thomas J. *The First Freedoms: Church and State in America to the Passage of the First Amendment.* New York: Oxford University Press, 1986.

Delgado, Richard, and Jean Stefanic. *Must We Defend Nazis?: Hate Speech, Pornography, and the New First Amendment.* New York: NYU Press, 1997.

Downs, Donald A. *Nazis in Skokie: Freedom, Community and the First Amendment.* Notre Dame, IN.: Univ. of Notre Dame Press, 1985.

Dreisbach, Daniel B. *Real Threat and Mere Shadow: Religious Liberty and the First Amendment.* Westchester, IL.: Crossway Books/Rutherford Institute, 1987.

Emerson, Thomas I. *Toward a General Theory of the First Amendment.* New York: Random House, 1966.

Fletcher, Michael A. "Dissenters Find Colleges Less Tolerant of Discord Following Attacks." *Washington Post*, Oct. 30, 2001: A6.

Force, Peter, ed. *Tracts and Other Papers Relating Princially to the Origin, Settlement, and Progress of the Colonies in North America.* Washington, DC: Peter Force, 1844.

Ford, Paul Leicester, ed. *The Works of Thomas Jefferson.* New York: G.P. Putnam and Sons, 1905.

Garvey, John H., and Frederick Schauer. *The First Amendment: A Reader.* St. Paul: West Publishing Co., 1996.

Gates, Henry Louis Jr. "War of Words: Critical Race Theory and the First Amendment," in Gates, Henry Louis Jr., Anthony P. Griffin, Donald E. Lively, Robert C. Post, William B. Rubenstein, Nadine Strossen, and Ira Glasser. *Speaking of Race, Speaking of Sex.* New York: NYU Press, 1993.

Greenhouse, Linda. "A Nation Challenged: The Supreme Court." *New York Times*, September 29, 2001: B5.

Guild, Reuben Aldridge, ed. *Complete Writings of Roger Williams.* Providence, RI: Russell & Russell, 1963.

Hamowy, Ronald, ed. *Cato's Letters, or Essays on Liberty, Civil and Religious, and Other Important Subjects.* 2 vols., Indianapolis: Liberty Fund, 1995.

Harrison, Lowell H. *Kentucky's Road to Statehood.* Louisville, KY: University Press of Kentucky, 1992.

Kirtley, Jane, ed. *The First Amendment Handbook.* Arlington, VA: Reporters' Committee for Freedom of the Press, 1995.

Kurland, Philip B., ed. *Church and State: The Supreme Court and the First Amendment.* Chicago: University of Chicago Press, 1975.

Kurland, Philip B., and Ralph Lerner, eds. *The Founders' Constitution.* 5 vols., Chicago: University of Chicago Press, 1987.

Levy, Leonard W. *The Establishment Clause: Religion and the First Amendment.* Chapel Hill, NC: UNC Press, 1994.

Levy, Leonard W., ed. *Freedom of the Press from Zenger to Jefferson: Early American Libertarian Theories.* Indianapolis, IN: Bobbs-Merrill, 1966.

Lobdell, William. "Response to Terror." *Los Angeles Times*, Dec. 11, 2001: A1.

Lutz, Donald. *The Origins of American Constitutionalism.* Baton Rouge, LA: Louisiana State University Press, 1988.

Madison, James. *The Debates in the Federal Convention of 1787 Which Framed the Constitution of the United States of America.* New York: Prometheus Books, 1997.

Martin, Jerry, and Anne Neal. "Defending Civilization: How Our Universities are Failing America and What Can Be Done About It." *Report of the Defense of Civilization Fund, American Council of Trustees and Alumni.* Washington, DC: 2001, available at http://www.goacta.org/Reports/defciv.pdf.

Matsuda, Mari. "Public Response to Racist Speech: Considering the Victim's Story," in Mari Matsuda, Charles R. Lawernce III, Richard Delgado, Kimberle Williams Crenshaw. *Words That Wound: Critical Race Theory, Assaultive Speech, and the First Amendment."* Boulder, CO: Westview Press, 1993.

Murphy, Paul L. *The Shaping of the First Amendment, 1791 to the Present.* New York: Oxford University Press, 1992.

Myers, Marvin, ed. *The Mind of the Founder: Sources of the Political Thought of James Madison.* Hanover, NH: University Press of New England for Brandeis University Press, 1981.

Nelson, Harold L., ed. *Freedom of the Press from Hamilton to the Warren Court.* Indianapolis, IN: Bobbs-Merrill, 1967.

Padover, Saul K. *The Complete Jefferson*. New York: Duell, Sloan & Pearce, 1943.

Padover, Saul K. *The Complete Madison*. New York: Harper & Bros., 1953.

Rubenstein, William. "Since When Is the Fourteenth Amendment Our Route to Equality? Some Reflections on the Construction of the 'Hate-Speech' Debate from a Lesbian/Gay Perspective," in Gates, Henry Louis Jr., Anthony P. Griffin, Donald E. Lively, Robert C. Post, William B. Rubenstein, Nadine Strossen, and Ira Glasser. *Speaking of Race, Speaking of Sex*. New York: NYU Press, 1993.

Schemo, Diana Jean. "A Nation Challenged: The Campuses," *New York Times*, Nov. 25, 2001: B1.

Shiffrin, Steven H., and Jesse H. Choper. *The First Amendment: Cases, Comments, Questions*. 3d ed. St. Paul, MN: West Group, 2001.

Sunstein, Cass R. *Democracy and the Problem of Free Speech*. New York: The Free Press, 1993.

Van Alstyne, William W. *First Amendment: Cases and Materials*. Westbury, New York: Foundation Press, 1995.

Washington, H. A., ed. *The Writings of Thomas Jefferson*. Washington, D.C.: Taylor and Maury, 1854.

Unsigned editorial. *Montreal Gazette*, Oct. 10, 2001: C1.

Index

access to public facilities, 272–77
access to public support, 277–91, 368–71
accommodation, 216–57
activist approach, 371–72
Adams, John, 13, 33
affirmative approach, 363–66
Alien and Sedition Acts, 13–14, 33–34
American Council of University Trustees and Alumni, 395–96
"as applied" challenge, 28
assembly, 340–44
association, 145, 150–63, 368–71

Bacon, Francis, 9
"bad tendency" test, 36, 38–41, 46, 51
Baptist Association of Danbury, Connecticut, 10–11
bigamy, 218–19
Bill for Establishing Religious Freedom, 9
Black, Hugo, 7, 44–45, 167–68, 172–73, 297
Blackmun, Harry, 119, 124, 206–7, 210, 262–63, 325–26
Blackstone, William, 14
Brandeis, Louis, 39–40, 43, 57
Brennan, William, 44, 55, 73–76, 79, 87, 98–99, 132–33, 151–52, 177–78, 297
Breyer, Steven, 125
broadcast media, 97–98, 100, 333–39
Burger, Warren, 76–79, 82, 96–97, 164, 172–74, 177, 194, 204, 237–39, 249–50, 325

Calvinism, 8–9
campaign contributions, 123–26
Cardozo, Benjamin, 5
categorical approach, 46–48
Cato's Letters, 31–32
children, 85–89, 97–99, 101–2
chilling effect, 25, 72–73, 102

Clark, Thomas, 193
"clear and present danger" test, 38, 40–46
coercion, 194–95, 200–2, 207, 209–10, 216
commercial speech, 118–22
compelled association. *See* association
compelled speech, 145–50
Comstock Act, 36
Congress of Industrial Organizations, 27
content neutrality, 59–60, 73, 94–95, 110, 122
continuing offense doctrine, 82–83
core speech, 56–57

Debs, Eugene, 39
Douglas, William, 6, 24, 44–46, 75, 77–78, 297
Dworkin, Andrea, 373, 380

Easterbrook, Frank, 379–80
Emerson, Donald, 15, 23–24, 362
equality, equal protection, 60, 372–94
Espionage Act of 1917, 37–38
establishment, Establishment Clause (*see also* religion, subsidies for; religion, endorsement), 164–217
expression, 55–58
expressive conduct, 26, 127–45

facial challenge, 28
fairness doctrine, 333–39
Federal Flag Protection Act, 138
Federalists, 13
fighting words, 48–50, 56
Fortas, Abraham, 130–31
Frankfurter, Felix, 86, 166, 168
Franklin, Benjamin, 12–13, 32
free exercise, Free Exercise Clause, 164, 167, 183, 194, 200, 204, 216–17, 218–57

Garrison, William Lloyd, 35
Gates, Henry Louis, Jr., 6, 382
government as speaker, 259–72

Hamilton, Alexander, 34
Hamilton, William, 32–33
Hand, Learned, 43
Harlan, John Marshall, 44, 75, 172–73
hate speech, 109–18
high wall separation, 167, 171
Holmes, Oliver Wendell, Jr., 38–40, 51, 57–58, 364–67

incidental benefits. *See* neutrality
incidental burdens, 26
indecency, 89–106
Industrial Workers of the World, 36–37
Internet, 84, 99, 102–06

Jefferson, Thomas, 9–14, 34, 165–66, 168

Kennedy, Anthony, 65, 89, 100, 189, 206–07, 210, 216–17, 255–56, 258–59, 267–71, 278–79, 284–85, 291, 380
Kentucky Resolution, 33

libel (*see also* seditious libel; privacy), 72, 74, 76, 109, 120, 301–21
limited forums, 66–70
Lincoln, Abraham, 35–36
Lovejoy, Elijah, 35

MacKinnon, Catharine, 373, 380
Madison, James, 9–13, 33–34, 165
Marshall, Thurgood, 177, 228–29, 251
Marshall, William P., 384
Massachusetts *Body of Liberties of 1641*, 8, 11
Matsuda, Mari, 381
McCarren Act, 42
McCarthy, Joseph, 42
McReynolds, James, 224
Milton, John, 8
Murphy, Frank, 231–32

negative approach, 366–68
neutrality, 141, 167, 182–83, 187–88, 193, 216, 218
newsgathering, limits on, 321–38
nude dancing, 138–44

obscenity, 36,38, 46, 51, 55, 73, 74–79
O'Connor, Sandra Day, 96, 122, 141–42, 152, 154, 179, 182, 187, 189, 205, 206, 216, 394
overbreadth, 25, 72–73, 85, 87. 102, 109

panhandling, 65
PATRIOT Act, 394–95
petition, 344–61
Powell, Lewis, 94, 120, 149, 308, 323
preferred rights, 5, 41
press, freedom of, 292–339
prior restraint, 292–301
privacy, 5, 11, 24, 27, 80–85, 89, 98, 100, 301–21
public forum, 27, 57–66
Puritans, 7–8

radio. *See* "broadcast media"
Rehnquist, William, 55, 62–63, 69–70, 96, 116–17, 119, 126–26, 187–89, 202–3, 214, 216, 248, 260–63, 312–13, 326
religion, definition of, 225–30
religion, endorsement of, 188–216
religion, subsidies for, 168–89
reporter's privilege, 328–33
Roberts, Owen, 220
Rubenstein, William, 382–83
Rutledge, John, 231

Scalia, Antonin, 63, 65, 78–79, 100–1, 110–11, 116–18, 126, 140–41, 143, 179, 183, 189, 195, 200, 202, 214–16, 250–51, 229, 257, 276, 287, 346–47, 353–54, 360

school funding. *See* religion, subsidies for.

secondary effects, 26, 56, 141–44
seditious libel, 31, 34, 38
sexual harassment, 106–9
Smith Act, 41, 43–44
Souter, David, 141, 143–44, 158, 288
speech–plus, 25, 127–28
Star Chamber, 7
Stevens, John Paul, 63, 64, 94–95, 97–98, 102, 126, 201–2, 323–25
Stewart, Potter, 75, 95, 148–49, 322–24
Stone, Harlan, 41

television. *See* broadcast media
Terrorism Information and Prevention System, 396
Thomas, Clarence, 100–1, 285–287
time, place and manner, 27, 59–60, 62, 64, 66
Tucker, Thomas, 12

unifying principles, 6, 15–23, 362–63

Valladingham, Clement, 35
viewpoint neutrality, 73, 95
Vinson, Fred, 41, 43
Virginia Resolution, 33–34

Warren, Earl, 44
White, Byron, 86–87, 124, 171, 177, 333
Williams, Roger, 8, 10
Wilson, James, 12

Zenger, John Peter, 32–33, 34, 74

Teaching Texts in Law and Politics

David Schultz, *General Editor*

The series Teaching Texts in Law and Politics is devoted to textbooks that explore the multidimensional and multidisciplinary areas of law and politics. Special emphasis is given to textbooks written for the undergraduate classroom. Subject matters addressed in this series include, but are not limited to: constitutional law; civil rights and liberties issues; law, race, gender, and gender orientation studies; law and ethics; women and the law; judicial behavior and decision-making; legal theory; comparative legal systems; criminal justice; courts and the political process; and other topics on the law and the political process that are of interest to undergraduate curriculum and education. Single-author and collaborative studies, as well as collections of essays are included.

To order other books in this series, please contact our Customer Service Department at:
    800-770-LANG (within the U.S.)
    (212) 647-7706 (outside the U.S.)
    (212) 647-7707 FAX

or browse online by series at:
    WWW.PETERLANG.COM